Business English
At Work

Instructor's Annotated Edition

Susan Jaderstrom
Santa Rosa Junior College
Petaluma, California

Joanne M. Miller

DISCARDED

**Glencoe
McGraw-Hill**

New York, New York   Columbus, Ohio   Woodland Hills, California   Peoria, Illinois

TABLE OF CONTENTS

Glencoe/McGraw-Hill

A Division of The **McGraw·Hill** *Companies*

Instructor's Annotated Edition of *Business English at Work*

Send all inquiries to:

Glencoe/McGraw-Hill
936 Eastwind Drive
Westerville, OH 43081

ISBN 0-02-802539-3

2 3 4 5 6 7 8 9 027 05 04 03 02 01 00 99

PREFACE

Welcome to *Business English at Work*—a complete teaching package for you and learning package for your students. You and your students are going to embark on an exciting journey through the world of English grammar, spelling, and punctuation. Working with these concepts, you and your students will be fascinated with the activities and the exercises that relate to the secondary learning topics—a totally new teaching and learning approach relating business English to the world of work.

Business English at Work is designed to help your students meet the challenges of a changing world, one in which the correct usage of English is tantamount to getting and holding a job. *Business English at Work* is designed to help you meet the needs of your students through the presentation of concepts on grammar, punctuation, capitalization, and proofreading—to name a few. The checkups that follow each presentation are enhanced with additional practice and worksheet applications both in the text and on the Student CD-ROM.

Text Features Included in the *Instructor's Annotated Edition*

Business English at Work uses a variety of text and margin features to present concepts of interest and importance to your students in their study of business English. Student text features that are included in the *Instructor's Annotated Edition*:

SECONDARY LEARNING

A two-page chapter opener presents the **Secondary Learning Concepts** around which the examples and applications of the chapter are written. Topics such as references, telecommunications, customer service, the World Wide Web, time management, electronic mail, cultural diversity, ergonomics, ethics, job skills, and coping strategies will relate the activities and exercises to the particular grammar, spelling, or punctuation concept being discussed.

TERMS TO REMEMBER

The **Terms to Remember** provide an opportunity for students to add new vocabulary words and definitions (which are found in the Glossary) to their growing language base. The Terms to Remember are related specifically to the Secondary Learning Concepts presented in each chapter.

OBJECTIVES

The **Learning Objectives** provide goals for structuring the students' learning activities and exercises so they know ahead of time what you will evaluate them on.

LOOKING AHEAD
Pretest

The **Looking Ahead Pretest** exercise in each chapter gives you the chance to test your students early and see how much they already know. You can then plan to spend more time on the concepts that they don't know.

Concepts and rules are presented individually in the chapters so that you can focus on them selectively to meet students' needs; thus students can see the concepts and rules applied in numerous examples.

LOOKING BACK

Posttest

The **Looking Back Posttest** exercise for each chapter helps you decide whether the students have acquired the concepts and rules that were presented in the chapter material.

The **Checkups** are a major feature of this text, being provided immediately after various concepts are covered, just when students need the reinforcement.

The **Do This/Do Not Do This** feature emphasizes a related grammar or punctuation rule. Students will like this interesting tie-in to rules made easy.

The **Practice Exercises and Worksheets** at the end of each chapter provide ample opportunities for your students to increase their skills in the concepts and rules of grammar, proofreading, writing, capitalization, and punctuation that were presented in the chapter.

Diagramming Exercises are provided to give your students a graphical hook for remembering how the parts of speech are used and how they relate to each other. Students will enjoy these fun exercises. The diagramming exercises on the Student CD-ROM are interactive and exciting to complete.

The **Online Activities** presented in each chapter will direct the students to the Internet for some interesting tours of various Websites.

ONLINE EXERCISES

You may want to follow any online activity you assign with a trip to the Glencoe/McGraw-Hill Website for *Business English at Work* by using the following address to access this special site for students: http://www.bew.glencoe.com

The **Appendix** contains a **Glossary** of the Terms to Remember with pertinent definitions and usage. The Appendix also contains the **Spelling Rules** and special **Word Usage** material. In addition, a thorough **Index** is provided to help locate concepts and rules that you may want to review with the students from time to time.

INSTRUCTOR SUPPORT

Special features in the *Instructor's Annotated Edition*:

- **Go To Transparency/PowerPoint**—These special icons offer suggestions for when to use Transparencies/PowerPoints to enhance student learning.

- **Instructor Notes**—Notes provided throughout the text direct you to helpful teaching hints in the *Instructor's Annotated Edition* (IAE) or on the Instructor CD-ROM. The IAE contains a page-for-page answer key for all activities, with the answer keys shown in color for ease of reading.

Instructor Ancillaries:

- The **Instructor CD-ROM** packaged with the IAE supports you as follows:

    1. The *Computerized Test Bank* and *ExamView Test Generator* provide almost 2000 test questions in multiple-choice and true-false formats. ExamView allows you to select a pretest, chapter test, midterm, final, or part test. Alternate tests, which can be randomized, are provided as part of the ExamView program.

    2. The *PowerPoint* slides present the concepts and rules in a readable, usable fashion that will provide interest and motivation to students.

    3. The *Student CD-ROM Exercises* are included both with and without answers so that you can print the exercises for at-the-moment practice or testing.

    4. *Course Outlines (Syllabi)* give you practical teaching schedules for using *Business English at Work* in a variety of settings.

    5. *Expanded Teaching Suggestions* provide additional methods and techniques for using the text that make the material more useful to the student, as well as making teaching easier for you.

- The **Instructor Transparency Package** has 160 color transparencies to support the learning concepts and enhance your presentations.

WEBSITE

A separate section of the Website is reserved for our instructors of *Business English at Work*. The Website contains additional testing, exercises, valuable teaching hints, research studies, and other information. To access this Website enter the following URL address at your Internet browser location:

> http://www.bew.glencoe.com/instructor

Follow the onscreen directions and enter the password as directed at the Website: glen/bew

We enjoyed developing this exciting program for you and your students. Please feel free to contact the authors at their e-mail addresses:

    Susan Jaderstrom: susan_jaderstrom@msn.com
    Joanne Miller: jmiller34@juno.com

Software support is provided by Glencoe/McGraw-Hill as follows:
Software Support
800-437-3715
8:00-6:00 EST

Customers can contact us at:
    http://www.epgtech.com
    epgtech@mcgraw-hill.com

SCANS CORRELATION WITH BUSINESS ENGLISH AT WORK CHAPTERS

SCANS Foundation Skill/Competency		Business English at Work Chapters 1-18																	
FOUNDATION SKILLS		1	2	3	4	5	6	7	8	9	10	11	12	13	14	15	16	17	18
Basic Skills																			
Reading	F-B-1	✓	✓	✓	✓	✓	✓	✓	✓	✓	✓	✓	✓	✓	✓	✓	✓	✓	✓
Writing	F-B-2	✓	✓	✓	✓	✓	✓	✓	✓	✓	✓	✓	✓	✓	✓	✓	✓	✓	✓
Arithmetic/Mathematics	F-B-3																		✓
Speaking	F-B-4																✓		
Listening	F-B-5	✓	✓	✓	✓	✓	✓	✓	✓	✓	✓	✓	✓	✓	✓	✓	✓	✓	✓
Thinking Skills																			
Thinking Creatively	F-TS-1	✓	✓	✓	✓	✓	✓	✓	✓	✓	✓	✓	✓	✓	✓	✓	✓	✓	✓
Making Decisions	F-TS-2	✓	✓	✓	✓	✓	✓	✓	✓	✓	✓	✓	✓	✓	✓	✓	✓	✓	✓
Solving Problems	F-TS-3	✓	✓	✓	✓	✓	✓	✓	✓	✓	✓	✓	✓	✓	✓	✓	✓	✓	✓
Seeing Things in the Mind's Eye	F-TS-4																		
Knowing How to Learn	F-TS-5	✓	✓	✓	✓	✓	✓	✓	✓	✓	✓	✓	✓	✓	✓	✓	✓	✓	✓
Reasoning	F-TS-6	✓	✓	✓	✓	✓	✓	✓	✓	✓	✓	✓	✓	✓	✓	✓	✓	✓	✓
Personal Qualities																			
Individual Responsibility	F-P-1																✓	✓	✓
Self-Esteem	F-P-2																✓	✓	
Sociability	F-P-3											✓							
Self-Management	F-P-4	✓					✓					✓							
Integrity	F-P-5													✓					✓
COMPETENCIES																			
Resources																			
Allocating Time	C-R-1						✓					✓							✓
Allocating Money	C-R-2																		✓
Allocating Materials	C-R-3											✓							
Allocating Space	C-R-4											✓							
Allocating Staff	C-R-5																		
Interpersonal Skills																			
Working on Teams	C-IS-1											✓						✓	
Teaching Others	C-IS-2																	✓	
Serving Customers	C-IS-3			✓															
Leading	C-IS-4														✓				
Negotiating	C-IS-5																		
Working with Culturally Diverse Others	C-IS-6								✓										
Information																			
Acquiring/Evaluating Data	C-I-1	✓	✓	✓	✓	✓	✓	✓	✓	✓	✓	✓	✓	✓	✓	✓	✓	✓	✓
Organizing/Maintaining Files	C-I-2																		
Interpreting/Communicating	C-I-3			✓	✓			✓								✓		✓	
Using Computers to Process Data	C-I-4	✓	✓	✓	✓	✓	✓	✓	✓	✓	✓	✓	✓	✓	✓	✓	✓	✓	✓
Systems																			
Understanding Systems	C-S-1											✓							
Monitoring/Correcting Performance	C-S-2	✓	✓	✓	✓	✓	✓	✓	✓	✓	✓	✓	✓	✓	✓	✓	✓	✓	✓
Designing/Improving Systems	C-S-3																		
Technology																			
Selecting Equipment/Tools	C-T-1	✓					✓	✓			✓		✓						
Using Technology for Specific Tasks	C-T-2	✓	✓	✓	✓	✓	✓	✓	✓	✓	✓	✓	✓	✓	✓	✓	✓	✓	✓
Maintaining/Troubleshooting	C-T-3																		

CHAPTER 1

1-1 Go to the Instructor CD-ROM for additional teaching suggestions and lesson plans. Chapters 1 through 3 are overview chapters and are general in content. If time is limited, Chapter 1 may be omitted. The *Looking Ahead* exercise may be used as a pretest, as an individual practice exercise at the end of a chapter, or as quiz material.

1-2 The chapter examples and exercises relate to the secondary learning topic, which is "References Online." Encourage the students to ask questions about the subject matter and to use online or traditional references to locate answers.

1-3 Collect references to display.

1-4 Teaching Suggestions
- Take students to a media reference area.
- Demonstrate electronic references.
- Have students review three reference manuals or three dictionaries by listing pluses and minuses for use in an office.

1-5 Dictionary information is taken from *Random House Webster's Unabridged Dictionary*. Stress the ways that dictionaries vary, and show specific examples.

1-6 Tell students that the dictionary entry shown in Figure 1 is only one dictionary example.

1-7 Syllabication differs among dictionaries. Syllabication also differs between dictionaries and reference manuals.

1-8 Recommend that students maintain an ongoing troublesome word list.

1-9 Suggestions for using checkup exercises: Use them as classroom exercises, as homework, or as examples for presenting the concepts. Prepare transparencies of the exercises along with the answers so students can quickly check their materials.

1-10 Answers to Checkup 1-1 will vary according to the dictionary used. You may prefer to grade or discuss the Syllabication and Part(s) of Speech columns only.

1-11 Students may use this pronunciation exercise as a group activity. After they pronounce the words, they check the dictionary for pronunciation.

1-12 The authors strongly recommend that each student purchase a reference manual. If this is not feasible, provide several for use in the classroom or multimedia center.

1-13 If you are using the *The Gregg Reference Manual*, refer to the chart "A Quick Guide to Key Topics by Paragraph Number." If you're using another reference manual, you'll probably find similar reference topics with their page or paragraph numbers.

1-14 Answers that are specific to *The Gregg Reference Manual* are indicated. Remember, answers will vary if students use other reference manuals.

1-15 Thesauri formats and information vary. The more recent editions include computer terminology.

1-16 The text uses *online* and *workstation*. You may find different spellings in the reference materials and in the workplace.

1-17 In Checkup 1-3, you may omit using the word division manual. You may also use this Checkup as a syllabication exercise.

1-18 Ask your colleagues and friends to gather printed material with proofreading errors. Have students practice finding errors in copy.

1-19 Show students how to use grammar check and spell check software applications.

1-20 Refer to the section on spelling in *The Gregg Reference Manual* for the definitions and correct use of words that sound alike or that are often misused.

1-21 Checkup 1-6 provides an excellent spell check demonstration or practice exercise.

1-22 Additional practice exercises are available on the Instructor CD and the Student CD.

1-23 Proofreading activities in the first several chapters consist of comparing copy and indicating differences.

1-24 A PowerPoint presentation describing communication on the Internet is available with this text on the Instructor CD-ROM.

1-25 Keep in mind that all Internet Websites may change or be deleted. You may want to check any site before you assign the activity to students.

1-26 *Netiquette* is the combination of the words *net* and *etiquette.* The word means *network etiquette*, which is the proper behavior on the Internet. The key to proper netiquette is to be positive and thoughtful.

    Flame is a derogatory comment intended to insult.

    Smiley is the use of punctuation marks and other symbols or characters to portray moods.

1-27 Students may print a map of their home with their name printed on the map. URL for the postal information page through Yahoo:
http://www.yahoo.com/Reference/Postal_Information/
URL for the United States Postal Service: http://www.usps.gov/
URL for BlastMap:
http://www.mapblast.com

CHAPTER 2

2-1 You may omit this chapter and proceed directly to Chapter 3, which discusses sentences, or to Chapter 4, which begins the study of the parts of speech. In Chapter 2, the chapter examples and exercises relate to the secondary learning topic, which is "Telecommunications." Encourage students to ask questions about the subject matter and to use online or traditional references to locate answers.

2-2 This chapter is an introduction to the parts of speech. The examples and exercises relate to very basic rules.

2-3 Stress the importance of using the correct terminology.

2-4 Stress that words may function as more than one part of speech. A word's label as a part of speech depends on its use within the sentence.

2-5 Prepare and use a transparency to identify parts of speech in different occupational areas.

2-6 The major emphasis in the section on nouns is the recognition of nouns as persons, places, things, activities, ideas, or qualities, and the identification of common and proper nouns.

2-7 Ask students to list as many common nouns as they can identify in the room.

2-8 Use a reference manual, current articles (especially articles about telecommunications), and online sources to obtain other words for the various categories of nouns.

2-9 Proper nouns in Checkup 2-1 will vary. Words such as *a* and *the* should not, of course, appear with the rewritten word unless the words are part of the proper noun. A class discussion of this exercise is an easy way to check students' understandings.

2-10 Stress that the pronoun *it* should not be used as a substitute for nouns that refer to people.

2-11 Another term for *helping verbs* is *auxiliary verbs.*

2-12 Stress that adjectives modify nouns and pronouns only; adverbs modify verbs, adjectives, and other adverbs.

2-13 Another question that adverbs answer —usually with adverbial clauses and phrases—is *why?*

2-14 In Sentence 3, *were* is a linking verb. *Satisfied* is an adjective modifying *We.*

2-15 Remind students to identify linking verbs. See Sentences 2 and 5.

2-16 As an extra practice exercise, ask students to locate the coordinating conjunctions in the secondary learning paragraphs and in the overview paragraphs at the beginning of the chapter, or in any checkup activity in the chapter.

2-17 Only a few of the more frequently used prepositions are listed.

2-18 Interjections are used in informal e-mail messages and in advertising copy.

2-19 The interjection *Oh* may not always be followed by an exclamation point. *Oh* is sometimes followed by a comma.

2-20 The proofreading exercises in this chapter continue to involve words and phrases.

2-21 Sentence writing does not begin until Chapter 3.

2-22 *USA Today* was chosen as the newspaper to search because of the frequency of articles on telecommunications and the easy-to-use search engine.

2-23 Check online sites carefully before assigning them to students. Be aware that site information and options may change. Some sites charge a fee to access articles. Omit this exercise or substitute another site, if you wish.

2-24 Students will pick different terms to read.

CHAPTER 3

3-1 The chapter examples and exercises relate to the secondary learning topic, which is "Customer Service." Encourage students to ask questions about the subject matter and use online or traditional references to locate the answers.

3-2 This chapter is an overview of the parts of a sentence. You may omit this chapter and proceed directly to Chapter 4, which is an introduction to nouns.

3-3 Teaching Suggestions:
- Ask students to bring in examples of inverted order sentences, indirect questions, courteous requests, dependent clauses, run-on sentences, and so on.
- Divide students into groups. As an ongoing project, have each group organize a news sheet for the class. These news sheets might consist of helpful business English hints that students develop, errors found in readings and the Internet (similar to the Slip-ups found in the textbook), new vocabulary, and so on. The title of one of their news sheets might be "Did You Know?"
- Additional teaching suggestions may be found on the Instructor CD-ROM.

3-4 Stress the importance of Questions 1 and 2 in identifying sentences. On their own, Questions 3 and 4 do not identify sentences.

3-5 Stress the importance of locating simple subjects. Once the complete subject is found, the rest of the sentence is the predicate.

3-6 Stress the difference between compound subjects and complete subjects. Review adjectives and adverbs as modifiers.

3-7 To make it easier to identify simple predicates, have students place prepositional and infinitive phrases in parentheses.

3-8 Stress compound predicate identification. If students understand compound predicates, they are less likely to confuse them with compound sentence structures.

3-9 Stress the *to whom?* and *from whom?* questions in identifying indirect objects.

3-10 Direct objects and indirect objects are also completions of verbs and may be referred to as complements.

3-11 Relate the word *complete* to *complement*.

3-12 Ask students to identify phrases in the secondary learning paragraphs printed at the beginning of this chapter.

3-13 Use the common definitions of *dependent* and *independent* to show the relationship to dependent and independent clauses.

3-14 Emphasize that the subject or verb may be plural in a simple sentence; however, the sentence still contains only a single subject or a single verb.

3-15 See Chapter 16 for more detailed explanations of the use of commas in compound and complex sentences.

3-16 The coordinating conjunctions used throughout the text are *and, or, nor,* and *but.*

3-17 Diagramming is introduced in this chapter. As each part of speech is introduced, it is added to the base line. You may choose to disregard the sections on diagramming in future chapters. If you use diagramming as a teaching tool, relate it to solving a puzzle and have some fun with it.

3-18 This proofreading exercise changes from those in Chapters 1 and 2 to give students another way to proofread. Most proofreading is done by checking copy against an original or another source. The first sentence in each exercise is always the correctly written one.

3-19 The format changes to give students another way to proofread—side-by-side checking. The material in the first column is correct.

3-20 Students need to identify the type of sentence to write. Some directions indicate a simple or compound subject, but allows students to decide the type of predicate to use—simple or compound.

3-21 Check online sites carefully before assigning them to students. Be aware that site information and options may change.

3-22 Have students print their lists and/or summarize this site, if you wish.

3-23 For additional writing practice, have students write more than one sentence per exercise.

3-24 The *Looking Back* section may be used as quiz material or as an additional practice exercise. The *Looking Ahead* section of the chapter may be used as a pretest, as another practice exercise, or as quiz material.

CHAPTER 4

4-1 The chapter examples and exercises relate to the secondary learning topic for Chapter 4, which is "The Internet." Encourage students to ask questions about the subject matter and to use online or traditional references to locate answers.

4-2 Teaching Suggestions:
- Ask students to identify and list all the common nouns and proper nouns that they see in the room.
- Use the nouns in the text copy "Classes of Nouns" for practice in identifying common and proper nouns. For example, a proper noun for *assistant* might be *Kelley*.
- Additional teaching suggestions may be found on the Instructor CD-ROM.

4-3 Activities such as "talking" and "printing" are included in the list of classes of nouns. Students frequently see these gerunds as verbs. Additional information concerning gerunds is found in Chapter 11.

4-4 Refer to *The Gregg Reference Manual* or another available manual for additional examples of common and proper nouns.

4-5 This section of the chapter includes a review of these terms: direct object, indirect object, complement (predicate noun), object of a preposition, and singular and compound subjects.

4-6 Point out the differences and similarities between predicate nouns and appositives. Predicate nouns are subject complements; they follow linking verbs and rename the subject. Predicate adjectives follow linking verbs and describe the subject. Appositives follow another noun and rename the noun. See Instructor CD-ROM for additional examples.

4-7 Collective nouns are covered in greater depth in Chapter 8 (pronoun/antecedents) and Chapter 11 (subject-verb agreement).

4-8 For additional writing practice, have students use the words in Checkup 4-3 (Exercise 2) in sentences.

4-9 Recommend that students refer to their dictionaries to find the preferred spellings of irregular plural nouns.

4-10 Present the section on subject-verb agreement before having students use the words in Checkup 4-4 in sentences.

4-11 Refer to *The Gregg Reference Manual* or another available reference manual for additional nouns ending in *s* that may have singular meanings and for nouns that have no plural forms.

4-12 Refer to *The Gregg Reference Manual* or another available reference manual for nouns that are never singular.

4-13 Dictionaries vary in their listings of preferred plural forms of foreign nouns. When discussing foreign nouns, indicate that many English nouns derived from another language end in *is* for singular and *es* for plural.

4-14 Note that the instructions in Checkup 4-4 (Exercise 2) require the preferred spellings as the answers.

4-15 Refer to *The Gregg Reference Manual* or another available reference manual for abbreviations of measurements.

4-16 The diagramming section of the chapter may be omitted. No practice or end-of-chapter worksheets include diagramming questions.

4-17 Have students identify (not diagram) the other parts of speech in these sentences for additional practice.

4-18 Proofreading completed business and personal documents against printed copy is a more common activity for business English students than marking copy with proofreaders' marks. For this reason, checking one copy against correct material is the basis for proofreading in the first several chapters.

4-19 Check all online exercises before you assign them to be sure the sites are still available. You may ask students to print the definitions from this exercise for class discussion.

4-20 Cyberspace: Coined by sci-fi writer William Gibson in his novel *Neuromancers* in the early 1980s. Refers to everyone and everything on the Internet.

4-21 From a Monty Python sketch titled *Spam*. The term is used to describe excessive information.

CHAPTER 5

5-1 The chapter examples and exercises relate to the secondary learning topic for Chapter 5, which is "The World Wide Web." Encourage students to ask questions about the subject matter and to use online or traditional references to locate answers.

5-2 Chapters 4 and 5 may be presented individually, or they may be combined.

5-3 Teaching suggestions:
  • Collect examples of the incorrect use of the possessive form from such sources as student writing samples, newspapers, and magazine articles.

  • Check current dictionaries or reference manuals to obtain the most up-to-date forms of compound nouns.

  • Additional teaching suggestions may be found on the Instructor CD-ROM.

5-4 Refer to *The Gregg Reference Manual* or another reference manual for additional examples of compound nouns.

5-5 Indicate that the word *online* is an example of a word that appears more frequently in current readings as one word rather than in its initial hyphenated form.

5-6 Refer to *The Gregg Reference Manual or another reference manual* for words that have two plural forms. In this case, *courts-martial* is the preferred form.

5-7 Refer to *The Gregg Reference Manual.* The nouns *chief of police* and *vice president* are not hyphenated.

5-8 Refer to *The Gregg Reference Manual* for the plurals of compounds ending in *ful.*

5-9 Refer to *The Gregg Reference Manual* for examples of compound titles.

5-10 Refer to *The Gregg Reference Manual* for compounds that have two recognized plural forms.

5-11 Emphasize that nouns in the nominative and objective cases are the same, but that the nouns change in form with the possessive case. You may find some authorities who use the term *subjective case* to mean the nominative case.

5-12 Limit examples for the objective case to direct objects, indirect objects, objects of a preposition, and objects of infinitives.

5-13 For an additional exercise, have students identify the specific uses in each case; for example, direct object, object of a preposition, subject, etc. The answers follow:
  1. direct object, object of a preposition, object of a preposition
  2. subject, direct object
  3. possessive
  4. possessive, object of infinitive
  5. subject, object of preposition
  6. subject, direct object, direct object

5-14 Refer to *The Gregg Reference Manual* for additional examples of singular possessives.

5-15 Stress that it is the owner that takes the possessive form—not the item owned. Emphasize the importance of asking *How many own?*

5-16 Use the following explanation for making a plural noun that ends in *s* possessive.
Situation A: *More than one girl owns books.*
　1. Make the owner (*girl*) of the books plural (*girls*).
　2. Note that the plural ends in *s.*
　3. Add only an apostrophe to make the plural possessive (*girls'*).
Situation B: *More than one secretary has a vacation.*
　1. Make the owner (*secretary*) of the vacation plural (*secretaries*). Note the change in spelling.
　2. Note that the plural ends in *s.*
　3. Add only an apostrophe to make the plural possessive (*secretaries'*).

5-17 Use the following explanation for making a plural noun that does not end in *s* possessive.
Situation: *More than one businessman has appointments.*
　1. Make the owner (*businessman*) of the appointments plural (*businessmen*).
　2. Note that the plural *businessmen* does not end in *s.*
　3. Add an apostrophe and *s* to make the plural possessive.

5-18 Define plurals and possessives very clearly for students. Students often confuse a plural word ending in *s* with the possessive form.

5-19 The word *its* is the clue that the noun *book* is singular. The possessive form is *book's.*

5-20 Refer to *The Gregg Reference Manual* or another available reference manual for rules on organization, association, and company names.

5-21 Use the telephone directory or Web page sites to identify the use of the apostrophe in the name of an organization or association.

5-22 The diagramming section of this chapter may be omitted. No practice or end-of-chapter worksheets include diagramming sentences.

5-23 *ISP* is an abbreviation for Internet service provider. You will more than likely have only one ISP; therefore, the noun is singular. The possessive form is *ISP's.*

5-24 For additional practice, require students to state the rules for possessive forms.

5-25 Caution students to read the sentence carefully. The magazines *do not belong* to the "latest computer."

5-26 Check online sites carefully before assigning the activities to students. Be aware that site information and options may change.

CHAPTER 6

6-1 The chapter examples and exercises relate to the secondary learning topic for Chapter 6, which is "Time Management." Encourage students to ask questions about the subject matter and to use online or traditional references to locate answers.

6-2 Capitalization authorities vary. Since it is impossible to include every rule or exception to the rule in the text, refer to *The Gregg Reference Manual* or another reference manual for more detailed explanations.

6-3 Teaching Suggestions:
 • Obtain a company or office desk manual that includes terms used by the organization. Emphasize the importance of following company practices even if they differ slightly from a text or dictionary.
 • Additional teaching suggestions may be found on the Instructor CD-ROM.

6-4 Refer to *The Gregg Reference Manual* or another reference manual for additional examples of imaginative names and nicknames.

6-5 Explain that certain substitutions for proper nouns such as "The Windy City" for Chicago have evolved through the years. People often use such substitutions in informal communications.

6-6 Refer to a current dictionary to check the capitalization of words that once were capitalized but because of common use have lost their identification with certain associated nouns.

6-7 Refer to *The Gregg Reference Manual* or another reference manual for information on nouns and pronouns. Emphasize that the company letterhead, invoice, or sales material identifies the way the firm wants its name written.

6-8 Refer to *The Gregg Reference Manual* or another reference manual for examples of organizational units.

6-9 Remind students that titles for lower-ranking government officials may vary depending on their use of context in a written communication. Refer to *The Gregg Reference Manual* or another reference manual for occasions to capitalize lower-ranking titles.

6-10 Refer to *The Gregg Reference Manual* or another reference manual for a distinction between official and occupational names.

6-11 Additional rules for publications include capitalizing short verbs and prepositions that function as adverbs. The word *to* in an infinitive phrase is not capitalized.

6-12 Ask students to supply names of such published words as book chapters, magazine articles, movies, television programs, newspapers, books, and magazines.

6-13 Remind students that *The Office Professional* is the name of the magazine. The word *magazine* is not a part of the title.

6-14 Discuss the capitalization of the word *English* in business English versus business communication in specific course titles or in general use.

6-15 Clarify the capitalization of seasons when they appear in specific events.
   The Penney Winter White Sale starts Monday. (specific event)
   Be sure to register for fall semester classes. (an ongoing period of time)
   Be sure to register for the Spring 2000 semester classes. (specific year included)

6-16 Remind students that some common nouns have capitalized abbreviations. All abbreviations should be written in full the first time they are used.

6-17 Ask students to suggest trademarks, brand names, and specific products that should be capitalized. In general correspondence, the product itself is not capitalized. However, some companies may capitalize their own products within their firms or they may capitalize the product for advertising purposes.

6-18 Refer to *The Gregg Reference Manual* or another reference manual for explanations of capitalizing after a colon.

6-19 Be aware that the word *roman* may be capitalized in dictionaries and some reference manuals.

6-20 Postal authorities strongly recommend the use of all caps in large mailings. The traditional format of initial caps and lowercase letters is still acceptable and may be read by electronic equipment.

6-21 No diagramming exercise appears in Chapter 6. Diagramming will continue in Chapter 7.

6-22 Check online sites carefully before assigning the activities to students. Be aware that site information and options may change.

CHAPTER 7

7-1 The chapter examples and exercises relate to the secondary learning topic for Chapter 7, which is "Electronic Mail." Encourage students to ask questions about the subject matter and to use online or traditional references to locate answers.

7-2 Teaching Suggestions:
• Refer students to the student notes for quick reviews or easy references.
• Record some correct pronoun phrases or sentences on tapes. Then have students listen to the tapes and practice correct pronoun usage. For example: "This is she." "May I tell Mary who is calling, please."
• Additional teaching suggestions may be found on the Instructor CD-ROM.

7-3 An understanding of nominative, objective, and possessive cases can make the study of pronouns much simpler.

7-4 Sentences that begin with the word *It* are considered weak sentences.

7-5 In this chapter, *subject complement* is used in place of *predicate noun* and *predicate pronoun*.

7-6 Another change might be a passive construction. *He was found to be the offensive writer of e-mail messages.* The infinitive *to be* requires an objective case pronoun when a noun or pronoun immediately precedes the words *to be*. For example, How could she ever have thought Lisa *to be* me? (Objective case is necessary, not the nominative case.)

7-7 Use these questions to identify direct and indirect objects.

   Gave what?   *instruction manual*   To whom?   *her*
   Offered what?   *service*   To whom?   *us*

7-8 Remind students that *except* and *between* may function as prepositions as well as conjunctions.

7-9 The section on subjects or objects of infinitives may be omitted; no exercise requires this information.

7-10 Emphasize that possessive pronouns do not have apostrophes.

7-11 Remind students that *mines* is not an acceptable possessive pronoun.

7-12 Emphasize the differences between the use of contractions and possessive pronouns (*it's, its; your, you're; their, they're; who's, whose; there's, theirs*). Remind students to select the word that makes sense in a sentence.

7-13 Have students attach verbs to each of the pronouns in the chart. They will easily see that attaching *gave* after the pronoun *me* is not correct.

7-14 Checkup 7-4 demonstrates the various uses of pronouns. Use the checkup as a class activity. Discuss the pros and cons, netiquette, and legitimate uses of electronic mail.

7-15 The names of the miscellaneous pronouns need to be recognized but not memorized.

7-16 Intensive and reflexive pronouns are covered under the heading "Compound Personal Pronouns."

7-17 Indicate that demonstrative pronouns function as pronouns and adjectives.

7-18 Some indefinite pronouns function as adjectives, but they are not included in this chapter.

7-19 Remind students that interrogative and relative pronouns are similar, but they have different functions in a sentence.

7-20 *Who, whom,* and *whose* are briefly introduced, but a more detailed explanation with additional practice exercises follows in the next section.

7-21 Restrictive and nonrestrictive clauses are discussed in more depth in Chapter 16.

7-22 Refer to a manual such as *The Gregg Reference Manual* for additional information concerning the use of *which*.

7-23 Use the suggestions in the student text for determining when to use *who* or *whom*.

7-24 The subject and object of an infinitive are not included in this discussion.

7-25 For extra diagramming practice, use the sentences with compound subjects and objects from Chapter 3.

7-26 The diagramming section of the chapter may be omitted. No practice or end-of-chapter worksheets include diagramming sentences.

7-27 Remind students that the word *except* functions as a preposition in this sentence.

7-28 Proofreaders' marks are introduced for the first time. Encourage students to use a colored pen or pencil for marking errors on documents.

7-29 Demonstrate the use of e-mail.

7-30 Check online sites carefully before assigning the activities to students. Be aware that site information and options may change.

CHAPTER 8

8-1 The chapter examples and exercises relate to the secondary learning topic for Chapter 8, which is "Cultural Diversity." Encourage students to ask questions about the subject matter and to use online or traditional references to locate answers.

8-2 Teaching Suggestions:
- Discuss various cultural differences and how biased behavior may be offensive.
- Additional teaching suggestions may be found on the Instructor CD-ROM.

8-3 See Question 8 in *Looking Ahead*. The subject *Kristen* is singular and requires the singular verb *was*. The intervening phrase does not affect the verb.

8-4 Encourage students to follow the steps for pronoun and antecedent agreement outlined in the text.

8-5 First- and second-person pronouns create few problems regarding antecedent agreement for person. Third-person pronouns need to be emphasized.

8-6 The use of *his* or *her* and *he* or *she* is widely used. If the sentence can be reworded or the subjects and objects made plural, recommend that students do so.

8-7 Checkup 8-2 provides an additional short writing practice. Each chapter has a set of Terms to Remember. These terms may be used as extra dictionary practice exercises or used in writing exercises.

8-8 Emphasize that the antecedent that is closer to *or* or *nor* determines whether the pronoun is singular or plural. This rule *only* applies to the words *or* or *nor*. The rule does not apply when *and* connects two antecedents.

8-9 Refer to a manual such as *The Gregg Reference Manual* for additional examples using antecedents joined by *and, or,* or *nor*.

8-10 Explain the use of an article (*a, an, the*) before each title in a sentence to indicate two titles and two persons or the omission of the second article to indicate only one title and one person.

8-11 A sentence with a plural subject and a singular subject joined by *or* or *nor* will be less awkward if the sentence is rephrased so that the plural antecedent is closer to the pronoun.

8-12 Refer to a manual such as *The Gregg Reference Manual* for additional information on collective nouns. Explain the difference in pronoun use when the group acts as one body and when the members of a group act individually.

8-13 Refer to *The Gregg Reference Manual* for additional examples and references for organizational and company names.

8-14 Recommend that students memorize the indefinite pronouns that can be used as single or plural pronouns.

8-15 Refer to a manual such as *The Gregg Reference Manual* for additional information on intervening phrases.

8-16 The diagramming section of the chapter may be omitted. This diagramming exercise involves adjectives. Stress the importance of diagramming the simple subject, verb, and object before adding adjectives.

8-17 The items in Exercise 2 cover material presented in the reference pronoun clarity section and in the pronouns requiring special attention section. These sentences require careful analysis. Students will need assistance with the unclear reference items.

8-18 In addition to just underlining errors, students will now be asked to insert any omitted words or marks of punctuation. The second paragraph is the paragraph that will have the errors if there are errors.

8-19 Encourage students to respond to the cultural diversity survey.

8-20 The exercise provides another writing opportunity as well as a proofreading exercise. Have students prepare a final copy of this document and e-mail or send it with an accompanying memo to you.

8-21 Have students e-mail their sentences to you.

8-22 Check online sites carefully before assigning them to students. Be aware that site information and options may change.

CHAPTER 9

9-1 The chapter examples and exercises relate to the secondary learning topic for Chapter 9, which is "Problem Solving and Decision Making." Encourage students to ask questions about the subject matter and to use online or traditional references to locate answers.

9-2 Chapters 9, 10, and 11 cover the study of verbs.

9-3 Teaching Suggestions:

- Some people may misuse certain verbs more than others. Examples are *have went* for *have gone, done* for *did, bidded* and *costed* for *bid* and *cost,* and *seen* for *saw.* Prepare your own tape using such words in sentences correctly.
- Additional teaching suggestions may be found on the Instructor CD-ROM.

9-4 Remind students that when the word *to* precedes a verb, it indicates an infinitive. Infinitives do not function as verbs.

9-5 Explain the terms *transitive* and *intransitive* by using direct objects.

9-6 Students may have problems with *to be* verb forms. Ask students to respond in unison or individually and to identify pronouns that can be placed before forms of *to be.* For example, say the word "is" or "was." Students would respond "he, she, it."

9-7 Recommend that students memorize the five sense verbs (*feel, look, smell, sound, taste*) and the six additional linking verbs (*appear, become, grow, remain, seem, stay*).

9-8 Stress that some helping verbs may be used alone such as in the sentences "I *have* a problem" or "She *did* her work without assistance."

9-9 Before students study verb tense, they should recognize the principal parts of verbs—present, past, past participle, and present participle. Use the words *form* or *part* of a verb rather than *tense* at this stage of presentation. Present, past, and future tense will be covered in Chapter 10.

9-10 Several spelling rules are necessary since some regular verbs require changes in spelling. Emphasize that these verbs are still regular verbs in spite of changes due to spelling. The exercises on spelling rules are on the Student's and Instructor's CD-ROMs. The spelling rules are located in the appendix.

9-11 Dictionaries vary, but many will not show the *ed* or *ing* endings for regular verbs such as *succeed* or *attempt.* If a change occurs in the spelling, however, the *ed* and *ing* endings are likely to be shown. Have students locate words such as *solve, carry, plan,* and *refer* in a dictionary.

9-12 *Label,* as well as *cancel,* is an exception. While *labeled, labeled,* and *labeling* are preferred, *labelled, labelled, labelling,* are acceptable. The same is true for the word *cancel.*

9-13 Encourage students to memorize only those past parts or past participles with which they have trouble.

9-14 At the beginning or end of a class, provide additional practice in identifying the parts of a verb. For example, say the word "ring"and add "past." Students respond, "rang." Use another verb to identify *past* or ask for another verb part. Keep the pace moving.

9-15 You may want to direct the students now to the checkup for sentences using *lay, lie; set, sit; raise, rise* on the Student's CD-ROM that accompanies this text.

9-16 The past form of the verb *lie* causes problems because it is the same as the present form of *lay;* therefore, it sounds as if it should be present tense.

9-17 The verb *lies* is used correctly in the Slip-up. The possible double meaning of the word *lies* as a verb or noun is the issue in this sentence.

9-18 All words in the sentences may be diagrammed.

9-19 This chapter introduces the proofreaders' marks for *delete, delete and close up,* and *insert comma.*

9-20 One grading method for Practice 3A (Proofreading) is to allow 20 points—5 points for the sentence error identification and 15 points for the proofreading exercise. There are 15 errors in the proofreading exercise. Allowing $1/2$ point instead of 1 point is another alternative.

9-21 Check online sites carefully before assigning them to students. Be aware that site information and options may change.

CHAPTER 10

10-1 The chapter examples and exercises relate to the secondary learning topic for Chapter 10, which is "Computer Software." Encourage students to ask questions about the subject matter and to use online or traditional references to locate answers.

10-2 Teaching Suggestions:
- Review irregular verbs daily. Stress such problem verbs as *went, gone, did, done, saw, seen, break, bring, begin, grow, have,* and *be.*
- Use current business magazine articles to demonstrate how writers use the active voice.
- Additional teaching suggestions may be found on the Instructor CD-ROM.

10-3 For additional practice, students may correct the sentences in the *Looking Ahead* exercise.

10-4 Demonstrate the use of *be* verb forms as linking or helping verbs. Demonstrate the use of *do* and *have* as main verbs or helping verbs.

10-5 Place various tenses of verbs on the chalkboard or on transparencies.

10-6 Remind students that most *plural* nouns end in *s*; however, verbs are the opposite. Most *singular* verbs end in *s*.

10-7 Additional examples of words that fall under these rules may be found in the spelling exercises rules in the appendix and in the exercises on the Student's CD-ROM.

10-8 Checkup 10-3 combines the past and present tenses and also includes forms of the verbs *do* and *be*.

10-9 Many writers no longer make the distinction between the verbs *shall* and *will*.

10-10 Using the perfect and progressive tenses allows students to vary their writing styles.

10-11 Remind students that the only helping verbs used with the perfect tense are *has, have, had, shall have,* or *will have*.

10-12 Checkup 10-5 provides another opportunity to review past and present participles. Omit this exercise if you do not plan to teach the perfect tenses.

10-13 Remind students to use the *to be* forms—*am, are, is, was, were, be, been*—with the present participle to form the progressive tense.

10-14 Omit Checkup 10-6 if you do not cover progressive and emphatic tenses.

10-15 Use the indicative and imperative sentences in Chapter 3 for extra practice sentences as you review the indicative and imperative moods in this chapter.

10-16 Refer to a reference manual such as *The Gregg Reference Manual* for a detailed explanation of the subjunctive mood.

10-17 Review subjects and direct objects in Chapters 2 and 3 before presenting verbals. Gerunds and infinitive phrases have several functions. Participles and participial phrases function as adjectives.

10-18 Gerunds also function as subject complements and appositives. To help students remember to use the possessive form before the gerund, stress the meaning of the sentences. For example, it is not "we appreciate you"; it is "we appreciate your teaching."

10-19 Emphasize that the sentences with gerund phrases must also have a verb or verbs or verb phrases. In Sentence 5, the verb phrase *is giving* consists of a present participle *giving* and a helping verb *is*. This is not a gerund.

10-20 Refer to a reference manual such as *The Gregg Reference Manual* for a discussion of commas after introductory participial expressions.

10-21 Explain the way to correct a dangling participle. If the statement has a verbal introduction, be sure the subject is doing the action of the verbal. Prepare a list of sentence beginnings using participles. Have students complete them using correct subjects.

10-22 Refer to a reference manual such as *The Gregg Reference Manual* for a discussion of commas after introductory infinitive phrases.

10-23 Emphasize that sentences with infinitive phrases must also have a verb/verb phrase or verbs/verb phrases. Students confuse infinitives with verbs and with prepositional phrases.

10-24 Refer to a reference manual such as *The Gregg Reference Manual* for a good explanation of splitting an infinitive.

10-25 All words in the sentences may be diagrammed. Doing the exercise will help students differentiate between gerunds and participles more clearly.

10-26 If the perfect and progressive tense sections are not covered, omit Questions 1, 3, 4, 7, and 9 in A and 2 in B.

10-27 Students may use proofreaders' marks to insert items or make corrections.

10-28 This chapter introduces the proofreaders' marks for *insert period* and *delete space*.

10-29 In Practice 3A, there are five sentence error identification items and a proofreading exercise with 15 points. See Chapter 9 for a suggested grading plan.

10-30 Check online sites carefully before assigning them to students. Be aware that site information and options may change.

10-31 When students are familiar with locating Websites, require some written work. For example, ask students to list two interesting items about one or two of the commercial sites. You may want students to use active voice, to write in present tense, to use verbals, and so on.

10-32 If the perfect and progressive tense sections are not covered, omit Question 5 in Section A and Question 3 in Section B.

10-33 If the perfect and progressive tense sections are not covered, omit Questions 1, 3, 4, 7, and 10.

CHAPTER 11

11-1 The chapter examples and exercises relate to the secondary learning topic, which is "Teamwork." Encourage students to ask questions about the subject matter and to use online or traditional references to locate answers.

11-2 Teaching Suggestions:
- Identify some dialectical, colloquial, or frequently misused phrases from your geographical area. Make tapes showing appropriate or logical substitutions for misused phrases.
- Additional teaching suggestions may be found on the Instructor CD-ROM.

11-3 Point out the differences in forming noun plurals versus verb plurals. Verbs do not have an *s* or *es* added to their plural forms; nouns do. Add *s* or *es* only to singular verbs used with third-person singular subjects.

11-4 Refer to a reference manual such as *The Gregg Reference Manual* for an explanation of using a plural verb after *you*.

11-5 Stress to the students that they should identify the subject of a sentence first; then they should check to see that the verb agrees with the subject.

11-6 *Essential* prepositional phrases should *not* be set aside by commas. *Non-essential* prepositional phrases should be set aside by commas.

11-7 Refer to the section on intervening phrases and clauses in *The Gregg Reference Manual* for a more detailed explanation of handling positive and negative subjects in the same sentence.

11-8 In sentences with a plural subject and a singular subject joined by *or* or *nor*, recommend placing the plural subject closer to the verb.

11-9 Review all the linking verbs.

11-10 Remind students that the compound pronouns *anyone*, *everyone*, and *someone* are two words when they are followed by an *of* phrase.

11-11 Remind students that prepositional phrases must be considered to determine subject-verb agreement when the pronouns *all, any, more, most, none,* and *some* are used. This is an exception to the general rule to disregard intervening prepositional phrases between the subject and verb.

11-12 In formal writing, *none* is a singular pronoun. In most of today's writing, *none* is plural if it means "none of them." *None* is singular if it means "none of it." *No one* is singular, and it means "not one single person."

11-13 Remind students that using phrases such as "members of a committee" or "members of a team" sounds less awkward than using a collective noun with a plural verb.

11-14 In this text, we are recommending the use of a singular verb with company, institution, and organization names.

11-15 Remind students that prepositional phrases must be considered with fractional amounts such as *the/a majority of, a part of, a portion of, a percentage of* or *one-half of.* Such phrases are exceptions to the general rule for disregarding intervening prepositional phrases between the subject and verb.

11-16 Finding the subject in a question may be easier if the question is rephrased as a statement.

11-17 Additional sentences with the word *statistics* include:

Statistics *is* often an unpopular course. The company's statistics *are* questionable.

11-18 All words in the sentences may be diagrammed. Work through the examples with the students.

11-19 For additional practice, have students identify simple subjects in Practice 1A.

11-20 In Item 8, Practice 2A, the subject *analyses* is plural; therefore, a plural verb is necessary.

11-21 In Item 9, Practice 2A, the word *every* with a compound subject makes a singular verb necessary.

11-22 In Item 10, Practice 2A, the expression a *percentage of* precedes a plural noun. The sentence requires a plural verb.

11-23 In Item 11, Practice 2A, *technical personnel* and *support* is considered one unit and requires a singular verb.

11-24 The proofreading exercise requires students to edit the copy and insert proofreading marks. A correct copy is not available for them to use.

11-25 Students should find the errors in this proofreading exercise. See Chapter 9 for a suggested grading plan.

11-26 For additional writing practice, have students select another task to write about.

11-27 Check online sites carefully before assigning them to students. Be aware that site information and options may change.

11-28 For additional writing practice, have students write two or three sentences about one or both of the sites visited.

11-29 Remind students that a present tense verb is required in the sentences.

CHAPTER 12

12-1 The chapter examples and exercises relate to the secondary learning topic for Chapter 12, which is "Ergonomics." Encourage students to ask questions about the subject matter and to use online or traditional references to locate answers.

12-2 Teaching Suggestions:
• Ask students to list as many nouns as they can, or have them use their dictionaries to find nouns.
• Additional teaching suggestions may be found on the Instructor CD-ROM.

12-3 For additional practice in identifying nouns being modified, have students list the adjectives followed by the noun being modified in parentheses; for example, *four* (colors), *different* (colors).

12-4 In Question 5, *oriental* does not require capitalization. Since it has become so commonly used, it no longer functions as a proper adjective.

12-5 Interrogative pronouns are not included in the chapter. The words *which* and *what* are interrogative pronouns that may also function as interrogative adjectives when they modify nouns. Writers today use *which* or *that* to introduce an essential clause.

12-6 Emphasize that *them* is never used as an adjective. Demonstrate differences between *these/that*, and *these/those* by pointing to different items around the classroom.

12-7 Remind students that the initial sound (not the first letter) of the noun following *a* or *an* determines whether to use *a* or *an*.

12-8 Remind students that *a*, *an*, and *the* are used before adjectives that modify nouns as well as directly before nouns (e.g., a soundproof room, a room.)

12-9 Explain the difference between two separate people doing two different things and one person serving in two capacities. The repetition of the articles *a*, *an*, and *the* helps determine this distinction.

12-10 Emphasize the use of a dictionary when working with compound adjectives. See a reference manual such as *The Gregg Reference Manual* for lists of compound adjectives.

12-11 To determine whether two words act as one thought in modifying a noun, separate the two. Use an example such as *first-class design*. Is it a *first* design? Is it a *class* design? Neither represents the intent in the sentence. It is a *first-class* design.

12-12 Refer to a reference manual such as *The Gregg Reference Manual* for additional examples of numbers with nouns and also exceptions to the general rule.

12-13 When introducing comparisons, use items student can see:

> *tall, taller, tallest* with students in classroom
> *large, larger, largest* with equipment or furniture

12-14 The examples emphasize *more* and *most*. Show how *less* and *least* are used also.

> *less* interesting, *least* interesting
> *less* intensive, *more* intensive
> *less* successful, *more* successful

12-15 Emphasize the inaccuracy of using two comparative forms such as *more heavier* or *more quicker*.

12-16 Demonstrate the inappropriate addition of *er* or *est* to such words as *attractive* or *successful*. You would not use "attractiver" or "successfulest."

12-17 Suggest that students memorize the list of irregular adjectives.

12-18 Demonstrate absolute adjectives with "a full cup" or a "round table" or a "straight line."

12-19 Note that *wrong* does not have the comparative and superlative blanks filled in. *Wrong* is an absolute adjective.

12-20 Check *The Gregg Reference Manual* or another available manual for references to other special adjectives.

12-21 All words in the sentences may be diagrammed.

12-22 For additional practice, have students identify the words being modified by the adjectives.

12-23 The proofreading exercise involves checking a copy with errors against a correct copy. Two additional proofreaders' marks are included in this exercise— *double space* and *insert hyphen*. See Chapter 9 for a suggested grading plan.

12-24 Check online sites carefully before assigning them to students. Be aware that site information and options may change.

12-25 For additional writing practice have students write two or three sentences about one or both of the sites visited.

12-26 For additional practice, have students identify the words being modified by the adjectives.

CHAPTER 13

13-1 The chapter examples and exercises relate to the secondary learning topic for Chapter 13, which is "Ethics and Etiquette." Encourage students to ask questions about the subject matter and to use online or traditional references to locate answers.

13-2 Teaching Suggestions:
- Discuss the *Do This/Do Not Do This* examples. If students have special problems with any of the examples, prepare additional sentences that illustrate the points made.

- Additional teaching suggestions may be found on the Instructor CD-ROM.

13-3 Always encourage students to ask one of the adverb identification questions— *how* (in what manner), *when, where,* and *to what extent* or *degree.*

13-4 Use sentences from the adverb section in Chapter 2 as additional exercises or examples.

13-5 Remind students that *very* modifies *precisely* and *precisely* modifies *outlined.*

13-6 Review predicate adjectives before discussing when to use adjectives and when to use adverbs in sentences.

13-7 At times, adjectives may also follow verbs such as *get, grow, keep, prove, remain,* and *turn.*

> proven *innocent*   turned *warm*
> remain *silent*   get *emotional*

13-8 Remind students that *looked* is a linking verb. *Looked* does not indicate action in this sentence.

13-9 Use Chapter 12 (Adjectives) as a guide for comparisons. Show the similarities and the differences in comparisons between adjectives and adverbs.

13-10 Refer to a reference manual such as *The Gregg Reference Manual* for examples of absolute adverbs that may be modified.

13-11 Remind students that the contraction *can't* is formed from *cannot.*

13-12 Some additional practice sentences that illustrate double negatives follow. Have students correct these sentences as you say them orally. Be sure to point out to the students that the following sentences are grammatically incorrect:

> *No one* at the meeting said *nothing.*
> We *don't* have *no* homework tonight.

13-13 Positioning the word *only* is difficult for some students. Ask students to collect sentences in which the words *only, also, nearly,* or *just* are used. Discuss these sentences in class. Show how these words can change the meaning of a sentence when positioned in different locations.

13-14 Checkup 13-9 includes sentences that may be used to show how meanings change when words such as *only* and *nearly* are placed in different locations.

13-15 Review the definitions of dependent and independent clauses. An adverb clause is one type of dependent clause. A dependent clause cannot stand on its own. Compare adverb and adjective clauses. Adjective clauses begin with such words as *who, that, which,* and *whose.*

13-16 Conjunctive adverbs are discussed in Chapter 15 rather than with the study of adverbs in this chapter. Additional subordinating conjunctions are also discussed in Chapter 15.

13-17 Identify the position for an adverb clause—before an independent clause or after it. Look at the examples. Have students interchange the position of the adverb clause within a sentence. Place the adverb clause before the independent clause and then after the independent clause to give students practice with the placement of the comma. This activity will help students "hear" which placement is best.

13-18 Emphasize the use of *well* (healthy) as an adjective. Also emphasize the use of *well* as an adverb, which answers the question *how.* Students may have trouble with the use of *good* after the linking verb *feel,* so remind them that *good* functions as an adjective when it follows the sense verb *feel.*

13-19 Recommend that students substitute the word *very* for *real* or *really.* If *very* fits, use the adverb *really.*

13-20 Recommend that students substitute the word *certainly* for *sure* or *surely.* If *certainly* fits, use the adverb *surely.*

13-21 All words in the sentences may be diagrammed.

13-22 The proofreading marks are already in this copy. Require students to key the proofreading exercise correctly. Accept handwritten copy only from someone who has no keyboarding skills. Grading plans may vary. The same grading plan as described in Chapter 9 may apply. Additional deductions for keyboarding errors may be made as well. You may wish to give a certain grade or assign a number of points (5 or 10). You may wish to assign 10 points if the document is correctly keyed and 0 points if it has any errors.

13-23 Check online sites carefully before assigning them to students. Be aware that site information and options may change.

13-24 For additional writing practice, have students identify several similarities that appear in the corporate codes of ethics that they were asked to read.

CHAPTER 14

14-1 The chapter examples and exercises relate to the secondary learning topic for Chapter 14, which is "Leadership." Encourage students to ask questions about the subject matter and to use online or traditional references to locate answers.

14-2 Teaching Suggestions:
- Use the paragraphs of the Secondary Learning or Overview for practice in identifying prepositions, prepositional phrases, and objects of prepositions.
- Have students write sentences using prepositions such as *to, among, between, in,* and *into.*
- Additional teaching suggestions may be found on the Instructor CD-ROM.

14-3 Remind students that some prepositions may also function as other parts of speech.
outside the door (preposition)
an *outside* chance (adjective)
go *outside* (adverb)

14-4 In Sentence 5, *directory* is the object of the preposition about. *Entrepreneurs* is the object of the preposition *of.*

14-5 *Compound preposition* is the term used in this text for a phrase such as *in spite of, in regard to, by means of* that contains more than one preposition.

14-6 In Sentence 4, note that the preposition *between* applies to both the words *thought* and *action.*

14-7 Note that the preposition *by* applies to the activities: (nouns) *volunteering, teaching,* and *helping.*

14-8 Emphasize that prepositional phrases do not contain verbs; infinitive phrases do include verbs.

14-9 Refer to Chapter 7 for additional practice sentences that use the objective case of pronouns.

14-10 In this text, the authors prefer that sentences be revised so they do not end with a preposition. However, if the placement of the preposition elsewhere in a short sentence or question is awkward, ending with a preposition is acceptable.

14-11 Refer to *The Gregg Reference Manual* or another reference manual for additional examples of unnecessary prepositions.

14-12 The example answer in Item 6 shows the preferred revision. It is acceptable to end short sentences or questions with a preposition if the revision is awkward.

14-13 Have students write sentences to help them understand the uses of *beside/ besides, among/between, different from, like/as, off/of/from, in/into,* and *to/too/ two.*

14-14 The word usage review exercises in the Instructor CD include the words *beside* and *besides.* Use the sentences for additional practice.

14-15 *Between* is sometimes used in situations with more than two persons or things. See *The Gregg Reference Manual* or another reference manual for other examples.

14-16 The word *different* should be followed by *from* when *from* connects an object to another word or set of words in a sentence. *Different* should be followed by *than* when a clause follows the word *than.*

14-17 The idiomatic phrases selected for this chapter are commonly used phrases and involve only verb and preposition combinations.

14-18 Encourage students to refer to their reference manuals for the correct idiomatic expressions.

14-19 All words in the sentences may be diagrammed.

14-20 In Sentence 3, the preposition *for* applies to both *asking* and *bargaining. For* does not have to be repeated.

14-21 In Sentence 5, the expression *agreed upon* is also acceptable.

14-22 The new proofreaders' mark that is introduced is . . . . Stet, which means *don't delete.*

14-23 The proofreading marks are already in this copy. Refer to the suggestions in Chapter 13 of the Instructor CD-ROM for general use and grading.

14-24 Check if the items in the Suggested Reading List in the proofreading exercise are in your library. Have students use these materials to write paragraphs that identify the characteristics of a good leader, define leadership, suggest ways to develop leadership qualities, or describe individuals who are leaders.

14-25 Check online sites carefully before assigning them to students. Be aware that site information and options may change.

14-26 Harry Truman's middle name is S. Since the "S" is not a middle initial, a period is not required.

14-27 The concept of emotional intelligence is interesting. If you use the Online Exercise, have students write paragraphs indicating reasons for their agreement or disagreement with their emotional intelligence results. After they have written their paragraphs, have students underline prepositional phrases or objects of prepositions. As a review, ask students to identify adjectives or nouns. If they have been diagramming sentences, have them diagram these sentences.

CHAPTER 15

15-1 The chapter examples and exercises relate to the secondary learning topic for Chapter 15, which is "Stress and Coping Strategies." Encourage students to ask questions about the subject matter and to use online or traditional references to locate answers.

15-2 Teaching Suggestions:
- Use the section entitled "Phrases and Clauses" in Chapter 3 to obtain additional practice materials. Be sure to review with students the meanings of a phrase and a clause before teaching conjunctions.
- Additional teaching suggestions may be found on the Instructor CD-ROM.

15-3 Dependent clauses are introduced by relative pronouns (*that, which, who, whom*) and subordinate conjunctions such as *although, when, if, because, where, while, after,* and *since.*

15-4 Remind students that an independent clause is a sentence.

15-5 Remind students that compound sentences can also consist of two independent clauses connected by a semicolon.

15-6 Conjunctive adverbs are sometimes studied with adverbs. In this text, conjunctive adverbs are placed here in the chapter about conjunctions because of their function as a connector. (See page 428.)

15-7 You may find the words *for, so,* and *yet* treated as coordinating conjunctions in some textbooks. Only the conjunctions *but, and, or,* and *nor* are presented as coordinating conjunctions in this chapter.

15-8 If one of the clauses in a compound sentence is very short (4-5 words or less), the comma before the coordinating conjunction may be omitted. Some authorities indicate that it is never wrong to use a comma with a short clause.

15-9 *As . . . as* and *so . . . as* are sometimes listed as correlative conjunctions. See the section entitled "Cautions in Using Conjunctions" (p. 432) for the positive and negative uses of these expressions.

15-10 Review subject and verb agreement with students.

15-11 Remind students to use *not only, but also.* Do not use *not only, but.*

15-12 Subordinating conjunctions were introduced in Chapter 13 in the section on adverb clauses. Remind students to look for a verb in a dependent clause.

15-13 Refer to *The Gregg Reference Manual* or another reference manual for instances when a dependent clause at the end of a sentence is preceded by a comma.

15-14 Have students verbalize the statements in the *Do This/Do Not Do This* examples to hear the correct versions.

15-15 Another term that is often used to describe a conjunctive adverb is *transition word* or *expression.* See *The Gregg Reference Manual* for a list of transitional expressions.

15-16 A comma is used after a conjunctive adverb of two or more syllables when the conjunctive adverb joins two independent clauses. A comma is not necessary after one-syllable conjunctive adverbs such as *then, still, thus, so, yet,* or *hence* that connect two independent clauses. Remind students that a semicolon does not always precede a transitional expression.

15-17 You may use more than one way to correct a sentence that is not parallel; however, the connections must involve the same parts of speech.

15-18 The distinction between *as . . . as* and *so . . . as* is not so important as it was in the past.

15-19 All words may be diagrammed.

15-20 The proofreaders' mark for *align text vertically* is introduced in this chapter.

15-21 The proofreaders' marks are already in this copy. Refer to the suggestions for general use and grading in Chapter 13 in the Instructor CD-ROM.

15-22 Check online sites carefully before assigning them to students. Be aware that site information and options may change.

15-23 Sentences 6, 7, and 8 in the *Looking Ahead* and *Looking Back* exercises include sentences that are not written correctly. (Only one of the answers in each group is correct.) Have students identify the errors in the remaining sentences, or use the remaining sentences as review exercises.

CHAPTER 16

16-1 The chapter examples and exercises relate to the secondary learning topic for Chapter 16, which is "Job Search and Career Development." Encourage students to ask questions about the subject matter and to use online or traditional references to locate answers.

16-2 Teaching Suggestions:
- Use sentences from other textbooks, and have students identify the types of commas used. Use the extra exercises on the Instructor's CD-ROM for additional practice or quizzes. If the students have the CD-ROM that accompanies this textbook, assign various exercises for practicing the skills needed.
- Additional teaching suggestions may be found on the Instructor CD-ROM.

16-3 The declarative sentence is also referred to as an *indicative sentence.*

16-4 Another way to help students to remember to place a period after a courteous request is to have them identify the sentence as one requiring *action.* Sentences that require an *answer* are direct questions and end with a question mark.

16-5 Decimal points and ciphers are not necessary in even amounts of money. However, in tabulations, the decimal points and ciphers are necessary.

16-6 The presence of the zero makes the decimal point more visible and allows the reader to see the decimal point more clearly.

16-7 Avoid using abbreviations in most written documents. However, on business forms, abbreviations are often used. If used, abbreviations should be written accurately.

16-8 Remind students that abbreviations for both singular and plural forms of measurements are the same.

16-9 *The Gregg Reference Manual* includes many examples of the use of periods with abbreviations. Students need to become familiar with many of these abbreviations in order to understand current material.

16-10 In the name Harry S Truman, no period is needed after *S* because *S* is his complete middle name.

16-11 Remind students that it is incorrect to use both a title and a professional designation to identify a person. For example, do not use *Dr. Helen Wind, M.D.*

16-12 Remind students that commas are not necessary to separate a seniority designation from a name unless the person wants commas used.

16-13 Shortened words such as *demo, reps,* or *info* may appear in informal documents; however, these words should not be used in correspondence with clients, customers, or other professionals.

16-14 Refer to a reference manual such as *The Gregg Reference Manual* for examples of foreign expressions.

16-15 If this text is also used as the text for a punctuation class, be certain to review the question mark and exclamation point in Chapter 3.

16-16 Some English books and reference manuals present *for, yet,* and *so* as coordinating conjunctions. This textbook indicates four coordinating conjunctions (*and, or, nor, but*).

16-17 In this text, the arbitrary cutoff for a short sentence is four words. According to some authorities, it is not wrong to use a comma when either or both clauses are short. In the exercises in this textbook, commas are not necessary and answers will reflect this. Emphasize the importance of being consistent.

16-18 Students frequently ignore the word *that* when they are identifying dependent clauses. Remind students that dependent clauses cannot stand alone. Also remind students that they should not use a comma before a coordinating conjunction that joins two dependent clauses.

16-19 Use samples of company letterhead or the telephone directory to determine if there is a trend in your area for using or omitting a series comma in a company name.

16-20 Remind students that to use both *etc.* and *such as* in the same sentence is redundant. See the example in the *Do This/Do Not Do This* feature.

16-21 Independent adjectives are also called *coordinate adjectives.* Remind students that both revisions (interchanging adjectives and placing the word *and* between the adjectives) must be satisfactory before a comma is necessary.

16-22 See Question 4. If Dan is the *only* brother you have, use commas to set *Dan* aside. For the answer to Question 4, it was assumed that you have other brothers.

16-23 Remind students that parenthetical expressions may appear at different points in a sentence. Parenthetical expressions may also be considered interrupting expressions.

16-24 In this text, a comma is used after all introductory expressions.

16-25 Refer to *The Gregg Reference Manual* for examples of essential and nonessential phrases that introduce dependent clauses.

16-26 Review prepositional phrases in Chapter 14 and infinitive and participial phrases in Chapter 10.

16-27 In this text no commas are placed in numbers such as 2790.

16-28 Remind students that commas are not necessary in dates with months and years only. Commas are not necessary before and after the word *Inc.* or before and after seniority designations unless the company or person prefers a comma. Some authoritative sources may indicate that the commas are optional, or some may even require commas with the above-listed items.

16-29 All words may be diagrammed. Always begin diagramming with the simple subject, simple predicate, and object.

16-30 For additional practice, have students give explanations and/or make corrections.

16-31 The reasons for the "No" answers are as follows:

   3. The sentence has no period at the end.

   4. The nonrestrictive phrase *which some say are unfair* needs to be set aside by commas.

   7. A comma is necessary after the word *asked* to introduce the quote.

   8. *Knowledge* and *skills* make up the compound subject. The compound subject is joined by the coordinating conjunction *and.* Do not place a comma before the coordinating conjunction that joins the subjects of the sentence.

   9. A comma is necessary before the tag question *don't you.* A question mark only—not a period and a question mark—follow the question.

  10. *Inc.* does not need to be set aside by commas. However, if it is the preference of the firm to use commas, the commas should be placed before *and* after *Inc.* The date needs to have a comma after the day.

16-32 Expand Practices 1A and 2A and End-of-Chapter Worksheets Practices 1B and 2B by having students state the reason for using commas in each of the items. Use the extra exercises on the Instructor and Student CD-ROMs.

16-33 The proofreading exercise involves editing. Students will put in their own proofreaders' marks. If time permits, students should key the documents in an appropriate format. There are 15 errors in the proofreading exercise. Grading may, therefore, be consistent with proofreading sections in previous chapters.

16-34 Check online sites carefully before assigning them to students. Be aware that site information and options may change.

16-35 The reasons for the "No" answers are as follows:

   2. The sentence, which is an indirect question, should end with a period, not a question mark.

   4. There are no periods in CEO.

   7. A comma is necessary after the introductory phrase *to sell yourself.*

   8. A comma is necessary after the introductory phrase *if you prepare for an interview.*

CHAPTER 17

17-1 The chapter examples and exercises relate to the secondary learning topic for Chapter 17, which is "Business Communication." Encourage students to ask questions about the subject matter and to use online or traditional references to locate answers.

17-2 Teaching Suggestions:

- Recommend that students use colored pencils, markers, or pens (fine points are important) to insert punctuation marks.

- Have students write sentences using selected marks of punctuation. These sentences may also involve words in the spelling and word usage sections in the appendix and on the CD. For example, assign a sentence using a semicolon or one using a colon and the word *last* or *latest.* Assign a sentence using a colon with the topic of *listening.*

- Additional teaching suggestions may be found on the Instructor CD-ROM.

17-3 *The Gregg Reference Manual* is the basic source for the rules for using the other punctuation marks covered in this chapter.

17-4 Remind students that if they are not sure about using a semicolon between independent clauses, they can write each clause as a separate sentence.

17-5 The term *transitional expression* rather than *conjunctive adverb* is used in some reference manuals. The semicolon links two clauses. One of these clauses may have a conjunctive adverb in it.

Conjunctive adverbs do not have to be the first word in a clause. Conjunctive adverbs do not automatically require a semicolon before them. For example,

The speaker, however, arrived late.

17-6 Additional examples of conjunctive adverbs appear in Chapter 15.

17-7 Distinguish between essential information and nonessential information following an introductory clause. If the information is essential, use a colon; if the information is not essential, use a semicolon.

17-8 Refer to *The Gregg Reference Manual* or another reference manual for rules concerning capitalization after colons.

17-9 Discuss the placement of lists and introductory statements that can or cannot stand on their own.

17-10 Some authoritative sources use the semicolon for lists such as those presented in the examples. In this text, a colon precedes essential information or explanations. A semicolon precedes nonessential information or explanations.

17-11 Periods and commas are *always* placed inside quotation marks. Semicolons and colons are *always* placed outside quotation marks.

17-12 Words introduced by expressions such as *the term* or *the word* may be set aside with quotes; however, most of these words are now placed in italics instead. When words are defined, the word is often italicized, and the definition is placed in quotes.

17-13 Explain the placement of question marks with quotation marks. Have students identify the question. Then ask these questions: Is the question a part of the quote only? (If yes, the question mark goes inside the quotes). Does the question apply to the entire sentence? (If yes, the question mark goes outside the quotes).

17-14 Possessive forms always present problems for some students. Students often have problems forming the plural possessives of the words *men, women,* and *children.* Remind the students that the possessive form for all of these words is formed by adding an *apostrophe* and *s* (*'s*).

> man, woman, child
> man's, woman's, child's
> men, women, children
> men's, women's, children's

17-15 Compound numbers are most frequently found at the beginning of a sentence or in a legal or formal business document.

17-16 In this text, a hyphen is inserted in a written fraction used as a noun or as an adjective.

17-17 Refer to Chapter 12 for additional examples of compound adjectives. Since word usage changes, stress the importance of using a current dictionary to check whether a compound adjective should or should not be hyphenated.

17-18 The syllable breaks in words shown in a dictionary are not always acceptable in business documents. Try to keep the word division rules to a minimum.

17-19 Instruct the students that they should not substitute dashes for other marks of punctuation too frequently in business writing.

17-20 These reminders may help students:
- If a sentence precedes a list, use a colon after the sentence.
- If a list precedes the sentence, use a dash after the list.

17-21 Dashes may set aside essential and nonessential material. Parentheses set aside only nonessential material. In some exercises, your personal interpretation of the material may suggest an interchange of the two punctuation marks.

17-22 Have students use underlining to indicate material that should be set in italics.

17-23 Review the difference between complete published works (books, newspapers, movies, and so on) and materials within such works (articles, chapters, sections, and so on).

17-24 All words may be diagrammed. Always begin by diagramming the simple subject, simple predicate, and object. Then locate the prepositional phrases since these are usually easy for students to identify. Proceed with simple adjectives. Continue breaking the sentence into its parts.

17-25 Encourage students to use dictionaries (especially for compound adjectives) and their text material. In this exercise, it would be helpful for students to identify the specific rule that is applied. See the teaching suggestions at the beginning of this chapter.

17-26 Sentences 5 and 7 may be punctuated with a semicolon or with a dash.

17-27 In Sentence 8, the question mark goes inside the quotation mark. Only the quoted material is a question.

17-28 In Sentence 9, the word *vice president* is written without a hyphen. Some dictionaries may use a hyphen in *vice president.*

17-29 In Sentence 10, the semicolon is placed outside the single quote.

17-30 The proofreading exercisc involves editing. Students must put in their own proofreading marks. If time permits, have students key the document in an appropriate format. Grading remains consistent with the proofreading exercises in other chapters.

CHAPTER 18

18-1 The chapter examples and exercises relate to the secondary learning topic for Chapter 18, which is "Doing Business on the Internet." Encourage students to ask questions about the subject matter and to use online or traditional references to locate answers.

18-2 Teaching Suggestions:
- Remind students that consistency in writing numbers is important. Using an up-to-date reference manual such as *The Gregg Reference Manual* will aid students in following a consistent pattern.
- Use current financial reports to show the importance of alignment of figures and the placement of dollar signs.
- Additional teaching suggestions may be found on the Instructor CD-ROM.

18-3 Refer to *Looking Ahead*, Question 4. Some reference manuals may show that *August, 1998* is acceptable. In this text, the comma between a month and year is omitted.

18-4 Use examples to show the meaning of related and unrelated numbers: *5* pages out of *50* (related numbers); *12* Websites in *three* days (unrelated numbers).

18-5 In this text, the comma is omitted in four-digit numbers such as *1029* and *2115.* The exercises will reflect this practice.

18-6 Explain the use of ZIP Codes, including the 9-digit codes. Stress accuracy in using correct addresses on all correspondence.

18-7 Demonstrate ways that students can rephrase sentences that begin with numbers of more than two words. Remind students that hyphenated words, such as *twenty-eight,* count as one word.

18-8 Use examples of invitations that you or your students may have received to such functions as weddings or graduations to demonstrate the formal use of dates.

18-9 Sentence 4 may also be written as *In the nineties, many companies restructured to control their production costs.*

18-10 Remind students that numbers to the right of the decimal point should not have commas. Emphasize the importance of the zero before the decimal point when the decimal stands alone. The zero makes it easier to recognize the number as a decimal.

18-11 Use the financial page of a newspaper to explain how to read financial quotations. The sentences will be more meaningful to the student.

18-12 Some reference manuals state that fractions used as adjectives should be hyphenated and that fractions used as nouns should not be hyphenated. In this text, hyphens appear in fractions used as both adjectives and nouns.

18-13 Refer to the sections of *The Gregg Reference Manual* entitled "No. or # With Figures" and "Nouns With Numbers or Letters" for a list of items that do *not* require the word *No.* for clarity. These may vary in other reference manuals.

18-14 Indicate that indefinite numbers are less specific than approximate numbers. Approximate numbers are nearly exact; for example, *about 100, less than ten,* and *more than 15.* Indefinite numbers are general in nature and are not easily counted; for example, *millions of account numbers* and *hundreds of entries.*

18-15 Review the formats in which measurements appear: 7 by 9 inches, 7 × 9 inches, and 7" × 9". When measurements are used as adjectives, a hyphen is necessary.

18-16 A list of roman numerals is available in most reference manuals. Have students practice writing some of the roman numerals. Note that *roman* is lowercase. Some reference manuals and dictionaries may capitalize *roman.*

18-17 Recommend that students avoid shortening inclusive numbers unless they are used frequently in some types of documents. The clarity of the sentence is improved when all figures are written in full.

18-18 Note the three accepted ways to write telephone numbers. All forms are acceptable in the exercises; however, it is usually simpler to identify one form for class use.

18-19 Point out the redundant nature of the expressions *9 a.m. in the morning* or *2 p.m. in the afternoon.*

18-20 Remind students that a hyphenated word counts as one word.

18-21 Point out that time periods used as specific business references are written in figures (even with the numbers 1–10) rather than words. Some examples include:

40-hour week	*6 percent* discount
30-year mortgage	*2/10, n30*
9-month note	*3-year* loan

18-22 All words may be diagrammed. This diagramming exercise is a review of material covered in previous chapters.

18-23 Expand Practice Exercises 1A and 2A and End-of-Chapter Worksheets Practices 1B and 2B by having students list the rule number or reason for the number usage in each item in the exercise.

18-24 Remind students that four-digit numbers do not require commas ($3000).

18-25 The proofreading exercise requires students to use proofreaders' marks to indicate errors in the copy. If time permits, have students key the document in appropriate format. There are 15 errors in the proofreading exercise. Grading remains consistent with the proofreading exercises in other chapters.

18-26 Check online sites carefully before assigning them to students. Be aware that site information and options may change.

18-27 Remind students that the item asks for general use. This requires all numbers to be present (pages 121-134).

18-28 Note other acceptable formats for telephone numbers.

800-555-3784
800/555-3784

In the phone number (800) 555-3784, a space is needed after the parentheses.

To use the various ancillaries and components provided with *Business English at Work,* the following information will be helpful:

Using the Instructor CD-ROM:

To open and save document files (such as Word or PowerPoint) from the Instructor CD-ROM, you may use one of two options:

1.   Open the file from the CD-ROM, select the Save As option, and save the file to your hard drive.

2.   Using Windows Explorer (Windows 95/98), copy one or more files from the CD-ROM to a folder on your hard drive. Select (highlight) the files you just copied. Pull down the File menu, select Properties, and turn off the Read-only attribute.

To access ExamView:

Installation and Startup Instructions are provided on the Instructor CD-ROM. The ExamView Test Generator is located in a special section on the CD-ROM. You may decide to print the Installation and Startup Instructions before you access ExamView.

Using the Student CD-ROM:

Complete Getting Started Instructions are provided on the Instructor CD-ROM to enable you to access the grammar skills exercises on the Student CD-ROM. Additional grammar and spelling exercises are located on the Student CD-ROM. To access these:

1.   Using Windows Explorer (Windows 95/98), click on BENGLISH

2.   Click Template. The contents of Template will allow you to select the specific chapter you wish by clicking on that chapter from the list.

These additional exercises are also located on the Instructor CD-ROM with and without the answers for you to use for practice or quizzes.

Using the Transparencies (Acetates):

A color transparency (acetate) package is available separately to correlate with *Business English at Work* chapters. You may choose to use the transparencies or the PowerPoints, which are included on the Instructor CD-ROM.

Business English
At Work

Susan Jaderstrom
Santa Rosa Junior College
Petaluma, California

Joanne M. Miller

Glencoe
McGraw-Hill

New York, New York   Columbus, Ohio   Woodland Hills, California   Peoria, Illinois

PHOTO CREDITS Cover Ned Shaw/Stock Illustration Source; 1 Gary Kaemmer/Image Bank; 2 Graham French/Masterfile; 28 Lester Lefkowitz/Stock Market; 52 Tom Tracy/The Photo File; 85 SuperStock; 86 Pamela Hamilton/Image Bank; 112 Keith Ballinger/Masterfile; 138 Matthais Kulka/Stock Market; 176 Dennis Novak/Image Bank; 208 Miao Wang/Image Bank; 239 Elle Schuster/Image Bank; 240 Felix Clouzot/Image Bank; 266 Tecmap/Westlight; 300 John Hartman/Stock Connection; 327 Peter Holst/Image Bank; 328 Nick Merrick/Hedrich Blessing, Ltd.; 360 SuperStock; 390 Chase Swift/Westlight; 418 Jeff Schultz/Alaska Stock; 447 Dennis O'Clair/Tony Stone Images; 448 Frozen Images, Inc.; 482 IFA/Leo De Wys Inc.; 518 John Lund/The Photo File.

Library of Congress Cataloging-in-Publication Data

Jaderstrom, Susan.
    Business English at work / Susan Jaderstrom, Joanne M. Miller.
        p. cm.
    Includes index.
    ISBN 0-02-802538-5
    1. English language--Business English--Problems, exercises, etc.
I. Miller, Joanne.   II. Title.
PE1115.J27   1999
808'.06665--dc21   98-23673
                                                            CIP

Glencoe/McGraw-Hill

A Division of The McGraw·Hill Companies

Business English at Work

Send all inquiries to:

Glencoe/McGraw-Hill
936 Eastwind Drive
Westerville, OH 43081

ISBN 0-02-802538-5

1 2 3 4 5 6 7 8 9 027 05 04 03 02 01 00 99 98

TABLE OF CONTENTS

Dear *Business English at Work* Student

Today's marketplace demands that workers have excellent skills in English. The development of these skills—grammar, spelling, punctuation, word choice, and sentence writing/revising to name a few—will be the major focus of this textbook. Many employers actually measure the competence of job applicants in many of these skills before making offers of employment. You are beginning a course of study with a textbook that has been designed just for you with these necessary competencies in mind.

When you successfully complete *Business English at Work,* you will have an advantage when you apply for a position or a promotion in the workplace. Why, you ask, will that be so?

This textbook was developed not only to present basic English concepts but also to tie these concepts to skills used in customer service, telecommunications, time management, electronic mail, leadership, ergonomics, coping strategies, and online research. You will have the opportunity to complete Internet exercises and to access the Glencoe/McGraw-Hill special site for *Business English at Work* on the World Wide Web. With the real-world applications in this textbook and the optional CD-ROM for more practice on your English skills, you will have a competitive edge!

Best wishes as you continue your studies and prepare for life in a fast-paced, demanding business environment. You can be sure that *Business English at Work* will go with you as you head into the future.

We welcome the opportunity to be an important part of your preparation for the world of work.

Sincerely

E. Addison Ellis III
E. Addison "Buzz" Ellis, III
President, Glencoe/McGraw-Hill

PREFACE

Welcome to the *Business English at Work* text and to an exciting journey through the world of English grammar, spelling, and punctuation. Working with these concepts, you will be mesmerized with the activities and the exercises that relate to the secondary learning topics—a totally new learning approach relating business English to the world of work.

Business English at Work is designed to help you meet the challenges of a changing world, one in which the correct usage of English is tantamount to getting and holding a job.

STUDENT TEXT FEATURES

Business English at Work uses a variety of text and margin features to present concepts of interest and importance to your study of business English.

Text features in the student edition include:

A two-page chapter opener presents the **Secondary Learning Concepts** around which the examples and applications of the chapter are written. Topics such as references, telecommunications, customer service, the World Wide Web, time management, electronic mail, cultural diversity, ergonomics, ethics, job skills, and coping strategies will relate the activities and exercises to the particular grammar, spelling, or punctuation concept being discussed.

Terms to Remember provide you an opportunity to add new vocabulary words with their definitions (which are found in the Glossary) to your growing language base. The Terms to Remember are related specifically to the Secondary Learning Concepts presented in each chapter.

The **Learning Objectives** provide goals for you to structure your learning activities and exercises toward, so that you know ahead of time on what you will be evaluated.

The **Looking Ahead Pretest** exercise gives you the chance to test yourself and see how much you already know. You can then plan to spend more time on the concepts that you don't know.

Concepts and rules are presented individually in the chapters so that you can focus on them selectively, then see the concepts and rules applied in numerous examples.

LOOKING BACK

Posttest

The **Looking Back Posttest** exercise helps you decide whether you have acquired the concepts and rules that you studied in the chapter material.

The **Checkups** are a major feature of this text, being provided immediately after various concepts are covered, just when you need the reinforcement.

The **Do This/Do Not Do This** feature illustrates a related grammar or punctuation rule.

The **Practice Exercises and Worksheets** at the end of each chapter provide ample opportunities for you to increase your skills in the concepts and rules of grammar, proofreading, writing, and punctuation that were presented in the chapter.

Diagramming Exercises are provided to give you a graphical hook for remembering how the parts of speech are used and how they relate to each other.

The **Online Activities** presented in each chapter will direct you to the Internet for some interesting tours of various Websites. You may

ONLINE EXERCISES

want to follow any online activity with a trip to the Glencoe/McGraw-Hill Website for *Business English at Work* by using the following address to access this special site for students:

http://www.bew.glencoe.com

The **Appendix** contains a **Glossary** of the Terms to Remember with pertinent definitions and usage. The Appendix also contains the **Spelling Rules** and special **Word Usage** material. In addition, a thorough **Index** is provided to help locate concepts and rules that you may want to review from time to time.

Margin features in the student edition include:

Tie in to
Reference Manual

* **Tie in to Reference Manual**—A special icon directs you to *The Gregg Reference Manual* for additional examples related to your text.

* **Notes**—Special reminders to enhance your learning are provided in appropriate places.

* **Punctuation and Capitalization Alerts**—Special icons and inserts give you specific and related information that will help you punctuate and use capitalization elements correctly. These reminders stand out from the copy for your quick and ready reference when you need them, not later after the concept has already been discussed.

Punctuation ALERT!

Capitalization ALERT!

GO TO CD-ROM
CHECKUP 1-1

- **Go To CD-ROM Checkups**—These special icons direct you quickly to additional practice exercises. The CD-ROM is an optional (but highly recommended) component that provides optimum instruction based on the concepts and rules contained in your text.

- **Slip-Ups**—Another special icon will highlight an actual instance of the misuse of business English. While these may bring a smile to your lips or even a laugh, keep in mind that this course is designed to help you avoid such "slip-ups" in your communication.

COMPONENTS OF THE PROGRAM

This first edition of *Business English at Work* is a complete, well-rounded program that includes the following components:

- **Text-Workbook** with ample examples, exercises, practices, and worksheets to establish a usable foundation in grammar, proof-reading, writing, and punctuation. The activities and exercises throughout each chapter are directly related to the Secondary Learning Concepts.

- **CD-ROM** with additional exercises and practices that relate to the concepts and rules presented in the text. Exercises that relate directly to the Checkups in the text are provided for extra practice or self-tests. Most of these exercises are interactive, giving you the opportunity to respond and be evaluated. Each chapter has exercises correlated with the textbook chapter Checkups. Other practice exercises are provided for additional reinforcement. As you complete each exercise, you may choose to print your exercise results. The CD-ROM is an optional (but highly recommended) component of the *Business English at Work* program.

WEBSITE

A separate section of the Website is reserved for you. This section contains online practice tests, crossword puzzles, additional learning exercises, and other World Wide Web links to stimulate your research efforts. Access to this Website is gained by entering the following URL address at your Internet browser location:

http://www.bew.glencoe.com

We have enjoyed developing this exciting program for you. Good luck in your studies using *Business English at Work*. Please feel free to contact us at our e-mail addresses:

Susan Jaderstrom   susan_jaderstrom@msn.com
Joanne Miller   jmiller34@juno.com

ACKNOWLEDGMENTS

The following educators have contributed significantly to the development of this text by their reviews and valuable comments. We thank them for their input.

Debbie Brockett
Arkansas Valley Technical Institute
Ozark, Arkansas

Janet Caruso
Briarcliffe College
Bethpage, New York

Gloria Cockerell
Collin County College
Plano, Texas

Phyllis J. Donovan
Bryant & Stratton Business Institute
Buffalo, New York

Carolyn K. Hayes
Brevard Community College
Cocoa, Florida

Arlene Iftiger
Victor Valley College
Victorville, California

Eleonore Ingram
Topeka Technical College
Topeka, Kansas

Elizabeth D. Kerbey
San Jacinto College Central
Pasadena, Texas

Joanne M. Landry
Massasoit Community College
Brockton, Massachusetts

William Mark Lewis
Western Business College
Portland, Oregon

Barbara J. Loudon
Lansing Community College
Lansing, Michigan

Carol G. Martin
Chattanooga State Technical
  Community College
Chattanooga, Tennessee

Diane Penn-Mickey
Northern Virginia Community College
Woodbridge, Virginia

Dean C. Rehm
Skadron College
San Bernardino, California

Carolyn Roberts
San Jacinto College
Houston, Texas

Mary Rowe
Miami-Dade Community College
Miami, Florida

Tani Theel Stempson
Southeast Community College
Lincoln, Nebraska

J. M. Vulgan
ECPI Technical College
Roanoke, Virginia

William H. Wray
ECPI Technical College
Roanoke, Virginia

Acknowledgements

CHAPTER 1

Resources to Improve Vocabulary, Proofreading, and Spelling

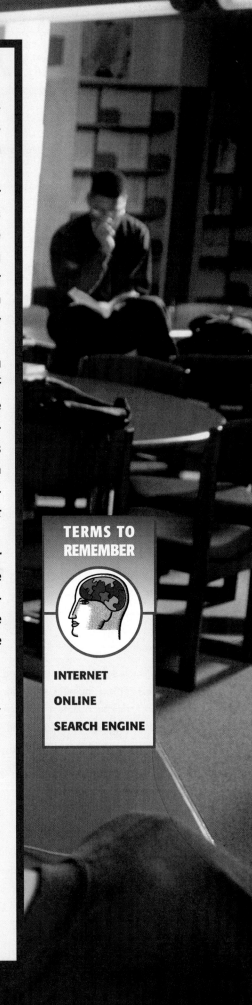

REFERENCES ONLINE

Rarely does an effective writer compose without using reference resources. These resources include books, such as a dictionary or a reference manual, and electronic resources, such as a computer spell checker or the Internet.

The Internet has become an indispensable resource for many writers. The Internet links the writer to common resources such as dictionaries as well as thousands of diverse and obscure references throughout the world. A major advantage of using the Internet is being able to immediately look up a reference at any time of the day or night without leaving the computer. In addition, some of the references available on the Internet may not be found in the typical library or bookstore.

If you know the location of an Internet resource site, you can go directly to that site. However, if you are uncertain of the location of a resource, you can find references on the Internet by using a search engine. A search engine is a service that helps organize various Internet sites into categories such as business, reference, or recreation. An Internet search engine, for example, can access specialized online dictionaries to help you define foreign or technical words that may not be listed in your desk-side dictionary.

Many writers use the Internet to search for quotations or to look up biographies of famous people. Some people use online references to plan trips, make hotel and airline reservations, locate maps, and to read the weather forecast. The broader your understanding of reference materials, the more likely you will find these tools to be indispensable to you.

TERMS TO REMEMBER

INTERNET

ONLINE

SEARCH ENGINE

OBJECTIVES

After you have studied this chapter and completed the exercises, you will be able to do the following:

1. Use a dictionary to answer questions about spelling, syllabication, pronunciation, parts of speech, and definitions.
2. Use an office reference manual and a word division manual.
3. Select appropriate synonyms for words or ideas.
4. Apply proofreading procedures in comparing documents.
5. Use proofreaders' marks to identify changes in the text.
6. Identify ways to improve your spelling and use of words that you commonly confuse or misuse.

LOOKING AHEAD

Pretest

Directions: *In the space provided, write the letter of the correct answer.*

1. What two parts of speech does the word *terminal* represent?
   a. adjective and verb
   b. noun and verb
   c. noun and adjective
   d. noun and adverb

   1. _____c_____

2. What is the meaning of the word *font*?
   a. an Internet connection
   b. Web-site advertising jargon
   c. keyboard character
   d. typeface size and style

   2. _____d_____

3. To what does the abbreviation *CD-ROM* refer?
   a. a person
   b. a thing
   c. a place
   d. none of the above

   3. _____b_____

4. Which of the following items are *not* found in an office reference manual?
   a. punctuation and number writing rules
   b. e-mail message illustrations
   c. word histories
   d. abbreviations

   4. _____c_____

5. What does the proofreaders' mark ⌀ mean?
   a. change the copy
   b. add a number
   c. delete copy
   d. add a space

   5. _____c_____

6. Which set of words is spelled correctly?
   a. delete, bulletin, retreival, cursor, access
   b. delete, bulleten, retreival, curser, access
   c. delete, bulletin, retrieval, cursor, access

   6. _____c_____

7. Which word in parentheses is correct?
   My peers are *(already, all ready)* using online resources for their
   English research papers.
   a. already
   b. all ready

   7. _____a_____

8. Which word is the best substitute for the underlined word in the following sentence?
   Amber followed the <u>sequence</u> of directions as she installed her new electronic
   reference software.
   a. arrangement   c. method
   b. order   d. design

   8. _____b_____

O V E R V I E W

Everyone appreciates error-free, well-written communications. Aren't you impressed when you can immediately understand a set of instructions? Don't you appreciate receiving mail with your name and address spelled correctly? A company's status as well as the writer's increases when documents appear without errors. To produce such error-free documents, an experienced writer never guesses about a writing detail but uses writing aids such as a current dictionary, a thesaurus, and a reference manual. An experienced writer knows the importance of careful proofreading.

In this chapter, you will explore various reference sources and practice suggested proofreading techniques. You will find that maintaining a "troublesome word list" in which you list difficult spelling words, sound-alike words, and new vocabulary words is helpful. These actions will get you started and help you develop business English confidence so that you, too, can produce impeccable documents.

TYPES OF REFERENCES

To help you develop as a writer, you will want to keep your reference materials where you can access them quickly and easily. Be certain to check the publication dates because information changes quickly, and outdated references become limited in value. Helpful references for studying business English include the dictionary, the thesaurus, and an office reference manual. Computerized reference versions are available on CD-ROMs, the Internet, or as functions of application software.

See Instructor's Notes 1-1 and 1-2 in IAE.

Go to Transparency/PowerPoint 1-1a, 1-1b, and 1-2.

Dictionaries

Dictionaries are the most frequently used references for accurate information. They are regularly revised by highly trained specialists who research and monitor the changes in the English language. Dictionaries vary in size and volume. Pocket dictionaries are easy to carry, but they lack detail. Unabridged dictionaries cover volumes of word entries and information, but they are cumbersome to use because of their size and weight. College-edition (desk) dictionaries with copyright dates of five years or less are satisfactory for most students. The title of several college-edition dictionaries include these:

Random House Webster's College Dictionary

The American Heritage Dictionary

Webster's New World College Dictionary

Specialized dictionaries for such fields as medicine, law, and engineering are helpful to the people working in those areas.

1-3 Collect references to display.

1-4 Take students to a media reference area. Demonstrate electronic references. Ask students to review three references or three dictionaries.

Go to
Transparency/PowerPoint 1-3a
and 1-3b.

1-5 Dictionary information is taken from *Random House Webster's Unabridged College Dictionary*. Dictionaries vary in the presentation of entries.

1-6 The dictionary entry shown in Figure 1 is only one dictionary example.

Figure 1 Sample dictionary entry.

From RANDOM HOUSE WEBSTER'S UNABRIDGED DICTIONARY by Copyright © 1997, 1996, 1993, 1987 by Random House, Inc. Reprinted by permission of Random House, Inc.

1-7 Syllabication differs among dictionaries and between dictionaries and reference manuals.

Punctuation
ALERT!

Use a hyphen to separate syllables when a word must continue on the next document line.

Even if you have been using a dictionary for years, you may have neglected to take advantage of all the information that a word entry offers. In addition to the usual spelling, definitions, pronunciation, and syllabication, a dictionary may include information such as parts of speech functions, word usage notes, irregular grammatical forms, word origins, synonyms, and antonyms.

To locate a word in the dictionary, check the word's spelling letter by letter. Use the two guide words at the top of each dictionary page to save searching time. The guide words represent the first and last words on the page. Each entry, which appears in bold type, is listed in alphabetic order between the two guide words.

To understand your dictionary's markings and abbreviations, review the introductory pages before the alphabetic entries. You will also want to check the way your dictionary presents information. Figure 1 illustrates the way one dictionary presents a word entry. The numbered items correlate with the text descriptions.

① ② ④ ③ ⑤

doc•u•ment (*n.* dok' yə mənt ; *v.* dok' yə ment'), *n.* **1.** a written or printed paper furnishing information or evidence, as a passport, deed, bill of sale, or bill of lading; a legal or official paper. **2.** any written item, as a book, article, or letter, esp. of a factual or informative nature. **3.** *Archaic.* evidence; proof. --*v.t.* **4.** to furnish with documents. **5.** to furnish with references, citations, etc., in support of statements made: *a carefully documented biography.* **6.** to support by documentary evidence: *to document a case.* **7.** *Naut.* to provide (a vessel) with a certificate giving particulars concerning nationality, ownership, tonnage, dimensions, etc. **8.** *Obs.* to instruct. [1400-50; late ME (<AF)<L *documentum* example (as precedent, warning, etc.), equiv. to *doc-* (s. of *docēre* to teach) + *u-* (var. or -i-i-before labials) + *-mentum -MENT*] -- doc•u•ment•a•ble (dok' y ment t b l, dok' y men' -), *adj.* - doc'u•'ment' er, n. --*Syn.* **6.** corroborate, verify, substantiate, validate.

⑥ ⑧ ⑦

Spelling.   Pronounce each of the word's syllables and sounds. See Reference 1 in Figure 1. If an entry has more than one correct spelling, the preferred spelling is listed first in many dictionaries.

Syllabication.   A boldfaced dot separates an entry into its parts or syllables. See Reference 2 in Figure 1. If an entry already has a hyphen, that hyphen replaces the boldfaced dot; the dot continues to separate the remaining syllables.

    self-ex • plan • a • to • ry　　　**ed • i • tor-in-chief**

If no dot or hyphen appears *between* words, assume they are two separate words.

    busi • ness card　　　**guide words**

Pronunciation.   The pronunciation appears in parentheses after the word entry. Use the explanatory notes for pronouncing words.

These explanatory notes are found in the introductory pages or at the bottom of every other dictionary page. See Reference 3 in Figure 1.

Stress (Accent) Marks.   A bold (primary) accent mark indicates that a syllable receives the greatest stress in pronunciation. The lighter (secondary) stress mark indicates less stress. See Reference 4 in Figure 1. These accent marks help you to pronounce unfamiliar words.

Parts of Speech.   Abbreviations for the parts of speech are in italics and appear after the pronunciation guide. If a word represents more than one part of speech, the correct label appears before *each* definition. Common abbreviation labels include the following:

adj.	=	adjective	*prep.*	=	preposition
adv.	=	adverb	*pron.*	=	pronoun
conj.	=	conjunction	*v.*	=	verb
interj.	=	interjection	*v.i.*	=	verb intransitive
n.	=	noun	*v.t.*	=	verb transitive

Your dictionary may also designate plural (*pl.*) and singular (*sing.*), definite articles (*def.art.*) and indefinite articles (*indef.art.*), and prefixes (*pref.*) and suffixes (*suff.*). You will find these parts of speech labels helpful in determining correct word usage. See Reference 5 in Figure 1.

Definitions.   Many word entries have more than one meaning, and the definitions may be different parts of speech. Definitions appear in consecutive order with the most common part of speech listed first. Within each part of speech section, the most frequently used definition is usually listed first. See Reference 6 in Figure 1.

1-8 Recommend that students maintain an ongoing troublesome word list.

Word History (Etymologies).   The symbol < designates the source of a word. The symbol means "from" and shows that a word comes from another language or another word. This information often appears in brackets [<] at the end of the definition. See Reference 7 in Figure 1.

Status Labels.   Several labels describe words that are no longer or never were standard English. The introductory pages of your dictionary include such descriptions. See Reference 8 in Figure 1. Some commonly used status labels include:

If you see an unfamiliar word in the examples or the text, use your dictionary to check the definition. Place the word on your troublesome word list. Maintain your list on cards, in a notebook, on disk, or by using some other efficient method.

obsolete (obs) [No longer in general use.]

colloquial dialect (coll dial) [Characteristic of ordinary or familiar conversation or writing rather than formal speech or writing; used by speakers in a specific geographic or social setting.]

informal (inf) [Not likely to occur in formal, prepared speech or carefully edited writing except when used intentionally to convey a casual tone.]

slang [Very informal usage; used in formal speech and writing only for special effect.]

archaic [Commonly used in an earlier time but rarely used today.]

nonstandard [Not conforming to the speech or grammar of educated persons; often regarded as a mark of low social status.]

Dictionary information may vary in other dictionaries or reference manuals. Further, all dictionary information does not apply to every entry. For example, the following dictionary information does not apply to the entry *document* in Figure 1. Another entry, however, may include one or more of these designations as well as those illustrated in Figure 1.

Irregular Grammatical Forms (Inflected Forms). A dictionary lists principal parts for irregular verbs (e.g., *break, broke, broken, breaking*), irregular plurals of nouns (e.g., *child, children*), and irregular adjective and adverb comparatives (e.g., *good, better, best*). The listing may not include the parts for regular forms. You will learn more about these forms in later chapters.

Abbreviations. In some dictionaries, abbreviations appear as normal word entries. Some abbreviations are capitalized, while others are lowercase. In other dictionaries, abbreviations may appear in a section titled "Abbreviations."

USPS   p.m.   M.B.A.

Synonyms and Antonyms. Synonyms represent words that mean the same or almost the same as the entry word. Antonyms are words that are opposite in meaning. Synonyms or antonyms, although limited in scope, appear at the end of the word entry.

A synonym for the adjective *sensitive* is responsive.

An antonym for the verb *appears* is vanishes or disappears.

CHECKUP 1-1

A. Directions: *Use a dictionary to find the following information for each of the Terms to Remember at the beginning of the chapter: correct syllabication; two guide words that appear at the top of the dictionary page on which you locate these terms; and part(s) of speech each term represents. Write your answers on the lines provided. If you cannot find a word in your dictionary, circle the word. The word may be so new that it does not appear, or you may be using a small dictionary that does not contain all the words needed.*

See Instructor Note 1-9 and 1-10 in IAE.

	Word	Syllabication	Guide Words	Part(s) of Speech
Ex.:	dictionary	**dic tio nary**	**dictatorship, diethylcarbamazine**	**N**
1.	Internet	In ter net	answers will vary	N
2.	online	on line	answers will vary	Adj
3.	search engine	search en gine	answers will vary	N
4.	reference	ref er ence	answers will vary	N

B. Directions: *Use a dictionary (printed or electronic) to locate the definitions of the following words. Write the definitions in the space provided.*

Ex.: reference (n.)

a source of information to which a reader is referred

1. ghostwriter (n.)

   a person who writes a speech, book, etc., for another who is presumed to be

   the author

2. caret (n.)

   a mark made in written or printed matter to show the place where something

   is to be inserted

3. icon (n.)

   picture image or other representation

4. multimedia (n.)

   simultaneous combined use of several media at once, such as films, slides,

   flashing lights, and music

5. pursuance (n.)

   the following of some plan or course of action

C. Directions: *Place the primary accent mark in these words that have been divided into syllables. Use a printed or electronic dictionary.*

Ex.: dic′tio nary

    1. ref′er ence   **3.** re ferred′   **5.** mil len′ni um

    2. di rec′to ry   **4.** in dis pen′sa ble

Pronunciation

D. Directions: *Practice pronouncing the following words. Use a printed or electronic dictionary for reference.*

See Instructor Note 1-11 in IAE.

    1. interrogate (v.)   **3.** versatile (adj.)   **5.** harass (v.)

    2. thesaurus (n.)   **4.** emphatic (adj.)   **6.** obscure (adj.)

Spelling

E. Directions: *In the space provided, correct the spelling of these words. Use your printed or electronic dictionary for reference.*

1.	paralell	parallel	4.	scaner	scanner
2.	reciept	receipt	5.	opticle	optical
3.	acess	access	6.	resulution	resolution

GO TO
CD-ROM
CHECKUP 1-1

Office Reference Manuals

An office reference manual contains detailed references to such topics as the following:

See Instructor Note 1-12 in IAE.

    Abbreviations   Business document formats

    Capitalization rules   Commonly misspelled and misused words

Go to Transparency/PowerPoint 1-4a and 1-4b.

Grammar usage
Punctuation rules
Spelling rules
Word division

Number usage
Proofreading and editing
Technology and document production
Written communication styles

Although several reference manuals (you may already have one) are available, this textbook follows a widely used reference manual, *The Gregg Reference Manual,* Glencoe/McGraw-Hill, by William A. Sabin. At times, you will be asked to use a reference manual for more detailed explanations. To save time in locating information in a reference manual, carefully read the directions for finding items. You will usually find these directions in the introductory pages of the reference manual.

CHECKUP 1-2

Tie in to Reference Manual

See Instructor Note 1-13 in IAE.

1-14 Answers that are specific to *The Gregg Reference Manual* are indicated. Answers will vary if students use other reference manuals.

Directions: *Use a reference manual such as* The Gregg Reference Manual *to complete the following exercises.*

Ex.: In which section of the manual will you find a listing of all topics covered in the manual?

In the Contents

1. What are the first five section titles? Use the space below to list them.

   a. Punctuation: Major Marks

   b. Punctuation: Other Marks

   c. Capitalization

   d. Numbers

   e. Abbreviations

2. What is the difference in meaning between *desert* and *dessert*?

   a. desert to abandon (v.); barren land (n.); a deserved reward (n.)

   b. dessert last course of a meal

   c. To what section did you refer? **Words That Sound Alike or Look Alike in** *The Gregg Reference Manual.* **A similar reference would be found in other manuals.**

3. Locate and write the abbreviations of these terms:

   a. United States Department of Agriculture USDA

   b. inch in or in.

4. Give an example of the correct way to write amounts of money under a dollar.
   50 cents

5. Identify two functions of a dash.
   Answers will vary, but they may include the following: to emphasize single words, to use in place of parentheses, to indicate an afterthought.

GO TO CD-ROM
CHECKUP 1-2

Thesaurus and Other References

The repetition of words causes boring writing. Your dictionary includes synonyms (words with similar meanings). However, to expand your word choices, use a thesaurus, which is a book of words and their synonyms. A thesaurus gives suggestions for similar substitute words, their parts of speech, and often a brief definition or an example of the word used in context. *Roget's II: The New Thesaurus* and *Bartlett's Roget's Thesaurus* are examples of two such reference books.

A word division manual is an alternative to a large dictionary. This manual gives a quick reference to spelling and hyphenation. However, it does not include definitions and other features of a dictionary.

Company or personal guide sheets also help you remember words that give you trouble. Differences may exist, however, between your text or reference manual and a guide sheet. For example, you would use the company's guide sheet to determine the preferred style for *workstation* or *work station* and *online* or *on-line* .

Electronic dictionaries and electronic thesauri consist of material that is similar to the printed references. Upon activating a program's function, the program checks for the word you want to change and displays the information on the screen; you select a word to substitute by highlighting the word or its appropriate letter.

Go to Transparency/PowerPoint 1-5.

1-15 Thesauri formats and information vary. The more recent editions include computer terminology.

Differences may exist between rules for dividing words into syllables, as shown in the dictionary, and rules for word division, as shown in a word division manual. For example, the word mostly *can be divided into two syllables; however, this word should not be divided at the end of a written line.*

1-16 This text uses *online* and *workstation*. You may find different spellings in the reference materials and in the workplace.

See Instructor Note 1-17 in IAE.

CHECKUP 1-3

A. Directions: Use a thesaurus to find two synonyms for each of these words.

Ex.: expansive (adj.) __broad, general, outgoing__

1. orientation (n.) __bearing, familiarization, introduction__

2. justify (v.) __excuse, explain away, rationalize, defend__

3. information (n.) __data, facts, knowledge__

4. copy (v.) __duplicate, imitate, replicate, reproduce__

5. visible (adj.) __visual, apparent, viewable__

B. Directions: Use a word division manual. Divide the words into syllables and then write them in the space provided.

Ex.: company **com pa ny**

1. address __ad dress__
2. knowledge __knowl edge__
3. mouse __mouse__

4. data base __da ta base__
5. description __de scrip tion__

GO TO CD-ROM
CHECKUP 1-3

Go to
Transparency/PowerPoint 1-6.

Proofreading a document is as important as creating it. Documents that are carelessly and hurriedly proofread cause embarrassment and uncomfortable explanations for companies and individuals. To avoid these situations, use your reference manual and dictionary whenever you have a question about word usage or grammatical accuracy. As you proceed through the text, you will have many opportunities to practice identifying errors, applying specific proofreading procedures, and using proofreaders' marks.

Types of Errors

The following list gives you the most common types of errors you will find in proofreading someone else's work or your own. Check for these errors as you proofread:

Format Errors

1. Check page numbers. Be sure they are in consecutive order.
2. Check enumerations. The numbers and letters need to be consecutive with no omissions or double items.
3. Compare labels on illustrations with the text references. They must agree.
4. Review spacing between headings and before paragraph indentions. The spacing should be consistent throughout the document.

Keyboarding Errors

1. Check for transposed letters and figures.
2. Recognize that errors occur in typical spots. Check the following very carefully:
   - Long words (Look for missing syllables.)
   - Words with double letters
   - Titles or proper names
   - Headings that use all capital letters
   - Addresses
   - Quotations, parentheses, and brackets—both beginning *and* ending marks
   - Word endings—keying *ing* for *in*
3. Check the number of zeros in figures, and be certain decimal points are in the correct location. Check all numbers at least twice.

Grammar, Usage, and Style Errors

1. Check capitalization, punctuation, and number usage as well as correct grammatical construction. Use your reference manual, dictionary, or word division book to clarify a question. *Never guess!*
2. Be sure all sentences are complete.
3. Eliminate slang or trite expressions in business documents.
4. Change words that are overused. Check your thesaurus to find a replacement for the repeated word.

SLIP-UP

Job application of a bookkeeper: "I am very conscientius and accurite." Source: Robert Half International Inc. [Note: Does the bookkeeper mean *conscientious* and *accurate*?]

Go to
Transparency/PowerPoint 1-7.

5. Check the accuracy of words that sound alike but have different meanings. For example, *their* and *there* and *stationery* and *stationary*.

Missing these elementary types of errors in proofreading is a definite sign of carelessness.

Proofreading Procedures

Proofreading on a computer screen is different from proofreading printed copy. In both cases, however, you should proofread your copy at least twice. Here are some proofreading procedures to use when proofreading printed copy:

Go to
Transparency/PowerPoint 1-8.

See Instructor Note 1-18.

Proofreading by Yourself

1. Read material from right to left rather than left to right, which is the normal reading pattern. This procedure requires you to concentrate on each word.

2. Read the copy word for word. When you see an unfamiliar word, read the copy character by character.

3. Slow down your rate of reading. To do this, use a ruler and your finger. As you read each word, place the ruler below each line on your final copy; place your finger below each word on your original copy. You cannot proofread carefully by skimming material.

4. Select a time and place to proofread when and where there is little or no noise and activity around you.

5. If possible, proofread copy after you have taken a break from the project. Often you will find that mistakes seem to glare at you when you come back to the project after a break.

Proofreading With Another Person

1. Try to proofread with a coworker when you have technical and legal documents or material that will be published. One person reads aloud from the original document; the second person checks the new copy. Change tasks every 15 minutes to avoid boredom and lack of concentration.

2. Be sure to read aloud all capital letters and marks of punctuation. Be consistent when you read numbers; for example, the number *29,450* is read *two nine comma four five zero.*

3. Ask a coworker to proofread your work. Agree to do the same when your coworker has work that requires proofreading.

Electronic Proofreading

Spell check features allow you to check for misspelled words on material that has been keyboarded on a computer. The spell check function checks your copy and highlights the words that do not match those in its dictionary. You then make the appropriate correction in the text from a list of alternate choices. Remember that you are always the decision maker.

Go to
Transparency/PowerPoint 1-9.

Grammar and style check applications point out your grammatical usage errors but only within each program's limitations. On the basis of the suggestions made, you must make the corrections. Be

---

aware that grammar checks vary in capacity and depth of their rules. To use the grammar checks effectively, you must have a clear understanding of the English language.

When proofreading copy on a computer screen, follow these suggestions:

1. Proofread material in blocks or paragraphs as you proceed through a document. Check that your material makes sense; read it word for word. Proofread the entire document again when you finish it.

2. Use the eraser side of a pencil as a pointer on your computer screen. Place a ruler below each line on your original as you compare copy.

3. Use the spell check feature of your software. This feature points out the obvious errors; however, a spell checker does not recognize words that are spelled correctly but used incorrectly in context; for example, *than* for *then* or *an* for *and*.

4. Check references to page numbers within the text especially if you revise or move copy around in a document. Check for spacing inconsistencies after you make corrections and revisions.

5. Visualize how the finished product will appear on paper.

6. Add words to your software dictionary that are unique to your personal or business communications.

7. Take frequent 60-second breaks to rest your eyes as you proofread lengthy documents.

Become aware of the types of errors you make as you key material. Then make a special effort to avoid these kinds of errors.

Proofreaders' Marks

Proofreading often identifies errors that need to be corrected or changes that need to be made to the document. Proofreaders' marks are standardized symbols that allow you to quickly mark errors and changes that are needed. You will find a chart of proofreaders' marks printed on the inside back cover of this textbook or in your reference manual.

CHECKUP 1-4

Directions: *Use the proofreaders' marks on the inside back cover of your textbook to answer the following questions in the space provided.*

Ex.: / What does this proofreaders' mark mean?   **make a lowercase letter**

1. What do the following proofreaders' marks mean?

   a. ⌐ delete _____

   b. # insert space _____

   c. ⱽ insert apostrophe _____

   d. ⌐ move left _____

2. Which proofreaders' mark will you use to correct the following situations?

   a. Capitalize the first letter of a word   ≡

   b. Create a new paragraph   ¶

   c. End a sentence with a period   ⊙

   d. Insert a comma   ⋀

**GO TO
CD-ROM**
CHECKUP 1-4

When a business communication is not proofread carefully, misspelled words and errors in keyboarding usually go unnoticed. These errors are distracting to the reader of the communication. The reader sees these errors, loses his or her concentration, and often becomes disinterested in the purpose of the document or transaction. Although the spell checker will catch many errors in spelling, you need to master spelling skills.

In the appendix of this textbook, you will be introduced to spelling rules and additional words from lists of the most frequently misspelled words. Practice exercises that will develop your skills may be found on the student CD-ROM.

Spelling Improvement Techniques

If you experience spelling difficulties, your problems will not disappear overnight or even by the time you finish this course. The following techniques, however, offer suggestions for improvement; your task is to continually practice these techniques.

Frequently Misspelled Words. Maintain a troublesome words list consisting of words that you constantly must check in the dictionary. Keep the list on 3 × 5 cards, in a notebook, or in any other convenient format. Use your list regularly to help you master the words. When you master a word, cross it off your list.

You may find it helpful to memorize troublesome words or to include them on your troublesome word list.

Spelling Rules. Spelling rules are located in the appendix. Keep in mind that there are exceptions to the rules. Exceptions usually include mispronounced words or often confusing spellings of words; for example, *dying* and *dyeing.*

Learning Resource Center. Your college or school may have a media resource center that offers assistance with individual spelling problem areas. Someone in the center may even assess your skills to determine specific areas of difficulty. Do not be reluctant to ask your instructor for other self-help aids.

Memorization. Sometimes memorizing words is the best technique for remembering the spelling or definition of troublesome words. Focus on five words a week. Practice the words until you can spell them correctly and also use them accurately in a sentence. A good source for these words is on the student CD-ROM.

Listen to a newscast, use the online research sources such as magazine article reprints, or obtain words from other classes. Select words from these sources and practice spelling them.

Mnemonic Devices. A mnemonic is a memory device. Here are a few examples to use with troublesome spelling words.

Think of a goose with a feather loose.

I want a piece of pie.

I put the <u>dent</u> in the superinten<u>dent</u>'s truck.

Did you <u>attend</u> the <u>dance</u>? (attendance)

It's never alwrong or never alright; it's always <u>all</u> <u>wrong</u> or always <u>all</u> <u>right</u>.

Pronunciation. Misspellings often occur because words are not spelled as they sound; for example in the word, *phenomenal,* the *ph* sounds like *f.* If you depend on the pronunciation of words to aid you in spelling, you can expect trouble.

On the other hand, incorrect pronunciation also causes spelling errors; for example, *incidently* (which is not correct) should be pronounced *incidentally.* Sometimes a syllable gets left out of a word; for example, *convenient* becomes *convenent* (which is not correct).

Dictionary Use. Use a dictionary when you question the spelling of a word. Always use the preferred spelling of the word, which is the one listed first in most dictionary entries (e.g., *judgment,* also *judgement*). Check the meaning of the word and note its pronunciation.

1-19 Show students how to use grammar check and spell check software applications.

GO TO CD-ROM
CHECKUP 1-5

CHECKUP 1-5

Directions: Each word below has one missing letter. Write the letter in the space provided. Check your dictionary (printed or electronic).

Ex.: act **o** r

1. gramm **a** r
2. man **e** uver
3. priv **i** lege
4. li **c** ense
5. sc **h** edule

6. curs **o** r
7. di **a** gnostic
8. brow **s** er
9. fa **c** simile
10. bro **c** hure

COMMONLY MISUSED WORDS

Commonly confused words (homonyms) are spell checker demons. The words sound alike but have different spellings and meanings. An example of commonly confused words is *it's* and *its.* The spell checker checks the spelling of the word but does not highlight the misused word if it is spelled correctly. In addition to commonly confused words, some words are often misused in communications. An example is the confusion between the use of *fewer* and *less.* Understanding the commonly confused and misused words and the way to use them in a document will increase the quality of your proofreading skills.

In the appendix, you will find examples of these commonly confused and misused words. A reference manual, such as *The Gregg Reference Manual*, will be helpful for the Word Usage Review. You will have practice opportunities using the student CD-ROM.

1-20 Refer to the section on spelling in *The Gregg Reference Manual* for definitions and correct use of words that sound alike or that are often misused.

CHECKUP 1-6

Directions: In the following sentences, you have a choice of two words that are frequently confused or misused. Select the correct word and write it in the space provided. Use *The Gregg Reference Manual* or another reference manual as a guide. If you are using a manual that omits these words or does not include some of these words, you may use your dictionary.

1-21 Checkup 1-6 provides an excellent spell check demonstration or practice exercise.

Ex.: The revised CD-ROM (*edition, addition*) will be in stores next week.   **edition**

1. Our Internet service provider (*formerly, formally*) had an office on Hastings Avenue.   formerly

2. My impatience did not (*faze, phase*) the hotline operator when I called for help.   faze

3. Excessive browsing through unrelated travel information was a (*waste, waist*) of time.   waste

4. (*Whether, Weather*) and travel information are available on the Internet, but I find the (*latter, later*) more enjoyable.   Weather, latter

5. What (*kind of, kind of a*) dictionary are you using?   kind of

GO TO
CD-ROM
CHECKUP 1-6

The following illustrates words or phrases that you should use in the place of those in the second column. This feature, which will appear regularly in this text, will give you additional aid in choosing words.

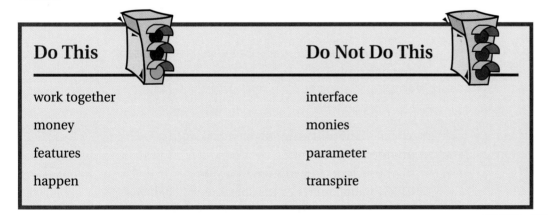

Do This	Do Not Do This
work together	interface
money	monies
features	parameter
happen	transpire

Use words most people readily understand!

PRACTICE

1-22 Additional practice exercises are available on the Instructor CD and the Student CD.

PRACTICE 1A

Chapter Review

Directions: In the space provided, write the letter of the correct answer.

1. Which statement is correct when dividing the word *self confidence* into syllables?
   a. A hyphen appears after *self.*
   b. A boldfaced dot appears after *self.*
   c. A primary stress mark appears after *self.*
   d. A primary stress mark appears after the last syllable.

   1. ___a___

2. A reference book that gives suggestions for similar substitute words is a(n)
   a. Office manual
   b. Electronic dictionary
   c. Dictionary
   d. Thesaurus

   2. ___d___

Proofreading

Directions: Use the proofreaders' marks located on the inside back cover of your text to answer the following questions. In the space provided, write the letter of the correct answer.

1. What does the proofreaders' mark ¶ mean?
   a. Begin a new paragraph.   c. Move copy to the left.
   b. Insert a space.   d. Move copy to the right.

   1. ___a___

2. Which proofreaders' mark should you use to indicate capitalization?
   a. #∧
   b. ∩
   c. ≡
   d. ∧

   2. ___c___

3. Which proofreaders' mark should you use to insert an apostrophe?
   a. • • •
   b. ∨
   c. ∧
   d. ＝

   3. ___b___

4. Which of the following statements is *not* a good proofreading practice?
   a. Read your copy from right to left.
   b. Read unfamiliar words character by character.
   c. Allow the electronic spell checker to do all your proofreading.
   d. Request another person to help you proofread.

   4. ___c___

NAME _____

Word Usage

Directions: *Select the correct word and write it in the space provided. You may use your reference books if you need help.*

1. My manager was (*formally, formerly*) promoted to vice president in the Global Network Division.

   1. _____formally_____

2. (*Never the less, Nevertheless, Never theless*), we bought the CD-ROM dictionary.

   2. ___Nevertheless___

3. ExploreNet provides Internet (*access, excess*), net-working, consulting, and programming services.

   3. _____access_____

4. I used (*fewer, less*) reference resources than Susan.

   4. _____fewer_____

5. We offer our tenants ten free hours of Internet (*access, excess*) time.

   5. _____access_____

6. A sizable waiting list of Internet users is (*eager, anxious*) to apply for service.

   6. _____eager_____

7. The manager (*complimented, complemented*) Makil on her research for the presentation.

   7. __complimented__

8. (*To, Too*) use my program, I'll need only 8 megabytes of RAM.

   8. _____To_____

Definitions

Directions: *Use your dictionary to select the definition for the underlined word. In the space provided, write the letter of the correct answer.*

1. A <u>nominal</u> charge for using e-mail seems appropriate.

   1. ___b___

   a. substantial
   c. tentative
   b. small
   d. normal

2. Our sales representatives had <u>phenomenal</u> records this month.

   2. ___d___

   a. fair
   c. poor
   b. average
   d. extraordinary

3. All the <u>futile</u> attempts to get online were irritating.

   3. ___b___

   a. numerous
   c. usual
   b. ineffective
   d. speedy

Parts of Speech

Directions: *Select the part of speech that each underlined word represents. In the space provided, write the letter of the correct answer.*

1. Which part of speech does the word *quickly* represent?

   1. ___d___

   a. noun
   c. adjective
   b. verb
   d. adverb

PRACTICE

2. Which part of speech does the word *suite* represent?   2. ___a___
   a. noun   c. adjective
   b. verb   d. adverb

Spelling

Directions: *Check the underlined word. If the word is correct, write **Yes** in the space provided. If it is not correct, write the word correctly.*

1. You are able to check facts with an electronic   1. ___thesaurus___
   dictionary, a <u>thesarus</u>, an atlas, or an almanac.

2. The bill for the Internet installation must be   2. ___paid___
   <u>payed</u> within 10 days if you want to receive the
   2 percent discount.

3. The last electronic traffic jam prevented   3. ___Yes___
   me from <u>receiving</u> my e-mail for four hours.

4. I hope you will find an <u>occasion</u> to use one   4. ___Yes, available___
   of the bulletin board services currently <u>avalable</u>.

5. By browsing the Internet, we found that A.B.   5. ___Yes, excellent___
   Travel <u>offered</u> an <u>excellant</u> air travel discount.

**GO TO
CD-ROM
PRACTICE 1
EXERCISES**

PRACTICE 2A

Proofreading

Directions: *Interpret the proofreaders' marks and rewrite the following sentences correctly. If necessary, refer to a reference manual or the inside back cover of your textbook.*

1. Real Estate offers a interesting and challenging careers.

   <u>Real estate offers an interesting and challenging career.</u>

2. Your vacation will begin at 1 PM Friday.

   <u>Your vacation will begin at 1 p.m. Friday.</u>

3. PhoneBase includes more than 100 milion telephone listigns in five
   CD-<u>Roms</u>.

   <u>Phone Base includes more than 100 million telephone listings on five</u>

   <u>CD-ROMs.</u>

4. Software applications becáme obsolecsent very quickly.

   <u>Software applications become obsolescent very quickly.</u>

5. We've found definitions of computer terms ~~through~~ the internet.

   <u>We have found definitions of computer terms on the Internet.</u>

NAME _____

Parts of Speech

Directions: Use your dictionary to identify the part or parts of speech each of these words represent. Use the following abbreviations: **N** (noun), **Pron** (pronoun), **VT** (verb transitive), **VI** (verb intransitive), **Adj** (adjective), **Adv** (adverb), **Prep** (preposition), **Conj** (conjunction). Write your answers in the space provided.

1. delivery   N
2. function   N, VI
3. demand   VT, VI, N
4. literate   Adj, N

5. input   N, Adj, VT
6. constructive   Adj
7. nor   Conj
8. because   Conj, adv

Synonyms

Directions: Use a thesaurus to substitute simple, commonplace words for those underlined in the sentences below. Write your answers in the space provided.

Answers will vary.

1. We are doing everything possible to <u>expedite</u> the delivery of your computer.

   1. speed up, hurry, hasten

2. CD-ROM drives have become <u>standard</u> features on desktop computers.

   2. common

3. The Internet is a great way to <u>disseminate</u> my product information.

   3. advertise, distribute

4. Sara and I had <u>dissimilar</u> requirements for completing our research.

   4. different

5. Locating information quickly on the Internet is possible when you <u>utilize</u> the correct search tools.

   5. use

6. His face was <u>impassive</u> when we told him about the network problems.

   6. indifferent, emotionless

GO TO
CD-ROM
PRACTICE 2
EXERCISES

PRACTICE 3 A

Proofreading

Directions: The following words and phrases describe printed or online references. Proofread and compare the words and phrases in Column A with those in Column B. If they are the same, write **Yes** in the space provided. If they are not the same, write **No**.

See Instructor Note 1-23 in IAE.

COLUMN A	COLUMN B	
1. forums	forms	1. No
2. thesaurus	thesarus	2. No
3. CD-ROMs	CD-Roms	3. No

**GO TO
CD-ROM**
PRACTICE 3
EXERCISES

4. subject index	subject index	4. Yes
5. latest weather reports	lastest weather report	5. No
6. service provider	service providor	6. No
7. toll-free hotline	toll free hot line	7. No
8. grammar check software	grammer check softwar	8. No
9. news.announce.newusers	new.announce newusers	9. No
10. bulletin board services	bulleten board services	10. No

PRACTICE 4A

WRITING

Assignment: *Prepare a list of ten words to describe an ideal business English class.*

Answers will vary. _____

_____

_____

_____

_____

_____

_____

_____

**GO TO
CD-ROM**
PRACTICE 4
EXERCISES

See Instructor Notes 1-24 and
1-25 in IAE.

ONLINE *EXERCISES*

To complete the following exercises, you need access to a computer with an Internet connection and a Web browser. A Web browser is a program that lets you view and explore information on the World Wide Web. Examples of Web browsers are Netscape and Microsoft Explorer.

In the following exercise, you will go directly to a Web page. To get to the Web page, you will key a Uniform Resource Locator, abbreviated as URL. The URL is the standard way to give the address of any resource on the Internet. All URLs include punctuation marks such as periods (.), slashes (/), tildes (~), underlines (_), and letters. Remember to use the exact spacing, punctuation marks, and letters of the URL.

Objective: *Use online dictionaries to look up meanings of computer terms.*

PRACTICE

NAME _____

ONLINE **EXERCISES**

See Instructor's Note 1-26 in IAE.

1. With your Internet browser on the screen, key the following URL in the location text box. (The location text box already has an address beginning with http://. Click on this box to highlight it. Key the new address over the top of the existing address. The existing address will disappear as you key in the new one.)

   http://www.onelook.com

   Press the **Enter** key on your keyboard.

2. You will be on the **OneLook Dictionaries** Web page. This dictionary searches general and specialized English dictionaries simultaneously.

3. Key **netiquette** in the **Enter Word** box, and click on **Look It Up**.

4. A series of links appears (the word *netiquette* is in blue). These links connect you to online computer dictionaries. Click on a link to *netiquette* and read the definition.

5. Use the **Back** button (left corner of your browser) to return to the page of links for *netiquette.* Click on several links until you feel you have a good understanding of the word.

6. Print one definition of **netiquette** by clicking on the **File** menu and selecting **Print**. Click **OK.** Hand in your printout.

7. Click the **Back** button until you return to the **OneLook Dictionaries Search** page.

8. Delete the word *netiquette;* enter the word **flame.** Click on **Look It Up.** Read the definition. Print a copy of the definition.

9. Look up **smiley;** click on **smiley** and read the definition. Give one example of a smiley.

10. Look up another word that means the same as *smiley.* Print a copy of the definition of that word.

Use exact punctuation when keying an Internet address.

NAME _____

PRACTICE 1B

Chapter Review

Directions: In the space provided, write the letter of the correct answer.

1. Which of the following statements is not a good electronic proofreading practice? 1. _____d_____
   a. Read copy word for word.
   c. Proofread in blocks.
   b. Take frequent breaks to rest your eyes.
   d. Increase your rate of reading.

2. Which item is a correct description of a word division manual? 2. _____d_____
   a. Lists substitute words
   c. Gives definitions
   b. Provides parts of speech
   d. Shows spelling

Proofreading

Directions: Use the proofreaders' marks located on the inside back cover of your text to answer the following questions. Write the letter of the correct answer in the space provided.

1. What does the proofreaders' mark / mean? 1. _____b_____
   a. Insert a space.
   c. Align vertically.
   b. Lowercase a letter.
   d. Start a new paragraph.

2. Which proofreaders' mark should you use to insert a comma? 2. _____a_____
   a. $\wedge$
   c. $\odot$
   b. $\vee$
   d. $\vee$

Definitions

Directions: Use your dictionary to select the definition for the underlined word. In the space provided, write the letter of the correct answer.

1. Searching for the word on the Internet was <u>ingenious</u>. 1. _____b_____
   a. not smart
   c. difficult
   b. clever
   d. time consuming

2. The advertised speed for using that search engine turned out to be <u>hyperbole</u>. 2. _____b_____
   a. fantastic
   c. authentic
   b. exaggeration
   d. factual

Parts of Speech

Directions: Select the part of speech that each underlined word represents. In the space provided, write the letter of the correct answer.

1. Which part of speech does the word *diagnose* represent in the following sentence? 1. _____b_____
   Please <u>diagnose</u> our Internet connection problem.
   a. noun
   c. adjective
   b. verb
   d. adverb

2. Which part of speech does the word *expanded* represent in the following sentence? 2. _____c_____
   Our <u>expanded</u> store hours increased sales by 3 percent.
   a. noun
   c. adjective
   b. verb
   d. adverb

NAME _____

PRACTICE 2B

Proofreading

Directions: *Interpret the proofreaders' marks and write the following sentences correctly. If necessary, refer to a reference manual or the inside back cover of your textbook.*

1. Ellen is cancelling her subscription to the magazine *Personal Computing* because does not have time to read it.

    Ellen is canceling her subscription to *Personal Computing* because she does not have time to read it.

2. Even 16 Megabytes of RAM (random access memory) are not enough to run some of our Graphics Programs.

    Even 16 megabytes of RAM (Random-Access Memory) will not run some of our graphics programs.

3. Joanne usually arrives at Work at 6 P.M. and checks her e-mail immediately

    Joanne usually arrives at work at 6 p.m. and checks her e-mail immediately.

4. He said, I will install your modem next week

    He said, "I will install your modem next week."

6. Internet Service provided by cable is hundreds times faster then a phone line.

    Internet service provided by cable is hundreds of times faster than using a phone line.

Parts of Speech

Directions: *Use your dictionary to identify the part or parts of speech these words represent. Use the following abbreviations:* **N** *(noun),* **Pron** *(pronoun),* **VT** *(verb transitive),* **VI** *(verb intransitive),* **Adj** *(adjective),* **Adv** *(adverb),* **Prep** *(preposition),* **Conj** *(conjunction). Write your answers in the space provided.*

1.	confident	Adj	5.	barely	Adv
2.	photocopy	N, VT	6.	and	Conj
3.	surge	N, VI, VT	7.	unhesitating	Adj
4.	domain	N	8.	from	Prep

Synonyms

Directions: *Use a thesaurus to substitute simple, commonplace words for those underlined in the sentences below. Write your answers in the space provided.*   *(Answers will vary.)*

1. The directions for installing our latest reference software seemed <u>ambiguous</u> to me.

    1. ____unclear, vague____

2. Ben faced <u>innumerable</u> decisions when he returned from vacation.

    2. ____many____

3. The hard drive was <u>decimated</u> by the virus.

    3. ____destroyed____

4. Joshua found the Internet connection problem <u>enervating</u>.

    4. ____draining____

5. Karen's <u>fulsome</u> comments at staff meetings got on my nerves.

    5. ____excessive, insincere, sickening____

6. Her <u>perfunctory</u> response to my question was disappointing.

    6. ____indifferent, routine____

Resources to Improve Vocabulary, Proofreading, and Spelling

NAME _____

PRACTICE 3B

Proofreading

Directions: *The following words and phrases describe printed or online references. Proofread and compare the words and phrases in Column A with those in Column B. If they are the same, write* **Yes** *in the space provided. If they are not the same, write* **No**.

	COLUMN A	COLUMN B		
1.	computer graphics	computer graphic	**1.**	No
2.	desktop publishing	desk top publishing	**2.**	No
3.	enhanced keyboard	enhanced key board	**3.**	No
4.	graphical user interface	graphical use interface	**4.**	No
5.	groupware	groupware	**5.**	Yes
6.	laser printer	lazer printer	**6.**	No

Writing

Directions: *Select five new terms you heard or saw recently in other classes, on television or radio, or in newspapers. Check the dictionary for the definitions. Write the definitions using words you understand.*

Answers will vary. _____

_____

_____

_____

 ONLINE **EXERCISES**   See Instructor Note 1-27 in IAE.

Objective: *Use an online reference to look up postal information and create a map.*

1. With your Internet browser on the screen, key:
   http://www.cedar.buffalo.edu/adserv.html in the Location text box and press **Enter.**
   Refer to the previous Online Exercise if you need to refresh your memory on using the Web.
2. When the National Address Server Web page appears, enter the following in the address box: (The personal name used does not matter.)
   Your name
   Your street address
   Your city, state, and ZIP Code
3. Click on **Process this Address.**
4. Print your name and address by clicking **Print** on the **File** menu.
5. Obtain a map of your address by clicking on **Map** from **MapBlast!**
6. Print out a map of your address.

LOOKING BACK

Posttest

Directions: In the space provided, write the letter of the correct answer. When necessary, use the appropriate reference materials to obtain your answers.

1. Which Internet addresses are the same?
   a. http://www.tollfree.edu.net/dir800/
      http://www.toll.freeedu.net/dir800/
   b. http://www.tollfree.edu.net/dir800/
      http://www.tollfree.edu.net/dir800/
   c. htp://www.tollfree.edu.net/dir800/
      htp://www.tollfree.educnet/dir800/
   d. http://www.toll.free.ednet.dir800/
      http://www.toll.free.ednet/dir800/

   1. _____b_____

2. What is the meaning of the word *tortuous?*
   a. painful   c. evil
   b. winding   d. unfortunate

   2. _____b_____

3. Which set of words is spelled correctly?
   a. recieve, begining, a lot, creditor, benefitted
   b. recieve, begining, alot, crediter, benefited
   c. receive, beginning, a lot, creditor, benefited
   d. receive, beginning, a lot, crediter, benefited

   3. _____c_____

4. What does the proofreaders' ⌒) mark mean?
   a. transpose   c. add a space
   b. capitalize   d. delete

   4. _____d_____

5. What two parts of speech does the word *design* represent?
   a. adjective and verb   c. noun and adjective
   b. verb and noun   d. adverb and noun

   5. _____b_____

6. Which word is the correct one?
   To update our technological equipment, we invested a considerable amount of (*capital, capitol*).
   a. capital
   b. capitol

   6. _____a_____

7. Which word is the best substitute for the underlined word in the following sentence?
   Abridged dictionaries are often easier to use.
   a. smaller   c. condensed
   b. online   d. computerized

   7. _____c_____

8. Which of the following items is *not* found in most office reference manuals?
   a. proofreaders' marks   c. word usage
   b. word history   d. word division

   8. _____b_____

CHAPTER 2

Overview of Parts of Speech

TELECOMMUNICATIONS

Imagine our personal lives without telephones. Imagine a company trying to conduct business without its telecommunication systems. Even though we may become exasperated with messages such as "If you wish to know your account balance, press 2 now," and "I am away from my desk, but your call is important to me," the various telecommunication devices are integral parts of our lives.

Millions of people use cellular phones, modems, pagers, voice mail, and fax machines to keep in touch with family, friends, and business associates. Using technology to transmit information over distances is telecommunications. The demand for telecommunication devices is on the rise as people discover the benefits for both business and personal uses.

Because of the wide variety of telecommunication products available and their reasonable prices, telecommuting is a way of life for many people. Telecommuters work where they please and keep in touch by using technology. The technology may include wearing a pager; using a cellular phone; faxing from a computer, printer, or fax machine; sending e-mail by a modem through a computer; and accessing voice mail from anywhere in the world. The telecommuting trend will accelerate with the arrival of newer, more user-friendly technology designed specifically for mobile employees.

OBJECTIVES

After you have studied this chapter and completed the exercises, you will be able to do the following:

1. Recognize the importance of the terminology used in studying grammar.
2. Identify nouns, pronouns, verbs, adjectives, adverbs, conjunctions, prepositions, and interjections.

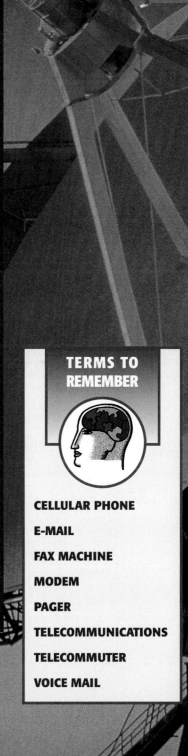

TERMS TO REMEMBER

CELLULAR PHONE

E-MAIL

FAX MACHINE

MODEM

PAGER

TELECOMMUNICATIONS

TELECOMMUTER

VOICE MAIL

LOOKING AHEAD

Pretest

Directions: *In the space provided, write the part of speech of each underlined word. Use the following abbreviations:* **N** *(noun),* **Adv** *(adverb),* **Pron** *(pronoun),* **C** *(conjunction),* **V** *(verb),* **Prep** *(preposition),* **Adj** *(adjective),* **I** *(interjection).*

1. Brian read all the sales <u>literature</u> on faxes and modems.　　　　1. __N__

2. <u>We</u> bought our equipment from Cellphone Inc.　　　　2. __Pron__

3. After I <u>added</u> additional megabytes of RAM, I installed the fax software.　　　　3. __V__

4. Callers appreciate quick and <u>courteous</u> responses to their telephone calls.　　　　4. __Adj__

5. She organizes her material <u>thoroughly</u> for telephone calls.　　　　5. __Adv__

6. All occupations need people who are honest <u>and</u> loyal.　　　　6. __C__

7. I definitely had no interest <u>in</u> a demonstration of the higher-priced cellular phone.　　　　7. __Prep__

8. <u>Oops</u>! I dialed the wrong number.　　　　8. __I__

9. <u>Your</u> computer has been moved to the new office.　　　　9. __Pron__

10. The scanner <u>and</u> the video were stolen from the storage room on Saturday.　　　　10. __C__

11. Many people who work in the telecommunications field <u>use</u> their laptops at home and at work.　　　　11. __V__

12. The <u>local</u> telephone company has been advertising for communication workers.　　　　12. __Adj__

13. That company lost its communication <u>network</u> when the fire destroyed the wiring.　　　　13. __N__

14. Computer users ultimately benefit by having their equipment updated <u>regularly</u>.　　　　14. __Adv__

15. After the power was restored <u>in</u> the building, the computer system needed to be rebooted before we could begin work.　　　　15. __Prep__

OVERVIEW

As you looked at the chapter title, you probably wondered why you needed to study the parts of speech. Do you need to know how to correctly use nouns, pronouns, conjunctions, etc., in order to write clearly?

Assume you called a computer hotline operator and received directions such as "Check the 'thingamajig' on the right, press the 'dingathong' a few times, and then move the 'whatchamacallit' over, and you'll be set." You would be confused—perhaps irritated—about the way your problem was handled.

The same problem exists when you are unaware of the parts of speech and the way they function in a sentence. A noun is not a "thingamajig"; it's a noun. A noun has the specific function of naming a person, place, thing, activity, idea, or quality in a sentence. The other parts of speech have specific functions as well. If you violate the major rules of the language, you may offend or irritate the reader. A customer, for example, may even lose trust in your information if your writing is unclear and imprecise.

Other fields such as medicine, law, police science, and human services have their respective vocabularies. The English language also has a set of terms, which are called the parts of speech, to organize its many words and groups of words into constructive patterns. The eight parts of speech are the *noun*, *pronoun*, *verb*, *adjective*, *adverb*, *conjunction*, *preposition*, and *interjection*. To identify each part of speech, you must determine the function of each word in a sentence. This understanding of correct grammar leads to clearer writing and gives you confidence when you proofread copy and correct errors. Each of the eight parts of speech will be discussed briefly in this chapter with more thorough discussions in future chapters.

PARTS OF SPEECH

Nouns

Nouns name people, places, things, activities, ideas, or qualities. You will use nouns in almost every sentence you write. Nouns may be plural or singular.

Proper and Common Nouns.   Some of the nouns in the following list begin with capital letters. These nouns are *proper nouns;* all others are *common nouns.* Proper nouns refer to a *specific* person, place, or thing. Common nouns refer to general names and are not capitalized.

People:	Maria, clients, nurse, salesperson, team
Place:	New Mexico, University of Wisconsin, AT&T, office, hospital
Things:	pager, telephones, dictionary, directory, technology
Activities:	moving, running, calling, formatting, faxing
Ideas or Qualities:	motivation, efficiency, capitalism, promptness, privacy

See Instructor Notes 2-1 and 2-2 in IAE.

Go to Transparency/PowerPoint 2-1, 2-2, 2-3a, 2-3b, 2-4, and 2-5.

2-3 Stress the importance of using the correct terminology.

2-4 Stress that words may function as more than one part of speech.

2-5 Prepare and use a transparency to identify parts of speech in different occupational areas.

See Instructor Note 2-6 in IAE.

Capitalization **ALERT!**

Capitalize all proper nouns.

2-7 Ask students to list as many common nouns as they can identify in the room.

Examine the common and proper nouns listed below. The common nouns represent general names; the proper nouns are specific names.

Common Nouns	Proper Nouns
woman	Lynn
state	Washington
college	Piedmont College
continent	Africa

In Chapters 4 and 5, you will study other types of nouns and the ways they function in sentences.

CHECKUP 2-1

(Answers will vary.)

2-8 Use a variety of resources to obtain other words for the categories of nouns.

See Instructor Note 2-9 in IAE.

Directions: Substitute a proper noun for the common noun that is underlined in the following sentences. In the space provided, correctly write the proper noun.

1. One <u>student</u> plans to major in both communications and speech therapy.   <u>Patrick</u>

2. I called a <u>company</u> for price information on plain paper faxes.   <u>The Paper Factory</u>

3. The <u>magazine</u> carried several articles on the increased use of cellular phones.   <u>Cellular News</u>

4. Judy contacted a <u>client</u> about a telephone courtesy presentation.   <u>Mr. Payne</u>

5. An <u>instructor</u> gave me the telephone number for a tutor.   <u>Ms. Varca</u>

6. Let's attend a telecommunications trade show in the <u>city</u>.   <u>Austin</u>

GO TO CD-ROM CHECKUP 2-1

Nouns are persons, places, things, activities, ideas, or qualities. Pronouns are words that take the place of nouns.

Pronouns

Pronouns are substitute words for nouns. Like nouns, they may be singular or plural. If you use pronouns correctly, your sentences will be clearer and less cumbersome. You can decrease the repetition of a noun by substituting a pronoun to obtain the same meaning.

Do This

Jane informed *her* coworkers that *she* is retiring.

Do Not Do This

Jane informed Jane's coworkers that Jane is retiring.

Personal Pronouns.   Although there are several other categories of pronouns, the examples in this chapter involve personal pronouns. You will study other pronouns with different functions in Chapter 7. Here are the personal pronouns:

I	me	my	mine					
you	your	yours						
he	she	it	him	her	his	hers	its	
we	us	our	ours					
they	them	their	theirs					

Personal pronouns, with the exception of *it,* can substitute for nouns referring to people. The pronoun *it* can only substitute for a thing, a place, or an animal. The following examples show a simple distinction:

Alice answered the telephone.
<u>She</u> **answered the telephone.**
(The pronoun *she* is a substitute for Alice—a person.)

Alice answered the telephone.
Alice answered <u>it.</u>
(The pronoun *it* is a substitute for telephone—a thing.)

The following sentences illustrate the use of personal pronouns. Each personal pronoun is underlined.

<u>I</u> **finished the telephone usage analysis on Tuesday.**
The amount of time to learn the system overwhelmed <u>me.</u>
<u>They</u> **used the network to plan <u>their</u> sales strategy.**
<u>You</u> **can buy a telephone from any store that <u>you</u> choose.**

The following sentences illustrate the use of nouns and personal pronouns.

As <u>Amy</u> left <u>her</u> office, <u>she</u> asked the receptionist to transfer calls to voice mail.
(The pronoun *her* and the pronoun *she* refer to Amy.)

When the <u>supervisors</u> requested input concerning the use of the telephone during business hours, <u>they</u> did not expect the large return of responses.
(The pronoun *they* refers to the noun *supervisors.*)

Your study of pronouns continues in Chapters 7 and 8.

SLIP-UP
"The telephone pole was approaching. I was attempting to swerve out of its way when it struck my front end."
Statement on an insurance form.
Note: Could a telephone pole approach a car and strike the front of it?

2-10 Stress that the pronoun *it* should not be used as a substitute for nouns that refer to people.

Refer to your reference manual for additional information about nouns and pronouns.

CHECKUP 2-2

Directions: Identify the personal pronouns in the following sentences. Write your answers in the space provided.

1. If students attend class regularly, they should have good notes.   <u>they</u>

2. I like to work the early morning shift because I still have the afternoon free to e-mail my friends.   <u>I I my</u>

3. Some of the more recent fax machines allow us to fax and input our data.   <u>us our</u>

**GO TO
CD-ROM**
CHECKUP 2-2

4. Successful telemarketers learn as much as possible about potential customers before they call.

they

5. Use this button to answer another incoming call while you put the previous caller on hold.

you

6. Almost all the computer magazines that we buy have telecommunications articles in them.

we them

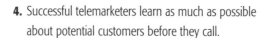

CHECKUP 2-3

Directions: *Use the following sentences from the Secondary Learning paragraphs to check your knowledge of nouns and pronouns. In the space provided, write **N** if the underlined word is a noun. Write **P** if the word is a pronoun.*

1. Telecommuters work where they please and keep in touch by using technology.

N P N

2. Using technology to transmit information over distances is telecommunications.

N N

3. The telecommuting trend will accelerate with the arrival of newer technology designed specifically for mobile employees.

N N

4. Imagine our personal lives without telephones.

P N N

**GO TO
CD-ROM**
CHECKUP 2-3

Go to
Transparency/PowerPoint 2-6.

Verbs

Verbs are words that show action, show a state of being, or help main verbs. You will use verbs in every sentence you write. Verbs give your statements power and add meaning.

Action Verbs. Most verbs are action words, and they are usually the main verb in a sentence. Action verbs indicate what someone or something does. Here are some action verbs:

think   sell   answer   write   call   retrieve

When you add a verb to a sentence, you can see the meaning develop. The following noun and pronoun do not mean much when they stand alone, but understanding develops when a verb is added.

Bill	(noun)	Bill calls.	(noun and verb)
We	(pronoun)	We answer.	(pronoun and verb)

Linking Verbs. Verbs also can be words that show *a state of being* or a condition. Since this type of verb provides a "link" between the parts of your statements, they are appropriately called *linking verbs.* Linking verbs do not indicate action. The various forms of *to be* are the most commonly used linking verbs.

Linking verbs include am, is, are, was, were, been, and being.

am   is   are   was   were   been   being

Larry <u>is</u> our new telephone installer.

He <u>was</u> too exhausted to attend our final meeting.

Diana and Benson <u>are</u> outstanding employees.

A discussion of other linking verbs follows in Chapter 9.

Helping Verbs.   Helping (auxiliary) verbs help in the formation of another verb. They "assist" and precede the main verb. Here are some examples of helping (auxiliary) verbs.

2-11 Another term for *helping verbs* is *auxiliary verbs.*

am	is	are	was	were	been	being
has	have	had	having	shall	should	will	would
can	could	do	does	did	may	might	must

The form of the main verb may change when you add helping verbs.

Main Verb	Helping Verb	Main Verb With Helping Verb
work	will	Karen will work.
include	might	It might include. . . .
interview	have	We have <u>interviewed</u>.
call	are	They are <u>calling</u>.
receive	had	He had <u>received</u>. . . .

Your study of verbs continues in Chapters 9, 10, and 11.

CHECKUP 2-4

Directions: *Check your knowledge of action, linking, and helping verbs by identifying the underlined verbs. Use the following abbreviations:* **A** *(action verb),* **L** *(linking verb),* **H** *(helping verb). Some sentences may have more than one answer.*

1. The combined fax, printer, and copier product line <u>began</u> with a discussion in our basement.   _____A_____

2. She <u>asked</u> specific questions about the product's warranty.   _____A_____

3. Don <u>wrote</u> the original bid, and Carrie <u>revised</u> it.   _____A A_____

4. Key locks on cellular phones <u>will</u> <u>discourage</u> unauthorized users.   _____H A_____

5. Telecommuting <u>is</u> attractive to workers with young families.   _____L_____

6. The Federal Communications Commission <u>has</u> <u>established</u> new standards for operations.   _____H A_____

7. I <u>have</u> <u>received</u> five voice mail messages since I <u>arrived</u> this morning.   _____H A A_____

8. The new phone options <u>are</u> very expensive for our small firm.   _____L_____

9. I <u>wrote</u> the incorrect telephone number and address.   _____A_____

10. Some telephone directories <u>list</u> business e-mail addresses.   _____A_____

**GO TO
CD-ROM
CHECKUP 2-4**

Go to
Transparency/PowerPoint 2-7.

2-12 Stress that adjectives modify nouns and pronouns only; adverbs modify verbs, adjectives, and other adverbs.

SLIP-UP
"The ladies of the church have cast off clothing of every kind. They can be seen in the church basement Saturday."
Announcement in a church bulletin. Note: Shouldn't the announcement refer to *castoff* clothing and refer to the clothing as *it* rather than *they*?

Adjectives

Adjectives modify (describe) nouns and pronouns and often limit their meanings. Adjectives answer these types of questions: What kind? How many? Which one?

What kind?

<u>potential</u> customers	<u>clear</u> messages
<u>experienced</u> salesperson	<u>large</u> desk

(The question *What kind?* describes a noun or pronoun.)

How many?

<u>two</u> employees	<u>several</u> copies
<u>numerous</u> responses	<u>frequent</u> interruptions

Which one?

<u>newest</u> machine	<u>incoming</u> call
<u>last</u> report	<u>original</u> proposal

(The questions *How many?* and *Which one?* limit the meaning of nouns.)

Adjectives clarify the meaning of a sentence and make the message more precise and often more interesting. These examples show how adjectives add clarity and preciseness to a sentence. The underlined words are adjectives.

McHenry & Co. shipped the desks.

McHenry & Co. shipped the <u>executive</u> desks.

(The word *executive* specifies "the kind" of desk that is being shipped.)

McHenry & Co. shipped the <u>five</u> <u>executive</u> desks that we ordered.

(Adding the words *five* and *executive* answers the questions *How many?* and *What kind?* The adjective *five* limits the number of executive desks that are being shipped.)

Adjectives With Nouns. Most adjectives that modify nouns appear *before* the nouns; however, some adjectives that modify nouns appear *after* linking verbs.

In the following sentences, the adjectives are underlined.

Our <u>new</u> manager bought an <u>expensive</u> speakerphone.

(The adjective *new* describes "which" manager and *expensive* describes the "kind of" speakerphone.)

A speakerphone is <u>expensive</u>.

(The adjective *expensive*, which follows the linking verb, describes the noun *speakerphone*.)

The workload was <u>heavy</u> last week.

(The adjective *heavy* describes the noun *workload*.)

Adjectives With Pronouns. Adjectives also modify pronouns. When adjectives modify pronouns, they *follow* the linking verb.

They were <u>competent</u> and <u>reliable</u>.

(The adjectives *competent* and *reliable* follow the linking verb *were* and describe the pronoun *they*. The adjectives answer the question *What kind?*)

You were <u>wise</u> to interrupt the abusive caller.
(The adjective *wise* follows the linking verb *were* and describes the pronoun *you*. This adjective indicates "what kind" of person you are.)

Additional information regarding adjectives appears in Chapter 12.

CHECKUP 2-5

Directions: Insert an adjective wherever you see a blank line. Write your answer in the space provided.

(Answers will vary.)

1. A _____ light indicates an incoming call. _flashing_____

2. A _____ voice conveys a favorable impression in a company. _pleasant_____

3. Answer all _____ calls on the first or second ring. _phone_____

4. When you answer the telephone for others, you must take _____ messages _accurate_____

5. Do not give _____ information to strangers when they call. _any_____

6. Our manager purchased an _____ portable computer. _expensive_____

**GO TO
CD-ROM**
CHECKUP 2-5

Go to
Transparency/PowerPoint 2-8.

Adverbs

You just learned that adjectives modify nouns and pronouns. Other words may also require description. Adverbs usually give additional information about the main verb, but they also modify adjectives or other adverbs. The following sentences illustrate how adverbs modify main verbs, adjectives, and other adverbs:

We <u>often</u> receive wrong numbers.
(The adverb *often* modifies the main verb *receive*.)

The buzzer on our phone was <u>too</u> loud.
(The adverb *too* modifies the adjective *loud*.)

She works <u>very</u> efficiently.
(The adverb *very* modifies the adverb *efficiently*.)

Adverbs answer these questions: *In what manner? Where? When? To what extent?* The following examples show the part of speech the adverb modifies and indicate the type of question that is being answered. All adverbs are underlined.

In what manner?
Jane analyzed the estimates <u>carefully</u>.
(The adverb *carefully* modifies the verb *analyzed* and answers the question *In what manner?*)

Few organizations <u>effectively</u> control their communication costs.
(The adverb *effectively* modifies the verb *control* and answers the question *In what manner?*)

Where?

Most of our customers live <u>here</u> in the city.
(The adverb *here* modifies the verb *live* and answers the question *Where?*)

We moved our telecommunication workshop dates <u>forward</u>.
(The adverb *forward* modifies the verb *moved* and answers the question *Where?*)

When?

NSP will install a second phone line <u>soon</u>.
(The adverb *soon* modifies the verb *install* and answers the question *When?*)

The president of our company visits each branch office <u>annually</u>.
(The adverb *annually* modifies the verb *visits* and answers the question *When?*)

To what extent?

Our inventories <u>sharply</u> decreased during the recent Communication Workers of America strike.
(The adverb *sharply* modifies the verb *decreased* and answers the question *To what extent?*)

2-13 Another question that adverbs answer—usually with adverbial clauses and phrases—is *Why?*

The buzzer on our phone was <u>too</u> loud.
(The adverb *too* modifies the adjective *loud* and answers the question *To what extent?*).

Do This	Do Not Do This
convert	convert over
cooperate	cooperate together
finish	finish up or finish off
refer	refer back

Do not use an adverb to express a meaning already contained in the verb.

You will study the comparison of adverbs and the ways that adverbs function in sentences in Chapter 13.

CHECKUP 2-6

A. Directions: *Identify the word each underlined adverb modifies. Write the word and the part of speech it represents—**V** (verb), **Adj** (adjective), or **Adv** (adverb)—in the space provided.*

Ex: We attend sales meetings <u>weekly</u>.   **attend**   **V**

1. We had a <u>fairly</u> long discussion about the future of telecommunications.   long   Adj

2. The number of users of BTE Airfones has jumped <u>dramatically</u>.   jumped   V

3. We were completely satisfied with the service from AJ Electronics.

satisfied   Adj

2-14 In sentence 3, *were* is a linking verb. *Satisfied* is an adjective modifying *We*.

4. Public Internet access may be coming very soon to a hotel in your city.

soon   Adv

5. Customer satisfaction rates decrease when callers cannot get problems solved immediately.

solved   V

B. Directions: *Identify the underlined word as an* **Adj** *(adjective) or an* **Adv** *(adverb). Write your answer in the space provided.*

2-15 Remind students to identify linking verbs. See sentences 2 and 5.

Ex: An ideal telecommuter needs limited supervision.   **Adj Adj**

1. We seldom repair answering machines.   Adv

2. Our workload is heavy during a new product introduction.   Adj

3. What is the appropriate communication system for our situation?   Adj

4. Angry callers create uncomfortable office situations.   Adj

5. Jake thought that the client was very interested in purchasing a speakerphone, but Jake was quite disappointed.   Adv Adv

GO TO CD-ROM
CHECKUP 2-6

Conjunctions

Conjunctions are connectors. They are not power words and do not add extra meaning to your statements. They simply connect words, phrases, or clauses to make your writing seem less abrupt. This chapter introduces the most frequently used type of conjunction, which is the *coordinating conjunction*. Associate it with coordinating a wardrobe; you want to put similar items together so that they match. When you use coordinating conjunctions, you will join similar items or thoughts of equal rank. You may use more than one conjunction in a sentence. Some common coordinating conjunctions are *and, or, but,* and *nor.* These examples show how the conjunctions join similar ideas.

Go to Transparency/PowerPoint 2-9.

> My fax is old and unreliable.
> My fax is old but still reliable.
> The staff and management completed and returned their self-evaluation reports.
> I must call my travel agent to make an airline reservation for June 4 or 5.

Chapter 15 includes a more detailed discussion of conjunctions.

See Instructor Note 2-16 in IAE.

Prepositions

You just learned that conjunctions are connecting words; now you will be introduced to another part of speech that also connects—the preposition. You will be amazed to see how much you use prepositions

Go to Transparency/PowerPoint 2-10.

as connectors. Here are some frequently used prepositions. There are many more, and you will study them in Chapter 14.

about	above	after
among	at	before
behind	by	down
from	in	inside
into	near	of
off	on	over
through	to	under
up	upon	with

2-17 Only a few of the more frequently used prepositions are listed.

Prepositions appear before a noun or pronoun. The term for the noun or pronoun that follows a preposition is the *object of the preposition*. The following examples show prepositions and the objects of the prepositions:

with me
(*With* is the preposition; the pronoun *me* is the object of the preposition.)

from Hilary
(*From* is the preposition; the proper noun *Hilary* is the object of the preposition.)

for callers
(*For* is the preposition; the noun *callers* is the object of the preposition.)

through Alabama
(*Through* is the preposition; the proper noun *Alabama* is the object of the preposition.)

Remember that prepositional phrases begin with a preposition and end with a noun or pronoun.

A group of words that connects nouns and pronouns to other words is a *prepositional phrase*. A prepositional phrase consists of a preposition, the object of the preposition, and the modifiers of the object of the preposition. You may find more than one preposition or prepositional phrase in a sentence. In the following examples, the prepositional phrases are underlined:

The USPS is testing its electronic postmark service in Atlanta.
(In the prepositional phrase *in Atlanta, in* is the preposition, and *Atlanta* is the noun.)

Employees increase communication costs when they use a business phone for personal calls.
(In the prepositional phrase *for personal calls, for* is the preposition, *calls* is the noun, and *personal* is an adjective modifying calls.)

Telecommuting is a work alternative, which allows an employee to complete normal work functions at home or in centers in local communities.
(In the prepositional phrases *at home, in centers,* and *in local communities, at, in,* and *in* are prepositions. *Home, centers,* and *communities* are nouns, and *local* is an adjective modifying the word *communities*.)

Chapter 2

Chapter 14 includes a detailed list of prepositions and shows how they are used with certain nouns and pronouns.

Interjections

An interjection consists of one or two words and shows an emotion or a strong reaction to something that has occurred. You will use very few interjections in formal communications. Interjections may be appropriate in advertising copy or in informal messages where they express feelings of congratulations, disapproval, or enthusiasm.

An exclamation mark usually follows an interjection. Here are some examples of interjections:

Good!	**Great Job!**	**Ha!**
Impossible!		**Nonsense!**
No Way!	**Oh!**	**Oh,**
Oh, No!	**Oops!**	**Wonderful!**
Ouch!	**Wow!**	**Yes!**

Great job! Our team efforts resulted in an expanded contract with Telecom.

(*Great job!* is an illustration of a congratulatory reaction.)

Ouch! May's telemarketing contacts were considerably below April's.

(*Ouch!* represents disapproval.)

Wow! I was very impressed with your presentation at the teleconference workshop.

(*Wow!* shows enthusiasm for something that occurs.)

Oh, so that's the answer.

(The interjection *oh* may be followed by a comma.)

Go to Transparency/PowerPoint 2-11.

2-18 Interjections are used in informal e-mail messages and in advertising copy.

Punctuation
ALERT!

Use an exclamation point after interjections.

2-19 *Oh* is sometimes followed by a comma.

CHECKUP 2-7

Directions: *In the space provided, write the part of speech of each underlined word. Use the following abbreviations:* **C** *(conjunction),* **I** *(interjection),* **Prep** *(preposition or prepositional phrase).*

1. My supervisor is ambitious but respected.   C

2. We research and test every telephone we manufacture.   C

3. Call accounting gives managers detailed reports about departmental telephone use.   Prep

4. Oh no! Here's another incorrect area code for Texas.   I Prep

5. Our office assistant answers the phone for five team participants.   Prep

6. We interviewed five candidates for the position.   Prep

GO TO CD-ROM
CHECKUP 2-7

PRACTICE

PRACTICE 1A

Directions: In the space provided, write the letter of the appropriate part of speech that each underlined word represents.

1. My supervisor told <u>her</u> to limit personal e-mail messages at the office.
   a. noun
   b. verb
   c. pronoun
   d. conjunction

   1. ___c___

2. A fax broadcast feature allows a business to <u>simultaneously</u> send one fax to many customers.
   a. noun
   b. adjective
   c. verb
   d. adverb

   2. ___d___

3. Live television newscasts and radio programs <u>are</u> already available online.
   a. verb
   b. conjunction
   c. adverb
   d. preposition

   3. ___a___

4. President Jones addressed the opening <u>session</u> of our teleconferencing workshop.
   a. noun
   b. adjective
   c. verb
   d. adverb

   4. ___a___

5. The company will ask businesses to pay an <u>extra</u> fee for e-mail listings in telephone directories.
   a. noun
   b. adverb
   c. adjective
   d. preposition

   5. ___c___

6. If you need to contact a person who is traveling on a ship, call the marine operator <u>or</u> satellite network.
   a. adjective
   b. conjunction
   c. adverb
   d. preposition

   6. ___b___

7. Travelers use fax <u>and</u> voice mail to make reservations and travel plans.
   a   pronoun
   b. conjunction
   c. adverb
   d. preposition

   7. ___b___

8. Businesses that cater <u>to</u> personal needs will prosper.
   a. verb
   b. conjunction
   c. adverb
   d. preposition

   8. ___d___

9. Both the modem and upgraded software were less <u>expensive</u> than we anticipated.
   a. noun
   b. adverb
   c. adjective
   d. preposition

   9. ___c___

10. Two cable companies <u>reported</u> deficits during the past year.
    a. noun
    b. adjective
    c. verb
    d. adverb

    10. ___c___

**GO TO
CD-ROM**
PRACTICE 1
EXERCISES

PRACTICE 2A

Parts of Speech

*Directions: In the space provided, write the part of speech of each underlined word. Use the following abbreviations: **N** (noun), **Pron** (pronoun), **V** (verb), **Adj** (adjective), **Adv** (adverb), **C** (conjunction), **Prep** (preposition), **I** (interjection).*

1. When I returned to the hotel <u>room</u>, I <u>saw</u> the message-waiting light flashing <u>on</u> the <u>telephone</u>.

   1. __N, V, Prep, N__

2. If <u>you</u> plan to upgrade your telephone <u>equipment</u>, obtain <u>several</u> quotes for service <u>and</u> prices.

   2. __Pron, N, Adj, C__

3. <u>We</u> need <u>motivated</u> and <u>reliable</u> telecommuters <u>in</u> our firm.

   3. __Pron, Adj, Adj, Prep__

4. Fax-on-demand <u>allows</u> you to dial the source, press the desired document <u>code</u>, <u>and</u> key in the number to request <u>documents</u>.

   4. __V, N, C, N__

5. Orders <u>are</u> left <u>at</u> <u>night</u> as voice messages <u>and</u> are retrieved and input the <u>next</u> day.

   5. __V, Prep, N, C, Adj__

6. <u>Use</u> only <u>prepaid</u> calling cards purchased <u>from</u> <u>honest</u> companies.

   6. __V, Adj, Prep, Adj__

7. The <u>founders</u> <u>of</u> our telecommunications company <u>had</u> neither vision nor <u>initiative</u>.

   7. __N, Prep, V, N__

8. Although we don't advise <u>it</u>, <u>we</u> know that home-based businesses can function <u>with</u> <u>one</u> phone line.

   8. __Pron, Pron, Prep, Adj__

Common Nouns

Directions: In the space provided, write an appropriate common noun for each proper noun listed below.

1. Houston   __city__   3. Jacob   __name__
2. September __month__   4. Ohio   __state__

Personal Pronouns

Directions: In the space provided, write an appropriate personal pronoun that will substitute for the word or words in parentheses. In addition, write an appropriate personal pronoun to fill in the blank.

1. (Jane) responded to _____ voice mail calls.

   __She__   __her__

NAME _____

2. (Mr. Sundby) thought _____ should attend the National Teleconference Association meeting.

He   I, we, he, you, they _____

3. (Todd) answered _____ phone.

He   his _____

Action Verbs

(Answers will vary.)

Directions: Substitute an action verb for the blank line in the following sentences. Write your answer in the space provided.

1. His cellular phone bill _____ when he started calling France daily.

    1. increased

2. Two thirds of new cellular phone customers _____ the phones for personal reasons.

    2. purchase

3. Michael _____ at the chance to design the company Web page.

    3. jumped

Adjectives

(Answers will vary.)

Directions: In the spaces provided, add an adjective to the following nouns.

1. urgent   message   3. telephone   callers

2. cable   service   4. happy   employees

Adverbs

(Answers will vary.)

Directions: Substitute an adverb for the blank line in the following sentences. Write your answer in the space provided.

1. Everyone in our office must be _____ trained in correct telephone etiquette.

    1. adequately

2. The telephone consultant is resigning _____ .

    2. immediately

3. Our inventories have _____ diminished.

    3. greatly

Prepositions or Conjunctions

(Answers will vary.)

Directions: In the spaces provided, write an appropriate preposition or conjunction to complete each of the following sentences.

1. Contact your local telephone office _____ informational brochures.

    1. for or about

2. Many _____ the phone companies are aiming services _____ small business owners.

    2. of at

3. New developments _____ telecommunications will benefit small _____ large businesses.

    3. in and

4. I went _____ the telecommunications exhibit, _____ I could not see everything _____ one day.

4. ____to__but__in____

5. Either Pete _____ Brad will call you _____ Monday.

5. _____or__on_____

GO TO
CD-ROM
PRACTICE 2
EXERCISES

PRACTICE 3A

PROOFREADING

See Instructor Note 2-20 in IAE.

*Directions: Proofread and compare the words and phrases in Column A with those in Column B. If they are the same, write **Yes** in the space provided. If they are not the same, write **No**.*

	Column A	Column B	
1.	deregulation	deregulation	1. Yes
2.	numerous accessories	numberous accesories	2. No
3.	toll-free number	toll free number	3. No
4.	distinctive ringing	distinctive ringing	4. Yes
5.	least-cost routing	least-cost route	5. No
6.	variety of battery options	variety of battery option	6. No
7.	DT-306, DT-326, and DT 346 models	DT-306, DT-336, and DT-346 models	7. No
8.	built-in pager	built-in pager	8. Yes
9.	36 hours of standby time	36 hours of standby time	9. Yes
10.	Federal Communications Commission (FTC)	Federal Communicatioins Commissioin (FTC)	10. No

GO TO
CD-ROM
PRACTICE 3
EXERCISES

PRACTICE 4A

WRITING

*Directions: For each of the following questions, list a common noun and a proper noun. For example, if a friend of yours named Sally Galimba has a cellular phone, friend is the common noun and **Sally Galimba** is the proper noun.*

(Answers will vary.)

2-21 Sentence writing does not begin until Chapter 3.

		Common Noun	Proper Noun
1.	Who has a cellular phone?	friend	Sally Galimba
2.	Who has a pager?	daughter	Arlene
3.	Who has a fax machine?	neighbor	Sam
4.	Who uses e-mail?	coworker	Sue
5.	Who telecommutes?	friend	Gloria

GO TO
CD-ROM
PRACTICE 4
EXERCISES

PRACTICE

See Instructor Note 2-22 in IAE.

 ONLINE **EXERCISES**

To complete the following exercises, you need access to a computer with an Internet connection.

Objective: *Search for an article in* USA Today *that describes one of the Terms to Remember. Note: You may incur charges to access articles on this Website.*

1. With your Internet browser on screen, key:

   http://www.usatoday.com in the location text box of your screen.

   Press the **Enter** key on your keyboard.

2. You will be on the Web page for the newspaper *USA Today.*

3. Locate the **Search** listing on the *USA Today* Web page. The Search listing will be at the left of the Web page. Click on **Our site**.

4. Select the **News** database by clicking on it.

5. In the description box, key in one of the Terms to Remember, such as **cellular.**

6. Click on **Begin Search.** The search engine for *USA Today* will locate all the articles that contain the word *cellular.*

7. When the list of documents appears, click on an article that looks interesting.

8. Print a copy. You print a copy by clicking on **File** (left side of your Internet browser), **Print,** and **OK.**

9. Click the **Back** button until you return to the Search screen.

10. Enter another Term to Remember in the description box, find another article, and print it.

Punctuation ALERT!

Use exact punctuation when keying an Internet address.

2-23 Check online sites carefully before assigning them to students. Some sites charge a fee to access the articles. Omit this exercise or substitute another site if you wish.

NAME _____

PRACTICE 1B

Chapter Review

Directions: In the space provided, write the letter of the appropriate part of speech that each underlined word represents.

1. Telecommuting <u>helps</u> employers meet trip reduction ordinances.
   a. noun **b.** verb **c.** adjective **d.** adverb

   1. ___b___

2. <u>Your</u> WorldLink card can be used from any phone in the world.
   a. noun **b.** verb **c.** adjective **d.** pronoun

   2. ___d___

3. The accident rate between using hands-free phones and hand-held phones is not <u>statistically</u> significant.
   a. noun **b.** verb **c.** adjective **d.** adverb

   3. ___d___

4. Brazil, Israel, <u>and</u> Switzerland have banned the use of hand-held phones while driving.
   a. noun **b.** conjunction **c.** preposition **d.** adjective

   4. ___b___

5. Most businesses prefer to hold <u>major</u> negotiations face-to-face instead of through teleconferencing.
   a. noun **b.** adjective **c.** adverb **d.** verb

   5. ___b___

6. The long-range impact of teleconferencing <u>on</u> business travel is unclear.
   a. noun **b.** adjective **c.** preposition **d.** conjunction

   6. ___c___

7. The <u>San Jose Hilton</u> in Silicon Valley has Internet access.
   a. noun **b.** adjective **c.** adverb **d.** verb

   7. ___a___

8. TeleCom <u>quickly</u> reacted to customer complaints about busy signals.
   a. noun **b.** adjective **c.** adverb **d.** verb

   8. ___c___

9. College students <u>rapidly</u> fill telecommunications positions.
   a. noun **b.** adjective **c.** adverb **d.** verb

   9. ___c___

10. Outsourcing has made it less attractive <u>for</u> full-time employees to request home telecommuting jobs.
    a. noun **b.** adjective **c.** preposition **d.** verb

    10. ___c___

PRACTICE 2B

Parts of Speech

Directions: In the space provided, write the part of speech of each underlined word. Use the following abbreviations: *N* (noun), *Pron* (pronoun), *V* (verb), *Adj* (adjective), *Adv* (adverb), *C* (conjunction), *Prep* (preposition), *I* (interjection).

1. Tens of thousands <u>of</u> technology <u>workers</u> in <u>California</u> <u>carry</u> cellular phones on hikes <u>and</u> use laptop computers at night.

   1. _____Prep, N, V, C_____

2. <u>Some</u> companies <u>insist</u> that their <u>employees</u> use air phones.

   2. _____Adj, V, N_____

3. A pager will help <u>you</u> stay <u>in</u> touch when you <u>are</u> on the <u>road</u>.

   3. _____Pron, Prep, V, N_____

4. <u>Amazing!</u> Some of the <u>smartest</u> executives in business feel buried by a <u>technology</u> <u>avalanche</u>.

   4. _____I, Adj, Adj, N_____

END-OF-CHAPTER WORKSHEETS

5. The best-known computer chip is the Pentium, which packs millions of transistors on a silicon wafer.

    5. _____ N, N, Prep, Adj _____

6. Cable TV and phone companies are quickly rushing to build new capabilities into their networks.

    6. _____ Adv, Adj, Prep, N _____

7. Deregulation is allowing new competition in local and long-distance phone services.

    7. _____ V, N, Prep, C _____

8. Technology users ultimately benefit from fast changes by getting better products and services for less money.

    8. _____ N, Adv, Adj, N _____

9. She believes that telecommuting can be a problem for those telecommuters who do not have the right tools.

    9. _____ Pron, N, Adj, N _____

10. The goal of a recently launched Website is to enable associates to communicate with each other electronically.

    10. _____ Prep, Adv, V, N _____

Common Nouns

Directions: *In the spaces provided, write an appropriate common noun for each proper noun listed below.*

1.	Canada	1.	country
2.	St. Louis	2.	city
3.	Trump Tower	3.	building

Personal Pronouns

Directions: *In the space provided, write an appropriate personal pronoun that will substitute for the word or words in parentheses. In addition, write appropriate personal pronouns to fill in the blank lines.*

1. (George Mono) provides a company Website so that _____ and other employees can download copies of contracts.

    1. _____ He he _____

2. (Teresa Herrea) takes the bus to the square, and _____ checks in at the Telecommuting Center where _____ works.

    2. _____ She she she _____

3. (Betty) ordered a new wireless phone, and TeleTech mailed _____ within one day.

    3. _____ She it _____

Action Verbs

Directions: *In the space provided, write an action verb to complete each sentence.* *(Answers will vary.)*

1. Some hotels _____ a fax machine, scanners, and laser printers.

    1. _____ provide _____

2. IBM _____ the first business computer in 1954.

    2. _____ introduced _____

3. Computerized highway signs _____ of accidents ahead.

    3. _____ warn _____

NAME _____

Adjectives

Directions: Add an adjective to the following nouns in the spaces provided.   *(Answers will vary.)*

1. <u>electronic</u>   device

2. <u>space</u>   travelers

3. <u>luxury</u>   hotel

Adverbs

Directions: Substitute an adverb for each blank line in the following sentences. Write your answer in the space provided.   *(Answers will vary.)*

1. Computers are _____ being improved, and new uses are being found for them.
2. The view from the _____ renovated hotel gives a panoramic view of the city.
3. She uses her cellular phone _____ in airports.

1. ____constantly____
2. ____recently____
3. ____frequently____

Prepositions or Conjunctions

Directions: In the spaces provided, write an appropriate preposition or conjunction to complete each sentence.

1. The $1.50 per page cost to fax _____ most hotel rooms is less expensive than sending a document _____ overnight mail.

2. A survey _____ hotel managers in Canada, the United Kingdom, _____ the United States shows technology has had a tremendous impact on hotel operations.

3. The company offer of free technology had much to do _____ Anna's willingness to work at home.

4. If a voice mail system cannot deliver a message, the system stores it _____ the computer's memory _____ later delivery.

5. Modern fax machines are often compatible _____ cellular phones.

1. ____from by____
2. ____of and____
3. ____with____
4. ____in for____
5. ____with____

PRACTICE 3B

Proofreading

Directions: The following words and phrases describe items in the field of telecommunications. Proofread and compare the words and phrases in Column A with those in Column B. If they are the same, write **Yes** in the space provided. If they are not the same, write **No.**

	Column A	Column B	
1.	hand-held, battery-run flip-top portable	hand-held, battery run flip-top portable	1. No
2.	e-mail address	email address	2. No
3.	laptop computers	laptop computors	3. No
4.	high-speed Internet access	high-speed Internet access	4. Yes
5.	wireless personal communications service	wireless personnel communications service	5. No

NAME _____

6.	www.phonemiser.com	www. phonemiser/com	**6.**	No
7.	fax-on-demand	fax-on-demand	**7.**	Yes
8.	corporate support center	Corporate Support Center	**8.**	No
9.	palm-size flip variety wireless phone	palm-size flip variety wireless phone	**9.**	Yes
10.	1-800-789-4903	1-800-798-4903	**10.**	No

Writing

Directions: *Use three adjectives to describe your business English class. Write your answers in the spaces provided.*   *(Answers will vary.)*

This business English class is _____**interesting**_____ , _____**informative**_____ , and _____**helpful**_____ .

Directions: *Use adverbs to fill in the blanks.*

1. My friends are _____ funny.

2. I like to have my questions answered _____ .

3. We _____ receive the answers to our questions.

1. _____**very**_____

2. _____**promptly**_____

3. _____**usually**_____

ONLINE EXERCISES

Objective: *Explore the International Teleworking Association Website.*

1. With your Internet browser on the screen, key:

   http://www.telecommute.org/ in the location text box and press **Enter.**

2. Read about TAC, which is an organization for telecommuters.

3. Click on the **FAQ's** section. You will be on a page that discusses the questions people ask when investigating telecommuting as a work option.

4. Read about telecommuting.

See Instructor Note 2-24 in IAE.

LOOKING BACK

Posttest

Directions: *In the space provided, write the part of speech of each underlined word. Use the following abbreviations:* **N** *(noun),* **Adv** *(adverb),* **Pron** *(pronoun),* **C** *(conjunction),* **V** *(verb),* **Prep** *(preposition),* **Adj** *(adjective),* **I** *(interjection).*

1. In the Silicon Valley, <u>unions</u> are rare, strikes <u>are</u> infrequent, <u>and</u> productivity is <u>high</u>.   1. <u> N V C Adj </u>

2. The <u>Internet</u> <u>repeatedly</u> breaks down as phone lines sag under a flood <u>of</u> <u>new</u> users.   2. <u>N Adv Prep Adj</u>

3. People can use <u>digital</u> cameras to view <u>and</u> print photos <u>on</u> their home computers.   3. <u> Adj C Prep </u>

4. A television <u>set</u> can be used <u>for</u> Web surfing from a <u>comfortable</u> chair.   4. <u> N Prep Adj </u>

5. Hair dryers <u>and</u> free local phone calls are more   5. <u> C Prep Adj </u>

   popular than in-room fax machines <u>at</u> <u>most</u> hotels.

6. Internet phones <u>look</u> like <u>regular</u> phones, <u>but</u> Internet phones allow you to   6. <u> V Adj C C </u>

   send <u>and</u> receive electronic mail.

7. Phone companies <u>face</u> <u>incredible</u> competition <u>from</u> cable television <u>operators</u>.   7. <u> V Adj Prep N </u>

8. A committee has been formed <u>by</u> the <u>American Hotel and Motel Association</u>   8. <u>Prep N Adj Adj</u>

   to address the <u>technology</u> needs of <u>business</u> travelers.

9. <u>Ouch!</u> I caught <u>my</u> finger in my <u>printer</u>.   9. <u> I Pron N </u>

10. The in-room hotel fax machine <u>amazingly</u> <u>gets</u> only one minute <u>of</u> use <u>each</u> day.   10. <u>Adv V Prep Adj</u>

CHAPTER 3

Sentence Development

CUSTOMER SERVICE

Do you return to a store where the sales staff ignore you? Do you enjoy calling a company that offers only a voice mail option? Do you shop at a store where you cannot return a purchase? If you are like most customers, you want to spend your money with companies that provide the best customer service.

Excellent customer service means that you, the consumer, deserve and expect attention to your needs. You want sales employees to listen to your questions and to respond efficiently and effectively. If you have a problem, you expect courteous, immediate assistance. Because you are a busy person, you desire quality products, convenient store hours, toll-free numbers, liberal return policies, and Websites.

Effective businesses know that they never get a second chance to make a first impression. These businesses place a high priority on customer service training and have a highly visible commitment to quality service. Their employees are enthusiastic and productive and take pride in helping customers.

OBJECTIVES

TERMS TO REMEMBER

CONSUMER

CUSTOMER SERVICE

QUALITY SERVICE

WEBSITES

After you have studied this chapter and completed the exercises, you will be able to do the following:

1. Demonstrate knowledge of terms used in sentence construction.
2. Use correct ending punctuation for statements, questions, commands, and exclamations.
3. Identify simple, compound, and complete subjects.
4. Identify simple, compound, and complete predicates.
5. Recognize direct objects, indirect objects, and other complements.
6. Identify normal and inverted sentence order patterns.
7. Differentiate between phrases and clauses.
8. Identify simple, compound, complex, and compound-complex sentences.
9. Identify complete sentences, fragments, and run-on sentences.
10. Diagram simple subject, simple predicate, and direct object portions of a sentence.

LOOKING AHEAD

Pretest

Directions: In the space provided, write the letter of the correct answer.

1. What term does the following statement define? *A group of words arranged in complete thoughts so that the words make sense.*
   - **a.** direct object
   - **b.** complement
   - **c.** sentence
   - **d.** complete predicate

   1. _____c_____

2. What mark of punctuation should follow this sentence? *Will you please contact us tomorrow*
   - **a.** question mark
   - **b.** period
   - **c.** exclamation mark
   - **d.** quotation marks

   2. _____b_____

3. What is the complete subject in this sentence? *Our managers and salespeople must possess outstanding problem-solving skills.*
   - **a.** outstanding problem-solving skills
   - **b.** problem-solving skills
   - **c.** managers and salespeople
   - **d.** Our managers and salespeople

   3. _____d_____

4. What is the simple predicate in this sentence? *I finally received the sales totals.*
   - **a.** received
   - **b.** finally received
   - **c.** I finally received
   - **d.** received the sales totals

   4. _____a_____

5. What is the direct object in the following sentence? *The brochure generated 120 requests for information.*
   - **a.** brochure
   - **b.** generated
   - **c.** information
   - **d.** requests

   5. _____d_____

6. Which sentence pattern does this statement represent? *Sales letters require strong first paragraphs to attract readers.*
   - **a.** the subject-verb pattern
   - **b.** the subject-linking verb-complement pattern
   - **c.** the subject-verb-object pattern
   - **d.** inverted order sentence

   6. _____c_____

7. Which statement describes a clause?
   - **a.** A clause contains a subject but no verb.
   - **b.** A clause contains a verb but no subject.
   - **c.** A clause contains a subject and a verb.
   - **d.** A clause contains neither a subject nor a verb.

   7. _____c_____

8. Which sentence formation does this statement represent?
   Today's customers have limited time to shop, but they require personalized assistance.
   - **a.** simple sentence
   - **b.** compound sentence
   - **c.** complex sentence
   - **d.** inverted sentence

   8. _____b_____

9. What does this group of words indicate? *We found no problems.*
   - **a.** a dependent clause
   - **b.** a complete sentence
   - **c.** sentence fragment
   - **d.** a run-on sentence

   9. _____b_____

10. Which statement concerning sentence diagramming is correct?
   - **a.** A diagram shows how words relate to each other.
   - **b.** A diagram makes it difficult to understand the meaning of a sentence.
   - **c.** A diagram makes it difficult to punctuate a sentence.
   - **d.** A diagram shows where special editing marks are placed in the copy.

   10. _____a_____

OVERVIEW

If you have tried to set up or have watched someone else set up a computer, you know how important it is to properly connect the monitor and printer to the computer. You have been told or have experienced the need for sufficient memory to run the application software. You know that modems and faxes have to be installed and connected properly to run effectively. In other words, all the parts must be considered and correctly put together to make your computer work. This same principle is true with the parts of speech. Each part of speech represents a valuable part of the whole sentence, but the parts must be connected appropriately for the sentence to serve its purpose and make sense.

In Chapter 2, you were introduced to the parts of speech. As you proceed through this chapter, you will see how these parts fit into sentence patterns, and you will learn the definitions of some additional terms. Note how each new term adds to the meaning and clarity of a sentence.

SENTENCE IDENTIFICATION

Sentences are words correctly arranged so that the words comprise *complete* statements or ideas that make *sense*. Each complete sentence begins with a capital letter and ends with an ending mark of punctuation.

Read the Questions for Sentence Identification that follow. With every group of words, you can determine if the words make a sentence by answering all four questions. The answers to all four questions should be "yes." If the answers to Questions 1 and 2 are "yes," proceed with Questions 3 and 4. If the answers to Questions 1 and 2 are "no," then you know immediately that the group of words is not a sentence.

Questions for Sentence Identification

1. Do the words make sense?
2. Do the words indicate a complete thought?
3. Does the group of words begin with a capital letter?
4. Does the group of words end with a period, question mark, or exclamation point?

Now look at the following groups of words:

All customers appreciate helpful salespeople.

(Ask yourself the four Questions for Sentence Identification. Your answers should all be "yes." This is a sentence.)

See Instructor Notes 3–1, 3–2, and 3–3 in IAE.

Go to
Transparencies/PowerPoints 3-1a, 3-1b, 3-1c, and 3-2.

Good writing begins with good reading.

Use a capital letter for the first word of a new sentence.

3–4 Stress the importance of Questions 1 and 2 in identifying sentences.

Go to
Transparency/PowerPoint 3-3.

Use an ending mark of punctuation such as a period, question mark, or exclamation point to end a sentence.

when the sales meeting is over

(Ask yourself the four questions. All your responses should be "no." This is *not* a sentence.)

All salespersons helpful appreciate customer.

(This group of words does not make sense or indicate a complete thought; therefore, it is *not* a sentence.)

CHECKUP 3-1

Directions: In the space provided, write **Yes** if the groups of words that follow are sentences. Write **No** if the words are not sentences. If the answer is **No,** explain why by writing the number(s) from the Questions for Sentence Identification that apply.

Ex: and that callers are directed immediately.   No (1, 2, 3)

1. Poor customer service damages a company's reputation.   Yes

2. I enjoy shopping.   Yes

3. unconditional service guarantees   No (1, 2, 3, 4)

4. Many salespeople seem to enjoy their work.   Yes

5. Service can be guaranteed in many ways.   Yes

6. the better we get at meeting customers' expectations.   No (1, 2, 3)

7. Next on the agenda.   No (1, 2)

8. Lee is working on a study to determine the attention that consumers give to coupons.   Yes

**GO TO
CD-ROM
CHECKUP 3-1**

PURPOSES OF SENTENCES

Go to
**Transparencies/PowerPoints
3-4a and 3-4b.**

Sentences have four different purposes and can be classified as follows:

- Statements (*declarative sentences*)
- Questions (*interrogative sentences*)
- Commands and requests (*imperative sentences*)
- Exclamations (*exclamatory sentences*)

Use a period at the end of statements.

Statements

Statements end with periods. These sentences are explanations or statements of facts and opinions.

Explanations

You need a well-prepared presentation that sells your product quickly.

Facts

We recently revised our sales manual.

Opinions

I prefer salespeople who are accurate and fast.

Questions

Direct questions end with question marks. *Indirect questions* may sound like questions, but they are declarative sentences and end with periods.

Use a question mark as the ending mark of punctuation for direct questions.

Direct Questions

Are your competitors increasing their television advertising?

Indirect Questions

She asked whether I planned to send her a copy of the new sales campaign.

Use a period as the ending mark of punctuation for indirect questions.

Commands and Requests

Command sentences express *direct commands,* or they express *courteous requests* that imply action. Both end with periods. The pronoun *you* is understood even though it is not always stated.

Use a period as the ending punctuation mark for command and courteous request sentences.

Direct Commands

Contact your sales representative if you need assistance.
(The subject of the sentence is *you.*)

Courteous Requests

Would you please get the client's signature on the sales contract.
May I please have your daily contact summaries by Friday.
(The courteous requests sound like questions, but they end with periods.)

To help you decide whether to use a period or a question mark, analyze the response you expect. If you want an answer "in words" to a question, use a question mark. If you want an "action" from the person you are addressing, use a period for a courteous request.

How is your new sales campaign progressing?
(The question needs an answer in words. Use a question mark to end the sentence.)

Will you please send me a report on the progress of your new sales campaign.
(You expect to receive the report; you do not expect the response, "Yes, I will send you a report." Use a period to end the sentence.)

Exclamations

Exclamations express strong reactions and end with exclamation marks. Business writers infrequently use exclamatory sentences.

Use an exclamation point as the ending punctuation mark for exclamatory sentences.

The customer is always right!

You won!

Directions: *In the space provided, identify the purpose of each of the sentences by writing one of the following abbreviations: **S** (statement), **DQ** (direct question), **IQ** (indirect question), **DC** (direct command), **CR** (courteous request), **E** (exclamatory sentence). Write one of the following punctuation marks at the end of the statement: period (.), question mark (?), exclamation point (!).*

1. Why not take a few minutes to thank your customers for their support

1. CR .

2. Some companies offer unconditional service guarantees

2. S .

3. Does your information system tell you which products are in great demand

3. DQ ?

4. Proofread the sales brochure copy, and return it to me by Monday

4. CR .

5. What is your reaction to a sales clerk who carries on a personal phone conversation while you wait for assistance

5. DQ ?

6. Will you please contact our marketing manager in Tokyo

6. CR .

7. What a great sales presentation

7. E !

8. I wonder if our sales commissions will increase

8. IQ .

9. Word-of-mouth advertising is an effective way to gain new clients

9. S .

10. Use last year's sales quotas as the basis for comparison

10. DC .

GO TO CD-ROM
CHECKUP 3-2

PARTS OF A SENTENCE

Go to
Transparency/PowerPoint 3-5.

Sentences have two parts—the *subject* and the *predicate*. The main word in a subject is often a noun (person, place, thing, idea, activity, or quality) or a pronoun (noun substitute). The main word in the predicate is the verb (action or *to be* form).

Subject

The subject of a sentence indicates *who is speaking, who is spoken to,* or *who or what is spoken about.* The last category offers the most choices for subjects.

Who is speaking?
I plan to contact my customers at least once a month.
We requested copies of the article, "The Best Sales Presentation Ideas."
(The subject is typically *We* or *I*, the *person or persons speaking.*)

Who is spoken to?
You may try our product in your home for one week.
(The subject is *you*, the *person being spoken to.*)

Who or what is spoken about?

Salespeople play important roles in closing sales.
(The subject is *salespeople*, or *who is being spoken about*.)

Guarantees show customers that you respect them and value their support.
(The subject is *guarantees*, or *what is spoken about*.)

Simple and Compound Subjects

A *simple subject* is the main word of the subject. Two or more main words in a subject comprise a *compound subject*. The words *and* and *or* (conjunctions) often connect the main words in a compound subject.

Simple Subjects

We use individualized goal plans to motivate our sales representatives.
(*We* is the main word and the *simple subject*, and the word *We* indicates *who is speaking*.)

Superior service brings customers back for additional purchases.
(*Service* is the main word of the subject. *Service* is the *simple subject* and indicates *what is spoken about*.)

3–5 Stress the importance of locating simple subjects.

Go to
Transparency/PowerPoint 3-6.

Compound Subjects

Banbury Textiles and McDonough Manufacturing use testimonial letters written by current clients.
(*Banbury Textiles* and *McDonough Manufacturing* are the main words that form the *compound subject* and indicate *who is spoken about*.)

Free consultations and estimates attract customers.
(*Consultations* and *estimates* are the main words that form the *compound subject*. These words indicate *what is spoken about*.)

Go to
Transparency/PowerPoint 3-7.

You may be wondering why it is important to identify the simple and compound subjects. These subject forms determine the verb you will use in your sentences. The time you spend identifying simple and compound subjects now will help you avoid errors in sentence structure later.

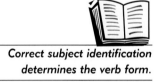

Correct subject identification determines the verb form.

CHECKUP 3-3

Directions: *In each of the following sentences, underline the simple subject once or the compound subject twice.*

1. They are projecting a sales increase of 14 percent.

2. Our representative will demonstrate our newest personal information manager (PIM) software tomorrow.

3. Cameras and film will be on sale for our preferred customers next week.

**GO TO
CD-ROM
CHECKUP 3-3**

4. <u>Elizabeth Franson</u> and <u>I</u> would like to discuss the opening that we have on our sales force.

5. <u>Customers</u> do not appreciate being kept "on hold" for toll calls to "help" lines.

6. Buying <u>habits</u> are changing as greater numbers of consumers shop at home.

Complete Subjects

Simple or compound subjects plus any of their modifiers comprise the complete subject of a sentence. Modifiers such as adjectives and adverbs describe other words.

**Go to
Transparency/PowerPoint 3-8.**

See Instructor Note 3-6 in IAE.

Review adjectives and the questions they answer (see Chapter 2).

Some customers choose products based on service and reliability rather than on price.

(The simple subject is *customers*. The word *some* modifies *customers* and indicates "how many" customers. *Some customers* is the complete subject.)

All objections and product complaints require attention.

(The compound subject is *objections* and *complaints*. The word *all* modifies *objections*; the word *product* modifies *complaints*. *All objections and product complaints* is the complete subject.)

CHECKUP 3-4

Directions: *In each of the following sentences, place parentheses ( ) around the complete subject. Underline the simple subject once or the compound subject twice.*

Ex.: (A service <u>guarantee</u>) informs customers that a firm is serious about doing things right the first time.

1. (CRI <u>Technology</u> and <u>TeleVideo Productions</u>) produce customer service training films.

2. (Most major <u>hotels</u> and <u>airlines</u>) reward their loyal customers.

3. (CD-ROM phone <u>books</u>) provide an inexpensive way to develop lists of prospective customers.

4. (<u>I</u>) cannot find out what the customer needs if I am doing all the talking.

5. (Active community <u>support</u> and employee <u>participation</u>) help gain exposure for your company.

6. (The <u>university</u> and the technical <u>college</u>) offer noncredit courses for improving sales techniques.

7. (Customer <u>feedback</u>) helps you correct problems.

8. (One women's apparel <u>shop</u>) offers discounts to loyal customers.

**GO TO
CD-ROM
CHECKUP 3-4**

Predicates

Once you have found the complete subject, the remainder of the sentence is the predicate. The verb is the easiest part of speech to recognize in the predicate.

The predicate adds meaning and clarity to the subject and tells *what the subject is doing or what the subject is.*

Frequent flier programs <u>encourage passenger loyalty.</u>
(The complete subject is *Frequent flier programs.* The remainder of the sentence is the predicate.)

Software companies <u>distribute products to customers for testing in the workplace.</u>
(The complete subject is *Software companies.* The remainder of the sentence is the predicate.)

John <u>developed several effective promotional messages for nonprofit organizations.</u>
(The complete subject is *John.* The remainder of the sentence is the predicate.)

Microsoft Corporation <u>sends product-development teams into companies to determine how they use software.</u>
(The complete subject is *Microsoft Corporation.* The remainder of the sentence is the predicate.)

Simple and Compound Predicates

A single verb is the *simple predicate* in a sentence. Two or more verbs form a *compound predicate.*

Simple Predicates
Mary <u>listens</u> carefully.
(The complete subject is *Mary.* The simple predicate is the verb *listens.*)
I <u>sell</u> software and computer supplies.
(The complete subject is *I.* The simple predicate is the verb *sell.*)
Our sales publications <u>are</u> attractive.
(The complete subject is *Our sales publications.* The simple predicate is the verb *are.*)

Compound Predicates
I <u>read</u> the warranty and <u>accepted</u> its provisions.
(The complete subject is *I. Read* and *accepted* are the verbs and the compound predicate.)
Our sales manager and a sales representative <u>listen</u> to our customers' complaints and <u>correct</u> all product deficiencies.
(The complete subject is *Our sales manager and a sales representative. Listen* and *correct* are the verbs and the compound predicate.)
Several companies <u>have eliminated</u> commissions and <u>placed</u> people on salaries.
(The complete subject is *Several companies. Have eliminated* and *placed* are the verbs and the compound predicate.)

Remember that a subject indicates who is speaking, who is spoken to, and who or what is spoken about.

Go to
Transparencies/PowerPoints
3-9a and 3-9b.

See Instructor Note 3-7 in IAE.

Verbs are action words or to be forms.

3-8 Stress compound predicate identification.

Note the use of the helping verb **have.**

A compound subject has two or more subjects. A compound predicate has two or more verbs.

CHECKUP 3-5

Directions: *In each of the following sentences from this chapter's Secondary Learning paragraphs, underline the simple predicate once* or *the compound predicate twice.*

1. Effective business managers <u>know</u> that they never get a second chance to make a first impression.
2. Their employees <u>are</u> enthusiastic and productive and <u>take</u> pride in helping customers.
3. These businesses <u>place</u> a high priority on customer service training and <u>have</u> a highly visible commitment to quality service.
4. You <u>want</u> sales employees to listen to your questions and to respond efficiently and effectively.

GO TO
CD-ROM
CHECKUP 3-5

Go to
Transparency/PowerPoint 3-10.

Complete Predicates

The complete predicate consists of a verb or verbs and all the modifiers that limit or describe the verbs.

> **Satisfied customers <u>create goodwill for your firm.</u>**
> (The complete subject is *Satisfied customers.* The simple predicate is *create.* The complete predicate is *create goodwill for your firm.*)

> **A restaurant trainer <u>may use videos or satellite television programs for training.</u>**
> (The complete subject is *A restaurant trainer.* The simple predicate is *may use.* The complete predicate is *may use videos or satellite television programs for training.*)

> **The National Retail Federation <u>offers seminars and conducts workshops in small retail stores.</u>**
> (The complete subject is *The National Retail Federation.* The compound predicate is *offers* and *conducts.* The complete predicate is *offers seminars and conducts workshops in small retail stores.*)

CHECKUP 3-6

Directions: *In each of the following sentences, place parentheses ( ) around the complete predicate. Underline the simple predicate once* or *the compound predicate twice.*

1. Timing (<u>becomes</u> your greatest advantage in reaching new markets.)
2. Large retailers (<u>use</u> electronic inventory systems to avoid running out of stock.)
3. Lawn Care, Inc., (<u>processes</u> all customer communications within 24 hours.)
4. (<u>Plan</u> and <u>rehearse</u> a new product demonstration.)
5. Consumers (<u>spend</u> more money when taxes are low and jobs are secure.)
6. Johnson and Johnson (<u>rewards</u> new ideas, <u>develops</u> them, and <u>evaluates</u> the end results.)
7. Sidewalk sales (<u>originated</u> during the early years of retailing.)
8. Six hundred field representatives (<u>counsel</u> and <u>assist</u> clients in a 12-state area.)

GO TO
CD-ROM
CHECKUP 3-6

OBJECTS AND COMPLEMENTS

You have now identified two parts of a sentence—the subject and the predicate. Another part of the sentence is the object, which is one way to complete the verb. Not all verbs will have objects. You will study additional material about verbs and objects in Chapter 9.

SLIP-UP

Headline in the *Maine Sunday Telegram:* "Neighbors Asked to Stop Barking"

Direct Objects

A direct object is a noun or a pronoun. A direct object provides one way to complete the verb by answering the questions *whom* or *what* after the verb. A direct object is *not* the subject of a sentence.

Go to Transparency/PowerPoint 3-11.

> **Laurie sells <u>homes</u> for a living.**
> Verb: *sells*
> Sells "what?": *homes*
> (Sells "whom" is not appropriate since homes are things.)
> Direct object: *homes*
>
> **My supervisor and coworkers congratulated <u>me</u> at the sales awards banquet.**
> Verb: *congratulated*
> Congratulated "whom?": *me*
> Direct object: *me*

Indirect Objects

A sentence cannot have an indirect object without having a direct object. An indirect object, like a direct object, is a noun or a pronoun and is *not* the subject of a sentence. The indirect object answers the questions *to whom*? or *for whom*? Typically, an indirect object precedes the direct object. Verb forms such as *give, offer, wish, ship, make, refuse, present,* or *send* usually precede an indirect object.

Go to Transparency/PowerPoint 3-12.

See Instructor Notes 3-9 and 3-10 in IAE.

> **The administrative assistant gave the sales <u>staff</u> several messages.**
> Verb: *gave*
> Direct Object: *messages*
> "To whom" are the messages given?: *staff*
> Indirect object: *staff*
>
> **We shipped <u>you</u> the reference manual last week.**
> Verb: *shipped*
> Direct object: *manual*
> "To whom" was the manual shipped?: *you*
> Indirect object: *you*

Subject Complements

Subject complements are predicate nouns or predicate pronouns that follow linking verbs such as *am, are, is, was,* and *were.* Linking

Linking verbs do not show action.

vers are not action verbs, but they have subjects. Subject complements rename or describe these subjects.

3-11 Relate the word *complete* to *complement*.

Complements Renaming Subjects (Predicate nouns)

Karen Daniels is <u>our new regional sales manager</u>.

(The complement *our new regional sales manager* renames *Karen Daniels*.)

We were the <u>top sales winners</u>.

(The complement *the top sales winners* renames *we*.)

The last person to contact the customer was <u>she</u>.

(The complement *she* renames *the last person*.)

Predicate Complements

Predicate complements are predicate adjectives that follow linking verbs and modify the subject in the sentence.

Complements Describing Subjects (Predicate adjectives)

Billboard advertising is <u>expensive</u>.

(The complement *expensive* describes *billboard advertising*.)

Anonymous survey cards are <u>not useful</u>.

(The complement *not useful* describes *anonymous survey cards*.)

Sales training video use is <u>popular</u>.

(The complement *popular* describes *sales training video use*.)

CHECKUP 3-7

Directions: *Identify the function of the underlined word or words in each sentence. In the space provided, write the abbreviation that identifies the function: direct objects (**DO**), indirect objects (**IO**), or complements (predicate nouns, pronouns, adjectives) (**C**).*

1. Database software assists sales <u>representatives</u> in maintaining client addresses and information.   DO

2. Sweetwaters Restaurant sent local food <u>editors</u> news releases of their new menus.   IO

3. Some sales brochures contain <u>testimonials</u> from satisfied customers.   DO

4. R. J. McDermid presented <u>Shermer and Associates</u> the Malcolm Baldrige National Quality Award.   IO

5. The Menominee Chamber of Commerce office processes <u>inquiries</u> within two days.   DO

6. Our salespeople are <u>intelligent</u> and <u>creative</u>.   C

**GO TO
CD-ROM**
CHECKUP 3-7

SENTENCE ORDER

You have already worked with sentences that are in a normal word pattern. The subject appears first and the predicate follows.

Varying the sentence order is a way to make sentences more interesting. When the predicate or part of the predicate is placed before the subject, the sentence is in inverted order. To identify the subjects of sentences in inverted order, try to change the order of the sentence to the normal subject-verb pattern. Correctly identify the simple subjects when sentences are in inverted order—these subjects determine the verb forms to use.

Go to Transparencies/PowerPoints 3-13a and 3-13b.

There/Here Sentences

The adverbs *here* and *there* are never subjects of sentences. When these words begin a sentence, the subject will always follow the verb.

There are several <u>causes</u> for lower customer satisfaction ratings.
Verb: *are*
Simple subject: *causes*
   (The subject *follows* the verb.)

Here is my monthly expense <u>report</u>.
Verb: *is*
Simple subject: *report*
   (The subject *follows* the verb.)

The adverbs here and there are not subjects of sentences.

Questions

Must we train people to be pleasant to customers?
   (Change the sentence into normal order.)

We must train people to be pleasant to customers.
Verb: *must train*
Simple subject: *We*

How much is a new customer worth?
   (Change the sentence into normal order.)

A new customer is worth how much?
Verb: *is*
Simple subject: *customer*

Sentences Beginning With Prepositional Phrases

On the counter are the most recent customer satisfaction surveys.
   (The subject follows the verb. Change the sentence into normal order.)

The most recent customer satisfaction surveys are on the counter.
Verb: *are*
Simple subject: *surveys*

Within the Target® retail system exist many opportunities for courteous employees to receive promotions.
   (The subject follows the verb. Change the sentence into normal order.)

Many opportunities exist for courteous employees to receive promotions within the Target ® retail system.
Verb: *exist*
Simple subject: *opportunities*

Sentence Development

CHECKUP 3-8

Directions: In the space provided, write **N** if the sentence is in normal order or write **I** if the sentence is in inverted order. Underline the simple subject once and the simple predicate twice.

1. Near the edge of Disney World lie the two visitor relations training centers. ___I___

2. You know the importance of delivering quality service when it is your own business. ___N___

3. Here are seven suggestions for improving customer relations. ___I___

4. What are the quotas for next month? ___I___

5. There are people who prefer to do their shopping in smaller malls. ___I___

6. Our customers appreciate our lower prices. ___N___

GO TO CD-ROM
CHECKUP 3-8

PHRASES AND CLAUSES

Prepositional phrases do not include a verb. Infinitive phrases begin with to and include a verb.

Go to Transparency/PowerPoint 3-14.

SLIP-UP
Newspaper headline: "Two Sisters Reunited After 18 Years in Checkout Counter."
Source: Internet

Learning grammar becomes more challenging when you add phrases and clauses to your writing. However, your writing also becomes more interesting.

Phrases

A phrase is a sequence of words that has neither a subject nor a predicate. *Prepositional phrases* begin with prepositions such as *of, in, at,* and *for* and end with a noun or pronoun. They do not include a verb. *Infinitive phrases* begin with *to* and include a verb form. Phrases cannot stand alone.

Prepositional Phrases	Infinitive Phrases
of our clients	to cancel the contract
in your move	to share their ideas
at our store	to run these ads
for them	to concentrate

When determining the subject in a sentence, do not consider prepositional or infinitive phrases. You may wish to place parentheses around your phrases as you identify subjects and verbs.

Each (of the sales managers) gives a brief report (at our district association meeting.)
Simple subject: *Each*
Verb: *gives*
(Both phrases in parentheses are prepositional phrases. Do not consider the prepositional phrase *of the sales managers* when selecting the subject.)

Chapter 3

A salesperson needs a helpful attitude (to provide quality service.)
Simple subject: *Salesperson*
Verb: *needs*
(The phrase is an infinitive phrase and is not the main verb.)

Additional information about phrases and subject selection appears in Chapter 11.

See Instructor Note 3-12 in IAE.

Clauses

A clause, like a phrase, is a sequence of words, but a clause has *both* a subject and a predicate. A clause that is a complete sentence can stand alone, which makes it an *independent clause*. A *dependent clause* is *not* a complete sentence and cannot stand alone. A dependent clause must be joined to an independent clause to make sense.

See Instructor Note 3-13 in IAE.

Go to Transparencies/PowerPoints 3-15a and 3-15b.

Independent Clauses

Point-of-Sale (POS) software provides information regarding sales activity by a salesperson.
(The sentence has a subject and a predicate, is a complete thought, and makes sense. When the sentence has a subject and a predicate and can stand alone, it is an independent clause.)

All customers appreciate helpful, pleasant salespersons.
(The sentence can stand alone and is an independent clause.)

Being independent means you can do something without help. An independent clause can stand on its own without help. Being dependent means you rely on someone else for help. A dependent clause relies on an independent clause for its help.

Dependent Clauses

When we complete our sales training,
(The words cannot stand alone but require an independent clause [complete sentence] to make sense.)

dependent clause — independent clause
When we complete our sales training, we will have a party.

After you have lost an account,
(The words cannot stand alone but require an independent clause to make sense.)

dependent clause — independent clause
After you have lost an account, find out why you lost it.
(The subject *you* is understood in the independent clause.)

independent clause — dependent clause
My supervisor gave me the names of two new clients before she left for London.
(Note the placement of the dependent clause.)

When a dependent clause *introduces* an independent clause, place a comma at the *end* of the dependent clause. No comma is necessary when the dependent clause is at the end of the sentence. Additional information concerning dependent clauses and commas appears in Chapter 16.

Place a comma after dependent clauses that *introduce* independent clauses.

If the refrigerator was damaged in moving, our standard guarantee still applies.

(Note the comma at the end of the dependent clause.)

Because they are often the first contacts customers have with firms, receptionists must have excellent communication skills.

(Note the comma at the end of the dependent clause.)

Receptionists must have excellent communication skills **because they are often the first contacts customers have with firms.**

(No comma is placed before or after the dependent clause when it appears at the end of the sentence.)

CHECKUP 3-9

Directions: *In the space provided, write* ***I*** *if the group of underlined words is an independent clause; write* ***D*** *if the group of words is a dependent clause. If the words are phrases, write* ***P***.

1. They based award ratings <u>on performance.</u>   P

2. <u>The fee is $120 to run this ad for three days.</u>   I

3. Obtain testimonials <u>from people</u> with local community credibility.   P

4. <u>Your service must be superior,</u> or your merchandise must be different from your competitors' goods.   I

5. <u>If Golden Rule Oil Company is late with an oil delivery,</u> the customer gets the oil free.   D

6. We have an unstated guarantee that our employees will do anything <u>to make customers happy.</u>   P

**GO TO
CD-ROM**
CHECKUP 3-9

SENTENCE FORMATIONS

The number of clauses in a sentence determines whether the formation is a simple sentence, a compound sentence, a complex sentence, or a compound-complex sentence. By using different sentence formations, you can add variety to your writing.

Simple Sentences

See Instructor Note 3-14 in IAE.

Go to
Transparencies/PowerPoints
3-16 and 3-17.

A simple sentence has one complete subject and one complete predicate. The subject, the predicate, or both may be compound. Although the subject or verb may be plural in number, it is still only a single subject or a single verb. In the following examples, the subjects are underlined once. The verbs are underlined twice.

Simple Subject-Single Verb

Our advertising <u>campaigns</u> usually <u>succeed</u>.

Compound Subject-Single Verb

<u>Vicki</u> and <u>I</u> <u>enjoyed</u> your comments about the new direct marketing campaign.

Simple Subject-Compound Verb

Professional <u>salespeople</u> <u>listen</u> to customer objections and <u>find</u> ways to handle them.

Compound Subject-Compound Verb

My <u>realtor</u> and <u>banker</u> <u>understood</u> my situation and <u>worked</u> for my benefit.

Compound Sentences

A compound sentence consists of two independent clauses (simple sentences) connected by a coordinating conjunction. Use coordinating conjunctions to connect two independent clauses of equal importance. Each independent clause has its own subject(s) and its own predicate(s). A comma separates the two independent clauses and appears *before* the coordinating conjunction.

Go to
Transparency/PowerPoint 3-18.

Words such as and, or, nor, *and* but *are coordinating conjunctions (see Chapter 2).*

See Instructor Notes 3-15 and 3-16 in IAE.

> **Scott did not buy our product, <u>but</u> he recommended our service to several others in his club.**

Independent clause 1: Scott did not buy our product.

Independent clause 2: He recommended our service to several others in his club.

(The two independent clauses are joined by the coordinating conjunction *but* to form a compound sentence. Place a comma *before* the coordinating conjunction.)

> ─── independent clause ─── ─── independent clause ───
> **We offer 90-minute service training classes, <u>and</u> we always have waiting lists for them.**

(The two independent clauses are joined by the coordinating conjunction *and* to form a compound sentence. Place a comma *before* the coordinating conjunction.)

Punctuation ALERT!

Use a comma to separate two independent clauses. The comma appears before the coordinating conjunction.

Complex Sentences

A complex sentence consists of an independent clause and a dependent clause. The dependent clause cannot stand alone; it depends on the independent clause for meaning. When you want to stress one idea more than another, use the complex sentence. The independent clause receives greater emphasis than the dependent clause receives.

Go to
Transparency/PowerPoint 3-19.

> ── dependent clause ── ── independent clause ──
> **When our competition increased, we concentrated on improving our customer service.**

(The emphasis is on the independent clause.)

Go to
Transparency/PowerPoint 3-20.

dependent clause   independent clause

Before I called on Northgate Industries, I practiced my presentation.

(The emphasis is on the independent clause.)

Compound-Complex Sentences

A compound-complex sentence consists of more than one independent clause and one or more dependent clauses.

dependent clause   independent clause

Because Geoff is rude to customers, he causes problems in our department, and we are getting irritated with his behavior.
independent clause

(The sentence contains two independent clauses and one dependent clause.)

dependent clause   independent clause

After her sales presentation, Dana planned to return to Seattle immediately, but the bad weather delayed her flight.
independent clause

(The sentence contains two independent clauses and one dependent clause.)

Sentence Fragments

Go to
Transparency/PowerPoint 3-21.

Sentence fragments may be words, phrases, or dependent clauses. They cannot stand alone even though some fragments may contain subjects and predicates. You will see fragments written incorrectly with a capital letter and a period. In many cases, you can attach a fragment to a sentence that precedes or follows it.

The next customer appreciation day.

(The fragment does not express a complete thought and does not have a predicate.)

Asked for sales assistance.

(The fragment does not express a complete thought and does not have a subject.)

Sentences must have subjects and predicates, make sense, and express complete thoughts.

Run-On Sentences

Go to
Transparency/PowerPoint 3-22.

Run-on sentences are complete sentences with period or comma faults. Two sentences "run" together, which makes it difficult to grasp the meaning of the material. Correcting run-on sentences involves (1) adding a comma and a coordinating conjunction such as *and, or,* or *but*; (2) using a semicolon; or (3) making two separate sentences.

Run-on Sentences—No Punctuation Between Clauses

I want to accept the sales job in Porterville the family wants to stay here.

Corrections

I want to accept the sales job in Porterville, but the family wants to stay here.

(Add a comma and a coordinating conjunction between the two independent clauses.)

I want to accept the sales job in Porterville; the family wants to stay here.

(Use a semicolon to separate the two independent clauses.)

I want to accept the sales job in Porterville. The family wants to stay here.

(Use a period to separate the two independent clauses.)

Run-On Sentences—Comma Splice

Every year we conduct a customer survey, our customers tell us what products they would like for us to offer.

(A comma without a coordinating conjunction between two independent clauses is referred to as a comma splice and results in a run-on sentence.)

Corrections

Every year we conduct a customer survey, and our customers tell us what products they would like for us to offer.

(Add a comma and a coordinating conjunction between the two independent clauses.)

Every year we conduct a customer survey; our customers tell us what products they would like for us to offer.

(Use a semicolon to separate the two independent clauses.)

Every year we conduct a customer survey. Our customers tell us what products they would like for us to offer.

(Use a period to separate the two independent clauses.)

CHECKUP 3-10

Directions: In the space provided, write one of the following abbreviations to identify each of the sentences listed below: **S** (simple sentence), **D** (compound sentence), **X** (complex sentence), **C** (compound-complex sentence), **F** (fragment), **R** (run-on sentence).

1. Because so much of our business is outside the United States, we need someone with international sales experience.   X

2. Don't focus solely on new customers work to increase sales to old ones.   R

3. The migration to suburbs creates problems for downtown merchants.   S

4. When customers open charge accounts.   F

5. CRI Productions uses videos to train employees, it's expensive.   R

6. Although Jordan just started working for us, he has done a remarkable job.   X

7. When customers have product complaints, they need someone who will listen, and they require immediate attention.   C

8. Every salesperson has an individual sales plan, and those who exceed their goals receive monetary rewards.   D

GO TO
CD-ROM
CHECKUP 3-10

DIAGRAMMING SENTENCES

See Instructor Note 3-17 in IAE.

A diagram is a line drawing or example that explains the parts or operation of something. A *sentence diagram* shows the parts of a sentence and the relationship of all the words to one another. The diagramming process is similar to putting together the parts of a puzzle. You begin with the major parts of the sentence—the simple subject, simple predicate (verb), and the direct object. Follow these beginning steps for diagramming sentences.

Ryan sells insurance.

1. Draw a horizontal line with a vertical line through it.

2. Write the simple subject (Ryan) to the left of the vertical line; write the simple predicate to the right.

   Ryan | sells

3. Draw another vertical line on the base line after the verb. This line does *not* cross the horizontal line.

   Ryan | sells |

4. Write the direct object to the right of this second vertical line.

   Ryan | sells | insurance

CHECKUP 3-11

Directions: *In the space provided below, diagram the following sentences. Use only the simple subject, simple predicate, and direct object.*

1. All product complaints require attention.

   complaints | require | attention

72

Chapter 3

2. We will send the reference manual.

We	will send	manual

3. Customer feedback has caused improvements.

feedback	has caused	improvements

4. I read the warranty.

I	read	warranty

5. My supervisor congratulated me.

supervisor	congratulated	me

**GO TO
CD-ROM
CHECKUP 3-11**

PRACTICE

NAME _____

PRACTICE 1A

Directions: In the space provided, write the letter of the item that identifies the under-lined word or words in each of the following sentences.

1. Top sales performers are <u>ambitious</u> and <u>innovative</u>.   1. __d__
   a. indirect object   c. compound predicate
   b. complete predicate   d. complement

2. <u>Our program is designed to increase sales, but it achieves this through higher levels of customer service.</u>   2. __b__
   a. simple sentence   c. complex sentence
   b. compound sentence   d. inverted sentence order

3. <u>Will you please explain to your customers that we are discontinuing these items.</u>   3. __d__
   a. indirect question   c. statement
   b. direct question   d. courteous request

4. <u>to the front of the store</u>   4. __a__
   a. phrase   c. inverted sentence order
   b. independent clause   d. command

5. <u>Will consumers' buying habits change with electronic shopping?</u>   5. __b__
   a. indirect question   c. simple sentence
   b. direct question   d. complex sentence

6. <u>Hallmark Cards</u> installed kiosks in shopping malls to allow shoppers to create their own greeting cards.   6. __c__
   a. compound subject   c. complete subject
   b. direct object   d. complement

7. <u>Because of consumer advertising supplements, the average newspaper weighs 50 percent more today than it did ten years ago.</u>   7. __c__
   a. simple sentence   c. complex sentence
   b. compound sentence   d. normal sentence order

8. Individual, Inc., <u>delivers</u> news stories to its customers by fax or electronic mail.   8. __d__
   a. simple subject   c. complement
   b. compound predicate   d. simple predicate

9. <u>If a customer has a problem,</u> he or she can call the store, and a service representative will resolve the matter.   9. __c__
   a. independent clause   c. dependent clause
   b. phrase   d. complete subject

10. <u>After the holiday sales, I needed several days of vacation, but I needed the extra money even more than the time off.</u>   10. __d__
    a. simple sentence   c. complex sentence
    b. compound sentence   d. compound-complex sentence

GO TO
CD-ROM
PRACTICE 1
EXERCISES

PRACTICE 2A

A. Directions: *In each of the following sentences, underline the simple or compound subject once and the simple or compound predicate twice. When appropriate, write an unstated subject in the blank at the beginning of the sentence.*

Ex: <u>You</u>_____ <u>Focus</u> on the value of your product.

1. _____ Our <u>customers</u> <u>demand</u> faster deliveries.

2. _____ The <u>FDA</u> <u>restricted</u> food-labeling procedures to protect consumers.

3. <u>You</u>_____ <u>Answer</u> the phone by the second ring.

4. _____ The <u>Better Business Bureau</u> and the <u>U.S. Postal Service</u> <u>are</u> sources for information about unknown clients.

5. _____ What <u>are</u> your sales <u>goals</u>?

B. Directions: *Place one of the following punctuation marks at the end of each statement: period (.), question mark (?), exclamation point (!). Write your answer in the space provided.*

1. Is there a service I can provide that my competitors are not offering   1. __?__

2. Listen more and talk less when you deal with customers   2. __.__

3. People don't mind paying more when they know the product is superior   3. __.__

4. A patient asked if I would reschedule her appointment   4. __.__

5. Will you please share your most memorable sales experience with our group   5. __.__

C. Directions: *In the following sentences, underline a direct object once and/or an indirect object twice. Circle the predicate nouns or predicate adjectives (complements).*

1. Our nine-member team sold <u>products</u> with a value of $6.2 million.

2. Interior Designs hired <u>me</u>.

3. After reviewing our database entries, we found outdated <u>addresses</u>.

4. Johnson Printing sends <u>customers</u> monthly satisfaction <u>surveys</u>.

5. First-rate customer service is a (prerequisite) for any company's success.

PRACTICE

NAME _____

D. Directions: *Write* **Yes** *in the space provided if the sentences that follow are in normal order. Write* **No** *if they are not in normal order. Underline the simple subject once and the simple predicate twice in all sentences.*

1. Have you built a strong sales team?

2. This information system will tell you what your customers want.

3. Which new markets will your home business target?

4. There are specialized courses in which creative ways to retain customers are taught.

5. Here is an extra bonus for finding all those customer referrals.

1. __No__

2. __Yes__

3. __No__

4. __No__

5. __No__

E. Directions: *If the word groups below are independent clauses, write* **Yes** *in the space provided. If they are dependent clauses and cannot stand alone, write* **No.** *Then complete the clause to make it a complete sentence.*

(Answers will vary.)

1. As growing numbers of consumers order from catalogs.

   No. As growing numbers of consumers order from catalogs, we will need more customer service representatives.

2. One of the first divisions that downsizing affects is employee training.

   Yes

3. AmericTrend involves current users of their products in new product surveys.

   Yes

4. If a business takes its customers for granted.

   No. If a business takes its customers for granted, it may lose business.

5. Shopping malls attract local consumers and tourists.

   Yes

F. Directions: *Rewrite the following groups of words correctly. Punctuation marks may be necessary.*

(Answers will vary.)

1. Customer service is more than an eagerness to please it is also customer satisfaction.

   Customer service is more than an eagerness to please; it is also customer satisfaction.

2. I apologize for the inconvenience our Super Bowl stock disappeared within an hour of delivery.

   I apologize for the inconvenience; our Super Bowl stock disappeared within an hour of delivery.

Chapter 3

3. We appreciate your business. Whether you're a lifetime customer or a newcomer.

   <u>Whether you're a lifetime customer or a newcomer, we appreciate your</u>

   <u>business.</u>

4. Bryant and Stoker eliminated commissions, and placed salespeople on salary.

   <u>Bryant and Stoker eliminated commissions and placed salespeople on salary.</u>

5. Business owners may use different training methods but they should make a commitment to improve customer relations.

   <u>Business owners may use different training methods, but they should make</u>

   <u>a commitment to improve customer relations.</u>

GO TO
CD-ROM
PRACTICE 2
EXERCISES

PRACTICE 3A

PROOFREADING

*Directions: Proofread and compare the two sentences in each group. If they are the same, write **Yes** in the space provided. If they are not the same, write **No**. Use the first sentence as the correct copy. If you find errors in the second sentence, underline them.*

See Instructor Note 3-18 in IAE.

1. Ask yourself, "What would make me buy from this company?"

   Ask yourself, <u>What</u> would make me buy from this <u>company</u>?'

   1. __No__

2. Prospective clients ignore you or tune you out if your voice is flat and monotonous.

   Prospective clients ignore <u>your</u> or <u>tune out</u> if your voice is flat and monotonous.

   2. __No__

3. Here are the complete results of the survey.

   Here are the complete results of the survey.

   3. __Yes__

4. Servicio, Inc., provides translating services to many companies in the United States.

   Servicio, Inc., provides translating services to many companies in the United States.

   4. __Yes__

   See Instructor Note 3-19 in IAE.

5. A private sale for our account customers only will be held at 7 p.m. Monday. | A private sale for our charge account customers only will be held at 7 <u>a.m.</u> Monday.

   5. __No__

GO TO
CD-ROM
PRACTICE 3
EXERCISES

PRACTICE

NAME

PRACTICE 4A

WRITING

3-20 Students need to identify the type of sentence to write.

(Answers will vary.)

Assignment: *In the space provided, complete the following exercises.*

1. Write a simple sentence describing a company with excellent customer service. Underline the simple subject once and the simple predicate twice.

   I like shopping at The Gap®.

2. Write a sentence with a compound subject describing a product or service you enjoy using. Underline the compound subject once and the simple or compound predicate twice.

   A fun atmosphere and good food are the reasons I like to eat at Friday's®.

3. Write a question about customer service. Underline the simple subject once and the simple predicate twice.

   Do you know whether Pepsi® has a Website?

4. Write a complex sentence about poor customer service. Underline the simple or compound subject once and the simple or compound predicate twice. Circle the dependent clause.

   Since I lost my receipt, the customer service representative told me that I could not return the jeans.

**GO TO
CD-ROM
PRACTICE 4
EXERCISES**

3-21 Check online sites carefully before assigning them to students.

ONLINE EXERCISES

Many businesses have Websites for their customers. A Website is a method of providing immediate customer service. To complete the following exercises, you need access to a computer with an Internet connection.

**Punctuation
ALERT!**

Use exact punctuation when typing an Internet address.

Objective: Visit a customer service Website.

1. With your Internet browser on the screen, key:

   http://www.gap.com in the location text box. Then, press **Enter.**

2. You will be on the Website for Gap clothing. Explore the site.

3. Answer the following questions about The Gap Website:

   • Can you order items online? If so, is there any information about having a secure Website?

NAME _____

ONLINE *EXERCISES*

- Does the company have an e-mail address? If so, what is the address?

- What features make this Website interesting?

4. Visit the following customer service Websites. List the interesting customer service features on each site.

Levi Strauss	**http://www.levi.com**
Southwest Airlines	**http://www.iflyswa.com**
Microsoft	**http://www.microsoft.com**
Coca-Cola Company	**http://www.coke.com**

3-22 Have students print their lists and/or summarize these sites, if you wish.

NAME _____

PRACTICE 1B

Directions: *In the space provided, write the letter of the item that identifies the underlined word or words in each of the following sentences.*

1. Some businesses may prefer advertising in the newspaper, and others may choose to create Websites. **1.** _____ c _____
   - **a.** simple sentence
   - **b.** compound predicate
   - **c.** compound sentence
   - **d.** complex sentence

2. We offer customers a money-back guarantee. **2.** _____ a _____
   - **a.** indirect object
   - **b.** direct object
   - **c.** simple subject
   - **d.** compound subject

3. Our representatives are extremely competent professionals. **3.** _____ c _____
   - **a.** indirect object
   - **b.** complete predicate
   - **c.** complement
   - **d.** compound predicate

4. Won't you please make certain the doors are locked and the alarm is set before you leave each evening. **4.** _____ d _____
   - **a.** indirect question
   - **b.** direct question
   - **c.** statement
   - **d.** courteous request

5. Greta asked if we had any customer complaints about our store hours. **5.** _____ a _____
   - **a.** indirect question
   - **b.** courteous request
   - **c.** inverted sentence order
   - **d.** direct question

6. If they send coupons to satisfied customers **6.** _____ c _____
   - **a.** phrase
   - **b.** independent clause
   - **c.** dependent clause
   - **d.** statement

7. Miscommunication frequently occurs in the business world because of poor message taking. **7.** _____ b _____
   - **a.** simple subject
   - **b.** simple predicate
   - **c.** complement
   - **d.** compound predicate

8. The tone of your voice is especially important on the telephone. **8.** _____ b _____
   - **a.** compound subject
   - **b.** complete subject
   - **c.** direct object
   - **d.** indirect object

9. When conducting business, should you obey the law or your own sense of ethics? **9.** _____ b _____
   - **a.** indirect question
   - **b.** direct question
   - **c.** command
   - **d.** courteous request

10. Gump's window display received public exposure and garnered interest in the Humane Society. **10.** _____ c _____
    - **a.** simple and complete predicates
    - **b.** simple predicate
    - **c.** compound predicate
    - **d.** complete predicate

NAME _____

PRACTICE 2B

A. Directions: *In each of the following sentences, underline the simple or compound subject once and the simple or compound predicate twice. When appropriate, write an unstated subject in the blank at the beginning of the sentence.*

1. _____ Creativity and originality characterize successful advertising campaigns.
2. You _____ Give your full attention to a customer.
3. _____ The receptionist answers the phone and screens the calls.
4. _____ People remember the last thing they hear in a sales presentation.
5. _____ An expert initial greeting creates goodwill.

B. Directions: *Place one of the following punctuation marks at the end of each statement: period (.), question mark (?), and exclamation point (!). Write your answer in the space provided.*

1. If you are friendly, your customers tend to be friendly   1. _____._____
2. Why do you think it is important to have a positive attitude   2. _____?_____
3. Always be courteous, no matter how busy you are   3. _____._____
4. Will you please send the information to the committee   4. _____._____
5. Use voice mail to leave a message if the party you are calling is unavailable   5. _____._____

C. Directions: *In the following sentences, underline a direct object once and/or an indirect object twice.*

1. You can show interest in customers by listening to their concerns.
2. The manager added additional salespeople during the holidays.
3. Broderbund sends customers software upgrade coupons.
4. Customers appreciate good service.
5. When you need more information about the products, ask the salesperson.

D. Directions: *Write **Yes** in the space provided if the sentences that follow are in normal order. Write **No** if they are not in normal order. Underline the simple subject once and the simple predicate twice in all sentences.*

1. Have you checked our sales figures for this month?   1. ____No____
2. Here is the discount coupon that Karen wanted.   2. ____No____
3. Across from the credit department offices is the customer complaint desk.   3. ____No____
4. Tim's message explained why he was unable to attend the meeting.   4. ____Yes____
5. There are two new sales representatives on the staff at Ryder Technology.   5. ____No____

E. Directions: *If the word groups below are independent clauses, write **Yes** in the space provided. If they are dependent clauses, write **No** and complete the clause to make it a complete sentence.* (Answers will vary.)

1. If there are more than two people in a room with a speakerphone

   No. If there are more than two people in a room with a speakerphone, close the door.

2. Write and record a greeting for your own voice mailbox.

   Yes

3. If you are going to be out of the office, let someone know where you may be reached.

   Yes

Name _____

4. When clients are not treated properly, they take their business elsewhere.

Yes _____

5. Before you pick up your phone.

No. Before you pick up your phone, be prepared to take a message. _____

F. Directions: *Rewrite the following groups of words correctly. Punctuation marks may be necessary.*　　　*(Answers will vary.)*

1. If your job involves taking calls from unhappy callers you have a difficult job

If your job involves taking calls from unhappy callers, you have a difficult job. _____

2. Put people before paperwork help the customer first.

Put people before paperwork, and help the customer first.　　Put people before paperwork; help the customer first.

3. When a customer has a problem. Address it quickly.

When a customer has a problem, address it quickly. _____

4. Your attitude is contagious, and will infect the customer.

Your attitude is contagious and will infect the customer. _____

5. Never promise what you can't deliver honesty is always the best policy.

Never promise what you can't deliver; honesty is always the best policy. _____

Practice 3B

Proofreading

Directions: *Proofread and compare the two sentences in each group. If they are the same, write* **Yes** *in the space provided. If they are not the same, write* **No.** *Use the first sentence as the correct copy. If you find errors in the second sentence, underline them.*

1. How does a company create an environment where customer service will flourish?

How does a company create a environment where customer service will flourish?

1. _____ No _____

2. Nothing makes a customer happier than a follow-up call a few days after a major purchase.

Nothing makes a customers happier than a follow-up call a few days after a major purchase.

2. _____ No _____

3. A first encounter—whether it's with the gardener, receptionist, or company president—can make or break a sale.

A first encounter—whether its with the gardener, receptionist or company president—can make or break a sale.

3. _____ No _____

4. When a customer has a problem, address it quickly.

When a customer has a problem, address it quickly.

4. _____ Yes _____

5. Hewlett Packard technician Patrick Mufaska has a sign in his workstation that reads, "The job that ate my brain."

Hewlett Packard technician Patrick Mufaska has a sign in his workstation that reads, "The job that ate my brain".

5. _____ No _____

NAME _____

WRITING

Assignment: *Complete the following exercises.*   (Answers will vary.)

1. Write a simple sentence describing a company with poor customer service. Underline the simple subject once and the simple predicate twice.

   The only office supply store in town closes at 5 p.m.

2. Write a sentence with a compound predicate describing a product or service you enjoy using. Underline the simple or compound subject once and the compound predicate twice.

   Dayton's® wraps packages and accepts returns without receipts.

3. Write an exclamatory sentence about customer service. Underline the simple subject once and the simple predicate twice.

   The customer is always right!

4. Write a compound sentence about good customer service. Underline the simple or compound subject once and the simple or compound predicate twice.

   See's Candies® has a great selection of chocolates, and they always give samples.

See Instructor Note 3-23 in IAE.

ONLINE *EXERCISES*

To complete the following exercises, you need access to a computer with an Internet connection.

Objective: *Visit a customer service Website.*

You will visit the Amazon Website, which is a cyberspace bookstore. This site offers millions of books online as well as links to interesting book-related sites.

1. With your Internet browser on the screen, key:

   http://www.amazon.com in the location text box. Then, press **Enter**.

2. Locate **Keyword Search** on the Amazon home page (not Search on your Internet browser) and click on it.

3. Key in the name **Tom Peters**.

4. Click on **Go!**

5. Select a book that looks interesting and read a description.

The purpose of visiting this site is to explore the effects of online shopping on customer service. You may wish to have students search for additional authors or books. You may ask students to write a few sentences about their selections.

Sentence Development   83

LOOKING BACK

See Instructor Note 3-24 in IAE.

Posttest

Directions: *In the space provided, write the letter of the correct answer.*

1. What term does the following define? *A noun or pronoun that completes the verb.*   1. ____c____
   a. subject
   c. direct object
   b. sentence
   d. complete predicate

2. What mark of punctuation should follow this sentence? *Will you please return the*   2. ____b____
   merchandise in the envelope provided
   a. question mark
   c. exclamation mark
   b. period
   d. quotation marks

3. What is the complete subject in this sentence? *The expectations of taxpayers and utility*   3. ____d____
   customers are greater than ever before.
   a. greater than ever before
   c. The expectations
   b. customers
   d. The expectations of taxpayers and utility
       customers

4. What is the simple predicate in this sentence? *Customer support representatives usually*   4. ____b____
   offer three or four choices to callers.
   a. usually
   c. usually offer
   b. offer
   d. Customer support representatives usually offer

5. What is the direct object in the following sentence? *The switchboard operator sets the*   5. ____b____
   mood for the call.
   a. sets
   c. rest
   b. mood
   d. call

6. Which sentence pattern does this statement represent? *Facial expression and body language*   6. ____b____
   are significant nonverbal signals.
   a. the subject-verb pattern
   c. the subject-verb-object pattern
   b. the subject-linking verb
   d. inverted order sentence
       -complement pattern

7. Which statement is *not* correct?   7. ____c____
   a. Infinitive phrases begin with *to.*
   c. Prepositional phrases include verbs.
   b. Phrases cannot stand alone.
   d. Phrases have neither subjects nor predicates.

8. Which sentence formation does this statement represent? *Answering machines have*   8. ____b____
   been available for years, and now voice mail has arrived in businesses.
   a. simple sentence
   c. complex sentence
   b. compound sentence
   d. inverted sentence

9. What does this group of words indicate? *Place people before paperwork.*   9. ____b____
   a. dependent clause
   c. a sentence fragment
   b. a complete sentence
   d. a run-on sentence

10. Diagram the following sentence.
    Bob sells telephones.

Bob	sells	telephones

PART 2

Reviewing Nouns and Pronouns

CHAPTER 4

Noun Functions and Plurals

THE INTERNET

The Internet, also known as the Net, is a massive worldwide network of computers. This network is rapidly becoming an important method of communications. Through the Internet, you can communicate with other people by using electronic mail. You can also research information, download computer programs, participate in discussion groups, play games, and shop.

Even the most farsighted Internet pioneers did not predict the enormous growth and the tremendous impact the Net has had on global communications. Experts even have difficulty calculating how many millions of people use the Internet daily from either their homes or their workplaces. The increased popularity of the Internet has caused a flood of investment and innovation. Advertisers are experimenting with ways to use the Internet to sell their products, and most companies are finding that a presence on the Internet is a necessity for competing in business.

Futurists predict that computers and the Internet will be everywhere, affecting everything we do. Futurists also believe that the Internet will be as readily available for communications as electricity is today. Your study of business English is vital to your ability to communicate effectively through computers and on the Internet, not only today but also in the future.

OBJECTIVES

After you have studied this chapter and completed the exercises, you will be able to do the following:

1. Identify proper and common nouns.
2. Identify functions of nouns in sentences.
3. Recognize the differences among singular, plural, and collective nouns.
4. Form plurals of singular nouns, numbers, letters, and abbreviations.
5. Form plurals of foreign and irregular nouns.
6. Diagram sentences having complements and appositives.

TERMS TO REMEMBER

DOWNLOAD

GLOBAL COMMUNICATIONS

NET

NETWORK

OBJECTIVES

LOOKING AHEAD

Pretest

Directions: In the space provided, write the letter of the correct answer.

1. What is the function of a noun in a sentence?
   a. connects words
   b. modifies verbs
   c. expresses action
   d. names something

   1. _____d_____

2. Which line of proper nouns is correct?
   a. TVs, Grand canyon, New York city
   b. january, C's, Adelman Cleaners
   c. CD-ROMs, Dr. Walters, College of the Redwoods
   d. Randy Sabien, university of North Carolina, Pope and Talbot

   2. _____c_____

3. *Both students expressed an interest in the Internet demonstration.* In this sentence, the noun *interest* is the
   a. direct object.
   b. subject of the sentence.
   c. object of a preposition.
   d. indirect object.

   3. _____a_____

4. *Lionel Hawkes, the company's investment counselor, checks several online stock reports daily.* In this sentence, the noun *counselor* is
   a. the subject of the sentence.
   b. an appositive.
   c. in direct address.
   d. the complement.

   4. _____b_____

Directions: In the space provided, write the letter or letters of the correct plural nouns.

	a.	b.	c.	d.		
1.	sketches	businesses	prefixs	waltzs	1.	a, b
2.	proofes	chiefs	halfs	leaves	2.	b, d
3.	trolleys	vacancys	supplys	libraries	3.	a, d
4.	studios	concertoes	portfolios	memoes	4.	a, c
5.	basis	stimuli	formulas	criteria	5.	b, c, d
6.	bldg.	bu	CPUs	Ds	6.	b, c, d

OVERVIEW

Chapter 2 was an overview of the parts of speech and some of their functions in sentences. In this chapter, as well as in Chapter 5, you will learn about nouns. Since nouns are highly visible parts of sentences, pay close attention to their many functions. In addition to understanding how nouns are used in sentences, you will learn rules for forming the plurals of nouns.

CLASSES OF NOUNS

Nouns name persons, places, and things. Nouns can also identify activities, ideas, and qualities. A sentence may have more than one noun.

Persons
friend programmer Queen Elizabeth

Places
city lake Glacier National Park

Things
e-mail desk software

Activities
printing talking filing

Ideas and Qualities
freedom courage value

Go to Transparencies/PowerPoints 4-1 and 4-2.

See Instructor Notes 4-1, 4-2, and 4-3 in IAE.

Refer to the nouns section in Chapter 2 for additional examples.

Go to Transparency/PowerPoint 4-3.

4-4 Refer to *The Gregg Reference Manual* or another available manual for additional examples of common and proper nouns.

Refer to a reference manual, such as* The Gregg Reference Manual, *for additional information on common and proper nouns.

Common and Proper Nouns

All nouns belong to one of two classifications—common nouns or proper nouns. *Common nouns* refer to general persons, places, and things. Do not capitalize common nouns. *Proper nouns* refer to specific persons, places, or things. Capitalize proper nouns.

Common Nouns
magazine textbook corporation

Proper Nouns
Netscape® January University of West Virginia

Some nouns in trademarks or names of items containing proper nouns were previously capitalized; however, because they have become everyday words, words such as the following no longer require capitalization:

aspirin e-mail manila envelope

SLIP-UP
Jason Thompson, who had four RBIs in August, four RBIs in September, and one homer since July 26, smashed a blast off a poet high in the upper deck for his grand slam. Source: Richard Lederer. [Note: Is the noun *poet* or *pole*?]

Exercise 1

Directions: *Identify the nouns in the following list of words. Underline common nouns once and proper nouns twice. Some words may be used as nouns or as other parts of speech.*

GO TO
CD-ROM
CHECKUP 4-1
EXERCISE 1

1. attitude
2. heavy
3. studios
4. Colby
5. Orlando
6. connection
7. years
8. Becker & Associates
9. resign
10. electronic
11. modems
12. achievement
13. Seattle
14. footnote
15. Lake Superior
16. protection
17. shortest
18. Rodriguez
19. directories
20. professional

Exercise 2

Directions: *Locate the nouns in the first paragraph of the Secondary Learning material at the beginning of the chapter. List the common and the proper nouns under the appropriate headings.*

GO TO
CD-ROM
CHECKUP 4-1
EXERCISE 2

Common Nouns	Proper Nouns
network	Internet
computers	Net
network	Internet
method	
communications	
people	
mail	
information	
programs	
groups	
games	

FUNCTIONS OF NOUNS

See Instructor Note 4-5 in IAE.

Nouns appear in different locations in a sentence and assume various roles depending on their positions. In the following text, you will learn the uses of nouns and their placement in sentences. You will also see how nouns are used as appositives and in direct address.

Go to Transparency/PowerPoint 4-4a.

Review the discussion on compound and simple subjects in Chapter 3.

Nouns Used as Singular or Compound Subjects

Nouns often appear as *singular* or *compound subjects* of sentences. Their usual placement in the sentence is before the verb.

The **number** of Web ads will increase tremendously in the next five years.

(The common noun *number* is a simple subject.)

Lycos and **Yahoo!** are popular online search engines.

(The proper nouns *Lycos* and *Yahoo!* represent a compound subject.)

Nouns Used as Direct Objects

A direct object often involves a noun that receives the action of a verb. A direct object appears after the verb. Direct objects may be singular or plural.

> **The city ordered new computers.**
>
> (The common noun *computers* is the direct object.)

Nouns Used as Indirect Objects

An indirect object usually appears before a direct object and directly after a verb in a sentence. Indirect objects usually follow verbs such as *buy, sell, send, ask,* and *give.*

> **I sent Tony the updated figures for the network configuration.**
>
> (The proper noun *Tony* is the indirect object of the verb *sent. Tony* answers the question *To whom?*)

Nouns Used as Objects of Prepositions

A prepositional phrase consists of a preposition, the object of the preposition, which is a noun or pronoun, and its modifiers. More than one prepositional phrase may appear in a sentence.

> **I send a check to my Internet service provider every month.**
>
> (In the prepositional phrase *to my Internet service provider,* the preposition is *to* and the object of the preposition is *provider,* which is a noun.)

Nouns Used as Subject Complements (Predicate Nouns)

A subject complement (predicate noun) follows a linking verb and renames the subject.

> **Jane White is our technical information specialist.**
>
> (The subject complement [predicate noun] *specialist* renames the subject *Jane White.*)

Nouns Used as Appositives

The term *appositive* means one noun renames another noun or pronoun. The appositive immediately follows the noun it renames.

> **Jane White, our technical information specialist, recommended that we select a new service provider.**
>
> (The common noun *specialist* renames and follows the proper noun *Jane White.*)

SLIP-UP

Announcement in a church bulletin: Thursday Night Potluck Supper. Prayer and medication to follow. [Note: Should the nouns be *prayer* and *meditation*?]

Review the discussion on direct objects in Chapter 3.

Go to
Transparency/PowerPoint 4-4b.

Review the section on indirect objects in Chapter 3.

Review the section on objects of prepositions in Chapter 3.

Go to
Transparency/PowerPoint 4-4c.

Review the discussion on subject complements in Chapter 3.

4-6 Point out the differences and similarities between predicate nouns and appositives.

Go to Transparency/PowerPoint 4-4d.

Tim Dahill, our vice president of marketing, is attending an international sales meeting this week.

(The common noun *vice president* renames and follows the proper noun *Tim Dahill.*)

Nouns Used as Direct Address

A noun in direct address names the individual being addressed.

Lindsey, please check the events scheduled for next week.
(*Lindsey* is the proper noun and the person being addressed.)

You know, Liz, your research on the intranet project was invaluable.
(*Liz* is the proper noun and the person being addressed.)

CHECKUP 4-2

Directions: *For each of the underlined nouns in the sentences that follow, select its function from the following:* **Subj** *(subject),* **DO** *(direct object),* **IO** *(indirect object),* **OP** *(object of preposition),* **Comp** *(subject complement),* **App** *(appositive), or* **DA** *(direct address). In the space provided, write the abbreviation for the function.*

1. The new search engine's capabilities improved <u>service</u> to our users. — DO

2. Some large companies have investigated the <u>advantages</u> of intranets, which are basically Internets within the firms. — DO

3. Thanks, <u>Beth</u>, for your assistance in organizing the demonstrations by our service providers. — DA

4. "This Week on the Internet," a local weekly newspaper <u>column</u>, always has good advice. — App

5. Computers are popular <u>products</u> in cyberspace. — Comp

6. Our department submitted an <u>analysis</u> of the safety issues involved with online financial transactions. — DO

7. <u>Chuck</u> submitted a request for new <u>passwords</u> in his department. — Subj, OP

8. <u>Bruce</u>, please check last week's hits and follow up on the promising leads. — DA

9. The supervisor gave <u>Carrie</u> the promotion. — IO

10. Grant Morrison, Mrs. Chin's <u>assistant</u>, was formerly employed at Intel. — App

GO TO CD-ROM CHECKUP 4-2

PLURAL FORMS OF NOUNS

Singular and Plural Nouns

A *singular noun* names one person, place, thing, activity, idea, or quality. A *plural noun* names two or more persons, places, things, ideas, or qualities. To form the plural of most common and proper nouns, add *s* to the singular noun. Use a dictionary when you are not sure about the spelling of a plural noun.

Singular Nouns	Plural Nouns
code	codes
password	passwords
Crawford	the Crawfords

Go to
Transparency/PowerPoint 4-5.

Most dictionaries include only those plural noun forms that do not require simply adding an s or es.

Collective Nouns

A collective noun names a group of persons or things. If a group acts as a unit, the collective noun is singular. If the sentence implies that the members of a team, committee, etc., are acting individually, the collective noun is plural. The following words are examples of collective nouns:

committee	team
crew	jury
audience	family

The committee announced its choice of the Employee of the Year.

(The committee is acting as one group. In this sentence, *committee* is singular and requires the singular pronoun *its*.)

The department members received the questionnaires Friday and were asked to return their responses within a week.

(Department members will act individually, so the plural pronoun *their* is required.)

Go to
Transparency/PowerPoint 4-6.

4-7 Collective nouns are covered in greater depth in Chapter 8 (pronoun antecedents) and Chapter 11 (subject-predicate agreement).

CHECKUP 4-3

Exercise 1
Directions: *Underline each singular noun once and each plural noun twice. Circle each collective noun.*

1. You can get sidetracked easily when you search for information on the Internet.

2. Airline travelers dislike waiting in line and carrying tickets.

3. An online forum is usually devoted to a single topic.

4. The board decided to expand its foreign operations.

5. Netscape® allows users to navigate the Internet and browse the Web.

GO TO
CD-ROM
CHECKUP 4-3
EXERCISE 1

6. A "flame" is an angry online <u>message</u>.

7. If you spill <u>liquids</u> on your <u>computer</u>, you can harm it.

8. I used the Net to see if <u>jobs</u> are available in health <u>occupations</u>.

9. The (panel) prepared a comprehensive <u>report</u> of its <u>concerns</u>.

10. Reference <u>librarians</u> often provide search <u>services</u> for <u>cardholders</u>.

Nouns Ending in *ch, sh, s, x,* or *z*

Go to
Transparency/PowerPoint 4-7.

If a singular noun or surname (last name) ends in a *ch, sh, s, x,* or *z* sound, form the plural by adding *es.*

Singular Nouns	Plural Nouns
batch	batches
business	businesses
wish	wishes
fax	faxes
waltz	waltzes
Exceptions:	
quiz	quizzes
loch	lochs
Surname	**Plural Surname**
Gomez	the Gomezes
Fitch	the Fitches
Fox	the Foxes

Nouns Ending in *f, fe,* or *ff*

Go to
Transparency/PowerPoint 4-8.

Many singular nouns ending in *f, fe,* or *ff* require only adding an *s* for their plural forms. To form the plurals of other singular nouns ending in *f* or *fe,* change the *f* or *fe* to *ve* and add an *s.* Both forms are acceptable for a few nouns. Use the dictionary's preferred spelling, which is the first one listed.

Singular Nouns	Plural Nouns
proof	proofs
life	lives
staff	staffs
yourself	yourselves
wharf	wharves/wharfs

Do not change surname spellings when forming their plurals.

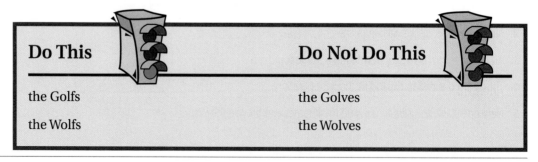

Do This	**Do Not Do This**
the Golfs	the Golves
the Wolfs	the Wolves

4-8 As an additional writing practice, have students use the words in sentences.

Exercise 2
Directions: *In the space provided, write the plural of the following nouns.*

1. loss — losses
2. inch — inches
3. chef — chefs
4. thief — thieves
5. virus — viruses
6. glitch — glitches
7. Sanchez — Sanchezes

8. tariff — tariffs
9. tax — taxes
10. bus — buses, busses
11. duplex — duplexes
12. blitz — blitzes
13. wharf — wharves, wharfs
14. half — halves

GO TO CD-ROM
CHECKUP 4-3
EXERCISE 2

Nouns Ending in *y*

When a noun ends in *y* and the letter before the *y* is a *vowel,* add an *s* to make the noun plural.

Go to
Transparency/PowerPoint 4-9.

Vowels are a, e, i, o, and u.

Singular Nouns	Plural Nouns
attorney	attorneys
holiday	holidays
Casey	the Caseys

When a noun ends in *y* and the letter before *y* is a *consonant,* change *y* to *i* and add *es* to make the noun plural.

Go to
Transparency/PowerPoint 4-10.

Singular Nouns	Plural Nouns
company	companies
copy	copies
entry	entries
quantity	quantities

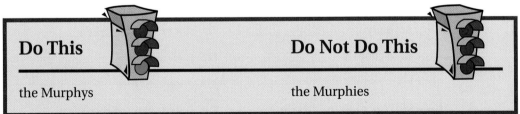

Do This

the Murphys

Do Not Do This

the Murphies

Do not change name spellings when forming their plurals.

Nouns Ending in *o*

When a noun ends in *o* and is preceded by a vowel, add an *s* to form the plural.

Go to
Transparency/PowerPoint 4-11.

Singular Nouns	Plural Nouns
portfolio	portfolios
video	videos
ratio	ratios

Noun Functions and Plurals

When a noun ends in *o* and is preceded by a consonant, add *s* or *es* to form the plural. Add an *s* to a singular musical term that ends in *o*. Some plural forms are acceptable with either *s* or *es*. When in doubt, refer to a dictionary for the preferred spellings.

Singular Nouns	Plural Nouns
logo	logos
memo	memos
macro	macros

Singular Nouns	Plural Nouns
veto	vetoes
potato	potatoes
echo	echoes

Singular Nouns (Musical)	Plural Nouns
piano	pianos
alto	altos

Singular Nouns	Plural Nouns
zero	zeros/zeroes
cargo	cargos/cargoes

CHECKUP 4-3

Exercise 3
Directions: In the space provided, write the plurals of the following nouns. Use a dictionary if you are uncertain about the plural forms. If more than one form is acceptable, write both forms of the plural.

1. community — communities
2. delay — delays
3. O'Riley — the O'Rileys
4. photo — photos
5. entry — entries
6. dictionary — dictionaries
7. stereo — stereos
8. hero — heroes
9. beneficiary — beneficiaries
10. ego — egos
11. smiley — smileys
12. solo — solos

GO TO CD-ROM
CHECKUP 4-3
EXERCISE 3

Go to Transparency/PowerPoint 4-12a.

4-9 Recommend that students refer to their dictionaries to find the preferred spellings of irregular plural nouns.

Irregular Noun Plurals and Special Nouns

Some singular nouns have irregular plurals. The plural forms change within the nouns or at the end of the nouns. Use a dictionary if you are not sure of the correct forms.

Singular Nouns	Plural Nouns
man	men
foot	feet
mouse	mice
goose	geese

Some nouns have the same singular and plural forms. These nouns do not need an *s* to make them plural.

Go to
Transparency/PowerPoint 4-12b.

Singular Nouns	Plural Nouns
sheep	sheep
species	species
Chinese	Chinese
series	series

Do This	Do Not Do This
Pronounce the word *corps* as "core" (sing.) or "cores" (pl.).	Do not pronounce the word *corps* as "corpse."

The spelling is the same for the singular and plural forms of corps.

Go to Transparency/PowerPoint 4-12c.

Some nouns that end in *s* look like plurals. Depending on their use, they may have singular meanings. Examples include the following:

news	physics	statistics
ethics	politics	economics

Most nouns that represent ideas or qualities have no plural forms.

honesty	patience	integrity

Some nouns are never singular.

proceeds	savings	
earnings	dues	credentials

4-10 Present the section on subject-verb agreement before having students use the words in Checkup 4-4 in sentences.

4-11 Refer to *The Gregg Reference Manual* or another available reference manual for additional nouns ending in *s* that may have singular meanings and for nouns that have no plural forms.

4-12 Refer to *The Gregg Reference Manual* or another available reference manual for nouns that are never singular.

CHECKUP 4-4

Exercise 1
Directions: *In the space provided, write the plural forms of the following nouns.*

1.	series	series	6.	courage	courage
2.	tooth	teeth	7.	gentleman	gentlemen
3.	athletics	athletics	8.	decency	decency
4.	trout	trout	9.	goods	goods
5.	woman	women	10.	foot	feet

GO TO CD-ROM
CHECKUP 4-4
EXERCISE 1

Foreign Nouns

Go to
PowerPoint 4-13.

4-13 Dictionaries vary in their listings of preferred plural forms of foreign nouns.

Foreign nouns may use foreign plural forms or English plural forms. Some nouns use both forms, although one form may be preferred over the other, or each form may have its own definition. Different dictionaries have different preferences. Use a dictionary if you are uncertain about a spelling.

Singular Foreign Nouns	Foreign Plurals	English Plurals
syllabus	syllabi (pref.)	syllabuses
analysis	analyses	
appendix	appendices	appendixes (pref.)
index	indices (math)	indexes (books)
criterion	criteria (pref.)	criterions
memorandum	memoranda	memorandums (pref.)
phenomenon	phenomena (pref.)	phenomenons
curriculum	curricula	curriculums (pref.)

CHECKUP 4-4

4-14 Note that the instructions in Checkup 4-4 require the preferred spellings as the answers.

**GO TO
CD-ROM**
CHECKUP 4-4
EXERCISE 2

Exercise 2
Directions: *In the space provided, write the **preferred** plural form of the following nouns. If a noun has two acceptable plural forms with **different** meanings, write **both** meanings with the plural forms. Use your dictionary if you are uncertain about forming foreign noun plurals.*

1. bureau ___bureaus (pref.)___
2. prospectus ___prospectuses___
3. antenna ___antennas (radio), antennae (insect)___
4. formula ___formulas (pref.)___
5. referendum ___referendums (pref.)___
6. matrix ___matrices (pref.)___
7. crisis ___crises___
8. diagnosis ___diagnoses___

Abbreviations

Go to
PowerPoint 4-14.

Most abbreviations form their plurals by adding *s* to the singular. Abbreviations should be used sparingly in formal writing. They should be used in business writing when the emphasis is communicating in a brief form.

Singular Abbreviations	Plural Abbreviations
Ave.	Aves.
acct.	accts.
PC	PCs
No.	Nos.
mo.	mos.
yr.	yrs.

Measurements

Most measurement abbreviations are the same in their singular and plural forms. No periods are necessary with measurement abbreviations.

Singular Abbreviations		Plural Abbreviations	
foot	ft	feet	ft
ounce	oz	ounces	oz
pound	lb	pounds	lb
kilometer	km	kilometers	km
bushel	bu	bushels	bu
		miles per hour	mph

Go to PowerPoint 4-15.

4-15 Refer to *The Gregg Reference Manual* or another available reference manual for abbreviations of measurements.

Refer to the measurement section in your reference manual.

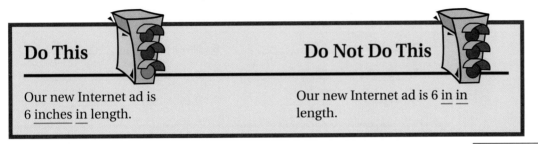

Do This	Do Not Do This
Our new Internet ad is 6 inches in length.	Our new Internet ad is 6 in in length.

Spell the word inches in full if the word in follows the word inches.

Numbers

Numbers expressed in figures form their plurals by adding an *s*. Numbers expressed in words form their plurals according to the rules for nouns.

Go to PowerPoint 4-16.

Singular Numbers	Plural Numbers
9	9s
1990	1990s
941	941s
thirty	thirties
four	fours

Letters

Capital letters form their plurals by adding *s*. To avoid confusion, add an apostrophe before the *s* to the plurals of *A, I, M,* and *U*. Without an apostrophe, *A's* would be *As*; *I's* would be *Is*; *M's* would be *Ms*; and *U's* would be *Us*. All lowercase letters form their plurals by adding apostrophe and *s*.

Go to PowerPoint 4-17.

Singular Letters	Plural Letters
D	Ds
CD-ROM	CD-ROMs
I	I's
M	M's
a	a's

Do This

All the A's in the advertising copy were difficult to read.

Do Not Do This

All the As in the advertising copy were difficult to read.

When the meaning is confusing or difficult to read, use 's to form the plural of a capital letter.

CHECKUP 4-4

Exercise 3

Directions: *In the space provided, write the plurals of the following abbreviations.*

**GO TO
CD-ROM**
CHECKUP 4-4
EXERCISE 3

1.	ck.	cks.	5.	dept.	depts.
2.	C (letter)	Cs	6.	HMO	HMOs
3.	yd	yd	7.	u (letter)	u's
4.	CPA	CPAs	8.	9 (number)	9s

DIAGRAMMING SENTENCES

4-16 The diagramming section of the chapter may be omitted.

The diagramming format continues with the placement of an appositive and a subject complement (the predicate noun.) To diagram a simple sentence with a subject complement (predicate noun), draw a slanted line after the verb. To diagram a simple sentence with an appositive, place the appositive in parentheses after the noun it modifies. In the examples and exercises that follow, diagram only those parts of a sentence that you have worked with in previous chapters or that are introduced in this chapter.

Subject Complement (predicate noun)

The Internet is a source of information.

Internet | is \ source

Simple subject: *Internet*
Linking verb: *is*
Subject complement: *source*

He is an experienced programmer.

He | is \ programmer

Simple subject: *He*
Linking verb: *is*
Subject complement: *programmer*

Appositive

DiscoverNet, the Internet service provider company, contacted me.

DiscoverNet (company) | contacted | me

Simple subject: *DiscoverNet*
Simple verb: *contacted*
Direct object: *me*
Appositive: *company*

Mrs. Baird, the team project leader, complimented Tina.

Mrs. Baird (leader) | complimented | Tina

Simple subject: *Mrs. Baird*
Simple verb: *complimented*
Direct object: *Tina*
Appositive: *leader*

CHECKUP 4-5

Directions: *In the space provided, diagram the following sentences. Diagram only the simple subject, simple verb, direct object, subject complement (predicate noun), and appositive.*

4-17 Have students identify other parts of speech in these sentences for additional practice.

1. Dave Jurasick, the new employee, required my assistance.

Dave Jurasick (employee) | required | assistance

2. My favorite Internet site is amazon.com.

site | is \ amazon.com

3. His organizational skills, a requirement for an accountant, impressed the interviewers.

skills (requirement) | impressed | interviewers

4. The LaserJet, my newest electronic purchase, was a welcome addition in my home office.

LaserJet (purchase) | was \ addition

5. Business Results, a local consulting firm, submitted a bid for 200 installations.

Business Results (firm) | submitted | bid

**GO TO
CD-ROM**
CHECKUP 4-5

PRACTICE

PRACTICE 1A

Directions: Select the correct plural form from the words in parentheses. Write the word in the space provided.

1. Do your state legislators have e-mail (*address, addresses*)?

1. ___addresses___

2. Internet (*TVs, TV's*) that provide e-mail and Web browsing features are still expensive.

2. ___TVs___

3. The committee's (*vetos, vetoes*) caused significant (*delayes, delays*) in our new online ad campaign.

3. ___vetoes, delays___

4. Glen expected more in-depth (*discussiones, discussions*) with (*folks, folkes*) who used the Internet (*chatboxs, chatboxes*).

4. ___discussions___
    ___folks___
    ___chatboxes___

5. Some filtering procedures give parents control over how their (*childs, children*) use online services.

5. ___children___

6. Does your e-mail system guarantee (*deliverys, deliveries*) or issue return (*receiptes, receipts*)?

6. ___deliveries___
    ___receipts___

7. Are you the type of person who handles (*crisis, crises*) calmly?

7. ___crises___

8. The (*Ruschs, Rusches*) asked for several (*analysis, analyses*) of online provider services.

8. ___Rusches___
    ___analyses___

9. I need more (*bookshelfs, bookshelves*) to hold my computer manuals.

9. ___bookshelves___

10. Networking is the small business tool of the (*1990's, 1990s*).

10. ___1990s___

11. The Yahoo! search engine directory shows more than 2000 health (*topices, topics*).

11. ___topics___

12. We discussed several (*hypothesis, hypotheses*), but we could not determine the cause for the network failure.

12. ___hypotheses___

13. We named Keith and Ben the (*heros, heroes*) of the day because they fixed our network problem so quickly.

13. ___heroes___

14. When we remodeled my home office, we used all oak wood (*finishs, finishes*) to create a comfortable, warm atmosphere.

14. ___finishes___

NAME _____

15. The (*Bradleys, Bradleyes*) use the Internet to obtain travel information.

15. _____Bradleys_____

16. E-mail messages seem to be replacing (*memoranda, memorandums*) as the form of interoffice communication.

16. __memorandums__
       (pref.)

17. A San Francisco hospital is making free (*videos, videoes*) of newborn (*babys, babies*) to transmit over Internet e-mail.

17. __videos, babies__

18. Most (*companys, companies*) do not make any profit in the first six (*months, monthes*) or one year.

18. _____companies_____
       _____months_____

19. A high school student designed the (*logos, logoes*) that we selected for our Web pages.

19. _____logos_____

20. Multimedia (*portfolioes, portfolios*) are necessary before interviewing with our company.

20. _____portfolios_____

GO TO
CD-ROM
PRACTICE 1
EXERCISES

PRACTICE 2A

A. Directions: *In the space provided, write the plural form of the underlined word or words.*

1. Both branch office <u>staff</u> are now on the company network.

1. _____staffs_____

2. The <u>Bush</u> and the <u>Truax</u> use America Online e-mail to keep in touch during the <u>holiday</u>.

2. _____Bushes_____
       _____Truaxes_____
       _____holidays_____

3. Successful Internet <u>company</u> concentrate more on serving customers and less on elaborate <u>graphic</u>.

3. __companies__
       __graphics__

4. One of the <u>criterion</u> for employment in a high-tech company is the ability to be flexible.

4. _____criteria_____

5. Our dormitory rooms are equipped with network connections to service <u>student</u> with their own <u>computer</u>.

5. _____students_____
       _____computers_____

6. Online opportunities for students include searching other <u>library</u> for materials and registering for <u>class</u>.

6. _____libraries_____
       _____classes_____

7. You can obtain payroll tax information from the Internet when you are ready to complete your firm's <u>940</u> and <u>941</u>.

7. __940s   941s__

8. Many <u>business</u> register their names on the Internet through an organization named Internic.

8. ___businesses___

9. Employers generally select nouns as keywords in their online employment <u>search</u> for <u>employee</u>.

9. ___searches___
___employees___

10. The best online real estate services usually provide <u>photo</u> of the interiors and exteriors of the <u>property</u>.

10. ___photos___
___properties___

11. Internet entrepreneurs find that products such as books, airline tickets, and <u>CD</u> are popular sales items.

11. ___CDs___

12. Only government <u>agency</u>, <u>university</u>, and large companies had Internet access in the <u>eighty</u>.

12. ___agencies___
___universities___
___eighties___

13. <u>Family</u> buy <u>thousand</u> of <u>PC</u> to use at home and to entertain their <u>child</u>.

13. ___Families___
___thousands___ ___PCs___
___children___

14. The *Mercury News* lost over a million <u>dollar</u> in ads as a result of the boycott.

14. ___dollars___

15. Dell uses the <u>alley</u> behind its <u>factory</u> for <u>delivery</u>.

15. ___alleys___ ___factories___
___deliveries___

16. Kelly found several <u>brand</u> of shampoo sold only on the Internet.

16. ___brands___

17. I found an interesting online article on <u>tornado</u>.

17. ___tornadoes (pref.)___

18. Drs. Cortez and Ransforth use the Internet to research many of their <u>diagnosis</u>.

18. ___diagnoses___

19. <u>Curriculum</u> are changing because of the research <u>capability</u> on the Internet.

19. ___Curriculums___
___capabilities___

20. Pat showed me a Web page displaying pictures of different <u>species</u> of fish.

20. ___species___

B. **Directions:** *For each underlined noun in these sentences that follow, select its function from the following:* **Subj** *(subject),* **DO** *(direct object),* **IO** *(indirect object),* **OP** *(object of preposition),* **Comp** *(subject complement),* **App** *(appositive) or* **DA** *(direct address). Write the abbreviation of the function in the space provided.*

1. The <u>shelves</u> were not strong enough to hold our computer references.

1. ___subj___

2. We ordered five <u>batches</u> of printing labels from <u>Computing Services</u>.

2. ___DO___
___OP___

3. The Internet has forced cooperation among <u>countries</u>.

3. ___OP___

NAME _____

4. Lynn, did you know that coffee cafes with Internet access are common throughout the United States?

4. ___DA___

5. Nuo Vang and Paula Olinski are the new language specialists in our Web design division.

5. ___Comp___

C. **Directions:** *Write two sentences using the plural forms of the following nouns. On line* a, *use the noun as the subject of the sentence. On line* b, *use the noun as the direct object of the sentence.*

Answers will vary.

1. company

   a. The manufacturing companies will close for a short vacation.

   b. The new law affected many companies.

2. network

   a. The TV networks covered the sporting events.

   b. The storm shut down the computer networks.

3. survey

   a. The surveys will give us some sales data.

   b. Please complete the surveys.

D. **Directions:** *Correct errors in plural forms, capitalization, and commas. Write each sentence correctly in the space provided.*

1. Nancy your promotion will become effective on june 1.

   Nancy, your promotion will become effective on June 1.

2. Sandy Atkins the administrative assistant for the sales area confirmed my two travel reservation to Kansas City.

   Sandy Atkins, the administrative assistant for the sales area, confirmed my

   two travel reservations to Kansas City.

**GO TO
CD-ROM**
**PRACTICE 2
EXERCISES**

PRACTICE 3A

PROOFREADING

Directions: *Proofread and compare the two sentences in each group. If they are the same, write* **Yes** *in the space provided. If they are not the same, write* **No.** *Use the first sentence as the correct copy. If you find errors in the second sentence, underline them.*

See Instructor Note 4-18 in IAE.

1. CDnow Inc. is a cyberstore that can offer every U.S. jazz album as well as thousands of imports.

1. ___No___

   CDNow Inc. is a cyberstore that can offer U.S. jazz albums as well as thousands of imports.

2. It has been only a few years since companies began doing business on the Internet.

     2. _____No_____

It has been only a few years since <u>companys</u> began doing business on the <u>Intranet.</u>

3. Online bill-paying services disburse funds within 24 hours.

     3. _____Yes_____

Online bill-paying services disburse funds within 24 hours.

4. Amazon, a popular bookstore on the Net, informs customers via e-mail when new books arrive.

     4. _____No_____

Amazon, a popular <u>bookstore, on</u> the Net, informs <u>customer</u> via e-mail when new books arrive.

5. Privacy issues and fraud are still major concerns with online banking.

     5. _____Yes_____

Privacy issues and fraud are still major concerns with online banking.

GO TO CD-ROM
PRACTICE 3 EXERCISES

PRACTICE 4A

WRITING

In the prewriting stage, you choose your topic (what you want to say), your purpose (how to say it), and your audience (to whom you want to say it).

The following procedures will help you in the prewriting process:

1. Identify several broad, general topics about which you might like to write. For example, you might identify the following:
   a. The Internet in Business   c. Internet Service Providers
   b. Education and the Internet   d. The Internet's Future

2. For this exercise, assume your selection is "Education and the Internet."

3. Identify several topics you might write about this general topic. List them under the general topic. For the general topic "Education and the Internet," you might use the following topics:
   a. How your classes have changed because of the Internet
   b. How you use the Internet in class
   c. How you think the Internet will continue to change education
   d. How you think young children will use the Internet to learn

4. Select one of the topics listed in Step 3.

NAME _____

Directions: In this writing assignment, use the topic in Step 4 above. Write three statements that express the points you want to make about this topic.

Answers will vary.

_____

_____

_____

_____

_____

GO TO
CD-ROM
PRACTICE 4
EXERCISES

ONLINE **EXERCISES**

Often new Internet terminology does not appear in printed dictionaries. When trying to find a meaning to an obscure term, one of the best places to start your search is the Internet. To complete the following exercises, you need access to a computer with an Internet connection.

Punctuation
ALERT!

Use exact punctuation when typing an Internet address.

Objective: *Increase your vocabulary and your familiarity with the World Wide Web by visiting a Web dictionary site.*

1. With your Internet browser on the screen, key: **http://www.onelook.com** in the location text box. Then, press **Enter** on your keyboard.

2. Key **cyberspace** in the **Enter word** box.

3. Click on **LOOK IT UP** (next to the word you keyed in).

4. Click on several of the hyperlinks to definitions of cyberspace. Write down your understanding of the word.

5. Press the **Back** button on your browser until you return to the OneLook Dictionaries search page.

6. Look up the definitions of the following words: *Internet, lurker, spam, newbie.*

7. Be prepared to discuss the terms in class. Your instructor may ask you to print the definitions for class discussion.

Internet: A worldwide network of computers. First developed in the 1960s.

Lurker: A person who reads the public discussions but does not participate.

Spam: Unwanted, irrelevant, or inappropriate messages sent to a public forum.

Newbie: New user of the Internet.

4-19 Check all online exercises before you assign them to be sure the sites are still available.

4-20 Cyberspace: Coined by sci-fi writer William Gibson in his novel *Neuromancer* in the early 1980s. Refers to everyone and everything on the Internet.

4-21 From a Monty Python sketch titled *Spam!* The term is used to describe excessive information.

NAME _____

PRACTICE 1B

Directions: *Select the correct plural form from the words in parentheses. Write the word in the space provided.*

1. Max registers for two evening (*class, classes*) each semester.
2. New York City has two (*YWCA's, YWCAs*).
3. We ordered two portable (*radioes, radios*) for emergency purposes.
4. Laurie asked for help using Yahoo! because she received so few (*matchs, matches*) to her (*inquiries, inquirys*).
5. Do more (*mans, men*) than (*womans, women*) use the Internet?
6. Many (*citys, cities*) have Web pages linked to local services.
7. We ordered several wireless (*mice, mouses*) for our laptop computers.
8. The two (*Cortezs, Cortezes*) who work in the accounting area are related.
9. The manager of the Montecito Center looked at three (*proofs, proofes*) of his business cards before choosing one.
10. The Web did not become popular until the (*1990s, 1990's*).
11. We worked with a design team for months to create the right (*icons, icones*) for our Web page.
12. Moniji Nursery presented five (*criterion, criteria*) that we had to meet if we planned to form a partnership.
13. The quality of sound coming over the Internet is as good as the (*stereos, steroes*) at home and in my truck.
14. We looked at three (sketchs, sketches) for our Web page.
15. The (*Duncans, Duncanes*) create animated Web pages.
16. Rex knew that (*parenthesis, parentheses*) could not be used in a Web address.
17. The total amount should have had two (*zeros, zeroes*) instead of three.
18. Toby researches the demographic profiles of (*municipalitys, municipalities*) and towns.
19. Ratings from Dun and Bradstreet help people make wise financial (*analysis, analyses*).
20. The (*CPA's, CPAs*) in Grand Rapids have met monthly since the early (*1980s, 1980's*).

1. _____classes_____
2. _____YWCAs_____
3. _____radios_____
4. _____matches_____
   _____inquiries_____
5. ___men, women___
6. _____cities_____
7. _____mice_____
8. _____Cortezes_____
9. _____proofs_____
10. _____1990s_____
11. _____icons_____
12. __criteria (pref.)__
13. _____stereos_____
14. _____sketches_____
15. _____Duncans_____
16. ___parentheses___
17. __zeros (pref.)__
18. __municipalities__
19. ____analyses____
20. __CPAs, 1980s__

PRACTICE 2B

A. *Directions:* *In the space provided, write the plural form of the underlined word or words.*

1. The <u>sheriff</u> from Sonoma and Napa <u>County</u> are discussing ways to use the Internet in law enforcement.
2. Five <u>city</u> joined to develop a county Website.

1. _sheriffs__Counties_
2. _____cities_____

NAME _____

3. Laurie purchased her <u>dish</u> from the Internet mall.   3. _____dishes_____

4. Online <u>dictionary</u> are easy to use and provide quick access to words and <u>definition</u>.   4. _dictionaries_ _definitions_

5. The payroll department would like us to file our <u>W2</u> electronically.   5. _____W2s_____

6. Nonie searched through five <u>batch</u> of printouts before finding the information from Richard Nelson Bolles's online job-hunting column.   6. _____batches_____

7. Fly Zone explains why <u>DJ</u> enjoy spinning music.   7. _____DJs_____

8. Infospace's People Search finds names, phone numbers, and street <u>address</u>.   8. _____addresses_____

9. The Contra Costa <u>Times</u> has an easy-to-use search page.   9. _____Times_____

10. We received so many <u>fax</u> that we added another dedicated fax line.   10. _____faxes_____

11. We spend several <u>hour</u> using the Internet each day.   11. _____hours_____

12. Joe debates <u>politics</u> on the PoliticsNow Website.   12. _____politics_____

13. All new employees are required to watch software instructional <u>video</u>.   13. _____videos_____

14. We found <u>piano</u> for sale at the Music Now site.   14. _____pianos_____

15. <u>Child</u> usually like the Global Show-n-Tell Museum.   15. _____Children_____

B. Directions: *For each underlined noun in the sentences below, select its function from the following:* **Subj** *(subject),* **DO** *(direct object),* **IO** *(indirect object),* **OP** *(object of preposition),* **Comp** *(subject complement),* **App** *(appositive), or* **DA** *(direct address). Write the abbreviation of the function in the space provided.*

1. <u>Eddie</u> posted three entries on the Website in an attempt to win a trip to Hawaii.   1. __Subj__

2. Louis Vucebcui is a food <u>enthusiast</u> who enjoys participating in food-related newsgroups on the Internet.   2. __Comp__

3. Family.com, a Disney-sponsored <u>site</u>, provides information for families.   3. __App__

4. Users never get a busy <u>signal</u> with satellite modems.   4. __DO__

5. We added several accessories to the laptop <u>computer</u>.   5. __OP__

PRACTICE 3B

PROOFREADING

The subject matter in the following sentences deals with the use of the Internet in business and personal use.

Directions: *Proofread and compare the two sentences in each group. If they are the same, write* **Yes** *in the space provided. If they are not the same, write* **No.** *Use the first sentence as the correct copy. If you find errors in the sentence, underline them.*

1. Women's Wire covers subjects relating to work, human interest, and self-improvement.   1. __No__

   Women's Wire covers subjects relating to work, human <u>interests,</u> and self-improvement.

2. Researchers go online to the Library of Congress, the Smithsonian, and major universities around the world.   2. __No__

   Researchers go online to the Library of <u>congress,</u> the Smithsonian, and major universities around the world.

NAME

PRACTICE 4B

WRITING

In the prewriting stage, you choose your topic (what you want to say), your purpose (how to say it), and your audience (to whom you want to say it). The following procedures will help you in the prewriting process:

1. Identify several broad, general topics about which you might like to write. For example, you might identify the following:
   a. The Internet in Business
   b. Personal Use of the Internet
   c. Internet Service Providers
   d. The Internet's Future

2. For this exercise, assume your selection is "Personal Use of the Internet."

3. Identify several topics you might write about this general topic. List them under the general topic. For the general topic "Personal Use of the Internet," you might use the following topics:
   a. The Web page you use the most
   b. The Web page that is the most entertaining
   c. The search engine you most frequently use
   d. Why you don't use the Internet

4. Select one of the topics in Step 3.

Directions: *In this writing assignment, use the topic you selected in Step 4. Write three statements that express the point you want to make about this topic.* *Answers will vary.*

_____

_____

_____

ONLINE *EXERCISES*

The Internet is filled with millions of Web pages. If you are searching for information, countless hours may be wasted trying to locate relevant sites. One of the best methods of finding useful sites is to read reviews by people who spend their time searching the Internet, writing about their findings, and categorizing the sites. To complete the following exercises, you need access to a computer with an Internet connection.

Objective: *To visit Websites reviewed by Yahoo! Internet Life.*

1. With your Internet browser on the screen, key:

   http://www.yil.com in the location text box. Press **Enter** on your keyboard.

2. This site contains numerous links to reviews of Web pages. You can search for sites or randomly read reviews. Click on three links that interest you.

3. Write three sentences about each Website visited. Indicate whether the site is relevant to you and whether you would visit the site again.

   Answers will vary. Students will have fun visiting this informative Website.

LOOKING BACK

Posttest

Directions: *In the space provided, write the letter of the correct answer.*

1. Which word is a collective noun?
   a. dictionary
   b. country
   c. disk
   d. team

   1. _____d_____

2. Which line of proper nouns is correct?
   a. PCs, Great falls, Black Hills
   b. The university of Texas, Pike's Peak, Disneyland
   c. Great America, Pima College, Kansas City
   d. America online, Des Moines, Southern Illinois University

   2. _____c_____

3. *The Shareware Search Engine searches for utilities based upon your criteria.*
   In this sentence, *utilities* is the
   a. direct object.
   b. complement.
   c. indirect object.
   d. object of the preposition.

   3. _____d_____

4. *Shelley Ling, the district manager, is responsible for our online advertising.*
   In this sentence, *manager* is
   a. the subject of the sentence
   b. an appositive.
   c. a direct address.
   d. the complement.

   4. _____b_____

Directions: *In the space provided, write the letter or letters of the correct plural nouns.*

1. a. matches	b. boxes	c. faxs	d. glasses	1.	a, b, d
2. a. proofes	b. cliffs	c. yourselfs	d. lives	2.	b, d
3. a. keyes	b. facilitys	c. entries	d. copys	3.	c
4. a. pianoes	b. ratios	c. logoes	d. potatoes	4.	b, d
5. a. analyses	b. memorandums	c. indexes	d. diagnosis	5.	a, b, c
6. a. accts.	b. lbs	c. C's	d. 1990's	6.	a

Noun Functions and Plurals

111

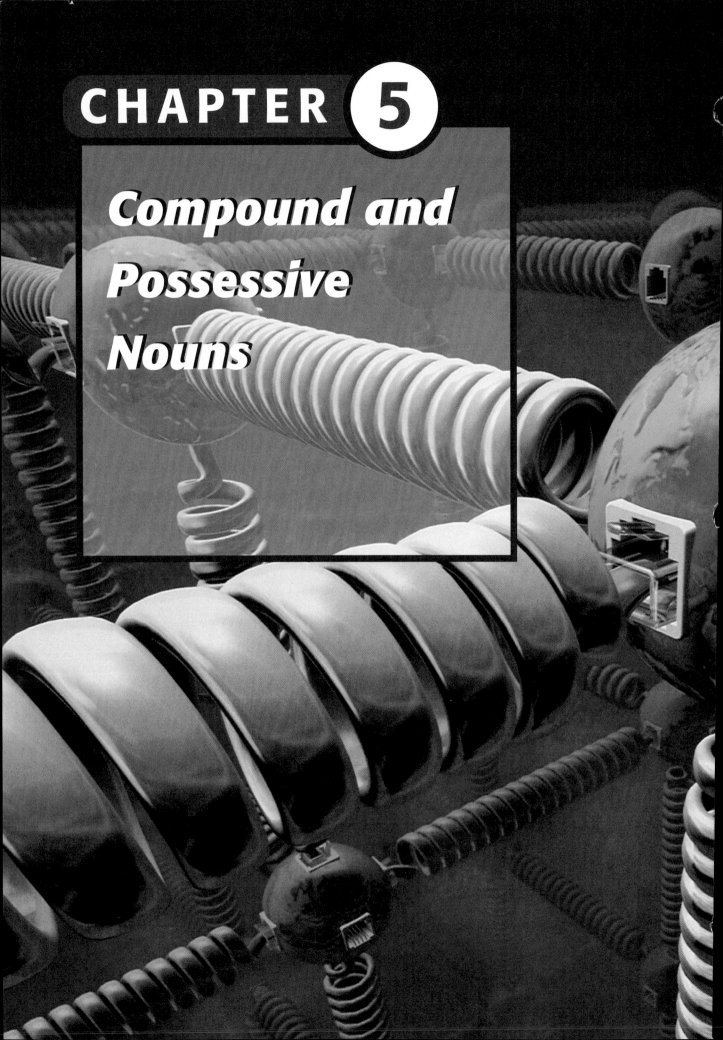

CHAPTER 5

Compound and Possessive Nouns

THE WORLD WIDE WEB

The World Wide Web is a graphical system on the Internet. A Website is a location where an individual, a university, a government agency, or a company stores Web pages. Millions of Websites offer information on everything from government documents to pictures of babies and pets.

The number of users of the World Wide Web is impossible to gauge. Predictions for the next five to ten years range widely from 200 million to 2 billion users. Some see the Internet as the world's biggest mall, where users participate in online auctions or shop for t-shirts or cars. Some spend time gossiping and socializing, while others use the Internet for research and education.

"Surf the Net" applies to browsing the vast storehouse of information on the World Wide Web. Searching the Internet is done by using search engines, which help categorize and find information. As more and more information is available on the Web, even search engines fail to bring order to the chaos. Many Internet users are feeling information overload.

The Web has changed forever how we communicate, access information, shop, and do research. In many career fields, a person's future success is enhanced by how effectively and productively he or she can use the extensive resources available on the Internet.

TERMS TO REMEMBER

INFORMATION OVERLOAD

"SURF THE NET"

WEB

WORLD WIDE WEB

OBJECTIVES

After you have studied this chapter and completed the exercises, you will be able to do the following:

1. Form plurals and possessives of compound nouns.
2. Recognize nominative, objective, and possessive cases of nouns.
3. Differentiate between plural and possessive forms of nouns.
4. Form possessives of singular, plural, and irregular nouns.
5. Identify correct forms of organization, association, and company names.
6. Form possessives of abbreviations, joint or separate ownership, and understood ownership.
7. Diagram sentences correctly.

LOOKING AHEAD

Pretest

Directions: *In the space provided, write the letter of the correct answer.*

1. *The firm gave Maria a new password.* In this sentence, what does the noun *Maria* illustrate?
   a. the nominative case
   b. the possessive case
   c. the objective and nominative cases
   d. the objective case

   1. ___d___

2. Which statement represents the correct possessive form?
   a. The firm's Internet exposure was very limited.
   b. The firms Internet exposure was very limited.
   c. The firm Internets' exposure was very limited.
   d. The firms Internet exposures' were very limited.

   2. ___a___

3. Which statement represents the correct possessive form?
   a. Mens and women's reactions to technological changes differ.
   b. Men's and women's reactions to technological changes differ.
   c. Mens' and womens' reactions to technological changes differ.
   d. Mens and womens' reactions to technological changes differ.

   3. ___b___

4. Which statement is written correctly?
   a. Web indexes' are important tools for searching sites' online.
   b. Web indexes are important tools for searching sites' online.
   c. Web indexes are important tools for searching sites online.
   d. Web indexes' are important tools' for searching sites online.

   4. ___c___

Directions: *In the space provided, write the letter or letters of the correct possessive or plural forms of nouns.*

1. a. write-offs
   b. money's order amount
   c. takeover's layoffs
   d. point of views

   1. ___a, c___

2. a. stockholder's meeting
   b. three CPA's recommendations
   c. Delgado's home
   d. Rob and Kathy's car

   2. ___c, d___

3. a. Kellogg's® cereals
   b. Pennsylvania Teacher's Association
   c. sale's meeting
   d. savings account balance

   3. ___a, d___

OVERVIEW

You possess or own things; for example, your car, your clothes, your class notes, and your business English textbook. Although you may indicate possession with such words as *own* ("I own."), *belong* ("It belongs to me."), and *of* ("this book of mine"), you may use a quicker and easier way—the apostrophe (') or apostrophe and *s* ('s). (An example of the apostrophe and *s* ['s] appears in the Slip-up on page 118.) In using the apostrophe to indicate possession, you should follow the rules presented in this chapter. Your knowledge of plural nouns (Chapter 4) will also be useful in recognizing the possessive case. Because of the changing nature of compound nouns, their plural and possessive features receive special attention in this chapter.

COMPOUND NOUNS

A compound noun consists of two or more words. Some compound nouns are written as one word. Some are written as hyphenated words. Others are written as two words. Sometimes compound nouns go through a change in form from two words to a hyphenated word to one word.

As a compound noun becomes more commonly used, it often becomes one word. Dictionaries may show spellings of compound nouns differently. Be sure to check a current dictionary if you are not certain about the correct form of a compound noun.

One-Word Compound Nouns

One type of compound noun consists of two or more words combined into one word. To form the plural of a one-word compound noun, follow the general rules for plurals.

One-Word Compound Nouns	Plural Forms
courthouse	courthouses
workstation	workstations
takeover	takeovers
printout	printouts
handful	handfuls
database	databases

(These compound nouns add *s* to form their plurals.)

businesswoman	businesswomen
chairman	chairmen

(These compound nouns have irregular plural forms.)

Margin notes:

See Instructor Notes 5-1, 5-2, and 5-3 in IAE.

Go to Transparencies/PowerPoints 5-1a, 5-1b, and 5-2.

5-4 Refer to *The Gregg Reference Manual* for additional examples of compound nouns.

See Instructor Note 5-5 in IAE.

Go to Transparency/PowerPoint 5-3.

The word *online* is an example of a word that appears more frequently in current readings as one word rather than in its previous hyphenated form (*on-line*).

If any plural form is unfamiliar, review the section in Chapter 4 for the rule you need. You may want to add the word and the plural to your list of difficult words.

Hyphenated Compounds With Nouns

Go to
Transparency/PowerPoint 5-4.

Some hyphenated compounds consist of a noun and another part of speech. To form the plurals of hyphenated compound nouns, make the *most important* word plural.

Hyphenated Compound	Plural Forms
brother-in-law	brothers-in-law
looker-on	lookers-on
court-martial	courts-martial (preferred)
cross-examination	cross-examinations
half-truth	half-truths

5-6 In this case, *courts-martial* is the preferred form.

(The underlined words are the most important ones.)

Hyphenated Compounds Without Nouns

Go to
Transparency/PowerPoint 5-5.

Some hyphenated compounds do not include noun elements. If the hyphenated compound word does not have a noun in it, add the *s* or *es* to the last word.

Compound Nouns	Plural Forms
write-off	write-offs
get-together	get-togethers
stand-in	stand-ins
free-for-all	free-for-alls
drive-in	drive-ins
run-through	run-throughs

(These hyphenated compounds do not have noun elements in them.)

Compound Nouns With Spaces

Go to
Transparency/PowerPoint 5-6.

Another common form of compound noun consists of two words. To form the plurals of compound nouns separated by spaces, make the most important words plural.

Compound Nouns	Plural Forms
style sheet	style sheets
hard copy	hard copies
floppy disk	floppy disks
vice president	vice presidents
editor in chief	editors in chief
fax machine	fax machines
chief of police	chiefs of police
rule of thumb	rules of thumb
account payable	accounts payable

5-7 The nouns *chief of police* and *vice president* are not hyphenated.

(The underlined words are the most important ones.)

CHECKUP 5-1

Directions: In the space provided, write the plural form of each word.

See Instructor Notes 5-8, 5-9, and 5-10 in IAE.

1. clipboard — clipboards
2. cupful — cupfuls
3. attorney-at-law — attorneys-at-law
4. vice admiral — vice admirals
5. letterhead — letterheads
6. layoff — layoffs
7. bulletin board — bulletin boards
8. disk drive — disk drives
9. backup — backups
10. department chairperson — department chairpersons
11. notary public — notaries public (pref.)
12. follow-up — follow-ups
13. block move — block moves
14. cross-examination — cross-examinations
15. half-gallon — half-gallons

GO TO CD-ROM CHECKUP 5-1

CASES OF NOUNS

The term *case* refers to the different functions of words in sentences. For noun and pronoun use, there are three cases: nominative, objective, and possessive. Nouns (or pronouns) that act as subjects of a sentence, as appositives, or as subject complements are in the *nominative* case. Nouns (or pronouns) that act as direct objects, indirect objects, objects of a preposition, or objects of infinitives are in the *objective* case. Further coverage of the nominative and objective cases appears in Chapter 7. The *possessive* case noun does not retain the same form as the nominative and objective forms; therefore, it requires special attention.

Go to Transparencies/PowerPoints 5-7a, 5-7b, and 5-7c.

See Instructor Note 5-11 in IAE.

See Instructor Note 5-12 in IAE.

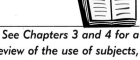

See Chapters 3 and 4 for a review of the use of subjects, complements, appositives, direct objects, indirect objects, and objects of prepositions.

The new Website coordinator began work yesterday.
(*Coordinator* [subject] is used in the nominative case.)

Jane is our new Website coordinator.
(*Coordinator* [subject complement] is used in the nominative case. *Coordinator* follows the linking verb *is* and identifies *Jane.*)

The department manager hired a new Website coordinator.
(*Coordinator* [direct object] is used in the objective case.)

We still have not had a meeting with the new Website coordinator.
(*Coordinator* [object of a preposition] is used in the objective case.)

I wanted to meet the new Website coordinator, but she was in a meeting.
(*Coordinator* is used as the object of the infinitive.)

Punctuation ALERT!

Use an apostrophe to form possessive nouns.

The new Website coordinator's job was demanding.

(*Coordinator* changes to *coordinator's*, which is used in the possessive case. An apostrophe and *s* added to the noun *coordinator* indicates the possessive form.)

CHECKUP 5-2

See Instructor Note 5-13 in IAE.

Directions: *In the space provided, indicate the case of the underlined word or words by writing one of the following abbreviations: **Nom** (nominative case), **Obj** (objective case), **Poss** (possessive case).*

1. Address your <u>complaints</u> about advertising <u>quality</u> directly to the <u>retailer</u>.   Obj, Obj, Obj

2. Web <u>users</u> require more sophisticated search <u>tools</u>.   Nom, Obj

3. We all pay for a <u>customer's</u> fraud.   Poss

4. The <u>magazine's</u> advertising revenue was not sufficient to continue <u>service</u>.   Poss, Obj

5. Many Web <u>pages</u> consist only of <u>pictures</u>.   Nom, Obj

6. Now <u>subscribers</u> can call a toll-free <u>number</u> and hear their e-mail <u>messages</u>.   Nom, Obj, Obj

GO TO CD-ROM CHECKUP 5-2

POSSESSIVE CASE NOUNS

A possessive case noun (or pronoun) shows that *someone* or *something* owns or possesses something else (another noun). A possessive case noun may also indicate a relationship between two nouns. An apostrophe and *s* (*'s*) or an apostrophe (*'*) indicates the possessive form of a noun.

> **Mr. <u>Sanborn's</u> computer was not powerful enough to support the new software.**
> (Mr. Sanborn owns the computer.)

> **Most supervisors appreciate their administrative <u>secretaries'</u> time management skills.**
> (The administrative secretaries possess the skills.)

> **<u>Sam's</u> friend recommended a successful Website and designer.**
> (Sam and friend indicates a relationship. Sam does not own or possess the friend.)

> **The <u>company's</u> employees quickly adapted to the updated network changes.**
> (Company and employees show a relationship. The company does not own or possess the employees.)

SLIP-UP

In a newspaper headline: Shot off woman's leg helps Nicklaus to 66.
Source: Richard Lederer.

Chapter 5

Possessive Singular Nouns

Form the possessive of a singular noun (one person, place, activity, thing, idea, or quality) by adding an apostrophe and s (*'s*). Always look for the possessor of an item. The possessor (a noun) receives the apostrophe and *s* designation, not the item possessed (also a noun). The possessors are underlined in the following examples.

Go to PowerPoint 5-8.

5-14 Refer to *The Gregg Reference Manual* for additional examples of possessive singular nouns.

See Instructor Note 5-15 in IAE.

Jack owns a book.

(The possessive form becomes *Jack's book.*)

Jack owns several books.

(Note that it does not make a difference if Jack owns one book or many books, the possessor is Jack. Jack is a singular noun, and the possessive form becomes *Jack's books.*)

A student owns a computer.

(*Student* is a singular noun; the possessive form becomes *student's computer.*)

A store owns many products.

(*Store* is a singular noun; the possessive form becomes *store's products.*)

The manager has a daughter.

(The *manager's daughter*)

A customer makes several payments.

(The *customer's payments*)

See a reference manual such as **The Gregg Reference Manual** *for additional examples regarding singular possessive formations.*

SLIP-UP

From a newspaper notice: I wish to thank anyone who so kindly assisted in my husband's death.
Source: Richard Lederer.

Possessive nouns modify another noun; therefore, they function as adjectives in sentences. The possessive noun usually appears immediately before another noun. In some cases, additional modifiers separate the possessive noun and the item being possessed.

An airline's record concerning on-time and safety information is available on the Internet.

(Two nouns appear consecutively. *Airline* is the possessor, and *record* is the item possessed. The possessive noun *airline* acts as an adjective indicating *what kind* of record.)

You can find out about an airline's on-time and safety record on the Internet.

(The two nouns are separated by the two modifiers, *on-time* and *safety.* The possessive noun *airline's* and the two modifiers act as adjectives indicating *what kind of* record.)

Note: Record *is the subject and therefore takes the singular verb* is.

Do not confuse a plural noun ending in *s* with a possessive form. One way to test whether you have a possessive noun is to interchange the two nouns and put the word *of* between them. If the *of* phrase sounds all right in a sentence, you have a possessive case noun. In the following examples, the possessive nouns are underlined:

John's suggestion seemed appropriate.

(The suggestion of *John* seemed appropriate.)

When I changed jobs, I lost one <u>week's</u> salary.

(When I changed jobs, I lost the salary *of one week*.)

The <u>equipment's</u> cost was a major selling point.

(The cost *of the equipment* was a major selling point.)

Remember to proofread a <u>Website's</u> address.

(Remember to proofread the address *of a Website*.)

CHECKUP 5-3

Directions: In the following sentences, underline the nouns that need apostrophes to show possession. Write these nouns correctly in the spaces provided.

1. the decision of our <u>committee</u> — committee's
2. the home page of the <u>company</u> — company's
3. the database of the search <u>engine</u> — engine's
4. the Internet service provider of <u>Todd</u> — Todd's
5. the complaints of the <u>customer</u> — customer's
6. the credit card of the <u>shopper</u> — shopper's
7. the sales of the <u>month</u> — month's
8. the profits of <u>Microsoft</u> — Microsoft's
9. the colleges of <u>Idaho</u> — Idaho's
10. the comments of the <u>editor</u> — editor's

**GO TO
CD-ROM
CHECKUP 5-3**

Possessive Plural Nouns

Form the possessive of a plural noun that ends in *s* or *es* by adding only an apostrophe.

To form a possessive plural noun, always make the singular noun plural before you form the possessive. Use the of phrase to determine whether you have a possessive noun.

See Instructor Note 5-16 in IAE.

Go to PowerPoint 5-9.

Singular Nouns	Plural Nouns	Plural Possessives
Girl	Girl<u>s</u>	Girls<u>'</u> books
Secretary	Secretarie<u>s</u>	Secretaries<u>'</u> vacations
Attorney	Attorney<u>s</u>	Attorneys<u>'</u> cases
Class	Classe<u>s</u>	Classes<u>'</u> requirements

Do This	Do Not Do This
All addresses of our clients are current.	All addresses' of our clients are current.
Our Websites have several interesting features.	Our Websites' have several interesting features.

(Do not use an apostrophe just because you see a word ending in *es* or *s*.)

Possessives of Irregular Plural Nouns

Form the possessive of a plural noun that does not end in *s* by adding an apostrophe and *s* (*'s*).

See Instructor Note 5-17 in IAE.

5-18 Define *plurals* and *possessives*.

Singular Nouns	Plural Nouns	Plural Possessives
Woman	Women	Women's ideas
Businessman	Businessmen	Businessmen's appointments

Do This

The new sales figures

Our earnings projections

My savings account balance

An economics class

Do Not Do This

The new sales' figures

Our earnings' projections

My savings' account balance

An economics' class

(Do not use an apostrophe with a descriptive adjective that ends in *s* and that provides identification only. Sometimes only a slight difference in wording will distinguish a descriptive adjective from a possessive.)

CHECKUP 5-4

To make a singular noun possessive, add apostrophe and s ('s). [boy's]
To make a plural noun that does not end in s possessive, add apostrophe and s ('s). [men's]
To make a plural noun ending in s possessive, add an apostrophe ('). [boys']

Directions: *Write the plural form for each noun on the first blank line. Write the plural possessive form for each noun on the second blank line.*

	Singular Nouns	Plural Nouns	Possessive Plurals
1.	copy	copies	copies'
2.	boss	bosses	bosses'
3.	browser	browsers	browsers'
4.	child	children	children's
5.	menu	menus	menus'
6.	directory	directories	directories'
7.	account	accounts	accounts'
8.	logo	logos	logos'
9.	proof	proofs	proofs'
10.	sketch	sketches	sketches'
11.	office	offices	offices'
12.	terminal	terminals	terminals'
13.	network	networks	networks'
14.	memorandum	memorandum	memorandums'
15.	month	months	months'

GO TO CD-ROM
CHECKUP 5-4

CHECKUP 5-5

Directions: *Underline plural nouns once and possessive nouns twice in the following sentences. If a possessive noun is required in the sentence, write the noun correctly in the space provided. If a sentence is correct, write* **Yes** *in the space provided.*

1. Did you know that the <u>firms finances</u> were in such a poor state?   firm's

2. <u>Fridays</u> computer planning meeting will have to be rescheduled.   Friday's

3. The Web provides <u>users</u> an inexpensive way to sell <u>products</u> and distribute information.   Yes

4. The <u>books pages</u> reflected that the writer had given considerable thought to its arrangement.   book's

5. The <u>Web Crawlers</u> limited database created frustration and loss of valuable research time.   Web Crawler's

6. The accountant was late in returning <u>Aprils</u> financial <u>statements</u>.   April's

7. Advertisers should recognize the <u>Webs</u> strength.   Web's

8. The first version of the <u>companys</u> software will support Macintosh <u>users</u>.   company's

9. Internal <u>Websites</u> or intranets are one of the fastest growing <u>technologies</u> throughout the world.   Yes

10. Too many fancy <u>gimmicks</u> in Website designs often result in turning a <u>viewers</u> attention elsewhere.   viewer's

---

5-19 The word *its* is the clue that the noun *book* is singular.

**GO TO
CD-ROM
CHECKUP 5-5**

Go to PowerPoint 5-10.

5-20 Refer to *The Gregg Reference Manual* for rules on organization, association, and company names.

See a reference manual such as The Gregg Reference Manual *for rules on forming possessives for organization, association, and company names.*

Separate and Joint Ownership

Use an apostrophe in all names of persons or companies to indicate *separate ownership* of an item or items. Use an apostrophe in the last of two or more names to show *joint ownership* of an item or items.

Richard's and Lee's reports
(Richard had a separate report or reports, and Lee had a separate report or reports.)

Richard and Lee's reports
(Richard and Lee had reports that belonged to them jointly.)

Netscape's and Microsoft's browsers
(Both Netscape and Microsoft have their own browsers.)

Jean and Andy's home office
(The home office is owned jointly by Jean and Andy.)

Organization, Association, and Company Names

The names of organizations, associations, and companies may contain words that are either possessive or descriptive terms. Use the form that the company, organization, or association displays on its logo, product, or letterhead. Some use an apostrophe and *s*; others do not.

See Instructor Note 5-21 in IAE.

Stokely's®	American Bankers Association
Kellogg's® Frosted Flakes	Citizens Political Committee
Bush's® baked beans	Pringles® potato chips
Vet's Club	The Greater Madison Convention
Reader's Digest®	and Visitors Bureau
Ladies' Home Journal®	
Wisconsin Sheriff's and Deputy Sheriff's Association	

CHECKUP 5-6

Directions: *Change each of the possessive case formats to an **of** phrase. Write your responses in the space provided.*

Ex. Beth and Michael's car is new.

the car of Beth and Michael

1. Bucholtz and Nardin's lawn care company has a very clever Website banner.

lawn care company of Bucholtz and Nardin

2. Thomas's and Marcy's opinions indicated that they had strong feelings about changing our marketing strategies.

opinions of Thomas and opinions of Marcy

3. The Future Secretaries Association's dues increased this year.

dues of the Future Secretaries Association

4. Yamika and Nobu's boutique won the Outstanding Website Design Award.

boutique of Yamika and Nobu

5. Badger Electric eliminated Charles's and Liane's positions when it merged with Prime Energy, Inc.

position of Charles and position of Liane

6. Did you attend the Chamber of Commerce's seminar at the local technical college last Thursday?

seminar of the Chamber of Commerce

GO TO CD-ROM CHECKUP 5-6

Compound Nouns

Form the possessive of a singular compound noun by adding an apostrophe and *s* ('s) at the end of the word.

printout's format	write-up's facts
takeover's announcement	credit card's expiration date

Go to PowerPoints 5-11a and 5-11b.

All compound nouns are made possessive at the end of the word or words.

Form the possessive of a plural compound noun that ends in *s* by adding only an apostrophe at the end of the word.

stockholders' dividends   newspapers' editorials
stand-ins' responsibilities   bookshelves' contents

Form the possessive of a plural compound noun that does not end in *s* by adding an apostrophe and *s* at the end of the word.

sisters-in-law's careers   chiefs of police's duties
editors in chief's columns   businessmen's remarks

Abbreviations

Go to PowerPoint 5-12.

Form the possessive of a singular abbreviation by adding an apostrophe and *s* (*'s*). Form the possessive of a plural abbreviation by adding only an apostrophe (').

FBI's investigation
CEO's decision
William T. Burns Jr.'s question
The Shefley Co.'s promotions
HMOs' restrictions (more than one HMO)
Ph.D.s' speeches (more than one Ph.D.)

Time and Amounts

Form the possessive of a noun expressing time or an amount in the same way as other nouns.

moment's delay   a dollar's worth
a week's vacation   two weeks' pay

Understood Possession

Use an apostrophe and *s* (*'s*) or an apostrophe (') to show possession of a noun that is understood but not stated.

Kathryn's suggestions were more detailed than Matt's.
(*Suggestions* is the missing but understood noun and refers to *Matt's suggestions.*)

This year's online sales increased 20 percent over last year's.
(*Online sales* [refers to last year's] is the missing but understood noun.)

CHECKUP 5-7

Directions: *Underline the incorrect possessive forms in the following sentences. Write the correct forms in the spaces provided. If the sentence is correct, write* **Yes** *in the space provided.*

1. The owner of Werewolf Internet Services has five year's experience   years'
   with commercial accounts.

Chapter 5

2. DRI's financial advice was research based, but a <u>competitors</u> was not.   competitor's _____

3. When our company merged with StarNet, some employees received three months' separation pay.   Yes _____

4. The district <u>attorney's</u> offices in both counties became involved in the dispute.   attorneys' _____

5. My son-in-law's employer is a cyberspace enthusiast.   Yes _____

6. A tool <u>bars'</u> icons give us commands at our fingertips.   bar's _____

7. Rhonda Steinmetz, <u>M.D.s'</u> online health advice has received favorable comments.   M.D.',s _____

8. The narrative on Cummings Inc.'s Web page was too lengthy.   Yes _____

9. This semester's interactive learning classes are more difficult than last <u>semesters.</u>   semester's _____

10. Her credit <u>cards'</u> expiration date made the online sale invalid.   card's _____

**GO TO
CD-ROM**
CHECKUP 5-7

DIAGRAMMING SENTENCES

In Chapter 3, you learned that a direct object appears on the same line as the simple subject and verb in diagrammed sentences. An indirect object appears under the verb. Note the slanted line and the horizontal connecting line under the verbs in the examples. The indirect object is written on the horizontal line. You will be asked to diagram only those parts of a sentence that you have worked with in previous chapters or that are introduced in this chapter.

5-22 The diagramming section of this chapter may be omitted.

The payroll department sent me my W-2 forms.

```
department | sent | forms
            \ me
```

Simple subject: *department*
Simple verb: *sent*
Direct object: *forms*
Indirect object: *me*

Place a possessive noun on a slanted line beneath the noun it modifies. The possessive noun functions as an adjective.

We hired Marty's friend to revise the layouts.

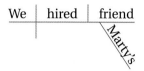

Simple subject: *We*
Simple verb: *hired*
Direct object: *friend*
Possessive noun: *Marty's*

CHECKUP 5-8

Directions: *In the space provided, diagram the following sentences. Diagram only the following parts: simple subject, verb, direct object, indirect object, appositive, subject complement, possessive noun.*

1. The company gave the university its unused equipment.

company	gave	equipment
	university	

2. Did Carole give you the message?

Carole	did give	message
	you	

3. They awarded our company the WebSite Progress designation.

They	awarded	designation
	company	

4. Janet's design included additional diagrams.

design	included	diagrams
Janet's		

5. Sheila brought me the preliminary cost figures.

Sheila	brought	figures
	me	

GO TO
CD-ROM
CHECKUP 5-8

NAME _____

PRACTICE 1A

Directions: *Select the correct word in parentheses, and write it in the space provided.*

1. I have one (*week's, weeks*) time to submit the new Web page.

   1. ___week's___

2. I wanted to check the (*travelers, travelers'*) guides before I asked for my travel (*agents', agent's*) advice.

   2. ___travelers'___
   ___agent's___

3. Activity on the Web has attracted the (*worlds, world's*) attention.

   3. ___world's___

4. Sites such as car dealers that offer specialized information are likely to draw (*consumers, consumers'*) who are looking for specific products.

   4. ___consumers___

5. (*Advertisers', Advertiser's*) messages should not be complicated or lengthy.

   5. ___Advertisers'___

6. Unlike some online (*provider's, providers'*) e-mail services, (*Juno's, Junos'*) is free.

   6. ___providers'___
   ___Juno's___

7. My supervisor always wants a summary of the (*days', day's*) important stories.

   7. ___day's___

8. Hypertext links within the (*news, new's*) article automatically took me to seven related items.

   8. ___news___

9. Successful companies need to provide different ways for (*feed back, feed-back, feedback*) such as 800 numbers, fax, or e-mail.

   9. ___feedback___

10. (*Visa and MasterCard's, Visa's and MasterCard's*) concerned standard for online (*credit-card, credit card, creditcard*) transactions should offer some protection to consumers.

    10. ___Visa and Mastercard's___
    ___credit card___

11. Club Web offers (*childrens', children's*) safety tips, games, and (*kids', kid's*) software.

    11. ___children's___
    ___kids'___

12. Most nonprofit (*company's, companies'*) names end with the extension .org.

    12. ___companies'___

13. Check your (*ISP's, ISPs'*) written policies if you are concerned about invasion of privacy.

    13. ___ISP's___

14. The (*paper's, papers'*) electronic edition arrives by e-mail around 5 p.m.

    14. ___paper's___

15. Two (*employees, employees'*) answer all (*clients', client's*) e-mail inquiries.

    15. ___employees___
    ___clients'___

5-23 ISP is the abbreviation for Internet service provider.

**GO TO
CD-ROM
PRACTICE 1
EXERCISES**

PRACTICE

PRACTICE 2A

A. Directions: Write the correct singular possessive form in the first blank, the plural form in the second blank, and the plural possessive form in the third blank.

		Singular Possessive	Plural Form	Plural Possessive
Ex:	assistant	assistant's	assistants	assistants'
1.	mailbox	mailbox's	mailboxes	mailboxes'
2.	attorney	attorney's	attorneys	attorneys'
3.	agency	agency's	agencies	agencies'
4.	child	child's	children	children's
5.	notary public	notary public's	notaries public	notaries public's (pref.)

B. Directions: In the space below each statement, correct the underlined error. Then write the rule that applies in your own words.

(Answers will vary for the rules. These responses are suggested answers.)

1. I can easily spend an <u>hours</u> time surfing Web sites.

   hour's   Nouns representing time form possessives in the same way as other nouns. An hour represents a singular noun. The singular possessive form is necessary.

2. Have you seen the Lands' End Website that advertises <u>womens</u> clothing?

   women's   *Women* is an irregular plural noun that does not end in *s;* therefore, the plural possessive form ends in *'s.*

3. The <u>editors'</u> in chiefs responses to IBM's announcement were all similar.

   editors in chief's   Plural compound nouns that do not end in *s* form their possessive forms by adding *'s* to the last word.

C. Directions: Underline the plural and possessive errors in the words in the following sentences. Write the words correctly in the space provided, inserting or deleting apostrophes as needed. If the sentence is correct, write *Yes* in the space.

See Instructor Note 5-24 in IAE.

1. *The Complete <u>Idiots</u> Guide to the Internet* was the first book I used to learn the functions of the Internet.   1. ___Idiot's___

2. New Web-based <u>programs'</u> written in the language of Java provide unlimited business applications.   2. ___programs___

3. The <u>Internets</u> security needs improvement for online payments.   3. ___Internet's___

NAME _____

4. I often read the latest <u>computer</u>' magazines to see what is new.

4. _computer_

See Instructor Note 5-25 in IAE.

5. Online reference <u>materials</u>' require frequent updates.

5. _materials_

6. Entertainment companies may charge subscription fees to <u>users</u>' of online games.

6. _users_

7. After four hours' work, she completed her research.

7. _Yes_

8. I read an interesting online report about the depletion of some of our <u>nations</u>' natural resources.

8. _nation's_

9. Horn and Harris's Department Store is having a <u>warehouse</u>' clearance sale.

9. _warehouse_

**GO TO
CD-ROM**
PRACTICE 2
EXERCISES

10. Fujitsu is one of the <u>worlds</u> largest software companies.

10. _world's_

PRACTICE 3A

PROOFREADING

Directions: *Proofread and compare the two sentences in each group. If they are the same, write* **Yes** *in the space provided. If they are not the same, write* **No.** *Use the first sentence as the correct copy. If you find errors in the second sentence, underline them.*

1. Amazon calls itself the "Earth's biggest bookstore."

1. _No_

Amazon calls itself the "<u>Earths</u>' biggest <u>bookstore</u>.

2. Even though we have an excellent catalog at our site, our customers must still dial our 800 number to place orders.

2. _No_

Even though we have an excellent catalog at our <u>sight,</u> our customers must still dial our <u>900</u> number to place orders.

3. The browser's color graphics were less clear than what I needed for my work.

3. _Yes_

The browser's color graphics were less clear than what I needed for my work.

Compound and Possessive Nouns

NAME _____

4. This year's trade show was 50 percent larger than last year's.   4. ___No___

This year's trade show was <u>500</u> percent larger <u>then</u> last <u>years</u>.

5. Alamo's Website gives its rental car customers suggestions for getting around in a strange city.   5. ___No___

<u>Alamo</u> Website gives <u>it's</u> rental car customers suggestions for getting around a strange city.

6. I like the Web pages that offer prizes or information, but I don't like those that are all pictures.   6. ___Yes___

I like the Web pages that offer prizes or information, but I don't like those that are all pictures.

7. Our lawyer told us that many online documents' legal points are incorrect or incomplete.   Our lawyer told us that many online <u>document's</u> legal points are incorrect <u>and</u> incomplete.   7. ___No___

8. It's easy to pick up a virus by downloading a file from the Internet.   <u>Its'</u> easy to <u>pickup</u> a virus by downloading a file from the <u>internet</u>.   8. ___No___

**GO TO
CD-ROM**
PRACTICE 3
EXERCISES

PRACTICE 4A

<u>WRITING</u>

The Writing Process: Drafting

You can begin drafting after prewriting. *Drafting* means to organize your sentences and put them into paragraph form. Using the topic and purpose, you can develop a theme, the point you want to make in the piece. The theme should be stated in a topic statement in the first paragraph. A paragraph consists of a topic sentence, which states a main idea related to the theme, and other sentences that support the main idea with details. Your audience, theme, and purpose will influence the style, or voice, of your writing, which gives it a particular "feel."

NAME _____

A. **Directions:** *For each item below, write a topic statement for a paragraph using the topic and purpose provided. Use a complete sentence.*

Answers will vary.

Ex: **Topic:** Using the Web. **Purpose:** To inform.

Using our college Web page gives me the opportunity to look up a list of

closed classes.

1. **Topic:** A complaint about public transportation. **Purpose:** To persuade.

Public transportation should be available for our students.

2. **Topic:** Fashions in clothing. **Purpose:** To describe.

Chartreuse and purple are the latest hot colors.

3. **Topic:** Your favorite animal. **Purpose:** To entertain.

My dog Nickels thinks he is a cat.

B. **Directions:** *For each item below, write three related sentences that provide details to support the stated topic sentence.*

Answers will vary.

1. English grammar is necessary for success in school. [Include at least one sentence using the possessive form of a noun. Underline the possessive noun.]

A student's grades will depend on his or her ability to write papers.

A student who is not proficient in English grammar will have a difficult

time writing papers.

Proficiency in English grammar gives students confidence.

2. Many students use (or don't use) the Internet in their classes. [Include at least one sentence using a compound noun. Underline the compound noun.]

Students who use the Internet for research can complete the research any

time of the day or night.

The information on the Internet is more up to date than information found

in a library.

I often use the Internet to access the database of information.

Knowing how to use the Internet increased my take home pay.

3. My English grammar has improved since enrolling in this class.

I have learned how to use nouns and pronouns correctly.

I enjoy diagramming sentences because it helps me see the relationship

among the parts of speech.

I am more confident about taking classes that require writing.

GO TO
CD-ROM
PRACTICE 4
EXERCISES

NAME _____

5-26 Check online sites carefully before assigning them to students.

Answers will vary.

Punctuation ALERT!

Use exact punctuation when typing an Internet address.

ONLINE EXERCISE

As the number of Web users grows, the demographics of the online population begins to look more like the mass population. New users feel confused choosing among the hundreds of thousands of Websites.

The longer people stay at a Website, the more opportunities for advertisers to get their messages noticed. Advertisers will pay to reach an audience that stays on the site long enough to absorb their ad messages. You will visit some of the consistently popular Websites.

Objective: *To examine a Website to determine the features that keep visitors staying longer than a few seconds.*

You will visit a Web page of a fast-growing community in cyberspace.

1. With your Internet browser on the screen, key:

   http://www.GeoCities.com in the location text box. Press **Enter** on the keyboard.

2. Observe the site. GeoCities has neighborhoods arranged around blocks containing 100 home pages each. GeoCities provides the structure and the tools, but just about all the content is created by GeoCities residents.

3. Time yourself as you move around looking at residents' home pages. When you leave GeoCities, note how much time you spent exploring.

4. List all the advertisers you can find throughout GeoCities. Be aware that advertisers pay to place banner ads on the home pages of members.

5. Write a topic sentence about your experience at GeoCities. Write two additional sentences describing your visit.

NAME _____

PRACTICE 1B

Directions: Select the correct word in parentheses, and write it in the space provided.

1. (*Mr. Marcusso's, Mr. Marcussos*) opinion is highly respected at work.
2. Rosario had two (*days', days*) notice to research Webcasting.
3. Several Internet firms are relocating to the Boston (*suburbs, suburbs'*).
4. Many (*companies', companies*) save crucial files on Zip disks.
5. Is it practical to do a complete online backup of (*today's, todays*) hard drives?
6. Our (*clients, clients'*) connect over the Internet by dialing into (*HP's, HPs*) network.
7. PointCast automatically downloads the latest (*versions, version's*) of its software.
8. Some (*firms, firms'*) have (*thousands, thousand's*) of people accessing the Internet every day.
9. (*Antonio's, Antonio*) and Heather's computers are on different floors of the building.
10. The Chicago Board of (*Trade's, Trades'*) Internet Advisory Committee meets monthly.

1. Mr. Marcusso's
2. days'
3. suburbs
4. companies
5. today's
6. clients, HP's
7. versions
8. firms, thousands
9. Antonio's
10. Trade's

PRACTICE 2B

Directions: Write the correct singular possessive form in the first blank, the plural form in the second blank, and the plural possessive form in the third blank.

	Singular Possessive	Plural Form	Plural Possessive
Ex: assistant	assistant's	assistants	assistants'
1. employee	employee's	employees	employees'
2. portfolio	portfolio's	portfolios	portfolios'
3. M.D.	M.D.'s	M.D.s	M.D.s'
4. modem	modem's	modems	modems'
5. post office	post office's	post offices	post offices'

A. Directions: In the space below each statement, correct the underlined error. Then write the rule that applies in your own words.

Answers will vary for the rules. These responses are suggested answers.

1. Infoseek's search engine as well as <u>Excites</u> finds specific information.

   Excite's. Excite is a singular noun. Excite also owns a search engine. The ownership is understood with Excite's.

2. <u>Magellans</u> People Find locates phone numbers and street addresses of U.S. and Canadian residents.

   Magellan's People Find belongs to the business Magellan.

3. Four11 bills itself as the largest directory of e-mail <u>addresses'</u>.

   Addresses is plural but not possessive.

END-OF-CHAPTER WORKSHEETS

NAME _____

B. Directions: *Underline the plural and possessive errors in the following sentences. Write the words correctly in the space provided, inserting or deleting apostrophes as needed. If the sentence is correct, write* **Yes** *in the space.*

1. This <u>weeks'</u> spam is about a vitamin supplement.
2. David tried to be removed from a <u>senders'</u> mailing list.
3. CyberPark has assorted card and board <u>games'</u>.
4. Nintendo <u>fan's</u> enjoy n64.com with its daily <u>new's</u> updates.
5. <u>Luckmans</u> Web Commander provides secure <u>business'</u> transactions on the Internet.
6. The Internet Reminder Service notified me of my <u>mother-in-laws</u> birthday.
7. Free online cards are available for <u>birthday's</u>, <u>graduation's</u>, and other <u>occasion's</u>.
8. Miramax provides you the opportunity to write a creative caption for the <u>months</u> movie scene.
9. <u>Dereks</u> Free Stuff Page has links to free samples and databases.
10. <u>Alex's</u> and Evelyn's son is a Web user enthusiast.

1. _____week's_____
2. ____sender's____
3. _____games_____
4. ___fans, news___
5. **Luckman's business**
6. __mother-in-law's__
7. _____birthdays_____
   graduations occasions
8. ____month's____
9. _____Derek's_____
10. _____Alex_____

PRACTICE 3B

PROOFREADING

Directions: *Proofread and compare the two sentences in each group. If they are the same, write* **Yes** *in the space provided. If they are not the same, write* **No.** *Use the first sentence as the correct copy. If you find errors in the second sentence, underline them.*

1. Net newbies are gravitating to Websites where they can find friends and feel comfortable.

   Net <u>newbies'</u> are gravitating to Websites where they can find friends and feel comfortable.

   1. _____No_____

2. If Websites do not capture Web surfers' interests within eight seconds, the surfers move on to other sites.

   If <u>a</u> Website do not capture Web <u>surfers</u> interests within eight seconds, the surfers move on to other <u>sights</u>.

   2. _____No_____

3. Women's Wire is a Web community for career-oriented women.

   Woman's Wire is a Web community for <u>career oriented</u> women.

   3. _____No_____

4. Nearly one-quarter of online users have purchased goods either on the Internet or through an online service.

   Nearly <u>one quarter</u> of <u>on-line</u> users have purchased goods either on the Internet or through an online service.

   4. _____No_____

5. PBS's Computer Chronicles will air a technical trivia game sponsored by Boston's Computer Museum.

   PBS' Computer Chronicles will air a technical trivia game sponsored by <u>Bostons</u> Computer Museum.

   5. _____No_____

PRACTICE 4B

WRITING

Directions: *For each item below, write a topic statement for a paragraph using the topic and purpose provided. Use a complete sentence.*   *(Answers will vary. Sample answers are given.)*

Ex: Topic: Chatting at a Website. **Purpose:** To inform.

Many Web pages add a way for Web surfers to chat.

1. **Topic:** A product you use and like. **Purpose:** To persuade.

I use Post-it® notes to mark the important parts of my books.

2. **Topic:** A happy time in your life. **Purpose:** To entertain.

Camp Hantesa evokes memories of good friends and great times.

3. **Topic:** Characteristics of a good teacher. **Purpose:** To describe.

A great teacher is one who encourages you to do your best.

Directions: *For each item below, write three related sentences that provide details to support the stated topic sentence.*   *(Answers will vary.)*

1. Knowledge of the Internet is important in my future. (Write at least one sentence using the possessive form of a noun. Underline the possessive noun.)

I can use the Internet's search engines to access information.

Such information can be used to learn about many subjects.

I will use this knowledge in my working career.

2. Some students do not take responsibility for their actions. (Write at least one sentence using a compound noun. Underline the compound noun.)

Some students fail to do their homework.

They often let other things get in their way of studying.

Instead of taking responsibility for their actions, they blame others.

3. Business English will help me succeed at work.

Most businesses use e-mail to communicate.

I know the e-mail I write will be judged according to its accuracy.

I want to learn business English in order to write grammatically correct memos and letters.

END-OF-CHAPTER WORKSHEETS

ONLINE *EXERCISE*

Objective: *To examine a Website to determine the features that keep visitors interested longer than a few seconds.*

You will visit a Web page of an extremely popular entertainment company.

1. With your Internet browser on the screen, key:

    http://www.disney.com in the location text box. Press **Enter** on the keyboard.

2. Observe the site. Disney has links to recent movies, amusement parks, and popular Disney characters.

3. Time yourself as you move around the Disney site. When you leave Disney, note how much time you spent exploring.

4. List all the advertisers you can find throughout the Disney site.

5. Write a topic sentence about your experience at Disney.com. Write two additional sentences describing your visit.

*L*OOKING *B*ACK

Posttest

Directions: *In the space provided, write the letter of the correct answer.*

1. *First Interstate Bank sent Larry to a Web design class.* In this sentence, what does the noun *Larry* illustrate?
   a. the nominative case
   b. the possessive case
   c. the objective and nominative cases
   d. the objective case

   1. _____d_____

2. Which statement represents the correct possessive form?
   a. The Video Store's Web page has 500 hits a day.
   b. The Video Stores' Web page has 500 hits a day.
   c. The Video Store Web's page has 500 hits a day.
   d. The Video Store Web page has 500 hits' a day.

   2. _____a_____

3. Which statement represents the correct possessive form?
   a. Monica and Meg's reactions to Internet research differ.
   b. Monica's and Meg's reactions to Internet research differ.
   c. Monicas' and Megs' reactions to Internet research differ.
   d. Monica and Megs' reactions to Internet research differ.

   3. _____b_____

4. Which statement is written correctly?
   a. Daily faxes' update our sales figures.
   b. Daily faxes update our sales figures'.
   c. Daily faxes update our sales figures.
   d. Daily faxes' update our sales' figures.

   4. _____c_____

Directions: *In the space provided, write the letter or letters of the correct possessive or plural forms of nouns.*

1. a. trade-offs
   b. brainstormings ideas'
   c. layoff's consequences
   d. notary's public

   1. _____a, c_____

2. a. a salesclerk's mistakes
   b. two HMO's doctors
   c. Ms. Lopez's application
   d. a companies' responsibilities

   2. _____a, c_____

3. a. Levi's jeans
   b. Childrens' Hospital
   c. days notice
   d. business checking account

   3. _____a, d_____

CHAPTER 6

Capitalization

TIME MANAGEMENT

Planning is an important process. Students say that planning helps them reduce stress and keeps them on time. Those students who plan are much more likely to have A and B averages than those who do not plan.

If you know how to plan, you have overcome procrastination and probably have all your paperwork under control. While you are in school, you have an opportunity to develop time management skills, which you can then apply to the workplace.

One of the most common roadblocks to managing time is procrastination. Procrastination means putting off doing tasks until a later time. Procrastination keeps you from starting or seeing a task through to completion and results in overwork, continual crises, and clutter. A procrastinator lacks planning skills and is unable to set priorities. To overcome procrastination, break projects into small tasks, and reward yourself at milestones in the process. Once you start a project, no matter how small the task, you are no longer procrastinating.

OBJECTIVES

After you have studied this chapter and completed the exercises, you will be able to do the following:

1. Use capitalization rules for proper nouns, first words in sentences, specific organizations, committees, government agencies, boards, and departments.
2. Apply capitalization rules for publications, events and holidays, acts, bills, laws, personal titles, and family titles.
3. Apply capitalization rules for academic degrees, languages, education levels and courses, and ethnic and religious designations.
4. Apply capitalization rules for time periods, seasons, and days and months, specific and general locations, and directions.
5. Apply capitalization rules for abbreviations, trademarks, brand names, and product names.
6. Apply capitalization rules for direct and indirect quotes, words after colons, and material within parentheses.
7. Identify appropriate items to capitalize in lists, outlines, business letters, and legal documents.

TERMS TO REMEMBER

PROCRASTINATION

PROCRASTINATOR

TIME MANAGEMENT

LOOKING AHEAD

Pretest

Directions: *Underline any capitalization errors in the following sentences. Write the words correctly in the space provided.*

1. trent always refers to his Follow-up File and Calendar to see what is on the schedule.

   Trent   follow-up file   calendar

2. The Salesperson knew that superintendent Ricci had a busy day; therefore, she outlined her Proposal quickly.

   salesperson   Superintendent   proposal

3. Neal Whitten is the author of the book *Becoming An Indispensable Employee In A Disposable World*.

   an   in   a

4. The Faculty at north central technical college spent many hours discussing Accreditation Standards.

   faculty   North Central Technical College   accreditation standards

5. The human resources department reserved redwood lodge in the Northern part of the State for a Fall retreat.

   Human Resources Department   Redwood Lodge   northern   state   fall

6. She said, "we have an ambitious, time-conscious Staff."

   We   staff

Directions: *In the space provided, write the letter of the correct answer.*

1. Which line has items that are all correct?
   a. Yavapai community college, Computer Design Course, business English
   b. Yavapai Community College, computer design course, Business English
   c. Yavapai Community college, Computer Design course, business English
   d. Yavapai Community College, computer design course, business English

   1. _____d_____

2. Which line has items that are all correct?
   a. passover, winter, thursday
   b. Passover, winter, thursday
   c. Passover, winter, Thursday
   d. Passover, Winter, Thursday

   2. _____c_____

3. Which line has items that are all correct?
   a. Invoice 2056B, page 95, room 218, Highway 161
   b. invoice 2056b, Page 95, Room 218, highway 161
   c. Invoice 2056B, page 95, Room 218, Highway 161
   d. Invoice 2056B, Page 95, Room 218, highway 161

   3. _____c_____

4. The correct capitalization usage for the salutation and complimentary closing is
   a. Dear Manager, Sincerely yours
   b. Dear Mr. Benton, Sincerely Yours
   c. dear Mr. Benton, Sincerely Yours
   d. Dear manager, Sincerely yours

   4. _____a_____

OVERVIEW

What is your reaction to a capitalized word as you are reading? Does it suggest something or someone specific or important? To indicate that importance, writers follow capitalization rules that have evolved through the years.

In this chapter, you will study some of these general rules so that you will know when to capitalize a word or use lowercase. Obviously, every rule cannot be studied; therefore, you will need to check your reference manual whenever you are in doubt. In addition, each career field may designate its own important words, or a company may list its capitalization rules in a company handbook.

CAPITALIZATION RULES

These rules cover the major areas that require capitalization. At several points throughout the chapter, you will be advised to refer to a reference manual for more detail.

First Word in a Sentence

Capitalize the first word in a sentence.

> **Time management skills are valuable in any career field.**
> **She managed her time efficiently.**

Proper Nouns

Capitalize proper nouns. Do not capitalize common nouns.

Proper Nouns	Common Nouns
Green Bay Unified School District	school district
Laurel Inn	motel
North High School	school
Salt Lake City	city
Tom Carrington	accountant
Yellowstone National Park	park
Germany	country
Putnam Heights Building	building
American Medical Association	association
Pomona Drive	street

See Instructor Notes 6-1, 6-2, and 6-3 in IAE.

Uppercase letters are capital letters.

Go to Transparencies/PowerPoints 6-1a to 6-1d, and 6-2a.

Proper nouns are specific names of persons, places, and things.

Personal Names

Capitalize the names or nicknames of specific persons. Use the capitalization and spelling that the owner of the name designates.

Elizabeth Nelson	Mary Ann, Maryanne, Mary Anne
Barry McMann	Luis Salazar, Louis Salazar
Hoang Duc Hien	Marcia Van Beek, Marcia van Beek
Patricia (Trish) Olson	Marcia VanBeek
Brandon Jackson (BJ)	Kaitlin (Katie)

Do This

Mr. Kauffman specifically asked Anne Wilson to complete the time management report.

Do Not Do This

Kauffman specifically asked Wilson to complete the management report.

Pronouns

Go to
Transparency/PowerPoint 6-2b.

Always capitalize the pronoun *I*. Do not capitalize other pronouns unless they appear at the beginning of a sentence.

I try to keep my desk organized.
Sherry and I included some time-saving hints in our company manual.
Their advice was to handle each piece of paper only once.

Geographic Locations

Capitalize the specific names of geographic locations. Capitalize the names of cities, states, countries, streets, parks, lakes, mountains, rivers, and regions. Do not capitalize general location names.

Do not capitalize the word city unless it is part of the city's name.

Specific Locations

Kansas City	Grand Canyon National Park
Arkansas	Himalaya Mountains
Austria	Black River
Kensington Avenue	Corn Belt
Lake Superior	

General Locations

their country	the mountains
our street	the river

Do This

New York City
the city of Cincinnati

Do Not Do This

New York city
the City of Cincinnati

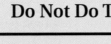

Do This	Do Not Do This
the state of Wyoming	the State of Wyoming
New York State	New York state
Buckeye State	Buckeye state

Proper Noun Substitutions

Capitalize informal substitutions for proper nouns and shortened versions of proper nouns. These substitutions are often referred to as imaginative names and nicknames.

Informal Substitutions	Shortened Versions
the First Lady	Big Blue (IBM)
Twin Cities (Minneapolis and St. Paul)	the Net (the Internet)
the Windy City (Chicago)	the Web (the World Wide Web)
French Quarter (New Orleans)	Rockies (the Rocky Mountains)

Proper Noun Derivatives

Capitalize adjectives formed from proper nouns. Do not capitalize words formed from proper nouns that are now commonly used and that are no longer identified with those nouns.

Slovenian food	china pattern
Spanish language	venetian blinds
Colombian coffee	manila folder
European descent	arabic numbers
Canadian winter	french fries
American lifestyle	
Bostonians	

Capitalize the word state only when it follows the name of the state or an informal name for the state. In legal documents, however, the State of Wyoming is correct.

6-4 Refer to The Gregg Reference Manual for additional examples of imaginative names and nicknames.

See Instructor Note 6-5 in IAE.

Go to Transparency/PowerPoint 6-2c.

See Instructor Note 6-6 in IAE.

Go to Transparency/PowerPoint 6-2d.

For additional examples of proper noun substitutions, see paragraphs illustrating imaginative names and nicknames in The Gregg Reference Manual or another manual you may have available.

CHECKUP 6-1

Directions: *Underline any capitalization errors in the following sentences. On the lines provided, write the words correctly. If the capitalization is correct, write **Yes.***

1. jani, kristen, and danielle always keep a Record of the time it takes them to complete a Task.

   Jani Kristen Danielle record task

2. andrew (andy) Wu, barney Mcmillan, and donna parks received Awards for submitting Timesaving Suggestions.

   Andrew (Andy) Barney McMillan Donna Parks awards timesaving suggestions

3. the time management seminars will be held in boston, massachusetts; richmond, vrginia; and charleston, south carolina.

   The Boston, Massachusetts Richmond, Virginia Charleston, South Carolina

---

Capitalization

4. I do not like to take work home on weekends.

Yes
_____

5. To relieve my stress, i walk in owen park during my Lunch Break.

I Owen Park lunch break
_____

6. people living in the united states feel more time pressures than people living in many european Countries.

People United States European countries
_____

7. Our next vacation will be in Mexico City or San Diego.

Yes
_____

8. When we attend the Conference in the windy city, we will visit several efficiency experts' Exhibits.

conference Windy City exhibits
_____

9. The state of Michigan tried to clarify overtime and compensatory time for its employees.

Yes
_____

10. Are Your daily tasks so time-consuming that you have little time for Planning?

your planning
_____

GO TO CD-ROM
CHECKUP 6-1

Go to Transparencies/
PowerPoints 6-3a and 6-3b.

See Instructor Note 6-7 in IAE.

Companies, Institutions, Organizations, and Clubs

Capitalize the first letters of all major words in names of companies, institutions, organizations, and clubs. Do not capitalize articles (*a, an, the*), conjunctions (*and, but, or, nor*), and prepositions with fewer than four letters (*of, in, on, by*) unless one of these words is the first word of the name. If available, use the official letterhead as a guide.

> Dickman and Rothstein Attorneys (company)
> Firstar Bank (company)
> the University of Michigan (institution)
> Palm Beach Junior College (institution)
> American Association of University Women (organization)
> United Way (organization)
> the Girl Scouts of America (organization)
> Future Business Leaders of America (club)
> Kiwanis International (club)

Do not capitalize words such as *company, club, institution,* or *organization* when used as general expressions.

> company profits
> our club's membership
> the objectives of the institution
> the organization's bylaws

Chapter 6

Departments, Committees, and Divisions

See Instructor Note 6-8 in IAE.

Go to PowerPoint 6-4.

Capitalize the specific names of departments, committees, project teams, or divisions within the organization with which *you* are associated. Do not capitalize names of departments, committees, project teams, or divisions if words other than *the* appear before them or if the names are not precise.

Refer to a reference manual such as The Gregg Reference Manual *for more examples of organizational units.*

> The Education and Training Department is offering time management courses.
>
> The Policy and Procedures Committee spent hours developing employee surveys.
>
> (The writer should know the precise name of the department or committee in the company where he or she works.)
>
> I'll check with someone in their advertising department to see if Cole can handle our new ad design.
>
> Will your advertising division have time to work on our new ad design?
>
> (The words *their* and *your* modify the organizational units in a general way.)
>
> Some type of review committee should be appointed to analyze overtime compensation.
>
> Ron does not have time to serve on another board of directors.
>
> (The names of the organizational units are not precise.)

Government Units

Go to PowerPoint 6-5.

Federal, state, county, and city government units should be identified accurately. The telephone directory is a good source for identifying these units. Federal agencies are listed under United States Government, while state, county, and city government units are listed under the states, counties, or cities in which these units are located. Use a reference manual to locate foreign government designations.

Capitalize specific official names of foreign, national, state, and local government units. Capitalize the names of agencies, divisions, departments, offices, commissions, and boards. Capitalize short forms of the names of government units.

British Empire	Texas Child Welfare Agency
World Health Organization	Wage Hour and Public Contracts Division
United States Senate	Railroad Retirement Board
the Congress	Department on Aging
the Nevada Legislature	Office of Consumer Affairs
Austin City Council	Traffic Commission
the House	the Senate

Do This	Do Not Do This
federal offices	Federal offices
federal government	Federal government
Federal Reserve Board	federal Reserve Board

Do not capitalize federal unless it is in the specific name of an agency.

CHECKUP 6-2

Directions: *Underline any capitalization errors in the following sentences. On the lines provided, write the words correctly. If the capitalization is correct, write* **Yes.**

1. Pat Halsted trains new employees for customer service positions at <u>people's</u> <u>state</u> <u>bank</u>.

   People's State Bank

2. Three employees from the trust department at <u>rohde</u> & <u>samuelson</u> <u>attorneys</u> received time off to attend a three-day workshop.

   Rohde Samuelson Attorneys

3. Reviewing federal and state tax regulations requires intense concentration.

   Yes

4. When I have some time off and can schedule <u>State</u> <u>Agency</u> appointments, I find that the offices are closed.

   state agency

5. The <u>accounting</u> <u>department</u> plans to begin the audit of <u>kerm</u> and <u>associates</u> of Waterloo, Iowa.

   Accounting Department Kerm Associates

6. I missed the deadline date for submitting my nomination papers for the <u>hendersonville</u> <u>city</u> <u>council</u> position.

   Hendersonville City Council

7. The <u>future</u> <u>business</u> <u>leaders</u> of <u>america</u> had too many objectives; therefore, the <u>Club</u> could not complete them during the year.

   Future Business Leaders America club

8. <u>huntington</u> & <u>associates</u> offers training in two-hour blocks, which the <u>Company</u> finds more effective than all-day training sessions.

   Huntington & Associates company

**GO TO
CD-ROM
CHECKUP 6–2**

Titles

Go to PowerPoint 6-6a.

See Instructor Note 6-9 in IAE.

Capitalize a social, professional, religious, academic, political, or military title that precedes a name.

Mrs. Lorna Evans	Professor Lloyd Blake
Dr. Lee Maxwell	Mayor Bob Jeffers
the Reverend Chris Myer	General Overhulzer

High-Ranking Government Officials.   Capitalize a title that follows the name of a high-ranking foreign, national, or state government official. Capitalize a title that is used to substitute for the complete name of a high-ranking government official.

Tommy Thompson, Governor of Wisconsin

the Prime Minister

the Chief Justice

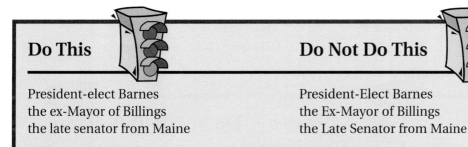

Do This	Do Not Do This
President-elect Barnes	President-Elect Barnes
the ex-Mayor of Billings	the Ex-Mayor of Billings
the late senator from Maine	the Late Senator from Maine

Do not capitalize such words as -elect, former, late, or ex- with titles.

Go to PowerPoint 6-6b.

Company, Institution, or Association Officials.   Do not capitalize the title of a company, institution, or association official that follows a name. Likewise, do not capitalize the title of a company, institution, or association official that is used as a substitute for a complete name unless practice or tradition indicates to the contrary.

Jerome Decker, president of Meridian Press

Lou Ballard, secretary of United Grocers

the president of AMOLCO Corporation

the secretary to the vice president

the treasurer of Teamsters Local 344

6-10 Refer to *The Gregg Reference Manual* for a distinction between official and occupational names.

General Occupational.   Do not capitalize occupational titles (teacher, writer, lawyer) used in a general way.

Go to PowerPoint 6-6c.

The attorney's comment about being on time embarrassed Warren.
A new state-of-the-art intranet is one of the chancellor's long-term objectives.

Title Substitutions.   Capitalize a title used as a substitute for a complete name in a direct address (except a title such as *sir, madam,* or *miss*). Capitalize a title used in place of a name in minutes or bylaws.

Capitalization

Direct Address

When will the bill be introduced, <u>S</u>enator?

<u>C</u>ommissioner, have you finished your response?

Wouldn't you agree, <u>s</u>ir, that managing one's time is important?

Bylaws and Minutes

The term of the <u>P</u>resident will be two years.

The duties of the <u>V</u>ice <u>P</u>resident shall include revising policies and pro-cedures.

Family Titles

Go to PowerPoint 6-7.

Capitalize the title of a family member when it is used by itself or when it is used in direct address. Capitalize the title of a family member when it precedes a name.

> I always wondered how <u>Mother</u> managed her time with five children to raise.
>
> I'll be late to work if I don't leave now, <u>D</u>ad.
>
> Did <u>A</u>unt Marge have her timesaving hints published?

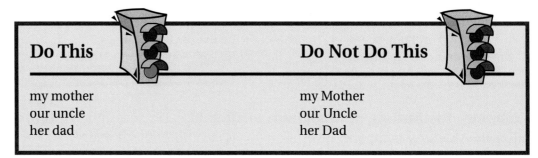

Do This	Do Not Do This
my mother	my Mother
our uncle	our Uncle
her dad	her Dad

Do not capitalize a family title when it is used with a possessive pronoun—my, your, our, his, her, their.

CHECKUP 6-3

Directions: *Underline any capitalization errors in the following sentences. On the lines provided, write the words correctly. If the capitalization is correct, write **Yes**.*

1. Rex Stout, the <u>Treasurer</u> of Minton Company, wrote a check for the project management software.

treasurer

2. Senator Arnie Carlson plans and thinks carefully before he votes on legislation.

Yes

3. One point that <u>professor</u> <u>enriquez</u> made was that we should review our long-term objectives periodically.

Professor Enriquez

4. Since my work at Green Door Graphics required so much overtime, I was not able to be the president of the Meadowview Parent-Teacher Association.

Yes

5. As the Administrative Assistant to Kay Johnson, Manager of Research and Planning, Terri finds that a "to do" list is very important.

administrative assistant   manager   research   planning

6. George McCann, Author of five time management books, was a former Attorney.

author   attorney

7. My Mother, aunt Dawn, and aunt Ruth plan and coordinate our family reunions each year.

mother   Aunt   Aunt

8. How much time were you planning to spend, Sir, with the President of the AOC?

sir   president

GO TO
CD-ROM
CHECKUP 6-3

Publications

Go to PowerPoints 6-8a and 6-8b.

See Instructor Note 6-11 in IAE.

Books, Magazines, and Newspapers.   Capitalize the first letters of all words with four or more letters in the title of a book, magazine, or newspaper. Place these titles in italics. Do not capitalize articles, conjunctions, or prepositions with fewer than four letters unless they are the first or last words in the title.

For a more detailed discussion of publications, see the sections of a reference manual that explain titles of literary and artistic works.

San Jose Mercury News (newspaper)
One-Minute Manager (book)
Travel and Leisure (magazine)

Robert's Rules of Order (book)
The Small Business Encyclopedia (book)
The Delta Pi Epsilon Journal (journal)

Do This

Time magazine
The New York Times newspaper

Do Not Do This

Time Magazine
The New York Times Newspaper

Other Published Works.   Capitalize the first letters of all the main words in works such as chapters in books, magazine articles, plays, musical productions, movies, documentaries, speeches, radio and television programs, and poems. Place quotation marks around these titles. Do not capitalize articles, conjunctions, or prepositions with fewer than four letters unless they are the first or last words in the title.

See Instructor Note 6-12 in IAE.

"Plural and Possessive Nouns" (chapter in a book)
"Anne of Green Gables" (play)
"Fly Away Home" (movie)
"Gettysburg Address" (speech)
"Daffodils" (poem)

"Are You Buying a Business or a Disaster?" (article in a magazine)
"Grease" (musical production)
"The Civil War Years" (documentary)
"Meet the Press" (television program)

Go to PowerPoint 6-9.

Events and Holidays

Capitalize the names of historical and current events, holidays, and special events.

the Great Depression	Fourth of July
World War II	Memorial Day
Public Safety Week	Toys for Tots
Save the Railroad Campaign	Festival in the Pines

Acts, Bills, and Laws

Go to PowerPoint 6-10.

Capitalize specific titles of laws, acts, codes, and amendments. Do not capitalize general names of laws, acts, codes, or amendments.

Specific Titles	**General Titles**
Child Safety Law 102	the building code
Drug-Free Workplace Act	several environmental bills
Family and Medical Leave Act	a constitutional amendment
Code of Criminal Procedure	
Health and Safety Code 11007	
the First Amendment	

CHECKUP 6-4

See Instructor Note 6-13 in IAE.

Directions: *Underline any capitalization errors in the following sentences. On the lines provided, write the words correctly. If the capitalization is correct, write* **Yes.**

1. Keep job and company details in your Desk Manual.

   desk manual

2. Sharon found some excellent timesaving tips listed in *The Office Professional* Magazine.

   magazine

3. The first speech was entitled "Identifying Time Wasters."

   Yes

4. We hope that the Family and Medical Leave Act will allow employees to spend the necessary time with family members who need them.

   Yes

5. Have you read the book *time management for dummies*?

   Time Management   Dummies

6. During my free time last evening, I watched the video "dancing with wolves."

   "Dancing With Wolves"

7. I receive overtime wages when I work on holidays such as thanksgiving and the fourth of july.

   Thanksgiving   Fourth   July

8. Listen to weau-tv "news at 6" for current events instead of taking time to read the *gazette evening news*.

   WEAU-TV "News   *Gazette Evening News*

**GO TO
CD-ROM**
CHECKUP 6-4

Chapter 6

Academic Degrees

Capitalize a specific academic degree that follows a person's name. Do not capitalize an academic degree used in a general way.

Go to
PowerPoint 6-11.

Traci Muldoon, Ph.D., prepared the master schedule of classes for next year.

She received her bachelor's degree from Piedmont Community College.

Languages

Always capitalize names of specific languages.

Go to
PowerPoint 6-12.

Bonnie speaks Spanish and English fluently.

Many of my business clients use French in their daily transactions.

Education Levels, Subjects, and Courses

Go to PowerPoint 6-13.

Capitalize a specific educational course title. Do not capitalize the general title of a course or area of study unless it is a language.

Specific Title	General Title
Records Management 221	a course in medical terminology
Bus. 201 WordPerfect 8.0	majoring in accounting

See Instructor Note 6-14 in IAE.

Do This

a course in business English
a major in Spanish history

Do Not Do This

a course in Business English
a major in spanish history

Do not capitalize general levels of education.

My daughter will be in kindergarten this fall; therefore, I will have to reschedule my workday.

All members of our family enrolled in university courses this semester.

Our community college offers courses at times that appeal to working adults.

Ethnic Designations

Capitalize the names of nationalities, ethnic groups, and races.

Go to
PowerPoint 6-14.

Caucasians	African-Americans	Native Americans
Hungarians	Germans	

Go to
PowerPoint 6-15.

Religious References

Capitalize the names of specific religious groups, religious days and books, names of churches, and any adjectives derived from religious terms.

Christians	Catholic missionaries
Easter	Judaism
Koran	First Presbyterian Church

CHECKUP 6-5

Directions: *Underline any capitalization errors in the following sentences. On the lines provided, write the words correctly. If the capitalization is correct, write* **Yes.**

1. I have decided to get a Degree in Business Administration, but first I have to arrange my schedule at the office.

   degree business administration

2. Jenny majored in human services and worked full time while she attended the university.

   Yes

3. In my Business Communications Class, I completed a research project on time management.

   business communications class

4. After the classroom building burned, we had to move the french and spanish classes to the first baptist church.

   French Spanish First Baptist Church

5. We needed more time to discuss the negative attitudes expressed toward the businesses in our community.

   Yes

6. When I started working on my Master's Degree, I found that my free time disappeared.

   master's degree

7. All High School students should be aware of how they spend their time.

   high school

8. George McDonald, ph.d., my instructor for office management 251, is always prompt in returning tests.

   Ph.D. Office Management

**GO TO
CD-ROM**
CHECKUP 6-5

Days and Months

Go to
PowerPoint 6-16.

Capitalize days of the week and months of the year.

Tuesday	April
Saturday	September

Chapter 6

Seasons

Do not capitalize the name of a season unless it is listed with a specific year or unless it is included in the specific name of an event.

See Instructor Note 6-15 in IAE.

> winter sales
>
> summers in the South
>
> registration in the fall and spring
>
> registration for the Spring 2001 semester
>   (*Spring* appears with a specific year.)
>
> Fall Arts and Crafts Fair
>
> Spring Fling
>   (In these examples, *Fall* and *Spring* are parts of the names of the events.)

Time Periods

Do not capitalize time periods, decades, or centuries used in a general way.

Go to PowerPoint 6-17.

> third-quarter report   the twenty-first century
> new millennium   the next century
> in the nineties

Punctuation ALERT!

Use periods with the abbreviations *a.m.* and *p.m.*

Do not capitalize *a.m.* or *p.m., noon* or *midnight,* or general times of the day.

> She was scheduled to arrive at 11 a.m.
>
> The plane landed at noon.
>
> I am not very productive by mid-afternoon.

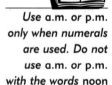

Use a.m. or p.m. only when numerals are used. Do not use a.m. or p.m. with the words noon or midnight or with general times of the day.

Do This	**Do Not Do This**
He finished the project at 12 p.m.	He finished the project at 12 p.m. noon.
or	
He finished the project at noon.	
The meeting begins at 9 a.m.	The meeting begins at 9 a.m. in the morning.
	or
	The meeting begins at nine a.m.

Compass Directions

Specific Regions.   Capitalize compass directions when they designate specific regions of a country. Capitalize derivatives of specific regions.

Go to PowerPoint 6-18.

> the Far East   in the East

the <u>M</u>idwest	<u>S</u>outh Carolina
<u>M</u>idwesterners	a <u>S</u>outherner
(derivative of *Midwest*)	(derivative of *South*)

General Compass Points. Do not capitalize general compass points or directions.

northern New Mexico	travel north on Wilson Avenue
east side of Cleveland	located east of Highway 12

Street Names. Capitalize compass points when they are part of a street name.

34 <u>N</u>orth Fulton Street	402 Belview Avenue <u>NW</u>

CHECKUP 6-6

Directions: *Underline any capitalization errors in the following sentences. On the lines provided, write the words correctly. If the capitalization is correct, write* **Yes.**

1. My best hours for completing homework are from 10 <u>P.M.</u> to <u>Midnight</u>.

p.m. midnight

2. We must receive the shipment of snowblowers by <u>friday</u>, <u>october</u> 1, in order to offer them at our annual <u>fall</u> Daze Sale.

Friday, October Fall

3. The <u>Annual</u> report is ready weeks ahead of schedule this year.

annual

4. My appointment calendar is filled from 8 <u>A.M.</u> to 5:30 <u>P.M.</u> on <u>tuesday</u> and <u>thursday</u>.

a.m. p.m. Tuesday Thursday

5. Inevitably when I'm in a rush, I forget about the <u>east</u> <u>elm</u> <u>street</u> detour.

East Elm Street

6. I talked to our builder recently, and he indicated that the late <u>Winter</u> <u>Snows</u> caused the construction delays.

winter snows

7. Billie Mae lives <u>North</u> of the city and spends an hour commuting each way.

north

8. The work ethic of many Midwesterners includes a respect for time.

Yes

9. Some employees who are asked to spend noon hours in training see this as time theft by management.

Yes

**GO TO
CD-ROM**
CHECKUP 6-6

10. Raymond C. Johnson is traveling in the <u>southwest</u> to promote his book *The Achievers*.

Southwest

Abbreviations

Capitalize an abbreviation representing a proper noun. Some common nouns also require capital letters for their shortened forms.

Go to PowerPoint 6-19.

See Instructor Note 6-16 in IAE.

Proper Noun Abbreviations

United States Postal Service	(USPS)
Northern States Power Company	(NSPC)
Occupational Safety and Health Administration	(OSHA)
Alaska (on envelope addresses)	(AK)

Common Noun Abbreviations

personal information manager	(PIM)
personal digital assistant	(PDA)
certified public accountant	(CPA)
Eastern standard time	(EST)
central processing unit	(CPU)
compact disk	(CD)

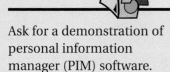

Do This	Do Not Do This
Ask for a demonstration of personal information manager (PIM) software.	Ask for a demonstration of PIM software.

Always identify the abbreviation in full the first time it is used before allowing it to stand alone in a written communication.

Nouns With Letters and Numbers

Capitalize nouns when they precede a number or letter. Do not capitalize the first letters of the words *line, paragraph, page, size,* and *verse* when they precede a number.

Go to PowerPoint 6-20.

Volume 10	page 1
Unit 3	size 8
Highway 5	paragraph 2
Invoice 203963	line 75
Flight 925	verse 6
Room 2B	

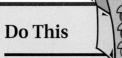 

Do This	Do Not Do This
The exhibit booth number is 14D.	The Exhibit Booth Number is 14D.

The word is separates the noun and number. Do not capitalize the noun or nouns that precede the letter or number when the two are separated by another word.

Trademarks, Brand Names, and Product Names

Go to PowerPoint 6-21.

See your reference manual for additional trademarks.

See Instructor Note 6-17 in IAE.

Capitalize trademarks or specific brand names. Generally, do not capitalize the type of product.

Trademark/Brand Names	Products
Magnavox®	stereo system
Maxwell House®	coffee
Dial®	soap
Kleenex®	tissues
Cutlass Cierra®	car
WordPerfect®	software
Wizard®	personal digital assistant
Parkay®	margarine
Macintosh®	computer

CHECKUP 6-7

*Directions: Underline any capitalization errors in the following sentences. On the lines provided, write the words correctly. If the capitalization is correct, write **Yes.***

1. We thought that we would save time by taking interstate 94 until we reached exit 70.

   Interstate Exit

2. Rod Stone uses personal information manager (PIM) software for scheduling.

   Yes

3. We are trying to meet the deadline that Osha gave us to correct our safety regulations.

   OSHA

4. I use software that includes Word for Windows for my Word Processing work and Excel for my Spreadsheets.

   word processing spreadsheets

5. AEC Software's program for project management scheduling is called FastTrack Schedule.

   Yes

6. Did you pay invoice 2096B, which included the software for the Sinclair Automated Time Clocks?

   Invoice automated time clocks

7. Please check section IX, paragraph 2, for timesaving steps recommended for real estate salespeople.

   Section

8. I noticed that ups guarantees timely arrivals, or customers receive refunds.

   UPS

GO TO CD-ROM CHECKUP 6-7

First Words

With Quotations.   Capitalize the first word of a direct quotation that is a complete sentence. Do not capitalize the first word of a quotation that cannot stand as a complete sentence. Do not capitalize the first word of the second part of an interrupted quotation.

Go to
PowerPoint 6-22.

Quotation Is Complete Sentence

When coworkers interrupted Sally, she said, "This project is needed in an hour. Let's get together later for lunch."

The speaker asked, "How many hours did you waste today?"

Quotation Is Incomplete Sentence

Do you know how your "free time" disappears?

Maria's desk was stacked with "unbelievable clutter."

Quotation Is Interrupted

"Your reservation will be guaranteed," the hotel reservations clerk said, "if you wish to use your credit card."

"I am going to use a master list," said the office manager, "and will update it at the end of each week."

With Colons.   Capitalize the first word that follows a colon if two or more complete sentences are involved. Do not capitalize the first word following a colon if the material that follows is not a complete sentence.

Go to
PowerPoints 6-23a and 6-23b.

See Instructor Note 6-18 in the IAE.

For additional examples of capitalizing after a colon, see sections on colon usage in your reference manual.

I have two major problems in budgeting my time: My projects need to be divided into smaller tasks. My tasks do not get prioritized.
(The colon is followed by two complete sentences.)

Ask yourself these timesaving questions: Am I doing the job at the right time? Can I delegate the job to someone else?
(The colon is followed by two complete questions.)

Time wasters include the following: procrastination, incomplete directions, and interruptions.
(The material following the colon is not a complete sentence.)

The team project leader requested these items: project objectives, potential problem areas, and time estimates.
(The material following the colon is not a complete sentence.)

Capitalize the first word of a sentence that follows a colon if the sentence states a formal rule (regulation) or needs added emphasis. Do not capitalize the first word of a sentence that follows a colon if the sentence simply expands or completes the first part of the sentence.

Remember: Divide a large project into manageable subsections.
(The sentence following the colon is one of emphasis. The first word in the sentence requires a capital letter.)

Here is the policy: All overtime hours must be approved by a supervisor.
(The sentence following the colon is a company regulation. The first word in the sentence requires a capital letter.)

Helen had one major goal for the week: she wanted to complete the five high-priority items on her "to do" list.

(The sentence following the colon completes the main thought expressed in the first sentence. The first word does not require a capital letter.)

Go to
PowerPoint 6-24.

Capitalize the first word in a vertical list following a colon.

The following time management tools will be helpful:
1. Current work analysis time log
2. Prioritized "to do" lists
3. Tickler file

Go to
PowerPoint 6-25.

Within Parentheses.   Capitalize the first word of a complete sentence that stands by itself in parentheses. However, do not capitalize the first word of a sentence in parentheses that is within another sentence.

Sentence Stands Alone

We need major revisions in our proposal for Magic Moments. (All six sections need correction.) Revisions are due by the end of the week.

Sentence Within a Sentence

Major revisions (all six sections need correction) are due by the end of the week.

Outlines

6-19   Be aware that the word *roman* may be capitalized in dictionaries and some reference manuals.

Go to PowerPoint 6-26.

Capitalize the main words in all headings preceded by a roman numeral. Capitalize the first letter in each word in second-level headings. Capitalize the first word and use lowercase for remaining words in third-level headings.

    I.   TIME MANAGEMENT (all caps)
         A. Master Lists (second-level heading)
         B. "To Do" Lists
         C. Electronic Aids
             1. Personal digital assistant (PDA) (third-level heading)
             2. Personal information manager (PIMs)

CHECKUP 6-8

Directions: Underline any capitalization errors in the following sentences. On the lines provided, write the words correctly. If the capitalization is correct, write **Yes.**

  1. Analyze the following items from your time log: Tasks to simplify, Tasks to modify, and Tasks to delegate.

    tasks tasks tasks

2. Use these headings on your weekly master list:

1. <u>week</u>

2. <u>activity</u>

3. <u>starting</u> date

4. <u>required</u> completion date

5. <u>estimated</u> amount of time

<u>Week Activity Starting Required Estimated</u>

3. "This software," the user remarked, "<u>Saves</u> me so much time in contacting potential sales leads."

<u>saves</u>

4. Improvements should be made in our training programs: <u>first</u>, reduce the time required for new employee training. <u>second</u>, hire workshop presenters who limit class time to four hours.

<u>First Second</u>

5. The speaker asked, "<u>is</u> anyone in the room a procrastinator?"

<u>Is</u>

6. Even more experienced workers need help in handling the "so much to do, no time to do it" problem.

<u>Yes</u>

7. Having a quiet work area for your home office (<u>A</u> separate room is preferable) improves efficiency.

<u>a</u>

8. The first day's lecture for my time management class follows this outline:

I. <u>Introduction</u>

　A. <u>definition</u>

　B. <u>importance</u> of <u>time</u>

II. <u>realistic</u> approaches

<u>INTRODUCTION Definition Importance Time REALISTIC APPROACHES</u>

GO TO CD-ROM CHECKUP 6-8

Business Letters, E-Mail Messages, and Website Addresses

Complimentary Closing. Capitalize only the first letter of the first word in a complimentary closing.

Go to PowerPoint 6-27.

<u>V</u>ery truly yours,
<u>S</u>incerely yours

Punctuation may be omitted after both the complimentary closing and the salutation. Do not mix punctuation styles by omitting punctuation after one and not the other.

Salutations.   Capitalize the first letter of a salutation or greeting and all nouns that follow. Capitalize the first letters of the main words in a salutation not directed to a specific individual.

Dear Mrs. Johnston: Dear Selection Committee:

Ladies and Gentlemen   Dear Manager:

Employees: (common e-mail greeting)

Inside Addresses.   Capitalize the first letters of major words in inside addresses.

Mr. Justin Rand, Treasurer
San Benito County Courthouse
125 Oak Street
Hollister, CA 99362

Go to PowerPoint 6-28.

E-Mail and Website Addresses.   Do not capitalize e-mail and Website addresses unless specifically indicated. Use the letters and symbols exactly as indicated by the correspondent or company.

http://167.8.29.7/weather/wfront
BitByte@gnn.com

Go to PowerPoint 6-29.

Addresses on Envelopes.   Capitalize all letters in all words in a mailing address on an envelope. Postal guidelines recommend that large mailings be done following this format (including no punctuation marks) to allow electronic equipment to read the addresses and speed mail delivery. Using initial capitals and lowercase letters in the inside address is also acceptable.

See Instructor Note 6-20 in IAE.

MR JUSTIN RAND TREASURER
SAN BENITO COUNTY COURTHOUSE
125 OAK STREET
HOLLISTER CA 99362

Go to PowerPoint 6-30.

Legal Documents

Amounts of Money.   Capitalize amounts of money written in words in legal documents. Do not capitalize the word after the hyphen in written numbers 21 through 99.

Nine Hundred Seventy-six Dollars ($976)
Fourteen Hundred Thirty-seven Dollars ($1437.00)

Resolutions.   Capitalize every letter in words such as *RESOLVED* and *WHEREAS*.

WHEREAS, we the members
BE IT RESOLVED that

Do This	Do Not Do This
Rydell vs. Bruhn	Rydell Vs. Bruhn
Rydell versus Brush	Rydell Versus Bruhn

Do not capitalize versus or vs. when referring to legal cases.

CHECKUP 6-9

*Directions: Underline any capitalization errors in the following sentences. On the lines provided, write the words correctly. If the capitalization is correct, write **Yes.***

See Instructor Note 6-21 in IAE.

1. An e-mail communication does not require the formal salutation of "Ladies And Gentlemen."

   and _____

2. The Website address for the Business Women's Network is HTTP://WWW.TPAG.COM/BWN.HTML.

   http://www.tpag.com/bwn.html _____

3. Omitting the ending punctuation from the salutation "dear Ms. Raymond" is a timesaver for some typists.

   Dear _____

4. The rental contract stated that we had to pay Eight hundred dollars ($800) by the first of each month.

   Hundred Dollars _____

5. The Simplified Letter Style omits such complimentary closings as Sincerely Yours and Yours Truly.

   yours truly _____

6. The last line of the inside address on the letter was Flagstaff, AZ 86001.

   Yes _____

GO TO CD-ROM
CHECKUP 6-9

PRACTICE

PRACTICE 1A

Directions: *Select the correct word in parentheses and write it in the space provided.*

1. We did not mail our order for (*Fall, fall*) merchandise until (*Tuesday, tuesday*).

   fall   Tuesday

2. The new personal information manager (*PIM, pim*) software from the (*Salt Lake Branch, Salt Lake branch*) arrived today.

   PIM   Salt Lake branch

3. Mr. Fredericks, our (*Business Instructor, business instructor*), asked an efficiency expert to speak to our (*Phi Lambda Theta Group, Phi Lambda Theta group*).

   business instructor   Phi Lambda Theta group

4. "Is it possible," asked my supervisor, "(*That, that*) this report will be finished by (*Noon, noon*)?"

   that   noon

5. Maintain a (*Time Log, time log*) to record the time that you spend on (*Club, club*) projects.

   time log   club

6. When (*President, president*) Tom Langdon conducted the meetings, he ended them promptly at 2 (*P.M., p.m.*).

   President,   p.m.

7. George-Ann Fay, who writes books on time management, was recently quoted by (*The Wall Street Journal, the wall street journal*).

   The Wall Street Journal

8. The catalog from (*Highsmith Microcomputer Company, highsmith microcomputer company*) includes many new gadgets for making our work simpler.

   Highsmith Microcomputer Company

9. We learned to prepare "to do" lists in our classes at the (*Business College, business college*).

   business college

10. During most years, (*Congress, congress*) tries to pass a budget before the (*Fourth of July, fourth of July*) holiday.

    Congress   Fourth of July

NAME _____

11. Which (*City, city*) is known as the (*City of Brotherly Love, city of brotherly love*)?

    city City of Brotherly Love

12. (*I, i*) learned an important bit of philosophy about wasted time from my (*Father, father*).

    I father

13. The (*Department of Public Instruction, department of public instruction*) was behind in acknowledging (*Grant Proposals, grant proposals.*)

    Department of Public Instruction   grant proposals

14. A time management tip that (*I, i*) use is labeling a (*Manila, manila*) folder with the project name as soon as I hear about the project.

    I manila

15. Traffic jams along (*State Street, state street*) or (*Highway 53, highway 53*) often make me late for appointments.

    State Street Highway 53

16. A note for (*fourteen hundred dollars, Fourteen Hundred Dollars*) ($1400) was due last Friday.

    Fourteen Hundred Dollars

17. Bob has his (*Master's, master's*) degree from (*Northwestern University, Northwestern university*).

    master's Northwestern University

18. The following activities may be time wasters: (*Frequent, frequent*) interruptions, (*Tardiness, tardiness*), and (*Lengthy, lengthy*) phone calls.

    frequent tardiness lengthy

19. Our (*Communications, communications*) course did not emphasize (*Time Management, time management*).

    communications time management

20. We were unhappy when our (*Instructor, instructor*) scheduled a test on Valentine's (*Day, day*).

    instructor Day

GO TO
CD-ROM
PRACTICE 1
EXERCISES

PRACTICE

NAME _____

PRACTICE 2A

Directions: *Underline any capitalization errors in the following sentences. On the lines provided, write the words correctly.*

1. For a fax message to reach <u>sydney</u>, <u>australia</u>, by 5 <u>P.M.</u>, you should send it by 2 <u>A.M.</u>

   Sydney, Australia   p.m.   a.m. _____

2. Some <u>Community</u> <u>Colleges</u> offer <u>Interactive</u> <u>Online</u> <u>Training</u> for those who don't have time to attend classes at the local <u>College</u>.

   community colleges   interactive online training   college _____

3. In his book *the joy of <u>working</u>*, <u>denis</u> <u>waitley</u> said, "<u>time</u> is an equal-opportunity employer."

   The Joy Working   Denis Waitley   Time _____

4. Eliot Burke, <u>Division</u> <u>Manager</u> for <u>seastrand</u> <u>properties</u>, believes that <u>Project</u> <u>Teams</u> should be limited to eight to ten people.

   division manager   Seastrand Properties   project teams _____

5. Mrs. <u>chao</u> asked her group to keep track of all office activities in 15-minute blocks from <u>april</u> 15 to <u>may</u> 1.

   Chao   April   May _____

6. The Personnel Screening and Review <u>committee</u> spent hours selecting the people we wanted to interview.

   Committee _____

7. Since spring vacation is less hectic than other times in the <u>recreation</u> <u>department</u>, I reorganized the <u>Files</u>.

   Recreation Department   files _____

8. The <u>University</u> offers several sections of <u>Business</u> <u>Communications</u> for <u>Juniors</u> and <u>Seniors</u>.

   university   business communications   juniors   seniors _____

9. After working so many overtime hours this <u>Winter</u>, <u>i</u> took my <u>Family</u> to <u>richland</u> <u>park</u> to hear the <u>u.s.</u> <u>air</u> <u>force</u> <u>jazz</u> <u>band</u>.

   winter I family Richland Park U.S. Air Force Jazz Band _____

10. My <u>Mother-in-Law</u> <u>judi</u> works for a <u>Seminar</u> <u>Bureau</u> and arranges <u>Time</u> <u>Management</u> <u>Workshops</u>.

    mother-in-law Judi seminar bureau time management workshops _

164   *Chapter 6*

NAME _____

11. Address Book, a <u>Shareware</u> <u>Program</u> which can be downloaded from <u>aol</u>, saves time for <u>Realtor</u> Lori Loken.

shareware program   AOL   realtor
_____

12. Pat uses a program called <u>lotus</u> <u>organizer</u>, which has an <u>Alarm</u> <u>Reminder</u>, <u>Address</u> <u>Book</u>, and <u>Calendar</u>.

Lotus Organizer   alarm reminder   address book   calendar
_____

13. The <u>caribbean</u> <u>association</u> of <u>professional</u> <u>secretaries</u> (<u>caps</u>) met in <u>july</u>, and members came from <u>jamaica</u>, <u>st. lucia</u>, and <u>trinidad</u>.

Caribbean Association   Professional Secretaries (CAPS)   July   Jamaica
_____

St. Lucia   Trinidad
_____

14. For a graph showing how executives spend their time, please see <u>table</u> 4, <u>Page</u> 209.

Table   page
_____

15. The citizens of <u>rusk</u> <u>county</u> anxiously awaited <u>judge</u> Tobin's decision on the Richmond <u>Versus</u> Wendt <u>Case</u>.

Rusk County   Judge   versus   case
_____

16. We will try to leave New York City after work on <u>friday</u> to travel <u>North</u> to spend a restful weekend at the <u>white</u> <u>briar</u> <u>hotel</u>.

Friday   north   White Briar Hotel
_____

17. After delaying her <u>Announcement</u> for three weeks, the <u>governor</u> of <u>new</u> <u>jersey</u> said she was seeking a <u>Fourth</u> <u>Term</u>.

announcement   Governor   New Jersey   fourth term
_____

18. I recently met Venetta Baker, M.A., the <u>Author</u> of 365 *ways for simplifying your work life*.

author   Ways   Simplifying Your Work Life
_____

19. Ben Larson, the <u>Project</u> <u>Manager</u> for <u>scarr</u> properties, <u>inc.</u>, says he schedules an extra 10 percent margin of time on each <u>Project</u>.

project manager   Scarr Properties, Inc.   project
_____

20. Here are several ways to avoid wasting time:
   1. <u>discourage</u> lengthy phone calls.
   2. <u>block</u> some quiet working time.
   3. <u>minimize</u> interruptions.

Discourage   Block   Minimize
_____

**GO TO
CD-ROM**
PRACTICE 2
EXERCISES

PRACTICE 3A

PROOFREADING

Exercise 1

*Directions: Proofread and compare the two sentences in each group. If they are the same, write **Yes** in the space provided. If they are not the same, write **No.** Use the first sentence as the correct copy. If you find errors in the second sentence, underline them.*

1. When a slowdown occurs, take advantage of
   that time to do things you can't complete during
   the regular time period.

   When a <u>slow</u> <u>down</u> occurs, take advantage of
   that time to do things you <u>cant</u> complete during
   the regular <u>Time</u> <u>Period</u>.

    1. <u>No</u>

2. If you follow the suggestions in the book, you will
   learn to analyze your workload, identify problems,
   delegate tasks, and reduce time spent on unnecessary
   jobs.

   If you follow the suggestions in the book, you will
   learn to <u>analyse</u> your workload, identify problems,
   delegate tasks, and reduce time spent on <u>unecessary</u>
   jobs.

    2. <u>No</u>

3. To set up a reminder file, you need 12 folders for the
   months, 31 folders for the days, and 1 folder for the
   next year.

   To set up a reminder file, you need 12 folders for the
   months, <u>30</u> folders for the days, and 1 folder for <u>the year.</u>

    3. <u>No</u>

4. At high-tech companies, the production of new
   products and intense competition require immediate
   training—not when the next college class is offered.

   At <u>High-Tech</u> <u>Companies</u>, the production of new
   products and intense competition <u>requires</u> immediate
   training—not when the next <u>College</u> <u>Class</u> is offered.

    4. <u>No</u>

5. If you are pressed for time, let your coworkers know
   your dilemma.

   If you are pressed for time, let your coworkers know
   your <u>dilemna</u>.

    5. <u>No</u>

Exercise 2

Directions: Compare the keyed version of the "to do" list with the original list. Underline the errors that you find in the second version. In the space provided at the end of the exercise, indicate the number of errors you found. (The letters A,B,C that you find after each task indicate the urgency of getting a particular task completed. "A" represents the most urgent tasks.)

JEFF DONOVAN, REALTOR
March 17, 20<year>

   1.   Compose mass mailing letter (C)
   2.   Follow up Redmon and Hendrick sales (A)
   3.   Close Daniels Ave. property (11 a.m.) (A)
   4.   Show Princeton lots (10 a.m.) (2 p.m.) (A)
   5.   Call for Kiwanis speakers (B)
   6.   Organize contracts for monthly report (C)
   7.   Obtain referrals (B)
   8.   Check listings (A)
   9.   Write new biographical sketch (B)
 10.   Proof brochure (B)

JEFF DONOVAN, REALTOR
March 17, 20<year>

1. Compose mass mailing letter (C)
2. Follow up Redmon and Hendrick sales (A)
3. Close Daniels ave. property (1 A.M.) (A)
4. Show Princeton lots (10 A.M.) (2 P.M.) (A)
5. Call for Kiwanis speakers (B)
6. Organize contracts for monthly report (C)
7. Obtain referals (B)
8. Check listings (A)
9. Write new Biogaphical sketch (C)
10. Proof brochure (B)

How many errors did you find?   __8__

GO TO
CD-ROM
PRACTICE 3
EXERCISES

PRACTICE 4A

WRITING

The Writing Process: Writing Effective Sentences

Use effective sentences to add interest and impact to your writing. As you create and combine sentences, vary the length of the sentences so that some are short and others are longer.

PRACTICE

NAME _____

A topic sentence introduces the subject of the sentence. When writing a topic sentence, make it specific enough to arouse the reader's interest. Also, write the topic sentence in a way that will "hook" your readers so that they will want to read further.

Directions: List three ways that you wasted time this week. Write a sentence for each of the time wasters indicating how you will avoid wasting time in the future. Vary the sentence length.

_____

_____

_____

Answers will vary.

**GO TO
CD-ROM**
PRACTICE 4
EXERCISES

See Instructor Note 6-22 in IAE.

**Punctuation
ALERT!**

Use exact punctuation when typing an Internet address.

ONLINE EXERCISES

Many American workers feel that they are rushed to do the things they have to do. Extremely happy workers are less likely to feel rushed and have more time for community activities. A goal of time management is to analyze your time, organize your life, and make short- and long-range goals. By efficiently planning and using your valuable time, perhaps you can feel in control of your life and have more time to do the things that you want to do.

Objective: To visit the Day-Timers Inc. Website, take a time management quiz, and find useful time management tips.

1. With your Internet browser on screen, key:

   http://www.daytimer.com in the location text box and press the **Enter** key on your keyboard.

2. Click on **Day-Timer Resource Center.**

3. Click on the **Interactive Skills Test.** This test rates your time management skill.

4. Print the results of the Skills Test.

5. Click on the back button of your Internet browser.

6. Click on **Library.** Search through the articles until you find one relevant to you. Print a copy of the article.

7. Click on the **Back** button of your Internet browser until you return to the Day-Timer Inc. home page.

8. Click on the section **studentzone.** Scroll through the page to see if you find anything of interest to you.

Chapter 6

NAME _____

PRACTICE 1B

Directions: *Select the correct word in parentheses and write it in the space provided.*

1. The instructor for the organizational management class will be Ormando Greco, (*Ph.D., ph.d.*).
   Ph.D. _____

2. Single parents like (*Leslie, leslie*) and (*Kim, kim*) find that job sharing is a solution for spending more time with their (*Children, children.*)
   Leslie Kim children _____

3. To save learning time, I bought (*Microsoft's, microsoft's*) Office Professional software.
   Microsoft's _____

4. If you want to see an impressive example of efficiency, go to (*Walt Disney World, walt disney world*) in (*Orlando, Florida; orlando, florida*).
   Walt Disney World Orlando, Florida _____

5. Delivery delays occur when mail addressed to Washington, DC, arrives in the (*state, State*) of Washington.
   state _____

6. We rushed the evidence to the offices of (*judge Ahrens, Judge Ahrens*).
   Judge Ahrens _____

7. Voting results in the (*East, east*) are known several hours before they are known in the (*west, West*).
   East, West _____

8. Renee arrives by 7 (*A.M., a.m.*) to plan her work day.
   a.m. _____

9. To organize your office, divide it into sections: (*Your, your*) desk, your bookcase, your computer workstation, and your files.
   your _____

10. Jerry reserved (*Thursday, thursday*) afternoon, (*September, september*) 9, to begin computerizing the filing system.
    Thursday   September _____

11. All (*Government, government*) offices close on Memorial (*Day, day*).
    government Day _____

12. On (*Chinese New Year, Chinese new year*), we are unable to do business in (*peking, Peking*).
    Chinese New Year Peking _____

13. Cheri Harris, (*president, President*) of the New Jersey League of Women Voters, schedules 30 (*minutes, Minutes*) twice a week for reading journal articles.
    president minutes _____

14. My (*Mother, mother*) sorts incoming e-mail by subject in order to read and reply to related mail at one time.
    mother _____

15. Barbara highly recommends the book (*Solutions For Time Management Problems, Solutions for Time Management Problems*).
    Solutions for Time Management Problems _____

Capitalization

NAME _____

PRACTICE 2B

Directions: Underline any capitalization errors in the following sentences. On the lines provided, write the words correctly.

1. In the book *Managing your Time*, Trevor Boutall recommends reviewing your progress toward your <u>Objectives</u> on a regular basis.

Your   objectives _____

2. Time is <u>Democratic</u> because we all have exactly the same amount every <u>Day</u>.

democratic   day _____

3. The new personal information managers (PIMs) let you post your <u>Daily Schedule</u> on the Web to allow colleagues to reach you at critical times.

daily schedule _____

4. When sending a similar e-mail message to several people, use the <u>Cut</u> and <u>Paste</u> commands just as you would in a <u>Word Processing Document</u>.

cut   paste   word processing document _____

5. Before Lisa leaves on a trip, she uses the following checklist:
   a.   <u>lock</u> the house.
   b.   <u>adjust</u> the thermostat and hot water heater.
   c.   <u>take</u> out the garbage.

Lock   Adjust   Take _____

6. If you are most alert and at peak energy in the <u>Morning</u>, do your most difficult or demanding work before 10 <u>A.M.</u>

morning   a.m. _____

7. Senator Diane Feinstein also served as the <u>Mayor</u> of San Francisco.

mayor _____

8. Trisha Mahoney, <u>Secretary</u> of <u>aauw</u>, does not clip newspaper or journal articles but instead does an <u>internet</u> search to find the most up-to-date information.

secretary   AAUW   Internet _____

9. Even though the <u>Company</u> discourages this practice, some employees still come to work on <u>veteran's day</u> and on <u>presidents' day</u>.

company   Veteran's Day   Presidents' Day _____

10. Kevin's car is equipped with a mini clipboard on the car dash so that he can write quick notes while he's making sales calls in the <u>Eastern</u> part of the <u>State</u>.

eastern   state _____

11. If a company's computers are connected by a <u>Network</u>, a <u>Software Organizer</u> may be used for <u>Electronic Group Scheduling</u>.

network   software organizer   electronic group scheduling ___

12. One of Parkinson's <u>Laws</u> states, "<u>any</u> task expands to fill the time allowed for it."

laws   Any _____

13. Use the following three-point introduction when phoning a business: <u>Your</u> name, <u>Affiliation</u>, and <u>Reason</u> for calling.

your   affiliation   reason _____

14. Mickey Jordan makes the following observation about creative people: <u>They</u> tend to keep things in stacks, in open spaces, or on chairs.

they _____

15. Personal information manager (PIM) software has been assisting disorganized businesspeople for more than a <u>Decade</u>.

decade _____

16. Day-Timer sponsors an <u>Organizational</u> <u>Seminar</u> each <u>Fall</u> and spring.

organizational seminar   fall _____

17. I believe <u>uncle</u> Craig received his <u>Master's</u> <u>Degree</u> from the University <u>Of</u> Arizona.

Uncle   master's degree   of _____

18. In Office Systems 202, we spent five weeks on <u>Time</u> <u>Management</u> topics.

time management _____

19. The Yahoo! <u>Search</u> turned up <u>One</u> <u>Million</u> Websites for the topic, but I finally found a useful URL at itstime.<u>COM</u>.

search   one million   com _____

20. When Karen first started using e-mail, she ended her messages with Sincerely <u>Yours</u>.

yours _____

PRACTICE 3B

PROOFREADING

Directions: *Proofread and compare the two sentences in each group. If they are the same, write **Yes** in the space provided. If they are not the same, write **No**. Use the first sentence as the correct copy. If you find errors in the second sentence, underline them.*

1. When you have a large project, break it into bite-size tasks to prevent procrastinating and feeling overwhelmed.
When you have a large <u>project break</u> it into <u>bit</u>-size tasks to prevent procrastinating and feeling overwhelmed.

1. _____ No _____

2. It is often difficult to say "No" to a request, especially if the person asking is in need of help.
It is often difficult to say <u>No</u> to a request, especially if the person asking is in need of help.

2. _____ No _____

3. Jeannette was asked to chair the Fundraising Committee for the northern Iowa chapter of PBL.
Jeannette was asked to chair the <u>fundraising</u> <u>committee</u> for the <u>Northern</u> Iowa chapter of PBL.

3. _____ No _____

NAME _____

4. When organizing your work area, discard the following items: outdated versions of manuals and catalogs, extra copies of documents, and information you never use.

When organizing your work area, discard the following items. Outdated versions of manuals and catalogs, extra copies of documents, and information you never use.

4. _____ No _____

5. Maricela Chavez, treasurer of our Hispanic Club, uses Lotus Organizer to keep a database of student members and manage a calendar of events.

Maricela Chavez, treasurer of our Hispanic Club, uses Lotus Organizer to keep a database of student members and manage a calendar of events.

5. _____ Yes _____

Directions: *Proofread and compare the two addresses and phone numbers. If they are the same, write **Yes** in the space provided. If they are not the same, write **No**. Use the first version as the correct copy. If you find errors in the second version, underline the errors.*

1. Utobia Systems Inc.
10881 Business Drive
Fontana, CA 92337
(909) 555-6866
Fax (909) 555-6877
1.888.4.UTOBIA

Utobia Systems Inc.
10881 Business Drive
Fontana, CA 92237
(909) 555-6866
Fax (909) 555-6877
1.555.4.UTOBIA

No _____

2. InFocus Systems, Inc.
Phone (503) 555-8888
Fax (503) 555-8631
1-800-555-6400
Europe Phone (31) 00 5623200
Europe Fax (31) 00 5624388
www.infocus.com/pcc

InFocus Systems, Inc.
Phone (503) 555-8888
Fax (503) 555-8631
1-800-555-6400
Europe Phone (31) 00 5623200
Europe Fax (31) 00 5624378
www.infocus.com/pcc

No _____

3. ViaGrafix Software Division
One American Way
Pryor, OK 74361
800/555-3223
918/555-7555
fax 918/555-6359
www.viagrafix.com
sales@viagrafix.com

ViaGrafix Software Division
One American Way
Pryor, OK 74361
800/555-3223
918/555-7555
fax 918/555-6359
www.viagrafix.com
sales@viagrafix.com
Yes _____

4. Polywell Computers, Inc.
1461 San Mateo Ave.
So. San Francisco, CA 94080 USA
Tel: (415) 555-7222
Fax: (415) 555-1974
E-Mail: info@polywell.com
(800) 555-9946
www.polywell.com

Polywell Computers, Inc.
1460 San Mateo Ave.
So. San Francisco, CA 94080 USA
Tel: (415) 555-7222
Fax: (415) 555-1974
E-Mail: info@polywell.com
(800) 555-9946
www.polywell.com
No _____

NAME _____

Directions: *Compare the keyed version of the "to do" list with the original list. Underline the errors that you find in the second version. In the space provided at the end of the exercise, indicate the number of errors you found. (The letters A, B, C that you find after each task indicate the urgency of getting a particular job completed. "A" represents the most urgent tasks.)*

KAREN MACAL, MARKETING MANAGER
February 14

1. Read article about Webcasting in *Newsweek* (C)
2. Call Roberto Gachet about meeting room setup (A)
3. Make arrangements with Jaylie for refreshments on Friday (A)
4. Proofread brochure before sending to printer (B)
5. Call Jane about lunch next week at 11:30 a.m. (B)
6. Make appointment for photograph before March 15 (B)
7. Send e-mail to Doug about budget priorities ($25,000 for new computers) (A)
8. Analyze results of sales incentive program (C)
9. Order a wireless mouse for presentations (C)
10. Write memo to reps about new products (B)

KAREN MACAL, MARKETING MANAGER
February 14

1. Read article about <u>webcasting</u> in *Newsweek* (C)

2. Call Roberto Gachet about meeting room <u>set up</u> (A)

3. Make arrangements with <u>Lydia</u> for refreshments on Friday (<u>B</u>)

4. Proofread brochure before sending to printer (B)

5. Call Jane about lunch next week at 11:30 <u>A.M.</u> (B)

6. Make appointment for photograph before March <u>25</u> (B)

7. Send e-mail to Doug about budget priorities (<u>$25,00</u> for new computers) (A)

8. Analyze results of <u>Sales Incentive Program</u> (C)

9. Order a wireless mouse for presentations (C)

10. Write memo to <u>Reps</u> about new products (B)

How many errors did you find?   <u>11</u>_____

PRACTICE 4B

WRITING

Directions: If you want to get a job done right, you have to do it yourself. Do you agree with this statement? Write three sentences that explain why you agree or why you do not agree with the statement. Vary the sentence length.   *Answers will vary.*

_____

_____

_____

_____

NAME _____

_____

_____

_____

 ## ONLINE *EXERCISES*

Objective: *To find useful time management tips.*

1. With your Internet browser on screen, key:

   http://www.tgon.com in the location text box. Press the **Enter** key on your keyboard.

2. You will be on The Get Organized! News home page. Click on **Resources** on the site until you find something of interest to you. Print the information.

LOOKING BACK

Posttest

Directions: *Underline any capitalization errors in the following sentences. On the lines provided, write the words correctly.*

1. <u>kay</u> feels <u>dylan</u> wastes time by reading <u>Junk</u> <u>Mail</u> and taking long <u>Breaks</u>.

   Kay   Dylan   junk mail   breaks

2. The <u>Committee</u> was surprised when <u>senator</u> Joe Blake accepted its invitation to speak at the <u>Seminar</u>.

   committee   Senator   seminar

3. Dr. Charles Hummell wrote the book *Tyranny <u>Of</u> <u>The</u> Urgent*, which is about the differences between urgent and important tasks.

   of the

4. She said, "<u>you</u> should use your scheduled work hours for company business."

   You

5. The <u>Winter</u> retreat for the <u>accounting</u> <u>department</u> is at <u>ravenwood</u> <u>lodge</u> in northern New Mexico.

   winter   Accounting Department   Ravenwood Lodge

6. The <u>Managers</u> at <u>asymetrix</u> sponsor the <u>syllabus</u> <u>conference</u> at Rohnert <u>park</u>, California.

   managers   Asymetrix   Syllabus Conference   Park

Directions: *In the space provided, write the letter of the correct answer.*

1. Which line has items that are all correct? 1. ___d___
   a. Golden west college, Multimedia Course, online Tutorial
   b. Golden West College, multimedia course, Online Tutorial
   c. Golden West college, Multimedia course, online Tutorial
   d. Golden West College, multimedia course, online tutorial

2. Which line has items that are all correct? 2. ___c___
   a. asians, halloween, summer, monday
   b. Asians, Halloween, summer, monday
   c. Asians, Halloween, summer, Monday
   d. Asians, Halloween, Summer, Monday

3. Which line has items that are all correct? 3. ___c___
   a. Volume X, page 23, room 226, Highway 101
   b. volume X, Page 23, Room 226, highway 101
   c. Volume X, page 23, Room 226, Highway 101
   d. Volume X, Page 23, Room 226, highway 101

4. Which line has the correct capitalization for a salutation and a complimentary closing? 4. ___d___
   a. Yours very truly, Dear selection committee
   b. Yours Very Truly, Dear Ms. Gronroos
   c. Yours Very Truly, dear ms. Gronroos
   d. Yours very truly, Dear Selection Committee

CHAPTER 7

Pronouns

ELECTRONIC MAIL

Electronic mail, also known as e-mail, is an online feature that lets you send a message from your computer to another computer, whether the other computer is next door or across the world. You receive messages in an electronic storage space called a mailbox, and each e-mail system has an electronic system administrator (or postmaster) that controls the e-mail.

E-mail is faster, less expensive, more convenient, and more spontaneous than traditional methods of communication. Voice mail is a more personal way of communicating because you can hear the tone of voice and the emotion of the speaker.

The elements of grammar, punctuation, and spelling are just as important for e-mail as they are for traditional means of communication. E-mail messages, however, are short and concise. Being aware of the proper behavior in sending and receiving e-mail is called "netiquette." Since communicating emotion online is difficult, avoid sarcasm or too much humor when composing your messages. Avoid responding in anger and always be courteous.

When using e-mail, be aware that deleted messages do not disappear completely. Many computer networks automatically back up all e-mail messages, and these messages may stay in the computer system for years. E-mail messages are not private; therefore, avoid sending sensitive information. An e-mail message is like an electronic postcard—it can be read, forwarded, and even changed by other people without your knowledge.

TERMS TO REMEMBER

ELECTRONIC MAIL

E-MAIL ADDRESS

MAILBOX

NETIQUETTE

OBJECTIVES

After you have studied this chapter and completed the exercises, you will be able to do the following:

1. Explain the function of a pronoun in a sentence.
2. Use nominative (subjective), objective, and possessive case pronouns correctly.
3. Differentiate between personal possessive pronouns and contractions.
4. Use compound personal pronouns correctly.
5. Recognize demonstrative and indefinite pronouns.
6. Recognize differences in the use of interrogative and relative pronouns.
7. Use *who* and *whom* correctly in sentences.
8. Diagram sentences correctly.

LOOKING AHEAD

Pretest

Directions: *In the space provided, write the letter of the correct answer.*

1. What is a pronoun?
   a. It is a connector.
   b. It is an action word.
   c. It is a noun substitute.
   d. It is a modifier of a noun.

   1. ___c___

2. Which statement is correct?
   a. Jack and myself attended the seminar on e-mail legal issues.
   b. Jack and me attended the seminar on e-mail legal issues.
   c. Me and Jack attended the seminar on e-mail legal issues.
   d. Jack and I attended the seminar on e-mail legal issues.

   2. ___d___

3. An appositive is:
   a. A subject complement.
   b. A possessive pronoun.
   c. A noun or noun phrase that identifies or explains the noun or pronoun preceding it.
   d. A noun or pronoun that identifies a verb used in a preceding sentence.

   3. ___c___

4. Which statement is correct?
   a. Your asked to give our director some information before you select your password.
   b. You're asked to give our director some information before you select your password.
   c. You're asked to give our director some information before you select you're password.
   d. Your asked to give our director some information before you select you're password.

   4. ___b___

5. Which statement is correct?
   a. Her mailbox was flooded with mail when she and Gretchen returned from vacation.
   b. I had answered my e-mail messages by the time her and Sally returned from lunch.
   c. The instructor is arranging an e-mail demonstration for we business majors.
   d. The newest e-mail virus concerned our programmers, Wendy and he.

   5. ___a___

6. Which statement is correct?
   a. I taught myself the e-mail software package.
   b. He expresses hisself very well.
   c. The managers theirselves acknowledged that the report was documented thoroughly.
   d. Jim and myself checked out the possibility of a virus.

   6. ___a___

7. Which statement is correct?
   a. Everyone whom was hired knew how to use the Internet.
   b. Everyone who was hired knew how to use the Internet.
   c. Everyone that was hired knew how to use the Internet.
   d. Everyone which was hired knew how to use the Internet.

   7. ___b___

8. Which statement is correct?
   a. This was the software analysis that we used.
   b. This here e-mail message is too long.
   c. Whose line of reasoning do you think is most logical—his or their's?
   d. Whose responsible for reviewing those e-mail messages?

   8. ___a___

9. Which statement is correct?
   a. To whose did you send the message?
   b. To whom did you send the message?
   c. To who did you send the message?
   d. Who did you send the message to?

   9. ___b___

10. Which statement is correct?
    a. Bud sends a report to Josh and I daily.
    b. Bud sends a report to I and Josh daily.
    c. Bud sends a report to Josh and myself daily.
    d. Bud sends a report to Josh and me daily.

    10. ___d___

O V E R V I E W

Although pronouns are substitutes for nouns, they have special characteristics of their own that require attention. In Chapter 2, you were introduced to personal pronouns, and you saw how pronouns helped you avoid the repetition of nouns. Your continued study of pronouns in Chapters 7 and 8 becomes more challenging since pronouns change in case, gender, number, and person more frequently than nouns. In addition to studying personal pronouns in greater depth,

you will learn about several other classifications of pronouns in this chapter.

Many people struggle with the use of the pronouns *who* and *whom*. In this chapter, you will learn how to determine which form is needed in a sentence. Another pronoun troublespot you will study is the use of contractions and possessive pronouns such as *it's* and *its*. When this type of error is not corrected, your writing and proofreading skills appear careless.

CASES OF PRONOUNS

Pronouns are words that substitute for nouns. Personal pronouns refer to persons or things. Like nouns, pronouns have three cases—*nominative, objective,* and *possessive.* The case of a personal pronoun depends on the pronoun's function in the sentence. As with nouns, a *first-person* pronoun refers to the one who is speaking. A *second-person* pronoun is the one spoken to, and a *third-person* pronoun is the one spoken about.

See Instructor Notes 7-1, 7-2, and 7-3 in IAE.

Go to
Transparencies/PowerPoints 7-1a, 7-1b, and 7-2.

Nominative (Subjective) Case Personal Pronouns

Use the nominative case (also called subjective case) when the pronoun is the subject of a verb, when it is a subject complement, or when it is in apposition to a subject. The following pronouns are in nominative case:

	Singular	Plural
First Person	I	we
Second Person	you	you
Third Person	he, she, it	they

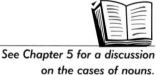

Review the section on personal pronouns in Chapter 2.

See Chapter 5 for a discussion on the cases of nouns.

Subject of Verb. Use the nominative case when the personal pronoun is the subject of a verb.

Go to
Transparency/PowerPoint 7-3.

> **He receives at least 50 messages daily.**
> (*He* is a third person pronoun and is the subject of the verb *receives.*)

Weak sentences (sentences with words that do not contribute substantially to the meanings of the sentences) often begin with It.

See Instructor Note 7-4 in IAE.

7-5 In this chapter, *subject complement* is used in place of *predicate noun* and *predicate pronoun*.

The most common linking verbs include am, are, is, was, were, been, and being. Linking verbs express a condition or state of being.

Subject complements rename or describe subjects. A predicate pronoun or a predicate noun is a subject complement.

See the paragraph(s) in a reference manual such as The Gregg Reference Manual to learn about pronoun usage with the infinitive to be.

Appositives identify or explain the nouns or pronouns immediately preceding them.

I use my e-mail frequently, but he prefers the telephone.

(*I* is a first-person pronoun and is the subject of the verb *use*. *He* is a third-person pronoun and is the subject of the verb *prefers*.)

You reach everyone quickly by sending e-mail messages.

(*You* is a second-person pronoun and is the subject of the verb *reach*.)

It takes only a few minutes to send most e-mail messages.

(*It* is a third-person pronoun and is the subject of the verb *takes*.)

Julie and she have developed new e-mail procedures.

(*She* is a third-person pronoun. *Julie* is a third-person noun. All nouns or pronouns in a compound subject must be in the nominative case.)

Subject Complement.   Use the nominative case when the personal pronoun is a subject complement (predicate noun, or predicate pronoun) and follows a linking verb.

The most experienced technician is he.

(*He* is the subject complement renaming *technician*. Use the nominative case pronoun *he*; do not use *him*.)

The persons selected were John and she.

(*John* and *she* are the subject complements for *persons*. Use the nominative case pronoun *she*; do not use *her*. In a sentence with a compound subject complement, both subjects must be in the nominative case.)

Appositive.   Use the nominative case for a personal pronoun that is in apposition to a subject.

The new employees—Danielle and he—received a list of current e-mail addresses.

(*Danielle* and *he* are in apposition to the subject *employees*. The phrase identifies the new employees. The subject *employees* is in the nominative case. *He* must be in the same case as the subject.)

Two nominees—you and she—are featured in our online newsletter.

(*You* and *she* are in apposition to the subject *nominees* and must be in the same case as the subject.)

See Instructor Note 7-6 in IAE.

Do This	Do Not Do This
The offensive writer of e-mail messages was found to be he.	The offensive writer of e-mail messages was found to be him.
Change in Structure They found him to be the offensive writer of e-mail messages.	*Use the nominative case only when the infinitive to be has no noun or pronoun immediately before it. In the sentence under Do This, note that the pronoun he (nominative) follows the infinitive to be. The sentence usually sounds less awkward with a change in structure as shown. In the sentence under Change in Structure, note that the objective case him is used correctly.*

When an appositive follows a pronoun, choose the case of the pronoun that would be correct if the appositive were omitted.

We employees spend a lot of time contacting customers by e-mail.

(If the appositive *employees* is omitted, the sentence is correct with the word *We* [nominative case]. *We spend a lot of time contacting customers by e-mail.* Do not use *us employees.*)

CHECKUP 7-1

Directions: In the space provided, write the appropriate code or codes to indicate the correct use of each underlined nominative case pronoun. Use the following codes: **S** (subject of a sentence), **C** (complement), **A** (appositive).

1. They use technology for fast, accurate communication.   S

2. You can reduce the number of junk e-mail messages received by calling your Internet service provider.   S

3. Could it have been he who sent the derogatory message about the company?   S, C

4. The new employees, Robin and she, need clearly written manuals that explain how to use the software.   A

5. She and I are checking the accuracy of our e-mail addresses.   S, S

6. We think e-mail is the most popular use of the Internet.   S

**GO TO
CD-ROM**
CHECKUP 7-1

Objective Case Personal Pronouns

Use the objective case when the pronoun is a direct or indirect object of a verb, an object of a preposition, or a subject or object of an infinitive. In addition, use the objective case when the pronoun is in apposition to a direct or indirect object or to the object of a preposition. The following pronouns are objective case pronouns:

	Singular	Plural
First Person	me	us
Second Person	you	you
Third Person	him, her, it	them

Direct or Indirect Object.   Use the objective case of personal pronouns when the pronouns are direct or indirect objects of verbs.

Have you asked him for a copy of the message?

(*Him* is an objective case pronoun used as a direct object.)

Unless files are essential or very short, do not attach them to e-mail messages.

(*Them* is an objective case pronoun used as a direct object.)

My supervisor gave her the instruction manual.

(*Her* is an objective case pronoun used as an indirect object.)

Direct objects answer the questions what? *or* whom? *Indirect objects answer the questions* to whom? *or for whom?*

See Instructor Note 7-7 in IAE.

JadeNet offered us free e-mail service for one month.
(*Us* is an objective case pronoun used as an indirect object.)

The e-mail etiquette presentation impressed Todd and me.
(Use the pronoun by itself as a check. The sentence *The e-mail etiquette presentation impressed me* makes sense. Use the objective case; do not use the nominative case *I*.)

Object of a Preposition.   Use the objective case when a personal pronoun is the object of a preposition.

The object of a preposition is the noun or pronoun in a prepositional phrase.

I received two e-mail messages from her today.
(*Her* is an objective case pronoun that is the object of the preposition *from*.)

Holly spoke with us about Internet service providers.
(*Us* is an objective case pronoun that is the object of the preposition *with*.)

My supervisor gave the e-mail instruction to Sherry and her.
(In compound objects, use the pronoun by itself as a check. The sentence *My supervisor gave the e-mail instruction to her* makes sense. Use the objective case; do not use *she*.)

Our clients have only good things to say about Byron and him.
(The sentence *Our clients have only good things to say about him* makes sense. Use the objective case; do not use *he*.)

See Instructor Note 7-8 in IAE.

Do This	Do Not Do This
Everyone except you and me had e-mail training.	Everyone except you and I had e-mail training.
The cost of the e-mail installation must be kept between you and me.	The cost of the e-mail installation must be kept between you and I.

Use an objective case pronoun with the prepositions except *and* between.

Appositive.   Use the objective case for a personal pronoun that is in apposition to a direct object, an indirect object, or an object of a preposition.

Please call an information services specialist, Hank or me.
(The pronoun *me* is used in apposition to the direct object, *specialist*. The object *specialist* is in the objective case. *Me* must be in the same case as the direct object *specialist*.)

The company offered two clients, Mrs. Riggs and her, free e-mail installations.
(The pronoun *her* [along with Mrs. Riggs] is used in apposition to the indirect object *clients*.)

Chapter 7

We received requests for e-mail installations from two clients, Mrs. Riggs and her.

(The pronoun *her* is used in apposition to the object of the preposition *clients*.)

When an appositive follows a pronoun, choose the case of the pronoun that would be correct if the appositive were omitted.

Carla sent e-mail messages to us managers.

(If the appositive *managers* is omitted, the sentence is correct with *us*. Use the objective case pronoun; do not use the nominative case pronoun *we*.)

Subject or Object of an Infinitive. Use the objective case when a pronoun is the subject or object of an infinitive.

Since she wrote the message quickly, Sonja asked me to proofread it.

(*Me* is the subject of the infinitive *to proofread*. The word *it* is the direct object of the infinitive *to proofread*.)

The supervisor told him to change the passwords.

(*Him* is the subject of the infinitive *to change*.)

My coworker always offers to help me.

(*Me* is the object of the infinitive *to help*.)

7-9 The section on subjects or objects of infinitives may be omitted; no exercise requires this information.

An infinitive is made up of a verb plus the word to *(e.g.,* to write*).*

CHECKUP 7-2

Directions: In the space provided, write the appropriate code or codes to indicate the correct use of each underlined objective case pronoun. Use the following codes: **DO** direct object), **IO** (indirect object), **OP** (object of preposition), **A** (appositive).

1. Please send them an updated e-mail address for me. _____IO, OP_____

2. Slow Internet access time irritates him. _____DO_____

3. If you hurt anyone's feelings with a written message, apologize to him or her. _____OP, OP_____

4. I thought Ed's message was meant for me. _____OP_____

5. Mrs. Ludwig gave you the responsibility for distributing new e-mail policies to all of us. _____IO, OP_____

6. The potential for e-mail abuse was evident to the two employees, Lupe and her. _____A_____

7. When a company monitors employees' e-mail, it must inform them. _____DO_____

8. She received a message that was intended for me. _____OP_____

9. The manager gave her the instruction manual for the new communication system. _____IO_____

10. The information systems managers, John and he, learned how to send messages to us quickly. _____A, OP_____

**GO TO
CD-ROM**
CHECKUP 7-2

Possessive Case Personal Pronouns

Go to Transparencies/PowerPoints 7-4a, 7-4b, and 7-4c.

7-10 Emphasize that possessive pronouns do not have apostrophes.

Possessive pronouns indicate ownership. The following pronouns are possessive case pronouns:

	Singular	Plural
First Person	my, mine	our, ours
Second Person	your, yours	your, yours
Third Person	his, her/hers, its	their, theirs

Preceding Nouns. Use the possessive pronouns *my, your, his, her, our,* and *their* to modify the nouns that follow. These possessive pronouns function as adjectives in sentences.

> **Her explanations for using the e-mail system were excellent.**
> (*Her* is a possessive pronoun that functions as an adjective modifying the noun *explanations.*)

> **We prefer to fax our correspondence.**
> (*Our* functions as an adjective modifying the noun c*orrespondence.*)

> **He writes clearly; therefore, his messages do not need corrections.**
> (*His* modifies *messages.*)

> **Choose your words wisely.**
> (*Your* modifies *words.*)

Separated From Nouns. Do not use the possessive pronouns *mine, yours, hers, ours,* and *theirs* as modifiers before nouns. These pronouns stand alone and are separated from the nouns to which they refer.

See Instructor Note 7-11 in IAE.

> **The responsibility is yours if a document is not transmitted.**
> (*Yours* is a possessive pronoun that refers to the noun *responsibility.* This possessive pronoun does not precede the noun to which it refers but stands alone.)

> **Hers was the only message longer than a page.**
> (*Hers* is a possessive pronoun that refers to the noun *message.*)

> **Are the e-mail reports ours or theirs?**
> (*Ours* and *theirs* are possessive pronouns that refer to the noun *reports.*)

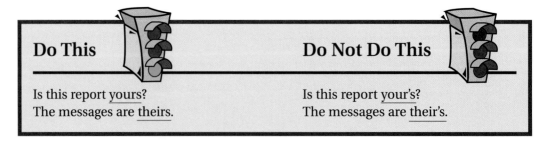

Do This	**Do Not Do This**
Is this report <u>yours</u>?	Is this report <u>your's</u>?
The messages are <u>theirs</u>.	The messages are <u>their's</u>.

Do not use apostrophes with possessive pronouns.

Contractions and Possessive Pronouns

7-12 Emphasize the differences between the use of contractions and possessive pronouns.

Several contractions and possessive pronouns sound alike and may cause writing difficulties. These pronouns and contractions may be confusing:

> its/it's   their/they're   theirs/there's   your/you're

It's/ Its.   Do not use the contraction *it's* (a shortened form for *it is*) in place of *its*, the personal pronoun.

> **It's too early to determine if I prefer using electronic mail or voice mail.**
> (*It's* is a contraction that means *it is*.)
>
> **The company announced its budget cuts through an intranet memo.**
> (*The company announced it is budget cuts* does not make sense. The possessive form *its* is necessary.)
>
> **I'm sure you will agree that it's easy to send e-mail messages.**
> (Contraction)
>
> **The USPS is examining its role in electronic mail service.**
> (Possessive case)

You're/Your.   Do not use the contraction *you're* (a shortened form for *you are*) in place of *your*, the personal pronoun.

> **When attaching files to messages, check that the person to whom you're sending the files can receive them.**
> (*You're* is a contraction that means *you are*.)
>
> **Does he really need to receive your e-mail message?**
> (*Does he really need to receive you are e-mail message?* does not make sense. The possessive form *your* is necessary.)
>
> **Print your e-mail address on your letterhead and business cards.**
> (Possessive case)
>
> **I understand you're thinking of becoming a full-time editor.**
> (Contraction)

They're/Their.   Do not use the contraction *they're* (shortened form for *they are*) in place of *their*, the possessive pronoun.

> **They're offering direct Internet access with e-mail capabilities.**
> (*They're* is a contraction that means *they are*.)
>
> **A survey showed that women managers prefer to compose their own correspondence.**
> (If you substitute *they are* for *their*, the sentence does not make sense; therefore, a possessive form is necessary.)

Go to PowerPoint 7-4d.

There's/Theirs.   Do not use the contraction *there's* (shortened form for *there is* or *there has*) in place of *theirs*, the possessive pronoun.

> **There's an attachment to my last e-mail message.**
> (*There's* is a contraction that means *there is*.)

The attachment with my last e-mail message was <u>theirs</u>.
(*There is* does not make sense in this sentence; therefore, the possessive form *theirs* is necessary.)

See Instructor Note 7-13 in IAE.

The summary that follows is a basic guide for using personal pronouns.

	Nominative Case		Objective Case		Possessive Case		
First Person (the one speaking)	I	we	me	us	my mine	our ours	
Second Person (the one spoken to)	you	you	you	you	your	yours	
Third Person (the one spoken about)	she	they	her	them	her hers	their theirs	
	he	they	him	them	his his	their theirs	
	it	they	it	them	its	their	theirs
Function	Subject Subject complement Appositive		Direct object Indirect object Object of preposition Appositive Object of infinitive Subject of infinitive		Possessive noun replacement Adjective		

CHECKUP 7-3

Directions: Select the correct word in parentheses, and write it in the space provided.

1. (*It's, Its, Its'*) easier to read printed copy than copy on a screen.   <u>It's</u>

2. E-mail communication ignores (*your, you're*) appearance, color, or gender.   <u>your</u>

3. (*They're, There, Their*) presence in the room while I'm entering data makes me nervous.   <u>Their</u>

4. I was puzzled by the message in (*my, mine*) e-mail inbox.   <u>my</u>

5. When a company owns the e-mail system, it may examine (*its, it's, its'*) employees' messages.   <u>its</u>

6. Robin uses (*her, her's*) free e-mail service daily.   <u>her</u>

7. (*You're, Your*) probably already familiar with e-mail in (*your, you're*) office.   <u>You're</u> <u>your</u>

8. Addie knew that the error was (*her's, hers*).   <u>hers</u>

GO TO CD-ROM CHECKUP 7-3

CHECKUP 7-4

Directions: Refer to the Secondary Learning material at the beginning of the chapter. Identify the nominative, objective, and possessive case pronouns found in the first two paragraphs. Place the pronouns in the appropriate columns listed below.

Paragraph 1:

Nominative	Objective	Possessive
you	you	your

Paragraph 2:

Nominative	Objective	Possessive
you		

7-14 Checkup 7-4 demonstrates the various uses of pronouns.

**GO TO
CD-ROM**
CHECKUP 7-4

MISCELLANEOUS PRONOUNS

In addition to personal pronouns, several other types of pronouns require study. These pronouns have specific classification names that may sound complicated. You will not be required to memorize these names, but you will need to recognize the classifications and use the pronouns correctly in sentences. In the text that follows, these types of pronouns will be presented: compound personal pronouns (intensive and reflexive pronouns), demonstrative pronouns, indefinite pronouns, interrogative pronouns, and relative pronouns.

See Instructor Note 7-15 in IAE.

Compound Personal Pronouns (Intensive and Reflexive Pronouns)

A compound personal pronoun consists of a personal pronoun and the suffix *self* or *selves*. Use a compound personal pronoun to add emphasis (intensive pronoun) or to refer to a previously named noun or pronoun (reflexive pronoun). The following pronouns are compound personal pronouns:

myself	himself	ourselves	themselves
yourself	herself	yourselves	
	itself		

Go to PowerPoints 7-5a, 7-5b, and 7-5c.

7-16 Intensive and reflexive pronouns are covered under the heading "Compound Personal Pronouns."

The words hisself, ourself(s), theirself, theirselves, yourselfs, *or* themself(s) *are not standard English words.*

Intensive Pronouns. Use the intensive compound personal pronoun to add emphasis to a noun or to another pronoun.

Linda <u>herself</u> assured us that the figures were accurate.

(The word *herself* is an intensive pronoun that emphasizes the noun *Linda*.)

I <u>myself</u> never thought that I'd use e-mail more than the fax.

(The word *myself* is an intensive pronoun that emphasizes another pronoun *I*.)

We ourselves see no reason to change software again.

(The word *ourselves* emphasizes the pronoun *We.*)

Reflexive Pronouns.   Use the reflexive compound pronoun to refer to a noun or pronoun previously used as the subject of a sentence.

I allowed myself sufficient time to respond to his message that criticized my actions.

(The reflexive pronoun *myself* refers to the subject *I.*)

The students taught themselves the details of using e-mail on the Internet.

(*Themselves* refers to the noun *students.*)

Don't criticize yourself for mistakes that are beyond your control.

(*Yourself* refers to the pronoun *you,* the understood subject.)

By noon, Katherine had convinced herself that her proposal was not going to be accepted.

(*Herself* refers to the noun *Katherine.*)

Do This	Do Not Do This
My supervisor expected Randy Sue and me to finish the mailing.	My supervisor expected Randy Sue and myself to finish the mailing.
Randy Sue and I will finish the mailing.	Randy Sue and myself will finish the mailing.

Before using a compound personal pronoun, be sure the noun or pronoun to which a compound noun refers is present in the sentence. Do not use a compound personal pronoun if a personal pronoun is adequate.

CHECKUP 7-5

Directions: *Select the appropriate pronoun in parentheses, and write it in the space provided.*

1. I have only (*me, myself*) and my oldest son to consider if I decide to start a new business in my home.   myself

2. Give (*yourselfs, yourselves*) a break, and review what you have accomplished.   yourselves

3. Please meet with George and (*I, me, myself*) to discuss the plan for improving e-mail communication.   me

4. Terry and (*I, me, myself*) decided to volunteer for the Software Selection Committee.   I

5. They satisfied (*theirselves, themselves, theirselfs, themselfs*) that they could meet the client's deadline.   themselves

6. He (*himself, hisself*) thought the e-mail policy concerning personal use was fair.   himself

GO TO
CD-ROM
CHECKUP 7-5

Chapter 7

Demonstrative Pronouns

Demonstrative pronouns designate specific persons, places, or things. The following pronouns are demonstrative pronouns:

Singular	Plural
this	these
that	those

Use demonstrative pronouns to point out specific persons, places, or things. When these demonstrative pronouns modify nouns, they function as adjectives.

We knew this was the individual we wanted to hire.

(The demonstrative pronoun *this* points out *individual,* a person.)

These are the messages we should have sent yesterday.

See Instructor Note 7-17 in IAE.

(The demonstrative pronoun *These* points out *messages,* which are things.)

We should have sent these messages yesterday.

(The demonstrative pronoun *these* functions as an adjective and answers the question *Which messages?*)

This company's research people surveyed the users of electronic mail.

(The demonstrative pronoun *this* functions as an adjective.)

Pronouns	Adjectives
these are	these messages
this was	this company's

Do This	Do Not Do This
This should be stored in your inbox.	This here should be stored in your inbox.
We were not expecting that message until Tuesday.	We were not expecting that there message until Tuesday.

Do not attach words such as here *and* there *to demonstrative pronouns or to demonstrative pronouns that function as adjectives.*

Indefinite Pronouns

Indefinite pronouns refer to persons, places, or things in a general way. They are not precise or exact. Additional information about the use of indefinite pronouns follows in Chapter 8. These pronouns are indefinite pronouns:

See Instructor Note 7-18 in IAE.

all	both	everything	nobody	others
another	each	few	no one	several
any	either	many	none	some
anybody	enough	more	nothing	somebody
anyone	everybody	most	one	someone
anything	everyone	neither	other	something

Use an indefinite pronoun to refer to nouns (persons, places, and things) spoken about in a general way. The nominative and objective cases are the same for indefinite pronouns.

Everyone needs a uniform list of emoticons (shortcut e-mail signs of emotions).
(*Everyone* is an indefinite pronoun that refers to people in a general way. In this sentence, *everyone* is the subject and is in the nominative case.)

If you plan to use emoticons (shortcut e-mail signs of emotion), give everyone a list of meanings.
(*Everyone* is an indefinite pronoun that refers to people in a general way. In this sentence, *everyone* is an indirect object and is in the objective case.)

Many of our employees are not managing their e-mail satisfactorily.
(*Many* is an indefinite pronoun that refers to people in a general way. In this sentence, *many* is the subject and is in the nominative case.)

Some think that they can write anything they want, and nobody will ever see it.
(*Some* and *nobody* are indefinite pronouns that do not refer to specific persons but to persons in general. In this sentence, *some* and *nobody* are in the nominative case. *Anything* is an indefinite pronoun that does not refer to a specific thing. In this sentence, *anything* is in the objective case.)

CHECKUP 7-6

Directions: Draw a line under each indefinite pronoun and circle each demonstrative pronoun. If necessary, refer to the lists for each type of pronoun.

1. (This) is my supervisor, Hal Thompson, who oversees everything from maintenance to advertising.

2. Someone is reading my e-mail messages.

3. A few agreed with the newest e-mail policy.

4. Be patient with (those) who are fearful of e-mail and technology in general.

5. Most of the e-mail addresses outside the United States end with country codes.

6. Some expect the receivers of e-mail messages to respond immediately.

7. E-mail allows users to send messages to anyone anywhere in the world in minutes.

8. Someone removed my mouse as a joke; I was not amused.

**GO TO
CD-ROM**
CHECKUP 7-6

Interrogative Pronouns

The word *interrogative* relates to forming questions. The following pronouns are interrogative pronouns:

Go to PowerPoint 7-6.

who	which	whoever
what	whom	whomever
whose	whatever	whichever

Use interrogative pronouns to form direct and indirect questions.

Direct Questions:

<u>Who</u> uses emoticons in e-mail messages?

To <u>whom</u> will you send that message?

<u>What</u> is the name of the e-mail system you have at home?

<u>What</u> happened to my first draft?

Indirect Questions:

I wonder <u>what</u> the new e-mail guidelines will be.

(*What* is used in an indirect question. An indirect question does not require a question mark.)

Bob asked <u>which</u> of the icons were used most frequently.

(*Which* is used in an indirect question. No question mark is necessary.)

Use a question mark at the end of a direct question and a period after an indirect question.

Relative Pronouns

The list of relative and interrogative pronouns is similar. *That* is the major addition to the list. The most frequently used relative pronouns are *who, whom, that,* and *which.* The following pronouns are relative pronouns:

See Instructor Note 7-19 in IAE.

who	which	whoever	whichever
whom	that	whomever	whose

Use a relative pronoun as a reference to a noun in an independent clause. A relative pronoun begins a dependent clause that cannot stand on its own.

We decided to hire Sue, <u>who</u> communicates very well.

(*Who* is a relative pronoun referring to *Sue.* The relative pronoun introduces the dependent clause *who communicates very well.*)

Refer to Chapter 3 for a review of dependent and independent clauses.

Who, Whom, Whose. The relative pronouns *who, whom,* and *whose* relate to people. These pronouns require different forms for each case.

See Instructor Note 7-20 in IAE.

Case	Pronoun
Nominative	who, whoever
Objective	whom, whomever
Possessive	whose

Additional help with these pronouns comes in a later section of this chapter.

That. The relative pronoun *that* relates to things and persons (only when a class or type of person is meant). The word *that* restricts the meaning of the sentence, making it necessary to the meaning of the sentence.

> **The firm <u>that</u> installed our intranet provides 24-hour hotline service.**
> (*That* is a relative pronoun referring to *firm.* The clause beginning with the word *that* is necessary to the meaning of the sentence. Not just any firm provides 24-hour service, but it is the firm *that installed our intranet* that provides 24-hour hotline service. No commas are necessary.)

> **She is the type of employee <u>that</u> answers all correspondence promptly.**
> (*That* refers to a *type* of person. The clause beginning with the word *that* is necessary since it identifies the type of employee. No commas are necessary.)

> **He received an e-mail message <u>that</u> someone had written in all capital letters.**
> (*That* refers to *message.* The clause beginning with the word *that* is necessary since it identifies which e-mail message. No commas are necessary.)

7-21 Restrictive and nonrestrictive clauses are discussed in more depth in Chapter 16.

7-22 Refer to a manual such as *The Gregg Reference Manual* for additional information concerning the use of *which.*

Which. The relative pronoun *which* refers primarily to things. The word *which* introduces nonrestrictive (nonessential) clauses. These clauses are not necessary to the meaning of a sentence.

> **Besides e-mail, the Internet provides newsgroups, <u>which</u> allow you to discuss shared interests with other users.**
> (*Which* is a relative pronoun that refers to *newsgroups.* The clause beginning with the word *which* adds interesting material, but it is not necessary to the meaning of the sentence. Commas are necessary to separate the nonrestrictive clause from the rest of the sentence.)

> **Your service provider, <u>which</u> is your Internet connection, transmits your message to the receiving machine.**
> (*Which* refers to *provider.* The clause is not necessary; therefore, it requires commas.)

CHECKUP 7-7

Directions: *Draw a line under each interrogative pronoun and circle each relative pronoun.*

1. E-mail information providers gather news and data (that) directly affect you.

2. Ms. Brown is the one (who) is going to the convention.

3. <u>Which</u> works better—Mail.Com software or Juno software?

4. My e-mail provider's address, (which) I thought I had lost, was in the folder.

5. Tracy Cook is the person (who) sent her résumé via e-mail.

6. <u>Whose</u> signature shall I place on this e-mail message?

7. Businesses should establish policies (that) discourage employees from cluttering their e-mail systems with personal messages.

8. <u>Who</u> told you emoticons were illegal?

GO TO CD-ROM
CHECKUP 7-7

USE OF *WHO, WHOM,* AND *WHOSE*

When you understand the nominative, objective, and possessive cases of pronouns, you will be able to use *who, whom,* and *whose* correctly in written documents.

See Instructor Note 7-23 in IAE.

Go to PowerPoint 7-7.

Who and whom are both interrogative pronouns and relative pronouns. Whose is the possessive form of who. Who is the nominative form, while whom and whose are the objective forms.

Who

Use the relative pronouns *who* or *whoever* to refer to persons. *Who* and *whoever* are nominative case pronouns. Use the nominative case when you can substitute *I, we, he, she,* or *they* in the clause beginning with *who* or *whoever.*

Managers <u>who</u> read employees' e-mail messages must be sure a policy gives them that right.
(Substitute *they* for *who* in the clause *who read employees' e-mail messages. They read employees' e-mail messages* makes sense; the nominative case pronoun *who* is correct.)

Matt Nelson, <u>who</u> is a sales manager for Kirtland Products, submitted his expense report by e-mail.
(Substitute *he* for *who* in the clause *who is a sales manager. He is a sales manager for Kirtland Products* makes sense. The nominative case pronoun *who* is correct.)

<u>Who</u> shall I say is calling?
(Rearrange the question to normal order [or a statement] and substitute *he. I shall say he is calling.* The nominative case *who* is correct.)

The person <u>who</u> uses simple words rather than lengthy expressions is usually a good communicator.
(*He uses simple words rather than lengthy expressions* makes sense. The nominative case *who* is correct.)

<u>Whoever</u> needs assistance always receives it from Karen.
(*He needs assistance* makes sense. The nominative case *whoever* is correct.)

See Instructor Note 7-24 in IAE.

Go to PowerPoints 7-8a and 7-8b.

Review direct objects, indirect objects (Chapter 3), and objects of prepositions (Chapter 2).

Whom

Use the relative pronouns *whom* or *whomever* to refer to persons. *Whom* and *whomever* are objective case pronouns. Use objective case pronouns when you can substitute *me, us, him, her,* or *them* as a direct or indirect object or as an object of a preposition. You can make this simpler by using just *him* and *them* as the substitute words. Both end in *m* as does the word *whom.*

> **Juanita Gomez, whom you met yesterday, left us her e-mail address.**
> (*Whom* is the object of the verb *met. You met her yesterday.*)
>
> **This is the person whom I saw reading my e-mail.**
> (*Whom* is the object of the verb *saw. I saw him reading my e-mail.*)
>
> **To whom was that last message addressed?**
> (*Whom* is the object of the preposition *to. That last message was addressed to him.*)
>
> **Bob Dawson, for whom we have great respect, was elected to the board of the International Internet Users Association.**
> (*Whom* is the object of the preposition *for. We have great respect for him.*)

Whose and *Who's*

Use the relative pronoun *whose* to show ownership. Do not use an apostrophe with this possessive form of the pronoun. Do not use the contraction *who's* (*who is, who has*) to show possession.

> **Do you know whose interpretation of the e-mail policy is correct?**
> (*Whose* indicates possession.)
>
> **We wonder whose technology will change the way we communicate ten years from now.**
> (*Whose* indicates possession.)
>
> **Who's going to inform the supervisor that his e-mail messages were returned with the wrong addresses?**
> (*Who's* is the contraction for *who is.*)

CHECKUP 7-8

Directions: Select the correct word in parentheses, and write it in the space provided.

1. Rhonda Patina, (*who, whom, whose*) is the regional sales manager for Lawson Communications, uses e-mail for impersonal messages only.   who

2. By (*who, whom, whose*) was this e-mail message signed?   whom

3. (*Who, Whom, Whose*) installed the intranet at Bentley Industries?   Who

4. Dan Dusquene is the service person (*who, whom, whose*) gave us the tip for storing messages.   who

5. (*Who, Whom, Whose*) e-mail address has numbers in it?   Whose

6. Ron Wilson, with (*who, whom, whose*) you talked on the phone,   whom
can advise us on employer liability and e-mail.

7. (*Who's, Whose*) the presenter for the Internet e-mail demonstration?   Who's

8. Is he the person (*who, whom, whose*) is writing the instructions   who
for using e-mail?

9. Mary, (*who, whom, whose*) I have known since high school, is now   whom
an assistant programmer.

10. Ann Doyle (*who, whom, whose*) manages RoyalNet, is the person to   who   whom
(*who, whom, whose*) I refer all my questions.

**GO TO
CD-ROM**
CHECKUP 7-8

DIAGRAMMING SENTENCES

To diagram a sentence with a compound subject, verb, or object, follow the examples below. You will be asked to diagram only those parts of a sentence that you have worked with in previous chapters or that are introduced in this chapter.

See Instructor Notes 7-25 and
7-26 in IAE.

*Review compound subjects,
verbs, and objects in Chapter 3.*

Compound Subject:
Clients and employees appreciate e-mail service.

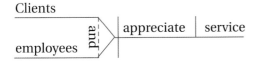

Compound Verb:
Our company purchased and installed an intranet system.

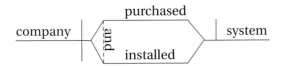

Compound Object:
He uses emoticons and abbreviations in his e-mail messages.

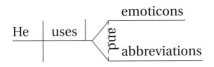

CHECKUP 7-9

Directions: *In the space provided, diagram only the following parts of the sentences: simple and compound subjects and verbs, compound objects, direct and indirect objects, appositives, subject complements, and possessive nouns.*

1. Terry and she misused their e-mail privileges.

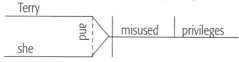

2. I use and enjoy my free e-mail software.

3. She gave us the e-mail policy and a list of acceptable emoticons.

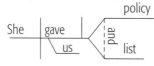

4. My instructor and my supervisor emphasized the importance of the subject line in e-mail messages.

5. You can send and receive e-mail as long as you have an Internet connection.

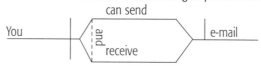

GO TO CD-ROM
CHECKUP 7-9

PRACTICE

NAME _____

PRACTICE 1A

Directions: Draw a line under the correct word in parentheses.

1. Computer users can send (<u>*their*</u>, *there, they're*) commercial ads through (<u>*their*</u>, *there, they're*) bulk e-mail providers.

2. (<u>*It's*</u>, *Its, Its'*) going to be a long time before (<u>*we*</u>, *us*) use e-mail at our home.

3. After (<u>*Todd and he*</u>, *Todd and him*) made (<u>*their*</u>, *there, they're*) decision, they gave (*we,* <u>*us*</u>) the new e-mail policy.

4. (<u>*We*</u>, *Us*) instructors wanted (*Ethan and her,* <u>*Ethan and she*</u>) to demonstrate e-mail to our students.

5. Everyone received the new e-mail policy except (<u>*me*</u>, *I*).

6. The instructor asked two former students, (*Juan and I,* <u>*Juan and me*</u>), for examples of company e-mail policies.

7. Jason Boyd is the employee (<u>*who*</u>, *whom*) has contributed the best e-mail ad design.

8. Juan Rodriguez, (*who,* <u>*whom*</u>) you hired last month, is an excellent translator for our foreign e-mail messages.

9. The new advanced electronic mail trainees—Eric, Sue, Beth, and (*I,* <u>*me*</u>)—will meet next week.

10. (*Them,* <u>*Those*</u>) employees (<u>*who*</u>, *whom*) want to discuss controversial issues via e-mail should investigate software with privacy options.

11. If Kendra cannot perform the work, the company will have to give (<u>*her*</u>, *she*) another job or dismiss (<u>*her*</u>, *she*).

12. (*Whose,* <u>*Who's*</u>) likely to read (<u>*your*</u>, *you're*) e-mail messages?

13. The representative (<u>*who*</u>, *whom*) installed the electronic mail program was patient with my coworker and (<u>*me*</u>, *I*.)

14. (<u>*He and I*</u>, *Him and I*) use our e-mail to keep in touch.

15. Once an e-mail disagreement starts, (*it's,* <u>*its*</u>, *its'*) intensity mushrooms quickly.

16. (<u>*Sam and I*</u>, *Sam and me*) worked on storage procedures for electronic and paper documents.

17. They sent two pages of new e-mail addresses to (*she,* <u>*her*</u>).

18. (*Her and me,* <u>*She and I*</u>) questioned sending the attachment since it had a copyright statement on it.

19. Be complete but concise in (<u>*your*</u>, *you're*) message.

20. (*Whose,* <u>*Who's*</u>) report should be submitted first—(<u>*theirs*</u>, *their's, theirs'*) or mine?

7-27 Remind students that the word *except* functions as a preposition in this sentence.

**GO TO
CD-ROM**
PRACTICE 1
EXERCISES

Pronouns

PRACTICE

PRACTICE 2A

A. **Directions:** *In the following sentences, underline all pronouns and contractions. If a pronoun or contraction is used incorrectly, circle it and write the correct word in the space provided. More than one error may appear in a sentence. If the sentence is correct, write* **Yes.**

1. Notify the online services you use to let them know you do not want you're name placed on mailing lists.

   1. _____your_____

2. I like receiving our company newsletters online because the news is current.

   2. _____Yes_____

3. Both of the assistants are careless in proofreading messages before they send them.

   3. _____Yes_____

4. Several of my coworkers delete all of they're messages when they become overwhelmed by information overload.

   4. _____their_____

5. Our instructor told me the subject line is very important in business documents.

   5. _____Yes_____

6. He and myself established the system to monitor our company's passwords.

   6. _____I_____

7. Send your message only to them who need a copy.

   7. _____those_____

8. He used the abbreviation FAQ (frequently asked questions) only for his internal correspondence.

   8. _____Yes_____

9. If you send material to clients whom have multiple e-mail addresses, record the address they use most frequently.

   9. _____who_____

10. We have been warned not to leave messages on our screens when we leave our desks.

    10. _____Yes_____

11. The company owns its computer system and most of the data in it.

    11. _____its_____

12. For them whom work at home, e-mail will save them time and money.

    12. _____those who_____

13. No one knows you do not have fancy envelopes and stationery when you send e-mail messages.

    13. _____Yes_____

14. Her and her supervisor spend at least 45 minutes daily reading their e-mail.

    14. _____She_____

15. Some abuse the e-mail system by sending nonwork-related messages to they're relatives.

    15. _____their_____

NAME _____

16. Emoticons are symbol combinations that get your emotions across when (your) using e-mail.

16. _____ you're _____

17. We ordered the catalogs that were advertised on the Website but mine never arrived; (hers') arrived a week ago.

17. _____ hers _____

18. My supervisor says he expects me to produce error-free documents.

18. _____ Yes _____

19. Betty has been an administrative assistant for years, and she prefers formal correspondence to e-mail.

19. _____ Yes _____

20. I like to read the headlines from "This is True," that is a free e-mail service.

20. _____ which _____

B. Directions: *The sentences below may have usage or punctuation errors. If the sentences are written correctly, write* **Yes** *in the space provided. If the sentence is written incorrectly, write it correctly in the space provided.*

Review restrictive and
nonrestrictive clauses.

1. Jon and him used the acronym RFC which means a request for comments at the end of their document.

Jon and he used the acronym RFC, which means a request for comments,

at the end of their document.

2. When you receive a message that makes you angry, do not respond immediately.

Yes

3. E-mail is good for reaching people which live in different time zones.

E-mail is good for reaching people who live in different time zones.

4. Somebody has to pay for free e-mail, and its the advertisers.

Somebody has to pay for free e-mail, and it's the advertisers.

5. Both Joe and myself were late for the meeting.

Both Joe and I were late for the meeting.

6. The e-mail message, that just arrived, was confidential.

The e-mail message that just arrived was confidential.

7. Usually, theirs at least one person in a company that can access any password.

Usually, there's at least one person in a company who can access any password.

8. Our service provider which Jane and me have used since 1995 is located on Tenth Avenue.

Our service provider, which Jane and I have used since 1995, is located

on Tenth Avenue.

GO TO
CD-ROM
PRACTICE 2
EXERCISES

9. The responsibility for composing the e-mail to Japan was their's.

The responsibility for composing the e-mail to Japan was theirs.

10. The employees selected for promotions were Jacob and her.

The employees selected for promotions were Jacob and she.

PRACTICE 3A

PROOFREADING

The subject matter in the following sentences deals with electronic mail and its impact on society.

A. ***Directions:*** *Proofread and compare the two sentences in each group. If they are the same, write **Yes** in the space provided. If they are not the same, write **No**. Use the first sentence as the correct copy. If you find errors in the second sentence, underline them.*

1. Check the newsgroups option of your Internet and look at news.admin.net-abuse.misc, which is a discussion group that focuses on various forms of Internet abuse.

 Check the newsgroup option of your Internet and look at newsadmin.net-abuse.misc which is a discussion group that focusses on various forms of Internet abuse.

 1. __No__

2. The Electronic Communications Privacy Act allows employers the right to read their employees' e-mail messages.

 The Electronic Communications Privacy act allows employers the right to read there employee's e-mail messages.

 2. __No__

3. Some companies do not approve of the use of emoticons such as :-) (smiley, when turned on its side) or abbreviations such as FYI (for your information).

 Some companies do not approve of the use of emotions such as :-) (smily, when turned on its side or abbreviations such a FYI (for your information.)

 3. __No__

4. For local e-mail access, look up Internet Services in the Yellow Pages of your telephone directory.

 For local e-mail access, look up Internet Services in the Yellow Pages of your telephone directory.

 4. __Yes__

5. Before you send your message, double check the receiver's address because one transposed letter can cause your message to go to someone else.

 Before you send you message, double check the receivers address because one transposed letter can cause your message to go to someone else.

 5. __No__

NAME _____

6. The NetUSA Global Mail Service allows travelers to dial   6. ___No___
   local access numbers in 900 cities to connect to a NetUSA
   mail server so that the travelers can obtain their e-mail.

   The NetUSA Global Mail Service allows <u>travellers</u> to dial
   local access numbers in <u>800</u> cities to connect to a <u>Net USA</u>
   mail server so that the travelers can obtain their e-mail.

7. Some critical internal e-mail messages that were thought   7. ___No___
   to be deleted have been accessed and used in court.

   Some critical internal e-mail <u>massages</u> that were thought
   to be deleted have been <u>acessed</u> and used in court.

B. **Directions:** *Compare the three Internet addresses in each group below. If they are the same, write* **Yes** *in the space provided. If they are not the same, write* **No.** *Use the first address as the correct copy. If you find an error in the second address, underline the error.*

1. info@abqcvb.org   info@abqcvb.org   1. ___No___
   gotoalaska@aol.com   gotoalaska@aol.com
   76521.2250@wco.com   76521.<u>25</u>@wco.com

2. wildland@alaska.net   wildland@alaska.net   2. ___Yes___
   ecaide@ecnet.com   ecaide@ecnet.com
   abbourget@cvfm.org   abbourget@cvfm.org

3. JTWINT84@juno.com   JT<u>WIN</u>84@juno.com   3. ___No___
   GTILLEMA@INTERLOC.com   GTILLEMA@<u>interloc</u>.com
   Cvtgact@cfvn.org   <u>Ctvgact</u>@cfvn.org

Using Proofreaders' Marks

Directions: *A coworker asks you to proofread a copy of an e-mail notice that will be distributed to all employees. Use the following proofreaders' marks, and mark the errors in the document below.*

7-28 Proofreaders' marks are used for the first time.

delete ⌐ʒ
capitalize ≡   insert ∧
lowercase /   change a word ʒ or ——————

From: Jerry <u>w.</u> Smithfield
         ≡

Date: May 31, 199-

To: All Employees

Subject: Company Use of Emoticons

During ∧*the* past month, I have ~~receded~~ *received* many e-mail messages that
have included ∧Abbreviated ̸Terms. In an effort to ~~be~~ be sure W̸e all
understand and us∧e the same abbreviations, please check the
accepted company terms listed below:

PRACTICE

GO TO CD-ROM
PRACTICE 3
EXERCISES

FAQ	= frequently asked questions
RFC	= request for comments
FYI	= for your information
IMO	= in my opinion
MSgS	= messages
NLT	= no later than

please use these abbreviations for internal e-mail messages only.

PRACTICE 4A

WRITING

Composing E-mail Messages

7-29 Demonstrate the use of e-mail.

Electronic mail is an established method of business and personal communication. The following guidelines help in writing e-mail messages:

- Practice the same rules of writing that you would follow if you were sending the correspondence through traditional channels. Use correct grammar, spelling, and punctuation.
- Include a descriptive subject line, but limit it to 25-35 characters.
- Write concisely and briefly. Eliminate unnecessary phrases and trite expressions.
- Keep line length to 60 characters.
- State important information immediately. Begin with your purpose and include important details.
- Eliminate abbreviations or jargon.
- Avoid using all-capital letters, which have the effect of "screaming" to the reader.
- Omit sarcasm and too much humor.

GO TO CD-ROM
PRACTICE 4
EXERCISES

Answers will vary.

Directions: Compose an e-mail message to a friend explaining why it is necessary to have good English skills. Use at least six pronouns in the message. Print a copy of your message for your instructor to evaluate.

NAME _____

ONLINE EXERCISES

Millions of people have e-mail addresses on the Internet. Because no "phone books" exist for these millions of international e-mail addresses, Websites that search for names and addresses are becoming increasingly popular. You will visit two "people finders" that search for home addresses, yellow- and white-page services, Internet phone numbers, and e-mail providers.

Objective: *To visit a search site and locate the e-mail address of a friend.*

1. With your Internet browser on the screen, key:

   http://www.whowhere.com in the location text box. Press the **Enter** key on your keyboard.

2. If you have an e-mail address, key your own name in the **First Name** and **Last Name** boxes. Click on **Find.**

3. If you do not know anyone with an e-mail address, click on **Phone** and **Address** of a person you know who is listed in a phone book. Click on **Find.**

4. With your Internet browser on the screen, key:

   http://www.four11.com in the location text box. Press the **Enter** key on your keyboard.

5. Try to locate someone you know by searching. Key in the information as it is indicated on your screen.

7-30 Check online sites carefully before assigning them to students.

Use exact punctuation when typing an Internet address.

Answers will vary.

END-OF-CHAPTER WORKSHEETS

NAME _____

PRACTICE 1B

Directions: Draw a line under the correct word in parentheses.

1. Advertisers can e-mail (*their, there, they're*) solicitations by using (*their, there, they're*) subscriber lists from PostMaster Direct.

2. (*It's, Its, Its'*) interesting to see the names that people select for (*their, there, they're*) e-mail addresses.

3. After (*Zack and he, Zack and him*) corresponded about Sara's dismissal, they questioned (*we, us*) about privacy issues.

4. (*We, Us*) employees wanted (*Zoe and her, Zoe and she*) to give us e-mail writing tips.

5. Everyone understood the abbreviation FAQs (frequently asked questions) except (*me, I*).

> 7-31 In sentence 5, the word *except* functions as a preposition.

6. The supervisor asked two computer technicians, (*Joe and I, Joe and me*), for help with forwarding e-mail messages home.

7. Sherri is the student (*who, whom*) had an internship at Intel last summer.

8. Carolina, (*who, whom*) is originally from El Salvador, is an expert in translating Spanish correspondence.

9. The most recently hired employees—Bianca, Jack and (*I, me*)—need e-mail training this week.

10. Companies (*who, that*) do not have an e-mail policy should immediately put one in place.

11. If Richard is ill again today, we will need to ask (*him, he*) for (*his, he*) e-mail password.

12. (*Whose, Who's*) responsibility is it to delete (*your, you're*) e-mail messages?

13. The programmer (*who, whom*) wrote our e-mail software was happy to explain it to my office mate and (*me, I*).

14. (*He and I, Him and I*) receive at least 20 e-mail messages a day.

15. (*It's, Its, Its'*) unlikely I will respond to every e-mail message.

16. (*Abby and I, Abby and me*) started at Adobe Systems on the same day.

17. Teresa gave several Web addresses to (*she, her*).

18. (*Him and me, He and I*) asked how to advertise by e-mail without spamming.

19. (*Your, You're*) message should include only one topic.

20. (*Whose, Who's*) directory did you consult—(*theirs, their's, theirs'*) or mine?

PRACTICE 2B

A. Directions: In the following sentences, underline all pronouns and contractions. If a pronoun or contraction is used incorrectly, circle it and write the correct word in the space provided. More than one error may appear in a sentence. If the sentence is correct, write Yes.

1. These small stack of messages is mine, but the big stack is his.	1.	This
2. Barb was careless, and she missed correcting the errors in several of her documents.	2.	Yes
3. You should not use e-mail to send confidential information to someone.	3.	Yes
4. They're messages were so general; there was nothing specific in them.	4.	Their
5. We thought e-mail technology would give we paralegals more time for researching cases.	5.	us

NAME _____

6. As you receive messages, scan them and respond to them immediately if possible.   **6.** _____Yes_____

7. She overuses the boring line "First the good news, then the bad" in her messages.   **7.** _____Yes_____

8. (You're) password on our e-mail system expires in a month, and (its) time for you to choose another.   **8.** ___Your it's___

9. I tried attaching a file to your e-mail message, but it did not work.   **9.** _____Yes_____

10. We do not want Sandy or (he) to have access to our passwords.   **10.** _____him_____

11. After the manager and (him) agreed, they told us about monitoring our e-mail messages.   **11.** _____he_____

12. A subject for each of your e-mail messages is necessary for Roberto and (I.)   **12.** _____me_____

13. It must have been (her) who left her password next to my computer.   **13.** _____she_____

14. The employees (whom) use the Internet must use it for business purposes only.   **14.** _____who_____

15. On April 22, we expect to receive (you're) payment for software you ordered from our Boston store.   **15.** _____your_____

B. Directions: *The sentences below may have usage or punctuation errors. If the sentences are written correctly, write* **Yes** *in the space provided. If the sentence is written incorrectly, write it correctly in the space provided.*

1. When asked for her suggestions, Katy used the acronym IMO which means "in my opinion."

When asked for her suggestions, Katy used the acronym IMO, which means "in my opinion."

2. If you wish to keep you're correspondence confidential, do not use e-mail.

If you wish to keep your correspondence confidential, do not use e-mail.

3. Sarcasm is difficult to understand by people which live outside the United States.

People who live outside the United States have difficulty understanding our sarcasm.

4. Somebody left me hundreds of unwanted messages, and its not any of my friends, which left me these messages.

Somebody left me hundreds of unwanted messages, and it's not any of my friends who left me these messages.

5. Both Kara and myself were annoyed by the announcement.

Both Kara and I were annoyed by the announcement.

PRACTICE 3B

PROOFREADING

The subject matter in the following sentences deals with electronic mail and its impact on society.

Directions: *Proofread and compare the two sentences in each group. If they are the same, write* **Yes** *in the space provided. If they are not the same, write* **No.** *Use the first sentence as the correct copy. If you find errors in the second sentence, underline them.*

1. According to the employee handbook, the corporation's electronic mail system is business property, and it's to be used for business purposes.   **1.** _____No_____

According to the employee handbook the corporation's electronic mail system is business property and its to be used for business purposes.

NAME _____

2. E-mail can be a creative and social tool that should be used to tell workers about important events.

    E-mail can be a creative and social tool <u>which</u> should be used to tell <u>worker's</u> about important events.

2. _____No_____

3. Because of the way e-mail is transmitted through the Internet, parts of it may remain on every intermediate host computer through which it passes.

    Because of the way e-mail is transmitted through the Internet, parts of it <u>it</u> may remain on every intermediate host computer through which it passes.

3. _____No_____

4. Many times my daughter e-mails me homework that I am asked to review.

    Many times my daughter e-mails me homework that I am asked to review.

4. _____Yes_____

PRACTICE 4B

WRITING

Composing E-mail Messages

Directions: *Compose an e-mail message explaining how you would use e-mail to communicate. Print a copy for your instructor to evaluate.*

Answers will vary.

_____

_____

_____

ONLINE *EXERCISES*

Objective: *To send electronic postcards.*

1. With your Internet browser on the screen, key:

    http://www.bluemountain.com in the location text box and press the **Enter** key on your keyboard.

2. Follow the directions to create and personalize a postcard.

3. With your Internet browser on the screen, key:

    http://www.123greetings.com in the location text box and press **Enter.**

4. This Website gives you an opportunity to create additional personalized postcards. Follow the directions to create your electronic postcard and send it.

Answers will vary.

LOOKING BACK

Posttest

Directions: *In the space provided, write the letter of the correct answer.*

1. Which of the following is *not* a pronoun?   1. ___c___
   a. its   c. for
   b. her   d. whomever

2. Which statement is correct?   2. ___d___
   a. Molly and myself researched international e-mail netiquette.
   b. Molly and me researched international e-mail netiquette.
   c. Me and Molly researched international e-mail netiquette.
   d. Molly and I researched international e-mail netiquette.

3. Which statement is correct?   3. ___d___
   a. Lisa sends e-mail computer virus alerts to Luke and I once a week.
   b. Lisa sends e-mail computer virus alerts to I and Luke once a week.
   c. Lisa sends e-mail computer virus alerts to Luke and myself once a week.
   d. Lisa sends e-mail computer virus alerts to Luke and me once a week.

4. Which statement is correct?   4. ___b___
   a. Your asked to verify you're password before you use e-mail.
   b. You're asked to verify your password before you use e-mail.
   c. You're asked to verify you're password before you use e-mail.
   d. Your asked to verify your password before you use e-mail.

5. Which statement is correct?   5. ___a___
   a. Her password had expired when she and Stan returned from vacation.
   b. Taylor had to answer an e-mail message before her and Stan went to lunch.
   c. The instructor is assigning e-mail accounts for we communication students.
   d. The lack of computer time concerned the managers, Denny and he.

6. Which statement is correct?   6. ___a___
   a. I taught myself how to attach e-mail documents.
   b. He becomes irritated with hisself when he forgets an e-mail address.
   c. The students theirselves recognized the importance of using e-mail.
   d. Melissa and myself are experts in searching for e-mail addresses.

7. Which statement is correct?   7. ___b___
   a. Everyone whom was enrolled in the class knew how to use e-mail.
   b. Everyone who was enrolled in the class knew how to use e-mail.
   c. Everyone that enrolled in the class knew how to use e-mail.
   d. Everyone which enrolled in the class knows how to use e-mail.

8. Which statement is correct?   8. ___a___
   a. This was the e-mail policy that we signed.
   b. This here e-mail policy needs to be signed.
   c. Whose password do you think is better—his or hers'?
   d. Who's e-mail message shall I respond to first?

9. Which statement is correct?   9. ___b___
   a. To whose did you e-mail the contract?   c.   To who did you e-mail the contract?
   b. To whom did you e-mail the contract?   d.   Who did you e-mail the contract to?

10. Which of the following is a possessive pronoun?   10. ___d___
    a. her's
    b. they're
    c. there's
    d. its

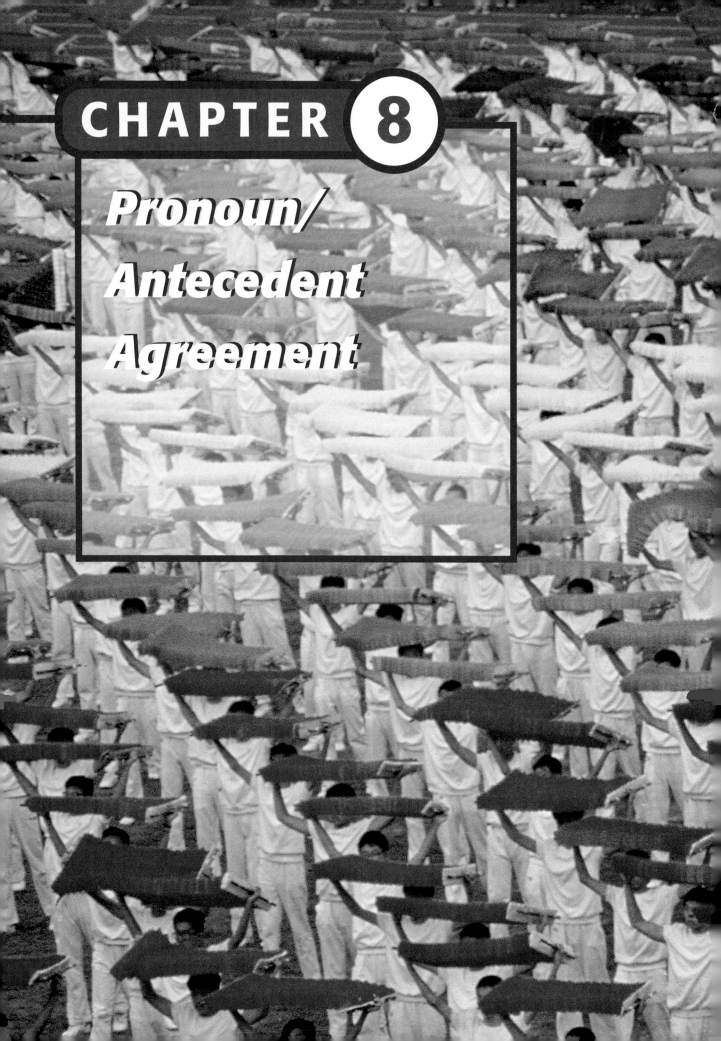

CHAPTER 8

Pronoun/ Antecedent Agreement

CULTURAL DIVERSITY

One factor leading to success in school or work is the acceptance of those who are "different" from you. *Cultural diversity* is the term used to name these differences. Cultural diversity is more than race or ethnicity, however. Cultural diversity also includes gender, age, religion, political orientation, physical size, and appearance. All these factors influence the cultural experiences and backgrounds of individuals and groups.

As life and work become more intertwined, people need a greater awareness of the ways that cultural heritage and background influence values, assumptions, and relationships. Some people do not realize that they exhibit biased behavior and may not be aware that their own behavior is offensive. Other people are aware of their biases and prejudices and know that their behavior offends others but still continue with derogatory jokes, comments, and actions. Still other people are willing to take action when they encounter inappropriate words or behaviors.

A good way to achieve an understanding of cultural diversity is to develop relationships with individuals who are culturally different. The more informed you are about different perspectives and lifestyles, the more marketable you will be in an increasingly diverse society and world. By appreciating the differences in others, you will be more successful in the diverse global workplace.

TERMS TO REMEMBER

CULTURAL DIVERSITY

CULTURAL HERITAGE

DEROGATORY

ETHNICITY

GENDER

OBJECTIVES

After you have studied this chapter and completed the exercises, you will be able to do the following:

1. Determine pronoun/antecedent agreement with reference to person, number, and gender.
2. Determine the correct use of singular or plural pronouns with compound subject antecedents.
3. Use the correct pronoun reference with collective antecedents.
4. Use appropriate singular and plural pronoun references with indefinite pronoun antecedents.
5. Correct unclear or dual pronoun references.
6. Identify explanatory phrases in determining antecedents.
7. Use correct pronoun forms with *than* and *as*.
8. Differentiate between one- and two-word indefinite pronouns.
9. Diagram sentences correctly.

LOOKING AHEAD

Pretest

Directions: In the space provided, write **Yes** if the pronoun and antecedent in the sentence are in agreement. If the pronoun is used incorrectly, underline the pronoun, and write the correction in the space provided.

1. Just because we have different backgrounds doesn't mean we have different goals.

   Yes

2. Whenever a diversity issue arises, a supervisor must look at <u>their</u> own attitudes.

   his or her

3. Educators and curriculum directors should develop new courses to help their students survive in a global market.

   Yes

4. When you plan to do business with a foreign company, you must participate in <u>their</u> traditions.

   its

5. Many poorly educated women obtain low-skilled service jobs to support <u>her</u> families.

   their

6. If we laugh at racial or gender jokes, <u>you</u> give our children the idea that this is acceptable behavior.

   we

7. My coworkers said that they had trouble communicating with foreign clients especially when <u>they</u> didn't know the language.

   The coworkers or the clients

8. Kristen, as well as Maria, was concerned about <u>their</u> child care costs.

   her

9. I think Ray still receives more money than <u>me</u>.

   I

10. <u>Every one</u> should be present for his or her cultural diversity orientation.

   Everyone

OVERVIEW

Now that you have been introduced to pronouns, you should use them correctly in sentences. Pronouns are not always specific in their meaning; therefore, they may cause problems when it is unclear as to whom or to what these pronouns are referring. You've probably experienced this frustration in following printed instructions such as those found in computer manuals or in assembling children's toys or furniture. Even when the parts are all there, you may not be sure to what the words *it* or *them* refer.

Your readers should not have to second-guess your intent or take a chance on what you actually mean by your pronoun references. In this chapter, you will determine ways to make these references clear. You will also study several additional pronoun troublespots.

PRONOUN/ ANTECEDENT AGREEMENT

An *antecedent* is the word or group of words to which a personal pronoun refers or that a personal pronoun replaces. A pronoun must give accurate and unmistakable reference to the noun or other pronoun it replaces. In other words, the pronoun must agree with its antecedent in *number* (singular, plural), *gender* (masculine, feminine, neuter), and *person* (first, second, third).

See Instructor Notes 8-1, 8-2, and 8-3 in IAE.
Go to Transparencies/PowerPoints 8-1a, 8-1b, and 8-2.

First *person refers to the one speaking,* second *person refers to the one spoken to, and* third *person refers to the one spoken about.*

Noun as Antecedent

Strong <u>individuals</u> understand <u>their</u> strengths and weaknesses.
(The antecedent is *individuals,* a third-person plural noun. The third-person plural pronoun *their* is necessary when referring to this antecedent.)

<u>Janet</u> remarked that <u>she</u> had benefited from affirmative action.
(The antecedent is *Janet,* a third-person singular noun. The third-person singular pronoun *she* is necessary when referring to this antecedent.)

Go to Transparency/PowerPoint 8-3.

Pronoun as Antecedent

<u>We</u> need a clear idea of what is expected of <u>us</u>.
(The antecedent is *we,* a first-person plural pronoun. The first-person plural pronoun *us* is necessary when referring to this antecedent.)

<u>He</u> expects to have <u>his</u> views considered by the board.
(The antecedent is *he,* a third-person singular pronoun. The third-person singular pronoun *his* is necessary when referring to this antecedent.)

Go to Transparency/PowerPoint 8-4.

Steps for Determining Antecedent Agreement

See Instructor Note 8-4 in IAE.

While you are learning to locate the antecedents and the referenced pronouns, follow these steps to be sure that these two areas are in agreement:

1. Identify the pronoun.
2. Decide to whom or to what the pronoun refers or what it replaces—the antecedent.
3. Identify the person (first, second, third); gender (masculine, feminine, neuter); and number (singular, plural) of the antecedent.
4. Identify the person, gender, and number of the referenced pronoun.
5. Determine if the person, gender, and number are the same for the pronoun and the antecedent. If they are, you have agreement. If they are not the same, you have a correction to make.
6. Continue the process with any remaining pronouns in the sentence.

Person

See Instructor Note 8-5 in IAE.

Refer to Chapter 7 for a chart of first-, second-, and third-person pronouns.

The three persons are *first, second,* and *third.* Follow the preceding steps to be sure you have pronoun and antecedent agreement in person.

First Person. Use a first-person pronoun if you have an antecedent that refers to the *person* or *persons speaking.*

I become angry when people laugh at my accent.
Identify the pronoun: *my*
Reference to: *I*
Antecedent: *I*—first person
Pronoun: *my*—first person
Agreement: yes

We perceive situations from our cultural backgrounds.
(The pronoun *our* refers to the antecedent *we* [another pronoun]. Both are first-person pronouns. They are in agreement.)

Second Person. Use a second-person pronoun if you have an antecedent that refers to the *person* or *persons spoken to.*

You may want to discuss your plans for decreasing employee tensions in the workplace.
Identify the pronoun: *your*
Reference to: *you*
Antecedent: *you*—second person
Pronoun: *your*—second person
Agreement: yes

When you show signs of insecurity, your credibility lessens in some people's eyes.
(The pronoun *your* refers to another pronoun *you.* Both are second-person pronouns. They are in agreement.)

Third Person. Use a third-person pronoun if you have an antecedent that refers to the *person* or *thing spoken about.*

> <u>Affirmative action</u> is not dead, but it is not as effective as <u>it</u> was in earlier years.
> Identify the pronoun: *it*
> Reference to: *affirmative action*
> Antecedent: *affirmative action*—third person
> Pronoun: *it*—third person
> Agreement: yes

> The women's movement focuses on the <u>career woman</u> and <u>her</u> problems in the workplace.

(The pronoun *her* refers to the antecedent *career woman.* Both are third-person pronouns. They are in agreement.)

> Many <u>managers</u> are out of touch with <u>their</u> employees' problems.

(The pronoun *their* refers to the antecedent *managers.* Both are third-person pronouns. They are in agreement.)

CHECKUP 8-1

Directions: Underline each antecedent once and its personal pronoun reference twice.

1. <u>Connie</u> indicated that it was <u>her</u> competence that employers appreciated.

2. Summer classes are usually smaller; therefore, <u>you</u> will have more opportunities to talk with <u>your</u> instructors.

3. <u>Women</u> often experience more pay discrimination than <u>their</u> male coworkers.

4. <u>People</u> should concentrate on what <u>they</u> have in common.

5. Terry resists <u>change</u> as well as the methods to bring <u>it</u> about.

6. <u>David Wing</u> earns <u>his</u> living explaining American customs to foreign businesspeople.

**GO TO
CD-ROM**
CHECKUP 8-1

Gender

The three genders are *masculine* and *feminine* (referring to persons) and *neuter* (referring to things). Follow the steps listed previously to be sure you have pronoun and antecedent agreement in gender.

Feminine and Masculine Gender. Use a *feminine* pronoun (*she, her*) when the pronoun definitely refers to a feminine antecedent. Use a *masculine* pronoun (*he, his, him*) when the pronoun definitely refers to a masculine antecedent.

Carol was used to working alone and finishing <u>her</u> work ahead of schedule.
Identify the pronoun: *her*
Reference to: *Carol*
Antecedent: *Carol*—third person, feminine gender
Pronoun: *her*—third person, feminine gender
Agreement: yes

Go to PowerPoints 8-5a and 8-5b.

<u>Marita</u> will begin to trust the system when <u>she</u> begins to feel included.
(The pronoun *she* refers to the antecedent *Marita*. Both are third person, feminine gender. They are in agreement.)

<u>Dennis</u> decided that <u>his</u> negative stereotypes of immigrants were inaccurate.
(The pronoun *his* refers to the antecedent *Dennis*. Both are third person, masculine gender. They are in agreement.)

What did <u>he</u> mean by <u>his</u> statement that Mary had an attitude problem?
(The pronoun *his* refers to the antecedent he. Both are third person, masculine gender. They are in agreement.)

Neuter Gender.   Use a neuter gender pronoun (*it, its*) to refer to an antecedent that represents things rather than persons.

The best way to solve a <u>problem</u> is to identify <u>its</u> cause.
Pronoun: *its*
Reference to: *problem*
Antecedent: *problem*—third person, neuter gender
Pronoun: *its*—third person, neuter gender
Agreement: yes

<u>Diversity training</u> is a waste of time if <u>it</u> is done hurriedly with no follow-through sessions.
(The pronoun *it* refers to the antecedent *diversity training*. Both are third person, neuter gender. They are in agreement.)

Regardless of the <u>message,</u> most foreign workers prefer to hear <u>it</u> in person.
(The pronoun *it* refers to the antecedent *message*. Both are third person, neuter gender. They are in agreement.)

See Instructor Note 8-6 in IAE.

Unknown Gender.   Use both masculine and feminine pronouns (*he or she, his or her*) when you do not know the gender of the antecedent or when you want to refer to a common gender antecedent such as *employee, instructor,* or *student.* Do not overuse these combinations. Make the pronouns and the antecedents plural, and rephrase the sentence if a sentence sounds awkward using both the masculine and feminine pronouns.

We planned to interview the candidate to see if he or she had the necessary language skills.

Pronouns: *he, she*
Reference to: *candidate*
Antecedent: *candidate*—third person, common gender
Pronouns: *he* and *she*—third person, masculine and feminine genders
Agreement: yes

Do you believe that how a person acts is how he or she wants to be treated?

(The pronouns *he* or *she* refer to the common gender antecedent person. All are third person. The antecedent *person* may be masculine or feminine. The pronouns *he* and *she* are appropriate. They are in agreement.)

Do you believe that how people act is how they want to be treated?

(Compare this sentence to the one above. The pronoun *they* refers to the antecedent *people*. Both are third-person pronouns. The sentence is less awkward, and it expresses the same message.)

The average salesperson is not successful unless he or she understands the customer's culture.

(The pronouns *he* and *she* refer to *salesperson*.)

Average salespeople are not successful unless they understand the customer's culture.

(The pronoun *they* refers to *salespeople*. Rephrasing the sentence eliminates the awkwardness of the *he* or *she* combination.)

Number

In addition to person and gender, you must be aware of pronoun number. The two choices are *singular* and *plural*. Follow the steps listed previously to be sure that you have pronoun and antecedent agreement in number.

Refer to the pronoun chart in Chapter 7.

Singular and Plural. Use a singular pronoun (*he, she, him, her, his, it*) if you use a singular antecedent. Use a plural pronoun (*they, their, them*) if you use a plural antecedent.

Heather claimed that management's failure to listen to her harassment complaint caused her to file a lawsuit.

Pronoun: *her, her*
Reference to: *Heather*
Antecedent: *Heather*—third person, singular form
Pronoun: *her*—third person, singular form
Agreement: yes

(The pronoun *her* refers to the antecedent *Heather.* Both are third-person singular forms. They are in agreement.)

Most employees expect to have their views considered.

(The pronoun *their* refers to the antecedent *employees.* Both are third-person plural forms. They are in agreement.)

Young workers may not realize the seriousness of their early drug abuse until they are older.

(The pronouns *their* and *they* refer to the antecedent *workers*. All are third-person plural forms. They are in agreement.)

Our cultural diversity committee made several recommendations, and management is seriously considering them.

(The pronoun *them* refers to the antecedent *recommendations*. Both are third-person plural forms. They are in agreement.)

CHECKUP 8-2

A. Directions: *Complete each sentence by adding a personal pronoun that agrees with the antecedent. Underline the antecedent.*

Ex.: Some people are not aware of how ____**their**____ behavior affects ____**their**____ coworkers.

1. Sue Chin believes ____her____ analytical abilities will make ____her____ successful.

2. Diversity does not refer to race and ethnicity only; ____it____ also includes age, gender, religion, and education.

3. Will the candidate and ____his or her____ spouse be able to survive a year in Malawi?

4. The first step was to ask employees to share ____their____ feelings about diversity.

5. Immigrant workers often feel ____they____ do not get the help ____they____ need when ____they____ first begin working in a U.S. firm.

6. Laura looked for traits that ____she____ had in common with ____her____ diverse group of friends.

7. Armando could not understand why ____his____ coworkers were displeased with ____his____ slower working pace.

8. Diversity training is not an event; ____it____ is an ongoing process.

9. When we stereotype individuals, we expect ____them____ to act according to those standards.

10. Companies are finding that ____they____ must share ____their____ goals and expectations with ____their____ employees.

B. Directions: *In the space provided, write a sentence using each of the following words from the Terms to Remember. Use examples of pronoun and antecedent agreement in each of your sentences.*

1. cultural diversity — Marvin discussed cultural diversity in his research paper.

2. cultural heritage — Debbie was proud of her cultural heritage.

3. derogatory — Arlene made a derogatory remark to her coworker.

4. ethnicity — Tamika was aware of her ethnicity.

5. gender — Roberto studied pronoun gender in his English class.

SLIP-UP

Sign in a Moscow hotel: If this is your first visit to the USSR, you are welcome to it. [Is the hotel giving the country away?]

See Instructor Note 8-7 in IAE.

Answers will vary.

GO TO CD-ROM CHECKUP 8-2

Compound Antecedents

Go to PowerPoint 8-6.

A compound subject consists of two or more persons, places, things, activities, ideas, or qualities. When the antecedent is a compound subject, the connecting word (*and, or, nor*) determines whether the pronoun is singular or plural.

Joined by *And.* Use a plural pronoun to refer to two or more antecedents (compound subject) joined by the word *and.*

> Massachusetts and Missouri allow their state employees to work four 10-hour days.
> (The plural pronoun *their* refers to two antecedents joined by *and.*)

> David and Inez realized that their work habits caused the team's delay.
> (*David* and *Inez* are third-person antecedents joined by *and.* These antecedents require the plural pronoun *their* for agreement.)

See Instructor Note 8-8 in IAE.

> Molly and Denise are presenting their diversity awareness workshop tomorrow.
> (*Molly* and *Denise* are third-person antecedents joined by *and.* These antecedents require the plural pronoun *their* for agreement.)

Use a singular pronoun reference when one person holds the two positions. Note that the article the appears before the first title only. The omission of an article before the second title indicates that this person is the diversity management director as well as the trainer.

Do This	Do Not Do This
The diversity management director and trainer scheduled his or her presentations.	The diversity management director and trainer scheduled their presentations.

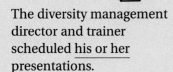

Do This	Do Not Do This
The diversity management director and the trainer scheduled their presentations.	The diversity management director and the trainer scheduled his or her presentations.

Use a plural pronoun when there are two positions held by two different people. Note that the article the appears before both titles. The repetition of the article indicates two people and two positions are involved.

See Instructor Notes 8-9 and 8-10 in IAE.

Joined by *Or* or *Nor.* Use a singular pronoun to refer to two singular antecedents joined by *or* or *nor.* Use a plural pronoun to refer to two plural antecedents joined by *or* or *nor.*

> Katie or Wanda will discuss the unfair treatment with her supervisor.
> (Two third-person singular feminine antecedents joined by *or* require a third-person singular feminine pronoun reference.)

Neither Dawn nor Simone seemed motivated by an increase in her paycheck.
(Two singular antecedents joined by *nor* require a singular pronoun reference.)

Neither diversity training classes nor social occasions accomplished their purpose of lessening racial tensions.
(Two plural antecedents joined by *nor* require a plural pronoun reference.)

Closed minds or unfair stereotypes take their toll on workers.
(Two plural antecedents joined by *or* require a plural pronoun reference.)

See Instructor Note 8-11 in IAE.

Joined by *Or* or *Nor*—Special Cases. Use a pronoun that agrees in number with the closer antecedent when a singular antecedent and a plural antecedent are joined by *or* or *nor*. Reword the sentence to make it sound less awkward when necessary.

Neither Cassie nor her coworkers were aware of their prejudices.
(The pronoun must agree with the closer antecedent, which is *coworkers*. *Coworkers* is plural; therefore, the necessary pronoun must also be plural.)

The division manager or the team leaders had to devise their strategies for hiring additional personnel.
(The pronoun *their* is closer to the antecedent *team leaders*.)

Neither the project workers nor the project leader was aware that his or her problems were caused by cultural differences.
(Even though this sentence is correctly written according to the *or/nor* rule, the sentence sounds awkward. Rewrite the sentence to place the plural antecedent closer to the pronoun.)

Neither the project leader nor the project workers were aware that their problems were caused by cultural differences.
(The rewritten sentence places the plural antecedent closer to the pronoun.)

CHECKUP 8-3

Directions: *Check the underlined word(s) for pronoun usage. If the pronoun is used correctly, write **Yes** in the space provided. If it is not used correctly, write the correct pronoun.*

1. Neither the supervisor nor the employees wanted to see their cultural diversity training opportunities discontinued.

   Yes

2. Mr. Brown and a student will be participating in his college's Cultural Awareness Day.

   their

3. Sue and her classmates misinterpreted their instructor's comments about cultural differences.

   Yes

4. Either June or Carolyn will be available to assist the new employee in any way <u>they</u> can.

<u>she</u>

5. Randy or Hank will speak about <u>their</u> experiences growing up in segregated Mississippi.

<u>his</u>

6. Neither the cultural diversity author nor the trainers were able to identify the sources for <u>his</u> statistics.

<u>their</u>

GO TO
CD-ROM
CHECKUP 8-3

Collective Antecedents

A collective antecedent refers to a group of people such as a committee, class, board, or jury. A collective antecedent is neuter in gender.

With Groups.   Use a singular pronoun reference when the collective antecedent is acting as a group. Use a plural pronoun reference when the members within the group are acting individually.

See Instructor Note 8-12 in IAE.

At <u>its</u> meeting, the <u>Cultural Awareness Committee</u> will make <u>its</u> recommendations.
(The collective antecedent, *Cultural Awareness Committee,* is acting as one group.)

Every <u>group</u> has a culture that identifies <u>its</u> values.
(The collective antecedent *group* is acting as one body.)

When a <u>team</u> finishes a major portion of <u>its</u> project, <u>it</u> should celebrate.
(The team is acting as a group in its celebration.)

The <u>faculty</u> were not unanimous in <u>their</u> voting to offer a program in cultural diversity.
(The members of the faculty acted individually in voting.)

A collective antecedent requires an analysis of the intent of the sentence. Is the antecedent acting as a group, or are the members of the group acting individually?

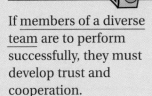

Do This	Do Not Do This
If <u>members</u> of a diverse <u>team</u> are to perform successfully, they must develop trust and cooperation.	If a <u>diverse team</u> are to perform successfully, they must develop trust and cooperation.

Reword a sentence if the plural pronoun sounds awkward. Instead, use members of such groups as the faculty, organization, firm, or board.

With Companies and Organizations.   In most cases, use a singular pronoun reference with antecedents that are companies and organizations.

StrideRight has a center that cares for the children as well as the elderly relatives of <u>its</u> workers.
(The company *StrideRight* requires a singular pronoun.)

Refer to the section on organizational and company names in a reference manual such as The Gregg Reference Manual for additional references.

Firstar International sent **its** managers to Switzerland for a trial work period.

(The company *Firstar International* requires a singular pronoun.)

See Instructor Note 8-13 in IAE.

The Museum of Black Inventors displays **its** photographs and documents in an interesting manner.

(The organization *The Museum of Black Inventors* requires a singular pronoun.)

Do This	Do Not Do This
The International Institute is offering its cultural survey to companies without charge. It hopes to receive some useful feedback.	The International Institute is offering its cultural survey to companies without charge. They hope to receive some useful feedback.

Use the pronoun consistently within a paragraph.

CHECKUP 8-4

Directions: Check the underlined word(s) for correct pronoun usage. If the pronoun is used correctly, write Yes in the space provided. If it is not used correctly, write the correct pronoun.

1. The Firefly Acts Company will present their interactive sessions on stereotypes and conflict.   _its_

2. TFC Corporation has to remind their employees to ask questions about how to do a task.   _its_

3. The Jones Company offers benefits to their employees worldwide.   _its_

4. The department demonstrated its ability to bounce back after several unfortunate multicultural incidents.   _Yes_

5. The firm realized how much their employees contributed to the bottom line.   _its_

6. How successful are the staff in its relationships with older workers?   _their_

GO TO CD-ROM

CHECKUP 8-4

Indefinite Pronoun Antecedents

Some indefinite pronouns are always singular; others are always plural. Several are either singular or plural depending on their context in the sentences. Indefinite pronouns are third-person pronouns. When indefinite pronouns are used as antecedents, appropriate third-person pronouns must be used in reference to them.

Indefinite Pronouns (always singular)		Indefinite Pronouns (always plural)	
another	many a	both	others
anybody	much	few	several
anyone	neither	many	
anything	nobody		
each	no one	**Indefinite Pronouns** (singular or plural)	
each one	nothing		
either	one	all	most
enough	other	any	none
every	somebody	more	some
everybody	someone		
everyone	something		
everything			

Third-person pronouns are he, she, it, they, them, his, her, him, hers, their, theirs, its.

Singular Indefinite Pronouns.

Use a singular personal pronoun reference when the antecedent is a singular indefinite pronoun. Ignore an intervening prepositional phrase when locating the antecedent. The words *each* and *every* often function as adjectives in sentences.

Prepositional phrases begin with a preposition and end with a noun or pronoun. Refer to Chapter 2 for a review of prepositions.

Everyone should appreciate his or her ethnic values.
(*Everyone* is a singular pronoun antecedent that requires the singular pronoun reference *his or her.*)

Neither of the two women testified against her supervisor.
(*Neither* is a singular indefinite pronoun that requires the singular pronoun reference *her.* Remove the prepositional phrase *of the two women* to determine the antecedent.)

Refer to the section on indefinite pronoun agreement in a reference manual such as The Gregg Reference Manual for additional examples.

No one should ever feel that his or her heritage is unimportant.
(*No one* is a singular indefinite pronoun that is always two words. No one requires the singular pronoun reference *his or her.*)

Every company needs legal advice when writing its sexual harassment policy.
(The singular indefinite pronoun *every* functions as an adjective in this sentence. *Company* is the antecedent, and it requires the singular reference pronoun *its.*)

Plural Indefinite Pronouns.

Use a plural personal pronoun reference when the antecedent is a plural indefinite pronoun. Ignore intervening prepositional phrases when locating the antecedent.

Both of the new workers handle their disabilities without problems.
(*Both* is a plural pronoun antecedent and requires the plural pronoun reference *their.* To locate the antecedent, eliminate the prepositional phrase *of the new workers.*)

Several of the new ethnic groups want to make their identities known in the workplace.
(To locate the antecedent, eliminate the prepositional phrase, *of the new ethnic groups. Several* is a plural pronoun antecedent and requires the plural pronoun reference *their.*)

Many of the foreign-born workers have done similar work in **their** home countries.

(*Many* is a plural pronoun antecedent and requires the plural pronoun reference *their*.)

Only a **few** of the applicants listed **their** ethnic backgrounds on the employment forms.

(*Few* is the plural pronoun antecedent and requires the plural pronoun reference *their*.)

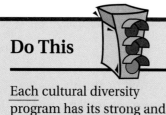

Do This	**Do Not Do This**
Each cultural diversity program has **its** strong and weak points.	**Each** cultural diversity program has **their** strong and weak points.

*Do not use a plural pronoun reference with a singular indefinite pronoun used as an adjective. In this sentence, **each**, a singular indefinite pronoun, is used as an adjective.*

See Instructor Note 8-14 in IAE.

Memorize the six indefinite pronouns that may be singular or plural. They are all, any, more, most, none, and some. Pay particular attention to the context of the sentence when you use these six pronouns.

Singular or Plural Indefinite Pronouns. Use an appropriate personal pronoun when the antecedent may be singular or plural. Determining whether the antecedent is singular or plural depends on the context of the sentence.

All of the legal material from the discrimination case is in **its** appropriate folder.

(*All* is an indefinite pronoun used as a singular antecedent. *All* refers to legal material [singular] and requires a singular pronoun [*its*] reference.)

All of the managers working in foreign countries received **their** employment instructions.

(*All* is an indefinite pronoun used as a plural antecedent. *All* refers to managers [plural] and requires a plural pronoun [*their*] reference.)

Most of the article is written, but **it** requires a check for gender bias.

(*Most* is an indefinite pronoun used as a singular antecedent. *Most* refers to *article* [singular] and requires a singular pronoun [*it*] reference.)

Most of the authors writing today have carefully checked **their** articles to avoid gender bias.

(*Most* is an indefinite pronoun used as a plural antecedent. *Most* refers to *authors* [plural] and requires a plural pronoun [*their*] reference.)

A. Directions: *Underline the antecedent in each of the following sentences. In the space provided, identify the antecedent as being singular or plural. Use* **S** *for singular antecedents, or* **P** *for plural antecedents.*

1. All of the workers have to understand basic instructions from their supervisors. ___P___

2. Everyone can learn to improve his or her interpersonal skills when dealing with culture clashes. ___S___

3. Several of my coworkers seem to live up to their own low expectations. ___P___

4. Both of the men hesitated to report their health-related problems to their supervisors. ___P___

5. A few of the smaller companies are recognizing that they need alternative work schedules for their employees. ___P___

6. Some of the workers presented their reports last Friday. ___P___

B. Directions: *In the space provided, rephrase the sentences to avoid the use of* **he or she** *and* **his or her.**   Answers will vary.

1. No one should feel that his or her contribution to the project is unimportant.

   The contribution of every person is important to the project.

2. Someone with a disability may need his or her workstation adjusted.

   Employees with disabilities may need their workstations adjusted.

3. Everyone should review his or her copy of the diversity policy in the handbook.

   All of us should review the diversity policy in the handbook.

4. If anybody would like to serve on the Cultural Diversity Committee, he or she should see Barb Johnson.

   Contact Barb Johnson if you would like to serve on the Cultural Diversity Committee.

**GO TO
CD-ROM
CHECKUP 8-5**

REFERENCE PRONOUN CLARITY

If you want your writing to be clear, you must make sure that the antecedent of a pronoun is clear and that a pronoun cannot possibly refer to more than one antecedent.

Use of *They, You, It*

Avoid the use of the pronouns *they, you,* and *it* unless you are very specific in identifying the antecedent. The following sentences are examples of faulty construction:

> **We never discuss religion because <u>they</u> become very opinionated.**
>
> (Substitute *my coworkers* or *my friends* for *they.*)

Before the meeting, they decided to picket the area.
(Substitute *union members* or *the employees* for *they*.)

The newer groups of immigrants tend to seek jobs where you do not need to speak English.
(Substitute *they, workers,* or *employees* for *you*.)

It says that the costs of training our future employees is going to increase.
(*It* is not specific. Substitute *the article* or *the report* for the pronoun *it*.)

Explanatory Phrases

See Instructor Note 8-15 in IAE.

Do not consider such explanatory phrases as *in addition to, as well as,* or *together with* when identifying an antecedent.

Support staff, as well as managers, can work in their homes rather than commute to the office.
(The antecedent is *support staff.* The phrase *as well as managers* is not considered.)

Managers, in conjunction with a trainer, should develop interactive diversity sessions for their project leaders.
(The antecedent is *managers.* The phrase *in conjunction with a trainer* is not considered.

Toni, as well as her sister, is working in her home rather than commuting to the office.
(The antecedent is *Toni.* The phrase *as well as her sister* is not considered.)

Unclear Reference

Reword a sentence if a pronoun seems to refer to more than one antecedent.

Supervisors who observe certain drug-related symptoms in their employees should report them to trained professionals.
(Are the supervisors reporting the symptoms, or are the supervisors reporting the employees?)
Rewritten:
Supervisors who observe certain drug-related symptoms in their employees should report these employees to trained professionals.
or
Supervisors who observe certain drug-related symptoms in their employees should report the symptoms to trained professionals.

The city of Cleveland publishes its multicultural guidebook every year. It has several ethnic points of interest.
(Does *it* refer to the city of Cleveland or the guidebook?)
Rewritten:
The multicultural guidebook that is published every year by the city of Cleveland includes several ethnic points of interest.
or
The city of Cleveland has several ethnic points of interest that are included in its yearly multicultural guidebook.

Companies send workers all over the world, but they give little thought to how <u>they</u> will make adjustments.

(Are the companies making the adjustments or are the workers going to be making the adjustments?)

Rewritten:

Companies send workers all over the world, but they give little thought to how <u>these workers</u> will adjust.

or

Companies send workers all over the world, but <u>these companies</u> give little thought to how they will help their workers adjust.

Lea had to keep reminding her boss that she had a Cultural Awareness Committee meeting this afternoon.

(Who had the meeting—Lea or her boss?)

Rewritten:

Lea had a Cultural Awareness Committee meeting this afternoon and had to keep reminding her boss that she would be leaving to attend the meeting.

or

Mrs. Ruiz, Lea's boss, had a Cultural Awareness Committee meeting this afternoon, and Lea had to keep reminding her about this meeting.

CHECKUP 8-6

Directions: *In the space provided, rewrite the sentences that are vague or unclear or that have incorrect reference pronouns. If the sentence is correct, write* **Yes.**

Answers will vary.

1. Adruf's emotional outburst and Tom's objections made me realize he had a point.
   Adruf's emotional outburst and Tom's objections made me realize <u>Adruf</u> had a point.
   Adruf's emotional outburst and Tom's objections made me realize <u>Tom</u> had a point.

2. MCI in conjunction with the International Institute of Minnesota started a training course for their newest Spanish-speaking bank tellers.
   MCI in conjunction with the International Institute of Minnesota started a training course for <u>its</u> newest Spanish-speaking bank tellers.

3. The manager told Jerry that he was not focusing on this particular problem.
   The manager was not focusing on this particular problem, and he told this to Jerry.
   The manager told Jerry that Jerry was not focusing on this particular problem.

4. They said that the number of working women with children under one year had increased.
   (The speaker, The researchers) said that the number of working women with children under one year had increased.

5. Conflict occurred because Jamie thought Shelley should do her share of the work.
   Conflict occurred because Jamie thought Shelley should share the workload.
   Conflict occurred because Jamie thought Shelley also should do Jamie's work.

6. The general managers as well as the union president voiced their objections about the gender job title discrepancies.
   Yes

GO TO CD-ROM
CHECKUP 8-6

Several pronoun areas require special attention.

Pronouns After *Than* and *As*

In an incomplete adverb clause using *than* or *as,* choose the case of the pronoun that you would use if the missing word were present.

> **I do not have the same language pronunciation difficulties <u>as you</u>.**
> (I do not have the same language pronunciation difficulties as you *have.*)

> **The employees at our European branch office are much more relaxed <u>than we</u>.**
> (The employees at our European branch office are much more relaxed than we *are.*)

> **In spite of her handicap, she can complete the work faster than <u>I</u>.**
> (In spite of her handicap, she can complete the work faster than I *can complete it.*)

> **My manager likes me better than <u>her</u>.**
> (My manager likes me better than *he likes* her.)

> **Discriminatory practices affected Juan more than <u>me</u>.**
> (Discriminatory practices affected Juan more than *they* affected me.)

One or Two Words

Write the words *every one* and *any one* as two words when they precede an *of* phrase. At all other times, write them as one word (*everyone, anyone*). *No one* is always two words.

> **<u>Everyone</u> is invited to hear Marshall speak about his year of work in Russia.**
> (There is no *of* phrase following *everyone. Everyone* is one word.)

> **<u>Every one</u> of the attendees enjoyed hearing Marshall speak about his experiences while working in Russia.**
> (*Every one* is two words. Note that these words precede an *of* phrase.)

> **If <u>anyone</u> has a concern with the gender equity policy, <u>he or she</u> should contact me by Friday.**
> (There is no *of* phrase following *anyone. Anyone* is one word. Note the singular pronoun reference *he or she.*)

> **<u>Any one</u> of these concerns will require attention by management.**
> (*Any one* is two words. Note that these words precede an *of* phrase.)

Each Other/One Another

Use *each other* when you refer to two persons or things. Use *one another* when you refer to more than two persons or things.

Before team members with diverse interests can work on the team's objectives, they must get to know <u>one another</u>.

Did it take time for the French and American workers to get to know <u>one another</u>?

Matt and I discovered that our biases interfered with our ability to listen to <u>each other</u> effectively.

CHECKUP 8-7

Directions: *Select the correct word in parentheses, and write it in the space provided.*

1. Stereotypes and prejudices cause many of us to have distorted visions of (*each other, one another*).   <u>one another</u>

2. A trait displayed by one person in a group does not mean that it is indicative of (*every one, everyone*) in the group.   <u>everyone</u>

3. Excessive bragging bothers my Asian friends as much as (*I, me*).   <u>me</u>

4. (*Anyone, Any one*) of several employees could have reported the drug use problem to the supervisor.   <u>Any one</u>

5. Robin is as capable as (*I, me*), but she didn't get the promotion.   <u>I</u>

6. You understand instructions better than (*her, she*).   <u>she</u>

GO TO CD-ROM
CHECKUP 8-7

DIAGRAMMING SENTENCES

Adjectives describe nouns or pronouns. Some pronouns function as adjectives in a sentence. Possessive nouns and pronouns also function as adjectives.

To diagram a sentence with an adjective, place the adjective on a slanted line beneath the noun or pronoun it modifies. *A, an*, and *the* also function as adjectives.

Different customs can create some awkward social situations.

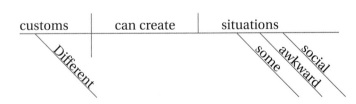

See Instructor Note 8-16 in IAE.

Review the diagramming of possessive nouns in Chapter 5.

Directions: *In the space provided, diagram the following sentences. Use all words in these sentences for diagramming.*

1. All college business majors take one cultural diversity course.

2. The negotiating committee disagreed and tabled the controversial material.

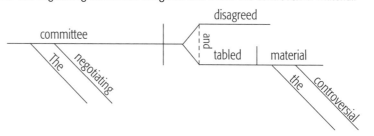

3. The company's sexual harassment policy was fair.

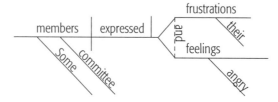

4. Most new employees accept the company's benefit package.

5. Some committee members expressed their frustrations and angry feelings.

GO TO
CD-ROM
CHECKUP 8-8

NAME _____

PRACTICE 1A

Directions: *In each of the following sentences, underline the antecedents once and the pronoun references twice.*

1. Charles Brown received one of the community service awards for his work in basic skills education.

2. Either the St. Louis Museum or the Washington Museum keeps its black history week activities on tape.

3. The U.S. Immigration and Naturalization Service released its statistics about Middle East immigrants.

4. One survey indicates that Texas, along with 12 other states, finds it must provide remedial education for government workers.

5. Tamiko appreciated having her supervisor greet her in Japanese.

6. You should learn at least 500 words in several languages if you get a job that requires interaction with foreign clients.

7. A supervisor should create an environment where people can show their true feelings.

8. J. J. Lewis, director of human resources, submitted his report on promotion and attrition rates.

9. A trainer should understand the type of disabilities he or she is likely to find in the workplace.

10. If you are working for a supervisor from another country, you should not expect constant complimentary feedback.

**GO TO
CD-ROM**
PRACTICE 1
EXERCISES

PRACTICE 2A

Exercise 1

Directions: *Complete each sentence by adding a personal pronoun that agrees with the antecedent. Underline the antecedent or antecedents in each sentence.*

1. Most of the African-American employees stated that ____they____ had graduated from inner-city schools.

2. Before receiving the company's sexual harassment policy, each employee had to sign for ____his or her____ copy.

3. The Texas Hotel and Motel Association in partnership with two colleges is promoting ____its____ Hispanic hospitality training program.

4. The United States, from ____its____ very beginnings, has been proud of ____its____ diversity.

5. An <u>instructor</u> brings <u>his or her</u> moral background into the classroom.

6. <u>Tim</u> had experience working with Native Americans, and it pre-pared <u>him</u> for interacting with other ethnic groups.

7. <u>Andy</u> or <u>Joe Yang</u> will share <u>his</u> feelings about adjusting to U.S. culture.

8. History indicates that the <u>United States</u> gained <u>its</u> strength because of <u>its</u> multicultural society.

9. How could diversity training help <u>Randy</u> and his <u>brothers</u> conduct <u>their</u> business more effectively?

10. The <u>Disney managers</u> who launched EuroDisney did not under-stand the difficulties <u>they</u> would have in duplicating Disney's home culture.

Exercise 2

See Instructor Note 8-17 in IAE.

Answers may vary.

Directions: In the space provided, rewrite those sentences that are vague or unclear or that have incorrect reference pronouns. If the sentence is satisfactory, write **Yes.**

1. They should provide counseling to all workers so that the workers can do their best work.

   <u>(Managers, Human resource directors, Supervisors) should provide</u>

   <u>counseling so that the workers can do their best work.</u>

2. If a good worker has consistent gender-based problems with a coworker, offer him or her the option of a transfer.

   <u>If a good worker has consistent gender-based problems with a coworker,</u>

   <u>offer the good worker the option of a transfer.</u>

3. A friend of mine told his supervisor that he needed to see his psy-chiatrist.

   <u>A friend of mine told his supervisor that he was making an appointment to</u>

   <u>see a psychiatrist.</u>

4. When I requested a transfer, they asked me for my reasons.

   <u>When I requested a transfer, (the supervisor, the manager, my coworkers)</u>

   <u>asked me for my reasons.</u>

5. Toby saw the harassment file on the desk and picked it up.

   <u>Toby saw the harassment file on the desk and picked up the file.</u>

NAME _____

6. Our teaching methods may not work for adults from other countries. It may even lead to conflict in our literacy classes.

   <u>Our teaching methods may not work for adults from other countries. These</u>

   <u>methods may even lead to conflict in our literacy classes.</u>

7. Some companies provide cultural training for their employees who
are assigned to work in other countries.

   <u>Yes</u>

8. Robert has more seniority than me.

   <u>Robert has more seniority than I.</u>

9. The affirmative action plan has the approval of every one.

   <u>The affirmative action plan has the approval of everyone.</u>

10. Kara felt that Renee was overreacting to the discrimination concerning her disability.

    <u>Kara felt that Renee was overreacting to the discrimination concerning</u>

    <u>Kara's disability.</u>

    <u>Kara felt that Renee was overreacting to the discrimination concerning</u>

    <u>Renee's disability.</u>

**GO TO
CD-ROM
PRACTICE 2
EXERCISES**

PRACTICE 3A

PROOFREADING

The subject matter in the following sentences involves cultural diversity topics.

*Directions: Proofread and compare the two sentences in each group. If they are the
same, write **Yes** in the space provided. If they are not the same, write **No**. Use the first
sentence as the correct copy. If you find errors in the second sentence, underline them;
insert any omitted words or marks of punctuation.*

See Instructor Note 8-18 in
IAE.

1. Businesspeople in some countries prefer lengthy
business meetings, but those in other countries want
quick closures to their transactions.

   1. <u>No</u>

   Businesspeople in some <u>counties</u> prefer <u>lengthly</u>
business meetings, but those in other countries
want quick closures to their transactions.

2. An American Management Association study indicates
that by the year 2000, only 15 percent of entry-level
workers will be native-born Caucasians.

   2. <u>No</u>

   The American <u>management association</u> study indicates that
by the year 2000, only 15 percent of entry-level workers
will be native-born Caucasians.

3. Studies show that merely studying about a culture does   3. ___No___
not change attitudes or reactions toward that group.

Studies show that merely studying about a culture does
not change attitudes or <u>reaction</u> toward that group.

4. To qualify as a disability under the Americans with   4. ___Yes___
Disabilities Act (ADA), a physical or mental condition
must limit a major life activity.

To qualify as a disability under the Americans with
Disabilities Act (ADA), a physical or mental condition
must limit a major life activity.

5. Small business owners can learn about diversity   5. ___No___
issues if they attend seminars at the community college
or if they participate in company-sponsored workshops.

Small <u>Business</u> <u>Owners</u> can learn about diversity issues
if they attend seminars at the community college or if
they <u>participate company-sponsered</u> workshops.

See Instructor Notes 8-19 and 8-20 in IAE.

Proofreading Exercise

Directions: Your work with a cultural diversity workshop presenter gives you an opportunity to proofread instructional materials. Proofread the following section of a cultural diversity pretest. (You may want to rate yourself on these points.) Make the necessary corrections using the proofreaders' marks that follow:

delete ⌒	make lowercase /
insert ∧	move to the left [
transpose ∩∪	move to the right]
capitalize ≡	space #

CULTURAL DIVERSITY AWARENESS SURVEY (DRAFT)

Directions: Use the scale that follows to respond to the questions below: A = Always   S = Sometimes   N = Never

1. I am a role model of hard work and open mindedness   1. _____
for my staf.

2. I can see things from other workers points of view.   2. _____

3. I handle conflict and job stresses well in my departmngt. 3. _____

4. i speak clearly and slowly when I'm explaining a task to   4. _____
a new employee.

5. I do not use slang and jargon when I speak to a visitor   5. _____
from another country.

6. I am able too motivate people through employee   6. _____
empowerment.

NAME _____

7. I am able to resolve problems with Employees from different backgrounds.

7. ____

8. I listen carfully to my employees and coworkers.

8. ____

9. I tolerate change well and initiate them when it appears to be the best solution.

9. ____

10. I am aware of International Events and customs.

10. ____

GO TO CD-ROM
PRACTICE 3
EXERCISES

PRACTICE 4A

WRITING

See Instructor Note 8-21 in IAE.

Answers will vary.

Directions: Use each of the following foreign expressions in a sentence. A sample sentence indicates one way that each of the foreign expressions may be used. Use a dictionary if you are uncertain about the meaning of a word.

1. fait accompli _____

Example: We realized that the merger was fait accompli.

2. incommunicado _____

Example: Richard was incommunicado while on vacation.

3. entrepreneur _____

Example: Sheila left her job to become an entrepreneur.

4. hombre_____

Example: We felt that Gregg was a tough hombre during salary negotiations.

5. maître d'hôtel _____

Example: The maître d'hôtel always gave us a booth at the restaurant.

6. hoi polloi _____

Example: I was among the hoi polloi during the parade.

7. status quo _____

Example: Our reorganization remains at status quo.

8. à la carte _____

Example: I prefer to order à la carte when I'm in a restaurant.

9. habeas corpus_____

Example: The habeas corpus was delivered on Friday.

10. nouveau riche_____

Example: He became one of the nouveau riche after the stock split.

GO TO CD-ROM
PRACTICE 4
EXERCISES

PRACTICE

NAME _____

ONLINE *EXERCISES*

See Instructor Note 8-22 in IAE.

Use exact punctuation when keying an Internet address.

Thousands of Websites are devoted to cultural diversity because of the importance of diversity in today's society. Some of the sites are helpful to businesses managing their diverse workforces. Other sites have links to every conceivable type of diversity found in the world.

Objective: *To visit a cultural diversity newsletter site.*

1. With your Internet browser on the screen, key:

   http://www.diversityhotwire.com in the location text box at the top left of your screen. Press the **Enter** key on the keyboard.

2. Click on **Diversity Challenges**.

3. Click on **Case Study**. Think about how you might handle the diversity situation presented.

4. If you'd like to read about other diversity situations and the responses, click on **View the archives and KJCG's responses.**

5. Click the **Back** button of your Internet browser until you are back to the Cultural Diversity Hotwire Web page, or click on Home Page on the screen.

6. Click on **Read the Article of the Month.** Read the article and make notes. Write a summary of the article after you leave the Website. Proofread your summary and circle any errors you made.

7. Click the **Back** button and visit other links on this Web page.

NAME _____

PRACTICE 1B

Directions: In each of the following sentences, underline the antecedents once and the pronoun references twice.

1. Jun Minorikawa was promoted because of her skills in negotiating Pacific Rim trade agreements.

2. The Society of Women Engineers and Women in Technology International offer their encouragement to women who have careers in science and technology.

3. Project HIRED released its report on clients with disabilities who secured permanent jobs.

4. San Francisco, as well as Singapore, provides its businesses with excellent locations for global ventures.

5. Mircea usually eats her lunch at a sushi bar on Fifth Avenue in New York City.

6. You should know that every large city provides you an opportunity to work with people from all over the world.

7. Tonya and Will realized that they were competing for the same promotion.

8. Jim Adamson, Maple's CEO, released his plan to provide better jobs for women.

9. An employee needs to communicate effectively with all customers whom he or she is likely to encounter.

10. If you are working in Paris, you should know that a dress code cannot be officially required of workers.

PRACTICE 2B

Exercise 1

Directions: Complete each sentence by adding a personal pronoun that agrees with the antecedent. Underline the antecedent or antecedents in each sentence.

1. Most of the Chinese employees stated that ____they____ speak Mandarin.

2. During the past month, several employees resigned ____their____ positions.

3. The Capital Training Foundation, along with the Township Chamber of Commerce, is promoting ____its____ occupational path program for high school students.

4. Tokyo is proud of ____its____ reputation as a center of technological innovation.

5. The extra travel took ____its____ toll on Kara's health.

6. Vera Esponda-Foster is head of diversity affairs at Pacific Bay and is widely recognized as a leader in ____her____ efforts to develop sensitivity workshops.

7. Some scientists say ____they____ know how to write computer programs, but ____they____ often struggle with office politics.

8. The cultural diversity coordinator said, "I want people to change ____their____ hearts, ____their____ perspectives, and ____their____ behaviors."

9. Lee Vyenielo or Kevin Vuong will speak with us about ____his____ company viewpoint.

10. Motorola used the Quick Start program to staff ____its____ manufacturing facility in Georgia.

Pronoun/Antecedent Agreement

NAME _____

Exercise 2

Directions: *In the space provided, correct those sentences that are vague or unclear or that have incorrect reference pronouns. If the sentence is satisfactory, write* **Yes.** *Answers may vary.*

1. They should offer sensitivity workshops to all employees so that the employees can change their behaviors.

   (Managers, Human resource directors, Supervisors) should offer sensitivity workshops so that employees can

   change their behaviors.

2. If an employee has completed diversity training and still makes inappropriate comments, terminate him or her.

   If an employee has completed diversity training and still makes inappropriate comments, terminate the

   employee.

3. Anyone of those suggestions should improve office morale.

   Any one of those suggestions should improve office morale.

4. When I refused to share an office with her, they asked me for my reasons.

   When I refused to share an office with her, (the supervisor, the manager, my coworkers) asked me for my reasons.

5. Several sensitivity trainers shared their experiences with each other.

   Several sensitivity trainers shared their experiences with one another.

PRACTICE 3B

PROOFREADING

Directions: *Proofread and compare the two sentences in each group. If they are the same, write* **Yes** *in the space provided. If they are not the same, write* **No.** *Use the first sentence as the correct copy. If you find errors in the second sentence, underline them; insert any omitted words or marks of punctuation.*

1. Most people want to be part of an organization in which they feel they are making a difference.
   Most people want to be part of an organzation in which they believe they our making a difference.

   1. No _____

2. Hans resented his managers asking him to behave like an American, to dress and groom like an American, to eat and drink like an American, and to speak the same language as an American.
   Hans resented his manager asking him to behave like an American, to dress and groom like an American, to eat and drink like an American, and to speak the same languages as an American.

   2. No _____

3. The U.S. Census Bureau predicts that by the year 2050 only half of the population will be non-Hispanic whites. Hispanics and Asians will account for over half of the population growth.
   The U.S. Census Bureau predicts that by the year 2040 only one-half of the population will be non-Hispanic whites. Hispanics and asians will account for over half of the population growth.

   3. No _____

4. SHPE is a nonprofit association that promotes the development of Hispanics in engineering, science, and other technical professions to achieve educational excellence and social equity.
   SHPE is a non-profit association that promotes the development of hispanics in engineering, science, and other technical professions to acheive educational excellence and social equity.

   4. No _____

END-OF-CHAPTER WORKSHEETS

NAME _____

Proofreading Exercise

Directions: *What does cultural diversity include? Here are some suggestions from a workshop group. The workshop trainer asked a student to write down the suggestions as they were being discussed. Proofread the following list. Use these proofreaders marks to correct the copy.*

delete	ꝺ	make lowercase	/
insert	∧	move to the left	[
transpose	∿	move to the right	]
capitalize	≡	space	#

Cultural diversity awareness

1. Age.
2. Male or female
3. Racial
4. experience work
5. education And training
6. Gender
7. Sex orientation

8. [Economic Status
9. Birthplace
10. Hometown
11. Social activities
12. Religion
13. Disability
14. Political disbeliefs

PRACTICE 4B

WRITING

Directions: *Write a sentence for each of the following biased words. Do not use the biased word but substitute another word or phrase that does not stereotype people by gender.*

Answers will vary.

Example: Stewardess
The flight attendant flew the San Francisco to Tokyo route twice a month.

1. businessmen — The executives (businesspeople) met yesterday.
2. fireman — My cousin is a firefighter.
3. manpower — We do not have enough staff to do the job.
4. repairman — The repair technician will be able to come tomorrow.
5. girl Friday — The receptionist is not in the office today.

ONLINE EXERCISES

Objective: *Visit the vast Web resources on cultural diversity.*

1. With your Internet browser on screen, key:

   http://www.careermosaic.com/cm/cm33.html in the location text box at the top left of your screen. Press the **Enter** key on the keyboard.

2. You will be on the Diversity Links for Women and Minorities page of the Website Career Mosaic.

3. Scroll down until you see links which are of interest to you. Click on a link and read the information available. Critique the link you choose. Prepare a short summary for your class if your instructor so directs.

LOOKING BACK

Posttest

Directions: In the space provided, write Yes if the pronoun and antecedent in the sentence are in agreement. If the pronoun is used incorrectly, underline the pronoun and write the correction in the space provided.

1. Just because we speak different languages doesn't mean that we cannot communicate.   Yes

2. Whenever a disagreement occurs, it is important for a manager to look at <u>their</u> method of solving conflicts.   his or her

3. The Affirmative Action Committee and the Diversity Committee work together to help their members appreciate people of various cultures.   Yes

4. When conducting business in other countries, you must know their protocols.   Yes

5. Many of the male immigrants work in low-paying occupations but still send money to <u>his</u> families back home.   their

6. If we do not know about other cultures, <u>you</u> may offend others and not realize that <u>your</u> behavior is offensive.   we   our

7. Our workers wanted new desk accessories to match their office decor.   Yes

8. Some of my coworkers, as well as my friend Selena, were concerned about their ability to speak English.   Yes

9. I think Bill has a better understanding of Chinese culture than <u>me</u>.   I

10. <u>Every one</u> needs to be aware of his or her rate of speech.   Everyone

PART 3

Reviewing Verbs

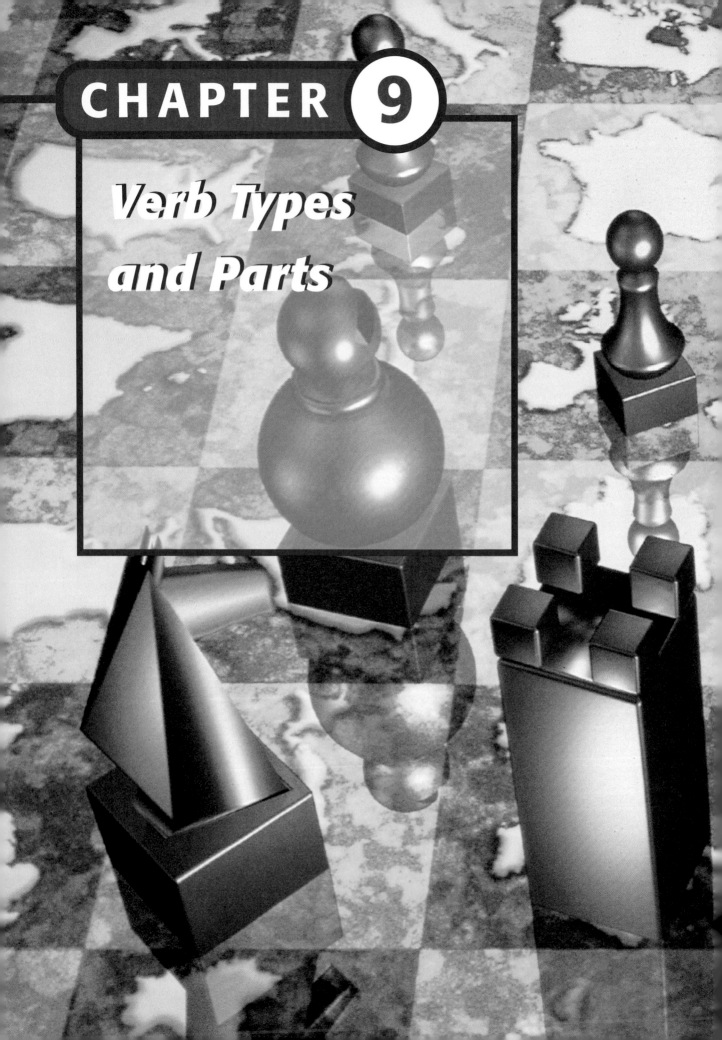

CHAPTER 9

Verb Types and Parts

PROBLEM SOLVING AND DECISION MAKING

Each day you make hundreds of decisions. Today you decided when to get up, what to wear, what to eat, and whether or not to read this book. You started a decision-making pattern when you were young and probably use that same pattern today. For most people, this decision-making pattern is successful. Poor decision makers, however, usually do not realize that their decision-making processes may be inadequate.

A popular process for making decisions involves identifying the problem, gathering information, listing and selecting the best solution, and evaluating the results. Your effectiveness in solving problems increases if you include opinions of others and generate multiple alternatives. Generating these alternatives is called *brainstorming*.

Some people avoid making decisions because they are afraid they will make a mistake. Their goal is to make the perfect decision, not realizing there is no such thing as the perfect decision. Every decision is a risk. Good decision makers know almost any decision can be changed or adjusted.

Because of the complexity of business decisions, more managers are relying on decision-making software to simplify the process. This software helps the decision maker organize thoughts, analyze multiple options, and make the best choice. One of the advantages of using decision-making software is documentation of the decision-making steps, which makes it easy to explain the process and decision to others. Using decision-making software is just one of the ways businesses are taking advantage of the power of their computers.

TERMS TO REMEMBER

BRAINSTORMING

DECISION-MAKING PROCESS

DECISION-MAKING SOFTWARE

OBJECTIVES

After you have studied this chapter and completed the exercises, you will be able to do the following:

1. Use action, linking, and helping verbs correctly.
2. Recognize the difference between transitive and intransitive verbs.
3. Recognize the parts of verbs—present, past, past participle, and present participle.
4. Identify regular and irregular verb forms.
5. Recognize spelling changes in parts of regular verb formations.
6. Use verb forms for *lie, lay; raise, rise;* and *set, sit* correctly.
7. Diagram sentences correctly.

LOOKING AHEAD

Pretest

Directions: *In the space provided, write the letter of the correct answer.*

1. In the sentence *Mr. Danson encouraged project teams to solve their own problems,* the verb *encouraged* is
   a. a linking verb.
   b. a helping verb.
   c. an action verb.
   d. an intransitive verb.

   1. ___c___

2. In the sentence *First impressions of a decision are important,* the verb *are* is
   a. a linking verb.
   b. a helping verb.
   c. an action verb.
   d. a transitive verb.

   2. ___a___

3. In the sentence *We have solved complex problems using expert system software,* the verb *have* is
   a. a linking verb.
   b. a helping verb.
   c. an action verb.
   d. an intransitive verb.

   3. ___b___

4. In the sentence *Expert systems help managers with their complex decisions,* the verb *help* is
   a. a linking verb.
   b. a helping verb.
   c. a transitive verb.
   d. an intransitive verb.

   4. ___c___

5. Which line consists of only irregular verb forms?
   a. require, identify, attempt
   b. become, build, choose
   c. form, outline, wish
   d. communicate, check, delay

   5. ___b___

6. Which verb represents the past participle form?
   a. wrote
   b. write
   c. written
   d. writing

   6. ___c___

7. Which word represents the past form of a verb?
   a. brought
   b. known
   c. gone
   d. done

   7. ___a___

8. Which present participle verb form is spelled correctly?
   a. notifying
   b. prefering
   c. wining
   d. supportting

   8. ___a___

9. Which verb requires an object?
   a. lie
   b. lay
   c. rise
   d. sit

   9. ___b___

10. Which of the following verbs is an intransitive verb?
    a. lay
    b. laid
    c. rise
    d. raise

    10. ___c___

OVERVIEW

A verb is an integral part of a sentence. You cannot write a clear, complete sentence without using a verb since the verb states what the subject does or is. Good writers select their verbs carefully and use them correctly.

A verb involves more form changes than any other part of speech; therefore, you have some new terms to learn. In this chapter, you will identify several kinds of verbs and also work with the four parts of verbs. Before you begin the study of verbs, you will find it helpful to review the parts of speech and the parts of a sentence that were introduced in Chapters 2 and 3.

VERB IDENTIFICATION

Verbs are words that express action or a state of being. In order to write effective sentences, you must use verbs correctly. The first step in your study of verbs is to identify the type of verb and its purpose in a sentence. The three types of verbs are *action, linking,* and *helping* (auxiliary) verbs.

See Instructor Notes 9-1, 9-2, 9-3, and 9-4 in IAE.

Go to Transparencies/ PowerPoints 9-1a and 9-1b.

Action Verb

Use an action verb to tell what someone or something (the subject) does. The action may be physical or mental.

Go to Transparency/PowerPoint 9-2.

We solved the problem.
(The subject is *we. Solved* is an action verb that indicates what the subject *we* did.)

Gerta summarized the committee's brainstorming ideas.
(*Summarized* is an action verb that indicates what the subject *Gerta* did.)

Always weigh the consequences of your decisions.
(*Weigh* is an action verb that indicates what the subject *you* [understood] should do.)

Review subjects in sentences in Chapter 3.

Action verbs include *transitive* and *intransitive verbs.* Your dictionaries identify verbs as transitive (*v.t.*) and intransitive (*v.i.*). Understanding the differences between transitive and intransitive verbs will also help you later in the chapter as you work with several frequently misused words.

9-5 Explain the terms *transitive* and *intransitive* by using direct objects.

Transitive Verb.   A transitive verb is an action verb that needs an object to complete the thought. The words following the verb answer the questions *What?* or *Whom?*

Go to Transparency/PowerPoint 9-3.

Review direct objects in Chapter 3.

Joe Bjiong assessed his competitor's products early in the decision-making process.

(*Assessed* is a transitive verb that requires an object to complete the thought. The object *products* answers the question *What is assessed?*)

We analyzed Solutions 1, 3, and 6 very carefully.

(*Analyzed* is a transitive verb that requires an object to complete the thought. The object *Solutions 1, 3, and 6* answers the question *What?*)

Pang Ju received an award for his conflict resolution research.

(*Received* is a transitive verb. The object *award* is a direct object that completes the thought.)

Intransitive Verb.   An intransitive verb is an action verb that does not require an object to complete the thought.

The managers listened carefully to the employees' concerns and problems.

(*Listened* is an intransitive verb. The intransitive verb *listened* does not require an object to complete the thought.)

Analytical thinking refers to an individual's problem-solving ability.

(*Refers* is an intransitive verb in this sentence. No object is necessary to complete the thought.)

His legal firm often refers its paralegals to our problem-solving seminars.

(*Refers* is a transitive verb in this sentence. The object *paralegals* is a direct object that completes the thought.)

Go to Transparency/PowerPoint 9-4.

CHECKUP 9-1

Directions: *Underline the transitive verbs once and the intransitive verbs twice. Write any direct objects in the space provided.*

1. The technique of brainstorming often generates unique solutions to problems.   — solutions

2. Conflict occurs in every relationship because no two people will always agree.   —

3. Small companies encounter difficulties when they ignore employee concerns.   — difficulties / concerns

4. Our approach to decision making usually works.   —

5. Workers need information about management's decisions.   — information

6. We examined the problem and asked several questions about the problem before we solved it.   — problem / questions   it

GO TO CD-ROM
CHECKUP 9-1

Linking Verb

Linking Verb—State of Being. Use a linking verb to connect the subject of the sentence with a subject complement (predicate noun, predicate pronoun) or with a predicate adjective. A linking verb does not indicate action. Some common state-of-being linking verb forms are forms of the verb *to be*: *am, is, are, was, were, be, been, being.*

> **Maria LaCosta <u>was</u> the principal speaker at the artificial intelligence conference.**
>
> (*Was* is a linking verb that connects the subject *Maria LaCosta* and the subject complement *the principal speaker*. The subject complement renames the subject. *Was* is not an action verb.)
>
> **Brainstorming sessions <u>are</u> usually eventful and lively.**
>
> (*Are* is a linking verb that links the subject *brainstorming sessions* and the predicate adjectives *eventful* and *lively*. The predicate adjectives describe the subject.)

Linking Verb—Other. Use a verb associated with the senses—*feel, look, smell, sound, taste*—as a linking verb. Additional linking verbs are *appear, become, grow, remain, stay,* and *seem*. Some of these linking verbs function as action verbs as well. To test whether a verb is a linking verb, use a *to be* verb form in place of one of the 11 verbs just listed. If the sentence makes sense with the substitute *to be* form, the verb is a linking verb.

> **She <u>remained</u> unconvinced of the value of brainstorming sessions.**
> (Substitute the word *was* for *remained*. *She was unconvinced of the value of brainstorming sessions*. The sentence makes sense with the substitution. In this sentence, *remained* is a linking verb. *Unconvinced* describes the subject *she*.)
>
> **The problem <u>appeared</u> more complicated than we had thought.**
> (Substitute *is* or *was*. In this sentence, *appeared* is a linking verb.)
>
> **All the possible solutions <u>looked</u> good for our needs.**
> (Substitute *are* or *were*. In this sentence, *looked* is a linking verb.)
>
> **We <u>looked</u> at all the possible solutions to the absenteeism problem.**
> (Substitute *are* or *were*. The sentence does not make sense with the substitution. In this sentence, *looked* is an action verb.)

CHECKUP 9-2

Directions: Underline action verbs once and linking verbs twice.

1. Decision making is often a team experience.
2. Poor decisions result when objectives are vague.
3. Mr. Larvik encouraged our open and frank discussions.
4. These decision-making steps sound complicated.
5. Carrie knew her problem-solving approach was too costly.
6. I identified my goals and set my priorities.

Go to
Transparency/PowerPoint 9-5.

Refer to Chapter 2 and Chapter 3 for a review of subject complements.

See Instructor Note 9-6 in IAE.

If the subject does something, the verb is an action verb. If the subject is renamed or described, the verb is a linking verb.

See Instructor Note 9-7 in IAE.

SLIP-UP
On Red Cross cards asking recipients to donate their blood: Give blood again. It will be felt for a lifetime.
Source: Richard Lederer.

**GO TO
CD-ROM**
CHECKUP 9–2

Helping Verb and Verb Phrase

See Instructor Note 9-8 in IAE.

Keep a list of the helping verbs in a convenient location. Then refer to these verbs when necessary.

Use a helping (auxiliary) verb with a main verb to form a verb phrase. The main verb in a verb phrase is always the last word in the phrase. Some helping verbs can function as main verbs and are used alone in such cases.

The following list of helping verbs will be useful in the remainder of this chapter and also in Chapter 10.

Helping Verbs

am	was	be	have	can	do
is	were	being	has	could	does
are		been	had		did
may	shall	will			
might	should	would			
must					

Success <u>may depend</u> on an individual's timely decision-making ability.
(*May* is the helping verb used with the main verb *depend* to form the verb phrase *may depend*.)

I <u>have</u> several decisions that I <u>must make</u> by Friday.
(*Have* is used alone as a main verb. *Must* is the helping verb used with the main verb *make*.)

Do This

We <u>used to be able to</u> discuss our problems rationally.

or

We <u>once could</u> discuss our problems rationally.

Do Not Do This

We <u>used to could</u> discuss our problems rationally.

We <u>use to</u> discuss our problems rationally.

Do not use the dialect form use to or used to could for once could or used to be able.

CHECKUP 9-3

Directions: Draw a line under each verb phrase and circle each helping verb.

Ex.: Barb's decision (was) accepted by her coworkers.

1. Work teams (must) resolve their problems promptly.
2. Sometimes conflict (can)(be) avoided if new information (is) supplied to the participants.
3. We (were) asked for a problem solution by the end of the week.
4. He (has) developed an effective action plan for union members.
5. Most people in work environments (have) encountered problem situations.

GO TO CD-ROM
CHECKUP 9-3

CHECKUP 9-4

Directions: *The sentences below are taken from the Secondary Learning paragraph. Underline the action verbs once and the linking verbs twice.*

1. A popular process for making decisions <u>involves</u> identifying the problem, gathering information, listing and selecting the best solution, and evaluating the results.
2. For most people, this decision-making pattern <u>is</u> successful.
3. Every decision <u>is</u> a risk.
4. Each day you <u>make</u> hundreds of decisions.
5. One of the advantages of using decision-making software <u>is</u> documentation of the decision-making steps.

**GO TO
CD-ROM**
CHECKUP 9-4

PARTS OF VERBS

Verbs are either *regular* or *irregular.* All regular and irregular verbs, with the exception of *be,* have four principal parts—the *present,* the *past,* the *past participle,* and the *present participle.* These principal parts are used to form verb tenses. An error in tense often occurs because of a failure to choose the correct principal part of the verb.

Definitions

Present. The first principal part of a verb is the present form, which refers to now or the present time.

> Expert systems **require** a knowledge base of rules and facts.
> (*Require* refers to the present time.)

> Members of our family business **discuss** the issues and then **take** a vote.
> (*Discuss* and *take* refer to the present time.)

Past. The second principal part of a verb refers to the past. The past verb part indicates that the action already took place. For most usage, this verb part is formed by adding *d* or *ed* to the present form of the verb. No helping verb is used with this principal part of the verb.

> We **discussed** many solutions to the problem.
> (*Discussed* is a verb that indicates the discussion already took place.)

> I **compared** the alternatives and **selected** the best solution for my needs.
> (*Compared* and *selected* are verbs that indicate the comparison and selection already took place.)

Past Participle. The third principal part of a verb is the past participle. To form the past participle of most verbs, add *d* or *ed* to the

See Instructor Note 9-9 in IAE.

Tense refers to the time (present, past, and future) indicated by a verb. You will work with verb tenses in greater depth in Chapter 10.

present part of the verb. The past participle requires a helping verb (*have, has,* or *had.*) A past participle combined with a helping verb indicates the action was completed. In a verb phrase, the past participle is always the last word of the phrase.

> **We have muddled through many problem situations without a clear plan.**
>
> (The past participle *muddled* and the helping verb *have* indicate the subject has already completed the action.)
>
> **Our committee members have reached a deadlock and both sides have refused to negotiate.**
>
> (The past participles *reached* and *refused* along with the helping verb *have* indicate the members have completed the actions.)

Present Participle. The fourth principal part of a verb is the present participle. A present participle is formed by using the present form of a verb plus *ing.* This verb form requires the use of a helping verb and indicates that there is continuing action involved. Some helping verbs are *is, are, was, were, can, could, have, has, had, should, would,* and *shall* or *will.*

> **We are considering an Executive Support System (ESS) for accessing relevant decision-making information.**
>
> (*Considering* is the present participle and consists of the present form *consider* plus *ing.* The required helping verb in this sentence is *are.* The combination *are considering* suggests a continuing action.)
>
> **John is outlining improvements for the next brainstorming session.**
>
> (*Outlining* is the present participle and consists of the present form *outline* plus *ing.* The combination *is outlining* suggests an ongoing action.)

Regular Verbs

Most verbs are regular verbs. If you check your dictionaries, you probably will not find the past, past participle, or present participle of a regular verb listed. In such cases, form these parts by adding *d, ed,* or *ing* to the present part of the verb.

Regular Verbs—General Formations. Add *d* or *ed* to the present part of most verbs to form the past or past participle. Add *ing* to the present part of most verbs to form the present participle.

Present Part	Past Part	Past Participle	Present Participle
assess	assessed	assessed	assessing
contribute	contributed	contributed	contributing
fail	failed	failed	failing
hang (death)	hanged	hanged	hanging
listen	listened	listened	listening
review	reviewed	reviewed	reviewing
solve	solved	solved	solving
support	supported	supported	supporting

Regular Verbs—*Y* Endings. Change the final *y* to *i* and add *ed* to form the past or the past participle of a verb that ends in *y* preceded by a consonant. The present participle retains the *y* before adding *ing*. Even though spelling changes occur with these verbs, they are regular verbs.

Present Part	Past Part	Past Participle	Present Participle
carry	carried	carried	carrying
identify	identified	identified	identifying
try	tried	tried	trying

Refer to Rule 20 in the spelling section of the appendix.

Refer to Rule 7 in the spelling section of the appendix.

See Instructor Note 9-10 in IAE.

Regular Verbs—One Syllable. Double the last consonant of a one-syllable verb that ends in one consonant preceded by *one* vowel before you add *ed* to form the past and past participle or *ing* to form the present participle. Even though spelling changes occur with these verbs, they are regular verbs.

Present Part	Past Part	Past Participle	Present Participle
plan	planned	planned	planning
stop	stopped	stopped	stopping
wrap	wrapped	wrapped	wrapping

Refer to Rule 9 in the spelling section of the appendix. Refer to your reference manual for other examples as needed.

Regular Verbs—Accented Syllables. Double the final consonant of a two-syllable verb accented on the *last* syllable that ends in a *single* consonant preceded by a *single* vowel when you add the suffix *ed* or *ing*. Even though spelling changes occur with these verbs, they are regular verbs.

Present Part	Past Part	Past Participle	Present Participle
ex cel´	excelled	excelled	excelling
oc cur´	occurred	occurred	occurring
pre fer´	preferred	preferred	preferring
re fer´	referred	referred	referring

See Instructor Note 9-11 in IAE.

CHECKUP 9-5

Directions: In the blank spaces, write the appropriate forms of the following regular verbs. The present part of the verb is given. Use a dictionary if you are not certain of a spelling or verb form.

	Present Part	Past Part	Past Participle	Present Participle
1.	accept	accepted	accepted	accepting
2.	ship	shipped	shipped	shipping
3.	label	labeled	labeled	labeling
4.	require	required	required	requiring
5.	control	controlled	controlled	controlling
6.	copy	copied	copied	copying
7.	attempt	attempted	attempted	attempting
8.	impel	impelled	impelled	impelling

See Instructor Note 9-12 in IAE.

GO TO CD-ROM
CHECKUP 9-5

Irregular Verbs

Irregular verbs do not form their past parts or past participles by adding *d* or *ed* to the present parts of the verb. The spellings and forms of irregular verbs do not follow a consistent pattern. To use these verbs correctly, memorize the forms, or check a dictionary whenever you are in doubt.

See Instructor Notes 9-13 and 9-14 in IAE.

Although there are more regular verbs than there are irregular verbs, many of the irregular verbs are commonly used. Here is a list of many of the irregular verbs:

Present Part	Past Part	Past Participle	Present Participle
be (am, is, are)	was, were	been	being
become	became	become	becoming
begin	began	begun	beginning
blow	blew	blown	blowing
break	broke	broken	breaking
bring	brought	brought	bringing
build	built	built	building
buy	bought	bought	buying
catch	caught	caught	catching
choose	chose	chosen	choosing
do	did	done	doing
draw	drew	drawn	drawing
drive	drove	driven	driving
eat	ate	eaten	eating
give	gave	given	giving
go	went	gone	going
grow	grew	grown	growing
hang (suspend an object)	hung	hung	hanging
have	had	had	having
hear	heard	heard	hearing
keep	kept	kept	keeping
lead	led	led	leading
leave	left	left	leaving
lose	lost	lost	losing
mean	meant	meant	meaning
ring	rang	rung	ringing
say	said	said	saying
see	saw	seen	seeing
send	sent	sent	sending
show	showed	shown	showing
spend	spent	spent	spending
take	took	taken	taking
teach	taught	taught	teaching
tell	told	told	telling
think	thought	thought	thinking
wear	wore	worn	wearing
write	wrote	written	writing

Do This	Do Not Do This
I have gone to my supervisor to explain the problem.	I have went to my super-visor to explain the problem.
I have done the evaluations of the four solutions.	I done the evaluations of the four solutions.
She had seen the film on conflict resolution before.	She seen the film on conflict resolution before.

Never use a helping verb with the verb went.

*Always use one of the helping verbs (*have, has, *and* had*) with the verbs* done *and* seen.

CHECKUP 9-6

Directions: In the blank spaces, write the appropriate forms of the following irregular verbs. The present part of the verb is given. Use a dictionary if you are not certain of a spelling or form.

	Present Part	Past Part	Past Participle	Present Participle
1.	fall	fell	fallen	falling
2.	bind	bound	bound	binding
3.	sing	sang	sung	singing
4.	run	ran	run	running
5.	withdraw	withdrew	withdrawn	withdrawing
6.	feel	felt	felt	feeling
7.	quit	quit	quit	quitting
8.	strike	struck	struck	striking
9.	bend	bent	bent	bending
10.	make	made	made	making

GO TO CD-ROM
CHECKUP 9-6

SPECIAL VERBS

Several pairs of verbs cause confusion. These verbs require special practice—*lay, lie; raise, rise;* and *set, sit.* To avoid misuse, remember that within each pair of the verbs just listed, one is transitive and the other is intransitive.

Go to PowerPoints 9-6a, 9-6b, 9-7a, 9-7b, 9-8a, and 9-8b.

See Instructor Note 9-15 in IAE.

Definitions

lay: to put or place an item somewhere
(Requires an object)

lie: to recline; to be located in a spot; to tell an untruth
(No object required)

Review the section on transitive and intransitive verbs at the beginning of this chapter.

raise: to lift up or bring something up
   (Requires an object)

rise: to get up
   (No object required)

set: to put or place something
   (Requires an object)

exception: the sun *sets*

sit: to be seated
   (No object required)

Special Verb Forms

These verb forms are *irregular* verbs.

Present Part	Past Part	Past Participle	Present Participle
lay	laid	laid	laying
lie	lay	lain	lying
set	set	set	setting
sit	sat	sat	sitting
raise	raised	raised	raising
rise	rose	risen	rising

The prioritized solutions <u>lay</u> on her desk for weeks.
(*Lay* is the past form of *lie. Lie* is an intransitive verb and does not require an object.)

Do you remember <u>laying</u> the agendas next to the copier?
(*Laying* is the present participle of *lay. Lay* is a transitive verb and requires an object [*agendas*].)

I <u>laid</u> the recommendations from the building improvement survey in a safe place.
(*Laid* is the past form of lay. *Lay* is a transitive verb and requires an object [*recommendations*].)

I will <u>set</u> the rules before we begin our discussion of the problem.
(*Set* is a transitive verb that requires an object [*rules*].)

The meeting will be long; therefore, <u>sit</u> in a chair that is comfortable.
(*Sit* is an intransitive verb and does not require an object.)

Did you <u>raise</u> the question or was it Jack who started the discussion?
(*Raise* is a transitive verb and requires an object [*question*].)

The discussion was controversial and voices often <u>rose</u> in protest.
(*Rose* is the past form of *rise. Rise* is an intransitive verb and does not require an object.)

I had <u>risen</u> at 5:30 a.m. because I thought we had an early morning negotiations meeting.
(*Risen* is the past participle of *rise. Rise* is an intransitive verb and requires no object.)

The verbs that have i as their second letter are intransitive and do not require an object.

See Instructor Note 9-16 in IAE.

See Instructor Note 9-17 in IAE.

SLIP-UP
Newspaper headline. President wins on budget, but more lies ahead. [Note: Is *lies* used as a noun or verb?]

CHECKUP 9-7

Directions: *Select the correct word, and write it in the space provided.*

1. Let's (*set, sit*) down to discuss the harassment complaint. _sit_

2. I had (*laid, lain*) the groundwork for our brainstorming session very carefully. _laid_

3. Our morale level (*raised, rose*) when the president indicated that the company would not be closing. _rose_

4. You should (*set, sit*) goals before you begin to make a decision. _set_

5. Please (*lay, lie*) your evaluations of the expert system software on my desk. _lay_

6. Some families experience monetary problems when landlords (*raise, rise*) rents. _raise_

**GO TO
CD-ROM
CHECKUP 9-7**

DIAGRAMMING SENTENCES

The sentences in this diagramming section will be a review of the areas covered in other diagramming sections in Chapters 3, 4, 5, 7, and 8. The numbers in parentheses indicate the chapters for your reference.

Simple subject (3)
Simple predicate—verb (3)
Direct object (3)
Appositive (4)
Subject complement (4)
Indirect object (5)

Possessive noun (5)
Compound subjects (7)
Compound verbs (7)
Compound objects (7)
Adjectives (8)

CHECKUP 9-8

9-18 All words in the sentences may be diagrammed.

Directions: *In the space provided, diagram the following sentences. Remember that* a, an, *and* the *function as adjectives.*

1. Our group leader set a discussion time limit.

| leader | set | limit |

Our   group   a   discussion   time

2. Child care and elder care are two major employee problems.

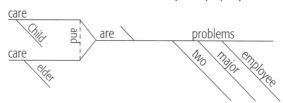

3. The committee's decision affected employee morale and job loyalty.

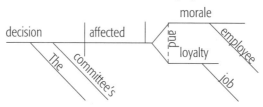

4. Mrs. Morrison, my supervisor, sent me the negotiation team's minutes and a new agenda.

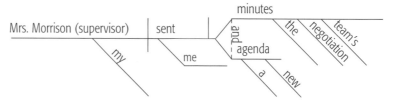

5. Rod and I discussed and evaluated Jane's recommended solutions.

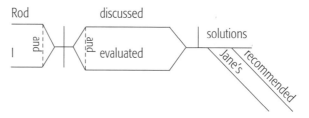

**GO TO
CD-ROM
CHECKUP 9-8**

NAME _____

PRACTICE 1A

A. Directions: *At the beginning of each sentence is a verb form. Select the correct verb form from those in parentheses and write it in the space provided.*

1. past participle   Les has (*gone, went*) to a seminar on decision making for health technicians.   **1.** __gone__

2. past   The hotel manager (*forgot, forgotten*) to include someone from housekeeping on the problem-solving team.   **2.** __forgot__

3. past   Our delayed decision (*cost, costed*) the company unnecessary expense.   **3.** __cost__

4. past participle   I thought I had (*became, become*) more tolerant of my coworkers' disorganization.   **4.** __become__

5. present participle   He is (*raising, rising*) some important issues for us to consider.   **5.** __raising__

6. past   Our present managers (*notified, has notified*) us about the final decision through e-mail.   **6.** __notified__

7. present participle   She is (*sitting, setting*) the dates and times for the brainstorming sessions.   **7.** __setting__

8. present   Write your solutions on cards and then (*lay, lie*) the cards in three piles—workable, possible, not workable.   **8.** __lay__

9. past, past   After a conflict (*has occurred, occurred*) in a negotiation meeting, Nancy (*laid, lay*) down to calm herself.   **9.** __occurred__   __lay__

10. past   He (*plan, planned*) to discuss the issue of excessive overtime with his supervisor.   **10.** __planned__

B. Directions: *Underline the verbs or verb phrases in each of the following sentences.*

1. He ignored the problems among the members of his staff.

2. A positive work environment improves worker morale and increases production.

3. Russ is making the problem more complicated than necessary.

4. Some workers are not comfortable when they must confront coworkers whose actions have upset them.

5. My favorite problem-solving technique involves "what if" questions.

**GO TO
CD-ROM**
PRACTICE 1
EXERCISES

PRACTICE

NAME _____

PRACTICE 2A

A. Directions: *In the space provided, identify the underlined verb or verbs by writing one of the following codes: A-T (action—transitive verb),   A-I (action—intransitive verb),   L (linking verb),   H (helping verb),   VP (verb phrase).*

1. My supervisor <u>is</u> an expert in leading brainstorming sessions.
 1. ___L___

2. Mr. Norvik <u>informed</u> his employees about the firm's decision-making process.
 2. ___A-T___

3. We took the time to reach a consensus before we <u>announced</u> our decision.
 3. ___A-T___

4. In emotional confrontations, sensitivity <u>seems</u> more important than the issues.
 4. ___L___

5. If your decision was unfair, <u>apologize</u> to those involved immediately.
 5. ___A-I___

6. One rule for brainstorming sessions <u>is</u> the elimination of the statement "That will never work."
 6. ___L___

7. If you look only at the symptoms of a problem, you <u>will</u> waste time solving a nonexistent problem.
 7. ___H___

8. When a coworker's action bothers you, <u>talk</u> with him or her before it becomes a serious problem.
 8. ___A-I___

9. When you <u>are</u> faced with a problem, consider all your alternatives.
 9. ___H___

10. Children <u>recognize</u> adult indecision and use it to their advantage.
 10. ___A-T___

B. Directions: *Each of the lines below includes one verb form. Fill in the remaining verbs in the spaces provided under each heading.*

	Present Part	Past Part	Past Participle	Present Participle
1.	<u>do</u>	did	<u>done</u>	doing
2.	<u>control</u>	<u>controlled</u>	controlled	controlling
3.	<u>meet</u>	met	met	<u>meeting</u>
4.	<u>drop</u>	<u>dropped</u>	dropped	dropping
5.	<u>sink</u>	sank	sunk	sinking
6.	<u>modify</u>	modified	modified	modifying
7.	infer	inferred	<u>inferred</u>	inferring
8.	keep	kept	kept	<u>keeping</u>
9.	freeze	<u>froze</u>	frozen	freezing
10.	<u>send</u>	sent	sent	sending

**GO TO
CD-ROM**
PRACTICE 2
EXERCISES

Chapter 9

PRACTICE 3A

PROOFREADING

The subject matter in the following sentences involves decision making and problem solving.

*Directions: Proofread and compare the two sentences in each group. If they are the same, write **Yes** in the space provided. If they are not the same, write **No**. Use the first sentence as the correct copy. If you find errors in the second sentence, underline them.*

1. Conflicts result when workers complain to their coworkers rather than to the person who can do something about the problem.

   <u>Problems</u> result when workers complain to their coworkers rather than to the <u>persons</u> who can do something about the problem.

   1. __No__

2. The more difficult problems you resolve, the more important you become to the organization.

   The more difficult problems you resolve, the more important you become to the organization.

   2. __Yes__

3. One of the best ways to get employee support is to give away the credit and ownership of your ideas.

   One of the best ways to get <u>employee's</u> support is to <u>give the</u> credit and ownership of your ideas.

   3. __No__

4. The major parts of a rule-based expert system are an expert knowledge base, a user interface, and an inference engine.

   The <u>mayor</u> parts of a <u>rule based</u> expert system are an expert knowledge base, a user interface, and an <u>inferance</u> engine.

   4. __No__

5. As you progress through the steps of problem solving, ask the question, "What is the best solution to the problem based on costs and feasibility?"

   As you progress through the steps of problem <u>solving ask</u> the question, "<u>what</u> is the best solution to the problem based on costs and <u>feasability</u>?"

   5. __No__

NAME _____

Proofreading Exercise

To assist you in solving your own problems, follow these steps:

Steps in Problem Solving

1.   Define the problem.

      Be certain the symptoms of the problem do not over-
      shadow the causes. This step is the most difficult.

2.   Identify solutions.

      Gather as many ideas as possible. Brainstorming is a
      method that often works since it encourages participants to
      be creative and spontaneous in their solutions.

3.   Select the best solution.

      List and rank the points you use to evaluate each idea.
      Each solution will have strengths and weaknesses.

4.   Evaluate the solution.

      Record the results of selecting your solution. If a similar
      problem occurs, you will have some of your work already
      accomplished.

See Instructor Notes 9-19 and 9-20 in IAE.

Directions: Use the following proofreaders' marks to make corrections in the copy that follows. Use the correct copy above as your guide.

Lowercase /	Move left ⌐	Insert letter ∧
Capitalize ≡	Move right ⌐	Insert comma ∧
Delete ꝺ	Insert space #	Transpose ∿
Delete and close up ꝺ		

Steps In Problem Solving

1.   Define the Problem.

      Be certain the symtoms of the problem do not overshadow
      the causes. This step isthe most difficult.

2.   identify solutions.

      Gather as many ideas as possible. Brainstorming.
      isa method that often works since it encourages partici-
      pants to be creative and spontaneous in thier solutions.

3.   Select the best solution.

      List and rank the points you use to evaluate each idea.
      Each solution will have strenths and have weaknesses.

4.   Evaluate the solution.

      Record the results of selecting your solution. If a similar
      problem occurs you will have some of your work
      already accomplished.

GO TO CD-ROM
PRACTICE 3 EXERCISES

PRACTICE 4A

WRITING

Directions: Solving problems involves a series of steps, which are listed below. Determine a problem you would like to solve. Write sentences to solve your problem. **Example:**

Answers will vary.

1. **Define the problem:**

   My car needs $1500 worth of repairs. The car is worth $2000. Should I repair the car or buy a new car?

2. **List three possible solutions:**

   1. Go to a mechanic and have the car checked for any potential problems. My concern is spending $1500 and then possibly spending more money for additional repairs.

   2. Withdraw money from savings and repair the car. My concern is that I may need the money in the savings account for other emergencies.

   3. Buy a new car. I could buy a used car for $1500. My concern is the mechanical condition of a used car.

   4. Ride my bike. I need to get more exercise anyway. My concern is what to do when I must go longer distances or what happens in bad weather.

3. **Select the best decision and defend it:**

   I will go to a mechanic and have the car examined for any potential problems. If it looks as if the $1500 is the only money I will need to spend, I will repair the car. If the car has other potential problems, I will get a new or used car. The bike option is too impractical for my lifestyle.

1. Define the problem:

   _____

2. List at least three possible solutions:

   _____

   _____

   _____

3. Select the best solution and defend it.

   _____

   _____

   _____

   _____

   _____

   _____

GO TO CD-ROM
PRACTICE 4 EXERCISES

PRACTICE

9-21 Check online sites carefully before assigning them to students.

Use exact punctuation when keying an Internet address.

ONLINE **EXERCISES**

Decision-making software helps analyze thousands of variables affecting decisions. The software takes the user step-by-step through a process to help make the best decision. Decision-making software is preferred when statistical analysis is necessary in making a good decision.

Objective: *To visit decision-making software sites.*

1. With your Internet browser on screen, key:

   http://www.arlingsoft.com in the location box. Press the **Enter** key on your keyboard.

2. Read about decision-making software. Click on the various links on this site.

3. Key the following in your Internet browser:

   http://www.inspiration.com and press the **Enter** key on your keyboard.

4. Inspiration Software is another decision-making tool. Read how Inspiration Software is used to collect and organize thoughts.

NAME _____

PRACTICE 1B

A. Directions: *At the beginning of each sentence is a verb form. Select the correct verb form from those in parentheses, and write it in the space provided.*

1. past participle	She has (*gave, given*) several excuses for not attending our planning meetings.	**1.**	given
2. past participle	Ross has (*drew, drawn*) the wrong conclusions about our postponement of the deadline.	**2.**	drawn
3. past	We (*payed, paid*) the price for failing to have a Website.	**3.**	paid
4. present	I noticed that Greg always (*sits, sets*) next to Karen at meetings.	**4.**	sits
5. past	The software engineer (*teached, taught*) us how to use the brainstorming software.	**5.**	taught

B. Directions: *Underline the verbs or verb phrases in each sentence.*

1. Good decisions <u>are based</u> on sound goals and objectives.

2. Hank Larson <u>is</u> a strong, independent decision maker.

3. Decision making <u>works</u> when it <u>is based</u> on objective evaluations of the information.

4. We <u>knew</u> that our employees <u>needed</u> additional decision-making practice.

5. Even when the final choices <u>are</u> obvious to you, explaining your reasoning to your supervisor <u>can be</u> difficult.

PRACTICE 2B

A. Directions: *In the space provided, identify the underlined verb or verbs by writing one of the following codes:* **A-T** *(action–transitive verb),* **A-I** *(action–intransitive verb),* **L** *(linking verb),* **H** *(helping verb),* **VP** *(verb phrase).*

1. The Chinese <u>developed</u> I Ching in 3000 BC to provide a more systematic process of decision making.	**1.**	A-T
2. A poor decision <u>is</u> reversible.	**2.**	L
3. Michelle <u>was</u> appointed our group leader.	**3.**	H
4. Your coworkers always <u>speak</u> very highly of your decisions.	**4.**	A-I
5. Todd <u>adjusted</u> the rules to keep peace in the group.	**5.**	A-T
6. Our work team rarely <u>misses</u> a deadline.	**6.**	A-T
7. Your information <u>appears</u> inaccurate.	**7.**	L
8. We <u>had</u> hoped for more time to gather our data.	**8.**	H
9. Brainstorming <u>encourages</u> group participation.	**9.**	A-T
10. A group of us <u>walk</u> around the parking lot during the lunch hour.	**10.**	A-I

NAME _____

B. Directions: *Each of the lines below includes one verb form. Fill in the remaining verbs in the spaces provided under each heading.*

Present Part	Past Part	Past Participle	Present Participle
1. begin	began	begun	beginning
2. drive	drove	driven	driving
3. fly	flew	flown	flying
4. make	made	made	making
5. wear	wore	worn	wearing

PRACTICE 3B

PROOFREADING

The subject matter in the following sentences involves decision making and problem solving.

Directions: *Proofread and compare the two sentences in each group. If they are the same, write* **Yes** *in the space provided. If they are not the same, write* **No.** *Use the first group of sentences as the correct copy. If you find errors in the second group of sentences, underline them.*

1. In business, 80 percent of decisions should be made immediately, 15 percent should take more time and thought, and 5 percent should not be made at all.

   In business, 80 percent of decisions should be made imediately, 10 percent should take more time and thought, and 5 percent should be made at all.

   1. _____No_____

2. Peter Drucker says, "People who don't take risks generally make about two big mistakes a year. People who do take risks generally make about two big mistakes a year."

   Peter Druker says "People who don't take risks generally make about two big mistakes a year. People who do take risks generally make about three big mistakes a year."

   2. _____No_____

3. When making decisions, avoid the impossible task of "getting all the facts."

   When making decisions, avoid the impossible task of "getting all the facts."

   3. _____Yes_____

4. When asking others for their opinions, just present the facts and issues, and let them tell you what they would do.

   When asking others for thier opinion, just present the facts and issues, and let them tell you what they would have done.

   4. _____No_____

5. Brainstorming involves listing every solution, no matter how far-out or crazy, that comes to mind.

   Brainstorming involves listing every solution, no matter how farout or crazy, that comes to mind.

   5. _____No_____

NAME _____

Proofreading Exercise

To assist you in solving your own problems, the following material summarizes some decision-making suggestions.

Suggestions for Decision Making

- Do not waste time trying to "gather all the facts."

- Consult with your supervisor, your coworkers, and others before the problem becomes unmanageable.

- Respect your intuition.

- Use brainstorming to generate ideas.

- Think of the best and worst possible outcomes of the decision.

- Strive for acceptance of the decision by group members.

- Inform others who will be affected by the decision.

- Change plans if a decision does not work.

Directions: *You are the recorder for a brainstorming session on suggestions for decision making. Use the following proofreaders' marks to make corrections in the copy that follows. Use the correct copy above as your guide.*

Delete ⟩	Delete and close up ⟩
Insert letter ∧	Lowercase /
Transpose ∩	Move left [
Capitalize ≡	Move right]
Insert comma ∧	Insert space #

Suggestions for Decision Making

- Don't waste time trying to "gather all the facts."

- Consult with your supervisor, your coworkers, and others before the problem becomes unmanageable.

- Respect your intuition or "gut feelings."

- Use brainstorming to generate ideas.

- think of the best and worst possible outcomes of the decision.

- Strive for acceptance of the decision by group members.

- Inform others who will be affected by the decision.

- Change plans if a decision does not work.

NAME _____

PRACTICE 4B

WRITING

Directions: Read the following case study. You are Lynn's coworker. Solve the problem by responding to the numbered items with complete sentences.   Answers will vary.

Lynn has worked satisfactorily for two years. She previously lived with her grandmother, who provided child care for Lynn's young son. Lynn's car became undriveable last month, and she has been unable to get it repaired. Therefore, she started riding the bus. The bus arrived at inconsistent times, which meant that Lynn has been late for her shift several times a week. You resent staying late to cover for Lynn.

Two weeks ago, Lynn's grandmother had a stroke and was hospitalized. Lynn no longer has child care. When Lynn's son was ill, she would bring him to work with her. Since her son is young, he would interrupt Lynn and her coworkers constantly during working hours. She has brought him to work three times in the last two weeks.

1. Define the problem: Answers will vary.

Lynn's personal problems are interfering with her ability to do her job. She needs reliable transportation, and

she needs help with child care.

2. Identify solutions: Answers will vary.

1. **Talk to Lynn. See if you can offer any assistance.**

2. **Talk to your supervisor.**

3. **Talk to your coworkers to see what they think you should do.**

3. Select the best solution and defend it: Answers will vary.

_____

_____

ONLINE *EXERCISES*

Objective: To visit a decision-making software site.

1. With your Internet browser on screen, key:
    http://www.sas.com in the location box at the top of your screen. Press the **Enter** key on your keyboard.
2. You will be at the SAS Institute Decision Making software site.
3. Click on the links to read about this decision-making software.

Objective: To visit an English grammar site.

1. With your Internet browser on screen, key:
    http://www.wsu.edu:8080/~brians/errors/index.html in the location box at the top of your screen. Press the **Enter** key on your keyboard.
2. You will be at Paul Brians' home page. Dr. Brians is a professor of English at Washington State University.
3. Read through the page and click on **Go to errors.**
4. On the Common Errors in English page, click on the following explanations:
    bring/take   lead/led   lie/lay   pole/poll
5. Put the words and definitions in your list of troublesome words.

LOOKING BACK

Posttest

Directions: *In the space provided, write the letter of the correct answer.*

1. In the sentence *Decision-making software helps users make decisions quickly,*
   the verb *helps* is
   a. a linking verb.
   b. a helping verb.
   c. an action verb.
   d. an intransitive verb.

   1. ___c___

2. In the sentence *Brainstorming is a method to increase your creativity,*
   the verb *is* is
   a. a linking verb.
   b. a helping verb.
   c. an action verb.
   d. a transitive verb.

   2. ___a___

3. In the sentence *Many software programs are devoted to creating business plans,*
   the verb *are* is
   a. a linking verb.
   b. a helping verb.
   c. an action verb.
   d. an intransitive verb.

   3. ___b___

4. In the sentence *Good decision makers identify possible solutions to problems,*
   the verb *identify* is
   a. a linking verb.
   b. a helping verb.
   c. a transitive verb.
   d. an intransitive verb.

   4. ___c___

5. Which line consists only of irregular verb forms?
   a. succeed, consider, assess
   b. carry, result, try
   c. confer, wrap, stop
   d. leave, hear, pay

   5. ___d___

6. Which verb represents the past participle form?
   a. know
   b. knew
   c. known
   d. knowing

   6. ___c___

7. Which word represents the past form of a verb?
   a. given
   b. begun
   c. wore
   d. been

   7. ___c___

8. Which present participle verb form is spelled correctly?
   a. begining
   b. clarifing
   c. conferring
   d. stoping

   8. ___c___

9. Which verb requires an object?
   a. lay
   b. lie
   c. sit
   d. rise

   9. ___a___

10. Which of the following verbs is an intransitive verb?
    a. raise
    b. set
    c. lay
    d. sit

    10. ___d___

CHAPTER 10

Verb Tense, Voice, and Mood —Verbals

COMPUTER SOFTWARE

Software is a set of electronic instructions that enables a computer to perform certain tasks. Most software is classified into two major categories: system software and application software. A major type of system software is operating system software such as Windows, which tells the computer how to use its own components. Application software tells the computer how to accomplish specific tasks such as word processing.

Operating system software exists primarily for the benefit of the computer. Application software does almost every task imaginable. Thousands of applications—from business to entertainment—are available. Commercial software firms range in size from a single, self-employed programmer to huge corporations like Microsoft and IBM.

The biggest legal problem affecting the computer industry is software piracy, which is the illegal copying or use of programs. Using pirated software is a felony. Many people who use the Internet think that all the data available on it is free; however, downloading software or reference materials may violate someone else's copyright. Because of the difficulty in developing effective antipiracy schemes, software developers rely on the law and on people's respect for the law to use computer programs and other materials legally.

OBJECTIVES

After you have studied this chapter and completed the exercises, you will be able to do the following:

1. Use the irregular verbs *be, have,* and *do* correctly.
2. Use the present, past, and future tenses of verbs correctly.
3. Demonstrate the use of the perfect tenses, progressive tenses, and emphatic tenses of verbs in sentences.
4. Differentiate between active and passive voices of verbs.
5. Identify the three ways to express verb mood.
6. Demonstrate the functions of verbals—gerunds, participles, infinitives—in sentences.
7. Diagram sentences correctly.

TERMS TO REMEMBER

APPLICATION SOFTWARE

COPYRIGHT

OPERATING SYSTEM SOFTWARE

SOFTWARE

SOFTWARE PIRACY

LOOKING AHEAD

Pretest

Directions: *Check the underlined word(s). If the word is correct, write* **Yes** *in the space provided. If it is not correct, write the word correctly.*

1. You <u>was</u> correct in your evaluation of our file management needs.

    1. _____ were _____

2. Accounting programs <u>saves</u> small business owners time and money.

    2. _____ save _____

3. We <u>done</u> the promotion for the new software well in advance of its release.

    3. _____ did _____

4. I am certain that software prices will <u>rise</u> soon.

    4. _____ Yes _____

5. I <u>had used</u> an outdated database package for several years before I got an updated version.

    5. _____ Yes _____

6. I <u>have sent</u> you a corrected copy of the manuscript.

    6. _____ Yes _____

7. Our company <u>produces</u> several accounting programs.

    7. _____ Yes _____

8. I move that the meeting <u>is</u> adjourned.

    8. _____ be _____

9. We appreciate <u>you</u> advising us to keep a record of our software expenses for tax purposes.

    9. _____ your _____

10. Writing a weekly software column <u>keeps</u> Maggie busy.

    10. _____ Yes _____

OVERVIEW

Now that you have studied the principal parts of regular and irregular verbs, you are ready to apply this knowledge to form the present, past, and future tenses of verbs. If you are still experiencing difficulty with the parts of verbs, make a list of those that you miss most frequently and memorize them.

You have probably heard the saying "It's the small things that make a difference." This saying can be applied to verbs as well. Knowing how to use the "small" verbs—*be, do,* and *have*—correctly is especially important.

As you learn about verb tenses, you will see why many writers prefer the active voice rather than the passive voice in writing business documents. Verbs also have moods. You are familiar with your own moods and how they affect what you do and feel. Mood also refers to the way verbs express their actions.

Some verb forms known as verbals look like verbs, but they function as nouns, adjectives, or adverbs in sentences. You will study gerunds, participles, and infinitives and learn to use these forms correctly.

IRREGULAR VERBS: *BE, DO, AND HAVE*

As you learned in Chapter 9, irregular verbs require extra study since there are no specific guidelines to follow when forming their parts. Three of the irregular verbs—*be, do,* and *have*—require additional special attention. You will find it helpful to memorize the parts of these three frequently used verbs.

See Instructor Notes 10-1, 10-2, 10-3, and 10-4 in IAE.

Go to Transparencies/PowerPoints 10-1a and 10-1b.

Verbs	Present Part	Past Part	Past Participle	Present Participle
(be)	am, is, are	was, were	been	being
(have)	have, has	had	had	having
(do)	do, does	did	done	doing

The following charts indicate the singular and plural verb forms of *be, do,* and *have* for first, second, and third persons. The present form of the verb is in the first set of parentheses. The past form is in the second set of parentheses.

Review regular and irregular verb forms in Chapter 9. Keep a list of those verbs with which you have difficulty.

Past participles and present participles require helping verbs. See Chapter 9 for a list of helping verbs.

Be

Singular

First Person:	I (am) (was)
Second Person:	you (are) (were)
Third Person:	he, she, it (is) (was)
	Mary (is) (was)

Plural

First Person: we (are) (were)

Second Person: you (are) (were)

Third Person: they (are) (were)

Mary and Tom (are) (were)

I was correct in the way I changed my password.

(*Was* is a linking verb used with *I*, a singular subject in first person.)

They were lab partners in the computer courses at Heald Business College last quarter.

(*Were* is a linking verb used with *they*, a plural subject in third person.)

She was experimenting with several new software programs.

(The verb phrase *was experimenting* consists of a present participle *experimenting* and a helping verb *was*. The verb phrase is used with *she*, a singular subject in third person.)

Do

Singular

First Person: I (do) (did)

Second Person: you (do) (did)

Third Person: he, she, it (does) (did)

Mary (does) (did)

Plural

First Person: we (do) (did)

Second Person: you (do) (did)

Third Person: they (do) (did)

Mary and Tom (do) (did)

The software technicians did the corrections for our program without charge.

(*Did* is the main verb used with *software technicians*, a third-person plural subject.)

We do the software preview tests in our Lexington plant.

(*Do* is the main verb used with *we*, a first-person plural subject.)

Sherry did not memorize her password.

(*Memorize* is the main verb, and *did* is the helping verb. Sherry is a third-person singular subject.)

Have

Singular

First Person: I (have) (had)

Second Person: you (have) (had)

Third Person: he, she, it (has) (had)

Mary (has) (had)

Plural

First Person:	we (have) (had)
Second Person:	you (have) (had)
Third Person:	they (have) (had)
	Mary and Tom (have) (had)

We _have_ partnerships with several leading independent software vendors.

(*Have* is the main verb used with we, a plural subject in first person.)

She _has_ a new password.

(*Has* is the main verb used with *she*, a singular subject in third person.)

They _have ordered_ another copy of the software instructions.

(The verb phrase *have ordered* consists of a past participle *ordered* and the helping verb *have*. The phrase is used with *they*, a plural subject in third person.)

CHECKUP 10-1

Directions: *Select the correct word, and write it in the space provided.*

1. We (*was, were*) at the computer products exhibition on Saturday. <u>were</u>

2. They (*do, does*) the programming research in the Dallas office. <u>do</u>

3. Nick (*had, have*) Quicken installed on his home computer. <u>had</u>

4. Gina (*did, done*) the artwork for the advertisement for our new database package. <u>did</u>

5. You (*was, were*) in the software design department <u>were</u>
   before I (*was, were*) hired. <u>was</u>

6. He (*has done, done*) a virus check on our software several times. <u>has done</u>

7. It (*is, are*) easy to forget software instructions if <u>is</u>
   you (*do, does*) not use the software regularly. <u>do</u>

8. You (*did, done*) the evaluation of the three software <u>did</u>
   packages in record time.

9. We (*has, have*) not received the updated documentation yet. <u>have</u>

10. She (*was, were*) learning two software programs concurrently. <u>was</u>

**GO TO
CD-ROM**
CHECKUP 10-1

VERB TENSE

In addition to describing "what happens" to a subject in a sentence, a verb indicates "when it happens." The tense of a verb helps to identify the time of an action or a state of being. Although a verb has several tenses, its principal ones are referred to as the simple tenses—the *present*, the *past*, and the *future*.

See Instructor Notes 10-5 and 10-6 in IAE.

Present Tense

Go to Transparency/PowerPoint 10-2a.

Be aware of the changes in verb forms when subjects are third-person singular.

Use the present tense to express a general truth or an action that is occurring now. Also, use the present tense to express an action that occurs regularly or habitually.

> **Dana completes the questionnaire quickly.**
> (*Completes* is a verb in the present tense that indicates an action occurring now.)
>
> **The new software program costs $900.**
> (*Costs* is a verb in the present tense that expresses a general truth.)
>
> **My supervisor makes all the decisions about software training.**
> (*Makes* is a verb in the present tense that indicates a regularly occurring action.)

With Singular Subjects.   Add *s* to a verb in present tense when the subject is a third-person singular noun (*company*) or a third-person singular pronoun (*he, she,* or *it*). Add *es* to the verb if it ends in *o, ch, s, sh, x,* or *z*.

> **Mark knows**   **he knows**
> (*Mark* is a third-person singular noun; *he* is a third-person singular pronoun. The present tense of the verb requires an *s*.)
>
> | | |
> |---|---|
> | **The sound echoes** | **it echoes** |
> | **Mr. Lawton teaches** | **he teaches** |
> | **the student misses** | **he or she misses** |
> | **a programmer finishes** | **he or she finishes** |
> | **the accountant faxes** | **he or she faxes** |
> | **the phone buzzes** | **it buzzes** |
>
> (Add *es* to verbs that end in *o, ch, s, sh, x,* or *z*.)

See Instructor Note 10-7 in IAE.

With Plural Subjects.   Do not add *s* or *es* to a verb in the present tense when the subject is a plural noun or a compound subject.

> | | |
> |---|---|
> | **we know** | **Mark and Lynn teach** |
> | **sounds echo** | **accountants fax** |

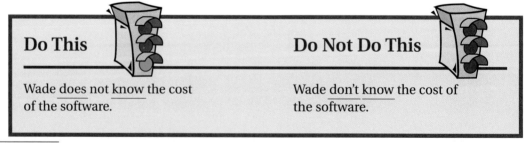

Do This	Do Not Do This
Wade does not know the cost of the software.	Wade don't know the cost of the software.

Use the singular form of do (does) with a singular third-person noun or pronoun.

Two examples of present tense verbs with first-, second-, and third-person subjects follow:

Present Tense Regular Verb: *Work*

	Singular Subject	Plural Subject
First Person:	I (work)	we (work)
Second Person:	you (work)	you (work)
Third Person:	he, she, it (works)	they (work)
	Kim (works)	

Present Tense Irregular Verb: *Build*

	Singular Subject	Plural Subject
First Person:	I (build)	we (build)
Second Person:	you (build)	you (build)
Third Person:	he, she, it (builds)	they (build)
	Ron (builds)	

CHECKUP 10-2

Directions: *Complete each sentence by writing the present tense of the verb in parentheses. Circle the subject in each sentence.*

1. (I) (*spend*) a lot of time installing software updates.
   spend

2. A user's (concern) with a new program (*deserve*) a response from the manufacturer.
   deserves

3. (Va Maoa) (*miss*) her old version of word processing software.
   misses

4. This (example) (*show*) how software can be applied to your operations.
   shows

5. Popular (software) often (*come*) with work-group features.
   comes

6. (You) (*receive*) excellent online tutorials with all our programs.
   receive

**GO TO
CD-ROM**
CHECKUP 10-2

Past Tense

Use past tense to express an action or condition that was started and completed in the past. Regular verbs require *d* or *ed* endings for their past tenses. Irregular verbs form their past tenses in various ways. Do not use a helping verb with a main verb to form the past tense.

Go to
Transparency/PowerPoint
10-2b.

Refer to Chapter 9 or your dictionary when you are not certain about the spelling of a verb in past tense. Most dictionaries include the spelling of irregular verb parts; they do not identify the parts of most regular verbs.

> Last week Mr. Sullivan <u>interviewed</u> ten candidates for the hotline technician's position.
>
> (*Interviewed* is a regular verb in past tense that indicates Mr. Sullivan already completed the action.)
>
> He <u>found</u> several clip art images and <u>used</u> them in the last issue of the newsletter.
>
> (*Found* is an irregular verb and *used* is a regular verb. Both are in past tense and indicate the actions took place in the past.)

Two past tense verbs in first, second, and third person appear below.

Past Tense Regular Verb: *Assist*

Use other verbs from the lists of regular and irregular verbs in Chapter 9 to practice forming past tenses.

	Singular Subject	Plural Subject
First Person:	I (assisted)	we (assisted)
Second Person:	you (assisted)	you (assisted)
Third Person:	he, she, it (assisted)	they (assisted)
	Jon (assisted)	

Do This	Do Not Do This
The intranet cost several thousand dollars to install.	The intranet costed several thousand dollars to install.

Costed *is not a verb form. Use the past tense* cost. *The present and past tenses for the verb* cost *are the same.*

No helping verbs are necessary with main verbs when forming the past tense.

Past Tense Irregular Verb: *Forget*

	Singular Subject	Plural Subject
First Person:	I (forgot)	we (forgot)
Second Person:	you (forgot)	you (forgot)
Third Person:	he, she, it (forgot)	they (forgot)
	Jon (forgot)	

Do This	Do Not Do This
They saw the newest contact management software.	They seen the newest contact management software.

Do not use the past participle form when you need a past tense verb. Seen *always requires a helping verb.*

CHECKUP 10-3

Review the to be *verb parts at the beginning of this chapter.*

See Instructor Note 10-8 in IAE.

Directions: *In the space provided, write the tense of the verb indicated in parentheses.*

1. We (*buy,* past) the software on the basis of its Best Buy rating.   bought

2. Our firm (*complete,* past) its analysis of accounting software packages.   completed

3. Project management software (*allow,* present) the user to break any   allows
   job into smaller tasks and track the progress of those tasks.

4. Leslie (*give,* past) some professional pointers on how to   gave
   use desktop publishing.

5. I (*be*, past) positive that my mailing labels (*be*, past) appropriate for my printer.   was   were

6. Clip art images (*be*, present) helpful to newsletter editors.   are

7. Accounting software (*do*, present) not replace a good accountant or a knowledge of basic bookkeeping.   does

8. A header (*appear*, present) at the top of a page, and a footer (*appear*, present) at the bottom of a page.   appears   appears

GO TO CD-ROM
CHECKUP 10-3

Future Tense

Use future tense to indicate an action or condition that will occur in the future. To form the future tense, use the helping verbs *will* or *shall* before the present part of the verb.

Go to Transparency/PowerPoint 10-3.

See Instructor Note 10-9 in IAE.

He will explain the integration of the two programs.
(*Explain* is the present part of the verb; *will* is the helping verb. *Will explain* is the verb phrase that indicates the explanation will be done in the future.)

Our software will arrive by Federal Express.
(*Arrive* is the present part of the verb; *will* is the helping verb. *Will arrive* is the verb phrase that indicates the software has not arrived but will arrive in the future.)

CHECKUP 10-4

Directions: Check the underlined word(s) for future tense usage. If the word(s) indicate future tense, write **Yes** in the space provided. If the word(s) do not indicate future tense, write your corrections in the space provided.

1. The Software Publishers Association will educate users about laws regarding computer software.   Yes

2. We used our desktop publishing program to produce brochures and newsletters.   will use

3. We will investigate several off-the-shelf accounting programs.   Yes

4. Our computer users' group reviewed its objectives.   will review

5. The software checked other users' calendars for free dates and times.   will check

6. The new software makes the payroll easier to prepare.   will make

GO TO CD-ROM
CHECKUP 10-4

See Instructor Notes 10-10 and 10-11 in IAE.

Review the past participles of regular and irregular verbs in Chapter 9. The perfect tenses require the helping verbs has, have, had, shall have, or will have.

Go to PowerPoint 10-4.

Perfect Tenses

In addition to the present, past, and future tenses (the simple tenses), there are three perfect tenses—the *present perfect*, the *past perfect*, and the *future perfect*.

Present Perfect Tense.   Use the present perfect tense to show that an action or condition that started in the past has just been completed or continues to take place up to the present. Use *has* or *have* with the past participle of a verb to form the present perfect tense.

> **Our firm has finished the testing of the software.**
>
> (*Has finished* is a verb phrase that consists of the past participle *finished* and the helping verb *has.* The verb phrase shows the action has recently been completed.)
>
> **We have found the instructions for installing the software difficult to understand.**
>
> (*Have found* is a verb phrase that consists of the past participle *found* and the helping verb *have.* The action in present perfect tense indicates the firm found the directions difficult to understand in the past and continues to find them difficult up to the present time.)

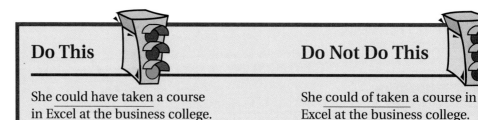

Do This	Do Not Do This
She could have taken a course in Excel at the business college.	She could of taken a course in Excel at the business college.

Do not use the preposition of as a substitution for the verb have.

Go to PowerPoint 10-5.

The verb will rather than shall appears in much of today's writing. Shall is commonly used in legal documents, however.

Go to PowerPoint 10-6.

Past Perfect Tense.   Use the past perfect tense to show that one action or condition began and was completed *before* another action in the past started. Use the helping verb *had* with the past participle of a verb to form the past perfect tense.

> **She had prepared her demonstration before the programmers made some major software changes.**
>
> (The action of preparing the demonstration was started and completed *before* another past action [that of the programmers] was completed.)
>
> **By the time *InfoWorld* published its evaluation, the manufacturer had increased the cost.**
>
> (The action by the manufacturer was started and completed before another past action [that of *InfoWorld*] was completed.)

Future Perfect Tense.   Use the future perfect tense to indicate an action or condition that will begin and end before a specific future time. Use the helping verbs *shall have* or *will have* before the past participle of a verb to form the future perfect tense.

He will have learned the software before next weekend.
(*Will have learned* is a verb phrase that consists of the past participle *learned* and the helping verbs *will* and *have.* The action of learning begins and ends before the future time of *next weekend.*)

By next year, all my software statistics will have become obsolete.
(*Will have become* is a verb phrase that consists of the past participle *become* and the helping verbs *will* and *have.* The action of becoming obsolete begins and ends before the future time of *next year.*)

An example of the perfect tense verbs—present, past, future—in first, second, and third person appears below.

Perfect Tense Irregular Verb: *See*

Present Perfect Tense

	Singular Subject	Plural Subject
First Person:	I (have seen)	We (have seen)
Second Person:	you (have seen)	you (have seen)
Third Person:	he, she, it (has seen)	they (have seen)
	Tom (has seen)	

Past Perfect Tense

	Singular Subject	Plural Subject
First Person:	I (had seen)	we (had seen)
Second Person:	you (had seen)	you (had seen)
Third Person:	he, she, it (had seen)	they (had seen)
	Tom (had seen)	

Future Perfect Tense

	Singular Subject	Plural Subject
First Person:	I (will [or shall]) have seen	we (will [or shall] have seen)
Second Person:	you (will have seen)	you (will have seen)
Third Person:	he, she, it (will have seen)	they (will have seen)
	Tom (will have seen)	

> Note that the present perfect tense uses *has* or *have.* *The past perfect tense uses* had, *and the future perfect tense uses* will have.

CHECKUP 10-5

Directions: *Fill in the blanks with the verb tense indicated. The first column gives you the present part of the verb with the subject in parentheses. See the example as a guide. Use your text if you are uncertain about a form.*

See Instructor Note 10-12 in IAE.

Present Part	Present Perfect	Past Perfect	Future Perfect
Ex. solve (he)	he has solved	he had solved	he will have solved
1. begin (I)	I have begun	I had begun	I will have begun
2. cover (it)	it has covered	it had covered	it will have covered

3. do (she)	she has done	she had done	she will have done
4. sample (they)	they have sampled	they had sampled	they will have sampled
5. break (you)	you have broken	you had broken	you will have broken
6. use (company)	a company has used	a company had used	a company will have used
7. carry (we)	we have carried	we had carried	we will have carried
8. see (Ryan)	Ryan has seen	Ryan had seen	Ryan will have seen

**GO TO
CD-ROM**
CHECKUP 10-5

See Instructor Note 10-13 in
IAE.

*Review the present participles
listed in Chapter 9.*

Progressive Tenses

The six progressive tenses follow the patterns of the simple and perfect tenses. These progressive tenses show continuing actions or conditions. The progressive tenses consist of the present participle (main verb ending in *ing*) and appropriate tenses of *to be* (*am, is, are, was, were, will be, shall be, have been, has been, had been,* or *will have been*).

Present Progressive Tense.   Use the present participle plus the helping verbs *am, is,* or *are* to form the present progressive tense. This tense involves an action or condition that is in progress at the present time.

> I <u>am using</u> a personal finance software program.

Past Progressive Tense.   Use the present participle plus the helping verbs *was* or *were* to form the past progressive tense. This tense involves an action or condition that was in progress at a time in the past.

> I <u>was using</u> a personal finance software program.

Future Progressive Tense.   Use the present participle plus the helping verb *will be* or *shall be* to form the future progressive tense. This tense involves an action or condition that will continue in the future.

> I <u>will be using</u> a personal finance software program.

Present Perfect Progressive Tense.   Use the present participle plus the helping verbs *have been* or *has been* to form the present perfect progressive tense. This tense describes a continuous action up to the present time.

> I <u>have been using</u> a personal software program since 1997.

Past Perfect Progressive Tense.   Use the present participle plus the helping verbs *had been* to form the past perfect progressive tense. This tense describes an action that was being completed at a specific time in the past.

> I <u>had been using</u> a personal finance software program until I learned an accounting program.

Future Perfect Progressive Tense. Use the present participle plus the helping verbs *will (shall) have been* to form the future perfect progressive tense. This tense describes an action that will continue to be in progress at a specified time in the future.

> By the end of this month, I <u>will have been using</u> a personal finance software program for at least three years.

Emphatic Tense

The present and past tenses have additional forms, called emphatic tenses, that add emphasis to the verb. Use the verbs *do* or *does* with the present part of a verb to form the present emphatic tense. Use the verb *did* with the present part of a verb to form the past emphatic tense.

> I <u>do make</u> an effort to read the ads for new software products.

(*Do* gives extra emphasis to the verb *make* and indicates present emphatic tense.)

> She <u>does place</u> an emphasis on software security.

(*Does* emphasizes the verb *place* and indicates present emphatic tense.)

> My manager <u>did show</u> me how to improve the formatting of the newsletter.

(*Did* emphasizes the verb *show* and indicates past emphatic tense.)

CHECKUP 10-6

Directions: *Underline the progressive or emphatic tense verbs in the following sentences. Using the codes below, indicate the number of the verb tense in the space provided. Refer to your text if you are uncertain about a form.*

See Instructor Note 10-14 in IAE.

1	=	present progressive tense
2	=	past progressive tense
3	=	future progressive tense
4	=	present perfect progressive tense
5	=	past perfect progressive tense
6	=	future perfect progressive tense
7	=	present emphatic tense
8	=	past emphatic tense

1. Tracey <u>is considering</u> the purchase of scheduling software for her catering business. **(1)**

2. They <u>will be doing</u> a software satisfaction survey throughout the week. **(3)**

3. We <u>did try</u> to obtain everyone's input concerning additional software needs. **(8)**

4. I <u>was reading</u> a computer magazine when my supervisor called. **(2)**

5. Selena <u>has been learning</u> several new software packages. **(4)**

6. They <u>do provide</u> excellent software training videos. **(7)**

7. Until this summer, the firm <u>had been hiring</u> computer software specialists. **(5)**

8. By the end of the summer, I <u>will have been working</u> as a data entry clerk for a year. **(6)**

**GO TO
CD-ROM**
CHECKUP 10-6

VOICE

Go to
PowerPoints 10-7 and 10-8.

An action verb may be in *active* or *passive* voice. Active voice means that the subject of a sentence performs the action. Passive voice means the subject receives the action. Use the *active* voice for most business writing. Use the *passive* voice if you want to draw attention to an act rather than to the person or thing performing the act. The passive voice consists of a past participle of the verb and one or more forms of the helping verb *be*.

We tested several new pieces of software.
(The subject *We* is performing the action. The verb *tested* is in active voice.)

Several new pieces of software were tested by us.
(*Pieces* is the subject being acted upon; *pieces* are not performing the action. The verb phrase *were tested* is in passive voice.)

Some computer applications require considerable computer memory.
(The subject *applications* is performing the action. The verb *require* is in active voice.)

Considerable computer memory is required for some computer applications.
(The verb is in passive voice.)

Business managers frequently use off-the-shelf accounting programs.
(The subject *managers* is performing the action. The verb *use* is in active voice.)

Off-the-shelf accounting programs are used most frequently by business managers.
(The subject *programs* is being acted upon. The verb is in passive voice.)

Several inappropriate software purchases were made in the past.
(Use the passive voice when you do not wish to identify the person who made the inappropriate purchases.)

The awards were announced at the annual Software Users' Association Conference.
(Use the passive voice. The awards are more important than the person who announced them.)

CHECKUP 10-7

A. Directions: In the space provided, write **A** if the action verb is in the active voice. Write **P** if the verb is in the passive voice.

1. A simple accounting package was recommended by my CPA.   P

2. We needed software for payroll and inventory control.   A

Chapter 10

3. Our firm paid $500 per person for training last year.   <u>A</u>

4. Large corporations hire consultants to locate the right company software.   <u>A</u>

5. Her presentation was supported by interesting graphics.   <u>P</u>

Directions: *Change the voice in the following sentences from passive to active. Write the corrected sentence in the space provided.*

1. The illegal software was downloaded from the Internet by Joseph.

Joseph downloaded the illegal software from the Internet.

2. The office suite software was purchased by Barbara.

Barbara purchased the office suite software.

3. One of the largest collections of shareware is held by the Public Software Library in Houston.

The Public Software Library in Houston holds one of the largest collections of shareware.

4. The new accounting software was highly recommended by Steve.

Steve highly recommended the new accounting software.

5. The software consultants were hired by Ashley.

Ashley hired the software consultants

**GO TO
CD-ROM**
CHECKUP 10-7

MOOD

The mood of a verb indicates whether the sentence is intended to make a statement, give a command, ask a question, express necessity, or express a wish or a statement contrary to fact. The three moods are *indicative, imperative,* and *subjunctive.*

See the discussion in Chapter 3 regarding indicative and imperative types of sentences.

Indicative Mood

Use the indicative mood to state facts or to ask direct questions.

See Instructor Note 10-15 in IAE.

We distributed the brochures to all the stores where our software is sold.
(The sentence makes a statement of fact.)

Are you familiar with personal information manager (PIM) software?
(The sentence is a question.)

Imperative Mood

Use the imperative mood to give instructions and commands or to make courteous requests. The subject of a verb in the imperative mood is *you,* which is usually omitted.

Return this software to the accounting department.
(*You,* the subject, is understood. *You* represents the person to whom the instruction is given. The sentence expresses a command.)

Will you please return this software to the accounting department.
(The instruction, *Will you please,* is a courteous request. The sentence requires action, not words, and needs a period rather than a question mark.)

Subjunctive Mood

Go to PowerPoint 10-9.

10-16 Refer to a manual such as *The Gregg Reference Manual* for an explanation of the subjunctive mood.

To Express Conditions Contrary to Fact. Use a subjunctive verb to express a condition that is contrary to fact or subject to an element of doubt. The verb *were* is used for *was*.

> **If I were you,** I would not revise the original document.
>
> (*If I were you* [I am not you] is contrary to fact. Do not use *If I was you.*)
>
> **If I were the purchasing agent,** I would pay attention to the employees' suggestions about software.
>
> (*If I were* indicates a phrase contrary to fact. You are not the purchasing agent.)

To Express a Wish. Use a subjunctive verb in sentences that begin with an expression of a wish.

> **I wish I were** more skilled in using my word processing software.
>
> (The sentence expresses a wish. Do not use *I wish I was.*)
>
> **He wishes he were** going to the netware demonstration workshop.
>
> (The sentence expresses a wish. Do not use *He wishes he was.*)

To State Motions. Use the subjunctive form in a clause beginning with *that*, which states a motion or formal proposal.

> **He moved that the meeting be adjourned.**
>
> (This is a motion, and it requires the subjunctive form of the verb *be* in the *that* clause. Do not use the verb *is.*)

CHECKUP 10-8

GO TO
CD-ROM
CHECKUP 10-8

*Directions: Identify the mood of the sentence by writing **IN** (Indicative mood), **IM** (Imperative mood), or **S** (Subjunctive mood) in the blank.*

1. If I were the project leader, I would ask management for more sophisticated project management software. — S

2. Are you aware of the legal implications in copying software? — IN

3. Please call our toll-free number to receive information on the accounting package. — IM

4. We wish we were able to answer your questions concerning netware systems. — S

5. Our desktop publishing software is not suitable for full-color documents. — IN

6. Check the software installation procedures carefully. — IM

Sometimes words that look like verbs function instead as nouns, adjectives, or adverbs. These verb forms are called verbals. The three verbals are *gerunds*, *participles*, and *infinitives*.

See Instructor Note 10-17 in IAE.

Go to PowerPoint 10-10.

See Instructor Note 10-18 in IAE.

Gerunds

A gerund is a verb form ending in *ing* that functions as a noun. A *gerund phrase* includes a gerund and any modifiers that are needed to make the meaning complete. Every word that ends in *ing* is not a gerund. Many words that end in *ing* are parts of verb phrases; others are participles. (See the section on participles that follows.)

Gerunds end in ing *and always function as nouns.*

Gerund Use.   Use a gerund as a subject (noun), object of a verb (noun), or object of a preposition (noun).

Using off-the-shelf software saves new business owners money.
(*Using off-the-shelf software* is a gerund phrase that functions as the subject of the sentence.)

Carla enjoyed designing software programs.
(*Designing software programs* is a gerund phrase that functions as the object of a sentence. The phrase answers the question, "Paula enjoyed what?")

Small companies often have problems with handling software changes.
(*Handling* is a gerund that functions as the object of the preposition *with*.)

Gerund Modifiers.   Use the possessive case of a noun or pronoun to modify a gerund.

We appreciated your teaching the introduction to computers course last quarter.
(*Teaching* is a gerund that functions as a direct object. In this sentence, the gerund *teaching* requires the possessive pronoun *your* before it. Do not use the pronoun *you*.)

I questioned his bringing the controversial topics into the discussion so quickly.
(Use the possessive case *his* to modify the gerund *bringing*; do not use *him bringing*.)

CHECKUP 10-9

Directions: In the following sentences, underline the gerund or gerund phrase once. Underline the main verb or verb phrase twice.

See Instructor Note 10-19 in IAE.

GO TO CD-ROM CHECKUP 10-9

1. Backing up software requires only a few minutes of time.

2. Maria enjoys designing integrated office suite programs.

3. Training new employees in the use of our groupware program requires time.

4. Small businesses should try using off-the-shelf software.

5. Reviewing sales literature is giving me some good ideas for buying software.

6. Records management software involves tracking active and inactive records.

Participles

A participle is a verbal that functions as an adjective. A *participial phrase* consists of a present, past, or perfect participle plus any additional modifiers; it also functions as an adjective. A *present participle* ends in *ing.* A *past participle* ends in *ed* for regular verbs and changes for irregular verbs. A *perfect participle* includes the word *having* before the past participle.

Review past and present participles in Chapter 9.

Use a participle or participial phrase as an adjective to modify a noun or a pronoun. Do not confuse a participle with a gerund that functions as a subject or an object of a sentence. Use a comma to set off an introductory participle or participial phrase.

> **Finding the software difficult to use, I selected another program.**
> *(Finding the software difficult to use* is a participial phrase that modifies the subject *I. Finding* is a present participle. Use a comma after the word *use* in the introductory participial phrase.)

See Instructor Notes 10-20 and 10-21 in IAE.

Punctuation ALERT!

Use a comma after an introductory participial phrase.

> **Assisted by the hotline operator, she was able to solve her problem.**
> (The participial phrase modifies *she,* the subject of the sentence. *Assisted* is a past participle. Use a comma after the participial phrase.)

> **Having reviewed the satisfaction surveys, I decided to purchase the software.**
> (The participial phrase modifies *I,* the subject of the sentence. *Having reviewed* is a perfect participial phrase. Use a comma after the participial phrase.)

> **We bought some used software for our children.**
> *(Used* is a past participle that modifies *software*).

> **The software cost $1000 plus handling charges.**
> *(Handling* is a present participle that modifies *charges.*)

SLIP-UP

Children on school buses weighing less than 10,000 pounds must be restrained. Source: Richard Lederer. [Note: Is the reference to the weight of the children or to the weight of the buses?]

284

Chapter 10

Directions: *Underline the participle or participial phrase in the following sentences. In the space provided, write the noun or pronoun that the participle or participial phrase modifies.*

1. <u>Using her spell-check feature</u>, Carla completed the daily crossword puzzle quickly.   <u>Carla</u>

2. Josh designed the <u>winning</u> logo for our new computer products store.   <u>logo</u>

3. <u>Putting aside my personal preferences</u>, I accepted the group's recommendation to change spreadsheet programs.   <u>I</u>

4. The <u>enlightening</u> speech created a great deal of discussion.   <u>speech</u>

5. I was concerned about the <u>broken</u> lock on a software storage cabinet.   <u>lock</u>

6. <u>Knowing my supervisor's previous reactions</u>, I hesitated asking for contact management software.   <u>I</u>

**GO TO
CD-ROM
CHECKUP 10-10**

Infinitives

An infinitive is a verbal that consists of the present part of a verb plus the word *to*. An *infinitive phrase* is the infinitive and its modifiers.

Use an infinitive or infinitive phrase as a noun, adjective, or an adverb. Do not confuse an infinitive phrase with a prepositional phrase. The infinitive phrase has the word *to* preceding the verb. Use a comma to set off an introductory infinitive phrase. Do not use a comma if the infinitive phrase is the subject of the sentence.

> **<u>To make a decision about a software purchase</u> requires a careful evaluation of each product.**
>
> (*To make a decision about a software purchase* is an infinitive phrase. The infinitive consists of the present tense of *make* plus the word *to*. The infinitive phrase in this sentence functions as a noun and is the subject of the sentence. This phrase does not require a comma.)

> **<u>To make a decision about software purchases</u>, evaluate each product carefully.**
>
> (The infinitive phrase is the same as in the example above, but it now functions as an adjective modifying *you* [understood subject]. A comma is necessary after the phrase.)

> **I wanted <u>to buy the least expensive word processing package available</u>.**
>
> (*To buy the least expensive word processing package available* is an infinitive phrase used as a noun—the direct object of the verb *wanted*. The phrase provides the answer to the question [*Wanted what?*].)

SLIP-UP

Sign in a hotel in Athens: "Visitors are expected to complain at the office between the hours of 9 and 11 a.m. daily." Source: Derek Davies.

10-22 Refer to a manual such as *The Gregg Reference Manual* for a discussion of commas after introducing phrases.

See Instructor Note 10-23 in IAE.

Punctuation ALERT!

Use a comma to set off an introductory infinitive phrase unless the infinitive phrase is the subject of the sentence.

See Instructor Note 10-24 in
IAE.

**If you will wait a minute, I will give you a software hotline number
to call.**

(*To call* is an infinitive used as an adjective, which modifies the noun
number.)

Do This	Do Not Do This
Our supervisor asked us to <u>proofread</u> our documents carefully.	Our supervisor asked us to carefully <u>proofread</u> our documents.
Acceptable	**Awkward**
<u>To deliberately evade</u> the issue of copying software is unwise.	<u>To evade</u> the issue of copying software <u>deliberately</u> is unwise.

Do not split an infinitive unless
it sounds awkward or loses
meaning in the process. A split
infinitive means that an adverb
appears between to and the
verb.

CHECKUP 10-11

*Directions: In the following sentences, underline the infinitive or infinitive phrase
once. Underline the main verb or verb phrase twice.*

1. Our company's accountants <u>advised</u> us <u>to buy accounts receivable, accounts payable, and
billing modules.</u>

2. You <u>know</u> that it <u>is</u> not hard <u>to get different software programs</u> <u>to "talk" to each other.</u>

3. She <u>used</u> a full-featured desktop publishing program <u>to produce the 200-page documentation.</u>

4. Our CPAs <u>examined</u> the software and <u>decided</u> <u>to install Personal Tax Edge.</u>

5. This software <u>permits</u> us <u>to streamline our ordering processes.</u>

6. Without our groupware installation, we <u>would have</u> to hire an additional employee.

**GO TO
CD-ROM**
CHECKUP 10-11

CHECKUP 10-12

*Directions: The sentences below are from the Secondary Learning paragraphs.
Underline the infinitive or infinitive phrase once, underline the gerund or gerund
phrase twice, and circle the participle or participial phrase.*

1. Software is a set of electronic instructions that enables a computer <u>to perform certain tasks.</u>

2. A major type of system software is (operating) system software such as Windows, which tells
the computer how <u>to use its own components.</u>

3. Application software tells the computer how to accomplish specific tasks such as word processing.

4. Using pirated software is a felony.

5. Many people who use the Internet think that all the data available on it is free; however, downloading software or reference materials may violate someone else's copyright.

GO TO
CD-ROM
CHECKUP 10-12

DIAGRAMMING SENTENCES

A *gerund* functions as a noun in a sentence and may be a subject or an object. To diagram a gerund, place it on a step. Place the gerund so that it curves along the lines. If the gerund is a subject, position it in the subject location. If the gerund is an object, position it in the object location.

They considered selecting the most expensive program. (object)

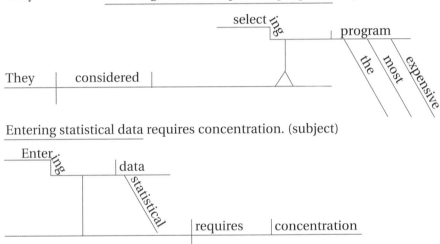

Entering statistical data requires concentration. (subject)

A *participle* functions as an adjective in a sentence. To diagram a participle or participial phrase, place it under the noun or pronoun it modifies. The participle curves along the line.

Completing their project, they contacted Sequent Software Company.

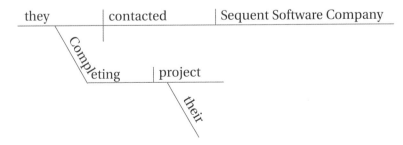

Verb Tense, Voice, and Mood—Verbals

CHECKUP 10-13

See Instructor Note 10-25 in IAE.

Directions: *Diagram the following sentences in the space provided.*

1. She denied copying Excel and Peachtree.

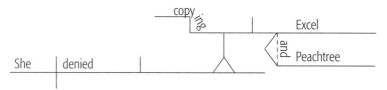

2. Using the WordPerfect thesaurus, I checked several synonyms.

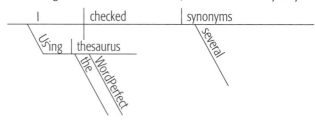

3. My supervisor approved subcontracting the software bid.

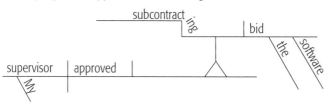

4. Using accounting software helps small business owners.

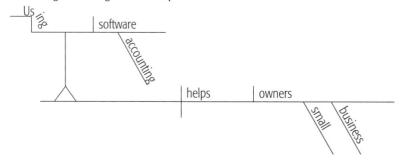

5. Working long hours, Sam finished the network installation.

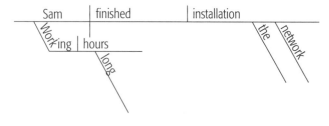

GO TO
CD-ROM
CHECKUP 10-13

Chapter 10

NAME _____

PRACTICE 1A

A. Directions: Select the correct word, and write it in the space provided.

1. I (*did, done*) the spreadsheet exercises during my lunch hour.

   1. _____did_____

2. The latest version of our accounting software (*cost, costed*) more than $1000.

   2. _____cost_____

3. The salesperson disliked (*me, my*) asking so many questions about the online banking software.

   3. _____my_____

4. All of our spreadsheet work requires (*concentrate, concentrated*) attention.

   4. ___concentrated___

5. He (*does, do*) try to provide online answers to software questions.

   5. _____does_____

B. Directions: In the space provided, write the letter of the item that describes or identifies the underlined verb or verbal.

1. *The CPA Software News* <u>has</u> always <u>prepared</u> excellent reviews of new accounting products.

   1. ___c___

   a. present tense
   b. past tense
   c. perfect tense
   d. progressive tense

2. I learned <u>to use</u> a database program in a college computer class.

   2. ___c___

   a. verb phrase
   b. gerund
   c. infinitive
   d. participle

3. The latest version of my integrated software program <u>contains</u> artificial intelligence devices called "office assistants."

   3. ___a___

   a. present tense
   b. past tense
   c. perfect tense
   d. future tense

4. The information management department <u>will be issuing</u> its first newsletter this week.

   4. ___c___

   a. present
   b. past tense
   c. progressive tense
   d. future tense

5. Most software outlets <u>will stock</u> the most popular programs.

   5. ___b___

   a. present tense
   b. future tense
   c. emphatic tense
   d. progressive tense

**GO TO
CD-ROM
PRACTICE 1
EXERCISES**

PRACTICE

PRACTICE 2A

See Instructor Note 10-26 in
IAE.

A. **Directions:** *At the beginning of each sentence is a verb form. In the space provided, write the tense of the verb indicated.*

1. present perfect

He (*master*) a variety of business software.

1. <u>has mastered</u>

2. present

I (*need*) to import a spreadsheet into another document.

2. <u>need</u>

3. present progressive

Some software trainers (*use*) computer-based programs in their classes.

3. <u>are using</u>

4. future progressive

SRC Graphics (*hire*) two new technical trainers next month.

4. <u>will be hiring</u>

5. past

Larry (*bring*) the training videotapes to the last department meeting.

5. <u>brought</u>

6. past

Rebates and sales (*decrease*) the prices of desktop publishing software.

6. <u>decreased</u>

7. past perfect

He (*prepare*) a list of the advantages of each piece of software that our firm was considering.

7. <u>had prepared</u>

8. future

The videotapes (*show*) Jeff how the software works.

8. <u>will show</u>

9. past perfect

I (*see*) an advertisement for VoiceType, but I could not remember the source.

9. <u>had seen</u>

10. present

Foreign-currency management (*be*) a helpful feature for companies in international sales.

10. <u>is</u>

NAME _____

B. **Directions:** *In the space provided, correct the sentences containing incorrect verb forms. Some sentences may have punctuation errors. If a sentence has no errors, write Yes.*

1. She wrote software instructions and designs advertising brochures for a major computer firm.

   <u>She wrote software instructions and designed advertising brochures for a</u>

   <u>major computer firm.</u>

   <u>She writes software instructions and designs advertising brochures for a</u>

   <u>major computer firm.</u>

2. Abe's Muffler Company has began to depend on billing software in its collection procedures.

   <u>Abe's Muffler Company has begun to depend on billing software for its</u>

   <u>collection procedures.</u>

3. Will you please select spreadsheet software that are compatible with other software packages?

   <u>Will you please select spreadsheet software that is compatible with other</u>

   <u>software packages.</u>

4. This accounting software is used by many home business owners.

   <u>Many home business owners use this accounting software.</u>

5. Keying statistical data hurriedly often causes errors in my spread-sheets.

   <u>Yes</u>

6. I was surprised at him learning the new version of the software so quickly.

   <u>I was surprised at his learning the new version of the software so quickly.</u>

7. The broke printer made it impossible to produce the labels for the mass mailing project.

   <u>The broken printer made it impossible to produce the labels for the mass</u>

   <u>mailing project.</u>

GO TO
CD-ROM
PRACTICE 2
EXERCISES

NAME _____

PRACTICE 3A

PROOFREADING

10-27 Students may use proofreaders' marks to insert items or make corrections.

*Directions: Proofread and compare the two sentences in each group. If they are the same, write **Yes** in the space provided. If they are not the same, write **No.** Use the first sentence as the correct copy. If you find errors in the second sentence, underline them.*

1. Off-the-shelf accounting packages usually include accounts receivable, accounts payable, and general ledger functions.

   Off-the-<u>shelf-accounting</u> packages <u>usualy</u> include <u>account</u> <u>recievable</u>, accounts payable, and general ledger functions.

   1. <u>No</u>

2. Microsoft's "office assistant" consists of action icons that provide suggestions and tips.

   <u>Microsofts'</u> 'office assistant' consists of action icons that <u>provides</u> suggestions and tips.

   2. <u>No</u>

3. SystemWizard is a diagnostic program that analyzes the peripherals attached to a PC.

   SystemWizard <u>are</u> a diagnostic program that analyzes the peripherals attached to a PC.

   3. <u>No</u>

4. When someone copies software illegally, other consumers pay the price.

   When someone copies software illegally, other consumers <u>will</u> pay the <u>prices</u>.

   4. <u>No</u>

5. Randy uses videos to learn how to take advantage of the newest software in the automotive repair business.

   Randy uses videos to learn how to take advantage of the newest software in the automotive repair business.

   5. <u>Yes</u>

NAME _____

Proofreading Exercise

If you are thinking about purchasing additional software, give the task careful consideration. The following material gives some suggestions for selecting software:

SOFTWARE SELECTION GUIDELINES

List the tasks you need to perform now or need to perform in the future.

Make a list of the features you want your software to have.

Review the sales literature, trade magazines, and consumer reports.

Discuss advantages of various programs with software dealers.

Determine the ease of learning the software.

Find out about user support. Is there an 800 hotline number to call?

Identify the computer hardware you are currently using. Will the software work on the equipment you now have?

Know your printer requirements and limitations.

Directions: *Use the following proofreaders' marks to make corrections in the copy below. Use the above copy as your correct guide.*

See Instructor Notes 10-28 and 10-29 in IAE.

lowercase /	move left ⌐
capitalize ≡	move right ⌐
delete ⌒	insert space # / ∧
transpose ∩	insert letter ∧
delete space ⌒	insert comma ⋀
insert period ⊙	delete and close up ⌒

SOFTWARE SELECTOIN GUIDELINES

⌐List the tasks you need to perform or need to perform in the future. *now#*

Make a list of the features you want your software to have.

Review the sales literature, Trade magazines, and consumer reports⊙

Discuss the advantages of various programs with software dealers⊙

Determine the ease of learning the software.

Find out about user support. is there an 800 hot line number to call?

Identify the computer hard ware you are curently using. Will the ⌐software work on the equipment you now have?

Know your printer requirements and limitations.

**GO TO
CD-ROM
PRACTICE 3
EXERCISES**

Verb Tense, Voice, and Mood–Verbals

NAME _____

PRACTICE 4A

WRITING

Answers will vary.

Directions: Write a paragraph describing the advantages of using word processing software to compose documents. Use action verbs and active voice.

[Word processing software offers you numerous advantages. You do not need to press Enter at the end of the line because the text wraps automatically to the next line. The spell check highlights errors and gives suggestions for changes. Changes are easy to make by inserting and deleting text.]

**GO TO
CD-ROM
PRACTICE 4
EXERCISES**

Use exact punctuation when
keying an Internet address.

10-30 Check online sites carefully before assigning them to students.

See Instructor Note 10-31 in IAE.

ONLINE EXERCISES

Many of the largest commercial software Websites receive millions of visitors a day. The goals of the Websites are to offer information software, to introduce new products, to provide downloadable software and upgrades, and to post job opportunities.

Objective: *To visit commercial software sites.*

1. With your Internet browser on screen, key:

    http://www.microsoft.com in the location box at the top of your screen. Press the **Enter** key on your keyboard.

2. You will be at the Microsoft Corporation Home Page. Go to places of interest.

3. Visit the following other commercial software sites:

    http://www.adobe.com

    http://www.sun.com

    http://www.netscape.com

    http://www.lotus.com

4. Print a site that provides information that you would like to share with the class.

NAME _____

PRACTICE 1B

See Instructor Note 10-32 in IAE.

A. Directions: *Select the correct answer, and write it in the space provided.*

1. The manager (*expect, expected*) to receive a multiuser discount on software.

1. _____expected_____

2. I wish I (*was, were*) using a larger computer monitor.

2. _____were_____

3. We disliked (*his, him*) complaining about using the old version of the desktop publishing program.

3. _____his_____

4. Suzanne (*does, do*) ask our opinion on page layout.

4. _____does_____

5. She (*has seen, seen*) demonstrations on patient billing software.

5. _____has seen_____

B. Directions: *In the space provided, write the letter of the item that describes or identifies the underlined verb or verbal.*

1. This 486 computer <u>is</u> no longer powerful enough for our software.
   a. present tense   c. future tense
   b. past tense   d. perfect tense

1. _____a_____

2. Janey learned <u>to pay</u> her bills with an online banking program.
   a. verb   c. infinitive
   b. gerund   d. participle

2. _____c_____

3. *PC Computing* <u>will be offering</u> a free CD with a subscription renewal.
   a. present   c. progressive tense
   b. past tense   d. future tense

3. _____c_____

4. <u>Recognizing the errors in the program</u>, we checked all the payroll figures again.
   a. verb phrase   c. gerund phrase
   b. infinitive phrase   d. participial phrase

4. _____d_____

5. <u>Organizing our customer database</u> has increased our efficiency.
   a. verb phrase   c. gerund phrase
   b. infinitive phrase   d. participial phrase

5. _____c_____

PRACTICE 2B

See Instructor Note 10-33 in IAE.

A. Directions: *In the space provided, write the tense of the verb indicated in parentheses.*

1. Rob (*design;* present perfect) our spreadsheet templates.

1. _____has designed_____

2. Our video store (*offer*; present) multimedia software that rates movies.

2. _____offers_____

3. Elementary science teachers (*recommend*; present progressive)
   The Magic School Bus as home enrichment.

3. _are recommending_

4. They (*promote*; future progressive) multimedia software during the holiday season.

4. _will be promoting_

5. I (*need;* future) a new operating system by next year.

5. _____will need_____

6. Kim (*leave;* past) her backup disks at home.

6. _____left_____

7. My supervisor (*order*; past perfect) group videoconferencing software while I was on vacation.

7. _____had ordered_____

Name _____

8. Analog telephone lines (*seem;* present emphatic) slow for using the Internet.

8. _____do seem_____

9. Our company (*advertise;* past) our new software during the Super Bowl.

9. _____advertised_____

10. We (*wait;* present perfect progressive) for the upgrade for six months.

10. _have been waiting_

B. Directions: *In the space provided, correct the sentences containing incorrect verb forms or follow the instructions in parentheses. Some sentences may have punctuation or grammar errors. If a sentence has no errors, write* **Yes.**

1. Some network software is priced according to the number of users. (Change to active voice.)

   The number of users determines the price of some network software.

2. He has went to the national computer exhibition in Minneapolis for the past five years.

   He has gone to the national computer exhibition in Minneapolis for the past five years.

3. Hurrying to meet the deadline, the annual report had several missing pages.

   Hurrying to meet the deadline, she omitted several pages from the annual report.

4. I wish I was able to feel comfortable using the Microsoft Natural keyboard.

   I wish I were able to feel comfortable using the Microsoft Natural keyboard.

5. Will you please recommend a keyboarding program that I can use at home?

   Will you please recommend a keyboarding program that I can use at home.

Practice 3B

PROOFREADING

Directions: *Proofread and compare the two sentences in each group. If they are the same, write* **Yes** *in the space provided. If they are not the same, write* **No.** *Use the first sentence as the correct copy. If you find errors in the second sentence, underline them.*

1. With Select Phone, you can find, count, locate, download, call, and mail anyone or any group of business or residential listings.

   With Select Phone, you can find, count, locate, download, call and mail anyone or any group of business or residential listings.

1. _____No_____

2. Claris Home Page is designed for novices to build a basic but professional-looking Website.

   Claris Home Page is designed for novices to build a basic but professional looking Website.

2. _____No_____

3. Dr. Solomon's Anti-Virus includes an SOS disk that lets you boot clean from a diskette, even if your operating system won't load.

   Dr. Solomon Anti-Virus includes an SOS disk that lets you boot clean from a diskette, even if your operating system will not load.

3. _____No_____

4. FileMaker Pro Server is a dedicated host that shares its database files with clients running FileMaker Pro on their workstations.

   FileMaker Pro Server is a dedicated host that shares its database files with clients running FileMaker Pro on their workstations.

4. _____Yes_____

5. Avery designed preset labels to work in Microsoft Word, WordPerfect, and LabelPro for output on laser or ink jet printers.

   Avery designed preset lables to work in Microsoft Word, Wordperfect, and LabelPro for output on lazer or ink jet printers.

5. _____No_____

NAME

Proofreading Exercise

The following material gives some preparation steps to follow before calling a software company for help:

Calling for Software Support

When you call for support, be at your computer, and have the appropriate product documentation available. Be prepared to give the following information:

The version number of the product that you are using.

The type of hardware that you are using, including network hardware, if applicable.

The exact wording of any messages that appeared on your screen.

A description of what happened and what you were doing at the time.

A description of how you tried to solve the problem.

Directions: *Use the following proofreaders' marks to make corrections in the copy below. Use the above copy as your correct guide.*

lowercase	/	move left	⌐
capitalize	≡	move right	⌐ #
delete	∂	insert space	∧
transpose	∩	insert letter	∧
delete space	⌒	insert comma	∧
insert period	⊙	delete and close up	∂

Calling for software Support

When you call for support, be at your computer, and have the appropriate product documentation available. Be prepared to give the following information:

The Version number of the product that you are using.

⌐ The type of hardware that you are using, including network hard ware, if applicable.

The exact wording of any messsages that appeared on your screen.

⌐A description of what happened and what you were doing at the time.

A description of how you treid to solve the problem.

PRACTICE 4B

WRITING

Directions: *Reflect on the first software that you used. Write a paragraph describing that software, what operating system it needed, and the differences between that software and the software you are using now. Use action verbs and active voice.* Answers will vary.

The first software I used was WordPerfect 5.1 for DOS on a 286 computer. I enjoyed using WordPerfect and

started writing directly at the computer instead of on paper. After learning Windows programs, I realized how

much memorization WordPerfect for DOS requires. The word processing features are basically the same except

the word processing programs today make documents look more professional with less effort from me.

NAME _____

ONLINE **EXERCISES**

Software piracy is a major concern of the computer industry, with billions of dollars in revenue lost each year. Software publishers and related organizations joined together to protect the software industry by forming the Software Publishers Association (SPA). The SPA provides information on software piracy and enforces software copyrights and trademarks.

Objective: *To visit the Software Publishers Association Website.*

1. With your Internet browser on screen, key:

   http://www.spa.org in the location box at the top of your screen. Press the **Enter** key on your keyboard.

2. Explore the site and answer the following questions on a separate sheet of paper.

   What is piracy?

   What is the liability for piracy?

   What is shareware?

   Is there a reward for reporting piracy?

This is an excellent site. Keep in mind that topics may change and information will therefore be updated and/or deleted. The following information is provided to you for use with your students. These numbers may change but are correct at the time of printing.

What is piracy?
The unauthorized use of software.
Purchasing a single-user license and loading the software on multiple computers or a server.
Making, distributing, and/or selling copies that appear to be from an authorized source.
Renting software without permission from the copyright holder.
Distributing and/or selling software that has been "unbundled," or separated, from the products with which it was intended to have been "bundled."
Downloading copyrighted software from the Internet or bulletin boards without permission from the copyright holder.

What is the liability for piracy?
If sued for civil copyright infringement, the penalty is up to $100,000 per title infringed. If charged with a criminal violation, the fine is up to $250,000 per title infringed and up to five years' imprisonment.

What is shareware?
Shareware is software that is passed out freely for evaluation purposes only. You must pay to keep the software. The evaluation time is usually 30 days.

Is there a reward for reporting piracy?
No. SPA feels it would compromise the nature of the reports taken and negatively affect the credibility of the source.

LOOKING BACK

Posttest

Directions: Check the underlined word(s). If the word is correct, write **Yes** in the space provided. If it is not correct, write the word correctly.

1. You <u>was</u> accurate in analyzing our data recovery needs.

2. Manufacturers of PC operating systems <u>design</u> newer, more capable versions each year.

3. He <u>done</u> the linking of Word with PowerPoint.

4. She <u>is</u> certain the lines between word processing and desktop publishing <u>will</u> continue to blur in the future.

5. We were amazed by <u>him</u> volunteering to develop our database queries.

6. Claris <u>sells</u> FileMaker Pro.

7. I had used Word for several years before I <u>learn</u> Access.

8. We <u>sent</u> our corporate logo online to a graphic artist.

9. I wish I <u>was</u> able to use CAD software.

10. Marvin <u>has</u> applied for a job as visual designer at Lucas Films.

1. _____were_____

2. _____Yes_____

3. _____did_____

4. _____Yes_____

5. _____his_____

6. _____Yes_____

7. _____learned_____

8. _____Yes_____

9. _____were_____

10. _____Yes_____

CHAPTER 11

Subject-Verb Agreement

TEAMWORK

Change is redefining the workplace. Factors such as global competition, information technology, and rising customer expectations are affecting businesses of all sizes. One of the ways organizations are responding to change is to focus on teams and teamwork.

Groups, committees, and task forces have existed for years. Within these organizations, individuals come together for a specific purpose—to produce a product or service.

A team, on the other hand, is a special designation for people who manage themselves. Team members clearly understand the tasks, and their top priority is getting the job done. A climate of trust and understanding exists because open and frank communication takes place. Team members share power and authority when possible, and much of the decision making is by consensus. The team evaluates its own effectiveness.

People on a team feel a strong bond with others on the team. Team members appreciate one another's differences and take pride in the contributions that they make to the organization. The businesses using the team model feel that teams produce an energetic and satisfying work climate.

TERMS TO REMEMBER

GLOBAL COMPETITION

SELF-MANAGING TEAMS

TEAM

TEAMWORK

WORK CLIMATE

OBJECTIVES

After you have studied this chapter and completed the exercises, you will be able to do the following:

1. Select single verbs that agree with single subjects and plural verbs that agree with plural subjects.
2. Identify phrases between subjects and verbs that do not affect the choice of the verb.
3. Use verbs that agree with subjects joined by *and, or*, and *nor* correctly.
4. Select linking verbs that agree with subjects.
5. Select verbs that agree with indefinite pronouns used as subjects.
6. Use verbs that agree with collective nouns.
7. Use verbs that agree with money, time periods, numbers, and measurements.
8. Use correct verbs with subjects in inverted sentences.
9. Use verbs that agree with plural nouns and gerund phrases.
10. Diagram sentences correctly.

LOOKING AHEAD

Pretest

Directions: *In the sentences below, underline the simple subject. Then select the correct verb, and write it in the space provided.*

1. <u>Mike</u> (*teach, teaches*) classes on team development for the American Management Association.

2. Groupware <u>functions</u> (*allow, allows*) organizations to share individual knowledge more efficiently.

3. The <u>survey</u>, along with the employees' comments, (*provide, provides*) a starting point for the safety committee.

4. Either <u>Nancy</u> or <u>Brandon</u> (*plan, plans*) to take my place on the search team for the new dean.

5. A vital <u>link</u> in a team's success (*are, is*) the professional level of support staff.

6. <u>Most</u> of the work group leaders (*schedule, schedules*) the times for meetings.

7. The <u>committee</u> (*know, knows*) that its recommendations must be based on reliable data.

8. In most teams, <u>three-fifths</u> of the time (*are, is*) spent in planning strategies.

9. Here (*are, is*) 35 additional <u>surveys</u> for our committee to tabulate.

10. The <u>news</u> (*has, have*) no bearing on the proposed acquisition.

1. <u>teaches</u>

2. <u>allow</u>

3. <u>provides</u>

4. <u>plans</u>

5. <u>is</u>

6. <u>schedule</u>

7. <u>knows</u>

8. <u>is</u>

9. <u>are</u>

10. <u>has</u>

OVERVIEW

As you identified subjects in Chapter 3, you were reminded that if you selected the correct subject you would find verb identification easier when you studied verbs. You will find this to be true as you study this chapter.

The verb in a sentence must be in agreement with its subject. In Chapter 10, you saw the changes that occurred in a verb with first-second-, and third-person subjects. A verb must also agree with its subject in number. A singular subject requires a singular verb. Likewise, a plural subject needs a plural verb. Not all sentences are that simple. Certain words or phrases are troublespots in subject-verb agreement. In this chapter, you will analyze some of these more troublesome agreement areas.

Good writers are very aware of subject-verb agreement. They know errors of this type can distract their readers.

SUBJECT-VERB AGREEMENT

A verb must agree with its subject in person (first, second, third) and number (singular, plural).

Singular Subject—Singular Verb

Use a singular verb with a singular subject. Add *s* or *es* to the present part of a verb when the subject is third-person singular. Use the simple subject to determine the correct verb form.

a manager supports	experience brings	she says
a team player shares	John agrees	he decides

(All the subjects are third-person singular and require singular verbs. The verbs require an *s* ending.)

he reaches	time goes	Shelly misses
Carri finishes	it taxes	telephone buzzes

(The subjects are third-person singular and require singular verbs. Verbs that end with the sounds of *ch, o, s, sh, x,* and *z* require *es* endings.)

Plural Subject—Plural Verb

Use a plural verb with a plural subject. A noun forms its plural by adding *s* or *es,* but this is not true with the plural form of a verb. Use the simple subject to determine the correct verb form.

the departments cooperate	members agree	we decide
the managers confer	they say	
team members compromise	they analyze	

(All the subjects are plural and require plural verbs. The plural verbs do not end in *s* or *es.*)

See Instructor Notes 11-1 and 11-2 in IAE.

Go to Transparencies/PowerPoints 11-1a, 11-1b, and 11-2.

Go to Transparency/ PowerPoint 11-3.

Refer to Chapter 10 for a review of singular verb formations.

An s or es added to a singular verb indicates the subject is third-person singular.

Go to Transparency/ PowerPoint 11-4.

See Instructor Note 11-3 in IAE.

Do not confuse the plurals of nouns and verbs. Plural verbs do not end in s or es. Refer to Chapter 10 for a review of plural verb formations.

Pronoun *You*—Plural Verb

See Instructor Note 11-4 in IAE.

Use a plural verb with both the second-person singular *or* second-person plural subject *you*.

> you <u>acknowledge</u>   you <u>learn</u>   you <u>are</u>
>
> you both <u>enjoy</u>   you <u>are</u> all invited

CHECKUP 11-1

Directions: In the sentences below, underline the simple subject. Then select the correct verb and write it in the space provided.

1. Our <u>supervisor</u> (*take, takes*) the time to explain the value of teamwork in an organization.   **takes**

2. Teamwork <u>success</u> (*depend, depends*) on keeping the lines of communication open.   **depends**

3. <u>Jason Rowe</u> (*serve, serves*) as our project coordinator.   **serves**

4. Our <u>project leader</u> (*know, knows*) his own communication style.   **knows**

5. As a member of the executive team, <u>you</u> (*need, needs*) effective time management skills.   **need**

6. Many <u>companies</u> (*stress, stresses*) the importance of teams.   **stress**

GO TO CD-ROM CHECKUP 11-1

SUBJECT-VERB AGREEMENT— SPECIAL CASES

In addition to the basic principles, subject-verb agreement also applies to numerous special cases. These cases involve intervening phrases; compound subjects; linking verbs; indefinite pronouns; collective nouns; amounts of money, numbers, and fractions; inverted sentences; and special nouns.

Intervening Words and Phrases—Prepositional Phrases

The verb must agree with the subject, *not* with the object of the prepositional phrase that may appear between the subject and the verb.

> **Five <u>members</u> of our team <u>work</u> in their home offices.**
> (*Members* is the plural subject; *team* is the object in the prepositional phrase *of our team.* The plural verb *work* agrees with the subject, not the object of the preposition.)

SLIP-UP

Newspaper typographical error: According to sources, negotiations between the school board and the teachers is at an impasse. The next step is *medication,* and this cannot be completed in time for any raises to be voted on at the March 3 school meeting. Source: Richard Lederer.

Refer to Chapter 2 for a review of prepositional phrases.

The notes from our supervisor keep our team motivated.
(*Notes* is the plural subject; *supervisor* is the object in the prepositional phrase *from our supervisor.* The plural verb *keep* agrees with the subject, not the object of the preposition.)

Intervening Words and Phrases—Other Modifying Phrases

When determining which verb to use, disregard modifying phrases that begin with words such as *along with, in addition to, together with, accompanied by, as well as,* and *in conjunction with.* These phrases modify the subject, but they do not change the subject in number and do not form a compound subject.

Zana, along with several other committee members, presents good ideas.
(*Zana* is the subject that must agree with the singular verb *presents.* The modifying phrase *along with several other committee members* does not make the subject plural nor does it form a compound subject.)

The project leader, together with his or her administrative assistants, assumes the responsibility for the final group report.
(*Project leader* is the subject that must agree with the verb *assumes.* The modifying phrase *together with his or her administrative assistants* does not make a compound subject.)

See Instructor Notes 11-5 and 11-6 in IAE.

Punctuation ALERT!

Do not use commas to set aside essential prepositional phrases from the rest of the sentence.

Go to PowerPoints 11-5a and 11-5b.

Punctuation ALERT!

Use commas to set aside modifying phrases such as *along with, in addition to, together with, including, accompanied by, as well as,* and *in conjunction with* when they are placed between the subject and the verb.

See Instructor Note 11-7 in IAE.

Do This

Group interaction, not personal egos, is important in teamwork.

Do Not Do This

Group interaction, not personal egos, are important in teamwork.

Use a verb that agrees with the positive subject in a sentence where you find both a positive and a negative subject. In this sentence, group interaction is the positive singular subject, which requires the singular verb is.

CHECKUP 11-2

Directions: *Select the correct verb, and write it in the space provided. Identify the verb as singular (S) or plural (P).*

1. Robert, as well as Joan, (*collect, collects*) facts and figures before making contributions to the group.   collects (S)

2. The members of our team (*is, are*) more idea-oriented than action-oriented.   are (P)

3. Group disagreements of any kind (*make, makes*) me uncomfortable.   make (P)

GO TO
CD-ROM
CHECKUP 11-2

Go to PowerPoint 11-6.

Refer to Chapters 3 and 8 for a review of compound subjects.

Remember that a compound subject that refers to the same person or thing must have a singular verb.

Go to PowerPoint 11-7.

See Instructor Note 11-8 in IAE.

4. Our company, in conjunction with the local technical college, (*offer, offers*) workshops in teamwork and conflict resolution.

   offers (S)

5. Owners of small businesses in our country (*understand, understands*) the value of teamwork.

   understand (P)

6. My interest in management topics (*include, includes*) teamwork.

   includes (S)

Compound Subjects Joined by *And*

Use a plural verb with a compound subject joined by *and* or *both ... and.*

> **The project leader <u>and</u> group members <u>need</u> time to plan their strategies.**
> (The compound subject *leader* and *members* joined by *and* requires the plural verb *need*.)

> <u>Both</u> **Ann <u>and</u> Lindsay <u>continue</u> to place the blame on each other.**
> (The compound subject *Ann* and *Lindsay* joined by *both ... and* requires the plural verb *continue*.)

Use a singular verb with a compound subject that refers to the same person or thing.

> **My colleague and mentor <u>has</u> an article on teamwork in our next company newsletter.**
> (The subjects *colleague* and *mentor* refer to one person; therefore, the sentence requires the singular verb *has*.)

Compound Subjects Joined By *Or* or *Nor*

The verb should agree with the subject nearer the verb when a compound subject is joined by *or* or *nor* or by *either ... or* or *neither ... nor.*

> **Lynn or Dan usually <u>prepares</u> the committee assignments.**
> (*Dan*, a singular subject, is the part of the compound subject nearer the verb. The singular verb *prepares* must agree with this singular subject.)

> **Neither the chairperson nor the ad hoc committee <u>members</u> <u>were</u> available after the meeting.**
> (*Members*, a plural subject, is the part of the compound subject that is nearer the verb. The plural verb *were* must agree with this plural subject.)

> **Either the managers or the <u>assistant</u> <u>has</u> copies of the report.**
> The verb *has* agrees with the nearer subject *assistant*.

> **Less Awkward:**
> **Either the assistant or the <u>managers</u> <u>have</u> copies of the report.**
> (Sentences with singular and plural subjects usually sound better with plural verbs. Therefore, rearrange the subjects so that the plural subject *managers* is closer to the verb.)

Compound Subjects Preceded by *Many a, Many an, Each, Every*

Use a singular verb when the words *many a, many an, each,* and *every* immediately precede a compound subject connected by *and.* The subject that follows one of these four expressions is considered singular; the verb must agree.

Go to PowerPoint 11-8.

Every team member and project leader <u>needs</u> a sense of commitment toward the team's goals.

(*Every* precedes the compound subject *team member* and *project leader.* The combination of *every* and a compound subject requires the singular verb *needs.*)

Many a committee meeting and negotiation session <u>has</u> <u>resulted</u> in a waste of my time.

(*Many a* precedes the compound subject *committee meeting* and *negotiation session.* The combination of *many a* and a compound subject requires the singular verb.)

CHECKUP 11-3

Directions: Select the correct verb, and write it in the space provided.

1. Jeff and Rick (*find, finds*) the group process challenging.   _____find_____

2. Each group project and job assignment (*need, needs*) direction.   _____needs_____

3. Neither Ellen nor Marty (*are, is*) cooperating with the other team members.   _____is_____

4. Every team leader and team member (*has, have*) access to the groupware network.   _____has_____

5. Three mentors and a master teacher (*work, works*) with teams of student teachers at several middle schools.   _____work_____

6. Both the project team members and the executive board (*agree, agrees*) that the first recommendation is too expensive.   _____agree_____

7. Either the project leader or the support staff personnel (*prepare, prepares*) the agendas for the meetings.   _____prepare_____

8. My supervisor and team leader (*tries, try*) to encourage me to participate in the group discussions. (*Note:* The supervisor and team leader is one person.)   _____tries_____

9. Evaluation and feedback (*provide, provides*) ways to improve your communication skills within a group.   _____provide_____

10. Neither the observation nor the evaluations by management (*intimidate, intimidates*) our team.   _____intimidate_____

GO TO CD-ROM
CHECKUP 11-3

In addition to the forms of to be, *linking verbs* include the five sense verbs, look, taste, feel, smell, *and* sound *and six additional verbs* remain, stay, appear, seem, grow, *and* become.

See Instructor Note 11-9 in IAE.

Linking Verbs

A linking verb should agree with its subject, not its subject comple-ment (predicate noun or pronoun).

> **Four new members seem a large number to add to this committee.**
> (The plural verb *seem* is a linking verb, which must agree with the plural subject *members*, not with the subject complement *number*.)

CHECKUP 11-4

Directions: In the sentences below, underline the simple subject. Then select the cor-rect verb, and write it in the space provided.

1. The first <u>item</u> on the team's agenda (*was, were*) introductions.   **was**

2. Social <u>gatherings</u> (*are, is*) a good opportunity to become acquainted with other team members.   **are**

3. <u>Agendas</u> for all group meetings (*are, is*) an excellent means to stay on track.   **are**

4. Twenty team <u>members</u> (*remain, remains*) a hindrance for effective group discussions.   **remain**

5. Company support <u>groups</u> (*is, are*) a help for single mothers and caregivers.   **are**

6. Group <u>projects</u> always (*seem, seems*) a waste of my time.   **seem**

GO TO CD-ROM CHECKUP 11-4

Go to PowerPoint 11-9.

See Instructor Note 11-10 in IAE.

Refer to Chapters 7 and 8 for a review of indefinite pronouns and pronoun and antecedent agreement.

Indefinite Pronouns That Require Singular Verbs

Use a singular verb when the subject of a sentence is one of the fol-lowing singular indefinite pronouns:

anybody	either	neither	one
anyone	everybody	no one	somebody
anything	everyone	nobody	someone
each	everything	nothing	something

> <u>Someone</u> in our group **has** a copy of the notes from our last meeting.
> (The singular indefinite pronoun *someone* is the subject and requires the singular verb *has.*)

> <u>Everyone</u> **develops** his or her own style of leading a work team.
> (The singular indefinite pronoun *everyone* is the subject and requires the singular verb *develops.*)

Indefinite Pronouns That Require Plural Verbs

Go to PowerPoint 11-10.

Use a plural verb when the subject is one of the following plural indef-inite pronouns: *both, few, many, others,* and *several.*

Several of our committees meet twice a month.

(The plural indefinite pronoun *several* is the subject and requires the plural verb *meet*.)

Many of our firm's best decisions are the result of teamwork.

(The plural indefinite pronoun *many* is the subject and requires the plural verb *are*.)

Indefinite Pronouns That Require Singular or Plural Verbs

Use a singular *or* plural verb when the indefinite pronouns *all, any, more, most, none,* and *some* are used as subjects. The form of the verb depends on whether the pronoun refers to something singular or something plural.

See Instructor Notes 11-11 and 11-12 in IAE.

Most of our team players are more successful when they are free from stress.

(The indefinite pronoun and subject *most* refers to *players*, which is plural. For agreement, the verb *are* must be plural.)

Some of our decisions were based on advice from outside experts.

(The indefinite pronoun and subject *some* refers to *decisions*, which is plural. For agreement, the verb *were* must be plural.)

Some of our work depends on the research done by a team of experts.

(The indefinite pronoun and subject *some* refers to *work*, which is singular. For agreement, the verb *depends* must be singular.)

CHECKUP 11-5

Directions: *In the sentences below, underline the subject. Then, in the space provided, write the correct present tense form of the verb indicated in parentheses.*

Ex.: Some of our work (*be*) complete. _____**is**_____

1. Each of the project members (*possess*) strengths that will benefit the final outcome. _____possesses_____

2. Some of the dissension (*result*) from inaccurate information. _____results_____

3. Both of my friends (*attend*) the accounting study group meeting every day at 8 a.m. _____attend_____

4. One of the team's policies (*be*) to keep the communication free of sexist or profane remarks. _____is_____

5. Either of the two locations (*seem*) satisfactory for a group retreat. _____seems_____

6. Most of the options (*appear*) workable. _____appear_____

7. All of our team members (*enjoy*) working together. _____enjoy_____

8. Everyone (*plan*) to attend the picnic to celebrate the completion of the project. _____plans_____

GO TO CD-ROM

CHECKUP 11-5

See Instructor Note 11-13 in IAE.

Go to PowerPoint 11-11.

Collective Nouns That Require Singular Verbs

Use a singular verb to refer to a group as one unit.

This particular project <u>team</u> <u>seems</u> very result oriented.
(The subject *team* refers to a group that is acting as one unit. Therefore, *team* requires the singular verb *seems*.)

Our work <u>group</u> <u>spends</u> several sessions discussing new ways to approach our assignment.
(The subject *group* refers to one unit and requires the singular verb *spends*.)

Use phrases such as members of the team or team members to avoid the awkward construction of a collective noun with a plural verb.

Go to PowerPoint 11-12.

Collective Nouns That Require Plural Verbs

Use a plural verb to refer to group members acting as individual members of the group. To avoid the awkward construction of a collective noun with a plural verb, reword the sentence. Use phrases such as *members of the team (group)* or *team (group) members.*

The <u>team</u> <u>are</u> checking their calendars for available meeting dates.
(*Team,* the subject, is a collective noun. In this sentence, the team members are acting individually rather than as one group. The plural verb *are* is necessary.)
Less Awkward:
The (<u>members of the team</u>, <u>team members</u>) are checking their calendars for available meeting dates.

At S & C Graphics, the <u>support group</u> <u>assist</u> workers with drug or alcohol problems.
(*Support group,* the subject, is a collective noun. In this sentence, the support people are acting individually to assist workers rather than as one group. The plural verb *assist* is necessary.)
Less Awkward:
At S & C Graphics, (<u>members of the support group</u>, <u>support group members</u>) assist workers with drug or alcohol problems.

Publications

Go to PowerPoint 11-13.

Use a singular verb when the name of a publication such as a book, magazine, software, or newspaper is used as a subject.

<u>Team News</u> <u>is</u> the publication our company uses to share information among its 12 teams.
(*Team News* is a publication and requires the singular verb *is*.)

<u>Management Review</u>, a business publication, often <u>runs</u> a column on teamwork.
(*Management Review* is a publication and requires the singular verb *runs*.)

Companies, Institutions, and Organizations

Use a singular verb when the name of a company, an institution, or an organization is used as a subject of a sentence.

> Northwestern University <u>makes</u> teamwork a key issue in its curriculum.
>
> (*Northwestern University* is a singular subject that requires the singular verb *makes*.)
>
> Lutheran Hospital Counseling Services <u>recommends</u> the formation of employee support groups to prevent staff burnout.
>
> (*Lutheran Hospital Counseling Services* is a singular subject that requires the singular verb *recommends*.)

Go to PowerPoint 11-14.

See Instructor Note 11-14 in IAE.

Refer to a reference manual such as The Gregg Reference Manual *for options in using plural verbs. You will find this information in the section referring to collective nouns.*

CHECKUP 11-6

Directions: In the sentences below, underline the simple subject. Then select the correct verb, and write it in the space provided.

1. Our study <u>group</u> (*meet, meets*) in the cafeteria every Friday.   <u>meets</u>

2. <u>Silicon Logic Engineering</u> (*has, have*) two work teams that design computer chips for Synopsys.   <u>has</u>

3. My <u>class</u> (*include, includes*) students of all ages.   <u>includes</u>

4. The personnel screening <u>committee</u> (*are, is*) recommending four candidates.   <u>is</u>

5. <u>North Central Technical College</u> (*encourage, encourages*) its staff to organize support groups for students.   <u>encourages</u>

6. <u>Team Review</u> (*allow, allows*) a group of people to review and edit word processing and graphics files.   <u>allows</u>

GO TO
CD-ROM
CHECKUP 11-6

Money, Time Periods, Numbers, and Measurements

Use a singular verb with money, measurements, time periods, or numbers when referring to one total amount or unit.

Go to PowerPoint 11-15.

> Twenty minutes <u>is</u> all I can spend at the project meeting today.
>
> (*Twenty minutes* is a time period that refers to a total unit of time. Therefore, the singular verb *is* is required.)
>
> One hundred dollars <u>is</u> the registration fee for the leadership training workshop.
>
> (*One hundred dollars* is one total amount and requires the singular verb *is*.)
>
> Twenty square feet <u>is</u> the size of our committee's meeting room.
>
> (*Twenty square feet* is a total measurement and requires the singular verb *is*.)

Fractional Amounts—Singular Verbs

See Instructor Note 11-15 in IAE.

Use a singular verb with expressions such as *the majority of, a part of, a portion of, a percentage of,* or *one-half of* when the noun that follows the word *of* is singular.

> **The majority of the report deals with the committee's recommendations.**
> (The singular noun *report* follows the word *of.* The subject *majority* requires the singular verb *deals.*)

> **A large portion of our work session is set aside for questions.**
> (The singular noun *session* follows the word *of.* The subject *portion* requires the singular verb *is.*)

Fractional Amounts—Plural Verbs

Use a plural verb with expressions such as *a majority of, a part of, a portion of, a percentage of,* or *one-half of* when the noun that follows the word *of* is plural.

> **A large percentage of the questionnaires were not returned by the requested date.**
> (The plural noun *questionnaires* follows the word *of.* The subject *percentage* requires the plural verb *were.*)

> **One-half of the committee chairpersons on our campus use e-mail as a means of communication.**
> (The plural noun *chairpersons* follows the word *of.* The subject *one-half* requires the plural verb *use.*)

A Number/The Number

Go to PowerPoint 11-16.

Use a plural verb with the subject *a number* when *of* follows. Use a singular verb with the subject *the number.*

> **A number of the members of our work team are new to the group process.**
> (The subject *a number* followed by *of* requires the plural verb *are.*)

> **The number of women in project leadership roles is increasing.**
> (The subject *the number* requires the singular verb *is.*)

CHECKUP 11-7

Directions: In the space provided, write **Yes** if the subject and verb agree in the sentence. Write the correct verb in the space if the subject and verb do not agree.

1. Twenty dollars per team member are too much. _____ is _____

2. The number of survey responses were helpful in our team's decision. _____ was _____

3. Three-fourths of the union members agree with the committee's suggestions. _____ Yes _____

4. A majority of our team members work in their homes and go to the office only for scheduled meetings.   _____Yes_____

5. A large percentage of the final report still need to be checked by the project leader.   _____needs_____

6. Two months seem an appropriate amount of time to complete the project.   _____seems_____

GO TO CD-ROM
CHECKUP 11-7

Inverted Sentences

An inverted sentence is one in which the subject appears after the verb.

Sentences Beginning With *Here* and *There*. Locate the subject in a sentence that begins with *here* or *there*. The verb should agree with the subject.

> **There are six people on our interview team.**
> (The subject is *people*. *People* is plural and requires the plural verb *are*.)

> **Here are five additional points for the team to consider.**
> (The subject is *points*, which is plural and requires the plural verb *are*.)

> **In teamwork, there is no guarantee that you will receive personal credit for your ideas.**
> (The subject is *guarantee*, which is singular and requires the singular verb *is*.)

Questions. Locate the subject in a question and make the verb agree with the subject. The subject often appears between a helping verb and the main verb.

> **Was anyone from our team absent from the last meeting?**
> (The subject is *anyone*, which is singular and requires the singular verb *was*.)

> **Is groupware considered to be a useful communication tool for work groups?**
> (The subject is *groupware*, which is singular and requires the singular verb *is*.)

> **Why are you concerned about a change in the team's personnel?**
> (The subject is *you*. *You* always requires the plural verb are.)

Remember that here and there are never subjects.

If the subject is difficult to find, delete here or there and turn the statement around.

See Instructor Note 11-16 in IAE.

CHECKUP 11-8

***Directions:** In the sentences below, underline the simple subject. In the space provided, write **Yes** if the subject and verb agree. In the space provided, write the correct verb if the subject and verb do not agree.*

1. There are a considerable amount of dissension between the old and new team members.   _____is_____

GO TO
CD-ROM
CHECKUP 11-8

2. Do <u>you</u> enjoy solitary work more than you enjoy teamwork?   <u>Yes</u>

3. Here is some <u>ideas</u> to motivate people who work in groups.   <u>are</u>

4. There are different team <u>members</u> writing various sections of the report.   <u>Yes</u>

5. How do <u>companies</u> show their appreciation for the efforts of outstanding individual team members?   <u>Yes</u>

6. Has <u>Conrad</u> and <u>Blaine</u> reviewed our proposed changes?   <u>Have</u>

Special Nouns/Gerund Phrases

Go to PowerPoint 11-17.

Nouns Ending in *ics*. Use a singular verb with a noun that ends in *ics* when the noun refers to one topic of study or body of knowledge. Use a plural verb with a noun that ends in *ics* when the noun refers to more than one idea or item such as qualities or activities.

See Instructor Note 11-17 in IAE.

<u>Statistics</u> <u>is</u> a course that helps me analyze some of our work group's surveys.

(The subject *statistics* refers to one topic of study and requires the singular verb *is*.)

The <u>statistics</u> from employee surveys <u>are</u> important in our group's informal research.

(The subject *statistics* refers to numerous items and requires the plural verb *are*.)

<u>Economics 301</u> <u>is</u> a required course for international marketing students.

(The subject *Economics 301* refers to one topic of study and requires the singular verb *is*.)

The <u>economics</u> of third-world countries <u>require</u> some review before our consulting team can make a recommendation.

(The subject *economics* refers to more than one situation and requires the plural verb *require*.)

Go to PowerPoint 11-18.

Plural Nouns. Use a plural verb with nouns ending in *s* such as *assets, dues, earnings, goods, grounds, odds, proceeds, savings,* and *thanks* when these nouns are used as subjects.

The <u>grounds</u> upon which the teams' policies were formulated <u>are</u> the result of months of work.

(*Grounds* is the subject and always requires the plural verb *are*.)

The <u>odds</u> <u>were</u> against us, but we tried to get additional support staff for the project team.

(*Odds* is the subject and always requires the plural verb *were*.)

Review phrases in Chapter 10.

Go to PowerPoint 11-19.

Gerund Phrases. Use a singular verb when a gerund phrase is the subject of a sentence.

Establishing outstanding teams requires time and commitment.
(*Establishing outstanding teams* is a gerund phrase and is the subject in this sentence. This phrase requires the singular verb *requires*.)

Sharing decision-making responsibilities with employees is a difficult change for some managers.
(*Sharing decision-making responsibilities with employees* is a gerund phrase, is the subject in this sentence, and requires the singular verb *is*.)

CHECKUP 11-9

Directions: *Select the correct verb, and write it in the space provided.*

1. Learning to handle conflicts instead of avoiding them (*are, is*) a sign of professionalism.   <u>is</u>

2. Earnings (*has, have*) increased since the teams have been organized.   <u>have</u>

3. Office politics (*seem, seems*) to be ignored in this committee.   <u>seem</u>

4. Disagreeing with someone's comment (*do, does*) not mean this person will be angry with you.   <u>does</u>

5. The goods (*was, were*) late in arriving; therefore, our production team started three days late.   <u>were</u>

6. His leadership tactics (*concern, concerns*) management.   <u>concern</u>

GO TO CD-ROM
CHECKUP 11-9

DIAGRAMMING SENTENCES

The sentences in this section involve the infinitive (a verb preceded by the word *to*). To diagram the infinitive phrase used as a noun, place the word *to* on a diagonal line that extends slightly below the connecting horizontal line. Write the verb in the infinitive phrase on the horizontal line that connects to the diagonal line.

Review infinitive phrases.

Then place the infinitive phrase on a "stilt" in the appropriate position.

Laura prefers to ask thought-provoking questions. (infinitive phrase used as a direct object)

Laura | prefers | to ask | questions | thought-provoking

To become a project manager requires good communication skills.
(infinitive phrase used as a noun)

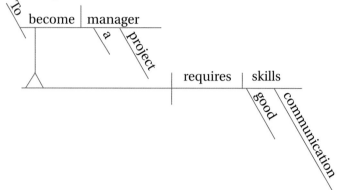

CHECKUP 11-10

See Instructor Note 11-18 in IAE.

Directions: *Diagram each sentence in the space provided.*

1. To complete the assignment will take ten people.

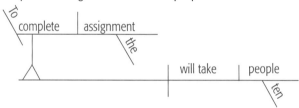

2. Our team expects to make a difference.

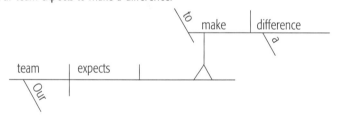

3. A team member needs to understand the team's purpose.

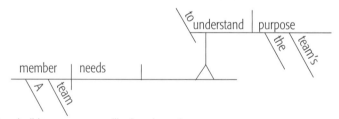

4. To rebuild team rapport will take a long time.

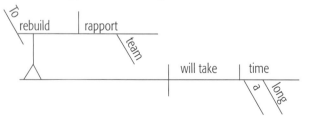

GO TO
CD-ROM
CHECKUP 11-10

PRACTICE 1A

Directions: *Select the correct verb, and write it in the space provided. Identify the verb as being singular (S) or plural (P).*

See Instructor Note 11-19 in IAE.

1. If you are in the hospitality industry, you really (*has, have*) to operate as a team.

1. ___have (P)___

2. No decision or recommendations (*was, were*) made.

2. ___were (P)___

3. Each of the work team leaders (*submit, submits*) a plan of action to his or her supervisor.

3. ___submits (S)___

4. Harvey Robbins (*include, includes*) some interesting points in his book *Why Teams Don't Work.*

4. ___includes (S)___

5. Our work group (*participate, participates*) in Casual Day on Fridays.

5. ___participates (S)___

6. Jane and David (*was, were*) team leaders of a task force to improve customer satisfaction ratings.

6. ___were (P)___

7. Some of our work (*depend, depends*) on the research done by the team of experts.

7. ___depends (S)___

8. She (*enjoy, enjoys*) working on team projects when all the members are dependable workers.

8. ___enjoys (S)___

9. A team member, through his or her contributions, (*gain, gains*) a feeling of personal accomplishment.

9. ___gains (S)___

**GO TO
CD-ROM
PRACTICE 1
EXERCISES**

10. RDC Plastics (*has, have*) a policy that allows only two strategic team members to fly on the same flight.

10. ___has (S)___

PRACTICE 2A

Directions: *In the sentences below, underline the simple subject. In the space provided, write **Yes** if the subject and verb are in agreement. Write the correct verb in the space if the subject and verb are not in agreement.*

1. Sometimes unintentional <u>remarks</u> become exaggerated in work group organizational meetings.

1. ___Yes___

2. Neither the project <u>manager</u> nor the <u>supervisors</u> has been informed of the cancellation of the job.

2. ___have___

3. <u>Everyone</u> on the team are cross-trained to substitute if someone is on vacation or becomes ill.

3. _____is_____

4. Our psychology <u>instructor</u> organizes discussion groups at least once a week.

4. _____Yes_____

5. <u>You</u> helps team members by communicating your expectations clearly.

5. _____help_____

6. A <u>team</u> of financial analysts manage my mutual fund.

6. _____manages_____

7. <u>Disagreements</u>, as well as progress, were communicated.

7. _____Yes_____

See Instructor Note 11-20 in IAE.

8. Their careful <u>analyses</u> of the situations was being appreciated by other team members.

8. _____were_____

See Instructor Note 11-21 in IAE.

9. Every team <u>member</u> and project <u>leader</u> are recognized for his or her efforts.

9. _____is_____

See Instructor Note 11-22 in IAE.

10. A large <u>percentage</u> of the discussions were positive.

10. _____Yes_____

See Instructor Note 11-23 in IAE.

11. Technical <u>personnel</u> and <u>support</u> are a big concern for us. (*Note:* Personnel and support comprise one thought unit.)

11. _____is_____

12. <u>Florence</u>, as well as Connie, support my position on raises.

12. _____supports_____

13. The <u>statistics</u> regarding on-time shipments supports Tom's recommendation.

13. _____support_____

**GO TO
CD-ROM
PRACTICE 2
EXERCISES**

14. A self-managing <u>team</u>, unlike a traditional group, improves the quality of planning.

14. _____Yes_____

15. Some <u>unions</u> and some union <u>members</u> suspects that self-managing teamwork is a "union-busting" tactic.

15. _____suspect_____

PRACTICE

NAME

PRACTICE 3A

PROOFREADING

*Directions: Proofread and compare the two sentences in each group. If they are the same, write **Yes** in the space provided. If they are not the same, write **No**. Use the first sentence as the correct copy. If you find errors in the second sentence, underline them; insert any omitted words or marks of punctuation.*

1. Management has formed a team of supervisors to study the issues of employee turnover and training.

   Management <u>have</u> formed a team of supervisors to study the <u>issue</u> of employee turnover and training.

   1. __No__

2. Our international sales team is experiencing an increase in sales in Poland, Hungary, and Czechoslovakia.

   Our international sales team <u>are</u> experiencing <u>a</u> increase in <u>slaes</u> in Poland, <u>Hungery</u>, and <u>Chzechoslovakia</u>.

   2. __No__

3. The best team leaders are self-starters who are enthusiastic about their responsibilities.

   The best team leaders are self-starters <u>whom</u> are <u>enthusastic</u> about their responsibilities.

   3. __No__

4. George Russell Jr., chairman of Frank Russell Co. in Tacoma, Washington, supports mountain climbing as a team-building exercise.

   George Russell <u>Sr.</u>, chairman of Frank Russell <u>Corp.</u> in <u>Seattle</u>, Washington<u>⌄</u> supports mountain climbing as a team-building <u>experience</u>.

   4. __No__

5. The concept of teamwork de-emphasizes individual achievement and encourages workers to learn from one another.

   The concept of teamwork <u>de-emphasises</u> individual achievement and encourages workers to learn from <u>each other</u>.

   5. __No__

**GO TO
CD-ROM**
PRACTICE 3
EXERCISES

Subject-Verb Agreement

PRACTICE

See Instructor Notes 11-24 and 11-25 in IAE.

Proofreading Exercise

Directions: *Review the proofreaders' marks listed below. Use these marks to make corrections in the copy that follows.*

Make lowercase /	Move left ⌐	Insert letter ∧
Capitalize ≡	Move right ⌐	Insert comma ∧
Delete ⸼	Insert space #	Transpose ∿
Delete space ‿	Insert period ⊙	
Delete and close up ⸚		

TO:⌐Anita Gregg∧Manager
            Benefits Division

FROM: Richard Chen, Vice president
            Human Services

DATE: April 21, 19—

SUBJECT: Employee Benefits Review

Please organize a team of employees(approximately 10-12) to review the current package of employee's benefits. The president has given our office the approval to send questionnaires to all employees to identify thier needs and concerns.

The team will be responsible for reviewing the questionnaires, tabulating the results, researching the the benefit options, and preparing recommendations for change. You should asses the strengths of each potential team member for his or her computer skills, analytical capabilities, or communication skills. Team members should be aware of a six- month time commitment to this project.

Please let me know the names of the team Members by May 1. I will then schedule a planing meeting with you and the team before May 15.

cg

PRACTICE 4A

WRITING

Directions: Listed below are some tasks that are important to groups. Select one task and write about the strengths you would bring to a group. Include skills that you have such as accounting, writing, or grammar. Relate these skills to the tasks.

Prepare budgets	Order supplies
Keep records	Train members
Keep work time	Select new members
Control quality	Orient new members
Assign jobs	Set goals
Solve technical problems	Discipline members

Keeping Records

I feel I am strong in keeping records. My accounting background has given me experience using Excel and QuickBooks. Other records I can keep are minutes of meetings because I have experience using Word. My records are always organized, and retrieval is fast and easy.

See Instructor Note 11-26 in IAE.

Answers will vary.

**GO TO
CD-ROM
PRACTICE 4
EXERCISES**

ONLINE **EXERCISES**

Consulting groups, organizations, and educational institutions closely study and watch workforce trends. Hundreds of Websites describe these workforce trends brought about by the rapid change in the marketplace.

Objective: *To visit an organizational consultant Website.*

1. With your Internet browser on screen, key:

   http://www.oeg.net/twk.html in the location box.

   Press the **Enter** key on your keyboard.

2. You will be on the teamwork page of the Organization Effectiveness Group.

3. Read the information about teamwork.

4. Click on the link to **Teamwork Model** in the second paragraph of the text.

5. You will be on the Teamwork Model page. Click on any area of the model for more information about teams.

6. Print any information you think the class may enjoy.

See Instructor Notes 11-27 and 11-28 in IAE.

Use exact punctuation when keying an Internet address.

NAME _____

PRACTICE 1B

Directions: *Select the correct verb, and write it in the space provided. Identify the verb as being singular (S) or plural (P).*

1. You (*determine, determines*) your own work schedule.

2. Either Sandy or Louis (*coordinate, coordinates*) our workshop.

3. Each of the employees (*have, has*) a job with interrelated tasks.

4. Lead workers (*coordinate, coordinates*) activities of their peers.

5. Our participation in "gainsharing" (*give, gives*) us a part of the increase in organization profits.

6. Samantha and Erin (*is, are*) on the employee involvement committee.

7. Many (*suggest, suggests*) evaluating a team's effectiveness periodically.

8. He (*feel, feels*) responsible and committed to our team's decisions.

9. Team members (*is, are*) skilled in involving active participation.

10. All members of the team (*participate, participates*) in the problem-solving process.

1. determine (P)
2. coordinates (S)
3. has (S)
4. coordinate (P)
5. gives (S)
6. are (P)
7. suggest (P)
8. feels (S)
9. are (P)
10. participate (P)

PRACTICE 2B

Directions: *In the sentences below, underline the simple subject. In the space provided, write **Yes** if the subject and verb are in agreement. Write the correct verb if the subject and verb are not in agreement.*

1. The number of women in management are increasing.

2. Neither Luis nor Pamela understand the limitations of our network.

3. Others in our company disagree with Richard and Charles.

4. Because of our success, Jennifer wants to be on our team.

5. Elizabeth Wilson, one of our vice presidents, communicate clearly and precisely.

6. Statistics indicates that large businesses are eliminating managers.

7. Many of the morale problems results from just a few disgruntled employees.

8. Patricia, Mary, and Tom makes decisions by consensus.

9. Getting to know employees as individuals are important for every supervisor.

10. Approximately 90 percent of our employees belongs to a union.

1. is
2. understands
3. Yes
4. Yes
5. communicates
6. indicate
7. result
8. make
9. is
10. belong

PRACTICE 3B

PROOFREADING

Directions: *Proofread and compare the two sentences in each group. If they are the same, write* **Yes** *in the space provided. If they are not the same, write* **No***. Use the first sentence as the correct copy. If you find errors in the second sentence, underline them; insert any omitted words or marks of punctuation.*

1. Self-managing teamwork is known by names such as autonomous work groups, work teams, self-directed teams, self-maintaining teams, business teams, self-leading teams, semiautonomous work groups, self-regulating groups, and many others.

    Self-managing teamwork is known by names such as autonomous work groups, work teams, self directed teams, self-maintaining teams, business teams, self-leading teams, semi-autonomous workgroups, self-regulating groups and many others.

    1. No _____

2. Quality Circles, a movement started by the Japanese, are groups of employees who voluntarily meet for an hour or more each week to solve a specific work problem.

    Quality Circles, a movement started by the Japanese, are groups of employees who voluntarily meet for an hour or more each week to solve a specific work problems.

    2. No _____

3. In a recent study of supervisors' attitudes toward employee involvement programs of all types, 72 percent of the supervisors viewed the programs as being good for their companies; 60 percent, good for the employees; but only 31 percent, beneficial to themselves.

    In a recent study of supervisors' attitudes toward employee involvement programs of all types, 72 percent of the supervisors viewed the programs as being good for their companies; 60 percent, good for the employees; but only 31 percent, beneficial to themselves.

    3. Yes _____

4. A controlling person with superior knowledge and ability may have an attitude that does not invite new ideas, challenge people, or stimulate a cooperative, supportive spirit.

    A controling person with superior knowledge and ability may have an attitude that does not invite new ideas, challenge people, or simulate a cooperative, supportive spirit.

    4. No _____

5. Drucker has suggested that 20 years from now the typical large business will have only half of the levels of management and a third of the number of managers that organizations have today.

    Drucker has suggested that 12 years from now a typical large business will have only half of the levels of management and a third of the number of managers that organizations has today.

    5. No _____

NAME _____

Proofreading Exercise

Directions: *Review the proofreaders' marks listed below. Use these marks to make corrections in the copy that follows.*

Make lowercase /	Move left ⌐	Insert letter ∧
Capitalize ≡	Move right ⌐	Insert comma ⋏
Delete ∂	Insert space #	Transpose ∩
Delete space ‿	Insert period ⊙	
Delete and close up ∂		

CHARACTERISTICS OF A SELF-MANAGING TEAM

The team performs a distinct task.

☐ Team members possesss a variety of skills related to the task.

Team members are interdependent.

The teams' focus is on the group rather than Individuals.

☐ Team members may rotate through the tasks.

the team has clear boundaries in terms of space and task responsi bilities.

The Team monitors and controls its work quantity and quality⊙

PRACTICE 4B

WRITING

Directions: *Describe the best group with which you have ever been involved. Discuss the characteristics of the group that made it productive and special.*   Answers will vary.

My best group involved a job that I held at Solano Community College. Four of us were in the group. We met

once a month to discuss progress in our positions. We rotated positions of group leader, recorder, and

refreshments provider. I enjoyed the rotations because I had experience developing agendas, chairing

meetings, recording discussions and actions, and creatively finding appropriate refreshments. We

accomplished a considerable amount of work, and I am glad that I had the experience of participating and

learning new skills.

_____

_____

_____

_____

_____

_____

NAME _____

ONLINE *EXERCISES*

1. With your Internet browser on screen, key:

   http://iwsp.human.cornell.edu/ in the location box.

   Press the **Enter** key on your keyboard.

2. You will be on the International Workplace Studies Program page of Cornell University. The International Workplace Studies Program (IWSP) conducts research on new ways of working.

3. Click on any of the links on this page to learn more about workplace trends.

4. If you wish to do other searches on teamwork, return to the home page of IWSP (**http://iwsp.human.cornell.edu**); click on the site for additional information or the site for tips on using the search engine. Follow the directions for additional searches.

LOOKING BACK

See Instructor Note 11-29 in IAE.

Posttest

Directions: *In the sentences below, underline the simple subject. Then select the correct verb, and write it in the space provided.*

1. <u>Carmen</u> (*analyze, analyzes*) statistics on workplace trends.
       1. <u>analyzes</u>

2. Task force <u>members</u> (*present, presents*) recommendations to our company next week.
       2. <u>present</u>

3. The <u>article</u>, as well as the Web resources, (*stimulate, stimulates*) our thinking about reorganizing our teams.
       3. <u>stimulates</u>

4. Neither <u>Stanley</u> nor <u>Julia</u> (*suggest, suggests*) changing the title of the report.
       4. <u>suggests</u>

5. Self-managing team <u>evaluations</u> (*is, are*) difficult to develop.
       5. <u>are</u>

6. <u>Many</u> of the managers (*like, likes*) the productivity benefits of teamwork.
       6. <u>like</u>

7. The <u>team</u> (*understand, understands*) that the sales brochure must be completed by Friday.
       7. <u>understands</u>

8. A large <u>percentage</u> of our employees (*enjoy, enjoys*) working in teams.
       8. <u>enjoy</u>

9. There (*is, are*) numerous <u>names</u> to describe teamwork.
       9. <u>are</u>

10. Randy's <u>politics</u> (*have, has*) splintered the group.
        10. <u>have</u>

PART 4

Reviewing Modifiers and Connectors

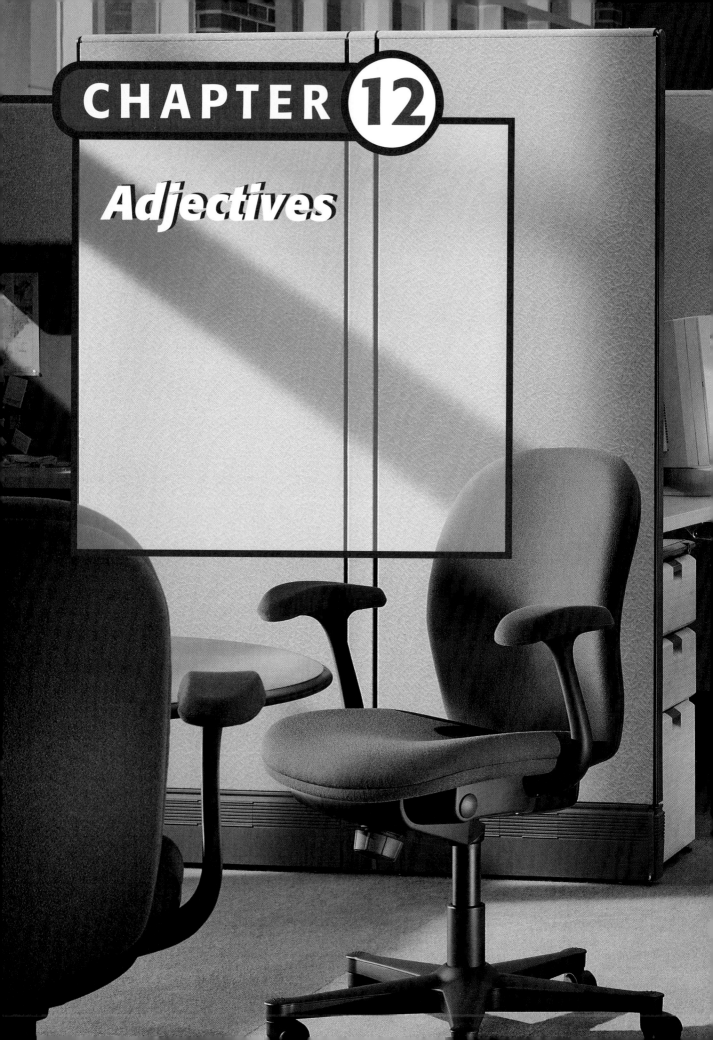

CHAPTER 12

Adjectives

ERGONOMICS

Ergonomics is the study of the relationship between the worker and the work environment. Ergonomic planners adjust the surrounding working conditions to meet the needs of the individual worker. Ergonomic planning includes an analysis of all workplace risk factors such as lighting, workstations, seating, monitors, work-rest cycles, and temperatures.

When a mismatch occurs between the worker and the physical requirements of the job, cumulative trauma disorder (CTD) or musculoskeletal disorder (MSD) sometimes occurs. Additional terms for CTD are repetitive motion injury or illness, repetitive strain injury or illness, or repetitive stress injury or illness (RSI). Usually CTDs occur when workers repeat the same motion each day, work in awkward positions, lift heavy objects, or use force to perform their jobs. CTDs comprise more than 100 different types of job-induced injuries and illnesses. Symptoms of CTD vary widely from minor aches and pains to crippling impairment such as carpal tunnel syndrome.

Work-related injuries cost employers billions of dollars in workers' compensation claims. Simple and inexpensive ergonomic solutions such as adjusting the height of a workstation or encouraging short breaks often will prevent needless CTDs from affecting workers. The Occupational Safety and Health Administration (OSHA) is responsible for providing education, research, and enforcement, and making rules to combat CTDs in the workplace. OSHA sponsors conferences, tracks ergonomic programs, reviews scientific literature, and investigates ergonomic cases.

OBJECTIVES

After you have studied this chapter and completed the exercises, you will be able to do the following:

1. Identify limiting, descriptive, possessive, proper, and demonstrative adjectives in sentences.
2. Use the articles *a, an,* and *the* correctly.
3. Hyphenate compound adjectives when appropriate.
4. Use the positive, comparative, and superlative degrees of adjectives correctly.
5. Identify nouns modified by adjectives, adjective phrases, and adjective clauses.
6. Determine the correct usage of commonly misused adjectives.
7. Diagram sentences correctly.

TERMS TO REMEMBER

CARPAL TUNNEL SYNDROME

CUMULATIVE TRAUMA DISORDERS (CTDs)

ERGONOMICS

OCCUPATIONAL SAFETY AND HEALTH ADMINISTRATION (OSHA)

REPETITIVE STRESS INJURY (RSI)

WORKERS' COMPENSATION

WORKSTATION

LOOKING AHEAD

Pretest

Directions: *In the space provided, write the letter of the correct answer.*

1. In the sentence *Our office furniture showroom was messy and crowded,* the adjectives are
   a. our, office, showroom, messy, crowded.
   b. office, furniture, showroom.
   c. office, furniture, messy, crowded.
   d. our, office, furniture, messy, crowded.

   1. ___d___

2. In the sentence *European decor has a definite charm,* the word *European* functions as a
   a. proper noun.
   b. proper adjective.
   c. possessive adjective.
   d. limiting adjective.

   2. ___b___

3. Which phrase represents the incorrect use of an article?
   a. an universal appeal
   b. an office window
   c. a blueprint
   d. an hour

   3. ___a___

4. In the sentence *Julia selected those colors for the employees' break room,* the function of *those* is that of
   a. an interrogative adjective.
   b. a possessive pronoun.
   c. a demonstrative adjective.
   d. a demonstrative pronoun.

   4. ___c___

5. Which compound adjective is *not* hyphenated correctly?
   a. first-class service
   b. point-of-sale transaction
   c. short term solution
   d. real estate office

   5. ___c___

6. The superlative adjective for *stunning* is
   a. stunninger
   b. stunning
   c. more stunning
   d. most stunning

   6. ___d___

7. In the sentence *We preferred the building blueprints that Lancaster Builders submitted,* which of the following is modified by the adjective phrase?
   a. building
   b. Lancaster Builders
   c. blueprints
   d. We

   7. ___c___

8. Which two sentences are *not* correct?
   a. We sold less bedroom furniture this year than we sold last year.
   b. We sold fewer bedroom furniture this year than we sold last year.
   c. We ordered further tests for radon detection.
   d. We ordered farther tests for radon detection.

   8. __b and d__

O V E R V I E W

Nouns and verbs provide the substance of a sentence, but writing would be very dull and vague without adjectives. When properly used, adjectives are the words that add the interesting details and color to sentences.

Wouldn't you be pleased if your supervisor wrote a letter of recommendation that described you as a dependable, intelligent, and energetic employee? Most of you would answer, "Yes." These adjectives certainly provide a favorable "picture" for a prospective employer. In this chapter, you will learn to create "pictures" in your writing by using adjectives that add variety, descriptive details, and specificity to your sentences.

TYPES OF ADJECTIVES

An adjective is a word that modifies (describes) a noun or a pronoun. Several adjectives often appear in one sentence. More than one adjective may describe one noun. An adjective answers these questions:

What kind?	red, new, exciting, durable
Which one?	this, that, these, those
How many?	one, few, 200, one-half, all, some
Whose?	his, Ryan's, companies'
	(Possessive pronouns and possessive nouns function as adjectives.)

Several types of adjectives, including limiting, descriptive, possessive, proper, and demonstrative, will be discussed in this chapter.

Limiting Adjectives

Limiting adjectives are numbers or words that indicate *how many*. Use a limiting adjective to limit the scope of the noun or pronoun.

We still need <u>three</u> workstations for the office on State Street.
(The adjective *three* indicates *how many* workstations are needed.)

<u>All</u> safety programs require the commitment of management.
(The adjective *all* indicates *how many* safety programs require commitment.)

Descriptive Adjectives

Descriptive adjectives answer the question *What kind?* They usually precede nouns or follow linking verbs.

See Instructor Notes 12-1 and 12-2 in IAE.

Go to Transparencies/PowerPoints 12-1a and 12-1b.

Refer to Chapter 2 for an introduction to adjectives.

Go to PowerPoints 12-2a and 12-2b.

Go to PowerPoint 12-3.

Refer to the list of linking verbs in Chapter 9.

Adjectives

Before Nouns. Use a descriptive adjective to tell something about (describe) a noun or a pronoun. Place a descriptive adjective as close as possible to the noun or pronoun it modifies.

> The <u>heating</u> system caused problems.
>
> (The descriptive adjective *heating* tells *what kind* of system. *Heating* appears before the noun it modifies.)
>
> I knew the <u>office</u> furniture that I bought at the auction was a <u>good</u> bargain.
>
> (The descriptive adjective *office* tells *what kind* of furniture. The adjective *good* tells *what kind* of bargain. Both adjectives appear before the nouns they modify.)

After Linking Verbs. Use a descriptive adjective after a linking verb to modify a noun or pronoun used as a subject. A descriptive adjective that follows a linking verb is one type of complement (predicate adjective).

> Excessive noise in the workplace is <u>annoying</u>.
>
> (The linking verb *is* connects the descriptive adjective *annoying* to the noun *noise.*)
>
> The total amount for the new carpeting seems <u>high</u>.
>
> (*Seems* is a linking verb connecting the descriptive adjective *high* to the noun *amount.*)

CHECKUP 12-1

See Instructor Note 12-3 in IAE.

Directions: Underline each descriptive adjective once. Circle each limiting adjective. Ignore a, an, *and* the.

1. The upholstery came in (four) different colors.

2. Tendinitis is (one) common type of <u>workplace</u> injury.

3. Workers need education about <u>proper</u> posture and <u>lifting</u> techniques.

4. The <u>new</u> furniture for the office is <u>sturdy</u> and <u>functional</u>.

5. A <u>thorough</u> investigation of worksites is <u>important</u> to identify the <u>various</u> hazards that affect the workers.

6. If you plan to order (some) furniture through a catalog, expect to wait (six) weeks for delivery.

GO TO CD-ROM
CHECKUP 12-1

Possessive Adjectives

Go to PowerPoint 12-4.

Possessive pronouns such as *my, her, his, your, its,* and *our* function as adjectives and are called possessive adjectives. Possessive nouns such as *Jack's* or *firm's* function as possessive adjectives also. Possessive adjectives answer the question *Whose?* Use a possessive adjective to modify a noun or pronoun.

Jane buys used furniture in good condition for <u>her</u> office at home.
(*Her* functions as a possessive adjective that answers the question *Whose office?*)

The <u>decorator's</u> hints about lighting showed us how to create some striking effects.
(*Decorator's* answers the question *Whose hints?*)

Proper Adjectives

Proper nouns or words derived from proper nouns also function as adjectives and are referred to as proper adjectives. Capitalize most proper adjectives as you would proper nouns. Do *not* capitalize proper adjectives when they lose their connections with the proper nouns from which they were derived. Proper adjectives answer the question *Which?*

The <u>January</u> office products catalog included several types of ergonomic chairs.
(*January* requires capitalization. *January* is a proper adjective that modifies the noun *catalog. January* answers the question *Which catalog?*)

Several <u>Canadian</u> firms sell reconditioned furniture that meets <u>OSHA</u> standards.
(*Canadian* modifies *firms* and *OSHA* modifies *standards*. Both *Canadian* and *OSHA* require capitalization.)

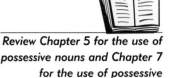

Review Chapter 5 for the use of possessive nouns and Chapter 7 for the use of possessive pronouns.

Refer to Chapter 4 for examples of proper nouns.

CHECKUP 12-2

Directions: *Underline the possessive and proper adjectives. In the space provided, identify the adjectives as possessive (**Pos**) or proper (**Prop**). Some adjectives may be both possessive and proper.*

Ex.: Mitch's desk had limited work surface space for his reference materials.
    Pos and Prop,
    Pos

1. <u>My</u> supervisor suggested that I use <u>my</u> copyholder.
    Pos, Pos

2. We hope to purchase some hand-carved <u>Mexican</u> furniture for <u>our</u> home office.
    Prop, Pos

3. <u>OSHA's</u> rules provide work environment guidelines for <u>American</u> companies.
    Pos and Prop
    Prop

4. He studied <u>British</u> architecture in <u>his</u> ergonomics class in college.
    Prop, Pos

5. The oriental rug was the focal point of <u>Ruth's</u> office.
    Pos and Prop

12-4 In sentence 5, the word *oriental* does not require capitalization.

GO TO CD-ROM CHECKUP 12-2

CHECKUP 12-3

Directions: *Use the second Secondary Learning paragraph for this exercise. Locate the limiting and possessive adjectives and write them in the appropriate columns. Do not include the adjectives* **a, an,** *and* **the.** *In parentheses, place the noun modified by each adjective.*

x

2. Those colors are the most effective for a room with no windows.

colors _____

3. Several building committee members stated that this grade of carpeting was best for heavily used areas.

grade _____

4. Those managers who purchase office furnishings must be aware of government regulations.

managers _____

5. We will have difficulty complying with that safety regulation.

regulation _____

6. I need that list of questions when I begin to look at computer equipment.

list _____

GO TO CD-ROM
CHECKUP 12-4

ARTICLES

Although the articles *a, an,* and *the* are less descriptive than words such as *strong* or *dull,* these articles are some of the most frequently used words in the English language. Articles always modify nouns.

A and *An*

Use *a* and *an* with singular nouns, not with plural nouns. Place *a* or *an* before any other adjective if two or more adjectives precede a noun.

> We plan to place <u>an</u> order for new furniture that will meet ergonomic standards.
>
> (The article *an* refers to *order,* a singular noun.)
>
> <u>A</u> large company cannot buy one type of chair for all its workers.
>
> (The article *a* refers to *company,* a singular noun.)

Guidelines for Using *A* or *An*

The initial sound (not the first letter) of the word that follows an article determines whether you will use *a* or *an.*

Go to PowerPoints 12-6a and 12-6b.

See Instructor Notes 12-7 and 12-8 in IAE.

Before Sounded Consonants.   Use *a* before words beginning with a consonant that is sounded.

<u>a</u> room   <u>a</u> hobby   <u>a</u> designer   <u>a</u> computer table

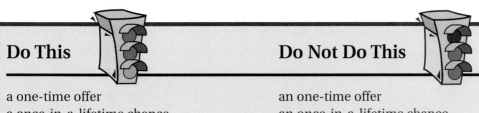

Do This	Do Not Do This
a one-time offer	an one-time offer
a once-in-a-lifetime chance	an once-in-a-lifetime chance

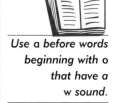

Use a before words beginning with o that have a w sound.

Before long *u*.   Use *a* before words beginning with the long sound of *u*.

a university	a union	a unique design
a unique design	a unilateral decision	

Before *a, e, i, o,* and short *u*.   Use *an* before words beginning with the vowel sounds *a, e, i,* and *o* and the short sound of *u*.

an oblong table	an unusual design
an interior designer	an accident
an X-ray	an f.o.b. order
(*X* is pronounced *ex.*)	(The letter *f* is pronounced *ef.*)

Before Silent *h*.   Use *an* before words beginning with silent *h*.

an hour ago	an honest sales staff
an honor	an honorarium

The

Use the article *the* with singular or plural nouns. Place *the* before any other adjective when two or more adjectives precede a noun.

> Our consultants evaluate your needs on the basis of the information sheet you complete.
>
> (The first *the* refers to *basis* and the second *the* refers to *sheet.* Both *basis* and *sheet* are singular nouns. *The* precedes *information,* a descriptive adjective that also modifies *sheet.*)
>
> The offices seem to have high noise levels.
>
> (*The* refers to *offices,* a plural noun.)

Repetition of Articles

See Instructor Note 12-9 in IAE.

Repeat an article before *each* noun when two persons, places, or things are involved. Do not repeat an article when only one person, place, or thing is intended.

> The facilities manager and the space planner proposed an open-office environment.
>
> (Two people—*the* facilities manager and *the* space planner—proposed an open-office environment.)
>
> The facilities manager and space planner proposed an open-office environment.
>
> (The same person [*the* facilities manager is also the space planner] proposed the open-office environment. *The* is not repeated before *space planner.*)
>
> Our designer thought the store and showroom was beyond our budget.
>
> (The combined store and showroom refers to one area. *The* is not repeated before *showroom.*)

Exercise 1

Directions: *In the space provided, write* a *or* an, *whichever is correct.*

1. OSHA report   _____an_____

2. showroom   _____a_____

3. eye-catching design   _____an_____

4. hour ago   _____an_____

5. uniform color scheme   _____a_____

6. hundred dollars   _____a_____

Exercise 2

Directions: *Select the correct word, and write it in the space provided.*

1. We need advice on (*a, an,*) wide variety of ergonomic issues.   _____a_____

2. The company adds (*a, an, the*) extra charge if you want (*a, an, the*) furniture delivered tomorrow.   __an   the__

3. We have seen (*a, an, the*) dramatic increase in injuries at our workplace.   _____a_____

4. (*A, An*) union member should be on (*a, an, the*) building committee.   __A   the__

5. (*An, The*) number one priority is (*a, an,*) adjustable chair.   __The   an__

6. We hired (*a, an*) consultant to advise us about our lighting concerns.   _____a_____

GO TO CD-ROM
CHECKUP 12-5

COMPOUND ADJECTIVES

Compound implies a combination of two or more parts. Compound adjectives combine two or more words to form *one* thought when they modify nouns. These words may be nouns, adjectives, participles, verbs, or adverbs. Many compound adjectives require hyphens.

Always use an up-to-date dictionary or reference manual to determine whether a compound adjective is two words or hyphenated. A dictionary entry showing a hyphenated compound adjective does *not* mean that the adjective is always hyphenated. Showing the hyphenation means that the compound adjective is hyphenated before a noun.

See Instructor Notes 12-10 and 12-11 in IAE.

Use an up-to-date dictionary or reference manual such as The Gregg Reference Manual *to determine whether a compound adjective is two words or hyphenated.*

Compound Adjectives—Hyphenated Before and After Nouns

Use a hyphen when these compound adjective combinations appear before or after a noun or in other locations in a sentence.

year-round	(noun + adjective)
price-conscious	(noun + adjective)
decision-making	(noun + participle)
work-related	(noun + participle)
high-ranking	(adjective + participle)
long-standing	(adjective + participle)
fast-paced	(adjective + noun + *ed*)
open-ended	(adjective + noun + *ed*)

Our water-repellent furniture for the lobby should last many years.
(*Water-repellent* is a combination of a noun plus an adjective that modifies *furniture*. The compound adjective *water-repellent* requires a hyphen.)

Our new furniture for the lobby was advertised as water-repellent.
(*Water-repellent* [noun plus adjective combination] appears after the noun and requires a hyphen.)

In this fast-paced office, employees should be receptive to stress-reducing suggestions.
(*Fast-paced* [adjective, plus noun, plus *ed* combination] and *stress-reducing* [noun plus participle combination] appear before nouns. Both of these compound adjectives require hyphens.)

Compound Adjectives—Hyphenated Only Before Nouns

Use a hyphen when these compound adjective combinations appear before a noun. Do not use a hyphen when these combinations appear in other locations in a sentence.

low-cost	(adjective + noun)
long-range	(adjective + noun)
well-known	(adverb + participle)
ever-increasing	(adverb + participle)
scaled-down	(participle + adverb)
make-or-break	(verb + verb)
drive-through	(verb + adverb)
up-to-date	(phrase)
state-of-the-art	(phrase)
end-of-the-year	(phrase)
off-the-shelf	(phrase)

We hope to receive some low-cost bids from local interior designers.
(*Low-cost* combines two separate words—an adjective and a noun—to form one compound adjective that modifies *bids*. The compound adjective *low-cost* requires a hyphen.)

We were surprised that the bid was submitted at such a <u>low cost</u>.

(In this sentence, the compound adjective *low cost* [adjective and noun] appears after the noun and does not require a hyphen.)

A <u>well-known</u> safety expert identified the principal causes of factory accidents.

(*Well-known* [adverb plus participle] appears before a noun and requires a hyphen.)

We needed <u>up-to-date</u> statistics verifying our safety record at the <u>end of the year</u>.

(*Up-to-date* is a phrase that appears before a noun and requires a hyphen. *End of the year* is a phrase that does not appear before a noun and does not require hyphens.)

Our <u>end-of-the-year</u> report showed a decrease in the number of employee accidents.

(*End-of-the-year* is a phrase that appears before a noun and requires a hyphen.)

Common Compound Adjectives

Do not use a hyphen when an adjective plus a noun combination is widely recognized as a concept or institution. Here are some common compound adjectives that do not require hyphens:

accounts receivable	post office	branch office
real estate	free trade	social security
high school	income tax	word processing

Decorators, Inc., recently completed designing the interior of a local <u>real estate</u> office.

(*Real estate* is a recognized adjective and noun combination and does not require a hyphen.)

To become a facilities planner, you need more than a <u>high school</u> education.

(*High school* is a recognized adjective and noun combination and does not require a hyphen.)

Numbers With Nouns

Use a hyphen to connect a number (words or figures) and a noun to form a compound adjective before a noun. The second element is always singular. Do *not* use a hyphen when the expression consisting of a number and noun *follows* the noun. This unit of measurement is singular or plural depending on the intent of the sentence.

See Instructor Note 12-12 in IAE.

a <u>6-foot</u> acoustical panel

(The second element *foot* is singular. The combination number and noun appears before a noun and requires a hyphen.)

an acoustical panel that is <u>6 feet</u> (plural)

(The number and noun follow the noun. No hyphen is necessary. The unit of measurement [*feet*] is plural.)

an <u>eight-point</u> proposal (*point* is singular)

a proposal that has <u>eight points</u> (plural)

Numerical Compound Adjectives

Use hyphens in the numbers between 21 and 99 when the numbers are written as words.

<u>Thirty-two</u> construction projects are in the Builders Exchange tour.

Our note to Inside Designs is for $18,223.00 (Eighteen thousand two hundred <u>twenty-three</u> dollars).

Series of Compound Adjectives

Use a hyphen in a series of compound adjectives even though the base noun does not follow each adjective.

The supervisors found the <u>one-</u>, <u>two-</u>, and <u>four-hour</u> tapes helpful for the employee safety workshops.

(The base noun *tapes* is not needed after each word in the series, but the hyphen after each word is necessary.)

"Self" Words

Use a hyphen when self is connected to another word to form a compound adjective.

self-help   self-management   self-evaluation

CHECKUP 12-6

Directions: In the following sentences, place the proofreaders' mark for inserting a hyphen (=̲) in the correct location. If a hyphen is incorrect, use the proofreaders' mark for delete (𝓭). Use a dictionary or reference manual if necessary.

1. The ergonomics consultant did a first class analysis of our furniture needs.

2. Betty suggested curvilinear tables for the small group conference rooms.

3. Some showrooms have 20,000 square foot areas to display complete workstations.

4. If you are trying to find a short term solution, rent or lease your office furniture.

5. KD Carpets was selling its fire resistant carpet at a low price.

6. After reading a recent branch office agenda, I noticed you were having a discussion on safety.

7. The training program was structured in a self study format.

8. The program featured equipment that was up to date.

GO TO
CD-ROM
CHECKUP 12-6

Most descriptive adjectives have three degrees of comparison—positive (*long*), comparative (*longer*), and superlative (*longest*). Absolute adjectives such as *round* and *square* are not capable of realistic comparison. Dictionaries provide information about adjective comparisons.

See Instructor Note 12-13 in IAE.

Positive Degree

Use the positive degree as the base form of the adjective to describe one person, place, thing, quality, idea, or one group of things.

light color   **large office**   **wide selection**

Daley's Office Products carries a **wide** selection of office furniture.

I have a **large** office.

Comparative Degree

Use the comparative degree to compare two people, places, ideas, qualities, or things.

lighter color   **larger office**   **wider selection**

Daley's Office Products carries a **wider** selection of office furniture than Dunn's Furniture.

My office is **larger** than yours.

Do This	Do Not Do This
The offices in the executive suite are <u>larger than the offices downstairs.</u>	The offices in the executive suite are <u>larger than downstairs.</u>

State comparisons precisely. The offices are not larger than the downstairs.

Superlative Degree

Use the superlative degree to compare more than two persons, places, or things.

lightest color   **largest office**   **widest selection**

Daley's Office Products carries the **widest** selection of office furniture I have ever seen.

My office is the **largest** one in the building.

SLIP-UP

Sign in a Maine shop: Our motto is to give our customers the lowest possible prices and workmanship. Note: Do they really give the lowest possible workmanship too?
Source: The Internet.

Guidelines for Forming Comparisons

One-Syllable Adjectives. Add *er* to the positive form of a one-syllable adjective to form its *comparative* degree. Add *est* to the positive form of a one-syllable adjective to form its *superlative* degree.

Refer to the spelling rule in the appendix for doubling consonants.

See Instructor Notes 12-14 and 12-15 in IAE.

Comparative			Superlative		
warm	+ er	warmer	warm	+ est	warmest
short	+ er	shorter	short	+ est	shortest
big	+ er	bigger	big	+ est	biggest

Two-Syllable Adjectives. Add *er* to the positive form of a two-syllable adjective, or add the words *more* or *less* before the positive form of a two-syllable adjective to form its *comparative* degree. Add *est* to the positive form of a two-syllable adjective, or add the words *most* or *least* before the positive form of a two-syllable adjective for its *superlative* degree. The sound often determines the choice.

Positive	Comparative	Superlative
narrow	narrower	narrowest
	or more narrow	*or* most narrow
quiet	quieter	quietest
	or more quiet	*or* most quiet
painful	more painful	most painful
	(*not* painfuler)	(*not* painfulest)
awkward	less awkward	least awkward

See Instructor Note 12-16 in IAE.

Three-Syllable Adjectives. Add the words *more* or *less* before the positive form of a three-syllable adjective for its *comparative* degree. Add the words *most* or *least* before the positive form of a three-syllable adjective for its *superlative* degree.

Positive	Comparative	Superlative
attractive	more attractive	most attractive
essential	more essential	most essential
efficient	less efficient	least efficient

Words Ending in *y*. Change the *y* to *i* and add *er* or *est* to form the *comparative* and *superlative* degrees.

Positive	Comparative	Superlative
friendly	friendlier	friendliest
busy	busier	busiest
heavy	heavier	heaviest

12-17 Suggest that students memorize the list of irregular adjectives.

Special Forms. Some irregular adjectives do not form their comparatives and superlatives in the normal way.

Positive	Comparative	Superlative
good	better	best
bad	worse	worst
little	less, lesser	littlest, least
many	more	most
much	more	most

Absolute Adjectives

The positive degree may be the only degree necessary for an adjective if it already expresses the highest degree. For example, if a table is oblong, it can't become more oblong or most oblong. Here is a list of some absolute adjectives:

See Instructor Note 12-18 in IAE.

Refer to a reference manual such as The Gregg Reference Manual for ways that some absolute adjectives may be modified.

circular	horizontal	straight
complete	ideal	supreme
correct	instantaneous	unanimous
dead	perfect	unique
empty	single	vertical
final	square	wrong

CHECKUP 12-7

Directions: *In the spaces provided, fill in the missing degree forms. One of the three adjective forms is already in correct order. All forms may not have missing degree forms.*

Positive	Comparative	Superlative
Ex.: **active**	**more active**	**most active**
1. stressful	more stressful	most stressful
2. bad	worse	worst
3. high	higher	highest
4. reputable	more reputable	most reputable
5. difficult	more difficult	most difficult
6. easy	easier	easiest
7. tall	taller	tallest
8. quiet	quieter	quietest
	or more quiet	*or* most quiet
9. supportive	more supportive	most supportive
10. wrong		

Go to Instructor Note 12-19 in IAE.

GO TO CD-ROM
CHECKUP 12-7

CHECKUP 12-8

Directions: *Select the correct word or words and write them in the space provided.*

1. To lower the noise levels, we purchased (*tall, taller, more tall*) acoustical panels.   taller

2. Which of these carpet samples is the (*more, most*) practical for a lobby area?   most

3. Of the two architects, who is (*better, best*)?   better

4. Your layouts are the (*more appealing, most appealing*) of any others in the display.   most appealing

5. The best way to monitor equipment noise is to buy (*quieter, more quieter*) equipment.   quieter

6. My office is always (*more warm, warmer*) than yours.   warmer

**GO TO
CD-ROM**
CHECKUP 12-8

ADJECTIVE CLAUSES AND PHRASES

Sometimes clauses and phrases modify nouns or pronouns. When a phrase modifies a noun or pronoun, it is an *adjective phrase*. An adjective phrase does not have a subject or a predicate and cannot stand by itself. When a clause modifies a noun or pronoun, it is an *adjective clause*. An adjective clause is a dependent clause that has a subject and predicate, but it is not a sentence and cannot stand by itself.

Adjective Clauses

Use the relative pronouns *who, whose, which,* and *that* to connect an adjective clause to the noun or pronoun that is modified. Place the adjective clause immediately after the noun that is described. Use commas to set aside the clause when it does not add to the meaning of the sentence (nonrestrictive clause). Do not use commas to set aside the clause when the clause is necessary (restrictive) to the meaning of the sentence.

Refer to Chapter 7 for a review of the correct use of that, which, *and* who.

SLIP-UP
We bought a bushel of apples from a roadstand farmer that was rotten. Note: Are the apples or the farmer rotten? Source: The Internet.

> **The employee who designs the best workstation will receive a prize.**
> (*Who* connects the adjective clause to the noun *employee*. The adjective clause *who designs the best workstation* describes the specific employee receiving the prize. The clause is necessary to the meaning of the sentence. No commas are necessary.)
>
> **The firm's main office, which is in South Carolina, compiled statistics on workplace injuries.**
> (*Which* refers to office. The clause is not necessary to the meaning of the sentence. Commas set the clause aside from the rest of the sentence.)

Adjective Phrases

When infinitive phrases, participial phrases, or prepositional phrases function as modifiers of nouns or pronouns, they are called adjective phrases.

Use a comma to set aside nonrestrictive phrases or clauses.

Having heard the statistics on carpal tunnel syndrome, I became more aware of this disorder's effects.

(*Having heard the statistics on carpal tunnel syndrome* is a participial phrase. In this sentence, it functions as an adjective phrase modifying the pronoun *I*.)

The lighting consultant from Acme Lighting was recommended highly.

(*From Acme Lighting* is a prepositional phrase. In this sentence, it tells *which* consultant and functions as an adjective phrase.)

To become acquainted with ergonomics, we searched the Internet.

(*To become acquainted with ergonomics* is an infinitive phrase. In this sentence, it modifies the pronoun *we* and functions as an adjective.)

Do This	Do Not Do This
Coming into the building, we saw the spectacular artwork.	Coming into the building, the artwork was spectacular.

The artwork was not coming into the building. The adjective phrase coming into the building *modifies the pronoun* we.

CHECKUP 12-9

Directions: In the space provided, write the word that is modified by the underlined adjective phrase or clause.

1. I did not agree with the ergonomics consultant who evaluated our facilities.

   consultant

2. The OSHA report that I must review is 55 pages.

   report

3. Richley Furniture, whose president is Dave Richley, specializes in office furniture for the physically handicapped.

   Richley Furniture

4. My new chair, which I just purchased last week, does not support my lower back.

   chair

5. Lu Cheng, who is my team leader, is concerned about employees taking sufficient rest breaks.

   Lu Cheng

6. Several executives in our company think that interior design is an expensive luxury.

   executives

GO TO CD-ROM

CHECKUP 12-9

Refer to a reference manual, such as The Gregg Reference Manual, *for additional examples of the words* fewer *and* less, farther *and* further, *and* latter, later, last, *and* latest.

See Instructor Note 12-20 in IAE.

Go to PowerPoint 12-7.

Several adjectives require special attention.

Fewer/Less

Use *fewer* with plural nouns that can be counted. Use *less* with singular nouns that refer to degree or amount or to things that cannot be counted.

> We noticed <u>less</u> noise since the construction workers left the area.
> (*Noise* is a noun referring to an amount which cannot be counted.)
>
> Langley Telemarketers had <u>fewer</u> cumulative trauma disorders last year than it had in the previous year.
> (The disorders may be counted.)

Farther/Further

Go to PowerPoint 12-8.

Use *farther* to refer to physical distance. Use *further* to mean additional.

> Your architectural firm is <u>farther</u> from our office than I had anticipated.
>
> Our Bloomington office is <u>farther</u> from office furniture stores than our Joliet office.
>
> <u>Further</u> help is available for workers suffering from repetitive-motion injuries.
>
> We will give the equipment survey <u>further</u> attention at the board meeting.

Latter/Later/Last/Latest

Go to PowerPoints 12-9a and 12-9b.

Use *latter* to refer to the second of two persons, places, or things mentioned. Use *later* to refer to time. Use *last* to refer to whatever follows everything else in a series. Use *latest* to refer to time (as in *most recent*).

> The <u>latter</u> set of statistics referred to work-related injuries.
>
> The <u>later</u> time for the safety committee meeting was not suitable for me.
>
> The <u>last</u> time we attended an ergonomics training class was two years ago.
>
> We just submitted the <u>latest</u> landscape plan for the front grounds.

CHECKUP 12-10

Directions: *Select the correct word, and write it in the space provided.*

1. Jill announced that no (*farther, further*) lighting options would be considered.

_____further_____

2. After looking at the (*later, latest*) designs, I selected the one that seemed the most conservative.

_____latest_____

3. We have had (*fewer, less*) accidents resulting from assembly line carelessness since we instituted safety workshops.

_____fewer_____

4. The (*last, latter*) book that I read on interior design was impressive.

_____last_____

5. I thought that the (*later, latter*) of the two building plans was creative and unique.

_____latter_____

6. He spends (*fewer, less*) hours at the office because he finds the environment depressing.

_____fewer_____

**GO TO
CD-ROM
CHECKUP 12-10**

DIAGRAMMING SENTENCES

In a sentence with an adjective clause, place the main clause in one diagram and the adjective clause beneath it in another diagram. Use a dotted line to connect the relative pronoun in the adjective clause to the modified noun or pronoun in the main clause.

Kathryn, who is our supervisor, plans to order new file cabinets.

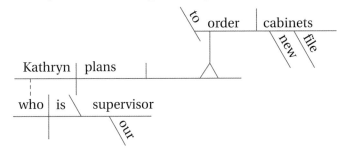

The carpet colors that I like are available.

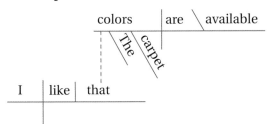

Adjectives

347

CHECKUP 12-11

See Instructor Note 12-21 in IAE.

Directions: *Diagram the following sentences in the space provided. All words in the sentences may be diagrammed.*

1. I need a new computer table that accommodates my height.

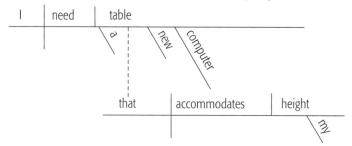

2. We bought a VDT screen that had low radiation emissions.

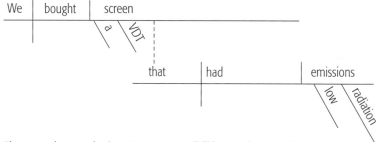

3. Those employees who have team responsibilities need some private space.

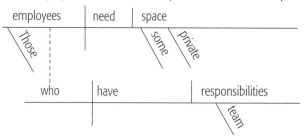

4. My supervisor is the person who orders the firm's office furniture.

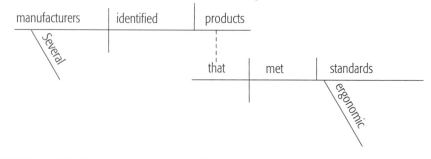

5. Several manufacturers identified products that met ergonomic standards.

GO TO CD-ROM
CHECKUP 12-11

NAME _____

PRACTICE 1A

A. Directions: *Select the correct word or words, and write them in the space provided.*

1. Have you received (*a, an*) application from Clarke Watson for the position of facilities coordinator?

   1. _____an_____

2. (*These, Them*) computer tables seem (*more sturdy, most sturdy*) than the ones at the discount stores.

   2. _____These_____
   _____more sturdy_____

3. We offer our employees (*a, an*) (*one hour, one-hour*) ergonomics training session.

   3. _____a_____
   _____one-hour_____

4. The (*well designed, well-designed*) chair is ideal for our employees.

   4. _____well-_____
   _____designed_____

5. I know that Blakely Decorators will give us the (*better, best*) design plan for our money.

   5. _____best_____

B. Directions: *In the following sentences, a noun or pronoun is underlined once. Place two lines under the adjective or adjectives that modify the underlined words.*

1. Sometimes lighting is overlooked in improving work environments.

2. I prefer that chair.

3. We plan to use this fabric for upholstering our office chairs.

4. Jane buys used furniture in good condition for her office.

5. Our firm allows workers to select their own seating.

**GO TO
CD-ROM**
PRACTICE 1
EXERCISES

PRACTICE 2A

Exercise 1

Directions: *Underline the adjectives in the following sentences. Ignore the articles* a, an, *and* the.

1. Our company requires increased rest breaks for computer operators.

2. After Franco uses my computer, the contrast control always needs some adjustments.

3. The building acoustics are excellent.

4. A good manager isolates noisy equipment and people from other workers.

5. This facility has a heating and cooling system with individual worker temperature controls.

See Instructor Note 12-22 in IAE.

NAME

Exercise 2

Directions: *In the space provided, correct the following sentences. Some sentences may have punctuation or grammatical errors.*

1. A 6 foot man requires a more different workstation than a petite woman.

A 6-foot man requires a different workstation than a petite woman.

2. Our Detroit architectural firm uses a first class database.

Our Detroit architectural firm uses a first-class database.

3. Chris Novelski who is our ergonomics coordinator recommended them chairs.

Chris Novelski, who is our ergonomics coordinator, recommended these chairs.

4. Thirty six percent of the employees with repetitive motion injuries lost at least 31 days of work.

Thirty-six percent of the employees with repetitive-motion injuries lost at least 31 days of work.

**GO TO
CD-ROM
PRACTICE 2
EXERCISES**

5. Companies can improve employee performance by shifting the angle between an computer screen and the user's eyes to eliminate glare.

Companies can improve employee performance by shifting the angle between a computer screen and the user's eyes to eliminate glare.

PRACTICE 3A

PROOFREADING

Directions: *Proofread and compare the two sentences in each group. If they are the same, write* **Yes** *in the space provided. If they are not the same, write* **No.** *Use the first sentence as the correct copy. If you find errors in the second sentence, underline them; insert any omitted words or marks of punctuation.*

1. OSHA's ergonomics program covers four major areas— worksite analysis, prevention, medical management, and training and education.

1.  No

OSHAs ergonomics program covers major four areas— worksite analysis, prevention, medical management, and training education.
(and)

NAME _____

2. Employers and employees should understand the
work patterns that may cause cumulative trauma
disorders (CTDs) or repetitive-motion disorders.

2. ___No___

Employers and employees should understand the
work patterns that͜cause cumulative trauma disorders
(CDT's) or repetitive-motion disorders.

3. Ergonomics centers on such work environment
areas as workstation design, safety devices, and
lighting to fit the employee's physical requirements.

3. ___No___

Ergonomics center on such work environment
areas as workstation design, safty devises, and
lighting to fit the employees' physical requirements.

4. Anyone whose job demands excessive repetitive
wrist and hand motion is a potential candidate
for CTS (carpal tunnel syndrome).

4. ___No___

Anyone whose job demands excessive repetitive
wrist and hand motions is a potential candidate
for CTS (carpol tunnel syndrome).

5. Many companies consider the design of physical
work spaces to be an important health and safety issue.

5. ___Yes___

Many companies consider the design of physical work
spaces to be an important health and safety issue.

Proofreading Exercise

The following list identifies some of the characteristics of an ergonomically
correct workstation.

See Instructor Note 12-23 in IAE.

ERGONOMIC WORKSTATIONS

1. Adjustable chairs.
2. Stable chairs with 5-leg bases.
3. Adjustable backrests.
4. Task lighting for reading printed copy.
5. Adequate space for equipment.
6. Adjustable working surfaces.
7. Antiglare screens on computer monitors.
8. Adequate wiring and cabling installations for electronic equipment.
9. Adequate storage space for supplies, backup tapes, and personal items.
10. Soothing colors on large wall areas.
11. Acoustic fabrics for noise reduction.
12. Clean ventilation system.

PRACTICE

Directions: Use the following proofreaders' marks to correct the copy below. Use the copy on page 351 as your correct guide.

Make lowercase /   Move left ⌐   Insert letter ∧
Capitalize ≡   Move right ⌐   Insert comma ⋏
Delete ⸤   Insert space #   Transpose ∪
Delete and close up ⸤   Delete space ⌣   Insert period ⊙
Double space ds ⌐   Insert hyphen ＿

ERGONOMIC WORK STATIONS

1. Adjustable chairs⊙
2. Stable chairs with 5-leg bases.
3. Adjustable backrests.
4. Task-lighting for reading *printed* copy.
5. Adequate space for equipment.
6. Adjustable working surfaces.
7. Anti-glare screens on computer monitors.
8. Adequate wiring and cabling installations for electronic equipment.
9. Adequate storage space for supplies, back-up tapes and personal items.
10. Soothing colors on large wall areas.
ds ⌐ 11. Acoustic fabrics for noise reduction.
     12. clean air ventilation system.

**GO TO
CD-ROM**
PRACTICE 3
EXERCISES

PRACTICE 4A

WRITING

Answers will vary.

Directions: Read the following case study. Write a paragraph describing your suggestions for helping Cathy.

Cathy does data entry at a computer eight hours a day. She takes a 15-minute break at 10:30 a.m., 30 minutes for lunch, and another 15-minute break at 3 p.m. She feels tingling and numbness in her hands. She often is clumsy and drops things. Cathy feels that her grip is getting weaker.

Cathy is probably experiencing warning signs of a cumulative trauma disorder. She is not taking enough breaks during the day. Cathy should tell her supervisor about her symptoms immediately. Then the supervisor can decide the way to make changes in her workstation. She should see a physician before her symptoms get worse. She should probably do some reading or research on the topic by obtaining materials from the local hospital, the Internet, or the library.

**GO TO
CD-ROM**
PRACTICE 4
EXERCISES

PRACTICE

NAME _____

ONLINE **EXERCISES**

Work-related injuries cost billions of dollars to businesses of all types and sizes. Numerous Web pages designed by individuals, consultants, and government agencies offer information about ergonomics and the prevention of work-related injuries.

Objective: *To visit an ergonomic consulting company Website.*

1. With your Internet browser on screen, key:

   http://www.advergo.com in the location box.

   Press the **Enter** key on your keyboard.

2. You will be at the Advanced Ergonomics, Inc. Web page.

3. Scroll down until you see **365 Ergonomic Tips and Tidbits for Office Workers** and click.

4. Explore the variety of different ergonomic tips. Print any tips which may be helpful in your occupation or future occupation.

See Instructor Notes 12-24 and 12-25 in IAE.

Use exact punctuation when keying an Internet address.

Adjectives

NAME _____

PRACTICE 1B

Directions: *Select the correct word or words, and write them in the space provided.*

1. The new safety manager seems (*most friendly, friendlier*) than Robert.

2. The meeting had a (*two-hour, two hour*) agenda.

3. You are fortunate if you have (*a, an, the*) adjustable chair and (*a, an, the*) nonglare work surface.

4. He uses a (*sony, Sony*) camcorder to analyze our keyboard movements.

5. Joan has the (*best, most best*) office.

6. Anthropometry is the study of the (*physical-dimensions, physical dimensions*) of the human body.

7. Of the two printers, we believe this one is (*more quiet, most quiet, quieter*).

8. Your document holder should have (*a, an, the*) dull matte finish to avoid glare.

9. Our health and safety manager recommends (*Magnitudes, Magnitude's*) ErgoSentry computer software.

10. (*Ninety five, Ninety-five*) employees responded to our survey about back pain.

1. **friendlier** _____

2. **two-hour** _____

3. **an a** _____

4. **Sony** _____

5. **best** _____

6. **physical dimensions**

7. **quieter** _____

8. **a** _____

9. **Magnitude's** _____

10. **Ninety-five** _____

PRACTICE 2B

See Instructor Note 12-26 in IAE.

A. *Directions:* *Underline the adjectives in the following sentences. Ignore the articles* a*,* an*, and* the*.*

1. Crown Delivery Service is contesting a $12,000 fine for failing to provide a safe and hazard-free workplace.

2. Dr. Myer's ErgoFree is a full-service ergonomics consulting company.

3. After work-site modifications, compensation claims dropped by 78 percent.

4. The increased use of flat, light-touch keyboards results in hand and arm injuries.

5. Jason Woo constantly complains about the ventilation noise.

6. The Medical Multimedia Group's Web page offered the latest information on CTD.

7. Some computer operators use T'ai Chi yoga to combat job-related injuries.

8. For most patients, the causes of their work injuries are unknown.

9. We wanted to read further research before switching to an alternative keyboard.

10. My monitor accumulates less dirt after the cooling vents are cleaned.

B. *Directions:* *In the space provided, correct the following sentences. Some sentences may have punctuation errors.*

1. OSHA which is located in Washington, D.C. has a ergonomic Web page.

   OSHA, which is located in Washington, D.C., has an ergonomic Web page.

2. My occupational physician's office is located just a one mile drive from here.

   My occupational physician's office is located just a one-mile drive from here.

3. The company's statistics indicated less repetitive stress injuries.

   The company's statistics indicated fewer repetitive stress injuries.

4. Fifty five percent of the poultry workers in the oklahoma plant have repetitive stress injuries.

   <u>Fifty-five</u> percent of the poultry workers in the <u>Oklahoma</u> plant have repetitive stress injuries. _____

5. The computer operator's monitor should be tilted to a 90 degree angle.

   The computer operator's monitor should be tilted to a <u>90-degree</u> angle. _____

PRACTICE 3B

PROOFREADING

Directions: *Proofread and compare the two sentences in each group. If they are the same, write **Yes** in the space provided. If they are not the same, write **No**. Use the first sentence as the correct copy. If you find errors in the second sentence, underline them; insert any omitted words or marks of punctuation.*

1. California became the first state in the nation to develop regulations to prevent work-related ailments such as carpal tunnel syndrome and other repetitive stress injuries.

   California became the first <u>State</u> in the <u>Nation</u> to develop regulations to prevent <u>work related</u> ailments such as <u>Carpal Tunnel Syndrome</u> and other repetitive stress injuries.

   1. <u>No</u> _____

2. OSHA estimates that some 2 million American workers suffer from RSI, with 300,000 new cases a year, costing about $20 billion a year in workers' compensation claims.

   OSHA estimates that some <u>2.5</u> million American workers suffer from RSI, with <u>300,0000</u> new cases a year, costing about $20 <u>million</u> a year in <u>worker's</u> compensation claims.

   2. <u>No</u> _____

3. Assembly-line workers, meat cutters, sewing machine operators, supermarket cashiers, carpenters, pianists, violinists, bank tellers, and baseball pitchers are just a few of the American workers plagued by job-related aches, pains, and nerve damage.

   Assembly-line workers, meat cutters, sewing machine operators, supermarket cashiers, carpenters, pianists, violinists, bank tellers, and baseball pitchers are just a few of the American workers plagued by job-related aches, pains, and nerve damage.

   3. <u>Yes</u> _____

4. Cumulative trauma disorders (CTDs) are not always caused on the job but can develop based on individual factors such as obesity, diabetes, pregnancy, and physical stresses occurring away from work.

   Cumulative trauma disorders (<u>CTD</u>) are not always caused on the <u>job,</u> but can develop based on ∧individual factors such as obesity, <u>diabetis</u>, pregnancy, and physical stresses <u>occuring</u> away from work.

   4. <u>No</u> _____

5. The National Aeronautics and Space Administration (NASA) recommends the following plants to improve indoor-air quality (IAQ): thin-leafed spider plant, Chinese evergreen, peace lily, philodendrons, golden pothos, ficus, mother-in-law's tongue, and English ivy.

The National Aeronautics and Space Administration <u>NASA</u> recommends the following plants to improve <u>indoor air</u> quality (IAQ): thin-leafed spider plant, Chinese evergreen, <u>Peace</u> lily, philodendrons, golden pothos, ficus, mother-in-<u>laws</u> tongue, and <u>english</u> ivy.

Proofreading Exercise

Workstations are a comprehensive system of furniture designed to allow flexibility in creating offices. Workstations are ergonomically designed to accommodate 95 percent of the population and include features such as adjustable desks, keyboard platforms and drawers, and file cabinets. The following list contains the workstation components and their estimated costs.

COMPUTER WORKSTATION

60-inch Computer Desk—Radius-edge Design	$404
48-inch Computer Desk	376
Corner Desk	550
Peninsula Top—Connects With Computer Desk	279
Support Column Kit—Peninsula Top	105
Peninsula Leg Kit—Peninsula Top	35
Hutch With Doors—Fits on Top of Computer Desk, 48"	335
Hutch With Doors—Fits on Top of Computer Desk, 60"	420
Articulating Keyboard Platform With Mouse Pad	328

Directions: *Use the following proofreaders' marks to correct the copy on page 357. Use the above copy as your correct guide.*

Make lowercase /	Move left ⌐	Insert letter ∧
Capitalize ≡	Move right ⌐	Insert comma ∧
Delete ⌐	Insert space #	Transpose ∩
Delete and close up ⌐	Delete space ⌒	Insert period ⊙
Double space *ds* ⌐	Insert hyphen = ∧	

COMPUTER WORKSTATIONS

60-inch Computer Desk—Radius Edge Design	$404
48-inch Computer Desk	376
Corner Desk	550
Peninsula Top—Conects With Computer desk	279
Support Column Kit—Peninsula Top	105
Peninsula Leg Kit—Peninsula Top	35
Hutch With Doors—Fits On Top of Computer Desk, 48"	363
Hutch With Doors—Fits on Top of Computer Desk, 60"	420
Articulating Key board Platfrom With Mouse pad	328

PRACTICE 4B

WRITING

Too much stress is related to increased blood pressure and increased risk of cumulative trauma disorders. Here are several events that can cause stress:

1. Death of a family member
2. Personal illness
3. Illness of a family member
4. Divorce or separation
5. Relocation
6. Addition to the family
7. Marriage
8. Change in working conditions
9. Job change
10. Financial problems
11. Company layoffs
12. Job termination

Directions: *Describe a stressful situation that may have occurred to you during the last year. This situation may be an event other than one from the above list. Describe the steps you took to cope with your stress.*

Answers will vary.

_____

_____

_____

_____

_____

_____

_____

_____

_____

_____

END-OF-CHAPTER WORKSHEETS

NAME _____

ONLINE *EXERCISE*

Objective: *To visit the Occupational Heath and Safety Administration (OSHA) Website.*

1. With your Internet browser on screen, key:

   http://www.osha.gov/ in the location box.

   Press the **Enter** key on your keyboard.

2. You will be at the OSHA Web page.

3. Click on the **Ergonomics** link. Read the general information about OSHA.

4. Click on the Back button to go back to the Home Page.

5. Click on HOT TOPICS.

6. Click on one of the topics that interests you.

LOOKING BACK

Posttest

Directions: *In the space provided, write the letter of the correct answer.*

1. In the sentence *Tendon inflammation resulting from repetitive work such as prolonged keyboarding may cause CTD,* the adjectives are
   a. Tendon, inflammation, repetitive, prolonged.
   b. Tendon, inflammation, work, prolonged.
   c. Tendon, repetitive, prolonged.
   d. Tendon, repetitive, work.

   1. ___c___

2. In the sentence *OHSA conferences present solutions to ergonomic problems,* the word *OSHA* functions as a
   a. proper noun.
   b. proper adjective.
   c. possessive adjective.
   d. limiting adjective.

   2. ___b___

3. Which phrase does *not* represent the correct use of an article?
   a. a safety hazard
   b. a honest mistake
   c. an unusual request
   d. a short rest break

   3. ___b___

4. In the sentence *We use those checklists to analyze workstation comfort,* the function of *those* is that of
   a. a descriptive adjective.
   b. a possessive pronoun.
   c. a demonstrative adjective.
   d. a limiting adjective.

   4. ___c___

5. Which compound adjective is *not* hyphenated correctly?
   a. long-term commitment
   b. office support function
   c. well-known cause
   d. fast paced environment

   5. ___d___

6. The superlative adjective for *complicated* is
   a. complicater.
   b. complicated.
   c. more complicated.
   d. most complicated.

   6. ___d___

7. In the sentence *Businesses implement ergonomic programs that reduce rates of injuries and illnesses,* which of the following is modified by the adjective phrase?
   a. businesses
   b. programs
   c. rates
   d. ergonomic

   7. ___b___

8. Which two sentences are *not* correct?
   a. We had fewer work-related injuries than we had last year.
   b. We had less work-related injuries than we had last year.
   c. We suggested farther research on antiglare monitors.
   d. We suggested further research on antiglare monitors.

   8. _b and c_

9. Which two sentences are *not* correct?
   a. Twenty five employees complained about the temperature.
   b. We completed a self-evaluation.
   c. Are you attending the one, two, or three day session?
   d. Did you distribute the branch office agenda?

   9. _a and c_

Adjectives

359

CHAPTER 13

Adverbs

ETHICS AND ETIQUETTE

As children, we developed many of our basic morals and values. We continue to reevaluate and readjust our value systems throughout our lives. As Dr. Albert Schweitzer said, "Ethics is the name we give to our concern for good behavior. We feel an obligation to consider not only our own personal well-being, but also that of others and of human society as a whole." The principles of right and wrong that guide our decisions affecting others are called ethics.

Surrounding us, however, is evidence of good people choosing to do what they know is wrong. Students cheat on tests or claim the work of others as their own. Employees manipulate budgets and expenses or steal office supplies for their personal use. People gossip, "play politics," or lie to customers.

All of us routinely face ethical dilemmas. Sometimes a clear choice exists between right and wrong. In other cases, we know what is right or wrong but feel concern for ourselves or our future when challenging the wrong action. We then compromise our values and justify our actions.

To help employees with ethical decision making, the majority of businesses provide frameworks for making ethical decisions. Ethical frameworks may include developing codes of conduct or sets of standards, supporting people in making ethical decisions, and training employees for their ethical responsibilities.

As employees carefully make decisions in an ethical environment, they take comfort in knowing how rightness, fairness, and goodness are defined within their organization. Ethical employees apply the rules of proper business etiquette and always treat their colleagues and customers with respect. An ethical business operates consistently and predictably with committed employees.

TERMS TO REMEMBER

BUSINESS ETIQUETTE

ETHICAL DECISIONS

ETHICAL DILEMMA

ETHICS

VALUE SYSTEM

OBJECTIVES

After you have studied this chapter and completed the exercises, you will be able to do the following:

1. Identify adverbs and the words they modify.
2. Differentiate between the use of adjectives and adverbs.
3. Recognize the importance of the placement of adverbs.
4. Form the comparative and superlative degrees of regular and irregular adverbs.
5. Recognize and correct double negatives and other incorrect uses of negative words.
6. Use special adverbs correctly.
7. Diagram sentences correctly.

LOOKING AHEAD

Pretest

Directions: *In the space provided, write the letter of the correct answer.*

1. In the sentence *Dishonest behavior has ramifications in virtually every society,* the adverb *virtually* modifies
   - **a.** a verb.
   - **b.** an adjective.
   - **c.** a noun.
   - **d.** an adverb.

   1. ___b___

2. In the sentence *Vance Motors always resolves its sales negotiations in a professional manner,* the adverb is
   - **a.** professional.
   - **b.** resolves.
   - **c.** always.
   - **d.** manner.

   2. ___c___

3. In the sentence *If you must leave a meeting, do so quietly,* the adverb answers the question:
   - **a.** How?
   - **b.** When?
   - **c.** Where?
   - **d.** To what extent or degree?

   3. ___a___

4. In the sentence *Emotionally disturbed people may have very distorted views of ethical behavior,* you will find
   - **a.** four adjectives and one adverb.
   - **b.** two adjectives and three adverbs.
   - **c.** four adjectives and no adverbs.
   - **d.** three adjectives and two adverbs.

   4. ___d___

5. Which one of the following sentences is correct?
   - **a.** Lois felt badly after she took the office supplies home.
   - **b.** Once the ethical issue was solved, we carefully outlined our next project.
   - **c.** Some managers act ethical at home, but they cheat at work.
   - **d.** We looked close at the company's environmental policy.

   5. ___b___

6. Which of the following lines correctly represents the *comparative* degree of adverbs?
   - **a.** more frequently; more slower
   - **b.** more likely; most strongly
   - **c.** calmlier; more widely
   - **d.** more precisely; sooner

   6. ___d___

7. Which of the following sentences is *not* correct?
   - **a.** You could not hardly believe such deceitful merchandising.
   - **b.** I have never understood the term *situational ethics.*
   - **c.** Mrs. Lyman calls a meeting only when she has a purpose for one.
   - **d.** Separating personal ethics from business ethics is not easy.

   7. ___a___

8. Which one of the following sentences is *not* correct?
   - **a.** Michaela does not work very well in a stressful environment.
   - **b.** Is low morale really a problem in your firm?
   - **c.** Yolanda was sure surprised with her appointment to the ethics committee.
   - **d.** Almost all difficult choices require an analysis of values.

   8. ___c___

Adjectives and adverbs have some similarities. Both modify other parts of speech, and both have degrees of comparison. Many adverbs have adjective bases. Sometimes making a choice between using an adverb or an adjective is confusing.

An adverb adds specificity to a sentence. Correct adverb use will help you express your thoughts more precisely and clearly. The different placements of an adverb such as *only* can change the meaning of a sentence. Using a double negative makes a sentence sound childlike or unintelligent. In this chapter, your study of adverbs will include the general use of adverbs as well as several confusing uses.

IDENTIFICATION OF ADVERBS

An adverb makes a sentence more precise. An adverb answers the questions *how, when, where,* and *to what extent or degree.* In addition to these questions, an adverbial clause often answers the question *why.* A later section covers adverbial clauses.

See Instructor Notes 13-1, 13-2, and 13-3 in IAE.

Go to Transparencies/PowerPoints 13-1a, 13-1b, and 13-2.

How? In what manner?	carefully, quickly, loudly, proudly, neatly, well
When?	yesterday, immediately, often, now, again, then, formerly
Where?	outside, there, down, forward, upward, away
To what extent? degree?	very, too, greatly, quite, gradually, rather, extremely

CHECKUP 13-1

Directions: *In the space provided, identify the type of question answered by each underlined adverb. Use the following codes: **A** (How?), **B** (When?), **C** (Where?), **D** (To what extent?).*

Ex.: Treat all company personnel <u>considerately</u>.   **A**

1. If someone is having trouble opening a door, move <u>quickly</u> to assist the individual.   A

2. Company personnel must go <u>outside</u> if they want to smoke.   C

3. If you ever lose your temper, apologize <u>immediately</u>.   B

4. The workers have <u>very</u> high morals and adhere to strict ethical standards.   D

5. If you borrow something, return it <u>promptly</u>.   B

6. My colleagues suggested that I step <u>forward</u> to report a policy violation.   C

GO TO CD-ROM
CHECKUP 13-1

FUNCTIONS OF ADVERBS

See Instructor Note 13-4 in IAE.

Refer to Chapter 2 for an introduction to adverbs.

Remember that in this sentence the word bow *is pronounced with a short o sound—similar to the word* how.

Review subject complements (predicate adjectives) in Chapter 9.

Both adjectives and adverbs are modifiers. Adjectives modify only nouns and pronouns. Adverbs modify verbs, adjectives, and other adverbs. Adverbs never modify nouns and pronouns.

Modify Verbs

Use an adverb to modify a verb. Place the adverb before or after the verb that is modified.

> **The law generally sets the minimum acceptable rules for measuring ethical behaviors.**
> (*Generally* is the adverb that modifies the verb *sets.* The adverb appears before the verb.)
>
> **Most Japanese businesspeople will bow slightly and then shake hands.**
> (*Slightly* is the adverb that modifies the verb *bow.* The adverb appears after the verb.)

Modify Adjectives

Use an adverb to modify an adjective. Place the adverb immediately before the adjective.

> **In some cases, it is truly difficult to separate individual ethics from business ethics.**
> (*Difficult* is an adjective that follows the linking verb *is. Difficult* modifies the subject *it. Truly* is an adverb that modifies the adjective *difficult.*)
>
> **We are extremely suspicious of any person who misuses his or her authority.**
> (*Extremely* is an adverb that appears before the adjective *suspicious* and modifies it.)

Modify Other Adverbs

Use an adverb to modify another adverb. Place the adverb immediately before the adverb being modified.

13-5 Remind the students that *very* modifies *precisely* and *precisely* modifies *outlined.*

> **Several employees wanted to have the protocol standards outlined very precisely.**
> (*Very* is an adverb that modifies another adverb *precisely. Precisely* modifies the verb *outlined.*)
>
> **The speaker at the ethics seminar spoke too rapidly.**
> (*Too* is an adverb that modifies another adverb *rapidly. Rapidly* modifies the verb *spoke.*)

Do This	Do Not Do This
Mary Jo is <u>polite</u>.	Mary Jo is <u>very</u>, <u>very</u> polite.
or	
Mary Jo is <u>very</u> polite.	

Do not use the phrase very, very. This is a redundant usage that adds nothing more to the meaning.

CHECKUP 13-2

Directions: *Underline the adverb(s) in each of the following sentences. In the space provided, write the word that is being modified by the underlined adverb. Then write the part of speech of the word being modified. Use the following codes:* **V** *(verb),* **Adj** *(adjective),* **Adv** *(adverb).*

Ex.: When businesses <u>knowingly</u> deceive customers, they are violating ethical standards.

    deceive (V)

1. The ethics of our colleagues may <u>strongly</u> affect our behavior at work.

    may affect (V)

2. The Social Venture Network (SVN) is a national organization of <u>socially</u> conscious business leaders.

    conscious (Adj)

3. A receptionist who understands confidentiality is <u>vitally</u> important to a firm.

    important (Adj)

4. Many businesses' community contributions reflect <u>positively</u> on their reputations.

    reflect (V)

5. When supervisors handle sensitive issues, they need to proceed <u>very</u> <u>cautiously</u>.

    cautiously (Adv)

    proceed (V)

6. The ethics workshop was <u>rather</u> long.

    long (Adj)

**GO TO
CD-ROM**
CHECKUP 13-2

FORMATION OF ADVERBS

You can form many adverbs from adjective root words. The following guidelines will help you identify adjectives and adverbs. These guidelines will also help you spell adverbs correctly.

Adjective Base Used to Form Adverbs

Add *ly* to an adjective root to form the majority of adverbs.

Adjective	Adverb
clear	clearly
honest	honestly
polite	politely

Noun Base Used to Form Adjectives Ending in *ly*

Use root words to identify words ending in *ly* as adjectives or adverbs. Although many adverbs end in *ly,* some adjectives also end in *ly.* Most of these adjectives are formed by adding *ly* to a noun root.

Noun	Adjective
cost	costly
elder	elderly
friend	friendly

Adverbs Formed From Adjectives Ending in *y*

Change the *y* to *i* and add *ly* to an adjective ending in *y* to form an adverb.

Adjective	Adverb
angry	angrily
ordinary	ordinarily
satisfactory	satisfactorily

Adverbs Formed From Adjectives Ending in *ible* or *able*

Drop the final *e* on adjectives that end in *able* or *ible* before adding the *y* to form the adverb.

Adjective	Adverb
acceptable	acceptably
considerable	considerably
sensible	sensibly

Adverbs Formed From Adjectives Ending in *ic*

Add *ally* to adjectives ending in *ic* to form the adverb.

Adjective	Adverb
automatic	automatically
basic	basically
specific	specifically

Other Adverbs

Although there are many adverbs that may be identified with the *ly* ending, there are other adverbs that do *not* end in *ly.* Following is a list that includes some of the other adverbs:

again	more	sometimes	not
almost	much	soon	

Remember to ask the questions how or in what manner, when, where, and to what extent or degree when you identify any adverb.

always	near	then
down	now	there
far	often	too
hard	once	up
here	quite	very
how	rather	well
inside	seldom	when
just	since	where

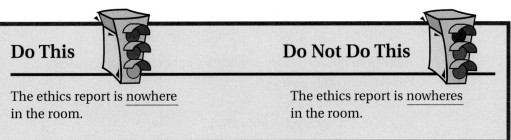

Do This

The ethics report is <u>nowhere</u> in the room.

Do Not Do This

The ethics report is <u>nowheres</u> in the room.

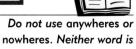

Do not use anywheres or nowheres. Neither word is correct English. Use anywhere or nowhere.

Do Not Hyphenate Adverbs Ending in *ly*

Do not hyphenate an expression made up of an adverb ending in *ly* and an adjective. These expressions are not compound adjectives (which often require hyphens) but adverbs followed by adjectives.

an <u>extremely</u> loud environment

a <u>universally</u> acceptable greeting

CHECKUP 13-3

Directions: *If a word in the following list is an adverb, write* **Yes** *in the space provided. If a word is not an adverb, write the correct adverb form. If the adverb is not correctly written, write it correctly.*

1.	short	shortly	**9.**	horrible	horribly
2.	always	Yes	**10.**	hasty	hastily
3.	intense	intensely	**11.**	seldom	Yes
4.	now	Yes	**12.**	immediate	immediately
5.	particularly	Yes	**13.**	again	Yes
6.	inside	Yes	**14.**	quite	Yes
7.	specific	specifically	**15.**	unfair	unfairly
8.	cautious	cautiously			

**GO TO
CD-ROM**
CHECKUP 13-3

See Instructor Note 13-6 in IAE.

Linking verbs include forms of be as well as seem, appear, grow, remain, stay, and become. Sense verbs include feel, look, sound, taste, and smell.

See Instructor Note 13-7 in IAE.

Making the correct choice of an adjective or an adverb is important in writing sentences. In most cases, the type of verb in the sentence indicates the need for an adjective or an adverb.

Verbs—Action Versus Linking

Use an adverb to modify action verbs. Use an adjective, not an adverb, after a linking verb to describe the subject.

> **Interest in the social responsibilities of businesses <u>increased considerably</u> this past year.**
> (The action verb *increased* requires the adverb *considerably* as a modifier. Do not use the adjective *considerable*.)

> **The malicious rumors <u>badly</u> <u>damaged</u> the supervisor's reputation.**
> (The action verb *damaged* requires the adverb *badly* as a modifier.)

> **The supervisor <u>felt</u> <u>bad</u> about the lack of an internal hiring practice.**
> (The adjective *bad* follows the sense verb *felt* and describes the subject *supervisor*. Do not use the adverb *badly*.)

> **The firm's pollution control options <u>seem</u> <u>limitless</u>.**
> (The linking verb *seem* requires the adjective *limitless*. *Limitless* describes the subject *options*.)

Verbs—Both Linking and Action

Clarify the intent of the sentence before making a decision about such verbs as *look, taste,* or *feel.* These verbs may be either action verbs or linking verbs. Use adverbs when these verbs are action verbs. Use adjectives when these verbs function as linking verbs.

13-8 Remind students that *looked* is a linking verb.

> **She <u>looked</u> <u>frantically</u> for another supplier after the fire occurred.**
> (The verb *looked* functions as an action verb and requires the adverb modifier *frantically*.)

> **Things <u>looked</u> <u>bad</u> for our company during the time of the strike.**
> (The verb *looked* functions as a linking verb and does not indicate action. The adjective *bad* describes the subject *things*. Do not use the adverb *badly*.)

> **He <u>appeared</u> <u>briefly</u> at the preliminary hearing.**
> (The verb *appeared* functions as an action verb and requires the adverb modifier *briefly*.)

> **She <u>appeared</u> <u>relieved</u> after she talked to her supervisor.**
> (The verb *appeared* functions as a linking verb and does not indicate action. The adjective *relieved* describes the pronoun *she*.)

Adjectives and Adverbs With the Same Form

Some adverbs and adjectives that have the same form include *fast, first, last, early,* and *right.* Use an adjective to modify a noun or pronoun. Use an adverb to modify verbs, adjectives, and other adverbs.

> **Be sure to arrive early.**
>
> (*Early* is an adverb that modifies the verb *arrive.*)
>
> **I prefer the early shift.**
>
> (*Early* is an adjective that modifies the noun *shift.*)

CHECKUP 13-4

Directions: *Select the correct word, and write it in the space provided.*

1. The human resources department monitors fair hiring practices (*close, closely*).   ___closely___

2. Corporate donations (*definite, definitely*) improve the cultural life of a community.   ___definitely___

3. Krogan Insurance responded (*quick, quickly*) to its workers' concerns.   ___quickly___

4. The mission statement that included a section on the firm's social responsibilities is (*perfect, perfectly*).   ___perfect___

5. His argument for more company responsibility for a clean environment was (*powerful, powerfully*).   ___powerful___

6. When you receive an invitation, respond to it (*prompt, promptly*).   ___promptly___

**GO TO
CD-ROM**
CHECKUP 13-4

CHECKUP 13-5

Directions: *List the adverbs in the third and the fifth paragraphs of the Secondary Learning section found at the beginning of the chapter.*

Paragraph 3	Paragraph 5
routinely	carefully
Sometimes	always
then	consistently
	predictably

**GO TO
CD-ROM**
CHECKUP 13-5

See Instructor Note 13-9 in IAE.

Rules for using the positive, comparative, and superlative degrees of adverbs are similar to those for adjectives.

Go to Transparency/PowerPoint 13-3.

Adverbs form comparisons in ways that are similar to those of adjectives. Adverbs also have three degrees of comparison—*positive, comparative,* and *superlative.* Some adverbs (absolute) do not allow comparisons. With the comparative degree, you compare two persons or things; with the superlative degree, you compare three or more persons or things.

Guidelines for Using Comparisons

One-Syllable Adverbs. Add *er* to the positive form of a one-syllable adverb to form its comparative degree. Add *est* to the positive form of a one-syllable adverb to form its superlative degree.

Positive	Comparative	Superlative
fast	faster	fastest
slow	slower	slowest
soon	sooner	soonest

I must leave soon.

(*Soon* modifies the verb *leave. Soon* is the positive form and indicates there is no comparison involved.)

Rick works faster than Gary.

(*Faster* modifies *works* and indicates the comparison of the two people, *Rick* and *Gary.* In this sentence the verb *works* does not appear with the subject *Gary* but is understood.)

Go to PowerPoint 13-4.

Two-Syllable Adverbs. Some two-syllable adverbs form their comparative and superlative degrees by adding *er* or *est* to their positive forms. Other two-syllable adverbs form their comparative and superlative degrees by placing *more* (*less*) or *most* (*least*) before the adverb. Sometimes, either method is correct.

Positive	Comparative	Superlative
often	more (or less) often	most (or least) often
smoothly	more smoothly	most smoothly
quickly	more quickly	most quickly
early	earlier	earliest

The complaint that we hear most often involves impolite employees.

(*Most often* modifies *hear* and implies a comparison of many complaints.)

Go to PowerPoint 13-5.

Three-Syllable Adverbs. Add the word *more* or *less* before the positive form of a three-syllable adverb to form its comparative degree. Add the words *most* or *least* before the positive form of a three-syllable adverb to form its superlative degree.

Positive	Comparative	Superlative
carefully	more carefully	most carefully
hurriedly	more hurriedly	most hurriedly

This safety device operates more reliably than any other device we've used.

(*Reliably* modifies the verb *operates* and indicates the comparison of two items. *More* modifies *reliably.*)

The third ethics policy is the most accurately documented.

(*Accurately* modifies the adjective *documented* and implies a comparison of many policies. *Most* modifies *accurately,* telling to what extent the policy is accurate.)

Irregular Adverbs

Use irregular comparisons for some adverbs.

Positive	Comparative	Superlative
well	better	best
badly	worse	worst

She works well under pressure.

(*Well* modifies the verb *works. Well* is the positive form and indicates there is no comparison involved.)

Can you think of a time that I behaved worse than I did today?

(*Worse* is the comparative form of *badly.* In this sentence, *worse* compares a time in the past with today.)

Absolute Adverbs

Some adverbs do not allow for comparisons. The list includes such adverbs as *no, now, past, there, here, too, very, partly, annually, basically,* and *sometimes.*

13-10 Refer to a reference manual such as *The Gregg Reference Manual* for examples of absolute adverbs that may be modified.

Some agree that we need additional ethics courses now.

(*Now* is absolute; you do not refer to *more now* or *most now* or *less now* or *least now. Now* tells when we need additional courses.)

Global Concepts gives ethics awards annually.

(*Annually* is absolute; you do not refer to *more annually, most annually, less annually,* or *least annually. Annually* tells when.)

CHECKUP 13-6

Directions: In the spaces provided, fill in the missing adverb degree forms.

Positive	Comparative	Superlative
Ex.: sweetly	more sweetly	**most sweetly**
1. casually	more casually	most casually
2. late	later	latest

**GO TO
CD-ROM**
CHECKUP 13-6

3. easily	more easily	**most easily**
4. efficiently	**more efficiently**	**most efficiently**
5. specifically	**more specifically**	most specifically
6. soon	**sooner**	soonest
7. accurately	more accurately	**most accurately**
8. well	**better**	best

CHECKUP 13-7

Directions: *Complete each sentence by writing the correct comparative or superlative form of the modifier indicated in parentheses.*

Ex.: Fraud occurs (*frequent*) when the economy is poor than when the economy is good. | **more frequently**

1. Some companies keep track of office supplies (*close*) than others. | more closely (less closely)

2. The revised hiring practices went into effect (*soon*) than we expected. | sooner

3. The (*careful*) identified ethical standards usually result in the least dissension. | most carefully

4. Try putting a smile in your voice to make it (*lively*). | more lively (livelier)

5. She thinks today's business students respond (*ethical*) than the students did five years ago. | more ethically (less ethically)

6. Of all the hours in the day, I work (*efficient*) in the morning. | most efficiently

**GO TO
CD-ROM**
CHECKUP 13-7

CAUTIONS FOR USING ADVERBS

Go to
Transparency/PowerPoint 13-6.

SLIP-UP

The Chevy Nova never sold well in Spanish-speaking countries. "No va" means "it does not go" in Spanish.
Source: *American Demographics* magazine.

Several adverbs require special attention. These include the use of negative words such as *never* and *not*, contractions, double negatives, and the placement of such adverbs as *nearly, merely*, and *only*.

Negative Words

A number of negative words are adverbs. These include *barely, hardly, never, no, not, nowhere*, and *scarcely*. The contraction *n't*, which means *not*, is also an adverb. A contraction is a word with one or more letters omitted.

Not **and** ***Never.*** Use *not* in a negative statement. In most cases, place the word *not* between the helping verb and the main verb in a sentence. Use *never* as a stronger word than *not* to mean "at no time." If *not* will suffice, refrain from using *never*.

> **Some people simply do not use good judgment in making decisions.**
> (*Not* is an adverb that modifies the verb phrase *do use*.)
>
> **Proper sales etiquette never goes out of style.**
> (*Never* is an adverb that modifies the verb *goes*. Never means "at no time" in this sentence.)

Contractions. Use an apostrophe to take the place of the missing letter or letters in such words as *aren't, doesn't, can't, wouldn't, hasn't, don't,* and *isn't*.

> **She doesn't expect support from management regarding her harassment claim.**
> (*Doesn't* is a contraction for *does not*.)
>
> **They didn't apologize for their rude behavior.**
> (*Didn't* is a contraction for *did not*.)

Double Negatives

A double negative is a sentence construction in which two negative words are used when one is sufficient. This combination gives the clause a positive meaning rather than the intended negative meaning.

Avoid double negatives in the same clause if the intent of the clause is supposed to be negative. Correct a double negative by deleting one of the negative words.

> **Incorrect Sentence:**
> I have not seen no evidence of unethical sales tactics in this store.
> **Corrected Sentences:**
> I have seen no evidence of unethical sales tactics in this store.
> I have not seen any evidence of unethical sales tactics in this store.
>
> **Incorrect Sentence:**
> She couldn't hardly believe the statistics about white-collar crime.
> **Corrected Sentences:**
> She could hardly believe the statistics about white-collar crime.
> She could not believe the statistics about white-collar crime.

Placement of *Only, Merely,* and *Nearly*

Place the adverb *only* immediately before the word or group of words it modifies. Place the adverbs *merely* and *nearly* as close as possible to the words modified. Clarify the intent of the sentence before using these adverbs. Sentence meanings may change with different placements.

> **Only Barry wants the code of ethics in the policies and procedures manual.**
> (Barry is the only person who wants the code of ethics in the policies and procedures manual.)

SLIP-UP
Newspaper advertisement for automobile repair service: Free pickup and delivery. Try us once, and you'll never go anywhere again.

13-11 Remind students that the contraction *can't* is formed from *cannot*.

Go to PowerPoint 13-7.

See Instructor Note 13-12 in IAE.

Go to PowerPoints 13-8a and 13-8b.

See Instructor Note 13-13 in IAE.

Barry wants <u>only</u> the code of ethics in the policies and procedures manual.
(Barry wants the code of ethics to be the one and only item in the policies and procedures manual.)

Barry wants the code of ethics in the policies and procedures manual <u>only</u>.
(Barry does not want the code of ethics to appear anywhere else but in the policies and procedures manual.)

CHECKUP 13-8

Directions: In the space provided, correct the following sentences. If the sentence is correct, write **Yes.**

Ex.: A ringing telephone should never go unanswered.   **Yes**

The sentence **A ringing telephone should not go unanswered** is also correct grammatically; however, using the word *not* makes the sentence weaker.

1. The company insists it never did nothing illegal with its price structuring.

   The company insists it did nothing illegal with its price structuring.

   The company insists it never did anything illegal with its price structuring.

2. It is'nt always easy to make a decision that will benefit the most people.

   It isn't always easy to make a decision that will benefit the most people.

   It is not always easy to make a decision that will benefit the most people.

3. The company managers were not looking forward to the newly announced merger.

   Yes

4. I can't hardly believe she was so rude to a client.

   I can hardly believe she was so rude to a client.

   I can't believe she was so rude to a client.

   I cannot believe she was so rude to a client.

5. I don't have no contact with top management.

   I have no contact with top management.

   I don't have any contact with top management.

   I do not have contact with top management.

6. Illegal insider trading couldn't never happen here.

   Illegal insider trading could not happen here.

   Illegal insider trading could never happen here.

**GO TO
CD-ROM
CHECKUP 13-8**

CHECKUP 13-9

Directions: In the space provided, write the word that is modified by the underlined word.

See Instructor Note 13-14 in IAE.

1. She used a PowerPoint presentation that <u>only</u> those people in the front rows could read.

   those

2. Ethical behavior should be the <u>only</u> acceptable behavior.

   acceptable

3. We know that it is <u>only</u> good manners to introduce new employees to the rest of the staff.

   good

4. He heard <u>only</u> negative viewpoints from his coworkers.

   negative

5. By putting our customers first, we gained <u>nearly</u> 50 accounts.

   50

6. In our firm, <u>only</u> top-level executives receive stock options.

   top-level

**GO TO
CD-ROM
CHECKUP 13-9**

ADVERB CLAUSES

When a clause modifies a verb, an adjective, or an adverb, it is an adverb clause. An *adverb clause* is a dependent clause that has a subject and a predicate. A dependent clause is not a sentence and cannot stand by itself.

See Instructor Note 13-15 in IAE.

Adverb Clauses

Use subordinating conjunctions such as *after, although, before, because, if, unless, when,* and *while* to introduce dependent adverb clauses. Place the adverb clauses as closely as possible to the words modified. Use commas after introductory adverb clauses that precede independent clauses. Generally, do not use commas to set aside adverb clauses that follow independent clauses.

See Instructor Notes 13-16 and 13-17 in IAE.

An independent clause has a subject and predicate and can stand alone.

Kayla always greets the guests <u>before a meeting begins</u>.
(*Before* connects the dependent adverb clause *before a meeting begins* to the independent clause *Kayla always greets the guests.* No comma is necessary since the adverb clause *follows* the independent clause.)

<u>When you answer the telephone</u>, ask for the name of the caller politely.
(*When you answer the telephone* is a dependent adverb clause that introduces the independent clause. Use a comma after the introductory adverb clause.)

Punctuation ALERT!

Use a comma after an introductory adverb clause. Generally, do not use a comma when the adverb clause follows an independent clause.

Adverbs

Directions: *In the following sentences, underline the adverb clauses once.*

1. Do not allow others to read the company's confidential materials while you are away from your desk.

2. After she attended the ethics class, she shared her notes with her supervisor.

3. When criticizing an employee, do so in private.

4. You must respect yourself before you can accept others' differences and opinions.

5. Because she was such a detail-oriented person, we expected her to find our errors.

6. Several of my coworkers voiced their approval when the manager announced the decision.

**GO TO
CD-ROM
CHECKUP 13-10**

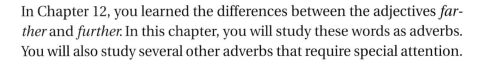

SPECIAL ADVERBS

In Chapter 12, you learned the differences between the adjectives *farther* and *further*. In this chapter, you will study these words as adverbs. You will also study several other adverbs that require special attention.

The definitions for the adverbs further *and* farther *are the same as those for the adjectives* further *and* farther, *but their functions in sentences are different.*

Farther/Further (Adverbs)

Use *farther* to refer to physical distance. Use *further* to mean additional or additionally.

> **To conduct business today, salespeople must travel farther from their homes. (adverb)**
> (*Farther* is an adverb that modifies the verb *travel.*)

> **We explained further our decision to move the production plant to South America. (adverb)**
> (*Further* is an adverb that modifies the verb *explained.*)

Good/Well

Use *good* as an adjective. Use *well* as an adverb. Use *well* as an adjective in reference to the state of someone's health.

> **I always feel good after I have helped someone.**
> (*Good* is an adjective that means in good spirits. *Good* modifies the pronoun *I.*)

> **The firm's family-leave proposal has worked very well during the past year.**
> (*Well* is an adverb that modifies the verb *has worked.*)

> **She knew that her child was not well, but she felt that she had to be at work.**
> (*Well* is an adjective that indicates the state of someone's health. *Well* modifies the noun *child.*)

See Instructor Note 13-18 in IAE.

Go to PowerPoint 13-9.

Most/Almost

Use *almost* as an adverb to mean "nearly." Use *almost* if the word *nearly* can be substituted satisfactorily. Use *most* as a limiting adjective to modify a noun. Also, use *most* as the superlative degree in a comparison.

Joan is <u>almost</u> finished with the ethics survey.

(*Almost* is an adverb that may be interchanged with the word *nearly*.)

<u>Most</u> managers treat employees fairly.

(*Most* is an adjective that modifies the noun *managers*.)

The union members liked the profit-sharing plan <u>most</u>.

(*Most* is an adverb that modifies the verb *liked* and indicates the superlative degree of comparison.)

Real/Really

Use *real* as a descriptive adjective to mean "genuine." Do not use *real* to modify another adjective. Use *really* as an adverb to mean "genuinely." Substitute *very* for the word *really* to determine if *really* is the correct word.

See Instructor Note 13-19 in IAE.

I never understood Penny's <u>real</u> reason for lying to her supervisor.

(*Real* is an adjective that modifies the noun *reason*.)

Ben gave a <u>really</u> good summary of his liberal views regarding the social responsibilities of business.

(*Really* is an adverb that modifies the adjective *good*. Substitute *very* for *really*. *Very* sounds satisfactory, which indicates *really* is the correct word.)

Sometime/Sometimes/Some Time

Use *sometime* as an adverb to mean "at some unscheduled time" or "in the future." Use *sometimes* as an adverb to mean "on some occasions." Use *some time* as a phrase in which the adjective *some* modifies the noun *time*. *Some time* designates an "amount of time."

We are going to review the basics of telephone etiquette <u>sometime</u> next week.

(*Sometime* is an adverb that modifies the adjective *next*.)

<u>Sometimes</u> we make inaccurate snap judgments.

(*Sometimes* is an adverb that modifies the verb *make*.)

To recover the stolen computer equipment will require <u>some time</u>.

(*Some time* is two words—the adjective *some* and the noun *time*.)

Sure/Surely

Use *sure* as an adjective. Use *surely* as an adverb to mean "without a doubt."

Go to PowerPoint 13-10.

13-20 Recommend that students substitute the word *certainly* for *sure* or *surely*.

They thought a child-care center on site was the <u>sure</u> solution for high absenteeism rates.

(*Sure* is an adjective modifying *solution*.)

Mary Ellen <u>surely</u> makes every attempt to be courteous to all clients.

(*Surely* is an adverb that modifies the verb *makes*.)

CHECKUP 13-11

Directions: Select the correct word, and write it in the space provided.

1. Rhonda handles her many responsibilities (*good, well*).   <u>well</u>

2. Scott (*sure, surely*) investigated the options for expanding sales in the eastern European countries.   <u>surely</u>

3. (*Almost, Most*) employees face tough ethical choices regularly.   <u>Most</u>

4. The stockholders were (*real, really*) pleased with the bottom line on our cash flow statement.   <u>really</u>

5. The safety figures looked (*good, well*) after the company added new equipment.   <u>good</u>

6. No one had anything (*farther, further*) to report.   <u>further</u>

**GO TO
CD-ROM
CHECKUP 13-11**

DIAGRAMMING SENTENCES

In sentences with adverbs, place the adverb on a slanted line below the word it modifies. In diagramming contractions, place the *n't* on a slanted line below the verb.

Adverb Modifying a Verb
Our receptionist greets clients professionally.

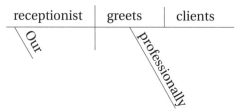

Adverb Modifying an Adjective
The clearly marked copy was our legal proof.

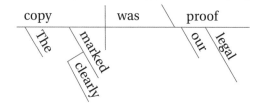

Adverb Modifying Another Adverb

Good manners very clearly reflect your company's image.

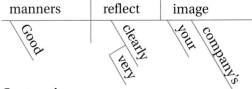

Contraction

Royalton Plastics didn't win the ethics award.

CHECKUP 13-12

Directions: *Diagram each sentence in the space provided. Use all words in the sentences.*

See Instructor Note 13-21 in IAE.

1. The company finally stopped its negative advertisements.

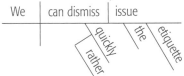

2. We can dismiss the etiquette issue rather quickly.

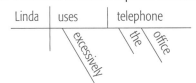

3. Linda uses the office telephone excessively.

Linda | uses | telephone

4. Socially responsible companies that treat their employees fairly are successful.

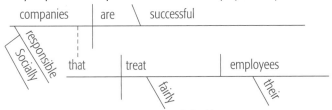

5. Senn Industries generously supports local charities.

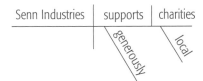

GO TO
CD-ROM
CHECKUP 13-12

Adverbs   379

PRACTICE

PRACTICE 1A

A. Directions: *Select the correct word, and write it in the space provided.*

1. When someone is introduced to you, shake hands (*firm, firmly*).

1. _____firmly_____

2. I felt (*bad, badly*) about the company reorganization.

2. _____bad_____

3. We rely on the integrity of (*almost, most*) everyone with whom we work.

3. _____almost_____

4. I took a (*real, really*) interesting class called Business Ethics and Social Responsibility.

4. _____really_____

5. Those who attended the Milton Friedman lectures (*sure, surely*) enjoyed them.

5. _____surely_____

B. Directions: *In the following sentences, a word or phrase is underlined once. Place two lines under each adverb that modifies the underlined word or phrase.*

1. Elizabeth is always courteous even when she is extremely busy.

2. Some unethical people want things now and are not willing to wait.

3. With proper checks and balances, it becomes very difficult to hide unethical acts.

4. The authority of superiors can greatly influence subordinates' ethical behavior.

5. We often judge people too harshly.

**GO TO
CD-ROM**
PRACTICE 1
EXERCISES

PRACTICE 2A

A. Directions: *Underline each adverb once. Draw two lines under each adjective. Ignore the articles* a, an, *and* the.

1. The speaker described ethical problems that he had experienced firsthand.

2. Sometimes we are too quick to judge people.

3. Speak directly into the phone and articulate clearly.

4. Do not ask callers to hold unless it is absolutely necessary.

5. We knew that the evidence against the devious client was largely circumstantial.

6. We inadvertently told Karen about the potential criminal investigation.

7. Administrative assistants should <u>not</u> discuss <u>confidential</u> <u>company</u> <u>business</u>.

8. I am <u>frequently</u> asked to contribute money for <u>office</u> celebrations that I <u>never</u> attend.

9. The <u>newly</u> <u>devised</u> <u>environmental</u> plan will be released <u>quite</u> <u>soon</u>.

10. <u>Your</u> <u>own</u> employees are <u>often</u> <u>crucial</u> to the success of the firm.

B. *Directions: In the space provided, correct the following sentences. If the sentence is correct, write* **Yes.**

1. Cultural diversity nearly exists in every workplace.

   Cultural diversity exists in <u>nearly</u> every workplace. _____

2. This book only deals with international customs and etiquette.

   This book deals with international customs and etiquette <u>only</u>. _____

   This book deals <u>only</u> with international customs and etiquette. _____

3. Kendra was sure pleased to be asked to join the ethics committee.

   Kendra was <u>surely</u> pleased to be asked to join the ethics committee. _____

4. Lee was real disturbed with the firm's false advertising.

   Lee was <u>really</u> disturbed with the firm's false advertising. _____

5. This company has always served us good, so I will not change suppliers.

   This company has always served us <u>well</u>, so I will not change suppliers. _____

GO TO
CD-ROM
PRACTICE 2
EXERCISES

PRACTICE 3A

PROOFREADING

Directions: Proofread and compare the two sentences in each group. If they are the same, write **Yes** *in the space provided. If they are not the same, write* **No.** *Use the first sentence as the correct copy. If you find errors in the second copy, underline them; insert any omitted words or marks of punctuation.*

1. Businesses, of course, must make profits, but they don't have to make these profits at the expense of their employees, customers, or society in general.

   1. ____No____

   Businesses, of course, must make profits, but they <u>do'nt</u> have to make these profits at the expense of their employees, customers, or society in general.

NAME _____

2. Diversity programs, family-leave policies, local
   community projects, and enforced safety regulations
   can simultaneously benefit employees as well as a
   company's bottom line.

   2. __No__

   Diversity programs, family-leave policies, local
   community projects, and enforced <u>safty</u> regulations
   can <u>simultaneous</u> benefit employees as well as <u>and</u> a
   company's bottom line.

3. We readily show respect by using such polite
   expressions as "please," "thank you," and
   "I appreciate your prompt response."

   3. __No__

   We <u>readly</u> show respect by using such polite
   expressions as "please," "thank you," and
   "I appreciate <u>you</u> prompt response."

4. Levi Strauss & Co. bases its approach to ethics upon
   six principles—honesty, promise-keeping, fairness,
   respect for others, compassion, and integrity.

   4. __No__

   Levi Strauss <u>and</u> Co. bases <u>their</u> approach to ethics <u>on</u>
   six <u>principals</u>—<u>honestly</u>, promise-keeping, fairness,
   respect for others, compassion, and integrity.

5. The Ethics Resource Center in Washington, D.C.,
   reports that almost all large corporations today
   have organized ethics programs.

   5. __No__

   The Ethics Resource Center in Washington, D.C.,
   reports that <u>most</u> all large corporations today
   have organized ethics programs.

Proofreading Exercise

*Directions: Your supervisor is giving a series of etiquette workshops on Minding Your
Manners, Minding Your E-mail Manners, and Minding Your Voice Mail Manners. The
draft that follows is one of the handouts that will be distributed at the workshop. Key
the document and make the corrections that are indicated by the proofreaders' marks.
If you are not certain about the use of a proofreaders' mark, use your reference manual.*

See Instructor Note 13-22 in
IAE.

MINDING yOUR VOICE MAIL MANNERS

To use Voice Mail to your advantage, here are some good manners
and business-like behaviors to follow:

1. ⌐Plan your message in advance. Write it out if necessary.

2. Identify yourself before you record your message. Do not
   assume that the receiver of the message can recognize your
   voice.

3. Do not use voice mail for messages that should be delivered in person such as evaluations, h iring decisions or disagreeable news.

4. Recognize the time limits on recorders. State the purpose of your call succinct.

5. ⌐ Indicate the type of response that you need. State a time
   └ when the receiver can reach you ⊙

6. Don't speak too fast. Spell names correctly and repeat numbers slow.

7. Try to time your messages for periods during the day when the receiver is likely to be avialable. Do not leave messages on Mon mornings since there maybe a backup from the week end.

8. Keep a written log of the messages that you leave and when you leave them.

GO TO
CD-ROM
PRACTICE 3
EXERCISES

PRACTICE 4A

WRITING

Occasionally you are involved in situations where ethics are a concern. In the classroom, you may see others cheating on tests or copying work from others and turning the work in as their own.

Directions: *Write a paragraph describing a specific ethical situation that you have encountered and have worked through at school or on the job.*

Answers will vary.

GO TO
CD-ROM
PRACTICE 4
EXERCISES

_____
_____
_____
_____
_____
_____
_____
_____
_____
_____
_____
_____
_____

PRACTICE

ONLINE *EXERCISES*

See Instructor Notes 13-23 and 13-24 in IAE.

Use exact punctuation when keying an Internet address.

Thousands of Web pages exist on ethics. You will find information on ethics and the law, gender ethics, ethical environments, educational ethics, ethics in medicine and science, computer ethics, and ethics in government. Hundreds of businesses and organizations publish their codes of conduct online.

Objective: *To read codes of conduct.*

1. With your Internet browser on screen, key:

   http://www.ethics.ubc.ca/resources/business in the location box.

   Press the **Enter** key on your keyboard.

2. You will be on the Centre for Applied Ethics Web page.

3. Links to corporate and business codes of ethics are available. Read at least two corporate codes of ethics.

4. Scroll through the Centre for Applied Ethics Web page.

5. Click on the various links to other ethics resources.

6. Write a summary of one of the codes of ethics for your instructor. Include similarities that you noticed in the codes that you read.

NAME _____

PRACTICE 1B

A. Directions: *Select the correct word or words, and write them in the space provided.*

1. Criticizing a competitor's product to a customer makes you look (*bad, badly*).

2. Rick said that he would have to be (*real, really*) sick before he would miss the awards banquet.

3. (*Sometimes, Some times*) I feel that my supervisor does not trust my judgment.

4. You (*sure, surely*) were aware that our company has an indoor smoking ban.

5. We could not decide which of the three alternatives would be the (*better, best*).

1.	bad
2.	really
3.	Sometimes
4.	surely
5.	best

B. Directions: *In the following sentences, a word or phrase is underlined once. Place two lines under each adverb that modifies the underlined word or phrase.*

1. Unethical managers view safety and health as strictly financial decisions.

2. She vaguely remembered the incident that involved tax evasion.

3. Jake and Peter argued heatedly about the proposed layoffs.

4. Decisions are sometimes overly influenced by financial considerations.

5. What are the really important things in your life?

PRACTICE 2B

A. Directions: *Underline each adverb once. Draw two lines under each adjective. Ignore the articles,* a, an, *and* the.

1. Managers in essentially authoritarian organizations often find little latitude to question policies.

2. The personal characteristics of managers greatly influence their reactions to moral standards.

3. Ethical codes are laws, regulations, and rules that have been carefully studied, interpreted, and recorded for easy reference.

4. Performance appraisals and product quality have ethical implications but frequently have few clear-cut answers.

5. We should examine all dilemmas objectively.

B. Directions: *In the space provided, correct the following sentences. Write* **Yes** *if the sentence is correct.*

1. Our ethics committee almost comprises members from every department.
   Our ethics committee comprises members from almost every department.

2. Disruption caused by conflict between groups nearly happens in every business.
   Disruption caused by conflict between groups happens in nearly every business.

3. Our manager only loses his temper with overseas shippers.
   Our manager loses his temper only with overseas shippers.

4. We were sure surprised when we heard about the incorrect reports.
   We were surely surprised when we heard about the incorrect reports.

5. Holly was real sad when she learned about the sexual harassment of Yolanda.
   Holly was really sad when she learned about the sexual harassment of Yolanda.

NAME _____

PRACTICE 3B

PROOFREADING

Directions: *Proofread and compare the two sentences in each group. If they are the same, write* **Yes** *in the space provided. If they are not the same, write* **No.** *Use the first sentence as the correct copy. If you find errors in the second sentence, underline them; insert any omitted words or marks of punctuation.*

1. One of the missions of the United States Office of Government Ethics is to prevent and resolve conflicts of interest and to foster high ethical standards.

    One of the misssions of The United States Office of Government Ethics is to prevent and resolve conflicts of interest and to foster high ethical standards.

    1. No

2. The Jefferson Center for Character Education has identified ten "universal values," which are honesty, integrity, promise-keeping, fidelity, fairness, caring for others, respect for others, responsible citizenship, pursuit of excellence, and accountability.

    The Jefferson Center for Character Education has identified ten "universal values," which are honesty, integrity, promise-keeping, fidelity, fairness, caring for others, respect for others, responsible citzenship, pursuit of excelence, and accountability.

    2. No

3. Unethical behavior among North American companies costs about $100 billion a year to investigate allegations, to resolve activities in question, and to put mechanisms in place to ensure that problems do not reoccur.

    Unethical behavior among North American companys cost about $100 billion a year to investigate allegations, to resolve activities in question, and to put mechanisms in place to insure that problems do not reoccurr.

    3. No

4. Elements of an effective business ethics environment may include codes of conduct, mission statements, training and awareness programs, frequent communication meetings, and an ethics office.

    Elements of an effective business ethics environment may include codes of conduct, mission statements, training and awareness programs, frequent communication meetings, and an ethics office.

    4. Yes

5. The fairness or justice approach to ethics originated in the teachings of the Greek philosopher Aristotle who said that "equals should be treated equally and unequals unequally."

    The fairness or justice approach to ethics originated in the teachings of the Greek Philosopher Aristotle who said that "Equals should be treated equal and unequals unequal".

    5. No

NAME _____

Proofreading Exercise

Directions: *You participated in a brainstorming session on determining ethical mistakes that employees make. The draft that follows is a list of reasons generated from the brainstorming. Key the document and make the corrections that are indicated by the proofreaders' marks. If you are not certain about the use of a proofreaders' mark, use your reference manual.*

EXAMPLES OF UNETHICAL BEHAVIOR

1. ⎡Falsifying expense reports
2. Taking long breaks
3. Misrepresenting Issues to others
4. Withholding information to "Protect" others
5. Covering up drug or alcohol abuse
6. Permitting sub-standard quality in product or service
7. covering up on the job accidents
8. Taking home office supplies

ds ⎡ 9. Blaming my supervisor for for my mistakes
   ⎣10. Divulging personal or confidential information

PRACTICE 4B

WRITING

Directions: *Write a paragraph describing the kind of person you consider unethical. Use a variety of sentence structures. You may use any of the behaviors in the exercise above in your paragraph. You may add any other unethical behaviors that you think should be emphasized.*

Answers will vary. _____

_____

_____

_____

_____

_____

_____

_____

_____

_____

_____

_____

_____

_____

_____

_____

NAME _____

ONLINE *EXERCISES*

Objective: *To visit the U.S. Office of Government ethics home page.*

1. With your Internet browser on screen, key the following:

   http://www.usoge.gov in the location box.

   Press the **Enter** key on your keyboard.

2. You will be on the U.S. Office of Government Ethics Web page.

3. Read at least two ethics program topics such as gifts between employees or gifts from outside sources.

4. Write a short paragraph telling how you feel about giving or receiving gifts at work.

Posttest

Directions: *In the space provided, write the letter of the correct answer.*

1. In the sentence *Joanne respectfully listened to Stephanie's concerns about her heavy workload,* the adverb *respectfully* modifies
   - a. a verb.
   - b. an adjective.
   - c. a noun.
   - d. an adverb.

   1. ___a___

2. In the sentence *Most customer service representatives patiently answer all questions,* the adverb is
   - a. most.
   - b. answer.
   - c. patiently.
   - d. all.

   2. ___c___

3. In the sentence *Our manager always models ethical standards,* the adverb answers the question:
   - a. How?
   - b. When?
   - c. Where?
   - d. To what extent or degree?

   3. ___d___

4. In the sentence *An extremely disgruntled employee often undermines a positive work environment,* you will find
   - a. four adjectives and one adverb.
   - b. two adjectives and three adverbs.
   - c. four adjectives and no adverbs.
   - d. five adjectives and two adverbs.

   4. ___d___

5. Which one of the following sentences is correct?
   - a. Tom felt badly when he realized the extent of the customer's anger.
   - b. The manager clearly insisted that employees be accountable for their actions.
   - c. Howard spoke about ethical responsibility but acted unethical.
   - d. We analyzed careful the cash report to find the shortage.

   5. ___b___

6. Which of the following lines represents the *comparative* degree of adverbs?
   - a. more hurriedly; best
   - b. more cautiously; most immediately
   - c. quicklier; more narrowly
   - d. more persistently; better

   6. ___d___

7. Which of the following sentences is *not* correct?
   - a. Rick could not hardly decide on the best solution for the problem.
   - b. She had nothing to say about the gossip in the office.
   - c. We claim overtime only if we work on Sunday.
   - d. Eliminating motives for unethical behavior is not easy.

   7. ___a___

8. Which one of the following sentences is *not* correct?
   - a. I do not work very good in an isolated environment.
   - b. Are you really trying to understand your manager's motivations?
   - c. We were surely amazed by the theft of the computers.
   - d. Almost all employees support our code of ethics.

   8. ___a___

CHAPTER 14

Prepositions

LEADERSHIP

A leader does not need to be a high-ranking person or a president of a company. A leader may sometimes be a follower at work yet a leader in the community. A person may not work but still show leadership ability by volunteering in an elementary classroom, teaching in a local literacy program, or helping with the organization of community events.

Decades of research have produced hundreds of definitions of leadership and thousands of research studies on leaders. Despite the attention on leadership, no specific formula exists that can distinguish leaders from nonleaders. Leaders may be outgoing or reserved, charismatic or boring, male or female, young or old.

One characteristic all leaders do possess, however, is that they have followers. People follow leaders because leaders have a clearly understood vision or direction. Leaders inspire others to commit to a vision by encouraging teamwork. Leaders are aware of their own strengths and compensate for their weaknesses. This capacity to inspire and to improve their own personal weaknesses is one characteristic that distinguishes leaders from followers.

Debate about whether leadership skills can be taught continues. Much of the current thinking about leadership contends that it can be divided into behaviors and abilities and taught with some degree of success. Most companies that undertake leadership training usually train all levels of employees and hope that employees become inspired to reexamine themselves, the organization, and other people in the organization.

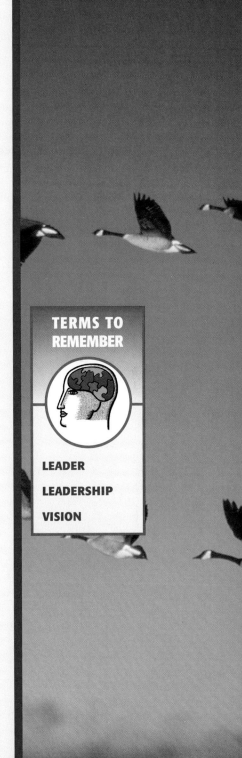

**TERMS TO
REMEMBER**

LEADER

LEADERSHIP

VISION

OBJECTIVES

After you have studied this chapter and completed the exercises, you will be able to do the following:

1. Identify prepositions.
2. Recognize prepositional phrases, objects of prepositions, and compound prepositions.
3. Differentiate between infinitive phrases and prepositional phrases.
4. Recognize the functions of prepositional phrases as adjectives and adverbs.
5. Determine inclusion, exclusion, and placement of prepositions.
6. Differentiate between commonly confused prepositions.
7. Use the correct idiomatic prepositional combinations.
8. Diagram sentences correctly.

LOOKING AHEAD

Pretest

Directions: *In the space provided, write* **T** *if the statement is true and* **F** *if the statement is false.*

1. The sentence *The American Management Association sponsors seminars on leadership in several cities throughout the United States* has four prepositions.

   1. ____F____

2. In the sentence *Some chief executive officers (CEOs) receive bonuses based on the company's profits,* the object of the preposition is *company's.*

   2. ____F____

3. In the sentence *Unfortunately, he used threats instead of education to motivate his subordinates, instead of* is a compound preposition.

   3. ____T____

4. In the sentence *Some leaders refuse to change course once they begin a project,* the phrase *to change course* is a prepositional phrase.

   4. ____F____

5. The preposition *at* is placed correctly in the sentence *Where is the job description for the sales manager at?*

   5. ____F____

6. Prepositional phrases modify nouns, pronouns, and verbs.

   6. ____T____

7. The word *among* is used correctly in the sentence *Hiring a family-business consultant may ease conflicts among family members.*

   7. ____T____

8. The sentence *My supervisor had no reason to be angry at me* is written correctly.

   8. ____F____

OVERVIEW

Imagine a desktop computer, printer, monitor, and keyboard without cables or cords. This scenario is similar to a sentence without connectors.

You have studied nouns and pronouns that identify persons, places, activities, ideas, and things, as well as verbs that indicate action. You learned that adjectives and adverbs modify various parts of speech. Now you will learn about the words that make the connections between all these various parts of speech. In this chapter, you will see how prepositions function as connectors in sentences.

Certain words and prepositions always appear together. Usage rather than rules determines these combinations. In order to make your writing indicate your precise intentions, you should pay particular attention to these combinations, as well as to several other prepositions that are often misused. Once you see how frequently prepositions are used, you will realize how indispensable they are in your writing.

IDENTIFICATION OF PREPOSITIONS

A preposition is a word that connects a noun or a pronoun (the *object* of the preposition) to another word or set of words in a sentence. A preposition shows the relationship between the object of the preposition and these other words.

See Instructor Notes 14-1, 14-2, and 14-3 in IAE.

Commonly Used Prepositions

about	behind	during	on	throughout
above	below	except	onto	to
across	beneath	for	opposite	toward
after	beside	from	out	under
against	besides	in	outside	underneath
along	between	inside	over	until
among	beyond	into	past	up
around	by	like	pending	upon
as	concerning	near	regarding	with
at	despite	of	since	within
before	down	off	through	without

> **SLIP-UP**
> Taken from a medical report: The patient was bitten by a bat as he walked down the street on his thumb.
> [Note: How many people have you seen walking down the street on their thumbs?]
> Source: Richard Lederer.

Prepositions and Prepositional Phrases

A prepositional phrase begins with a preposition and ends with a noun or pronoun called the object of the preposition. A prepositional phrase consists of a preposition, the noun or pronoun object, and any modifiers of the noun or pronoun object. A prepositional phrase cannot stand alone. More than one prepositional phrase often appears in a sentence.

Go to Transparencies/PowerPoints 14-1a, 14-1b, 14-1c, and 14-2.

Use a preposition to connect the object of the preposition (noun or pronoun) to another word or set of words in a sentence.

These managers know the risks <u>of leadership.</u>

(The preposition is *of.* The prepositional phrase is of *leadership.* The noun *leadership* is the object of the preposition.)

Self-awareness often helps people understand the leadership style that works best <u>for them.</u>

(The preposition is *for.* The prepositional phrase is *for them.* The pronoun *them* is the object of the preposition.)

The speed <u>of communication</u> is a leadership challenge that will continue <u>into the next century.</u>

(This sentence contains two prepositional phrases. In the prepositional phrase *of communication*, the preposition is *of* and the object of the preposition is *communication.* In the prepositional phrase *into the next century*, the preposition is *into*, and the object of the preposition is *century. The* and *next* are modifiers of the noun *century.*)

Phil did not change his leadership style when he moved <u>from the military</u> <u>to business.</u>

(Each of the two consecutive prepositional phrases has objects. The object of the preposition *from* is *military.* The object of the preposition *to* is *business.*)

Remember that a sentence can have several prepositional phrases.

CHECKUP 14-1

Directions: In the following sentences, circle each preposition and draw one line under each prepositional phrase.

1. Dundee Research hired managers (with) listening and nurturing skills.

2. Leadership is more what you do (for) other people than what you do (to) them.

3. Employees may feel uncomfortable (under) the leadership (of) a "Type A" personality.

4. She needs a four-year degree and an internship (for) a management position.

5. (For) information (about) the International Directory (of) Young Entrepreneurs, call (617) 555-4690.

6. (Without) integrity, a leader will have a difficult time obtaining loyalty (from) followers.

See Instructor Note 14-4 in IAE.

**GO TO
CD-ROM
CHECKUP 14-1**

See Instructor Note 14-5 in IAE.

Compound Prepositions

A compound preposition consists of a combination of words that is often considered as one preposition. A compound preposition connects the object of a preposition to another word or set of words.

Compound Prepositions

according to	in place of
ahead of	in regard to

along with	in spite of
apart from	instead of
because of	next to
by means of	on account of
in accordance with	on behalf of
in addition to	out of
in front of	with reference to

Use a compound preposition, when necessary, to connect the object of the preposition to another word or set of words.

Good managers give sufficient, positive feedback <u>instead of</u> only constant criticism.

(The prepositional phrase is *instead of only constant criticism.* The compound preposition is *instead of.* The object of the compound preposition is *criticism.*)

CHECKUP 14-2

Directions: *In the following sentences, circle the object of the preposition and draw one line under each prepositional phrase.*

1. Most people are uncomfortable with changes in the management of a firm.

2. According to our records, Charles became president in 1989.

3. Sometimes a member of the younger generation does not function well in the family business.

4. In most cases, putting your goals on paper bridges a gap between thought and action.

5. When you delegate work to someone, be sure that person understands the assignment.

6. When you generate trust in your employees, you create a receptive environment for your ideas.

See Instructor Note 14-6 in IAE.

GO TO CD-ROM
CHECKUP 14-2

CHECKUP 14-3

Directions: *Refer to the first paragraph from the Secondary Learning found at the beginning of the chapter. In the space provided, list the prepositional phrases in the paragraph. Circle the objects of the prepositions.*

of a company	by teaching
at work	in a local literacy program
in the community	by helping
by volunteering	with the organization
in an elementary classroom	of community events

See Instructor Note 14-7 in IAE.

GO TO CD-ROM
CHECKUP 14-3

CONSIDERATIONS IN IDENTIFYING AND USING PREPOSITIONS

Go to PowerPoint 14-3.

Making a distinction between prepositional phrases and infinitive phrases is necessary. Some prepositions may also function as other parts of speech; for example, the adverb. The use of a pronoun as an object of a preposition also requires review.

Infinitive Phrases/Prepositional Phrases

See Instructor Note 14-8 in IAE.

A prepositional phrase has a noun or pronoun as its object. There are no verbs in a prepositional phrase.

An infinitive phrase consists of the word *to* followed by a verb. A prepositional phrase does *not* contain a verb.

The assistant to the president decided to investigate expert system software.

(*To the president* is a prepositional phrase. A verb does not follow the word *to*. *To investigate expert system software* is an infinitive phrase. A verb follows the word *to*.)

Listen to yourself to see how clearly you present ideas.

(*To yourself* is a prepositional phrase. No verb follows the word *to*. *To see* is an infinitive phrase. A verb follows the word *to*.)

Prepositions and Adverbs

Go to PowerPoint 14-4.

The words *by, through,* and *in* can be used as adverbs without objects. When these same words take objects, they are prepositions.

This year the management buzz term "thought leadership" is in.

(*In* is an adverb that answers the question *Where?* No object follows the word *in.*)

Andersen Consulting is establishing a "thought leadership" center in Palo Alto.

(*In* is a preposition. In this sentence, it takes the object *Palo Alto.*)

Objects of Prepositions and Pronouns

Go to PowerPoint 14-5.

See Instructor Note 14-9 in IAE.

Refer to Chapter 7 for a review of the objective case of pronouns.

Objective case pronouns include *her, him, you, me, us, them, it,* and *whom.* Use the objective case of a pronoun as the object of a preposition.

The team leader gave the netware research material to Yolanda and her for processing.

(Omit *Yolanda* to see if the sentence sounds correct with the pronoun *her.* If it does, use the objective case pronoun *her.* The nominative case *she* is not a satisfactory substitution. *Yolanda* and *her* are the objects of the preposition.)

Between you and me, I would not wish to be a manager in that company.

(The objective case *you* and *me* is necessary after the preposition *between. You* and *me* are the objects of the preposition.)

A writer <u>about whom</u> few people have heard has written a book on leadership.

(Use the objective case pronoun *whom* as the object of the preposition.)

CHECKUP 14-4

Directions: *In the space provided, identify the underlined word or words in each of the sentences. Use the following codes:* **Prep** *(preposition),* **PP** *(Prepositional phrase),* **I** *(infinitive or infinitive phrase),* **Adv** *(adverb),* **OP** *(object of preposition).*

1. A new CEO needs to understand the goals <u>of the major stockholders.</u>   PP

2. My supervisor said he would wait <u>outside</u> for me.   Adv

3. People need <u>to know</u> they are doing a good job for the company.   I

4. If you let society place you in a role, you will never go <u>beyond</u> that role.   Prep

5. <u>During</u> the past few years, the autocratic style of management has not been popular.   Prep

6. When you are finished with the book on values, please return it to <u>Jane</u> or <u>me.</u>   OP

GO TO CD-ROM
CHECKUP 14-4

FUNCTIONS OF PREPOSITIONAL PHRASES

Prepositional phrases function as modifiers. A prepositional phrase that modifies a noun or pronoun functions as an adjective. A prepositional phrase that modifies a verb, adjective, or adverb functions as an adverb.

Adjective Function

Use a prepositional phrase as an adjective to modify a noun or a pronoun. In most cases, place the prepositional phrase after the word or words being modified or after a linking verb.

Once you have lost the trust <u>of your employees,</u> you will have a difficult time regaining it.

(*Of your employees* modifies the noun *trust* and answers the question *Whose trust?*)

The woman <u>with the president</u> is a leadership consultant.

(*With the president* describes the noun *woman* and answers the question *Which one?*)

Linda was <u>under considerable pressure</u> last week.

(*Under considerable pressure* describes the noun *Linda* and follows the linking verb *was.*)

Prepositional phrases that modify nouns and pronouns answer such questions as Who? How many? and What kind?

Adverb Function

Use a prepositional phrase as an adverb to modify a verb, an adjective, or another adverb.

He was a good leader who will be judged <u>by his effective leadership record</u>.

(*By his effective leadership record* modifies the verb *judged* and answers the question *How?*)

Benjamin Franklin rarely spoke <u>in public</u> but worked <u>behind the scenes</u> to accomplish his goals.

(*In public* and *behind the scenes* are prepositional phrases that modify the verbs *spoke* and *worked*. The phrases answer the question *Where?*)

The compliment was important <u>to me</u>.

(*To me* is a prepositional phrase that modifies the adjective *important*.)

CHECKUP 14-5

Directions: In the space provided, write the word or phrase modified by the underlined prepositional phrase. All prepositional phrases may not be underlined in this exercise.

1. <u>None of their children</u> wanted to assume a leadership role in the family business. — None

2. Make a list <u>of the drawbacks and benefits</u> of your decision. — list

3. Within many organizations, risk is not greeted <u>with enthusiasm</u>. — greeted

4. A positive outlook moves you <u>toward a problem-solving mode</u> of thinking. — moves

5. Power, like any other mark <u>of authority</u>, can be used in a negative way. — mark

6. Some employees consistently make negative remarks <u>about their</u> leaders. — remarks

GO TO CD-ROM
CHECKUP 14-5

PLACEMENT OF PREPOSITIONS

General Placement

Avoid ending a sentence with a preposition. Place a preposition before its object in the majority of sentences. If a sentence sounds awkward with this pattern, revise the sentence. An exception to this general placement of a preposition is with some short questions or sentences.

Allison had a clear-cut goal to strive <u>for</u>.

Revised Sentence:

Allison had a clear-cut goal <u>for</u> which to strive.

Mission statements often become too complicated for employees to relate <u>to</u>.

Revised Sentence:

Mission statements often become too complicated for employees to relate <u>to them</u>.

What is a leadership analysis good *for*?

(*For what is a leadership analysis good?* or *For what good is a leadership analysis?* are awkward questions. The example, which is a short question ending in a preposition, is acceptable. A revised question *Of what benefit is a leadership analysis?* is also satisfactory.)

Inclusion of Necessary Prepositions

Do not omit a preposition when it is needed. Use separate prepositions when words cannot be related to one object by the same preposition.

A family emergency prevented Harry <u>from</u> going to the leadership institute.

(Do not use *prevented Harry going.* The preposition *from* is necessary.)

What style <u>of</u> management do you prefer—participative or autocratic?

(Do not use *What style management.* The preposition *of* is necessary.)

Executives must <u>plan for</u> and <u>win acceptance of</u> new operations in the production department.

(Separate prepositions are necessary. Do not use *Executives must plan and win acceptance of new operations in the production department.*)

Omission of Unnecessary Prepositions

Omit prepositions that do not add clarity to the meaning of a sentence. Do not repeat a preposition in a sentence if phrases make sense by using the same preposition.

See Instructor Note 14-11 in IAE.

Refer to a reference manual such as The Gregg Reference Manual *for additional examples of unnecessary prepositions.*

The president's office is <u>near</u> the lobby.

(Do not use *near to the lobby.* The preposition *to* is not necessary.)

Our team leader would like <u>us</u> to finish the project before the holidays.

(Do not use *like for us to finish.* The preposition *for* is not necessary.)

Our president frequently speaks <u>at</u> Kiwanis and Rotary meetings.

(The preposition *at* does not need to be repeated before *Kiwanis* and *Rotary* since the same preposition [*at*] applies to both phrases.)

CHECKUP 14-6

Directions: *In the space provided, correct those sentences that are written incorrectly. Write* **Yes** *if the sentence is correct.*

1. She asked what leadership activities he was involved in.

She asked in what leadership activities he was involved.

---

2. Honeywell's goal is to get more employees to think like and act like owners.

   Honeywell's goal is to get more employees to think and act like owners.

3. The human resources director hires only those applicants who have graduated high school.

   The human resources director hires only those applicants who have graduated from high school.

4. A leader must have a clear understanding and a caring attitude toward employee needs.

   A leader must have a clear understanding of and a caring attitude toward employee needs.

5. Where can I get a copy of the policies and procedures manual at?

   Where can I get a copy of the policies and procedures manual?

6. How much middle management support can we count on?

   On how much middle management support can we count? (Preferred)

See Instructor Note 14-12 in IAE.

GO TO
CD-ROM
CHECKUP 14-6

CAUTIONS IN USING SPECIAL PREPOSITIONS

See Instructor Note 14-13 in IAE.

Some prepositions cause confusion. The following pairs require special consideration:

Beside/Besides

See Instructor Note 14-14.

Go to PowerPoint 14-6.

Use *beside* as a preposition to mean "by the side of" or "not connected with something." Use *besides* as a preposition to mean "in addition to" or "other than."

The person taking minutes should sit beside the chairperson.
(*Beside* means "by the side of" or "next to.")

The discussion on leadership values was beside the point at this time.
(*Beside* means the discussion was not connected with the material currently being discussed.)

Besides Maria, the manager appointed two other women to the team.
(*Besides* means "in addition to.")

Our union leader had several possible solutions besides the one we agreed upon.
(*Besides* means "other than.")

Among/Between

Go to PowerPoint 14-7.

See Instructor Note 14-15 in IAE.

In general, use the preposition *between* to refer to two persons, places, qualities, activities, ideas, or things. Use the preposition *among* to refer to more than two persons, places, qualities, activities, ideas, or things.

In our family business, my mother and father share decision-making responsibilities <u>between</u> them.

(*Between* refers to two persons.)

He is <u>among</u> those who believe that leadership requires a futuristic attitude.

(*Among those* suggests that more than two people are involved.)

Different From

Use the word *different* followed by the preposition *from* when *from* connects an object to another word or set of words in a sentence.

Go to PowerPoint 14-8.

See Instructor Note 14-16 in IAE.

To some, a leader is <u>different from</u> a manager.

(Use the preposition *from* after *different.* In this sentence, *from* connects the object *manager* to the rest of the sentence. Do not use *different than.*)

His leadership style is quite <u>different from</u> mine.

(Use the preposition *from* after *different.* In this sentence, *from* connects the object *mine* to the rest of the sentence. Do not use *different than.*)

Like/As

Use the preposition *like* to mean "similar to" or "resembling." Do not use a verb after the preposition *like.* Do not use *like* to join clauses. Use the conjunctions *as* or *as if* to join clauses.

Go to PowerPoint 14-9.

Jeremy looks <u>like</u> a leader.

(The preposition *like* is not followed by a verb and takes the object *leader.*)

Adam wants to be the president of the family's company just <u>like</u> his father.

(The preposition *like* is not followed by a verb and takes the object *father.*)

Jeremy looks <u>as if</u> he wants to be a leader.

(The words *as if* introduce the clause *he wants to be a leader.* The clause includes a subject and a verb.)

The negotiation process worked <u>as</u> it should.

(The word *as* introduces a clause *it should.* The clause includes a subject and a verb.)

Like takes an object (noun or pronoun) and is not followed by a verb.

Off/From

Do not use *off of* in prepositional phrases. Do not substitute *off* for *from* in certain phrases.

The supervisor had to keep reminding people to keep beverages <u>off</u> their computer desks.

(Do not use *off of their computer desks.*)

I got the leadership meeting notes <u>from</u> her.

(Do not use *off of* her as the prepositional phrase.)

The board of directors decided to borrow $1 million <u>from</u> the local bank.

(Do not use *off the local bank* as the prepositional phrase.)

In/Into

Go to PowerPoint 14-10.

Use *in* to indicate a "location or position within a place." Use *into* to indicate "movement or direction from outside to inside" or a "change of condition or form."

Ironically, those who avoid risks often seem to end up in leadership positions.

(*In* indicates a "position within someplace.")

Much of a leader's time is spent in meetings.

(*In* indicates a location.)

Would everyone please move into the lecture hall for Juan's presentation on motivation.

(*Into* indicates movement from outside the hall to the inside.)

To achieve a goal, break it down into small, concrete actions.

(*Into* indicates a change of form.)

To/Too/Two

Go to PowerPoints 14-11a and 14-11b.

Use the preposition *to* to indicate "toward." Also use *to* as an infinitive or as part of an infinitive phrase. Use *too* as an adverb to indicate an "excessive amount" or "also." Use *two* as an adjective to indicate the number (how many).

How do you react to setbacks and difficult situations?

(*To* is a preposition. No verb follows.)

Does he have the time and energy to develop the international markets?

(*To* is part of an infinitive phrase. A verb follows the word *to*.)

Many people in leadership positions speak too quickly.

(*Too* indicates excessively.)

Ryan was selected for leadership training, too.

(*Too* means "also.")

I am one of the two people to be selected for the management training program.

(*Two* is the number.)

CHECKUP 14-7

Directions: *Select the correct word, and write it in the space provided.*

1. Chairing a meeting is different (*from, than*) anything I have ever done.

   from

2. His leadership style is (*as, like*) mine.

   like

3. Estate planning (*among, between*) family business leaders is not a simple process.

   among

4. Few people know as much about leadership (*as, like*) Peter Drucker knows.

   as

5. Workers want to know how their jobs fit (*in, into*)
   the overall picture.

   into

6. We find leadership in many places (*beside, besides*)
   the CEO's office.

   besides

7. Allen had (*to, too, two*) many other commitments when
   he became our team leader.

   too

8. The finance director took my budget proposal (*off, off of*)
   today's agenda.

   off

IDENTIFICATION OF IDIOMATIC EXPRESSIONS

An idiom refers to an expression that has evolved from general usage through the years but which has no established rule for this usage. Many idioms involve a verb and preposition combination.

Following are some examples of these verb and preposition combinations along with brief definitions. Since the same verb may precede different prepositions, it is necessary to select the correct combination to express the meaning intended.

Refer to the sections on prepositions or word usage in your reference manual to determine the correct idiomatic expression to use.

accompanied by (a person)
accompanied by or with (an item)

The supervisor <u>accompanied by</u> his boss went to the president's office.

We noticed that the check was <u>accompanied with</u> a letter of appreciation.

adapted from (taken from another source)
adapted to (adjusted to)

They knew his management techniques were <u>adapted from</u> those he used in England.

Anna soon <u>adapted to</u> her new leadership role.

agree in (principle)
agree on (a plan)
agree with (a person)

We all <u>agreed in</u> principle that a leader has to be open-minded about changing technology.

The committee <u>agreed on</u> the need to increase the number of leadership seminars.

Kent <u>agreed with</u> me about some new ways to motivate employees.

angry at, angry about (a situation)
angry with (person)

I am still <u>angry about</u> the board's decision to limit overtime hours.

When Lucy is <u>angry with</u> someone, she delays her actions until she can think more clearly.

argue about (situation)
argue for (something)
argue with (person)
Several committee members <u>argued about</u> the wording of the mission statement.
Our team leader <u>argued for</u> additional support staff assistance.
I do not like to <u>argue with</u> my supervisor.

arrive at (time, specific location, conclusion)
arrive by (type of transport)
arrive in (general location)
I will <u>arrive at</u> the university to speak about leadership issues in the new millennium.
We plan to <u>arrive by</u> plane although we have scheduled our executives on different flights.
Hank plans to <u>arrive in</u> Tucson for a meeting with the Arizona branch managers.

concur in (an opinion)
concur with (a person)
Everybody on the board <u>concurred in</u> hiring Robin Malloy.
The owner of the firm <u>concurred with</u> us regarding our request for a refund.

CHECKUP 14-8

Directions: *Select the correct idiomatic expression, and write it in the space provided.*

1. The union could not (*agree on, agree to, agree with*) the compensation plan for part-time workers.

   <u>agree on</u>

2. We were (*angry with, angry about*) the lack of leadership training opportunities.

   <u>angry about</u>

3. I adapted my goals (*from, to*) those I outlined last year.

   <u>from</u>

4. Our speaker will arrive (*at, by, in*) the airport (*at, by, in*) 12:35 p.m.

   <u>at   at</u>

5. Although both plans had merit, I (*argued about, argued for, argued with*) the least expensive plan to implement.

   <u>argued for</u>

6. The manager (*concurred in, concurred with*) Betsy in her request for a salary increase.

   <u>concurred with</u>

GO TO
CD-ROM
CHECKUP 14-8

Other Idiomatic Expressions

Review the following idiomatic expressions carefully.

correspond by (means)
correspond to (show similarity)
correspond with (a person by writing)

Even in the executive offices, correspondence by mail is decreasing.

Fran's plan corresponded to the one management had envisioned.

Corresponding with international businesspeople requires careful use of the language.

enter in *or* **on (record)**
enter into (agreement)

Our insecure manager enters every infraction of the rules in a log book.

The two recruitment coordinators entered into a reciprocal agreement concerning the hiring of employees.

live at (address, place)
live in (area)
live on (amount)

Sometimes his family thinks he lives at the office.

Our firm encourages all managers to live in the city.

Union leaders tried to convince management that workers can't live on a minimum wage.

reconciled to (to accept)
reconciled with (to bring into agreement)

I am reconciled to the fact that I will not be promoted this year.

Our auditor insists on the reconciliation of our checkbook with the ledgers.

talk about (something)
talk for (time period)
talk to (tell something to someone or to an audience)
talk with (converse with an individual or small group)

At our fall meeting, the superintendent talked about the enrollment patterns for community colleges.

We talked for some time about the impending merger.

Have you talked to your manager about a leadership training program?

Our telecommunications network allows our branch managers in Akron and Waterloo to talk with each other.

wait at (location)
wait for (person, thing)
wait on (customer)

Please wait at the information desk for the human services director.

She waited for an answer to her leave request.

Never appear too busy to wait on a customer.

CHECKUP 14-9

Directions: *Select the correct idiomatic expression, and write it in the space provided.*

1. I (*waited at, waited for, waited on*) Terry to contact me about the meeting.

   waited for

2. Has the checkbook been (*reconciled to, reconciled with*) the bank statement this month?

   reconciled with

3. Our CEO (*entered in, entered into*) merger negotiations with another firm last March.

   entered into

4. Many of our managers (*live at, live in*) Cedarburg or Port Washington.

   live in

5. We (*correspond by, correspond with*) our three branch managers through e-mail.

   correspond with

6. The board chairman asked the CEO to (*talk about, talk to, talk with*) the stockholders at the annual meeting.

   talk to

**GO TO
CD-ROM
CHECKUP 14-9**

DIAGRAMMING SENTENCES

To diagram a prepositional phrase, place the preposition on a diagonal line under the word it modifies. Place the object of the preposition on a horizontal line that extends from the diagonal.

Prepositional Phrase as an Adjective

A leader must have a vision of the future.

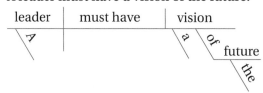

Prepositional Phrase as an Adverb

She completed an internship in management at Sacred Heart Hospital.

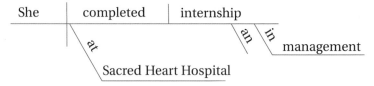

Directions: *In the space provided, diagram the following sentences.*

1. The workforce of the next decade will require a new type of leadership.

See Instructor Note 14-19 in
IAE.

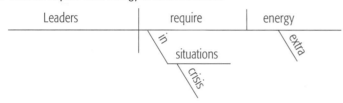

2. Leaders require extra energy in crisis situations.

3. Our managers consider all sides of a controversy.

4. The supervisor disliked any criticisms of his plans.

5. Participative leaders appreciate input from their employees.

GO TO
CD-ROM
CHECKUP 14-10

PRACTICE

PRACTICE 1A

A. **Directions:** *In the space provided, identify the underlined word or words in each of the sentences. Use the following codes:* **Prep** *(preposition),* **PP** *(prepositional phrase),* **I** *(infinitive or infinitive phrase),* **OP** *(object of a preposition),* **CP** *(compound preposition).*

1. My long-term goal is <u>to become</u> the president of a small company.

   1. _____I_____

2. We completed a leadership survey in the engineering <u>businesses</u> of Tulsa.

   2. _____OP_____

3. He thought of <u>himself</u> as a manager, not as a leader.

   3. _____OP_____

4. When employees care as much <u>about</u> company goals as the leader does, the company will prosper.

   4. _____Prep_____

5. <u>To grow</u>, try focusing on positive ways you can make changes.

   5. _____I_____

6. This is the best solution <u>in spite of</u> the many alternatives.

   6. _____CP_____

7. Max, who thrives <u>on</u> competition, knows the value of persistence.

   7. _____Prep_____

8. To improve the way you interact with people, change your attitude <u>toward them</u>.

   8. _____PP_____

9. What leadership literature have you read <u>in the past few months</u>?

   9. _____PP_____

10. <u>In addition to</u> moving expenses, our company paid our new manager's rent for two months.

    10. _____CP_____

B. **Directions:** *Select the correct word or words, and write them in the space provided.*

1. Sometimes it is difficult to tell the difference (*between, among*) a manager and a leader.

   1. _____between_____

2. (*To, Too, Two*) some managers, style is more important than anything else.

   2. _____To_____

3. My manager seems to be prejudiced against me and people (*as, like*) me.

   3. _____like_____

4. Management finally (*agreed to, agreed in, agreed with*) the terms of the union.

   4. _____agreed to_____

5. My (*anger with, anger about*) the injustice of the decision seemed justifiable at the time.

   5. _____anger about_____

**GO TO
CD-ROM
PRACTICE 1
EXERCISES**

Chapter 14

NAME _____

PRACTICE 2A

A. Directions: *Draw one line under each prepositional phrase. Circle the object of each preposition.*

1. He is the chairman of a (company) with (millions) of (dollars) in annual (sales).

2. Employees need a sense of (control) over their working (environments).

3. Do not try to reason with (people) when they are in the (middle) of an (outburst).

4. The CEO Institute provides solutions to management (problems) through peer (involvement) and (discussions).

5. A family owner needs to work on the (development) of leadership (qualities) in the next (generation).

B. Directions: *In the space provided, correct those sentences that are written incorrectly. Write **Yes** if the sentence is correct.*

1. How well do you listen and communicate with your subordinates?

   How well do you listen to and communicate with your subordinates?

2. To who do promotions go in your firm?

   To whom do promotions go in your firm?

3. They kept asking for and bargaining for additional safety measures.

   They kept asking and bargaining for additional safety measures.

   See Instructor Note 14-20 in IAE.

4. The long-range planning committee met over at the restaurant.

   The long-range planning committee met at the restaurant.

   See Instructor Note 14-21 in IAE.

5. We could not arrive by a conclusion so we agreed with another course of action.

   We could not arrive at a conclusion so we agreed on another course of action.

6. Running the family business requires dividing responsibilities among the three of us.

   Yes

7. Where are my books on leadership development at?

   Where are my books on leadership development?

8. We had to little time too complete the leadership style questionnaire.

   We had too little time to complete the leadership style questionnaire.

9. I have always felt that Mac did not listen to his workers like he should.

   I have always felt that Mac did not listen to his workers as he should.

10. Antonio plans to arrive at Cheyenne to talk at the regional managers.

    Antonio plans to arrive in Cheyenne to talk to the regional managers.

GO TO
CD-ROM
PRACTICE 2
EXERCISES

NAME _____

PRACTICE 3A

PROOFREADING

*Directions: Proofread and compare the two sentences in each group. If they are the same, write **Yes** in the space provided. If they are not the same, write **No**. Use the first sentence as the correct copy. If you find errors in the second sentence, underline them; insert any omitted words or marks of punctuation.*

1. Cargill, Inc., the country's largest privately held firm, has **1.** ___No___
   had a nonfamily CEO twice in the past 30 years.
   Cargill, Inc., the <u>countries'</u> largest <u>privately-held</u> firm,_∧^{has}
   had a nonfamily CEO twice in the past 30 years.

2. He interviewed for the position of manager of the **2.** ___No___
   executive development program at the University
   of St. Thomas in Minneapolis.
   He interviewed for the position of manager <u>for</u> the
   executive development program <u>in</u> the University
   of St. Thomas in <u>Minnesota</u>.

3. The Hugh O'Brian Youth Foundation (HOBY) helps **3.** ___No___
   high school sophomores learn leadership skills
   by allowing them to interact with those who
   run today's businesses.
   The Hugh <u>O"Brian</u> Youth Foundation (HOBY) <u>help</u>
   high school <u>sophmores</u> learn leadership skills
   by allowing them to interact with those who
   run <u>todays</u> businesses.

4. Business Cents Resources in Pittsburgh offers "day-camp" **4.** ___No___
   programs for children ages 3 through 16 to teach them
   about money, leadership, and other business topics.
   Business Cents <u>Resource</u> in Pittsburgh offers "day-camp"
   programs for children ages 3 <u>to</u> 16 to teach them
   about money, leadership, and other business topics.

5. One-fourth of the participants in a national family- **5.** ___No___
   business survey indicated that their next CEO
   may be a woman.
   One-<u>fifth</u> of the participants in a national family-
   business survey indicated that their next CEO
   may be a woman.

NAME

Proofreading Exercise

Directions: Your employer, Dr. Fred Tyler, asks you to prepare a final copy of a suggested reading list for his management classes. The draft that follows requires corrections. Key the document and make the corrections that are indicated by the proofreaders' marks. If you are not certain about the use of a proofreaders' mark, use your reference manual or the proofreaders' marks listed on the inside back cover of this textbook.

See Instructor Notes 14-22, 14-23, and 14-24 in IAE.

SUGGESTED READING LIST
MANAGEMENT 310
DR. FRED B. TYLER

Warren Bennis and Patricia Ward Beiderman, *Organizing Genius: Secrets of Creative Collaboration*, Addison-Wesley, New York.

David L. Bradford and Allan R. Cohen, *Managing For Excellence*, John Wiley & Sons, New York.

Paul Hershey, *The Situational Leader*, Warner Books, Inc., New York.

John P. Kotter, *the Leadership Factor*, The Free Press, New York.

James Lundy, *Lead, Follow, or Get Out of the Way*, Pfeiffer & Company, San Diego.

James Miller with Paul Brown, *The Corporate Coach*, Harper Business, New York.

Patricia Pitcher, *The Dramas of Leadership*, John Wiley & Sons, NY New York.

Joseph Quigley, *Vision: How Leaders Develop It, Share It, and Sustain It*, McGraw-Hill Inc., New York.

Perry M. Smith, *Taking Charge*, Avery Publishing Group Inc., Garden City Park, New York.

GO TO CD-ROM PRACTICE 3 EXERCISES

PRACTICE 4A

WRITING

Directions: Write a paragraph describing a person you believe to be a good leader. Describe the qualities that make this person a good leader.

Answers will vary.

GO TO CD-ROM PRACTICE 4 EXERCISES

PRACTICE

ONLINE *EXERCISE*

See Instructor Note 14-25 in IAE.

The Web has unlimited sites on leadership. Many of these sites are maintained by universities that have leadership educational programs for students. In addition, leadership consultants have Web pages offering services, seminars, tips, and advice on leadership.

One aspect of leadership success is understanding how your personality style relates to other personality styles. One well-known personality profile is The Keirsey Temperament Sorter by David Keirsey. David Keirsey maintains a Web page where you can take The Keirsey Temperament Sorter online, receive your score, and read more about your personality style.

Objective: *To complete The Keirsey Temperament Sorter and analyze the results.*

Use exact punctuation when keying an Internet address.

1. With your Internet browser on screen, key:

   http://www.keirsey.com in the location text box.

   Press the **Enter** key on your keyboard.

2. You will be on the Website for the Keirsey Temperament Sorter and Temperament Theory.

3. Click on the link to **Keirsey Temperament Sorter II, an online personality questionnaire.**

4. Answer the questions. When you are finished, click on **Score test.**

5. Print the **Keirsey Temperament Test Results.**

6. Click on **The Four Temperaments.**

7. Find your temperament, click on it, and read about your temperament type. Print it if you want a copy for your files.

NAME _____

PRACTICE 1B

A. Directions: *In the space provided, identify the underlined word or words in each of the sentences. Use the following codes:* **Prep** *(preposition),* **PP** *(prepositional phrase),* **I** *(infinitive phrase),* **OP** *(object of a preposition),* **CP** *(compound preposition).*

1. My goal is to become the best leader possible, both on the job and <u>in</u> my personal life.   **1.** Prep

2. I am leading the meeting <u>on behalf of</u> Terry.   **2.** CP

3. Margaret will not be accepted as a leader until she learns <u>to communicate clearly and directly.</u>   **3.** I

4. Virtually every organization is looking for women with strong leadership <u>abilities.</u>   **4.** OP

5. Support your supervisor or staff <u>through tough times</u>, and your loyalty likely will be reciprocated.   **5.** PP

B. Directions: *Select the correct word or words and write them in the space provided.*

1. We always place the tape recorder (*beside, besides*) the president's chair.   **1.** beside

2. If I had to choose (*among, between*) the two candidates, I would prefer Margaret's leadership style.   **2.** between

3. The final report is (*different from, different than*) the draft that I submitted to Cynthia.   **3.** different from

4. Patricia is taking several university courses to help her move (*in, into*) a leadership position.   **4.** into

5. All these committee meetings are taking up (*to, too, two*) much of my time.   **5.** too

PRACTICE 2B

A. Directions: *Draw one line under each prepositional phrase. Circle the object of each preposition.*

1. In spite of the delayed shipment, we still managed to retain the business of the largest customer in Canada.

2. Our managers encourage leadership development among employees at all levels of the organization.

3. The president hired Michael Wilson to establish the identity of a new division that is separate from the parent company.

4. Burt Nanus and Warren Bennis base their definition of leadership on five competencies or strategies.

5. We need to obtain the support of the board in addition to the approval of our department manager.

B. Directions: *In the space provided, correct those sentences that are written incorrectly. Write* **Yes** *if the sentence is correct.*

1. A successful leader makes a commitment to the organization and fosters that same kind commitment in other employees.

   A successful leader makes a commitment to the organization and fosters that same kind of commitment in other employees.

2. The president is always accompanied by her assistant when traveling in Japan.

   Yes

3. It looks like Tom will be promoted before the end of the month!

   It looks as if Tom will be promoted before the end of the month!

4. Beside the manager, no one has access to the master list of computer passwords.

   Besides the manager, no one has access to the master list of computer passwords.

5. Janie should plan for and decide the speakers for our annual meeting.

   Janie should plan for and decide upon (or on) the speakers for our annual meeting.

NAME _____

PRACTICE 3B

PROOFREADING

Directions: *Proofread and compare the two sentences in each group. If they are the same, write* **Yes** *in the space provided. If they are not the same, write* **No**. *Use the first sentence as the correct copy. If you find errors in the second sentence, underline them; insert any omitted words or marks of punctuation.*

1. Johnson & Johnson articulates its business principles in a document called "Our Credo," which clearly describes the company's responsibilities to customers, employees, communities, and stockholders.

   Johnson & Johnson articlates it's business principals in a document called "Our Credo," which clearly describes the company's responsibilities to customers, employees, communities, and stockholders.

   1. No _____

2. In 1982, Group President Jan Carlzon of Scandinavian Air System (SAS) gave all 16,000 employees gold watches for turning around company sales.

   In 1982, Group President Jane Carlzon of Scandinavan Air System (SAS) gave all 1,600 employees gold watches for turning around company sales.

   2. No _____

3. An important leadership skill is the ability to coach, which means helping an employee on the spot to improve his or her job performance.

   An important leadership skill is the ability to coach, which means helping an employee on the spot to improve his or her job performance.

   3. Yes _____

4. Some strategies for motivating employees include listening to complaints and ideas objectively, finding ways to recognize and reward good work, praising good performance in public, and counseling poor performers privately.

   Some strategys for motivating employees include listening to complaints and ideas objectivly, finding ways to recognize and award good work, praising good performance in public, and counsoling poor performers privately.

   4. No _____

5. Difficult people can be negative, irritating, and impossible to manage, but a good leader always tries to analyze challenging behavior and then takes appropriate action.

   Difficult people can be negative, iritating, and impossible to manage, but a good leader always tries to analyse challenging behavor and then takes appropriate action.

   5. No _____

Proofreading Exercise

See Instructor Note 14-26 in IAE.

Directions: *Your manager is preparing a list of leadership quotations. The following draft of quotes requires corrections. Key the document and make the corrections that are indicated by the proofreaders' marks. If you are not certain about the use of a proofreaders' mark, use your reference manual or the proofreaders' marks listed on the inside back cover of this textbook.*

LEADERSHIP QUOTATIONS

"You cannot push anyone up the ladder ~~unless he is willing to climb himself~~ Andrew Carnegei *(stet)*

"The buck stops here." Harry S. Truman ·

"You can only make others better by being goood yourself." Hugh R. Hanels

"treat people as if they were what they ought to be, and you help them becom what they are capable of being." Johann Wolfgang Von Goethe

]"Managers are people who do things right, and leaders are people who do the right thing." Warren Bennis

]"If you can dream it, you can do it." Walt Disney

["If we don't change our direction, we're likely to endup where we're headed."   Chinese proverb

NAME _____

PRACTICE 4B

WRITING

Directions: Write a paragraph describing a successful leadership experience you have had. Include your role and the results of your experience.
Answers will vary.

_____
_____
_____
_____
_____
_____
_____
_____
_____
_____
_____
_____
_____
_____
_____
_____
_____
_____
_____
_____
_____
_____
_____

NAME _____

See Instructor Note 14-27 in IAE.

ONLINE EXERCISES

Employers know that the most valued and productive employees are not necessarily those with the highest intelligence quotient (IQ). Daniel Goleman is the author of *Emotional Intelligence: Why It Can Matter More Than IQ for Character, Health, and Lifelong Achievement.* The premise of this book is that emotional intelligence, which includes empathy and resourcefulness, gives people a competitive edge in life.

Objective: *To complete The EQ Test and analyze the results.*

1. With your Internet browser on screen, key:

   http://www.utne.com/cgi-bin/eq in the location text box.

   Press the **Enter** key on your keyboard.

2. Scroll down and answer the questions.

3. When you are finished with the questions, click on **What's My Quotient?**

4. Read the information about your emotional intelligence.

LOOKING BACK

Posttest

Directions: *In the space provided, write **T** if the statement is true and **F** if the statement is false.*

1. The sentence *Most managers who understand participatory management techniques look for opportunities to apply the principles and practices within their own units* has three prepositions.

   1. _____F_____

2. In the sentence *Leaders demonstrate their commitment to ethics by their behavior*, the object of the preposition is *their*.

   2. _____F_____

3. In the sentence *Leaders need persistence and a willingness to take risks*, the phrase *to take risks* is an infinitive phrase.

   3. _____T_____

4. In the sentence *The manager's parking space is located in the underground parking lot beneath the building*, the phrase *beneath the building* is a prepositional phrase.

   4. _____T_____

5. The sentence *The promotion to vice president is between Betty and I* is written correctly.

   5. _____F_____

6. Prepositional phrases contain verbs.

   6. _____F_____

7. The word *like* is used correctly in the sentence *My manager said he wanted to hire another conscientious worker like me.*

   7. _____T_____

8. The idiomatic expression *agree in* is used correctly in the sentence *I agree in principle with my supervisor's decision.*

   8. _____T_____

9. The sentence *Please keep confidential memos off of your desk* is written correctly.

   9. _____F_____

10. The sentence *Where is my telephone directory at?* is written correctly.

    10. _____F_____

CHAPTER 15

Conjunctions

STRESS AND COPING STRATEGIES

Stress is emotional tension caused by everyday events in our lives. Certain occupations cause more stress than others, but most Americans feel that their jobs cause them stress. Researchers are showing links between stress and physical symptoms like tension, pain, and irritability. Stress may also be a cause of illnesses such as headaches, high blood pressure, and cancer.

Stress can be a negative force in our lives if we do not have adequate coping resources. Coping strategies involve exercise, healthful eating, and relaxation techniques. For many people, developing coping strategies means making lifestyle changes.

Exercise not only releases frustrations but also makes you feel better about yourself. Many working people say that they do not have time to exercise, but exercise opportunities are all around us. You can get off the bus a stop early, or park your car in the farthest space available and then walk to your workplace. You can take the stairs or walk briskly around the office. You can use an exercise bike while you watch television, or you can take a walk during the halftime of a televised sports event.

Proper nutrition helps stabilize your moods. By reducing your intake of caffeine, sugar, nicotine, and alcohol, you can reduce stress. Even though candy or soft drinks help increase your energy temporarily, they cause your blood sugar to drop, making you feel fatigued. Sources of long-lasting energy are fruits, vegetables, and whole grains.

Many people who are under stress do not take time to relax. Relaxation techniques involve activities that you like to do but do not take the time to do. Some people relax by listening to music, reading, or by doing deep-breathing exercises. Others find it uplifting to be around positive people who like to laugh.

TERMS TO REMEMBER

COPING STRATEGIES

IRRITABILITY

STRESS

TENSION

OBJECTIVES

After you have studied this chapter and completed the exercises, you will be able to do the following:

1. Identify clauses and sentences.
2. Use coordinating and correlative conjunctions correctly.
3. Use subordinating conjunctions and conjunctive adverbs correctly.
4. Use correct punctuation in sentences containing coordinating, correlative, or subordinating conjunctions, or conjunctive adverbs.
5. Identify correct parallel structure in sentences.
6. Distinguish between conjunctions and prepositions.
7. Use commonly confused conjunction expressions correctly.
8. Diagram sentences correctly.

LOOKING AHEAD

Pretest

Directions: *In the space provided, write the letter of the correct answer.*

1. The sentence *Things went well initially, but soon I was spending too much time at work* is an example of a
   a. simple sentence.
   c. complex sentence.
   b. compound sentence.
   d. compound-complex sentence.

   1. ___b___

2. In the sentence *We encourage our employees to leave the office at 5 p.m. or as close to 5 as possible,* the conjunction *or* is a
   a. coordinating conjunction.
   c. subordinating conjunction.
   b. correlative conjunction.
   d. conjunctive adverb.

   2. ___a___

3. Which sentence is written correctly?
   a. Either Lisa will contact a psychologist or participate in group counseling.
   b. Lisa will either contact a psychologist or participate in group counseling.
   c. Lisa will either contact a psychologist and either participate in group counseling.
   d. Either Lisa will contact a psychologist and either participate in group counseling.

   3. ___b___

4. In the sentence *Since I work from my home, I can set a routine that is comfortably paced,* the conjunction *since* is a
   a. coordinating conjunction.
   b. correlative conjunction.
   c. subordinating conjunction.
   d. conjunctive adverb.

   4. ___c___

5. Which of the following is an example of a conjunctive adverb?
   a. neither...nor
   c. when
   b. nevertheless
   d. like

   5. ___b___

6. Which sentence is punctuated correctly?
   a. Work, family relationships and financial problems are three leading causes of stress.
   b. Companies may offer anxiety, or depression treatments for their employees.
   c. Most managers think that they delegate effectively, but often fail to release their challenging projects.
   d. If you have been a victim in the downsizing of a company, you have experienced stress.

   6. ___d___

7. Which sentence is written correctly?
   a. I worked at CT Labs until I retired in 1998.
   b. To maintain your health, be sure and contact your doctor for regular checkups.
   c. Walking is exercise that is healthy, easy, and energizes you.
   d. Neither Aaron or Larry has been at work the past week.

   7. ___a___

8. Which sentence is written correctly?
   a. I have considered taking a stress management workshop and to apply for a new job.
   b. I can't help but think that I need to delegate more of my work.
   c. Being an office worker can be just as stressful as being a firefighter or a doctor.
   d. I read in a magazine where laughter has a positive effect on physical and mental health.

   8. ___c___

You will often find a need to connect your thoughts rather than present them in short choppy sentences. Within a sentence, you can join nouns, pronouns, verbs, adjectives, and adverbs. You can also join phrases, clauses, and even complete sentences.

In this chapter, you will learn how to connect these sentence parts or entire sentences. The expressions you connect must be grammatically equal; for example, nouns must be connected with other nouns or adjectives with other adjectives. This principle is known as parallelism and is a requisite for clear writing.

Before you begin your work with conjunctions, you will have an opportunity to review dependent and independent clauses as well as the types of sentence structures. When you complete this chapter, you will have finished your intensive study of basic grammar principles.

REVIEW OF CLAUSES AND SENTENCES

A brief review of the types of clauses and sentence formations is appropriate before you study the connecting function of conjunctions.

See Instructor Notes 15-1 and 15-2 in IAE.

Clauses

Independent Clauses. An independent clause (or main clause) can stand alone as a complete sentence. A clause has a complete subject and predicate.

Go to Transparencies/PowerPoints 15-1a and 15-1b.

> independent clause
> **Stress-related symptoms vary.**

(*Stress-related symptoms* is the complete subject, and *vary* is the complete predicate. These make a complete sentence and can stand alone.)

Refer to Chapter 3 for a review of independent and dependent clauses.

Dependent Clauses. A dependent clause (or *subordinate clause*) also contains a subject and a predicate; however, a dependent clause is not a complete sentence and cannot stand alone. A dependent clause requires an independent clause to make sense. A dependent clause may appear before or after an independent clause.

See Instructor Note 15-3 in IAE.

> dependent clause | independent clause
> **After I received my promotion, I began to delegate more of my work.**

(*After I received my promotion* is the dependent clause and has a subject and a predicate, but it cannot stand alone. The clause is not a complete thought, and it must depend on the independent clause *I began to delegate more of my work* to make sense. In this sentence, the dependent clause comes before the independent clause.)

> independent clause | dependent clause
> **I began to delegate more of my work after I received my promotion.**

(In this sentence, the dependent clause comes after the independent clause.)

Sentences

Simple Sentence.   A simple sentence consists of one complete subject and one complete predicate. The subject, the predicate, or both may be compound.

independent clause
Company leaders often set the workaholic pace in their firms.
(The sentence has a complete subject [*company leaders*] and a complete predicate [*often set the workaholic pace in their firms*].)

independent clause
Work and worry create tension and cause headaches in the workplace.
(The sentence has a compound subject [*work* and *worry*] and a compound simple predicate [*create* and *cause*]. The complete predicate is *create tension and cause headaches in the workplace*.)

Compound Sentence.   A compound sentence consists of two simple independent clauses connected by a conjunction such as *or, and, nor,* or *but.*

independent clause
Work pressures often cause stress, but

independent clause
family and financial concerns are additional causes.
(The conjunction *but* connects the two independent clauses.)

independent clause
Nick spends time with his family, and

independent clause
he never fails to attend his children's scheduled events.
(The conjunction *and* connects the two independent clauses.)

Complex Sentence.   A complex sentence contains an independent clause and one or more dependent clauses.

dependent clause
Although his team was ahead in its production goal,

independent clause
Bryan worried about the final outcome.
(The sentence contains an independent clause [*Bryan worried about the final outcome*] and a dependent clause [*Although his team was ahead in its production goal*].)

dependent clause   dependent clause
Because our supervisor challenges us and because he sets short-range

independent clause
goals, he decreases the tension involved in doing new tasks.
(The sentence contains an independent clause [*he decreases the tension involved in doing new tasks*]. The sentence also contains two dependent clauses—*Because our supervisor challenges us* and *because he sets short-range goals.*)

See Instructor Notes 15-4 and 15-5 in IAE.

Compound-Complex Sentence.   A compound-complex sentence contains more than one independent clause and one or more dependent clauses.

dependent clause
If managers do not develop time management techniques,

independent clause
their stress levels will increase;

independent clause
furthermore, their personal time will suffer.

(The sentence contains two independent clauses—*their stress levels will increase* and *furthermore, their personal time will suffer.* The sentence contains one dependent clause [*If managers do not develop time management techniques*].)

dependent clause   *independent clause*
After he recovered from his heart attack, he continued his same

independent clause
stressful routine; moreover, he failed to exercise.

(The sentence contains two independent clauses—*he continued his same stressful routine* and *moreover, he failed to exercise.* The sentence contains one dependent clause [*After he recovered from his heart attack*].)

CHECKUP 15-1

Directions: *Use the following codes to identify the sentences listed below:* ***S*** *(simple sentence),* ***D*** *(compound sentence),* ***X*** *(complex sentence),* ***C*** *(compound-complex sentence). Underline each independent clause once and each dependent clause twice.*

1. The supervisor was a patient teacher, and Angie felt very comfortable during her initial training.   D

2. While many workers experience stress in their lives, baby boomers feel the pressures especially at work.   X

3. A job loss causes a stressful situation.   S

4. Everyone is subject to burnout unless he or she recognizes the early symptoms.   X

5. Jane's daughter did not like her mother's hectic schedule, and she vowed to live her life differently.   D

6. When I became the department manager, I had to learn to delegate; otherwise, I would have become a frustrated workaholic.   C

**GO TO
CD-ROM**
CHECKUP 15-1

See Instructor Note 15-6 in IAE.

Go to PowerPoints 15-2a, 15-2b, and 15-2c.

See Instructor Note 15-7 in IAE.

SLIP-UP

Newspaper want ad: We will oil your sewing machine and adjust tension in your home for $1.00.
[Note: Now that's a bargain!]

See Instructor Note 15-8 in IAE.

Conjunctions join words, phrases, and clauses. Like prepositions, they show relationships. Conjunctions, however, do not have objects; prepositions do. All conjunctions are either *coordinating, correlative,* or *subordinating.* One function of the *conjunctive adverb* is that of a connector; therefore, it appears in this section.

Coordinating Conjunctions

A coordinating conjunction such as *and, or, but,* or *nor* joins words, phrases, or clauses that are equal in grammatical construction and importance.

Use *but* to express a contrasting idea. Use *and* to show an addition. Use *or* to indicate a choice. Use *nor* to make a second choice negative.

> **Telemarketers <u>and</u> others who work alone are potential stress victims.**
> (The conjunction *and* joins the noun *telemarketers* and the pronoun *others.* The conjunction shows an addition to the noun *telemarketers.*)

> **Owners of small businesses make <u>or</u> break their companies by their reactions to unexpected events.**
> (The conjunction *or* joins the verb *make* and the verb *break.* The conjunction indicates a choice between *make* or *break.*)

> **One employee sees the project as an exciting challenge, <u>but</u> another sees the project as an impossible task.**
> (The conjunction *but* joins two independent clauses. The conjunction indicates a contrasting idea.)

> **Jon and Kara did not view the conflict as a threat to their working relationship, <u>nor</u> did they discuss the issue.**
> (The conjunction *nor* joins the two independent clauses. The conjunction *nor* makes the second choice negative.)

Insert a comma before a coordinating conjunction that separates two independent clauses.

> **Burnout does not necessarily come from hard work, <u>but</u> it may result from a lack of enjoyment of the work.**
> (This compound sentence has two independent clauses. A comma is necessary before the coordinating conjunction *but.*)

> **People prefer to work with mature individuals, <u>and</u> one indication of maturity is self-control.**
> (This compound sentence has two complete clauses. A comma is necessary before the coordinating conjunction *and.*)

Do not use a comma before a coordinating conjunction that links two words or two phrases. Do not use a comma before a conjunction if the material following the conjunction is not a complete sentence.

Sometimes my personal calendar <u>and</u> daily planner make me depressed.

(No comma is necessary before the coordinating conjunction *and* that links two words—*calendar* and *planner*.)

Her job is to analyze office stress patterns <u>and</u> to conduct seminars on stress management.

(No comma is necessary before the coordinating conjunction *and* that links two infinitive phrases.)

Sherry did not enjoy new assignments <u>but</u> preferred her regular routine of work.

(No comma is necessary before the coordinating conjunction *but*. The phrase *but preferred her regular routine of work* is not a complete sentence.)

Gordy always praises his employees in public <u>but</u> reprimands them in private.

(No comma is necessary before the coordinating conjunction *but*. The phrase *but reprimands them in private* is not a complete sentence.)

Use commas to separate three or more words, phrases, or clauses in a series. Do not place a comma after the last item in a series. Include a comma before the coordinating conjunction.

Much of a manager's stress comes from the board of directors, shareholders, employees, or the media.

(This is a series of four items. Each item must be separated from the other with a comma. A comma is necessary before the coordinating conjunction *or*.)

The arguments, accusations, and inaccurate information created a stressful situation.

(This is a series of three items. Each item must be separated from the others with a comma. A comma is necessary before the coordinating conjunction *and*. Do not use a comma after the last item, *inaccurate information*.)

Separate all items in a series with a comma. Be sure to place a comma before the coordinating conjunction.

CHECKUP 15-2

Directions: *Underline the coordinating conjunctions. Use the proofreaders' mark ⋀ to insert a comma where it is appropriate.*

1. Meetings, paperwork⋀ <u>and</u> downsizing create the most stress for managers.

2. My manager delegates vendor <u>and</u> customer inquiries to Holly <u>or</u> me.

3. Sooner <u>or</u> later, you will find yourself in a stressful situation.

4. Kay always felt apprehensive about a new assignment <u>but</u> tried to cover her fears with a display of enthusiasm⋀optimism⋀<u>and</u> calmness.

5. Signs of burnout are chronic fatigue <u>and</u> disinterest in things you once enjoyed.

6. A project may not be done your way⋀<u>but</u> you must learn to delegate.

GO TO CD-ROM
CHECKUP 15-2

Correlative Conjunctions

Go to PowerPoint 15-3.

See Instructor Notes 15-9 and 15-10 in IAE.

Correlative conjunctions join words, phrases, and sentences of equal importance. Correlative conjunctions appear in pairs, and both parts receive the same attention. The common pairs used as correlative conjunctions are as follows:

both/and   neither/nor

either/or   not only/but also

whether/or

Use correlative conjunctions to join words, phrases, and clauses that are equal in construction and importance. Place the paired conjunctions as near as possible to the words they connect.

See Instructor Note 15-11 in IAE.

Neither he nor she causes your reactions; you do.
(The paired conjunctions *neither* and *nor* are of equal importance and work together. They appear next to the words they connect [*he*] and [*she*].)

A company focuses on stress not only because of a concern for its employees' health but also because of the effects of employee stress on its profit.
(The paired conjunctions *not only* and *but also* work together and appear next to the phrases they connect.)

Whether personal problems or work difficulties cause you stress, recognize the early burnout signs.
(The paired conjunctions *whether* and *or* are of equal importance and work together. They appear next to the words they connect [*personal problems*] and [*work difficulties*].)

CHECKUP 15-3

Directions: *Underline each conjunction. In the space provided, identify the conjunctions as coordinating (**Coord**) or correlative (**Corr**).*

1. Stress management therapy sessions often include nutrition suggestions and breathing exercises. — Coord

2. Either walking or exercising helps relieve tension and stress. — Corr, Coord

3. Kelly's aggressive behavior caused problems not only with her coworkers but also with the customers. — Corr

4. To decrease the amount of time spent reading communications, employees were asked to streamline both e-mail and voice mail messages. — Corr

5. Learning to set priorities or analyzing use of time can reduce the pressure that leads to stress. — Coord

6. My new venture is hard work, but it gives me a sense of satisfaction and pride. — Coord, Coord

**GO TO
CD-ROM**
CHECKUP 15-3

Subordinating Conjunctions

Another way to join expressions is with a subordinating conjunction. A subordinating conjunction introduces a dependent clause and links it to an independent clause. A dependent clause does not make sense by itself; it depends on the independent clause for meaning.

Go to PowerPoints 15-4a and 15-4b.

See Instructor Note 15-12 in IAE.

Refer to Chapter 13 for an introduction to subordinating conjunctions.

Following are some subordinating conjunctions grouped according to their meanings in sentences. Several appear in more than one column.

Time	Reason	Place
after	as	where
as long as	because	wherever
as soon as	in order that	
before	inasmuch as	
since	for	**Manner**
until	since	as
when	so that	as if
whenever	whereas	as though
while		

Condition	Concession	Comparison
as if	although	as much as
except	even though	than
if	though	
otherwise		
unless		

Use a subordinating conjunction to introduce a dependent clause. Place a comma after a dependent clause that begins a sentence. Generally, do not use a comma before a dependent clause that appears at the end of a sentence.

See Instructor Note 15-13 in IAE.

Although I lost money, I handled the stress of the cycles in the real estate market very well.

(*Although I lost money* is a dependent clause that cannot stand alone. The dependent clause appears at the beginning of the sentence and introduces an independent clause [*I handled the stress of the cycles in the real estate market very well*]. A comma is necessary after the dependent clause.)

When you think someone is overstressed, show your concern and understanding.

(*When you think someone is overstressed* is a dependent clause that indicates time and introduces an independent clause [*show your concern and understanding*]. The dependent clause cannot stand alone. A comma is necessary after the dependent clause.)

Too many of us become ill before we decide to change our habits.

(*Before we decide to change our habits* is a dependent clause and indicates time. The dependent clause cannot stand alone. The dependent clause appears at the end of the complete sentence and does not require a comma before it.)

See Instructor Note
15-14 in IAE.

Avoid the expression
"can't help but."

Do This	**Do Not Do This**
I can't help <u>worrying</u> that my job will be eliminated after the merger.	I can't help but <u>worry</u> that my job will be eliminated after the merger.

Avoid the expression
"but what."

Do This	**Do Not Do This**
I think that <u>perhaps</u> I should discuss this move with my family.	I don't know but what I should discuss this move with my family.

CHECKUP 15-4

**GO TO
CD-ROM
CHECKUP 15-4**

Directions: In each of the following sentences, underline the dependent clause. Circle the subordinating conjunction.

1. (Since) Taylor was unhappy with her hectic 55-hour workweek, she opened her own business.

2. Most employees should know (where) they stand.

3. Flextime makes it easier for employees to be home (when) their children get out of school.

4. (As) recent statistics indicate, the need to manage time is more urgent than ever.

5. Some companies don't lay off workers (because) they value their employees' loyalty and trust.

6. (If) these suggestions help you cope, let me know.

Go to PowerPoint 15-5.

See Instructor Note 15-15 in IAE.

Conjunctive Adverbs

A conjunctive adverb shows a relationship between two independent clauses of equal weight. The words are adverbs, but they also function as connectors.

Some common conjunctive adverbs are as follows:

consequently	nevertheless
furthermore	otherwise
hence	similarly
however	still
indeed	therefore
instead	thus
likewise	yet
moreover	

Use a semicolon before a conjunctive adverb when it joins two independent clauses. Use a comma after a conjunctive adverb of two or more syllables.

See Instructor Note 15-16 in IAE.

Most businesses take three to six months to recover from a major disaster; however, some businesses never recover their losses.
(*However* is a conjunctive adverb that connects the two independent clauses. In this sentence, a semicolon precedes the conjunctive adverb *however,* and a comma follows it.)

Our speaker suggested that we should not avoid stress; instead, we should let it work for us.
(In this sentence, the word *instead* functions as a conjunctive adverb that connects the two independent clauses. A semicolon precedes the conjunctive adverb *instead,* and a comma follows it.)

A supervisor's words are powerful; therefore, they can cause an employee some anxious moments.
(*Therefore* is a conjunctive adverb that connects the two independent clauses. A semicolon precedes the conjunctive adverb *therefore,* and a comma follows it.)

Punctuation
ALERT!

Use a semicolon before a conjunctive adverb when it joins two independent clauses. Use a comma after a conjunctive adverb of two or more syllables.

CHECKUP 15-5

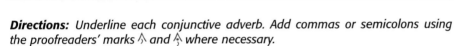

Directions: *Underline each conjunctive adverb. Add commas or semicolons using the proofreaders' marks ⋀ and ⋀̣ where necessary.*

1. Most businesses will not have to deal with serious disasters nevertheless managers need plans that will keep their firms operating during emergencies.

2. Avoid negative situations by associating with workers who provide stimulating conversation similarly refrain from joining the gossip enthusiasts.

3. My supervisor always comments on our work furthermore she knows how to make the work environment pleasant.

4. Jack's intention was to relieve the tense moment however his words did just the opposite.

5. Travel can be a major source of stress at any time moveover it is especially traumatic during the holidays.

6. I felt isolated and stressed working at home consequently I requested a transfer to a local branch office.

GO TO
CD-ROM
CHECKUP 15-5

CHECKUP 15-6

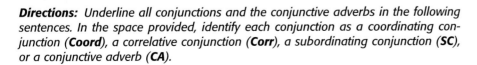

Directions: *Underline all conjunctions and the conjunctive adverbs in the following sentences. In the space provided, identify each conjunction as a coordinating conjunction (**Coord**), a correlative conjunction (**Corr**), a subordinating conjunction (**SC**), or a conjunctive adverb (**CA**).*

1. In my opinion, the mark of a great CEO is how he or she handles stress. _____Coord_____

2. Workers are beginning to take steps to make their lives simpler and less stressful; however, these are not easy tasks. _____Coord, CA_____

3. Whether a hurricane or a terrorist attack can immobilize our firm depends on our emergency action plan. _____Corr_____

4. Employees who are mentally and physically drained are not productive workers. _____Coord_____

5. If you find Monday mornings especially stressful, you have plenty of company. _____SC_____

6. Satisfied workers and productivity seem to correlate; however, some studies show no strong connection between satisfaction and performance. _____Coord, CA, Coord_____

GO TO CD-ROM
CHECKUP 15-6

CHECKUP 15-7

Directions: Read the Secondary Learning paragraphs 2 and 3 found at the beginning of the chapter. Then list the conjunctions and conjunctive adverbs that you find in those paragraphs in the space provided. All types of conjunctions may not appear in the paragraphs.

Coordinating Conjunctions	Correlative Conjunctions
and	not only/but also
but	
or	
and	
or	
or	

Subordinating Conjunctions	Conjunctive Adverbs
if	
while	

GO TO CD-ROM
CHECKUP 15-7

PARALLELISM

Parallelism is the linking together of similar grammatical parts in a sentence. To have parallel sentence structure, similar constructions need to be connected, such as nouns to other nouns, verbs to other verbs, or clauses to other clauses. Use coordinating conjunctions or correlative conjunctions to join parallel parts of a sentence.

Go to PowerPoint 15-6.

See Instructor Note 15-17 in IAE.

Correct:
To relieve work stress, Sylvia exercises daily, gets physical checkups yearly, and plays tennis several times a week.
(The three present tense verbs [*exercises, gets, plays*] are parallel in construction.)

Incorrect:

To relieve work stress, Sylvia exercises daily, gets physical checkups yearly, and is playing tennis several times a week.

(The phrase *is playing tennis several times a week* is not parallel to the verbs *exercises* and *gets*.)

Correct:

Having a home-based business eliminates rush-hour traffic <u>hassles</u> and department <u>meetings</u>.

(The two nouns [*hassles* and *meetings*] are parallel.)

Incorrect:

Having a home-based business eliminates rush-hour traffic hassles and going to department meetings.

(The phrase *going to department meetings* is not parallel to the noun *hassles*.)

Correct:

Jason is <u>overworked</u>, <u>irritable</u>, and <u>demanding</u>.

(The three adjectives are parallel in construction.)

Incorrect:

Jason is overworked, irritable, and demands too much from his staff.

(The phrase *demands too much from his staff* is not parallel to the adjectives *overworked* and *irritable*.)

Stress took its toll <u>both</u> on her health <u>and</u> on her family.

(The two phrases [*on her health* and *on her family*] connected by correlative conjunctions are parallel in construction.)

She thought <u>that</u> the coping strategies were working and <u>that</u> the department was decreasing its turnover rate.

(If necessary, repeat an introductory word. The word *that* introduces the two dependent clauses and makes the parallel construction clear.)

CHECKUP 15-8

Directions: *The following sentences are not parallel in construction. In the space provided, write the sentence correctly.*

1. Workers derive satisfaction from feeling valued and to be in control of their work.

   Workers derive satisfaction from feeling valued and <u>being</u> in control of their work.

2. My interests away from the office include reading, hiking, and I like to swim.

   My interests away from the office include reading, hiking, and <u>swimming</u>.

3. Workers with high-stress levels respond not only in ways that may be harmful to the company but also to themselves.

   Workers with high-stress levels respond in ways that may be harmful <u>not only</u> to the company but also to themselves.

4. After starting his own company, Andy had less stress, more flexible schedules, and spent more time with his family.

   <u>After starting his own company, Andy had less stress, more flexible schedules, and more time to spend with his family.</u>

5. Policies for using e-mail and how to reduce paperwork can relieve the tension from information overload.

   <u>Policies for using e-mail and hints (suggestions) for reducing paperwork can relieve the tension from information overload.</u>

   <u>Policies for using e-mail and for reducing paperwork can relieve the tension from information overload.</u>

6. The stress management counselor either advised spending less time at the office or finding another job.

   <u>The stress management counselor advised either spending less time at the office or finding another job.</u>

**GO TO
CD-ROM**
CHECKUP 15-8

CAUTIONS IN USING CONJUNCTIONS

Conjunctions do not have objects.

A number of words may be used as conjunctions and as prepositions; therefore, it is important to understand the functions of the conjunction. Several uses of confusing conjunctions also require clarification and special attention.

Conjunctions and Prepositions

Determine the appropriate function of a word in a sentence. Some words may be both prepositions and conjunctions; for example, _before, after, until, for, than,_ and _since._ Use a conjunction to connect clauses. Use a preposition when an object is expressed or understood; conjunctions do not have objects.

She will not accept the promotion <u>until</u> she discusses it with her family.
(In this sentence, _until_ is a conjunction. _Until_ connects the clause, _she discusses it with her family_ with the clause _She will not accept the promotion._

She will not accept the promotion <u>until</u> next month.
(In this sentence, _until_ is a preposition and takes the object _month._ No verb follows the preposition.)

Tom always leaves the office <u>after</u> I do.
(_After_ is a conjunction that connects the clause _I do_ with the clause _Tom always leaves the office._ Both clauses have a subject and a predicate.)

Tom always leaves the office <u>after</u> 5 p.m.
(_After_ is a preposition. _After_ takes the object _5 p.m._)

Try To, Be Sure To, Go To

Do not use expressions such as *try and, go and,* and *be sure and* when the infinitive form is needed. Use *try to, go to,* and *be sure to.*

> **I'd like some time alone to <u>try to determine</u> why I'm feeling so stressed.**
>
> (Use *try to,* not *try and.*)
>
> **<u>Be sure to inform</u> your supervisor if you need some time off because of personal problems.**
>
> (Use *be sure to,* not *be sure and.*)

As, As If, As Though, Like

Use the conjunctions *as, as if,* or *as though* to introduce a subordinate clause. The clause will have a verb in it. Use the preposition *like* to introduce a prepositional phrase. The prepositional phrase will not contain a verb.

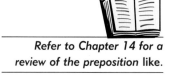

Refer to Chapter 14 for a review of the preposition like.

> **Megan acts <u>as if</u> she does not want help with the project.**
>
> (*As if* is a subordinating conjunction that introduces the clause *she does not want help with the project.* Note that the verb is *does want.*)
>
> **Managers make mistakes in their relationships with people <u>like</u> anyone else.**
>
> (*Like* is a preposition that takes the object *anyone else.* Note that there is no verb expressed after *like.*)

As . . . As, So . . . As, Equally As

Use *as . . . as* in positive comparisons. Use *so . . . as* in negative compari-sons. Do not use *equally as,* which is a redundant phrase.

See Instructor Note 15-18 in IAE.

> **My coping strategies are <u>as effective as</u> yours.**
>
> (*As effective* as indicates a positive comparison. Do not use the phrase *equally as effective as.*)
>
> **My coping strategies are <u>not so effective as</u> yours.**
>
> (*Not so effective as* indicates a negative comparison.)

Where, That

Do not use the conjunction *where* instead of *that* to introduce a clause that includes a reference to a location.

> **I read in the school newspaper <u>that</u> a stress management expert would be speaking at the next PTA meeting.**
>
> (Do not use *I read in the school newspaper where.*)

CHECKUP 15-9

Directions: Check the underlined word(s) for correct usage. If the word is correct, write **Yes** in the space provided. If it is not correct, write the word correctly.

**GO TO
CD-ROM**
CHECKUP 15-9

1. Our new manager is not <u>as</u> conscientious as her predecessor.   so

2. Some companies provide workers with tickets to functions <u>as</u> the symphony or sport events.   like

3. Try <u>and</u> exercise before leaving for work each morning.   to

4. He always acts <u>as if</u> he enjoys his job.   Yes

5. Her supervisor suggested that she go <u>and</u> see a depression therapy counselor.   to

6. I saw in *Time* magazine <u>where</u> research is being done on the effects of stress on heart disease.   that

DIAGRAMMING SENTENCES

You have already learned to diagram sentences with compound verbs, subjects, and objects.

Matt and Al organized a stress reduction seminar.

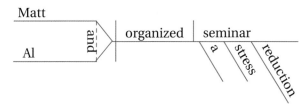

Matt developed and presented a stress reduction seminar.

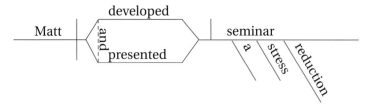

Matt presents stress reduction seminars and workshops.

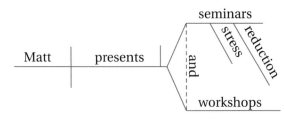

In addition to reviewing the diagramming of a conjunction used with nouns, verbs, and objects, you will learn to diagram sentences with compound adjectives and adverbs. Use a dotted line to connect two adjectives or two adverbs.

A heavy but steady workload challenges some workers.

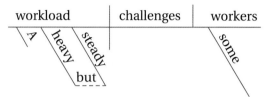

He implemented the changes quickly and easily.

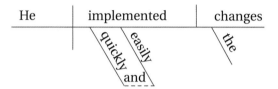

CHECKUP 15-10

Directions: *In the space provided below, diagram the following sentences. All words may be diagrammed.*

See Instructor Note 15-19 in IAE.

1. Most healthy and successful people are Type A and Type B personalities.

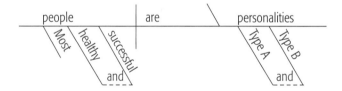

2. Work pressures and personal problems often cause stress-related illnesses.

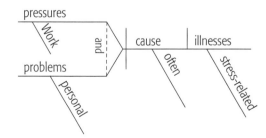

3. Pam eats carbohydrates in times of stress or work anxiety.

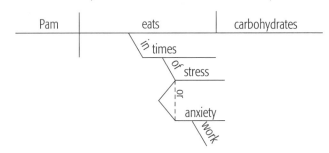

4. People with low self-esteem are comfortable with familiar and undemanding tasks.

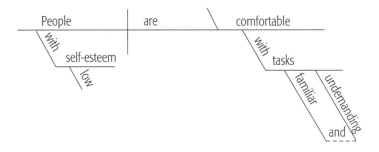

5. She has an enthusiastic but realistic work attitude.

GO TO
CD-ROM
CHECKUP 15-10

PRACTICE

NAME _____

PRACTICE 1A

A. Directions: *Select the correct word or words, and write them in the space provided.*

1. She neither asked for help (*or, nor*) confided in her coworkers.

   1. _____nor_____

2. You don't always get to choose what happens to you, (*but, and*) you can choose how to handle each situation.

   2. _____but_____

3. When she discovered her management style was (*like, as*) her supervisor's, she decided to change it.

   3. _____like_____

4. Should I sell the business or (*try and, try to*) restructure the way I run it?

   4. _____try to_____

5. Diane neither participates in office functions (*nor, or*) socializes with her coworkers.

   5. _____nor_____

6. I heard on the news (*where, that*) our division of Northern States Power may be moved.

   6. _____that_____

7. (*As, Like*) I indicated in my application letter, I am interested in a challenging job.

   7. _____As_____

8. (*Be sure and, Be sure to*) let me know when you plan to attend the stress workshop.

   8. _____Be sure to_____

9. Brett apologized to Kathy (*as, like*) I suggested.

   9. _____as_____

10. The stress I feel at work is not (*as, so*) great as the stress I deal with at home.

    10. _____so_____

B. Directions: *In the space provided, identify the type of conjunction represented by the underlined word. Use the following codes:* **Coord** *(coordinating conjunction),* **Corr** *(correlative conjunction),* **SC** *(subordinating conjunction),* **CA** *(conjunctive adverb). If the underlined word is* not *a conjunction, write* **No.**

1. Some stress keeps us alert, <u>but</u> too much can be disastrous.

   1. _____Coord_____

2. Family expectations sometimes cause people to work at jobs that they really don't <u>like</u>.

   2. _____No_____

3. These managers will not survive this high-stress environment <u>unless</u> they change their attitudes about time.

   3. _____SC_____

4. Indications of burnout include a loss of interest <u>not only</u> in activities outside the business <u>but also</u> in family events.

   4. _____Corr_____

5. Job security is not a sure thing for today's workers; <u>nevertheless</u>, those who can adjust to the insecurity move ahead.

   5. _____CA_____

**GO TO
CD-ROM
PRACTICE 1
EXERCISES**

Conjunctions

437

PRACTICE

PRACTICE 2A

Directions: *Underline the conjunctions and the conjunctive adverbs in the following sentences. Insert any missing commas or semicolons by using the proofreaders' marks ⋏ or ⋏.*

1. Flextime, job sharing <u>and</u> work-at-home arrangements are ways to help employees balance work <u>and</u> other parts of their lives.

2. Self-esteem is the way you think <u>and</u> feel about yourself, but it is not the way someone else thinks <u>or</u> feels about you.

3. She is unreceptive to emotional appeals, <u>however,</u> she will listen to facts <u>and</u> reason.

4. Caring for your pet will calm you <u>and</u> prevent the buildup of stress.

5. Low self-esteem is the cause of hostility <u>and</u> cynicism, <u>furthermore,</u> these two traits are factors in Type A-related heart disease.

6. <u>After</u> you have taken a vacation, ease into your old routine <u>and</u> activities slowly.

7. <u>Unless</u> home-based entrepreneurs make an effort to be around people, they can feel isolated <u>and</u> stressed.

8. <u>Not only</u> economic pressures <u>but also</u> time pressures create stress for real estate agents.

9. <u>Even though</u> I will have to work all weekend, I am going to complete the report.

10. <u>Neither</u> the working conditions <u>nor</u> the tasks are enjoyable.

Directions: *In the space provided, correct the following sentences. Check for errors in word usage, punctuation, and appropriate sentence structure. If the sentence is correct, write Yes.*

1. Ways to reduce stress include Yoga, meditation and exercising.

   <u>Ways to reduce stress include yoga, meditation, and exercise.</u>

2. After working at such a fast pace for years I began to experience stress insomnia and I was constantly tired.

   <u>After working at such a fast pace for years, I began to experience stress,</u>

   <u>insomnia, and constant fatigue.</u>

3. Whether an early riser or a night owl or not, maintain your high energy level by eating properly.

   <u>Whether an early riser or a night owl, maintain your high energy level by</u>

   <u>eating properly.</u>

4. When people know that they are valued they are more secure and produce more.

   <u>When people know that they are valued, they are more secure and productive.</u>

GO TO
CD-ROM
PRACTICE 2
EXERCISES

5. Some workers said that bad management was the cause of their stress however others blamed their stress on the difficulties in balancing their professional and personal lives.

Some workers said that bad management was the cause of their stress;

however, others blamed their stress on the difficulties in balancing their

professional and personal lives.

PRACTICE 3A

PROOFREADING

Directions: Proofread and compare the two sentences in each group. If they are the same, write Yes in the space provided. If they are not the same, write No. Use the first sentence as the correct copy. If you find errors in the second sentence, underline them.

1. When the International Survey Research Corporation completed a recent study, it found that 44 percent of the employees felt that their workloads were excessive.

   As the International Survey Research Corporation completed a recent study, it found that 45 percent of the employees felt that their workloads were excessive.

   1. __No__

2. Dr. Stephen Rechtschaffen is a pioneer in the wellness movement and the author of the book *Time Shifting*.

   Dr. Stephen Rechtschaffen is a pioneer in the wellness movement, and the the author of the book *Time Shifting*.

   2. __No__

3. According to a recent study, a majority of the 185,000 people interviewed experienced some feelings of depression on the first business day of the month.

   According to a recent study, a majority of the 185,000 people interviewed experienced some feelings of depression on the first business day of the month.

   3. __Yes__

4. Perhaps I could manage my stress more effectively if I read *The Overwhelmed Person's Guide to Time Management* by Ronni Eisenberg.

   Perhaps I could manage my stress more effectively as I read *The Overwhelmed Person's Guide to Time Management* by Ronnie Eisenberg.

   4. __No__

5. Rob Krakovitz, author of *High Energy*, says that the sound of an alarm clock "starts your day in distress by blaring you awake and putting your system into a panic."

   Rob Krakovitz, author of *High Energy*, says that the sound of a alarm clock "starts your day in distress by blaring you awake or putting your system in a panic."

   5. __No__

PRACTICE

See Instructor Notes 15-20
and 15-21 in IAE.

Proofreading Exercise

Directions: The draft that follows requires corrections. Key the list of coping strategies and make the corrections that are indicated by the proofreaders' marks. If you are not certain about the use of a proofreaders' mark, use your reference manual or the proofreaders' marks listed on the inside back cover of this textbook.

COPEING STRATEGIES

1. Exercise

   Remember that the exercise needs to be consistent but it does not have to be strenuous.

2. Visualization

   Think of positive solutions or of ways that successful people would solve the problem.

3. Diet

   Eat a low fat breakfast and watch your wt.

4. Meditation and yoga

   Try to get in touch with your inner self. *stet*

5. Asertiveness

   Learn to say "No" some times.

6. Luaghter

   learn to laugh at yourself.

7. Outside activities

   Learn a new skill and task, volunteer at an interesting location, or become involved with community activities.

8. Friendships

   Confide in a trusted friend away from the office.

**GO TO
CD-ROM
PRACTICE 3
EXERCISES**

PRACTICE 4A

WRITING

Answers will vary.

Directions: Describe the most stressful time you have had at work, school, and/or home during the past month.

I returned to school after ten years of staying at home with my children. I did not realize how much my life would change. I was worried about getting my homework done and still maintaining an orderly household. My children were used to elaborate dinner meals, which I no longer had the time to prepare. I started to leave the laundry for the weekends instead of doing it every day. During the first week, I was not able to sleep well, and I felt that my life was spinning out of control.

**GO TO
CD-ROM
PRACTICE 4
EXERCISES**

NAME _____

ONLINE *EXERCISES*

Numerous health-related sites are available on the Internet. People who have conquered illnesses, controlled weight, or discovered useful meditation and relaxation techniques are willing to share their successes with others. Some sites are scientific and research-based while others are personal stories and nonfactual accounts.

Objective: *To visit an online clinic.*

1. With your Internet browser on screen, key:

   http://www.mayohealth.org in the location text box.

   Press the **Enter** key on your keyboard.

2. You will be at the Mayo Clinic health education site.

3. Scroll down the Web page until you see a health-related item that is of interest to you. Click on that item and read the information.

4. This site also has search options. Enter a word such as fitness, diet, or nutrition in the search box and click on **Search.**

See Instructor Note 15-22 in IAE.

Use exact punctuation when keying an Internet address.

NAME _____

PRACTICE 1B

A. Directions: *Choose the correct word or words, and write them in the space provided.*

1. Loreen lost her temper (*because, as*) her manager called her during the weekend.

2. If you are frustrated with someone, write your grievances in a letter (*and, but*) don't mail the letter.

3. Neither excess anger (*or, nor*) stress is good for one's mental health.

4. (*As, When*) she realized she was trying to be perfect all the time, she was better able to handle her stress.

5. I am going to (*try and, try to*) arrive at work early tomorrow.

1. because _____
2. but _____
3. nor _____
4. When _____
5. try to _____

B. Directions: *In the space provided, identify the type of conjunction represented by the underlined word. Use the following codes:* **Coord** *(coordinating conjunction),* **Corr** *(correlative conjunction),* **SC** *(subordinating conjunction),* **CA** *(conjunctive adverb). If the underlined word is* not *a conjunction, write* **No.**

1. Anger can ruin relationships <u>or</u> destroy careers.

2. <u>If</u> you are feeling blue, wear a particularly comfortable shirt or bright scarf to brighten your spirits.

3. One of the best cures <u>for</u> frustration is exercise.

4. <u>Whenever</u> you exercise outdoors, carry personal identification.

5. Stretching before a workout increases aerobic capacity; <u>therefore</u>, you should stretch 5 to 7 minutes before exercising.

6. Men with higher fitness levels live longer <u>even though</u> they may be overweight.

7. Tap water contains <u>not only</u> calcium and magnesium <u>but also</u> other trace elements that protect the heart.

8. <u>Because</u> anger is cumulative, it can break down your immune system.

9. If you refuse to compromise <u>or</u> to modify your ideas, you are destined to fail at your job.

10. A fad diet requires you to eat huge quantities of only one food <u>or</u> type of food, or it suggests that you eat a very limited selection of foods at a specific time of the day.

1. Coord _____
2. SC _____
3. No _____
4. SC _____
5. CA _____
6. SC _____
7. Corr _____
8. SC _____
9. Coord _____
10. Coord _____

PRACTICE 2B

A. Directions: *Underline the conjunctions and the conjunctive adverbs in the following sentences. Insert any missing commas or semicolons by using the proofreaders' marks ⋀ or ⩘.*

1. When Ken travels for business⋀he finds that he suffers from separation stress⋀encounters language differences⋀and experiences travel-related sleep disorders.

2. Women who report high levels of job-related stress are often depressed⋀anxious⋀and socially isolated.

3. A large number of people are using alternative medicines such as acupuncture⋀massage therapy⋀or megavitamins⋀however⋀these alternatives could worsen some medical problems.

4. Since Lou's heart attack⋀he avoids stressful situations.

NAME _____

5. If you have a low degree of control over your job, you have nearly twice the risk of developing heart disease.

6. The wellness consultant suggested that we either develop a stress prevention program or offer seminars in coping strategies.

7. While many factors determine a person's tendency to exercise, recent research indicates that genetic factors may play a role.

8. Cigarette smoking, excessive body fat, and lack of exercise may be the predominate causes of stroke in people under the age of 75.

9. Stress is caused not only by work problems but also by home pressures.

10. Jenny enjoys her work but finds the pace hectic at times.

B. Directions: *In the space provided, correct the following sentences. Check for errors in word usage, punctuation, and appropriate sentence structure. If the sentence is correct, write* **Yes.**

1. Rachel stopped eating candy bars and cola.

   Rachel stopped eating candy bars and drinking cola. _____

2. Reducing your stress load and exercise help you sleep better at night.

   Reducing your stress load and exercising help you sleep better at night. _____

3. Confidence is a valuable ally in combating stress and it helps you feel that you will be successful.

   Confidence is a valuable ally in combating stress, and it helps you feel that you will be successful. _____

4. Ruth was experiencing not only difficult times at work but also increased demands at home.

   Yes _____

5. Healthful lifestyle habits and to have proper nutrition help build your energy reserves.

   Healthful lifestyle habits and proper nutrition help build your energy reserves. _____

PRACTICE 3B

PROOFREADING

Directions: *Proofread and compare the two sentences in each group. If they are the same, write* **Yes** *in the space provided. If they are not the same, write* **No.** *Use the first sentence as the correct copy. If you find errors in the second sentence, underline them; insert any omitted words or marks of punctuation.*

1. Dr. Randal Beaton, research associate professor at the University of Washington School of Nursing, says, "People who work in offices are stressed because their jobs offer little in the way of creativity, control or satisfaction."

   Dr. Randle Beaton, research associate professor at the University of Washington School of Medicine, says, "People who work in offices are stressed because their jobs offer little in the way of creativity, control or satisfaction."

   1. **No** _____

2. The U.S. Centers for Disease Control (CDC) designed a federal campaign to encourage more Americans to participate in regular exercise programs, and information on this campaign can be found at http://www.cdc.gov/nccdphp/dnpa/readyset.

   The U.S. Center for Disease Control (CDC) designed a Federal campaign to encourage more Americans to participate in regular exercize programs, and information on this campagn can be found at http://www.cdc.gov/nccdphp/dnpa/readyset.

   2. **No** _____

END-OF-CHAPTER WORKSHEETS

3. A new study concludes that working women with one or more children tend to have higher levels of the stress hormone cortisol than working women with no children; consequently, working women with children have an increased risk of cardiovascular disease.

3. No

A new study concludes that working women with one or more children tend to have higher levels of the stress hormone cortisle than working women with no children,consequently,working women with children have an increased risk of cardiovasculor disease.

4. Researchers at the University of California–Davis, School of Medicine, report that working more than 25 hours a week in the first trimester of pregnancy is associated with a three-fold increase in the risk of miscarriage compared with working fewer hours.

4. Yes

Researchers at the University of California–Davis, School of Medicine, report that working more than 25 hours a week in the first trimester of pregnancy is associated with a three-fold increase in the risk of miscarriage compared with working fewer hours.

Proofreading Exercise

When people are angry, they are at higher risk for illness and depression. Angry people see them-selves as victims and have not learned to express anger in a mature, reasonable way.

Directions: *The draft that follows requires corrections. Key the anger coping strategies and make the corrections that are indicated by the proof-readers' marks. If you are not certain about the use of a proofreaders' mark, use your reference manual or the proofreaders' marks listed on the inside back cover of this textbook.*

Managing Anger

1. Be aware of situations that make you angry at work, at home, or in your car.

2. Put yourself in the other person's place, and try to see his or her pt. of view.

3. Resist the urge to get into Name-calling.

4. Speak quietly, and calmly to keep the situation from escalating.

5. Practice relaxation techniques by focusing on something pleasant.

6. Write out what is bothering you, but don't give the list to the other person.

7. Walk away if you can't get your emotions under control.

8. Don't take anger out on yourself by over eating or drinking.

PRACTICE 4B

WRITING

Directions: *Describe the person in your life who gives (or gave) you the most stress.*

Answers will vary.

I worked with a very demanding coworker. She gave me the impression that she thought she was smarter than I

was and insisted that I do things the way she did. I tried to be polite and get along with her; however, the more

pleasant I was, the more demanding she became. I couldn't sleep or eat and thought about quitting my job.

NAME _____

ONLINE *EXERCISES*

Objective: *To visit a health and fitness magazine Website.*

1. With your Internet browser on screen, key:

   http://www.vitality.com in the location text box.

   Press the **Enter** key on your keyboard.

2. You will be at the *Vitality* magazine Website.

3. Click on **Vitality on Demand.**

4. Click on **Keyword Search.**

5. In the Keyword box, enter a coping strategy. Examples include fitness, exercise, nutrition, diet, caffeine, sleep, or relaxation. Press **Enter.**

6. You will see a listing of articles on the coping strategy you selected. Click on an article of interest to you.

LOOKING BACK

Posttest

See Instructor Note 15-23 in IAE.

Directions: *In the space provided, write the letter of the correct answer.*

1. The sentence *Jan's job is very stressful, but she uses relaxation techniques to help her cope with her stress* is an example of a
   a. simple sentence.
   b. compound sentence.
   c. complex sentence.
   d. compound-complex sentence.

   1. ___b___

2. In the sentence *If you speak quietly and calmly, other people are likely to lower their voices,* the conjunction *and* is a
   a. coordinating conjunction.
   b. correlative conjunction.
   c. subordinating conjunction.
   d. conjunctive adverb.

   2. ___a___

3. Which sentence is written correctly?
   a. She was either late or I was early.
   b. Either she was late or I was early.
   c. She either was late or I was early.
   d. She was late or either I was early.

   3. ___b___

4. In the sentence *Although I arrive early at work, I still do not finish my work,* the conjunction *although* is a
   a. coordinating conjunction.
   b. correlative conjunction.
   c. subordinating conjunction.
   d. conjunctive adverb.

   4. ___c___

5. Which of the following is an example of a conjunctive adverb?
   a. not only/but also
   b. furthermore
   c. if
   d. but

   5. ___b___

6. Which sentence is punctuated correctly?
   a. Anger may break down your immune system and cause heart disease, ulcers and depression.
   b. Focus your thoughts on something pleasant during boring meetings, or a slow-moving checkout line.
   c. If you are a workaholic you should reduce the energy drain you are placing on your body.
   d. Overstressed people often complain about being tired, and they frequently make mistakes in their work.

   6. ___d___

7. Which sentence is written correctly?
   a. Karen is not as energetic as Carla is.
   b. I read where 10 percent of the American people inherited a low tolerance for stress.
   c. Try to eat a healthy breakfast each day.
   d. Neither Luis or Sam attended the stress management seminars.

   7. ___c___

8. Which sentence is written correctly?
   a. Alcohol is a depressant for most people, and excessive intake can lead to restless sleep.
   b. Some people exercise with equipment as a stationary bicycle or a rowing machine.
   c. Be sure and leave yourself time each day to relax.
   d. I can't help but think that I need to spend more time with my family.

   8. ___a___

PART 5

Reviewing Punctuation and Number Use

CHAPTER 16

The Period and the Comma

JOB SEARCH AND CAREER DEVELOPMENT

Most people dread a job search because they dislike the feeling of not being in control. While you cannot control the economy or the hiring policies of companies, you can control your own job search.

The majority of jobs, as many as 80 percent by most estimates, are filled by networking. Networking involves asking friends and relatives for job leads and using sources available through college placement offices.

A résumé, cover letter, and the interview are factors that enter into a hiring decision. The résumé must be well organized and error free; it must include concrete examples of achievements. The cover letter gives new information that is not included on the résumé, shows how well you know the company, and demonstrates your knowledge of the English language. The cover letter asks for the interview and makes it easy for the interviewer to contact you.

The interview is the final step in the employment process—and the most crucial. Most interviewers make a judgment within the first three to five minutes of an interview. The best way to prepare for an interview is to find out as much as possible about the company and the person interviewing you. Companies are looking for well-prepared candidates with positive attitudes who can show how they will fit into an organization.

OBJECTIVES

After you have studied this chapter and completed the exercises, you will be able to do the following:

1. Use periods correctly at the end of declarative and imperative sentences, courteous requests, and indirect questions.
2. Identify miscellaneous uses of the period.
3. Use commas correctly between items in a series and in compound sentences.
4. Use commas correctly with independent adjectives.
5. Use commas correctly to set off appositive and parenthetical expressions.
6. Use commas correctly with introductory expressions.
7. Use commas correctly with nonrestrictive clauses.
8. Identify miscellaneous uses of the comma.
9. Diagram sentences correctly.

TERMS TO REMEMBER

COVER LETTER

JOB SEARCH

JOB TARGETS

NETWORKING

RÉSUMÉ

LOOKING AHEAD

Pretest

Directions: *Use the proofreaders' mark ⊙ to insert periods where necessary. Use the proofreaders' mark ∧ to insert commas.*

1. Kaitlin wanted to know the questions that most interviewers asked during interviews⊙

2. My most recent supervisor was K⊙R⊙Stonefield, CPA∧of Baker∧Strong & Lester∧Wilmington∧DE 19804.

3. A healthy economy creates more jobs∧but qualified people are still scarce⊙

4. The interviewer expressed an interest in the types of training, seminars∧or workshops that I had attended.

5. Several temporary agencies in our area offer computerized∧self-paced training programs for their employees⊙

6. Lynn Davis∧a career transition specialist∧reminded us about the importance of learning new skills.

7. Before Ken hired a new employee∧he prepared a list of detailed job qualifications.

8. Firstar Bank encourages all its employees∧regardless of age∧to take advantage of training opportunities.

9. Don't forget to check the public library information∧which is readily available and easily accessed⊙

10. You remember when I began working at the Thompson store on December 1∧1990∧in the city of Marshfield∧Wisconsin∧don't you?

OVERVIEW

You have learned to place words in a logical and meaningful order, and you are familiar with the grammatical terms used in the process of putting a sentence together. You are now ready to take the next step, which involves using the proper marks of punctuation. Punctuation marks often determine the exact meaning of a sentence; therefore, they cannot be placed whenever you pause for a breath or at your individual whim. Imagine this entire page without a mark of punctuation. Of course, you would agree that no one would understand the material. The same concept applies to each sentence. Punctuation details are essential in making your words flow smoothly and in clarifying the intent of your writing.

Many of the rules in this chapter have already been identified in the Punctuation Alerts throughout the previous chapters. In this chapter, you will review these marks of punctuation and also learn several new rules.

THE PERIOD

The period is the most frequently used punctuation mark. The period usually appears at the end of a sentence, but it has several other uses within a sentence.

Declarative Sentences

Use a period at the end of a declarative sentence.

> **Our company is an equal-opportunity employer.**
> (The sentence states a fact; a period is necessary.)

Imperative Sentences

Use a period at the end of a sentence that indicates a command or a strong suggestion. Such a sentence is called an imperative sentence.

> **Make a positive point in your cover letter about the recent training that you have received.**
> (The sentence is a suggestion and requires a period. *You* is the understood subject.)

> **Do not be late for an interview.**
> (The sentence is a command and requires a period. *You* is the understood subject.)

Courteous Requests

Use a period at the end of a sentence that makes a courteous request.

> **Will you please show me how to place my résumé on the Internet.**
> (The type of response requested is one of action [*show me*], not words.)

See Instructor Notes 16-1 and 16-2 in IAE.

Go to Transparencies/PowerPoints 16-1a and 16-1b.

See Instructor Note 16-3 in IAE.

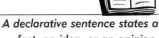

A declarative sentence states a fact, an idea, or an opinion.

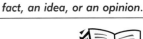

Refer to Chapter 3 for a review of the various sentence types.

See Instructor Note 16-4 in IAE.

A courteous request requires an action rather than an answer in words.

Indirect Questions

Use a period after an indirect question.

Go to Transparency/PowerPoint 16-2.

An indirect question does not require an answer.

I wonder how many applications have been submitted for the medical records technician position.

(This indirect question requires no specific answer. A period is necessary at the end of the sentence.)

Decimal Points

Use a period to separate dollars and cents. Do not place a period after a dollar amount if there are no cents involved. Use a period as a decimal point to express whole numbers and fractional amounts.

$3.99	$156.28	$11,928.32

(A decimal point is necessary between the dollar amount and the cents.)

$2	$900	$62,300

(No decimal point is necessary after a dollar amount without cents.)

0.005	0.05	2.5	37.8

(A period functions as a decimal point in fractional amounts.)

See Instructor Note 16-5 in IAE.

See Instructor Note 16-6 in IAE.

Refer to your reference manual for a list of abbreviated business expressions including measurements.

Abbreviated Words and Measurements

Use a period at the end of an abbreviated word. Do not use a period after a measurement that is abbreviated on most business or technical forms. Spell out measurements when they are used in general or nontechnical writing.

assn. = association	intl. = international
asst. = assistant	mfg. = manufacturing
bldg. = building	pd. = paid

(Periods are necessary after abbreviated words.)

ft = foot, feet	oz = ounce, ounces
gal = gallon, gallons	qt = quart, quarts
hr = hour, hours	yr = year, years

(No periods are necessary after abbreviations for measurements on invoices or other business forms.)

See Instructor Note 16-7 in IAE.

See Instructor Note 16-8 in IAE.

See Instructor Note 16-9 in IAE.

Go to PowerPoint 16-3.

Refer to the sections on abbreviations in your reference manual for additional examples of abbreviations with or without periods.

Small and Capital Letters

Use a period after each letter in abbreviations that consist of small letters. Do not use a period after each letter in most abbreviations that consist of all capital letters.

a.k.a. = also known as

c.o.d. = collect on delivery

f.o.b. = free on board (within sentences)

(Periods are necessary with abbreviations made up of small letters.)

CEO	=	chief executive officer
DNR	=	Department of Natural Resources (government)
FOB	=	free on board (on business forms)
HMO	=	health maintenance organization
PIN	=	personal identification number

Go to PowerPoints 16-4a and 16-4b.

Exceptions:

P.O.	=	post office
U.S.	=	United States
M.A.	=	Master of Arts
M.D.	=	Doctor of Medicine
B.C.	=	before Christ

(Use periods after each capital letter in abbreviations for certain academic degrees and other abbreviations.)

CHECKUP 16-1

Directions: _Use the proofreaders' mark ⊙ to insert periods where necessary. Use the proofreaders' mark ⌿ to delete unnecessary periods._

1. I was not sure whether the abbreviation for the word _association_ was _assoc_ or _assn._

2. I wonder how long it will take to find out if the position is mine.

3. I budgeted $200 for my job search activities.

4. Jamie said that I should call about the paralegal position A.S.A.P.

5. Will you please send rejection letters to these 30 job applicants.

6. The human resources manager indicated that there would be a 2.5 percent COLA after the second year of employment.

GO TO CD-ROM
CHECKUP 16-1

Personal Names and Corporate Names

Use a period after the initials or with abbreviations of most names. Do not use a period with a nickname. Use the same format that an individual uses in a signature or that a company uses on its letterhead as its official designation.

T. C. Robbins   **Thos. C. Robbins**   **Brown Bros.**
(A period is usually necessary after initials or with an abbreviation of a personal or company name.)

Tom Robbins   **Buzz Carey**
(A period is not necessary with a nickname.)

Harry S Truman   **AAA Travel Agency**
(Periods after initials are not necessary if the official signature or the name on the company letterhead does not include them.)

See Instructor Note 16-10 in IAE.

Titles, Academic Degrees, Professional Identification

See Instructor Note 16-11 in IAE.

Use a period after an abbreviation of a person's title.

| Mrs. | Ms. | Mr. | Dr. |

Dr. Peter Sandford applied for a position as a college curriculum director.

Use a period after each element in the abbreviation of an academic degree or professional identification.

| B.A. | Ph.D. | M.B.A. | M.D. |

(Periods are necessary after an abbreviated title.)

Helen Wing, M.D., spoke to our classes on Career Day.

(Periods are necessary after letters in professional designations.)

Anthony Doneli, M.B.A., explained ways to use a Web page for hiring employees.

(Periods are necessary after letters in academic degrees.)

Do This	Do Not Do This
Miss Reilley included a unit on finding a job in our keyboarding class.	Miss. Reilley included a unit on finding a job in our keyboarding class.

Do not use a period after Miss since it is not an abbreviation. Ms. is technically not an abbreviation, but it is used as one.

See Instructor Note 16-12 in IAE.

Seniority Designations

Use a period after an abbreviated seniority designation.

Jerome Madson Jr. is planning a career in tourism and hospitality.

(*Jr. is* a seniority designation and requires a period.)

James Redman III reviewed the top four recommendations of the interview committee.

(The seniority designation *III* does not require a period; it is not an abbreviation.)

See your reference manual for standard and ZIP Code abbreviations.

Geographic Locations

Use a period after an abbreviation of a country, state, or province unless the abbreviation appears in ZIP Code format.

Go to PowerPoint 16-5.

State or Province	ZIP Code Abbreviation	Standard Abbreviation
Alabama	AL	Ala.
New Jersey	NJ	N.J.
Ontario	ON	Ont.

(Periods are necessary with standard state and province abbreviations. Periods are not necessary after the abbreviations in ZIP Code format.)

Shortened Forms of Words

Do not use a period after a shortened word or a foreign word that is not an abbreviation.

See Instructor Notes 16-13 and 16-14 in IAE.

Go to PowerPoint 16-6.

info = information   rep = representative

specs = specifications   temp = temporary

(Periods are not necessary after shortened words that are not abbreviations.)

ad hoc   = for a particular purpose

in re *or* re = concerning

(Periods are not necessary with foreign words that are not abbreviations.)

Use shortened forms of words for informal writing only.

Refer to your reference manual for a list of foreign expressions.

Outlines and Lists

Use a period after the numbers or letters that identify items in an outline or list unless the numbers or letters are in parentheses.

I. CAREER PLANNING
   A. Job Resources
      1. Classified ads
         a. Advantages
           (1) Accessibility

(In this abbreviated outline, periods are necessary after all letters and numbers except the last item [(1)], which is enclosed in parentheses.)

Use periods after complete sentences, dependent clauses, and long phrases in a list or outline. Do not use periods after short phrases unless the phrases are necessary to complete the introductory statement.

Follow these basic interview rules:
1. Do not complain about a former employer.
2. Demonstrate a positive attitude.
3. Avoid discussing personal problems.
(Periods are necessary after these complete sentences.)

These characteristics will impress an interviewer:
1. A genuine smile
2. A sincere greeting
3. An interest in the company
4. A display of enthusiasm
(Periods are not necessary after short phrases listed on separate lines. The lead-in statement is complete.)

Before going on an interview, be sure to check on:
a. Time and date of interview.
b. Pronunciation of interviewer's name.
c. Location of interview.
(Each lettered item is necessary to complete the introductory statement. Periods at the end of each phrase are necessary.)

See Instructor Note 16-15 in IAE.

Directions: Use the proofreaders' mark ⊙ to insert periods where necessary. Use the proofreaders' mark ⌿ to delete unnecessary periods.

1. My interview is at 9 am with Dr Martin B Stein.

2. Willard Kline Jr was one of the finalists who returned for a second interview.

3. I addressed the thank-you note to Roger D Bennet, 3460 Third Avenue, Topeka, KS 91303.

4. Mrs Liz Alldred told me about a job opening at the TV station W E A Q.

5. Mr D T Garcia organized an ad hoc committee to improve the firm's outdated application forms.

6. For each job contact record the following information:
   1. Name, address, and phone number.
   2. Contact person.
   3. Position and responsibilities.

**GO TO
CD-ROM
CHECKUP 16-2**

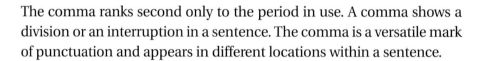

For a more thorough review, refer to your reference manual section on commas. Refer to Chapter 15 for a review of compound sentences.

See Instructor Note 16-16 in IAE.

The comma ranks second only to the period in use. A comma shows a division or an interruption in a sentence. The comma is a versatile mark of punctuation and appears in different locations within a sentence.

Compound Sentences

Use a comma to separate two independent clauses in a compound sentence. Place the comma before the coordinating conjunction (*and, or, nor, but*) that joins the two clauses.

> **An employee's interest in continuing education impresses employers, and they will often pay the worker's tuition.**
> (The sentence contains two independent clauses separated by the conjunction *and*. The comma appears before the conjunction.)

See Instructor Note 16-17 in IAE.

Omit the comma before the coordinating conjunction in a compound sentence if either or both of the two independent clauses are very short (four words or less). Do not omit the comma if it is necessary for clarity.

> **Make your objective realistic or eliminate this section of the résumé.**
> (The first clause is short. No comma is necessary before the coordinating conjunction *or*.)

> **Stevenson's offers high salaries but we offer better benefits.**
> (Both independent clauses are short [four words or less]. No comma is necessary before the coordinating conjunction *but*.)

John interviewed me, and Sara explained my tasks.
(*The comma before the conjunction* and *is necessary to avoid confusion about the number of people John interviewed.*)

Use a comma before the coordinating conjunction when a subject is not expressed (but implied) in one or both clauses in an imperative sentence. Do not use a comma if one of the independent clauses is very short.

Online résumé postings are popular ways to search for a job, but do not forget the value of direct company contacts.
(*The second clause is a command with the implied subject* you. *A comma before the coordinating conjunction is necessary to separate the two clauses.*)

Complete the application and return it to our office by September 20.
(*The first imperative clause is very short; therefore, no comma is necessary to separate the two clauses.*)

Do not use a comma before a coordinating conjunction that joins a compound subject, predicate, object, or subject complement.

Go to PowerPoint 16-7.

Lucy finds it difficult to ask character questions or to question the accuracy of a résumé.
(Or *is the coordinating conjunction that joins the two phrases* to ask character questions *and* to question the accuracy of a résumé. *No comma is necessary with two phrases.*)

An expert interviewer is a good listener and a perceptive evaluator of responses.
(And *is the coordinating conjunction that joins the two subject complements* listener *and* evaluator. *No comma is necessary.*)

The interviewers verified that candidates had the necessary work experience and that they had the licenses they claimed to have.
(*The subject of this sentence is* interviewers. *The compound object of the sentence is* that candidates had the necessary work experience *and* that they had the licenses they claimed to have. *No comma is necessary before the conjunction* and.)

See Instructor Note 16-18 in IAE.

CHECKUP 16-3

Directions: *Use the proofreaders' mark ∧ to insert commas where needed. Use the proofreaders' mark ⌀ to delete unnecessary commas.*

1. Job hunting is often hard work∧and it can be very frustrating when no interviews result.

2. Many employers realize the need to give references∧but they fear retaliation if the person fails to get the job.

3. Research a company⌀and then complete the application.

The Period and the Comma   457

GO TO
CD-ROM
CHECKUP 16-3

4. Be sure that your nails and hair are neat, and that your interview attire is basically conservative.

5. Fred continually upgraded his skills, but failed to receive the desired promotions.

6. Address your thank-you letter to the interviewer and include a statement about your continued interest in the job.

Series

Use commas to separate words, phrases, or clauses in a series. Be sure to include the comma before the coordinating conjunction.

A good résumé includes information about your education, skills, and experience.
(Commas separate words in a series. A comma is necessary before the coordinating conjunction *and*.)

This job requires knowledge of the insurance business, a community college degree, and previous office experience.
(Commas separate phrases in a series. A comma is necessary before the coordinating conjunction *and*.)

Prepare a list of questions, organize the questions according to priority, and take the list with you to the interview.
(Commas separate clauses in a series. The subject *you* is understood. A comma is necessary before the coordinating conjunction *and*.)

Do not use commas to separate items when each item is connected by a conjunction.

Are you looking at new career options or are you hoping for a promotion or are you thinking about a lateral move for more experience?
(All three questions can stand on their own. No commas are necessary to separate the clauses since conjunctions [*or*] already separate them.)

Use commas in a series of names in an organization exactly the way that the organization uses the commas on its letterhead or on another verifiable source. Do not use a comma before the ampersand (&) in the name of an organization unless the company itself does.

Gavin, Lokken, Holbrook, and Elkins interviewed five applicants for its administrative assistant position.
(In this example, the comma appears before the coordinating conjunction. A company's letterhead is the best format guide to use in punctuating names of organizations.)

Reinhart, Reynolds & Steinberg has a list of standard questions for its interviewers to ask potential employees.
(Do not use a comma before the ampersand [&] unless the company includes it on its letterhead.)

SLIP-UP

From a cover letter: "I have lurnt WordPerfect 6.0, computor and spreadsheat programs." [Note: The spell check and comma rules still have to be mastered.] Source: Robert Half, reported by Elaine McShulskis in HRMagazine.

See Instructor Note 16-19 in IAE.

Use an authoritative source such as company letterhead before writing the name of an organization if you are unsure of its correct usage.

Use a comma before and after the abbreviation *etc.* When *etc.* appears at the end of a sentence, use a comma before the abbreviation only. The abbreviation *etc.* means "and so forth" or "and others." Do not use the phrase *and etc.*

Go to PowerPoint 16-8.

See Instructor Note 16-20 in IAE.

> **Most people use classified advertisements, personal contacts, college listings, employment agencies, etc., as their basic sources of job-hunting information.**
>
> (*Etc.* implies that there are other sources. *Etc.* is a vague ending because it does not indicate the additional sources available. A comma is necessary before and after *etc.*)
>
> **To enhance our job hunting, we use classified advertisements, personal contacts, college listings, etc.**
>
> (A comma is needed before *etc.* but not after it.)

Do This	Do Not Do This
In preparing a résumé, avoid items <u>such as</u> past or desired salaries, reasons for leaving past positions, and health status.	In preparing a résumé, avoid items <u>such as</u> past or desired salaries, reasons for leaving past positions, health status, <u>etc.</u>
or	
In preparing a résumé, avoid past or desired salaries, reasons for leaving past positions, health status, <u>etc.</u>	

Do not use etc. if the expression such as has already been used in the sentence.

CHECKUP 16-4

Directions: Use the proofreaders' mark ∧ to insert commas where needed. Use the proofreaders' mark ⌐ to delete unnecessary commas or words. Treat company names as normal items in a series.

1. The firm sent its job announcement to the high schools, and to the community colleges, and to the newspapers.

2. Questions about age, race, sex, religion, national origin, etc., are prohibited on job application forms.

3. We have placed online ads for administrative assistants, salespeople, sales managers, etc.

4. Perrin, Gavin, Smith, and Lowry requires that each job candidate sign a reference check waiver.

GO TO CD-ROM

CHECKUP 16-4

SLIP-UP

I am loyal to my employer at all costs. Please feel free to respond to my résumé on my office voice mail. Source: The Internet.

See Instructor Note 16-21 in IAE.

Refer to Chapter 12 for additional information on independent adjectives.

---

5. More and more companies are providing elder care, adoption benefits, and child care options as a part of their benefits package.

6. Working as a temporary employee gave me an opportunity to keep my schedule flexible, to learn new skills, and to find a permanent home.

Independent Adjectives

Place a comma between independent adjectives that precede a noun unless they are already separated by a coordinating conjunction. To determine whether adjectives are independent, reverse their order or place the word *and* between the two adjectives. If both revisions sound satisfactory, place a comma between the two adjectives.

We need competent, courteous employees to serve our customers.
(Reverse the order of the two adjectives. *Courteous, competent employees* sounds satisfactory. Insert the word *and* between the two adjectives. *Competent and courteous employees* sounds satisfactory. A comma between the two adjectives is necessary.)

We need competent and courteous employees to serve our customers.
(A comma is not needed because *competent* and *courteous* are separated by the coordinating conjunction *and*.)

Finding the ideal employee in a dynamic, fast-paced industry is a challenge.
(Reverse the order of the adjectives. *Fast-paced, dynamic* industry sounds satisfactory. Insert the word *and* between the two adjectives. *Dynamic and fast-paced industry* sounds satisfactory. A comma between the two adjectives is necessary.)

Job enrichment can expand boring work into several new roles and responsibilities.
(Reverse the order of the adjectives. *New several* does not sound satisfactory. Insert the word *and* between the two adjectives. *Several and new* does not sound satisfactory. No commas are necessary.)

CHECKUP 16-5

Directions: Use the proofreaders' mark ⋀ to insert commas where needed. Use the proofreaders' mark ⌿ to delete unnecessary commas.

1. Read the local newspaper for information about the fastest growing, most profitable companies in your area.

2. Dennis has a self-assured, confident attitude about his future.

3. Some temporary workers prefer the freedom of temporary work to the requirements of consistent, permanent employment.

---

4. I had never worked on the two, outdated, computer programs that they gave me to use in my business, skills test.

5. Serious job hunters should search for a job at a steady, well-planned pace.

6. Wendy bought an attractive, new suit to wear for her job interviews.

GO TO
CD-ROM
CHECKUP 16-5

Appositives

Use commas to set off an appositive if it is not essential to the meaning of a sentence.

An appositive explains or identifies the nouns or pronouns it follows.

Rob McClellan, chief executive officer of McClellan and Associates, looks for candidates with international experience.

(*Rob McClellan* is the subject of the sentence. The appositive *chief executive officer of McClellan and Associates* adds information that is not necessary for the meaning of the sentence. The appositive requires commas to set it aside from the rest of the sentence.)

America's Job Bank, a job-search site on the Web, gave me some insights into the national job market.

(The appositive *a job-search site on the Web* is an explanation that is not necessary for the meaning of the sentence. The appositive requires commas to set it aside from the rest of the sentence.)

Do not use commas to set off an appositive that explains or clarifies the noun preceding it.

The book *Finding a Job on the Internet* contains practical advice about preparing résumés for online use.

(The appositive indicates *which* book and is essential for the meaning of the sentence. No commas are necessary to set off the appositive from the rest of the sentence.)

My business instructor Mr. Halvorsen wrote an excellent letter of recommendation for me.

(You may have more than one business instructor. *Mr. Halvorsen* identifies the specific instructor and is necessary for the meaning of the sentence. No commas are necessary to set off the appositive from the rest of the sentence. If Mr. Halvorsen is the only business instructor you have, his name should be set aside with commas.)

CHECKUP 16-6

Directions: *Use the proofreaders' mark ∧ to insert commas where needed. Use the proofreaders' mark ⌒ to delete unnecessary commas.*

1. Some hiring committees select a compromise applicant, one who neither totally pleases nor displeases anyone.

2. Emmett Lowry, president of a Trenton outplacement firm, carefully checks all business and professional references of job applicants.

See Instructor Note 16-22 in IAE.

GO TO CD-ROM CHECKUP 16-6

See Instructor Note 16-23 in IAE.

Refer to your reference manual for additional examples of parenthetical expressions. They may be called transitional expressions *or* independent comments *in your reference manual.*

3. I was not able to define the term "functional résumé" in my introductory careers course.

4. My brother, Dan, is also applying for a job at the Memorial Surgery Center.

5. Lori Robbins, the receptionist, introduced me to the members of the interviewing team.

6. Victory Medical Center, the largest employer in our city, always has openings for nurses.

Parenthetical Expressions

Parenthetical expressions interrupt a sentence. These side remarks do not add to the clarity of a sentence, and they are set aside by commas. Parenthetical words and phrases act as connectors, or they express a writer's opinion or explanation about the statement. Here is a partial list of parenthetical expressions:

after all	I believe
as a consequence	if any
as a matter of fact	in fact
as a result	it would seem
as you know	of course
believe me	on the contrary
consequently	therefore
for example	to be exact
however	unfortunately

Set off a nonessential parenthetical expression with commas.

There is, I am sure, an explanation for the delay in informing me of my employment test results.

(The parenthetical expression *I am sure* that appears within the sentence is not necessary for the meaning of the sentence. The parenthetical expression requires commas to set it aside from the rest of the sentence.)

Actually, I've always been satisfied with my temporary work assignments.

(The parenthetical expression *actually* is not necessary for the meaning of the sentence. The parenthetical expression requires a comma to set it aside from the rest of the sentence.)

A college degree, as you know, does not guarantee a job.

(The parenthetical expression *as you know* appears in the middle of the sentence, but it is not necessary for the meaning of the sentence. The parenthetical expression requires commas to set it aside from the rest of the sentence.)

CHECKUP 16-7

Directions: *Underline the parenthetical expressions. Use the proofreaders' mark ∧ to insert commas where needed.*

1. Several major newspapers∧in fact∧post their "Help Wanted" ads online.
2. Interviews∧in most cases∧last 30 to 45 minutes.
3. Many job hunters have little∧if any∧knowledge of the best ways to discuss the salary issue.
4. You realize∧I am sure∧that company Web pages can be valuable recruitment tools.
5. Videoconferencing∧by the way∧is a low-cost way to review many candidates.
6. This job candidate∧no doubt∧has good computer and communication skills.

**GO TO
CD-ROM**
CHECKUP 16-7

Introductory Expressions

Introductory expressions may be words, phrases, or clauses. Dependent clauses have subjects and verbs but cannot stand alone. Other introductory expressions include prepositional, infinitive, and participial phrases.

Dependent Clauses. Use a comma to separate an introductory dependent clause from the independent clause.

> **If you lost your job tomorrow, would you be able to get another job without too much trouble?**
> (The dependent clause *If you lost your job tomorrow* introduces the independent clause *would you be able to get another job without too much trouble.* A comma is necessary after the dependent clause.)

> **Although he was not hired for the information systems manager position, he was told about another opening in computer operations.**
> (The dependent clause introduces an independent clause. A comma is necessary after the dependent clause since it comes at the beginning of the sentence.)

Generally, do not use a comma when the dependent clause follows the independent clause or when it is necessary for the meaning of the sentence.

> **Be sure to request a letter of recommendation before you leave a job.**
> (The dependent clause *before you leave a job* appears at the end of the sentence. A comma is not necessary to separate the dependent clause from the rest of the sentence.)

> **Many people stay in their mediocre jobs because they are afraid of failure.**
> (The dependent clause appears at the end of the sentence. A comma is not necessary.)

Prepositional Phrases. Use a comma to set off an introductory prepositional phrase from the independent clause that follows.

See Instructor Note 16-24 in IAE.

Refer to Chapter 3 to review clauses and to Chapter 15 to review subordinating conjunctions.

See Instructor Note 16-25 in IAE.

A prepositional phrase consists of a preposition and its object. Refer to Chapter 14 for a review of prepositional phrases.

See Instructor Note 16-26 in IAE.
Go to PowerPoint 16-9.

Within ten months, she received a promotion to the position of office manager.

(The short prepositional phrase *Within ten months* introduces the independent clause *she received a promotion to the position of office manager.* A comma follows the prepositional phrase.)

From a job hunter's standpoint, online newsgroups are a good way to learn about a specific profession.

(*From a job hunter's standpoint* introduces the independent clause. A comma follows the prepositional phrase.)

An infinitive consists of a verb preceded by to. Refer to Chapter 10 for a review of infinitives.

Infinitive Phrases. Use a comma to set off an introductory infinitive phrase from the rest of the sentence. Do not use a comma when an infinitive phrase is the subject of a sentence.

To find qualified job applicants, more companies are using online services.

(*To find qualified job applicants* is the infinitive phrase that introduces the independent clause *more companies are using online services.* A comma is necessary after the introductory infinitive phrase.)

To find qualified applicants is a competitive task faced by most companies.

(In this sentence, *To find qualified applicants* is the subject of the sentence followed by the verb *is.* No comma is necessary after the word *applicants.*)

Refer to Chapter 10 for a review of participial phrases.

Participial Phrases. Use a comma to set off an introductory participial phrase from the rest of the sentence.

Disappointed about the lack of jobs in his field, Darrin decided to return to the community college for retraining.

(*Disappointed about the lack of jobs in his field* is the participial phrase that introduces an independent clause. The participial phrase modifies the subject *Darrin.* A comma is necessary after the participial phrase.)

Reviewing the job qualifications, I realized that I needed additional skills to obtain the position.

(*Reviewing the job qualifications* is the participial phrase that introduces an independent clause. The participial phrase modifies the subject *I.* A comma is necessary after the participial phrase.)

CHECKUP 16-8

Directions: *In the following sentences use the proofreaders' mark* ∧ *to insert commas where needed. Use the proofreaders' mark* ⌒ *to delete unnecessary commas.*

1. When you are introduced to the interviewer, greet him or her with a firm handshake.

2. After you are employed, proof of immigration status will be necessary.

3. To highlight your problem-solving ability, use action words such as *initiated* and *created.*

4. You probably willl not be happy in an autocratic environment⟋if you are a "free spirit."

5. Throughout your job search₍follow these steps to market your skills and attributes.

6. Surprised by the large number of job applicants₍Edie decided to allow the committee extra time to review applications.

GO TO CD-ROM CHECKUP 16-8

Nonrestrictive and Restrictive Adjective Clauses

A *nonrestrictive* (nonessential) adjective clause is not necessary for the meaning of the word it modifies. A nonrestrictive adjective clause usually begins with the word *which*. A *restrictive* (essential) adjective clause is necessary for the meaning of the word it modifies. A restrictive adjective clause usually begins with the word *that*. The words *who* and *whose* introduce either restrictive or nonrestrictive clauses.

Nonrestrictive Adjective Clauses.   Use commas to set off a nonrestrictive adjective clause from the rest of the sentence.

> **His personality test indicated that he had high empathy, which is a strong attribute for social workers.**
> (The nonrestrictive adjective clause *which is a strong attribute for social workers* modifies the noun *empathy*. The clause is not necessary for the meaning of the sentence and must be set aside with commas.)

> **Some temporary agencies use self-paced CD-ROM job search materials, which include workbooks and videotapes.**
> (The nonrestrictive adjective clause modifies the noun *materials*. The clause is not necessary for the meaning of the sentence and must be set aside with commas.)

Restrictive Adjective Clauses.   Do not set off restrictive adjective clauses from the rest of the sentence.

Go to PowerPoint 16-10.

> **Job applicants who indicate that they have spent more than nine months looking for a job are carefully checked and evaluated.**
> (The restrictive adjective clause *who indicate that they have spent more than nine months looking for a job* modifies the noun *applicants*. The clause restricts the meaning of the sentence by identifying which job applicants are being checked. No commas are necessary to set off the restrictive clause.)

> **Companies that continue to offer a wide array of benefit options attract high-caliber workers.**
> (The clause restricts the meaning of the sentence by clarifying *which* companies attract high-caliber workers. No commas are necessary to set off the restrictive clause.)

CHECKUP 16-9

Directions: In the following sentences, underline the restrictive or nonrestrictive adjective clauses. Use the proofreaders' mark ∧ to insert commas where needed. Use the proofreaders' mark ⌁ to delete unnecessary commas.

1. People, who are 40 years and older, will comprise more than half of our workforce by the year 2005.

2. Some firms are now producing employment tests, that evaluate an applicant's reactions in a real job.

3. My brother Stan, who works at a temporary agency, gave me some job-hunting tips.

4. At my second interview, which was held at Colby's Grille, the interviewer discussed many advantages of working for the firm.

5. We did not hire the job applicant, who sent us an outdated résumé.

6. I read Grant Parkinson's latest job search book, which outlined several ways to write a résumé for online use.

GO TO
CD-ROM
CHECKUP 16-9

SLIP-UP
Written in a cover letter:
"Please call me after 5:30 because I am self-employed, and my employer does not know I am looking for another job." [Note: Aren't you your own employer when you are self-employed?]
Source: Robert Half.

Miscellaneous Comma Usage

Contrasting Expressions.   Use commas to set aside a contrasting expression from the rest of the sentence. A contrasting expression often begins with the word *not* or *never.* A contrasting expression contradicts the noun or idea it follows.

> **The résumé, not the cover letter, is the place for job experience and education details.**
> (*Not the cover letter* is a contrasting expression. The contrasting expression requires commas to set it aside from the rest of the sentence.)

> **The position for which I'm interviewing is a new position, not an existing one.**
> (*Not an existing one* is a contrasting expression that is not necessary for the meaning of the sentence. The contrasting expression requires commas to set it aside from the rest of the sentence.)

Direct Address.   Use commas to set off the names of individuals who are being addressed directly.

> **We are happy to inform you, Taylor, that you have been selected as our new technical services representative.**
> (*Taylor* is the person being addressed. The individual's name requires commas to set it aside from the rest of the sentence.)

> **Kimberly, do you have any questions that you would like to ask the members of the committee?**
> (*Kimberly* is the person being addressed. The individual's name requires commas to set it aside from the rest of the sentence.)

Tag Questions.   Use a comma to separate a tag question from the rest of the sentence.

> **He has already reserved the conference room for interviews on Tuesday, hasn't he?**
> (The tag question *hasn't he?* requires a comma before it to separate the question from the rest of the sentence.)

> **We don't have to answer questions about our marital status, do we?**
> (The tag question *do we?* is separated by a comma from the rest of the sentence.)

Quotations.   Use a comma to introduce a direct quotation or set it off from other parts of a sentence. Do not use a comma to set off an indirect quotation.

> **She said, "Honesty on an application form is imperative."**
> (The comma after the word *said* is necessary before a direct quotation.)

> **"Honesty," she said, "is imperative on an application form."**
> (The commas are necessary to set aside a direct quotation from the other parts of a sentence.)

> **She said that honesty on an application form is imperative.**
> (No commas are necessary for this indirect quotation.)

CHECKUP 16-10

Directions: *Use the proofreaders' mark ⋀ to insert commas where needed. Use the proofreaders' mark ⌒ to delete unnecessary commas.*

1. Thank you for interviewing me, Mr. Decker.

2. Our firm has always had excellent results, never unfavorable, with preemployment psychological tests.

3. Jenni said, that Suyon Yee is planning to begin work on November 1.

4. You have never been fired from a job, have you?

5. The receptionist said, "Mrs. Barstow, the personnel manager, will be interviewing you."

6. Meghan, why are you interested in working for this firm?

GO TO
CD-ROM
CHECKUP 16-10

Dates.   Use a comma before and after the year when a date includes a month, day, and year. Do not use a comma if only the month and day or only the month and year are in a sentence.

> **I hope to have my first promotion by June 30, 2001, or at the latest December 31, 2002.**
> (Commas are necessary before and after the year *2001*. The month, day, and year are included in the sentence.)

Mrs. Melendez indicated that she would inform me by November 10 about my job status.

(No commas are necessary. Only the month and day are included.)

My last job interview was in October 1998 for a data entry position.

(No commas are necessary. Only the month and year are included.)

Addresses. Use commas to separate parts of an address or geographical location. Do not place a comma between a state name or a two-letter state abbreviation and the ZIP Code within a document or on an envelope. Within a document, use a comma after the ZIP Code to separate it from the material that follows.

I ordered two career books from Glencoe/McGraw-Hill, 936 Eastwind Drive, Westerville, OH 43081, last week.

(Each part of the address is set off by commas except the state and ZIP Code. A comma follows the ZIP Code to set it aside from the remainder of the sentence.)

Stratten Technology is opening a new plant in Raleigh, North Carolina, and plans to hire 750 new employees.

(The city *Raleigh* is set off from the state *North Carolina.* The comma after *North Carolina* sets the state off from the rest of the sentence.)

Occupational Designations, Academic Degrees. Use commas to set off occupational designations or academic degrees when they follow a person's name. Do not use both a personal or job title before a name and a job or academic degree designation after the name.

Austin Hugo, M.D., was one of the speakers at the new employee orientation.

(The occupational designation *M.D.* is set aside with commas. Do not use *Dr. Austin Hugo, M.D.*)

I enjoy my job with Leslie Perko, M.B.A.

(Do not use *Mrs. Leslie Perko, M.B.A.*)

Seniority Designations. Do not use commas to separate seniority designations from the name unless the person being referenced prefers to use commas.

Thomsen Electronics promoted Nathan Snyder Jr. to the position of manager of its South American operations.

(*Jr.* is a seniority title and does not require commas to separate it from the name.)

Thomsen Electronics promoted Nathan Snyder II to the position of manager of its South American operations.

(*II* is a seniority title and does not require commas to separate it from the name.)

Company Names. Do not use commas to separate *Inc.* or *Ltd.* from the rest of the company name unless the company's letterhead or other official source indicates commas are necessary.

Career Associates Inc. helps displaced workers find jobs.

(No commas are necessary to set off *Inc.* unless a company indicates a preference to include commas. You should check correspondence, letterheads, or other reference sources to determine this preference.)

Numbers. Use a comma in a whole number with more than four figures. Some offices prefer to insert a comma in a number such as 3,482. Do not use a comma in a policy, account, page, serial, model, or check number or in a house number in an address.

See Instructor Note 16-27 in IAE.

A research firm surveyed 30,500 businesses to determine future hiring practices.

(The number has more than four figures and requires a comma for ease in reading.)

We charge all expenses for hiring employees to account No. 6930.

(No commas are used in account numbers.)

CHECKUP 16-11

Directions: *Use the proofreaders' mark* ∧ *to insert commas where needed. Use the proofreaders' mark* ⌒ *to delete unnecessary commas.*

See Instructor Note 16-28 in IAE.

1. I was a part-time student at the community college between September, 1995, and June, 1998.

2. Evergreen Rehabilitation, Inc., hired Elizabeth Michaels, Ph.D., as its staff psychologist.

3. Please contact me at 69,150 Admiral Way, Bend, OR 97702.

4. On January 1, 1999, Douglas Seward, Jr., became the CEO of Bartingale, Inc.

5. The hospital administrator recommended that Alison Whitby, R.N., and Mike Ramos, M.D., become members of the hospital's interview committee.

6. From research for my interview, I knew the firm had produced 12,325 units last month.

GO TO
CD-ROM
CHECKUP 16-11

DIAGRAMMING SENTENCES

Each independent clause in a compound sentence receives separate attention in diagramming. Use vertical dotted lines separated by a solid horizontal line to connect the verbs in each independent clause. Write the conjunction on the solid horizontal line.

```
    developed
 ┌─────────────
 ┊
 └──── and ────
 ┊
    sent
 └─────────────
```

Jeanne is the chairperson of the interview committee and Antonio is the recorder.

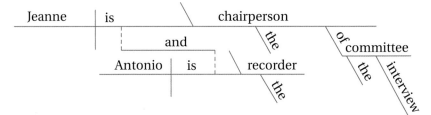

CHECKUP 16-12

See Instructor Note 16-29 in IAE.

Directions: *In the space provided below, diagram the following sentences. All words may be diagrammed.*

1. I can juggle a complicated schedule, and I handle pressure situations well.

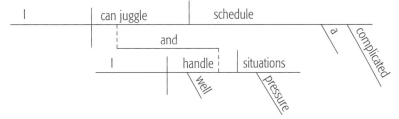

2. Lynn plans to attend college, but she needs a part-time summer job.

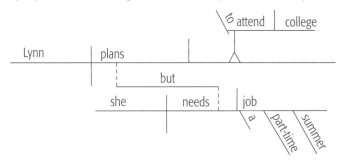

3. You can post your résumé online, or you can send us a copy.

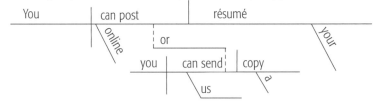

4. An interview is not an everyday event, and feelings of fear or unease are normal.

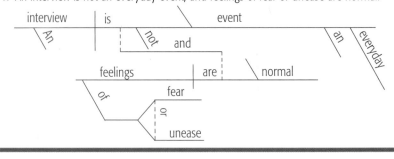

GO TO CD-ROM
CHECKUP 16-12

NAME _____

PRACTICE 1A

A. Directions: *If the sentence is punctuated correctly, write **Yes** in the space provided. If the sentence is not punctuated correctly, write **No**.*

See Instructor Notes 16-30 and 16-31 in IAE.

1. During the course of your career, you can expect to change employers a number of times.

1. __Yes__

2. To gauge an applicant's ability to solve problems, interviewers ask questions that require some analysis.

2. __Yes__

3. You are the one who must sell your skills, experience, and education

3. __No__

4. Basing hiring decisions on IQ tests, which some say are unfair leaves a company open to lawsuits.

4. __No__

5. No one can guarantee you a job, no matter how well you perform at school.

5. __Yes__

6. An untrained, inexperienced interviewer must not let preconceived ideas cloud his or her judgment.

6. __Yes__

7. She asked "What did you do when a coworker missed a deadline that caused your work to be late?"

7. __No__

8. Knowledge of market trends, and new skills is important if you want to look for a job.

8. __No__

9. You do know if an organization is democratic or autocratic don't you?

9. __No__

10. I have worked for Noland and Nichols, Inc. since December 1 1998.

10. __No__

B. Directions: *In the space provided, write the letter of the appropriate reason for each of the underlined commas. Some underlined commas may not be necessary.*

A = Commas set off a nonrestrictive clause.
B = Commas set off introductory phrases and clauses.
C = Commas set off parenthetical expressions.
D = Commas set off an appositive.
E = Commas separate a series.
F = Commas separate compound sentences.
G = Commas separate independent adjectives.
H = No comma or commas are necessary.

1. To find the position you want, approach your job hunt with a plan.

1. __B__

2. The job search workshop showed me how to develop a complete, comprehensive plan to approach the job market.

2. __G__

NAME _____

3. Maggie, for instance, should have left her boring job months ago.

3. ___C___

4. The interviewer asked every applicant to sign a comprehensive waiver, a form allowing the employer to contact all references.

4. ___D___

5. Job hunters, who fail to follow directions, will have trouble finding a job.

5. ___H___

6. Some applicants ask no questions, which makes interviewers think the job is of no interest to these interviewees.

6. ___A___

7. Should you accept the first salary figure that is offered, or should you negotiate salary during the job interview?

7. ___F___

8. She worked in a comfortable environment, received good benefits, and enjoyed her coworkers.

8. ___E___

9. Most professional associations conduct annual salary surveys, that they send to their members, or that they publish in special brochures.

9. ___H___

10. Attempting to meet the deadline for submitting her application, Sandra neglected to proofread her résumé carefully.

10. ___B___

**GO TO
CD-ROM**
PRACTICE 1
EXERCISES

PRACTICE 2A

See Instructor Note 16-32 in IAE.

Directions: Use the proofreaders' marks ⌄ and ⊙ to insert commas and periods where needed. Use the proofreaders' mark ⌿ to delete unnecessary marks of punctuation.

1. Are you looking for a new job, or just exploring additional careers?

2. Few management opportunities are available for investment representatives, commercial bankers, or consultants, without college degrees.

3. In recent years, it has become easier to change jobs, because health benefits and pensions are simpler to transfer.

4. A company is interested primarily in your ability to improve the company's operation, not in your former job titles.

5. To deduct job-hunting expenses on your income taxes, you will need itemized, detailed accounts and receipts.

6. Holly encourages applicants to talk about themselves, which gives them an opportunity to discuss more than their skills.

Chapter 16

NAME _____

7. As you prepare your résumé, be sure that your objective refers to your contribution to the company.

8. Use titles such as Mr. Ms. Mrs. Miss. etc. in a salutation for an employment cover letter.

9. Dunbar, Peterson, and Edwards has a paralegal position available in its office at 1206 Union Street, Alexandria, Minnesota.

10. Ben Collins, Jr., had limited experience in leading, and managing in the new team-based business environment.

11. The best references, usually, are those from past supervisors.

12. Sam wondered how many questions the interviewer would ask in his 30-minute, videoconference interview.

13. Will you please write N/A, (not applicable) in the blank, if a question does not apply to you.

14. Employers, by the way, report a lack of proficiency in written and oral communication skills.

15. Barbara knew what she enjoyed doing, but she had problems describing her strengths in a concise, positive way.

16. A friend of mine, Kerry Williams, MD, transferred to Lexington, Kentucky, in August 1998.

17. Having researched the company, I knew its reputation in the community.

18. The best time to visit a temp. service is Monday at 10 a.m. or Friday at 3 p.m.

19. You have read the book, *Finding a Job on the Internet*, haven't you?

20. Temporary agencies usually divide jobs into these employment groups:

    1. Office,

    2. Industrial,

    3. Medical,

    4. Technical,

GO TO
CD-ROM
PRACTICE 2
EXERCISES

The Period and the Comma

NAME _____

PRACTICE 3A

PROOFREADING

*Directions: Proofread and compare the two sentences in each group. If they are the same, write **Yes** in the space provided. If they are not the same, write **No.** Use the first sentence as the correct copy. If you find errors in the second sentence, underline them; insert any omitted words or marks of punctuation.*

1. A recent Gallup poll shows that one-third of college-educated people who are employed would select a different career if they could begin again.

   A recent Gallup <u>pole</u> shows that one-third of college-educated <u>people, who</u> are <u>employed,</u> would select a different <u>career, if</u> they could begin again.

   1. <u>No</u>

2. The Job Web at http://www.jobweb.org has job listings and links to job recruiters and professional associations.

   The Job Web at http://www.jobweb.org has job <u>listings, and</u> links <u>for</u> job recruiters and professional associations.

   2 <u>No</u>

3. Development Dimensions Intl., which is headquartered in Pittsburgh, Pennsylvania, prepares tests that simulate activities on the real job.

   Development Dimensions <u>Internl.</u>, which is headquartered in Pittsburgh, Pennsylvania, prepares tests that <u>stimulate</u> activities on the real job.

   3. <u>No</u>

4. Some employers think that applicants who hold part-time jobs and participate in several extracurricular activities while maintaining good grades make excellent employees.

   Some employers think that applicants <u>that</u> hold part-time jobs and participate in several extracurricular activities while maintaining good grades make excellent employees.

   4. <u>No</u>

5. Twenty-six states have laws that offer varying degrees of protection to employers who provide "good-faith" references and release truthful information about their former employees.

   Twenty-six states have laws that offer varying degrees of protection to employers <u>that</u> provide <u>good-faith</u> <u>references, and</u> release truthful information about their former employees.

   5. <u>No</u>

NAME _____

Proofreading Exercise

Before beginning a job search, review your goals, analyze your strengths and weaknesses, and determine the type of work that satisfies you. The questions in the following exercise provide the basis for your personal planning.

Directions: Use proofreaders' marks to correct the following copy. If you are not certain about the use of a proofreaders' mark, use your reference manual or the proofreaders' marks listed on the inside back cover of this textbook.

PERSONAL PLANING GUIDE LINES

1. What things are improtant to me?
2. What makes my current job meaningfull to me?
3. What do I want to be doing one year form now? three years from now?
4. What am I doing <u>now</u> to prepare myself to reach these goals?
5. What must I do by a year from now to prepare myself to reach these goals?
6. What negative things are occurring at work, or in my personal life now?
7. What positive things are occuring at work or in my personal life now?
8. What are my mayor attributes?
9. What skills do I need?
10. what type of competition will I encounter in the field in which I am most interested?
11. Where can I obtain the training or upgrade the skills that I need?
12. What is the future forthe field in which I am most interested?

See Instructor Note 16-33 in IAE.

> **SLIP-UP**
> On a résumé: "Instrumental in *ruining* entire operation for a Midwest chain operation." [Will he or she ruin our business as well?] Source: Robert Half.

GO TO CD-ROM
PRACTICE 3 EXERCISES

PRACTICE 4A

WRITING

Directions: Write a paragraph describing the characteristics of your ideal job. Include the type of work performed, the skills needed, the pay and fringe benefits, and the ideal working conditions.

Answers will vary.

My ideal job is working for a nonprofit agency. I like to help others, and I receive personal satisfaction from knowing that I have helped to change someone's life. This year I have volunteered for COTS, which is a nonprofit organization that helps homeless families. I want to work for COTS when I receive my Child Care Certificate from the college. I plan to work with young homeless children, helping them to feel secure and teaching them to play cooperatively with one another. In my college classes, I have learned how to recognize emotional problems in children and have developed strategies to help children cope with problems that they cannot control. I know how to structure play activities and how to encourage children to learn. The pay will be minimum wage with no benefits, but I am willing to accept those limitations.

GO TO CD-ROM
PRACTICE 4 EXERCISES

The Period and the Comma

NAME _____

See Instructor Note 16-34 in
IAE.

ONLINE **EXERCISES**

The Internet has more than 10,000 sites that deal with jobs, careers, or job hunting. You can research companies, post your résumé online, or find a placement professional to help you in your job search. Thousands of articles will help you write your résumé and cover letter, develop your job network, or give you advice on how to find a job.

Objective: _To visit career sites._

Punctuation ALERT!

Use exact punctuation when keying an Internet address.

1. With your Internet browser, key:

   http://www.careermag.com in the location text box.

2. Press the **Enter** key on your keyboard. You will be at the site of _Career Magazine,_ a comprehensive resource designed to meet the needs of job seekers. You can find job openings, a résumé bank, employer profiles, a career forum, and articles relevant to the job search.

3. Search for an article that looks interesting. Print it and share it with your instructor and classmates.

NAME _____

PRACTICE 1B

See Instructor Note 16-35 in IAE.

A. Directions: *If the sentence is punctuated correctly, write* **Yes** *in the space provided. If the sentence is not punctuated correctly, write* **No.**

1. Lateral movement, not upward movement, may be a way to develop new skills.   **1.** ___Yes___

2. She wondered how he passed the computer proficiency test without studying?   **2.** ___No___

3. Gary's yearly salary is between $20,000 and $30,000.   **3.** ___Yes___

4. My last interview for the position is with the C.E.O.   **4.** ___No___

5. Dr. Larry Kliner teaches a career class at Santa Barbara City College.   **5.** ___Yes___

6. Jason Navarro III applied for a position in Colorado Springs, Colorado.   **6.** ___Yes___

7. To sell yourself inform the employer about your qualifications in the cover letter.   **7.** ___No___

8. If you prepare for an interview you will sound more professional during your actual presentation.   **8.** ___No___

9. During an interview, don't test a new hairstyle, break in new shoes, or wear a new outfit for the first time.   **9.** ___Yes___

10. Over 25 percent of major U.S. corporations use lie-detector tests for some employees, and half of all supermarket chains require them.   **10.** ___Yes___

B. Directions: *In the space provided, write the letter of the appropriate reason for each of the underlined commas. Some underlined commas may not be necessary.*

      A = *Commas set off a nonrestrictive clause.*
      B = *Commas set off introductory phrases and clauses.*
      C = *Commas set off parenthetical expressions.*
      D = *Commas set off an appositive.*
      E = *Commas separate a series.*
      F = *Commas separate compound sentences.*
      G = *Commas separate independent adjectives.*
      H = *No comma or commas are necessary.*

1. Some job applicants, unfortunately, are not prepared for their interviews.   **1.** ___C___

2. Employers say that they want employees who are loyal, energetic, and reliable.   **2.** ___E___

3. If you belong to a job club, you will receive emotional support from other job seekers.   **3.** ___B___

4. Elizabeth McCarthy, assistant vice president, wants every interviewee to leave thinking he or she did well in the interview.   **4.** ___D___

5. Some companies interview outsiders only to compare them with workers within the firm, which does not seem fair.   **5.** ___A___

6. Conservative, professional clothing is always appropriate attire for a job interview.   **6.** ___G___

7. Written job descriptions can be helpful, but they may fail to stress what you will be expected to do most of the time.   **7.** ___F___

8. You will probably be unhappy in your job, if your working environment is unpleasant.   **8.** ___H___

9. A lack of opportunities can dampen interest in the work, and result in frustration and boredom.   **9.** ___H___

10. If you are considering the salary and benefits for a job in another geographic area, make an allowance for differences in the cost of living.   **10.** ___B___

The Period and the Comma

END-OF-CHAPTER WORKSHEETS

NAME _____

PRACTICE 2B

Directions: *Use the proofreaders' marks* ∧ *and* ⊙ *to insert commas and periods where needed. Use the proofreaders' mark* ⌐ *to delete unnecessary marks of punctuation.*

1. Networking is speaking out meeting new people and sharing professional job information.

2. Leaving a job with "class," creates good feelings and makes your supervisor think well of you.

3. Please complete the application and return it to our office at 6309 Adams Street, Anchorage AK 99516.

4. Henry Gronroos II has a reputation for expecting precise prompt responses from his employees.

5. Shirley please contact Terri Herndon MD for an interview on Monday October 5 1998.

6. The cover letter should use descriptive detailed phrases not general statements.

7. On the other hand if you want your résumé to look professional use a laser printer.

8. An effective job search method is to contact every friend and I mean every friend about any job vacancies.

9. Will you please describe your strengths and also your weaknesses ⊙

10. Jorin Smyth Ubach and Gallen usually hires one employee a month, doesn't it?

11. You may prefer full-time work but you may be able to find part-time work only.

12. Anne Von Sund is a friendly personable interviewer who makes interviewees feel that she likes them.

13. Some interview questions that employers ask determine your ability to think through a typical realistic job situation.

14. Before going on a job interview use the following methods to find out about the company:

    1. Read newspaper clippings articles etc at a library ⊙

    2. Ask questions from receptionists public relations people the personnel office etc ⊙

    3. Ask everybody you know if he or she knows anyone who works there ⊙

    4. Sign up with a local temp agency and ask to be placed in the organization ⊙

15. The American Accounting Association in Sarasota Florida publishes *Accounting Review* a journal describing trends in the accounting profession.

16. A new form of health coverage one that may increase in popularity involves a corporate medical center which is onsite and staffed by the company.

17. If you prefer bureaucratic management you might be very unhappy in a small entrepreneurial company.

18. In some cases however the interviewer will insist on discussing salary early in the interview.

19. Having been interviewed by a group I realize the importance of thinking about the answers before verbalizing them.

20. Job application cover letters addressed to a CEO are usually thrown out or sent to the human resources department.

NAME _____

PRACTICE 3B

PROOFREADING

Directions: *Proofread and compare the two sentences in each group. If they are the same, write* **Yes** *in the space provided. If they are not the same, write* **No.** *Use the first sentence as the correct copy. If you find errors in the second sentence, underline them; insert any omitted words or marks of punctuation.*

1. Richard Nelson Bolles, author of *What Color is Your Parachute?,* believes that all of us have handicaps; consequently, we must find employers who will overlook our handicaps and hire us.

   Richard Nelson Bolles, author of *What Color is Your Parachute?* believes that all of us have handicaps; consequently we must find employees, who will overlook our handicaps and hire us.

   1. No _____

2. The three basic résumé styles include the chronological, which focuses on time and job continuity; the functional, which is organized by functions, skills, and responsibilities; and the combination, which uses elements of both the chronological and functional styles.

   The three basic résumé styles include the chronologicle, which focuses on time and job continuity; the functional, which is organized by functions, skills, and responsibilities; and the combination, which is eliments of both the chronological and functional style.

   2. No _____

3. Some action verbs you might use on your résumé to emphasize efficiency and problem-solving skills include *expedited, improved, reorganized, revised, simplified,* and *streamlined.*

   Some action verbs you might use on your résumé to emphasize efficency and problem solving skills include: *expedited, improved, re-organized, revised, simplified,* and *streamlined.*

   3. No _____

4. *Standard & Poor's Register of Corporations, Directors, and Executives* (a.k.a. S&P) is a corporate directory available on CD-ROM covering more than 50,000 firms with brief financial information, names of major executives and directors, listings of new firms, etc.

   Standard & Poor's Register of Corporations, Directors, and Executives (a.k.a. S&P) is a corporate directory available on CD-ROM covering more than 50,000 firms with brief financial information, names of major executives and directors, listings of new firms, etc.

   4. Yes _____

5. Expect to face at least one of these types of interviews during your job search: group interviews with other applicants, interviews by a group, all-day interviews or multiple interviews, luncheon interviews, and job and performance assessment interviews.

   Expect to face at least one of these types of interviews during your job search: group interviews with other applicants, interviews by a group, all day interviews or multiple interviews, lunch interviews, and job and performance assessment interviews.

   5. No _____

Proofreading Exercise

Directions: *Use proofreaders' marks to correct the following copy. If you are not certain about the use of a proofreaders' mark, use your reference manual or the proofreaders' marks listed on the inside back cover of this textbook.*

END-OF-CHAPTER WORKSHEETS

NAME _____

INTERVIEWING

1. Prepare for the interview. Learn about the company, the position, and the salary range.
2. Dress appropriately. Wear professional, conservative clothing.
3. Arrive at least 15 minutes early. If you arrive earlier than 15 min. before the interview, use the time to relax and collect your thoughts.
4. Arrive alone. Never bring anybody with you to the interview.
5. BE aware of your behavior in the reception area. Do not smoke or eat or apply cosmetis or use a cellular phone or exhibit nervous mannerisms. *Do not*
6. ~~Don't~~ criticize former employers. Critical statements indicate that you may be difficult to work with and may raise questions about your discretion.
7. Be truthful about your accomplishments. Employers appreciate honesty, and you will be discovered sooner or later if you exaggerate.
8. Avoid talking about sensitive subjects. Sensitive subjects involve religion, politics, and sex.

PRACTICE 4B

WRITING

During a career search, you must be able to describe your achievements on your résumé and in your cover letter.

Directions: *Identify an achievement that you have accomplished. Use one of the following suggestions: paid work experience; volunteer work; school, classroom, or extracurricular activity; hobby; recreational activity; or a social relationship. Write a paragraph detailing how you made the achievement happen.*   Answers will vary.

I was on the tennis team in high school. Although I was not the best player on the team, I practiced long hours and

always tried my best, even during practices. When I was not playing in matches, I was supportive and encouraging to my

teammates. I was pleasantly surprised when the team voted me as its captain.

ONLINE EXERCISES

Objective: *To visit sites listing job openings.*

1. With your Internet browser on screen, key one of the following addresses:
   http://www.careermosaic.com
   http://www.helpwanted.com
   http://www.careers.org
   http://www.jobweb.org

2. Click any of the links to find information relevant to your job search.

3. Print a job listing that you would be interested in and could qualify to perform. Write a brief paragraph telling why you chose this particular job listing.

LOOKING BACK

Posttest

Directions: Use the proofreaders' mark ⊙ to insert periods where necessary. Use the proofreaders' mark ⋀ to insert commas.

1. Roger wondered whether he would be asked to return for a second interview⊙

2. Carolyn Lock⋀PhD⊙is a well-known career counselor and can be reached at 4893 Mountain Road⋀ Phoenix⋀AZ 85674⊙

3. Finding a job does not begin with writing a résumé⋀but it does begin with self-analysis.

4. Managers who are looking for work find newspaper advertisements⋀private employment agencies⋀and contacts with friends to be more productive than other job search methods.

5. During the interview⋀Ken used examples that indicated he was a creative⋀original problem solver.

6. The majority of jobs⋀as many as 80 percent by most estimates⋀seem to be filled by people who hear about the openings informally.

7. If you do informational interviews⋀you will have the knowledge to competently negotiate salaries.

8. Employment firms⋀particularly the smaller ones⋀will keep your résumé and cover letter on file⋀won't they?

9. Job clubs⋀which are support groups sponsored by community groups and government agencies⋀provide encouragement and reinforcement for those looking for jobs.

10. I applied for a job at T.J.Maxx⋀and I was finally hired on June 1⋀1998⋀in Carbondale⋀Illinois.

CHAPTER 17

Other Punctuation

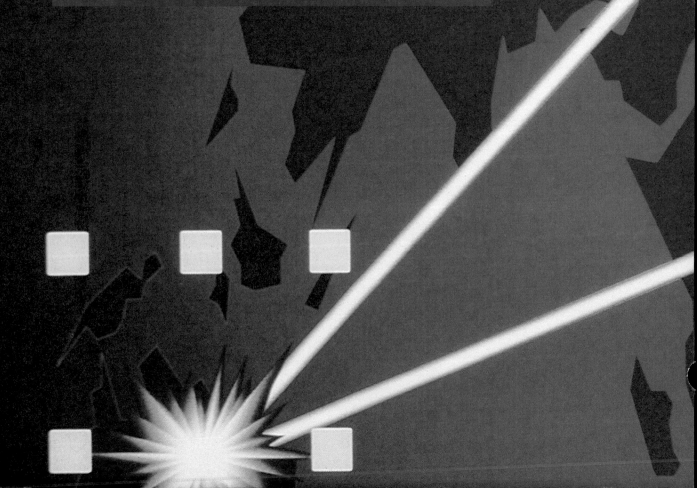

BUSINESS COMMUNICATION

Studying business English builds a foundation for your written and spoken communications. No matter what career you choose or how technologically advanced your workplace may be, the basic communication skills of writing, speaking, and listening remain essential. You increase your likelihood of on-the-job success by communicating effectively.

Workplace communication depends in part upon the written word. While you may not write formal reports or letters, you probably will join the ranks of millions of workers worldwide who use e-mail for quick and fast communication. Your choice of written words makes either a positive or negative impression on your reader and is a permanent record of your abilities.

Oral communication is another part of workplace communication. Most people fear public speaking. Even though your job may not require speaking in front of large groups, you definitely will communicate every day with customers and other employees. You probably will make presentations in small-group meetings. You must use proper grammar and be aware of not only what you are saying but also how you are saying it. The right choice of words enhances your ability to get along with others.

On the job, you will spend more of your time listening than you do reading, writing, or speaking; yet the average person remembers only about 25 percent of what he or she hears. In the workplace, avoiding distractions and listening for information such as dates, names, prices, and explanations are valued communication skills.

TERMS TO REMEMBER

COMMUNICATION

PERMANENT RECORD

OBJECTIVES

After you have studied this chapter and completed the exercises, you will be able to do the following:

1. Use semicolons and colons correctly.
2. Use quotation marks and apostrophes correctly.
3. Differentiate between the uses of hyphens and dashes.
4. Use parentheses and italics correctly.
5. Identify uses for ellipses, brackets, and asterisks.
6. Place adjacent marks of punctuation in correct order.
7. Use capital letters with other punctuation marks correctly.
8. Diagram sentences correctly.

LOOKING AHEAD

Pretest

Directions: *Check the following sentences for punctuation and capitalization errors. Rewrite the sentences correctly in the space provided. If the sentence is punctuated and capitalized correctly, write* **Yes**.

1. The letter is too curt, there is nothing personal about it.

   The letter is too curt; there is nothing personal about it.

2. "The rules for dropping courses, said the counselor, are in the college catalog in three places; Section 4, Section 5, and Section 12."

   "The rules for dropping courses," said the counselor, "are in the college catalog in three places: Section 4, Section 5, and Section 12."

3. Transparencies and slides do not hold a viewer's attention today.

   Yes

4. Lisa knew the importance of communicating any job related concerns to her project coordinator.

   Lisa knew the importance of communicating any job-related concerns to her project coordinator.

5. Discuss three or four major points five at the very most in your oral presentations.

   Discuss three or four major points—five at the very most—in your oral presentations.

6. Include the subject of your message in your e-mail correspondence. (you will get a better response with a specific subject line.

   Include the subject of your message in your e-mail correspondence. (You will get a better response with a specific subject line.)

7. I read several good suggestions about maintaining communication among workers in an article that appeared in The San Antonio Business Journal.

   I read several good suggestions about maintaining communication among workers in an article that appeared in *The San Antonio Business Journal*.

8. We played a communication game in which we had to complete the sentence, "Say it like a pro and listen . . . ."

   Yes

O V E R V I E W

Punctuation is more than knowing where to place a period and a comma. Although the other marks of punctuation presented in this chapter are not so frequently used as the period and comma, they can add variety and clarity to your sentences.

Semicolons and colons are additional ways to indicate pauses in your writing. Dashes, parentheses, and italics (or underlines) set off or emphasize information. Quotation marks, apostrophes, and hyphens are necessary for clarity. The remaining marks—ellipses, brackets, and asterisks—have specific uses also. By adding these other marks of punctuation to your knowledge of using periods, commas, and grammatical structure, you will have a sound foundation for writing.

The rules for these other punctuation marks provide consistency and standardization in their use; therefore, this area of punctuation requires study and practice.

THE SEMICOLON

A semicolon (;) is a mark of punctuation that indicates a pause. The semicolon is not so strong as a period, but it is stronger than a comma.

Independent Clauses

Use a semicolon to separate two closely related independent clauses that are not joined by a coordinating conjunction (*and, or, nor, but*).

Indicate the specific action you expect the reader of your memo to take; suggest only one action.

(The two closely related clauses are not separated by a coordinating conjunction. A semicolon is necessary to separate the two clauses.)

Conjunctive Adverbs

Use a semicolon to separate two independent clauses joined by a conjunctive adverb such as *however, nevertheless, therefore, moreover,* and *furthermore*. A comma usually follows a conjunctive adverb of two or more syllables.

The speaker arrived late; nevertheless, he had an effective multimedia presentation.

(The two independent clauses are joined by the conjunctive adverb *nevertheless*. A semicolon is placed before the word *nevertheless*, and a comma follows the word. This sentence could also be separated into two sentences: *The speaker arrived late. Nevertheless, he had an effective multimedia presentation.* The second sentence has a conjunctive adverb [*nevertheless*] followed by a comma and an independent clause.)

Go to Transparencies/PowerPoints 17-1a, 17-1b, and 17-2.

See Instructor Notes 17-1, 17-2, 17-3, and 17-4 in IAE.

Use a semicolon to separate two independent clauses that are not joined by a coordinating conjunction.

Go to Transparency/PowerPoint 17-3.

See Instructor Notes 17-5 and 17-6 in IAE.

Refer to Chapter 15 for a list of conjunctive adverbs.

We take great care in writing letters to make good impressions; however, we become very informal in writing e-mail messages and often leave poor impressions.

(A semicolon is placed before *however* to separate the two independent clauses. A comma follows the conjunctive adverb *however*.)

Enumerations and Explanations

See Instructor Note 17-7 in IAE.

Use a semicolon before such introductory expressions as *for example* (e.g.), *that is* (i.e.), or *namely* when they introduce enumerations, explanations, or examples that are not essential to the sentence. Place a comma after the expressions. (Refer to the section on colons for enumerations, explanations, or examples that are essential to the sentence.)

We are changing our holiday sales campaign; for example, we are sending out several gift catalogs rather than just one.

(The expression *for example* introduces an explanation that is not necessary for the meaning of the first independent clause. A semicolon is necessary before the words *for example,* and a comma follows.)

A manager should communicate his or her expectations to the teams; namely, his or her deadlines for reports to management and the format for the reports.

(*Namely* suggests an enumeration that is not necessary for the meaning of the independent clause. A semicolon is necessary before *namely,* and a comma follows.)

Series

Go to PowerPoint 17-4.

Use a semicolon to separate items in a series if any of the items already contain commas.

People have inquired about the intranet workshops that will be held in Cleveland, Ohio; Pensacola, Florida; Springfield, Illinois; and Little Rock, Arkansas.

(Each city and state combination already contains commas. A semicolon after each state name makes the sentence easier to understand.)

I will be judging students' speeches for Mr. Kendall's business communication class on Monday, May 15; Wednesday, May 17; and Wednesday, May 24.

(Each day and month combination already contains commas. A semicolon after each of the days makes it easier to read the dates.)

Directions: Use the proofreaders' mark ⋏ to insert semicolons and the proofreaders' mark ⋏ to insert commas where necessary.

1. Skimming a report gives you the essential meaning⋏the remaining sentences clarify these major ideas.

2. Something always seemed to block Amy's success⋏namely⋏her lack of communication skills.

3. I tried to explain the delay to my supervisor⋏she seemed too busy to listen.

4. The price for the communication texts did not include shipping costs⋏consequently⋏we must add this amount to your order.

5. His itinerary to present seminars on listening techniques includes Joliet⋏Illinois⋏Terre Haute⋏Indiana⋏and Grand Rapids⋏Michigan.

6. Both high schools have students who may be finalists in the city-wide essay contest⋏for example⋏students in the advanced-level writing classes.

**GO TO
CD-ROM**
CHECKUP 17-1

THE COLON

A colon (:) is a stronger mark of punctuation than a semicolon and a comma. The colon is not so strong as a period. The main function of a colon is to introduce lists.

Introduction to Lists

Use a colon to introduce lists after expressions such as *the following, as follows, these,* and *thus.* Capitalize the word following the colon when items begin on separate lines in a list. Capitalize the word after the colon when two or more complete sentences follow the colon. Do not capitalize the word after the colon when the material (other than an enumerated list) cannot stand alone or when the material explains the first clause.

See Instructor Note 17-8 in IAE.

Refer to a reference manual such as The Gregg Reference Manual *for additional guidelines for the capitalization of material following colons.*

> **A business letter consists of the following parts:**
> 1. **Date line**
> 2. **Inside address**
> 3. **Salutation**
> 4. **Message**
> 5. **Closing**
> 6. **Writer's name and title**
> 7. **Reference initials**

(The expression *the following* suggests that a list will appear. A colon is necessary after the introductory clause. The first word in each line requires a capital letter.)

Go to PowerPoint 17-5.

Before you begin to write copy for a Website, ask <u>these</u> questions:
What aspect of my service or product will benefit the viewer most?
How will it benefit the viewer?
(A colon is necessary between the introductory clause and the two questions. The sentence contains two complete sentences following the colon; therefore, the first word in each sentence requires a capital letter.)

My basic references for writing are <u>as follows:</u> a dictionary, a thesaurus, and an office reference manual.
(The expression *as follows* indicates a list will follow. A colon is necessary after the introductory clause. The items listed do not require capital letters because they cannot stand alone as a complete sentence.)

Incomplete Introductory Clauses

See Instructor Note 17-9 in IAE.

Do not use a colon after an incomplete introductory clause that introduces a list.

The office assistants attending the proofreading workshop are Ann Avery, Mary O'Neill, and Nelson Clark.
(The introductory clause *The office assistants attending the proofreading workshop are* preceding the list cannot stand on its own. No colon is necessary to introduce the list.)

Use a colon if the items in the list appear on separate lines.

The office assistants attending the proofreading workshop are:
Ann Avery
Mary O'Neill
Nelson Clark
(The introductory clause cannot stand on its own; however, since the individuals' names appear on separate lines, a colon is necessary after the word *are.*)

Illustrations and Explanations

See Instructor Note 17-10 in IAE.

Use a colon before expressions such as *namely, for example,* or *that is* when they introduce explanations that are *essential* to the meaning of the sentence.

Three communication minicourses will be offered at our college: namely, punctuation, grammar, and proofreading.
(The introductory clause suggests that an essential explanation is still to appear. The word *namely* identifies the specific courses. A colon precedes the word *namely,* and a comma follows it.)

Several types of lists will help you communicate your ideas: for example, bulleted lists, numbered steps, and modified bulleted lists.
(The introductory clause suggests that an illustration of the lists [essential material] is still to appear. A colon is necessary before the words *for example,* and a comma follows the words.)

Sentence Interruptions

Do not use a colon before a list if another sentence separates the introductory clause and list.

The basic items listed below are suggestions for writing a new product advertisement. All copy for product advertisements require the marketing director's approval.

Benefits

Features

Service

Ordering information

(A sentence interrupts the introductory clause and the list. No colon is necessary after the introductory clause or after the interrupting sentence.)

The following newsletter suggestions work for me. I have a more detailed explanation for each one if you are interested.

1. **Know your objectives.**
2. **Make it easy and quick to read.**
3. **Concentrate on content.**

(No colon is necessary because a sentence interrupts the introductory clause and the list.)

Time

Use a colon between the hour and minutes expressed in figures.

My business communication class begins at 10:30 a.m.

(A colon is necessary between the hour *10* and the minutes *30*.)

Salutations

Use a colon after the salutation in a business letter when using mixed punctuation (a colon after the salutation and a comma after the complimentary close.) Do not use a colon with open punctuation (no punctuation after the salutation or complimentary close).

Dear Manager:

(A colon is necessary after *Manager* in a letter using mixed punctuation.)

Dear Mr. Ramirez

(No colon is necessary after *Ramirez* if the letter uses open punctuation.)

CHECKUP 17-2

Directions: *Use the proofreaders' marks ⊙and ⊙to insert colons and periods where necessary. Use the proofreaders' mark ≡to capitalize letters when necessary. Use the proofreaders' mark ⌀ to delete unnecessary colons.*

1. The last speech class that I took gave me the confidence to do these two things ⊙ give a speech without notes and handle questions with ease.

2. In a letter with mixed punctuation, a salutation for a U.S. senator is as follows⊙

Dear Senator Feingold⊙

3. These businesses responded to our communication survey⊙

l̲e̲gal offices

m̲e̲dical and health facilities

f̲i̲nancial institutions

n̲o̲nprofit organizations

4. You may call the television station with your response to our viewers' questions anytime between the hours of 6⊙30 p.m. to 9⊙30 p.m.

5. Check the following paragraphs in *The Gregg Reference Manual* for suggestions on letter placement⊙The suggestions should be followed for all future assignments.

t̲o̲p margins

s̲i̲de margins

b̲o̲ttom margins

l̲e̲ngthening a short letter

s̲h̲ortening a long letter

6. The survey indicates two trends⊙first, presentation software is replacing the overhead projector. second, companies are investing money in training employees to use the software.

GO TO CD-ROM CHECKUP 17-2

QUOTATION MARKS

See Instructor Note 17-11 in IAE.

Refer to a reference manual such as The Gregg Reference Manual *for additional information about (or additional examples of) direct quotations.*

Commas separate the direct quote from the rest of the sentence.

Quotation marks (" ") identify someone else's words. Quotation marks also set aside parts of published works as well as special words or phrases.

Direct Quotations

Use quotation marks around a direct quotation. A direct quotation includes the exact words spoken or written by someone. Place periods and commas inside the closing quotation mark.

O. R. Mahmud said, "I want our brochure to show that our products are different from the others out there."

(The words between the pair of quotation marks are the exact words of the speaker. The period goes inside the closing quotation mark.)

"I have never analyzed my communication style," she said.

(This is a direct quotation. The comma goes inside the closing quotation mark.)

Indirect Quotations

Do not use quotation marks in an indirect quotation. An indirect quotation is a restatement of the original material. The words *whether* or *that* often introduce an indirect quotation.

I was very pleased when my supervisor told me that I had excellent writing skills.

(The clause *I had excellent writing skills* is not a direct quote by the supervisor and does not need quotation marks around it. The word *that* introduces the indirect quotation.)

The supervisor asked whether we had all completed our survey forms.

(*Whether we had all completed our survey forms* is not a direct quote. No quotation marks are necessary.)

Separated Quotations

Use two sets of quotation marks when a quotation is separated by intervening expressions such as *he said*. Do not capitalize the first word of the second part of the quoted material.

"Business correspondence," says Werner, "must be clearly written and interesting to read."

(The intervening expression [*says Werner*] separates the two parts of the quotation. Both parts require a pair of quotation marks. The word *must* does not require a capital letter.)

Parts of Published Works

Use quotation marks around the names of articles in newspapers and magazines. Use quotations around the titles of chapters in books.

I found an interesting article entitled "Communication Games" in one of my business magazines.

(The title of the article "Communication Games" requires quotes to indicate that it is part of a larger publication—a magazine.)

Our business English instructor assigned the exercises in Chapter 17, "Other Punctuation Marks."

(The chapter title "Other Punctuation Marks" requires quotes around it to designate that it is part of a larger publication—a book. The period goes inside the closing quotation mark.)

Technical or Unusual Expressions

Use quotation marks around technical or unusual expressions.

Leave enough "white space" on each page of your newsletter.

(The technical term *white space* requires quotation marks around it for emphasis.)

Do not use the expression "Thanking you in advance for your cooperation" because it is an obsolete phrase.

(The outdated expression *thanking you in advance for your cooperation* requires quotation marks around it.)

Go to PowerPoint 17-6.

Refer to a reference manual such as The Gregg Reference Manual *for a discussion on using quotation marks with the titles of literary and artistic works.*

Refer to a reference manual such as The Gregg Reference Manual *for information on using quotation marks to emphasize expressions.*

See Instructor Note 17-12 in IAE.

See Instructor Note 17-13 in IAE.

Special Effect Words

Use quotation marks around slang words or special effect words and phrases.

> **I think the newsletter column that features different employees each month is "cool."**
> (The slang word *cool* requires quotation marks around it.)

> **Darrin's e-mail messages are rude, and I would like to suggest that he apply some "netiquette" to his writing.**
> (The use of the word *netiquette* is intended for special effect and requires quotation marks.)

Instructions

Use quotation marks to highlight instructions introduced by the words *signed, entitled, marked, labeled,* and *headed.* Capitalize the first letter of the word or phrase.

> **I returned the files to Dan in an envelope marked "Confidential."**
> (The word *marked* introduces *Confidential,* an instruction that requires quotation marks around it.)

> **Please place all messages that must be answered by 4 p.m. in a folder labeled "Urgent."**
> (The word *labeled* introduces *urgent,* an implied instruction. *Urgent* requires quotation marks around it.)

Quotation Marks With Other Marks of Punctuation

Place a question mark or exclamation point inside the closing quotation mark when the question mark or exclamation point applies only to the quoted material.

> **The office assistant asked, "Did you want the e-mail addresses before noon?"**
> (The question applies to the direct quote; the question does not apply to the entire sentence. The question mark goes inside the closing quotation mark.)

> **"What a surprise!" exclaimed Mary when she heard that she had placed first in the speech contest sponsored by Kiwanis.**
> (The exclamation point refers to the direct quote; the explanation point does not apply to the entire sentence. The exclamation point goes inside the closing quotation mark.)

Place a question mark or exclamation point outside the closing quotation mark when the exclamation point or question mark applies to the entire sentence.

> **Are you sure that she said, "The PowerPoint workshop will be on Friday, not Thursday"?**
> (The question refers to the entire sentence. The question mark goes outside the closing quotation mark.)

Place semicolons and colons after the closing quotation mark.

Our instructor repeated, "Periods and commas go inside the closing quotation mark"; however, some of us had trouble remembering this rule.

(The semicolon goes after the closing quotation mark.)

The envelope containing the following items should be marked "Priority": budget committee minutes and agenda for Friday's meeting.

(The colon goes after the closing quotation mark.)

CHECKUP 17-3

Directions: *Use the appropriate proofreaders' mark* ⩔ *to insert quotation marks where necessary. Use the proofreaders' mark* ≡ *to capitalize letters where necessary. Use the proofreaders' mark* ⌒ *to delete unnecessary quotation marks.*

1. The team leader said "that the team's report would be used as the basis for improving communication."

2. I told my assistant that an envelope marked "personal" should not be opened.

3. "Speaking before large audiences," said our speech instructor, "is a skill that you can practice by listening to these motivational tapes at home."

4. Did Mary say, "I think listening skills are as important as speaking skills?"

5. My supervisor tends to "hit the ceiling" every time I misunderstand his directions.

6. I really do not like these "smileys" that everyone seems to be placing on e-mail messages.

7. She distributed the article "Listening is an Art" to the people attending the seminar.

8. I asked, "don't dashes and parentheses have similar functions in sentences?"

9. My mechanic gets this look of "Spare me," however, I attempt to communicate by mimicking the noises that my car makes when I start it.

10. "The news release must be on the editor's desk by this afternoon," said Gloria.

GO TO
CD-ROM
CHECKUP 17-3

THE APOSTROPHE

An apostrophe (') is used to indicate a missing letter in a contraction or a possessive. An apostrophe is also used in some plural forms.

Contractions

Use an apostrophe to show the omission of a letter or letters in a contraction.

I'm	= I + am	isn't	= is + not
couldn't	= could + not	we're	= we + are
they'll	= they + will	it's	= it + is

See Instructor's Note 17-14 in IAE.

Refer to Chapter 5 for a review of possessive forms of nouns.

Possessives

To form the possessive of a singular noun or an irregular plural noun, add an apostrophe and s ('s) to the noun. (An irregular plural noun does not end in s.) To form the possessive of a regular plural noun that ends in s or es, add an apostrophe only.

Singular Possessive	**Irregular Plural Possessive**
Jane's speech	women's issues
speaker's message	children's essays
writer's ideas	salespeople's body language

Plural Possessive
students' speeches
employees' newsletter
proofreaders' marks

Plurals

Do not use an apostrophe to form the plurals of words from other parts of speech used as nouns unless the word would be easily misread.

His newsletter article generated some pros and cons among the readers.
(The words *pros* and *cons* do not require an apostrophe and s ('s) for their plural forms. Their meanings are not likely to be misconstrued.)

She uses too many so's in her writing.
(The word *so's* requires an apostrophe to avoid a misreading.)

Lowercase Letters and Abbreviations

To form the plurals of lowercase letters and abbreviations with letters, add an apostrophe and s ('s). The apostrophe is used so that the resulting plurals are not confused with other words.

crossing t's and dotting i's   two letter a's
several c.o.d.'s

Numbers

Go to PowerPoint 17-7.

To form the plurals of numbers expressed in figures, add an s. Adding an apostrophe and s ('s) is not necessary.

in the 1990s   size 10s   four 4s
several 5s   two Form 941s   two No. 942s

Capital Letters and Abbreviations

Go to PowerPoint 17-8.

To form the plurals of the single capital letters *A, I, M,* and *U,* add an apostrophe and s ('s) to avoid misunderstandings in meanings.

A's   I's   M's   U's

Do not add an apostrophe and *s* (*'s*) to form the plurals of other singular capital letters.

four Ns   two Ks

To form plurals of abbreviations ending with capital letters, add *s* only.

CPAs   HMOs   PCs   M.A.s   Ph.D.s

Quotations Within Quoted Material

Use apostrophes (single quotation marks) around a quotation within a quotation. Place the period inside the closing apostrophe.

John M. Mora wrote, "A sentence longer than 30 words usually needs a 'brevity check.'"

(The words *brevity check* require single quotation marks to set them aside from the rest of the sentence. The period goes inside the single closing quotation mark.)

CHECKUP 17-4

Directions: Use the proofreaders' mark ⱽ to add an apostrophe where needed. Use the proofreaders' mark ꟿ to delete unnecessary apostrophes.

1. Margies address is easy to remember; it has two 5's followed by two 4's.
2. The speaker said, "Theres always a danger of getting too folksy in your business correspondence."
3. The plant secretaries English review class meets at 6:45 a.m. on Fridays.
4. Dora uses too many "you knows" in her conversations.
5. My supervisors handwriting is difficult to read because she doesnt cross her ts.
6. I have completed the registration packets for all the Ms.

GO TO CD-ROM
CHECKUP 17-4

THE HYPHEN

A hyphen (-) has a variety of uses in compound words and in numbers. A hyphen also indicates syllabication. Changes in word hyphenation sometimes occur over time. For example, in the past, *on-line* was the preferred spelling. Now *online* (no hyphen) is preferred. Use a current dictionary as a helpful reference.

Compound Numbers

Use a hyphen with compound numbers from *twenty-one* through *ninety-nine*.

See Instructor Note 17-15 in IAE.

Thirty-five messages arrived yesterday.
Two hundred seventy-five registrations have been received.

See Instructor Note 17-16 in IAE.

Refer to Chapter 12 for a review of the use of the hyphen in compound adjectives.

For compound adjectives that require hyphens, refer to your reference manual under the heading "Compound Adjectives."

See Instructor Note 17-17 In IAE.

SLIP-UP

Want ad: Christmas tag sale. Handmade gifts for the hard-to-find person. [Note: Is the person hard to find or is the gift hard to find?] Source: Internet.

SLIP-UP

Want ad: "3-year-old teacher needed for pre-school. Experience preferred." [Note: Exactly how much experience do you have when you are three?] Source: Internet.

Fractions

Use a hyphen to separate the numerator (top number in a fraction) from the denominator (bottom number) of a fraction written in words.

> **three-fourths** of the page
> **two-fifths** majority

Compound Adjectives

Use a hyphen in a compound adjective (two or more words) that precedes a noun. In most situations, do not hyphenate a compound adjective that follows the noun modified.

> He summarized the sensitive issue in a **well-written** memo.
> The memo is **well written**.
> She made a number of **off-the-record** comments.
> She asked that her comments be kept **off the record**.
> The **up-to-date** report contains many illustrations.
> The report is **up to date** and contains many illustrations.

Numbers and Nouns

Use a hyphen in an adjective consisting of a number and a noun that precedes the noun modified.

> **first-rate** job   the **two-letter** state abbreviation
> a **$25-a-month** charge   a **30-minute** presentation

Suspending Hyphens

When two or more hyphenated adjectives have a common element and this element is shown only with the last term, use a suspending hyphen after each of the incomplete adjectives to show a relationship with the last term.

> **12- to 15-hour** project
> **two- or three-column** newsletter
> **large- and small-scale** drawings
> **long- and short-term** assignments

Compound Nouns

Do not hyphenate well-known compound nouns acting as adjectives. If the compound noun does not appear as one word or as a hyphenated word in a dictionary, assume the word is written as two words.

> **public relations** consultant
> **high school** newsletter
> **accounts receivable** aged report
> **real estate** description

Adverbs

Do not place a hyphen after an adverb ending in *ly* that is combined with a present or past participle.

Refer to Chapter 10 for a review of participles.

an <u>extremely interesting</u> speaker
<u>hastily prepared</u> speech
<u>clearly documented</u> manuscript
<u>carefully edited</u> copy

Prefix *Re*

In most words beginning with *re,* the prefix *re* should not be followed by a hyphen. However, use a hyphen in those words beginning with *re* that look like other words with the same spelling but are different in meaning and pronunciation.

<u>re-sign</u>	resign	<u>re-mark</u>	remark
<u>re-collect</u>	recollect	<u>re-sort</u>	resort
<u>re-count</u>	recount		

Self Prefixes

Use a hyphen after the word *self* when it acts as a prefix.

<u>self-confidence</u>   <u>self-paced</u>

Range of Numbers or Letters

Use a hyphen to indicate a range of numbers or letters. The hyphen takes the place of the word *to.*

<u>10-12</u> years   March <u>12-16</u> Letters <u>A-C</u>

One Person With Two Functions

Use a hyphen to indicate dual functions performed by one person.

<u>owner-manager</u>   <u>director-producer</u>
<u>secretary-treasurer</u>   <u>teacher-counselor</u>

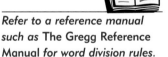

Refer to a reference manual such as The Gregg Reference Manual *for word division rules.*

See Instructor Note 17-18 in IAE.

Word Division

Avoid dividing a word at the end of a line; however, if you must divide a word, follow these rules. Use a hyphen to divide a word at the end of a line to show that it cannot be completed on that line. Place the hyphen at the end of the first line, not at the beginning of the second line. Divide words only between syllables. Always refer to a dictionary when you are not certain about the correct syllabication of a word.

continued	<u>con-tin-ued</u>
conference	<u>con-fer-ence</u>

Format. Leave three characters (one may be the hyphen) on the first line and carry the rest of the word to the second line. Carry at least three characters (the last may be a punctuation mark) to the second line. Avoid dividing words with fewer than six letters.

> **data   imply   party   eager   only   ready**
> (These words should not be divided. They have fewer than six letters.)
>
> **experience   ex-pe-ri-ence   secretary   sec-re-tary**
> (These words follow the rule that three characters [one may be a hyphen] must be left on a line with the remainder of the word carried to the next line.)

One-Syllable Words.   Do not divide one-syllable words. The addition of *ed* still leaves these words as one-syllable words.

> **first   length   think   cleared   marked   searched**

Abbreviations and Contractions.   Do not divide abbreviations or contractions.

> **dept.   AT&T   wouldn't   o'clock**
> **f.o.b.   ASCII   we'll   WYSIWIG**

Double Consonants.   Divide a word between double consonants if the base word contains a double consonant.

> **collect   col-lect   correspond   cor-re-spond**
> **difficult   dif-fi-cult**

One-Letter Syllables.   Do not divide a one-letter syllable at the beginning or the end of a word.

> **agenda   agen-da   enormous   enor-mous**
>
> Divide *after* a one-letter syllable that appears within a word.
>
> **category   cate-gory   regular   regu-lar**
> **similar   simi-lar**

Separately Sounded Vowels.   Divide between two separately sounded vowels that appear together in a word.

> **influential   in-flu-en-tial   create   cre-ate**

CHECKUP 17-5

Directions: Use the proofreaders' mark $\stackrel{=}{\wedge}$ to insert hyphens where needed. Use the proofreaders' mark to delete unnecessary hyphens.

1. That long three hour meeting of the budget committee created friction between the chairperson and the secretary treasurer.

2. You will find the e mail policies on pages 34 40 of the employee handbook.

3. We specialize in developing presentation materials for minority͞ͅand women-owned businesses.

4. At its last meeting, the budget committee authorized one͞ͅeighth of the total budget for a communications lab.

5. His well͞ͅorganized illustrations and easily͞ͅunderstood directions made the exercises simple to complete.

6. Marie purchased a self͞ͅstudy book that contained a step͞ͅby͞ͅstep guide to improve listening effectiveness.

GO TO CD-ROM
CHECKUP 17-5

CHECKUP 17-6

Directions: *In the space provided, rewrite the word and insert hyphens at those points where each word could be divided at the end of a line. Write **No** if the word should not be divided.*

1.	message	mes-sage
2.	communication	com-mu-ni-ca-tion
3.	courtesy	cour-tesy
4.	wouldn't	No
5.	portfolio	port-fo-lio
6.	aloud	No
7.	negative	nega-tive
8.	occurrence	oc-cur-rence
9.	watched	No
10.	mfg.	No

GO TO CD-ROM
CHECKUP 17-6

THE DASH

A dash (—) may be substituted for a comma, semicolon, colon, or parentheses only if there is a noticeable break in a sentence or if a word, phrase, or clause needs to be emphasized. Dashes may enclose essential as well as nonessential material. Do not use a dash just because you are not sure which mark of punctuation is correct.

En dashes and *em dashes* are available with most word processing software. En dashes are longer than a hyphen but not so long as em dashes. En dashes are used as substitutions for the word *to* in number sequences (20–25 years). Em dashes are used in all other places where a dash is necessary. Use two hyphens for a dash if your software does not have em dash capabilities.

See Instructor Note 17-19 in IAE.

Use the dash sparingly in formal writing.

Change of Thought

Use a dash to indicate a break or a change of thought in a sentence.

Listen attentively—with your eyes as well as your ears—so that people recognize your interest in their remarks.
(The dash sets aside a break *with your eyes as well as your ears.*)

Andrew's business plan—50 pages long—included his plans for the future of his company.
(The dash sets aside a change of thought.)

Parenthetical Comment

Use a dash to set off a parenthetical comment or an afterthought from the rest of the sentence.

Either during the first or second week in October—I cannot remember exactly—I wrote to you about our change of address.
(The dash sets aside *I cannot remember exactly,* which is a nonessential parenthetical expression.)

They agreed on all the final recommendations—every one of them!
(*Every one of them* is an afterthought and requires dashes to set it apart from the rest of the sentence.)

Repetitions and Reminders

Use a dash to set off repetitious statements or to emphasize a reminder.

Words left out of letters or misspelled names are common errors made by writers—errors that could be avoided.
(The word *errors* is repeated. A dash sets the word *errors* off from the rest of the sentence.)

Don't forget the orientation meeting—January 2 at 4 p.m.—with our new employees.
(*January 2 at 4 p.m.* is a reminder set off by dashes from the rest of the sentence.)

Summary Words

See Instructor Note 17-20 in IAE.

Use a dash before the words *these, they, any, all,* and *each* when these words are used as subjects to summarize a preceding list.

Accuracy, completeness, clarity, and conciseness—these are the goals that I try to remember when I am writing.
(The dash precedes the subject *these.*)

Listening, speaking, and writing—each represents a skill that managers and supervisors need.
(The dash precedes the subject *each.*)

CHECKUP 17-7

Directions: *In the following sentences, use the proofreaders' mark ∧ to insert dashes where needed.*

1. Terry had to give a sales presentation on a new product∧a presentation that required detailed diagrams and examples.

2. Sally wasted much of her time∧too much of it∧trying to write a perfect first draft of a report.

3. After the meeting, I had nothing to say∧nothing at all.

4. We have more than one hundred inquiries∧all in response to our Web page ad∧that we must answer.

5. The objective, the outline, and the format∧these need to be determined before you begin to write the report.

6. The chairperson's next tactic∧no one should be offended∧is to limit each individual's discussion time at our meetings.

GO TO CD-ROM
CHECKUP 17-7

PARENTHESES

Parentheses (( )), like dashes, enclose interruptions in sentences. However, parentheses set off only nonessential information. Using parentheses does not appear so abrupt as using dashes. Parentheses de-emphasize material; dashes emphasize material.

See Instructor Note 17-21 in IAE.

Nonessential Material

Use parentheses to set off nonessential material that is not intended to be part of the main statement. Do not capitalize the first word of material within the parentheses if it is a short complete sentence. Capitalize the first word of material within the parentheses if the sentence is lengthy.

Refer to a reference manual such as **The Gregg Reference Manual** *for examples of punctuation with parentheses.*

Lindsay Dotson (she was a Mansfield graduate) is now the public relations director for IPAL.
(The parentheses set aside *she was a Mansfield graduate,* which is nonessential material. The word *she* is not capitalized since it begins a short sentence that appears within a sentence.)

The director chose Marty as the team leader for the Crawford project. (His communication skills surpass those of the other members on the team.)
(The sentence in parentheses is lengthy. The first word *his* requires a capital letter.)

Other Punctuation

501

Lists

Use parentheses around numbers or letters that identify a list of items in the text copy.

The school referendum failed for these reasons: (1) lack of communication with the voters, (2) cost of computer facilities, and (3) increase in taxes.

(Parentheses make it easier to read numbered lists included in the text copy.)

1. Evaluate your presentation by asking these questions: (a) How did your audience react? (b) Were the visual aids effective? (c) What were the strengths of the presentation?

(Use letters if a number is already used in the sentence context.)

Outlines

Use parentheses for sections of an outline.

    I.   VISION AND MISSION
       A. Set Target Dates
          1. Status reports
             a. Organizational
                (1) Format
                   (a) Written outline
                   (b) Formal report
                (2) Frequency

(The parentheses around (1) and (2) and around (a) and (b) include the fifth and sixth subdivisions in this outline.)

Nonessential References and Directions

Use parentheses to enclose a nonessential reference or set of directions.

This article includes three samples of correct formats for business letters (Figures 6, 7, and 8).

(The material in parentheses is a nonessential reference notation.)

Please send the memo to all branch offices. (Be sure to use today's date.)

(The material in parentheses is a direction.)

Explanations

Use parentheses to enclose explanatory words or phrases.

The Association for Business Communication (ABC) met in San Antonio for the fall meeting.

(The letters in parentheses are the abbreviation of the Association for Business Communication.)

At our last meeting, the chairperson assigned accountabilities (who is responsible for each job) and established tentative due dates.

(*Who is responsible for each job* explains the meaning of the word *accountabilities.*)

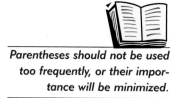

Numbers in Formal Documents

Use parentheses around figures that follow amounts written in words in legal or formal business documents.

In the last collection letter I received, you indicated that I owed three thousand two hundred dollars ($3,200).

CHECKUP 17-8

Directions: Use the proofreaders' mark ( ) to insert parentheses where necessary. Use the proofreaders' mark ≡ to capitalize letters where necessary. Use the proofreaders' mark ⌀ to delete unnecessary parentheses.

1. The terms of the contract give employees retroactive pay for (ninety) (90) days.

2. My former business communication instructor had high standards (she required correct grammar), which helped me become a good newspaper reporter.

3. Avoid these redundant expressions in your correspondence: (1) *each and every,* (2) *consensus of opinion,* (3) *refer back,* and (4) *true facts.*

4. Pressing the palms of your hands together tightly relieves tension. (try this the next time you give a speech.)

5. Companies hiring new graduates rated communication skills (see Table 10) high on their lists of employment requisites.

6. WYSIWYG (what you see is what you get) was a significant computer design feature that improved the communication process.

GO TO CD-ROM CHECKUP 17-8

ITALICS

Use italic type to emphasize words and phrases and to indicate titles of complete published works.

See Instructor Note 17-22 in IAE.

Definitions and Word Emphasis

Use italics to identify words that are being defined or highlighted.

The number of *fantastics* and *terrifics* in William's speech reflected a somewhat limited vocabulary.

(Italics are used to highlight the words *fantastics* and *terrifics.*)

The term *at-will* means that an employer can fire an employee as long as the reason is not illegal.

(Italics are used to identify the term *at-will* that is being defined.)

Published Materials

See Instructor Note 17-23 in IAE.

Use italics to identify complete published works such as titles of books, newspapers, magazines, and pamphlets. Use italics for titles of movies, plays, television and radio series, paintings, and sculptures. When you proofread, underline the phrase or word to be italicized.

The *Leader Telegram,* our local newspaper, featured several articles on public speaking.

(Italics are used to identify the newspaper *Leader Telegram,* which is a complete published work.)

The chapter "Oral Presentations" appears in the book *Communication Systems.*

(Italics are used to identify the book *Communication Systems,* which is a complete published work.)

ELLIPSIS MARKS

SLIP-UP

Excuse for missing work. "I've used up all my sick days . . . so I'm calling in dead!" Source: The Internet.

Ellipsis marks (…) indicate that part of a quoted sentence is omitted. The ellipsis marks also are used for highlighting information such as specific points in advertising copy.

Omissions

Use ellipsis marks to indicate omissions in quoted material. Use three spaced periods to designate omissions at the beginning or in the middle of a sentence. Use four spaced periods (or other ending punctuation) at the end of a sentence. Do not use more or fewer periods.

Barry advised, "Audiovisual aids enhance a speech. . . . To be effective, the visuals must be dynamic."

(Four spaced periods are necessary to identify the omission because it falls at the end of the sentence. One of the periods is the ending mark of punctuation.)

Barry advised, "Audiovisual aids enhance a speech . . . but require careful planning."

(Three spaced periods are necessary to identify the omission because it falls in the middle of the sentence.)

Displays

Use ellipsis marks to highlight specific points. Advertising displays often include ellipsis marks to identify points that the advertisers wish to emphasize.

An Action-Oriented Book That Will Help You
. . . Communicate Better With Supervisors
. . . Get Your Ideas Accepted
. . . Improve Your Presentation Skills

(Ellipsis marks [three spaced periods] introduce each emphasized line. Advertising copy often uses capital letters for each word.)

BRACKETS

Brackets ([ ]) are used when a separation is necessary in a sentence already enclosed in parentheses, when an error occurs in quoted material, or when an editorial comment is made in a quotation. Brackets are not used frequently in business documents.

Errors

Insert the word *sic* in brackets immediately after a misspelled word, grammatical error, or factual error made by the person quoted. *Sic* means "so" or "thus" and points out that the error was not made by the present writer but was present in the original version.

The job advertised in the Tuesday evening *Tribune* was for someone "with computer knowledge and good grammer [sic] skills."
(The word *grammar* is misspelled. The word was misspelled by the person who submitted the ad.)

The speaker ended his presentation by saying, "Listening skills are the key to effective management." [Applause indicated agreement.]
(The material in the bracket is not part of the quoted material but is the writer's interpretation of the applause.)

Parenthetical Expressions Within Parentheses

Use brackets to enclose a parenthetical expression within a statement that is already within parentheses. Place the shorter parenthetical expression in brackets and place the longer parenthetical statement in parentheses.

(Review Chapter 16 [commas] before you rewrite your report.)
(The parenthetical word *commas* is enclosed in brackets to set it aside from the rest of the material already in parentheses.)

THE ASTERISK

The main purpose of the asterisk (*) is to refer the reader to another location for a more detailed explanation or reference.

Use an asterisk to indicate that a footnote or explanation appears in a table or at the bottom of the page. Place an asterisk after a comma, semicolon, colon, or period.

> **The average manager spends 10 percent of his or her time writing and 15 percent reading.***
>
> (The asterisk indicates that the percentage is explained in another location. The asterisk is placed after the period.)

CHECKUP 17-9

Directions: Insert italics (underline), ellipsis marks, brackets, or asterisks where necessary. Use the proofreaders' mark ⌐ to delete unnecessary punctuation marks. If the sentence is correct, write **Yes** in the space provided.

1. The word <u>grammar</u> is often misspelled in job advertisements. _____

2. Our Satisfied Participants say: _____ Yes
  . . . Excellent Speakers
  . . . Useful Study Guides
  . . . Organized Presentations

3. The *Book of Lists** identifies speaking before a group as _____ Yes
  the top human fear in the United States.

4. The following books are useful in writing a business plan: <u>How to Write a Clear,</u> _____
  <u>Effective Business Plan</u> and <u>Business Plans That Win.</u>

5. Gossip flourishes when employees lose faith in administration . . . ⌐or when _____
  employees feel helpless.

6. (Please use 3- by 5-inch notes [Post-it Notes] to list agenda items.) _____ Yes

**GO TO
CD-ROM
CHECKUP 17-9**

DIAGRAMMING SENTENCES

See Instructor Note 17-24 in IAE.

The sentences for diagramming are a review of the rules you have studied in the past 16 chapters.

Directions: *In the space provided, diagram the following sentences. All words may be diagrammed.*

1. Supervisors need training in the communication of goals to front-line workers.

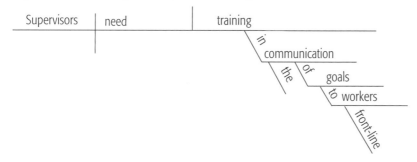

2. At the end of a meeting, identify those items that need future consideration.

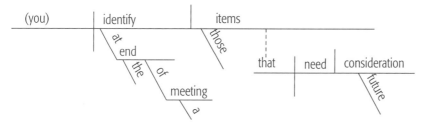

3. People often receive the nonverbal message and do not hear the words.

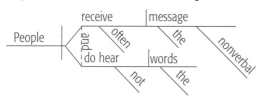

4. Corporate executives use factual reports for policy or action decisions.

5. My supervisor requires fact-based written and verbal communication from everyone.

**GO TO
CD-ROM
CHECKUP 17-10**

PRACTICE 1A

A. **Directions:** *Check the following sentences for punctuation errors. Rewrite the sentences correctly in the space provided. If the sentence is punctuated correctly, write* **Yes.**

1. The intranet carried an employee information announcement concerning up to date communication procedures.

   The intranet carried an employee information announcement concerning up-to-date communication procedures.

2. To improve your writing, obtain a copy of *The Elements of Style* by Strunk and White.

   Yes

3. In your next report, omit some of the I's.

   Yes

4. I checked out several books all on the topic of nonverbal communication from the public library.

   I checked out several books—all on the topic of nonverbal communication— from the public library.

5. "Public speaking is uncomfortable for many people, says Bill Menard, because it was never taught properly."

   "Public speaking is uncomfortable for many people," says Bill Menard, "because it was never taught properly."

6. Most people are not good listeners they are too busy thinking about what they are going to say next.

   Most people are not good listeners; they are too busy thinking about what they are going to say next.

7. Nonverbal communication consists of the following; (1) eye contact, (2) gestures, (3) mannerisms, and (4) body movement.

   Nonverbal communication consists of the following: (1) eye contact, (2) gestures, (3) mannerisms, and (4) body movement.

8. Heather's last e mail message was a reminder to attend the seminar on womens issues.

   Heather's last e-mail message was a reminder to attend the seminar on women's issues.

NAME _____

B. Directions: *In each of the following sentences, a mark or marks of punctuation are missing. In the space provided, write the code for the missing mark of punctuation. Then use proofreaders' marks to indicate the correct placement of the punctuation in the sentence. Use underlining to indicate italics.*

Semi = *Semicolon*	**Hy** = *Hyphen*
Col = *Colon*	**Dash** = *Dash*
QM = *Quotation Marks*	**Paren** = *Parentheses*
Apos = *Apostrophe*	**Ital** = *Italics*

1. Write a simple, straightforward document use declarative sentences.

   1. _____Semi_____

2. Did you know that many words used in formal report writing such as <u>sic</u> and <u>ibid</u> are Latin words?

   2. _____Ital, Ital_____

3. Most labor-law experts agree that a business needs an employee handbook one that clearly identifies policies, rules, and benefits.

   3. _____Dash_____

4. Liquid crystal display (LCD) portable projectors are perfect for speakers who enjoy making dynamic presentations.

   4. _____Paren_____

5. The clients name was misspelled again, said John.

   5. _____QM, Apos, QM_____

6. I thought her letter sounded self centered and arrogant.

   6. _____Hy_____

7. The term <u>layout</u> refers to the process of making a page look the way you want it to be.

   7. _____Ital_____

8. She thought my well intended compliment was insensitive.

   8. _____Hy_____

9. Every meeting has three stages planning, conducting, and evaluating.

   9. _____Col_____

10. Deb uses desktop publishing software to create slides she prints them on a color laser printer.

    10. _____Semi_____

**GO TO
CD-ROM**
PRACTICE 1
EXERCISES

PRACTICE 2A

Directions: *Use proofreaders' marks to make the necessary corrections in punctuation and capitalization. Use underlining to indicate italics. More than one correction in a sentence may be needed.*

See Instructor Note 17-25 in IAE.

1. Use the exact format of the company name as it appears in the companys letterhead for example Sean McQuinn & Sons.

2. These are questions that are often asked what is the role of the annual meeting in attracting investors? is the annual report a successful recruitment device for new investors?

PRACTICE

3. Some on the move executives need light weight equipment to deliver their high impact multimedia presentations.

4. The supervisors responsibility is to write an evaluation of the interns progress in meeting his or her on the job learning objectives.

See Instructor Notes 17-26, 17-27, 17-28, and 17-29 in IAE.

5. Almost three fourths of our high school students attend a community or four-year college however the number is less nationwide.

6. Although its possible to create an all purpose brochure, its more difficult to write copy for a general audience. (If budgets allow, create different brochures for different customers.)

7. Betty is a self taught writer its quite evident in her reporting.

8. Bon asked Is the equipment available for a presentation on Friday?

9. The officers of our family business include the following Rod Cole, president Maggie Cole, vice president Donna Weins, secretary treasurer.

**GO TO
CD-ROM**
PRACTICE 2
EXERCISES

10. Richard Koonce stated, too many managers practice mushroom management these managers control their employees by keeping them in the dark.

PRACTICE 3A

PROOFREADING

*Directions: Proofread and compare the two sentences in each group. If they are the same, write **Yes** in the space provided. If they are not the same, write **No**. Use the first sentence as the correct copy. If you find errors in the second sentence, underline them; insert any omitted words or marks of punctuation.*

1. NEC Technologies Inc. has a new LCD (liquid crystal display) projector line that weighs less than 16 pounds and has a built-in carrying handle.

   NEC Technologies Inc. has a new L.C.D. (liquid crystal display) projector line that weighs less than 6 pounds and has a builtin carrying handle.

   1. ___No___

2. Three courses in our administrative assistant program— Business English 140, Written Communications 40, and Report Writing 70—stress the importance of communication skills.

   Three courses in our Administrative Assistant program— Business English 140; Written Communications 40; and Report Writing 70—stress the importance of communication skills.

   2. ___No___

3. David Quigley of the advertising agency Quigley and Mather says that the headlines are read five times more than the material beneath them.

3. __No__

David Quigley o~~f~~ the advertising agency Quigley and Mather ~~said~~ that <ins>the</ins> headlines are read five times more than the material beneath them.

4. Over 1300 readers (over 18 years) were tested on editorial and ad copy, and the results showed that 98 percent of the readers misunderstood some part of the material they had read.

4. __No__

Over 1300 readers (over 18 years) were tested on editorial and ad copy, and the results showed that <ins>95</ins> percent of the readers <ins>mis-understood</ins> some part of the material they had read.

Proofreading Exercise

See Instructor Note 17-30 in IAE.

Listening is an important communication skill; however, very few people receive training in listening. The suggestions in the following proofreading exercise will help you improve your listening skills.

Directions: Use proofreaders' marks to edit the following information. If you are not certain about the use of a proofreaders' mark, use your reference manual or the proofreaders' marks on the inside back cover of this textbook.

LISTENING TECHNIQUES

1. Give the speaker your undivided attention. Concentrate on the message or instructions being given, not on the speaker's appearance or mannerisms.

2. Do not become so engrossed in taking notes that you miss the important concepts. (if you have good notes, you will be able to ask appropriate questions for clarification of a point or direction.)

3. Avoid letting your preconcieved ideas about a topic interfer with the message. You may not agree with the message, but you should not "tune it out."

4. Ask appropriate questions after a presentation or a set of instructions has been given. Save your questions, ask them at one time rather than interrupting periodically.

5. Review your notes at once. (Much of the message is lost immediately after hearing it.) Going over a set of notes helps reinforce what has been said and helps you remember the material.

GO TO
CD-ROM
PRACTICE 3
EXERCISES

**GO TO
CD-ROM**
PRACTICE 4
EXERCISES

PRACTICE 4A

WRITING

Directions: Observe the interactions among your classmates as they talk and sit together in different places, like the classroom, library, cafeteria, etc. Notice the space they maintain and how it differs from one person to another. Make notes on your observations. Write a paragraph or two on your observations and include what you believe are the reasons for the different space allocations that you observe.

Answers will vary.

ONLINE EXERCISES

Most professional communication organizations have Websites that explain their services and link their members to various communication resources. Examples of communication organizations include The American Communication Association (ACA), the Association for Business Communication (ABC), or the Society for Technical Communication (STC). In addition, educational institutions either post their course outlines and materials for communication classes on a Web page or offer communication courses totally online. You will find these resources more valuable than using the keywords *nonverbal communication* or *listening* in an online search.

Objective: *Test your knowledge of human communication.*

**Punctuation
ALERT!**

Use exact punctuation when keying an Internet address.

1. With your Internet browser on screen, key:
   http://www.cios.org/www/testme.htm in the location text box. Press the **Enter** key on your keyboard.

2. You will be at the test for human communication on the Communication Institute for Online Scholarship Web page.

3. Twenty-eight questions are listed, ranging from electronic communication to social history of communication. Click on a question to see if you can answer it correctly. When you have answered the question correctly, go on to another question.

4. If you would like to see what the Communication Institute for Online Scholarship main menu offers, click on **Return to CIOS main menu** at the bottom of the test page.

5. If you would like to link to other communication organizations, go to the following Web address:
   http://www.csufresno.edu/speechcomm/wscalink.htm

6. This is the site for the Western States Communication Association. Click on any communication organization that looks interesting to you.

NAME _____

PRACTICE 1B

A. Directions: *Check the following sentences for punctuation errors. Rewrite the sentences correctly in the space provided. If the sentence is punctuated correctly, write* **Yes.**

1. Some refer to caring about office ethics as taking the high road.

   Some refer to caring about office ethics as "taking the high road." (or *taking the high road*.)

2. Here is a copy of an actual—no kidding!—memo that my supervisor sent last week.

   Here is a copy of an actual (no kidding!) memo that my supervisor sent last week.

3. Some people leave their pagers on beep instead of vibrate, which is annoying during meetings.

   Some people leave their pagers on "beep" instead of "vibrate," which is annoying during meetings.

4. John has the habit of saying, "That reminds me. . ."

   John has the habit of saying, "That reminds me . . . ."

5. I am exhausted because I worked a 12-hour day yesterday.

   Yes

6. Our performance evaluation has a number of categories (creativity, initiative, teamwork, etc.) with spaces to indicate "strengths" and "growth opportunities."

   Yes

7. Anna was too self absorbed to actively participate in our conversation.

   Anna was too self-absorbed to actively participate in our conversation.

8. This three to four month research project is more interesting than I thought that it would be.

   This three- to four-month research project is more interesting than I thought that it would be.

9. Jack feels that it is unfair for people to suggest (As many have) that engineers are antisocial.

   Jack feels that is unfair for people to suggest (as many have) that engineers are antisocial.

10. Becoming a good listener means overcoming listening barriers; for example, not concentrating, becoming distracted, and talking instead of listening.

    Yes

B. Directions: *In each of the following sentences, a mark of punctuation is missing. In the space provided, write the code for the missing mark of punctuation. Then use proofreaders' marks to insert the correct punctuation in the sentence. Use underlining to indicate italics.*

Semi = Semicolon	**Hy** = Hyphen
Col = Colon	**Dash** = Dash
QM = Quotation Marks	**Paren** = Parentheses
Apos = Apostrophe	**Ital** = Italics

1. The book Woe is I is a survival guide for those who want a sensible, modern introduction to grammar usage.   **1.** _____Ital_____

2. When taking notes, concentrate on the key points for example, do not write everything that the speaker says.   **2.** _____Semi_____

3. ASAP(as soon as possible)appears on just about every e-mail that Lora sends.   **3.** _____Paren_____

NAME _____

4. The following months have only 30 days April, June, September, and November.

4. _____Col_____

5. Immediately and I mean immediately call 911 for any emergency that occurs.

5. _____Dash_____

6. When companies collect opinions of people who care about a decision, they are involved in a process that some call getting buy-in.

6. _____QM_____

7. Ralph is a strong willed, opinionated manager.

7. _____Hy_____

8. Frauka's manager replied, "That's why we need you to proofread all outgoing correspondence."

8. _____Apos_____

9. Please use the term businessperson instead of businessman.

9. _____Ital_____

10. When it's 9 30 in San Francisco, it is 12 30 in New York City.

10. _____Col_____

PRACTICE 2B

Directions: *Use proofreaders' marks to make the necessary corrections in punctuation and capitalization. Use underlining to indicate italics. More than one correction in a sentence may be needed.*

1. To emphasize an idea, place it first or last in your correspondence(letter, memo, email, or report.)

2. Scott said that his coworkers are not in his opinion busy enough.

3. The videoconference takes advantage of these types of media Audio, Graphics, and Video.

4. The term spamming refers to the sending of unwanted email.

5. Keep your written messages simple don't use more than two or three typefaces.

6. Many email messages do not need to be saved therefore delete electronic messages after reading them.

7. To improve the quality of our written correspondence, we are purchasing new laser printers consequently please notify Sally if you are still using a dot matrix printer.

8. Our products have higher than average sales in Seattle Washington Portland Oregon and Monterey California.

9. To make a form letter more personal, try the following hints :
> **1.** use personalized envelopes instead of labels.
> **2.** spell names correctly.
> **3.** use high grade paper and a laser printer.

10. In the article Understanding Foreign Correspondence, the writer stated that the French prefer a formal salutation such as Very Honored Mr. Professor Hermann.

11. Avoid overusing words that may irritate your listener, said Devron, such as you know or sort of.

12. Joy wondered "Whether we found her five page handout on voice mail too detailed."

13. Please read Chapter 3 in The Art of Communicating before 1 30 p.m. next Tuesday.

14. Our manager had the annoying habit of ending every staff meeting with the words do not forget to cross your t's and dot your i's.

15. During the 1990's, several HMO's underwent massive restructuring.

NAME _____

PRACTICE 3B

PROOFREADING

Directions: *Proofread and compare the two sentences in each group. If they are the same, write **Yes** in the space provided. If they are not the same, write **No**. Use the first sentence as the correct copy. If you find errors in the second sentence, underline them; insert any omitted words or marks of punctuation.*

1. When brainstorming ideas for a presentation, write one idea on a 3- x 5-inch index card or Post-it Note.
   When brainstorming ideas for a presentation, write one idea on a 3 x 5 inch index card or Post-It Note.

   1.____No____

2. Research studies indicate that people who cannot "read" other people's body language have difficulty adjusting their behaviors to improve relationships; consequently, these people are not always socially adaptable or popular.
   Research studies indicate that people who can't read other peoples body language have difficulty adjusting their behaviors to improve relationships; consequently these people are not always socially adaptable or popular.

   2.____No____

3. Although you cannot change your features (without the benefit of plastic surgery), you can control your attractiveness and social acceptance by establishing your own "style" of grooming, clothing, and accessories.
   Although you cannot change your features (without the benefit of plastic surgery) you can control your attractiveness and social acceptance by establishing your own style of grooming, clothing and accessories.

   3.____No____

4. The advertising slogan "Come alive with Pepsi" was translated in one country as "Bring your ancestors back from the dead."
   The advertising slogan "come alive with Pepsi" was translated in one country as "Bring your ancestors back from the dead."

   4.____No____

5. Our human resources specialist often says, "If I receive a résumé or cover letter with a typographical error or if it smells like cigarette smoke, I throw it away."
   Our human resources specialist often says, "If I receive a résumé or cover letter with a typographical error or if it smells like cigarette smoke, I throw it away."

   5.____Yes____

Proofreading Exercise

No matter what your career area, you will attend meetings. At some point in your working life, you may be asked to organize and chair meetings. The suggestions included in the following proofreading exercise will help you plan and conduct effective meetings.

Directions: *Use proofreaders' marks to edit the following information. If you are not certain about the use of a proofreaders' mark, use your reference manual or the proofreaders' marks on the inside back cover of this textbook.*

MEETING MANAGEMENT

1. Determine meeting objectives. What are you trying to accomplish? If their is know clear reason to meet, dont call a meeting.
2. Develop an agenda. If possible (And it generally is), see that every one receives an agenda before the meeting.
3. Appoint an facilitator. The facilitator does not necessarily have to be the person of the highest rank; he or she may be the person who owns the discussion issue or issues.

---

4. Establish ground rules. Ground rules encourage "straight" talk with no "dancing around the issues."

5. Establish the meeting length. Avoid the tendency to get "hung up" on trivial points, and never feel obligated to fill an alloted meeting time period after the goals have been accomplished.

6. Prepare written minutes. Always have someone take notes on the key points of the discussion, and distribute the minutes to the meeting participants (and other concerned parties) within 24 hours.

PRACTICE 4B

WRITING

Stereotyping means judging in a positive or negative way based upon an individual's perceptions. Examples of stereotyping include classifying all homeless people as lazy or people with poor grammar as dumb.

Directions: *Have you ever been stereotyped? Write about a personal experience when you felt someone had stereotyped you.*

Answers will vary.

Because I have dark hair and brown eyes, people try to guess my nationality. People often ask where my ancestors were

born. Since I do not want to be stereotyped by a nationality, I always respond to questions about my ancestry by saying

that I am an American.

ONLINE EXERCISES

Because communication problems are typically funny, many cartoonists draw cartoons around the theme of communications. Your teacher or other class members have probably brought cartoons to class to add humor to your business English class.

Objective: *To find a cartoon depicting a communication problem.*

1. With your Internet browser on screen, key:

   http://www.unitedmedia.com/comics/ in the location text box at the top of your screen.

   Press the **Enter** key on your keyboard.

2. You will be at the Comic Strip Website for United Media. The page provides links to over 20 comic strips. Click on a comic strip and find a cartoon which pertains to communication. You will definitely find communication jokes in the *Dilbert* and *Frank & Ernest* strips.

3. Print the cartoon and share it with the class.

Posttest

Directions: Check the following sentences for punctuation and capitalization errors. Rewrite the sentences correctly in the space provided. If the sentence is punctuated and capitalized correctly, write **Yes.**

1. Nonverbal cues are especially important in conveying feelings, some researchers maintain that a nonverbal message contributes more to the message than the spoken words.

   Nonverbal cues are especially important in conveying feelings; some researchers maintain that a nonverbal message contributes more to the message than the spoken words.

2. "Quadico strives for effective communication, said the speaker, and uses the following techniques when introducing a new employee benefits plan; written summaries, face to face training meetings, and videos."

   "Quadico strives for effective communication," said the speaker, "and uses the following techniques when introducing a new employee benefits plan: written summaries, face-to-face training meetings, and videos."

3. Your receiver's feedback lets you know if you have not communicated accurately.

   Yes

4. Many businesses offer in house training programs in communications.

   Many businesses offer in-house training programs in communications.

5. Spanish, Japanese, Chinese, Italian, and French these are the languages in our diverse workforce that have enriched my understanding of different cultures.

   Spanish, Japanese, Chinese, Italian, and French—these are the languages in our diverse workforce that have enriched my understanding of different cultures.

6. We use the Internet daily for our research. (see "Online Search Procedures" for information about using search engines.)

   We use the Internet daily for our research. (See "Online Search Procedures" for information about using search engines.)

7. *The MLA Style Manual* gives suggestions for citing online resources.

   Yes

8. Jenny Simpson said, "good listening supports effective relationships in the organization . . ."

   Jenny Simpson said, "Good listening supports effective relationships in the organization . . . ."

CHAPTER 18

Numbers

DOING BUSINESS ON THE INTERNET

During the Internet's first twenty years, government organizations and educational institutions were the major users. They used the Internet primarily to do research and to exchange information. These Internet users felt that the Internet was "above" commercial activity like marketing and advertising.

With the addition of colorful graphics and a point-and-click interface, interest in the Internet exploded dramatically in the 1990s. As millions of consumers started using the Internet, businesses began to see the relatively inexpensive potential for reaching new global customers. Today, businesses use the Internet for marketing, sales, and customer support. People shop online for about anything found in classified advertisements or in malls, including airline and concert tickets, boats, cars, jewelry, antiques, and t-shirts.

Integrating the Internet into an organization takes planning and strategizing. Businesses must carefully design and maintain their Web pages and immediately answer their customers' e-mail. Businesses also must provide security for customer information if interactive ordering is involved. If the design of the Web page and the quality of customer service are good, doing business on the Internet enhances communication and increases customer loyalty.

Some consumers, on the other hand, are complaining of online fraud. Unscrupulous people run scams to secure personal information or sell e-mail addresses and other demographic data to others. Many consumers are hesitant about making online purchases because they do not know what information is collected about them or by whom. Consumer Websites are now available to help avoid Internet scams, eliminate junk e-mail, and report instances of fraud.

TERMS TO REMEMBER

DEMOGRAPHIC

INTERACTIVE ORDERING

JUNK E-MAIL

POINT-AND-CLICK INTERFACE

SCAMS

OBJECTIVES

After you have studied this chapter and completed the exercises, you will be able to do the following:

1. Identify appropriate times to use words versus figures in expressing numbers.
2. Differentiate between cardinal and ordinal numbers.
3. Use numbers with addresses, ages, and dates correctly.
4. Use numbers in decimals, fractions, and measurements correctly.
5. Use numbers in amounts of money and percentages correctly.
6. Use numbers in telephone numbers, temperatures, time, and time periods correctly.
7. Diagram sentences with various parts of speech.

LOOKING AHEAD

Pretest

Directions: *Underline the errors in number usage in the following sentences. Write the corrections in the space provided. Write* **Yes** *if the numbers in a sentence are written correctly.*

1. Leath Furniture sold its supply of 89 office desk lamps in <u>6</u> days.

2. <u>37</u> financial institutions participate in our home-banking program.

3. You are the <u>3d</u> person to call us about the misplaced decimal point in our Website advertisement.

4. Lindfield, 32, left the company in <u>August, 1998,</u> to become part owner of a retail sporting-goods store.

5. Our accountant's fees increased 5 percent this year.

6. We had to refund <u>$300.00</u> to <u>seventy-five</u> customers.

7. The merger will give a pretax savings of $800 million to $1 billion a year.

8. One workshop begins at 8:30 a.m.; the other begins at 12 noon.

1. <u>six</u>

2. <u>Thirty-seven</u>

3. <u>third</u>

4. <u>August 1998</u>

5. <u>Yes</u>

6. <u>$300   75</u>

7. <u>Yes</u>

8. <u>Yes</u>

O V E R V I E W

Some people find numbers fascinating and enjoy working with them; others find them intimidating. Regardless of your feelings about working with figures, you should use them correctly in your written documents.

Numbers may be written in figures or in words. Figures are easier to read; however, numbers spelled out in words lend a formal touch to a document. The choice of using figures or words also may depend on whether the material is *technical* or *nontechnical*. The emphasis in this chapter is on numbers used in technical material, in business correspondence, and on business forms.

GENERAL RULES FOR WRITING NUMBERS

Several rules are so general that they should be emphasized before studying specific applications and exceptions.

Go to Transparencies/PowerPoints 18-1a and 18-1b.

See Instructor Notes 18-1, 18-2, and 18-3.

Numbers 1 Through 10

In general, use words to express the numbers one through ten.

> At our last meeting, our speaker identified <u>eight</u> advantages of Website advertising.

> Smart cards offer consumers flexibility because <u>one</u> card can be used for <u>three</u> or <u>four</u> functions.

SLIP-UP
Want ad in newspaper: For Rent: *6-room hated* apartment. Source: The Internet.

Do This	**Do Not Do This**
On a scale of <u>1</u> to <u>8</u>, our product was rated an <u>8</u>.	On a scale of <u>one to eight</u>, our product was rated an <u>eight</u>.

Numbers Above 10

Use figures for numbers above ten.

> I know that <u>20</u> states already require business taxes to be paid electronically.

> We just received <u>914</u> leads for potential customers.

When numbers are referred to as numbers, use figures; for example, scale of 1 to 8. This rule applies even though the figures involved are 1 through 10.

Go to Transparency/PowerPoint 18-2.

Approximate Numbers

Approximate numbers are nearly exact numbers. Express approximate numbers from one through ten in words. Express approximate numbers above ten in figures.

Go to Transparency/PowerPoint 18-3.

> About <u>ten</u> Internet service providers have offices in Tacoma.

> More than <u>30</u> firms a day are going into business on the Web.

Related Numbers

See Instructor Note 18-4 in IAE.

Adopt a consistent style for writing related numbers in a sentence. When related numbers, both above and below 10, are used in the same sentence, express all related numbers in figures. Do not express numbers ten and below in figures if the other numbers in the sentence are not related.

State Farm Insurance recently hired 3 new agents in Fort Collins, 4 in Colorado Springs, and 12 in Denver.

(When one number is above 10, the other related numbers are written in figures. In this sentence, the related items are the number of *new agents*.)

Out of the 15 questions on the product satisfaction questionnaire, only 5 questions gave us pertinent feedback.

(The numbers are related; both refer to *questions*.)

Experts say that questionnaires about product satisfaction should be limited to one page with no more than 15 questions.

(*One page* and *15 questions* are not related items. They should be written according to the general rules for writing numbers.)

Our bank's EasyPay accounting service has 900 clients, but only three employees monitor the transactions.

(The *900* clients and *three* employees are not related numbers. The general rules for writing numbers above and below 10 apply.)

Cardinal and Ordinal Numbers

The cardinal numbers are used in simple counting or in answer to *how many*. Write cardinal numbers as follows:

one	two	eleven	twenty-one
1	2	11	21

The uses for ordinal numbers appear within the specific rules and exceptions that follow in the next section.

The ordinal numbers are used to show the order of succession. Write ordinal numbers as follows:

first	second	eleventh	twenty-first
1st	2d	11th	21st

Third, duties should be divided so that one employee does not approve payments and also write checks.

(The ordinal number is *third*, and the cardinal number is *one*.)

The bank's latest home-banking services surpass the expensive first generation of programs.

(The ordinal number is *first*.)

Go to PowerPoints 18-4a and 18-4b.

Commas in Numbers

Use commas to set off whole numbers with five or more figures in three-digit groups beginning at the right.

15,620	132,469	5,675,298

Omit the comma in a whole number with only four digits. Use the comma if a number with only four digits is used in conjunction with numbers of five digits or more; for example, in a column.

See Instructor Note 18-5 in IAE.

3000   **8500**   **2050**

(No commas are necessary in four-digit whole numbers.)

  1,875
15,620
  3,000

(In this column of numbers, commas are necessary in the numbers *1,875* and *3,000* because the number *15,620* requires a comma.)

CHECKUP 18-1

Directions: *Underline the errors in number usage in the following sentences. Write the corrections in the space provided. Write **Yes** if the numbers in a sentence are written correctly.*

1. All 4 of the Internet directory services offer fax numbers and 3 offer electronic mail addresses.
   <u> four   three </u>

2. The Hall of Malls on the Internet lists over eighty-five malls.
   <u> 85 </u>

3. The bookkeeper made fifteen payments to fictitious companies before the 2 owners finally established some internal controls.
   <u> 15 two </u>

4. A brochure from Charter Bank listed 6 advantages of home-banking services.
   <u> six </u>

5. We have sixteen clients in Rochester and four in Alexandria.
   <u> 16 4 </u>

6. Car rental rates advertised on the Web should be checked fourteen, seven, and three days in advance to see if prices have been lowered.
   <u> 14 7 3 </u>

7. As a 2d source of financial information, check the business and economic section of your newspaper.
   <u> second </u>

8. As part of a pilot online program, People's Bank hopes to get one thousand customers and thirty merchants to participate.
   <u> 1000 30 </u>

**GO TO
CD-ROM**
CHECKUP 18-1

SPECIFIC RULES FOR WRITING NUMBERS

The type of writing that you do determines whether you use figures or words. Formal writing requires more numbers written as words. Most business correspondence includes material in which numbers require emphasis; therefore, more numbers are written as figures. The rules that follow involve those in general practice today.

Abbreviations

Use figures with abbreviations.

No. 2 pencil	Bldg. 10	Fig. 21	30 mph
5 in	2/10, n/30	18 m	20 gal

Addresses

House and Building Numbers.   Write house and building numbers in figures except for those identified as *One.* Do not use commas in house or building numbers.

152 Blanco Road	Building 118A
2531½ Dickens Drive	18294 Oakwood Parkway
One Mankato Avenue	

Street Addresses.   Use words (ordinal format) to express street names that contain the numbers 1–10. Use figures (ordinal format) to express numbered street names above 10.

19 Third Street	209 100th Street
3545 Tenth Avenue	1201 North 62d Street

Highway Numbers.   Use figures to identify highway numbers.

Interstate 80 (or) I-80	State Highway 10
U.S. Highway 1	County Road G12

ZIP Codes.   Use figures for all ZIP Codes. A nine-digit ZIP Code consists of the basic five digits followed immediately by a hyphen and another four digits. A nine-digit ZIP Code is also referred to as a ZIP+4 Code. Do not use commas with ZIP codes.

See Instructor Note 18-6 in IAE.

Flagstaff, AZ 86001	Kansas City, MO 64195-0404

Miscellaneous Address Numbers.   Use figures for suite numbers, mailstop codes, post office box numbers, and e-mail addresses.

Suite 27, Plaza Building
(Place on line above a street address.)

P.O. Box 4091 or Post Office Box 4091
(A post office box may be used in place of a mailing address.)

MSC 42
(Place the mailstop code on the line above the addressee's name.)

Miller14@juno.com
(Use exact spacing and punctuation in e-mail addresses.)

Age

Go to PowerPoint 18-5.

General Age.   Use words to express general age.

I was twelve when I began looking at products offered for sale on the Internet.
(The word *twelve* is used in a general, nontechnical format.)

Chapter 18

Now that Helen is in her <u>forties</u>, she is checking Websites for retirement investment suggestions.

(The word *forties* is used in a general, nontechnical format.)

Precise Age. Use figures to express age when the age appears immediately after the person's name or when the age is expressed in years, months, and days.

> Dan Kirkwood, <u>38</u>, is the new Website design coordinator.
> (The age is set off by commas when it appears after a name.)

> Our oldest sales representative is <u>64</u> years <u>2</u> months old.
> (Precise age requires figures.)

Legal Age. Use figures to express legal age.

> My son applied for his driver's license at the age of <u>16</u>.

> Pete did not want to retire at the age of <u>65</u>, but it was his company's mandatory retirement age.

Emphasis on Age. Use figures to emphasize age in general correspondence.

> We are advertising a new line of computer products with <u>5</u>- and <u>6</u>-year-old children in mind.
> (The ages *5* and *6* are in figures for emphasis.)

Anniversaries and Birthdays

Spell out ordinal numbers to express anniversaries that contain one or two words. (A hyphenated ordinal number counts as one word.) Use ordinal numbers in figures to express anniversaries that contain more than two words.

> the firm's <u>tenth</u> anniversary (one word)

> John's <u>thirty-fifth</u> birthday (one word)

> the company's <u>150th</u> anniversary (three words [*one hundred fiftieth*])

CHECKUP 18-2

*Directions: Underline the errors in number usage in the following sentences. Write the corrections in the space provided. Write **Yes** if the numbers in a sentence are written correctly.*

1. I requested the material from Mr. O'Brien at the following address:

   > MSC <u>4,912</u>
   > Mr. Lance O'Brien
   > Suite <u>Nine</u>, L.E. Phillips Building
   > <u>15,608</u> North <u>3d</u> Street
   > Columbia, SC <u>29,209</u>-1560

   MSC 4912   Suite 9   15608 North Third Street   29209-1560

2. Tim Collins, <u>thirty-nine</u>, decided that it was time to open his own company.

39
_____

3. We outgrew the production space at 967 North <u>Fifty-third</u> Street and moved into new facilities on State Highway <u>Eight</u>.

53d Street   State Highway 8
_____

4. The Money Store, a financial services company, says that it is the No. 1 lender of Small Business Association guaranteed loans.

Yes
_____

5. According to a recent survey, <u>twenty-eight-year-old</u> Web surfers were the most uncomfortable about sharing personal information for online target audience advertisements.

28-year-old
_____

6. Please send all inquiries about online banking to <u>1</u> Plaza Boulevard.

One Plaza Boulevard
_____

7. Through the years, accountants in their late <u>50s</u> have seen many changes in the handling of accounts payable.

fifties
_____

8. We just celebrated our <u>2d</u> successful year of online banking.

second
_____

GO TO CD-ROM
CHECKUP 18-2

Adjacent Numbers

Use a comma to separate adjacent numbers in a sentence when both figures are numbers or both are words.

> By the year <u>2000</u>, <u>40</u> percent of U.S. households may be shopping with debit cards.

Beginning of a Sentence

See Instructor Note 18-7 in IAE.

Use words to express numbers that begin a sentence. Use hyphens with the numbers 21 through 99 expressed in words. Reword the sentence if the beginning number consists of more than two words. A hyphenated word counts as one word.

> <u>Twenty-four</u> **inquiries to our Website advertisement surprised us.**
> (*Twenty-four* requires a hyphen. *Twenty-four* is written in words because it is at the beginning of a sentence. *Twenty-four* counts as one word.)
>
> **Awkward:**
>
> <u>Thirteen hundred twenty-eight</u> **people responded to our online personal information surveys.**
>
> **Improved:**
>
> **We received <u>1328</u> responses to our online personal information surveys.**

Chapter 18

Do This

Forty to fifty customers said they thought our Website was one of the best that they had seen.

Do Not Do This

Forty to 50 customers said they thought our Website was one of the best that they had seen.

Use words (forty to fifty) for related figures at the beginning of a sentence.

Consecutive Numbers

Generally, use words for the first number in consecutive numbers when one of the two numbers is part of a compound modifier.

four 12-story buildings   **twenty 5-page documents**
(The first numbers are written in words when they appear before compound modifiers.)

Use figures for the first of the consecutive numbers if the second number is shorter than the first when written out.

35 one-time hits   **900 two-page product reviews**
(The first numbers *35* and *900* are in figures; the second numbers *one* and *two* are shorter than *35* and *900* when written out in words.)

Dates

Go to PowerPoint 18-6.

Months, Days, and Years. Use cardinal numbers to express dates in month-day, month-year, or month-day-year order. Use commas to separate the year from the month and day. Do not use commas to separate a month and year when used without the day.

May 2   May 1999

August 29, 2000   August 2000

If you submit your payment by January 15, 1999, you will be eligible for a discount.
(Commas separate the year from the month and day in this introductory clause.)

Bruce referred to an article on online commerce in the November 1999 issue of the magazine.
(No commas are necessary when the date consists of a month and year only.)

Military and Foreign. Use cardinal numbers to express dates associated with military or foreign correspondence. Write dates in day, month, year sequence. Do not separate with commas.

2 May 1999   **29 August 2000**

See Instructor Note 18-8 in IAE.

Days Before Month; Days Alone.   Use ordinal numbers when the day comes before the month or stands alone and the emphasis in the sentence is on the figure. Use ordinal words when the purpose of the writing is more formal. The intent of the sentence determines the use of figures or words.

> **Online registration must be completed by the 3d of January.**
> (The emphasis in this sentence is on the date. Ordinal, not cardinal, numbers are necessary.)
>
> **Please contact us by the 21st.**
> (The day *21st* is used alone. The day is emphasized and requires an ordinal, not a cardinal, number.)
>
> **You are cordially invited to a reception for the new president of OnlineAlert on the third day of October 1999.**
> (The formal tone of writing requires ordinal words rather than figures.)

Legal Documents.   Use ordinal numbers to express dates appearing in legal documents.

> **October twenty-first**
> *or*
> **the twenty-first day of October**
> **Nineteen hundred ninety-nine**
> *or*
> **One thousand nine hundred ninety-nine**
> **WITNESS WHEREOF I have hereunto set my hand and seal the twenty-first day of October, in the year one thousand nine hundred ninety-nine.**

Refer to a legal handbook or reference manual for information on number style in legal documents.

Decades and Centuries

Decades.   Use words or figures to express decades.

> the 1990s   the nineties   the '90s
> during the years 1998–2008

Centuries.   Use words or figures to express centuries.

> the 1900s   the twenty-first century

CHECKUP 18-3

*Directions: Underline the errors in number usage in the following sentences. Write the corrections in the space provided. Write **Yes** if the numbers in a sentence are written correctly.*

1. 25 clients asked for assistance with personal finance planning in addition to tax planning this year.

   Twenty-five

2. I use the program Quicken to pay my bills on the <u>fifth</u> of each month.

5th

___

3. I am responsible for <u>5 2-page</u> articles for our Internet news magazine this year.

five 2-page

___

4. In the '90s, many companies restructured to control their production costs.

Yes;   *also*   In the nineties

See Instructor Note 18-9 in IAE.

___

5. Beginning <u>July, 1999</u>, <u>nine hundred seventy-five thousand</u> business taxpayers will be required to pay federal taxes electronically.

July 1999   975,000

___

6. This week, <u>two hundred twenty</u> people checked our Website.

220

___

7. Consumer debt has grown more than four times as fast as wages since <u>January 1 1995</u>.

January 1, 1995

___

8. Do you have any predictions to make regarding online banking for the twenty-first century?

Yes;   *also*   21st

___

9. We received purchase orders dated 05 September 1998 from the military.

Yes

___

10. "I checked the original legal document, and it was dated the 'twenty-first day of October,'" responded the lawyer in his letter of <u>October seven</u>.

October 7

___

GO TO
CD-ROM
CHECKUP 18-3

Decimals

Writing Decimals.   Use figures to express decimals.

1.326   115.2   89.3926

Using Zeros.   Place a zero before the decimal point if the decimal appears by itself. The zero sets the decimal apart and makes it easy to recognize the decimal as less than a whole number.

See Instructor Note 18-10 in IAE.

0.01   0.00923   0.59

Aligning Figures.   Align figures at the decimal point. Add a zero or zeros at the end of a decimal to justify a column of figures on the right.

9.5	35.95	4.000
102.7	2.50	12.500
		9.333

___

Financial Quotes

See Instructor Note 18-11 in IAE.

Use figures to express financial quotes.

Home Depot stock was up 3/8 and closed at 68.

Fractions

Go to PowerPoint 18-7.

See Instructor Note 18-12 in IAE.

Fractions on Their Own.   Use words to express fractions that stand alone. Use a hyphen between the numerator (top number in a fraction) and denominator (bottom number in a fraction).

two-thirds of our banking customers

one-half of the assets

one-eighth of a page

Fractions in Measurements.   Use figures to express fractions in measurements. Do not use an "of" phrase after fractions written in figures. Write out the fraction in words if an "of" phrase must follow the fraction. Do not use *st, ds,* or *ths* after fractions expressed in numbers.

7/8 ounce   *or*   **seven-eighths of an ounce**

3/4 pound   *or*   **three-fourths of a pound**

(Do not use *7/8ths of an ounce* or *7/8 of an ounce.* Do not use *3/4ths of a pound* or *3/4 of a pound.*)

Fractions and Whole Numbers.   Use figures when a fraction is written with a whole number. Do not use a hyphen between the whole number and the fraction.

2½ hours late   **5¼ pages**

Identification Numbers

See Instructor Note 18-13 in IAE.

Use figures to identify forms or items such as form numbers, model numbers, serial numbers, policy numbers, and invoice numbers. Do not use commas to separate the digits. The abbreviation *No.* is not necessary with most items identified by number if the item is preceded by a descriptive noun.

Form 940	**Diagram 1**
Pentium II	**Model 203-S5**
Policy 8342916429	**Chapter IX**
Invoice 3213	**Item 614695-D**

(The abbreviation *No.* is not necessary with these items.)

Catalog No. 9640	**Serial No. 9640**
License No. KUP 874	**Social Security No. 384-63-5058**

(The abbreviation *No.* is necessary to identify these numbers.)

Directions: *Underline the errors in number usage in the following sentences. Write the corrections in the space provided. Write **Yes** if the numbers in a sentence are written correctly.*

1. I just checked the Internet and learned that my favorite stock was at <u>56 and three-fourths</u>, which was lower than yesterday's <u>57 and one-half</u>.

   $56^3/_4$ $57^1/_2$

2. Consumer prices increased a moderate <u>.3</u> percent with little sign of inflation.

   0.3

3. Bowman Nutrition Services submitted its Form 941 electronically this payroll period.

   Yes

4. Only <u>1/3</u> of the consumers are confident about buying mutual funds on their own.

   one-third

5. My social security number appeared along with my grade on the door of <u>Room No. 248</u>.

   Room 248

6. By going online with my bank accounts, I save at least <u>one half</u> day a month working on bookkeeping tasks.

   one-half

7. The Web advertisement indicated that the material weighed just <u>1/4th of a pound</u>.

   1/4 pound *or*
   one-fourth of a pound

8. By the time I finished a draft of my Website material, I had <u>five and three quarters</u> pages.

   $5^3/_4$

GO TO
CD-ROM
CHECKUP 18-4

Indefinite Numbers

Use words to express indefinite numbers and amounts. Indefinite numbers are not easily counted or determined.

many thousands of requests   **a few hundred debit cards**

dozens of online scams   **thousands of dollars**

hundreds of credit card delinquencies

See Instructor Note 18-14 in IAE.

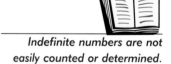

Indefinite numbers are not easily counted or determined.

Large Numbers

Use a combination of figures and words to express numbers in the millions or above. If several large numbers appear in a sentence, be consistent in the format.

2 million people   **1.5 billion items**

9.5 million words

Real estate brokers used the Internet and major online services to list 375,000 of the approximately 4,100,000 homes available for sale.
(The number *4,100,000* [instead of *4.1 million*] is used because of the related number *375,000*, which is less than a million. The format should be consistent.)

Measurements and Dimensions

Measurements.   Use figures (including the numbers 1 through 10) to express measurements used in a technical sense. These measurements include items such as yards, inches, feet, acres, pounds, ounces, gross, dozen, gallons, quarts, computer measurements, and miles. Do not use a comma to separate a measurement that consists of two parts.

75 yards (yd)	**6 quarts (qt)**	**5 pounds 3 ounces**
8 dozen (doz)	**15 miles (mi)**	**5 feet 11 inches**
16 megabytes (MB)		**1.2 gigabytes (GB)**

Dimensions.   Use figures to express dimensions.

12- by 15-foot room   **a room 12 by 15 feet**

or

12- × 15-foot room   **a room 12 × 15 feet**

or

12' × 15' room   **a room 12' × 15'**

We need a 6- by 8-foot window for our office.

(Hyphens are necessary when the dimension precedes a noun.)

The window in our office is 6 × 8 feet.

(No hyphens are necessary in the dimension when the dimension does not precede a noun. The word *feet* is not repeated after both numbers; it is needed only after the last measurement.)

The window in our office is 6' × 8'.

(The symbol for feet ['] is necessary after both numbers.)

Metric Measurements.   Use figures to express metric measurements. Use a space to mark off groups of three digits.

a trip of 480 km (kilometers)

about 25 kg (kilograms)

a distance of 100 000 m (meters)

CHECKUP 18-5

Directions: *Underline the errors in number usage in the following sentences. Write the corrections in the space provided. Write* **Yes** *if the numbers in a sentence are written correctly.*

1. LocalEyes provides lists of local businesses and currently has <u>11,500,000</u> listings.   <u>11.5 million</u>

2. If you converted these figures to meter measurements, your answer would be <u>20,000,000</u> square meters.   <u>20 000 000</u>

3. The Internet advertisement indicated that the weight of the item was <u>four pounds, six ounces.</u>   <u>4 pounds 6 ounces</u>

4. Each month <u>1000s</u> of firms analyze the effects of advertising on the Web. ⟶ <u>thousands</u>

5. Dunbar Research expects that <u>52,000,000</u> consumers will read Net advertisements by the year 2000. ⟶ <u>52 million</u>

6. The FTC estimates that scams can cause losses to consumers amounting to millions of dollars. ⟶ <u>Yes</u>

7. Dan submitted a preliminary Website design that was <u>seven inches by nine inches</u>. ⟶ <u>7 by 9 inches</u> / <u>7 × 9 inches</u> / <u>7″ × 9″</u>

8. If you request a copy of our newsletter advertised on our Website, you will receive a professional document printed on <u>twenty-pound</u> paper. ⟶ <u>20-pound</u>

See Instructor Note 18-15 in IAE.

GO TO CD-ROM
CHECKUP 18-5

Money

Amounts of Money Above $1.   Use figures to express amounts of money above $1. Do not use a decimal point or zeros after even dollar amounts within a sentence.

$2.98	$12.95	$429.63	$21,398.50
$25	$2000	about $50,000	

The invoice includes <u>$2000</u> plus the sales tax of <u>$100</u> for a total of <u>$2100</u>. (No decimal points or zeros are necessary after the even amounts of money [*$2000* and *$100*]. The normal end-of-sentence period follows the last amount [*$2100*].)

Amounts of Money in Columns.   Use zeros with even dollar amounts in a column of figures in which the other amounts contain cents.

> $ 505.00
> 1015.22
>   95.95

Foreign Money.   Generally, place the abbreviated identification of foreign money before the amount.

> DM1000 (German marks)   NKr1000 (Norwegian kroner)
> ¥10,000 (Japanese yen)   £ 10,000 (British pound)

Large Amounts of Money.   Combine figures and words to express amounts of money of $1 million or more. Use the *dollar sign* or the word *dollars,* but do not use both with one figure.

Preferred	Acceptable
$2 million	2 million dollars
$5½ million	5½ million dollars
$5.5 million	5.5 million dollars

(Do not use the redundant forms *$2 million dollars, $5½ million dollars, or $5.5 million dollars.*)

Related Amounts of Money.   Keep related amounts of money in the same format.

> We paid **$1,000,000** for the building on Main Street and **$2,780,000** for the one on Central Avenue.
>
> (Do not write *$1 million* and *$2,780,000,* or *1 million dollars* and *$2,780,000.* Use the same format within the sentence.)

Amounts of Money Less Than $1.   Use figures to express amounts below $1. Spell out the word *cents* after the amount.

> A stamp costs <u>33 cents</u>.
>
> The <u>55-cent</u> coupons add up at the grocery store.

Cents in a Series.   Do not use the dollar sign with an amount less than $1 unless it appears in a series or in a table in which the other figures require dollar signs.

> The sales taxes on our purchases were: **$3.21, <u>$.80</u>, $12,** and **$6.25.**
>
> (The amount *$.80* should be written in the same format as the dollar amounts with cents.)

Range of Amounts of Money.   Repeat the dollar sign or cent sign with each amount when a range of prices is expressed. Do not repeat the word *dollars* or *cents* with each amount.

> in the <u>$</u>25,000 to <u>$</u>40,000 range
>
> an increase from 32 to 33 <u>cents</u>

Amounts of Money in Legal Documents.   Use words to express amounts of money in legal or formal documents. Write the amount in figures, and place it in parentheses after the written expression. Use the word *and* before the cents in written expressions of money.

> Five Hundred Thousand Dollars ($500,000)
>
> Three Thousand Two Hundred Twenty-nine <u>and</u> 83/100 Dollars ($3,229.83)

Percentages

Exact and Approximate Percentages.   Use figures to express exact or approximate percentages. Write the word *percent* after the number.

> 0.5 percent   10 percent   6.5 percent   6½ percent
>
> nearly 65 percent   over 30 percent

Series of Percentages.   Write the word *percent* only at the end of the last number in a sentence with several percentages listed.

> We offer trade discounts of 10, 20, and 30 <u>percent</u> to our long-term customers.

CHECKUP 18-6

Directions: *Underline the errors in number usage in the following sentences. Write the corrections in the space provided. Write* **Yes** *if the numbers in a sentence are written correctly.*

1. We just bought a book for $20.95 and found that the same book was advertised on the Internet for $12.

   Yes

2. The Internet advertisement indicated that the product's cost of <u>$839.00</u> included the <u>five 1/2</u> percent sales tax.

   $839 5½

3. I purchased an excellent personal finance software program for approximately <u>forty dollars</u>.

   $40

4. An information request for a phone number can cost <u>85 cents</u>, <u>95 cents</u>, or $1.10, depending on the carrier.

   $.85 $.95

5. A grocery item can cost $1.62 or $1.69; however, customers are usually in a rush and do not notice the <u>seven-cent</u> difference.

   7-cent

6. According to one statistic, <u>ten</u> percent of Internet users go online to shop, and <u>79%</u> go online to browse.

   10 percent

   79 percent

7. The machines to read smart cards cost merchants <u>$500.00</u> to <u>1,000.00</u>.

   $500 to $1000

8. A Japan rail pass that is good for one week sells for ¥ 28,300 (<u>$230.00</u>).

   ($230)

9. Someone told me that online telephone directories are only about <u>seventy percent to eighty percent</u> accurate.

   70 to 80 percent

10. Consumer spending probably rose <u>.6%</u> in July.

    0.6 percent

**GO TO
CD-ROM**
CHECKUP 18-6

Political Divisions

Use words to identify political subdivisions such as congressional districts or precincts.

<u>Fifteenth</u> District representative   <u>Eighth</u> Precinct election returns

Publications

Use figures to express pages, paragraphs, lines, steps, notes, and verses in publications. Do not capitalize the words *page, line, verse, step, note,* or *paragraph* before the numbers.

Chapter <u>9</u>   Section <u>2</u>

page <u>15</u>, line <u>2</u>   paragraphs <u>401–470</u>

Ratios

Use figures to express ratios.

<u>2-to-1</u> ratio   *or*   a <u>2:1</u> ratio

See Instructor Note 18-16 in IAE.

Roman Numerals

In Outlines and Reports. Use roman numerals to subdivide items on outlines or reports. Align roman numerals at the right in an outline or list. Place a period after the numeral. You may see the word *roman* capitalized (*Roman*) in your workplace and in some reference manuals or dictionaries.

    I. PRODUCTIVITY TOOLS
    II. EFFECTIVE ADVERTISING DESIGN
    III. SOFTWARE HIGHLIGHTS

As Literary Divisions. Use roman numerals to indicate the major parts of complete literary works such as volumes or chapters.

    Volume XII   Chapter VI

As Lowercase Roman Numerals. Use lowercase roman numerals to indicate page numbers in prefaces or in other materials that precede text materials.

    The credits are on page ii of the introduction to the book

In Seniority Titles. Use roman numerals or arabic numerals for seniority titles depending on the individual's preference. Do not set aside seniority titles with commas unless the person referenced prefers the commas.

Refer to a reference manual such as The Gregg Reference Manual for a list of roman numerals.

Robert Hamilton III	*or*	Robert Hamilton 3d
Lance Ford II	*or*	Lance Ford 2d

Inclusive Figures

See Instructor Note 18-17 in IAE.

Do not shorten the second number in an inclusive set of figures unless page numbers or dates are used frequently in a document. Do not shorten inclusive numbers under 100.

    pages 146-50 (frequent use)   pages 46-50 (under 100)
    or
    pages 146-150 (general use)

    1996-99 (frequent use)   *or*   1996-1999 (general use)

Do not shorten the second number when the second number begins with a digit that is different from the first number.

    1990-2005   pages 518-624
    (Do not use the short forms of *1990-05* or *518-24*.)

Do not use a shortened form for the second number in any situation in which the first number ends in two or more zeros.

    2000-2005   pages 300-306
    (Do not use the short forms of *2000-5* and *300-6*.)

CHECKUP 18-7

Directions: *Underline the errors in number usage in the following sentences. Write the corrections in the space provided. Write* **Yes** *if the numbers in a sentence are written correctly.*

1. Wallace L. Ingram <u>the third</u> referred to the advantages of the Internet on page <u>ten</u> in his handout.

    <u>III or 3d 10</u>

2. People in the <u>12th</u> District voted against the sales tax referendum.

    <u>Twelfth</u>

3. A 2-to-1 ratio seems acceptable for our advertising purposes.

    <u>Yes or 2:1</u>

4. You will find your answer in paragraph <u>eight</u> of the prospectus.

    <u>8</u>

5. For a more detailed explanation, refer to the information in Chapter <u>ii</u>, lines <u>63-8</u>.

    <u>II 63-68</u>

6. This is the final outline for the seminar on small business technology:
<u>i</u> PRODUCTIVITY TOOLS FOR SMALL BUSINESS
<u>ii</u> NETWORKING FOR SMALL BUSINESS
<u>iii</u> THE INTERNET FOR SMALL BUSINESS

    <u>I. II. III.</u>

7. Companies became even more concerned with secure encryption methods in the years <u>1999-01</u>.

    <u>1999-2001</u>

8. Check page <u>VII</u> in the table of contents for the chapter about online banking.

    <u>vii</u>

GO TO CD-ROM
CHECKUP 18-7

Size

Use figures to express size. Do not capitalize the word *size* when it appears before the number.

    Apparently, the only clothing items on sale were <u>size 8</u> or <u>size 18</u>.

Symbols

    Use figures with symbols.
    5 @ <u>$100</u> (5 items at $100 each)
    <u>#10</u> (Number 10)

Telephone Numbers

See Instructor Note 18-18 in IAE.

Domestic Numbers. Use figures for most telephone numbers. If a company uses combinations of letters and numbers or all words, follow the company's exact format. Use diagonals, parentheses, periods, or hyphens to separate the area code from the rest of the number.

    212/555-1378   (212) 555-1378   212.555.1378   212-555-1378

International Numbers. Use figures for international telephone numbers. Separate the international access codes, country codes, city codes, and telephone numbers with hyphens.

011-47-2-22-826-090

Extensions. Use figures to identify an extension. Spell out *Extension* or abbreviate it (*Ext.*).

312-555-5476, Extension 66   or   312-555-5476, Ext. 66

Temperature

Use figures to express temperatures. Do not space between the number and the degree symbol or between the degree symbol and C (Celsius) or F (Fahrenheit).

80 degrees   80 degrees Fahrenheit   80°F   100°C

Time

In printed material, you may see a.m. and p.m. written in small capitals (A.M., P.M.).

With *a.m.* and *p.m.* Use figures with *a.m.* and *p.m.* Do not space within *a.m.* or within *p.m.* Do not use the word *o'clock* with *a.m.* and *p.m.*

We expected our order to arrive by 4:30 p.m.

With Colons and Zeros Omitted. Omit the colon and zeros with times that do not involve minutes (even when other expressions of time in the sentence include minutes).

Express mail should arrive by 10 a.m. or by 3:30 p.m.

With the Word *O'clock*. Use figures with *o'clock* to emphasize time. Use words with *o'clock* to set a formal tone; for example, in social invitations.

5 o'clock   or   five o'clock
9 o'clock at night (for emphasis)
nine o'clock at night (formal or social situations)

See Instructor Note 18-19 in IAE.

In Time Phrases. Do not use the expressions *in the morning, in the afternoon, in the evening,* or *at night* with *a.m.* or *p.m.*

Our office opens at 9 o'clock in the morning.
(Using *9 a.m. in the morning* is redundant.)

With *Noon* and *Midnight*. Express the terms *noon* and *midnight* in words. If other times in a sentence are written in figures, use *12 noon* or *12 midnight.*

I plan to take a business marketing class that begins at noon.
(The word *noon* may stand alone when no other time expressions are present.)

I plan to take a business marketing class that is scheduled from 12 noon to 1:50 p.m.
(The term *12 noon* is necessary because another time expression in figures is present.)

Time Periods

General Time Periods. Use words to express general time periods such as years, months, weeks, and days except when the time period requires more than two words.

See Instructor Note 18-20 in IAE.

> **During the past <u>twelve</u> years, I have seen many technological changes in the ways that companies transact business.**
>
> (The time period *twelve* consists of one word.)
>
> **By using the Internet, you can shop <u>365</u> days a year.**
>
> (The time period *365* would be more than two words if it were written in words.)

Business-Related Time Periods. Use numbers to indicate time periods associated with payroll periods, discounts, mortgage periods, loan payments, credit terms, and interest payments.

See Instructor Note 18-21 in IAE.

> **I found it easy to compute the amount of interest I would pay on a <u>15-year</u> mortgage.**
>
> (In this sentence, the term *15-year* is a business-related time period and requires numbers rather than words.)
>
> **To develop a global market for his products, Mike received a <u>4-year</u> loan from his bank.**
>
> (Even though the figure *4* is below *10,* it is a business-related time period and requires numbers rather than words.)

CHECKUP 18-8

Directions: *Underline the errors in number usage in the following sentences. Write the corrections in the space provided. Write* **Yes** *if the numbers in a sentence are written correctly.*

1. Business Results is presenting seminars on November 19 and 20 at <u>8:30 a.m. in the morning</u>, 12 noon, and <u>1 p.m. in the afternoon</u>.

   8:30 a.m.   1 p.m.
   _____

2. We had too many women's shoes in <u>Size eight</u> in our inventory.

   size 8
   _____

3. These were the items ordered:

5	#3078	@	$100.00
12	#4853	@	88.98
7	#2975	@	325.00

   Yes
   _____

4. One car manufacturer says that its <u>eight hundred</u> number draws fewer leads for potential customers than its Website.

   800 number
   _____

GO TO
CD-ROM
CHECKUP 18-8

5. A new Internet training center opened downtown, and its hours are <u>6 a.m. o'clock</u> to <u>10 p.m. o'clock</u>.

6 a.m. 10 p.m.

6. For a free catalog, call us at 1-800-555-6222, <u>X922</u>.

Extension 922 or Ext. 922

DIAGRAMMING SENTENCES

The following sentences for diagramming include a review of the rules you have studied in the previous chapters.

CHECKUP 18-9

See Instructor Note 18-22 in IAE.

***Directions:** In the space provided, diagram the following sentences. All words may be diagrammed.*

1. Over the past few months, banks have promoted their new home-banking services.

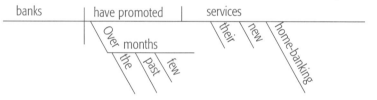

2. A directory *Venture Capital: Where to Find It* gives prospective business developers excellent ideas for sources of money.

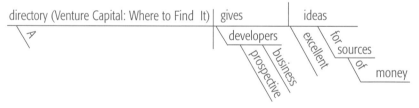

3. Typical banner ads that appear on Websites are quite expensive.

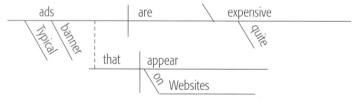

4. One company that advertised on the Web promised viewers a copy of its latest book on home health remedies.

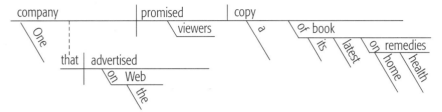

5. Buying advertised Website products requires some caution and common sense.

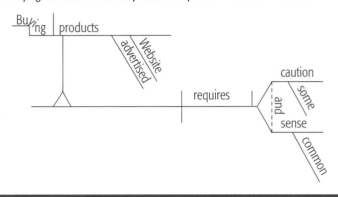

GO TO
CD-ROM
CHECKUP 18-9

PRACTICE

See Instructor Note 18-23 in
IAE.

PRACTICE 1A

A. **Directions:** *Underline the errors in number and word usage in the following sentences. Write the corrections in the space provided. Write* **Yes** *if the numbers and words in a sentence are written correctly.*

1. Credit card interest payments ranging from 18 to **1.** _____Yes_____
   30 percent are not tax deductible.

2. More than 67,000,000 Americans carry debit cards. **2.** ___67 million___

3. Most investors were surprised when the Dow   **3.** _____8000_____
   Jones Industrial Average reached the eight
   thousand mark.

4. Over a period of 10, 20, or 30 years, stocks seem **4.** _____Yes_____
   to perform more effectively than other investments.

5. By the nineteen hundred and eighties, American **5.** _____1980s_____
   manufacturers realized the impact that foreign
   competitors were having on their sales.

6. We received 3½ times the number of expected   **6.** _____Yes_____
   responses to our online advertising.

7. Printing costs for the brochure that we offered at **7.** ___16 cents___
   our Website increased $.16, and we can no longer
   send free copies.

8. Two-thirds of those responding to the survey   **8.** _____Yes_____
   indicated that they had not made purchases
   on the Internet.

9. Web advertising is well over the $1 billion   **9.** _$1 billion *or*_
   dollar amount.   _1 billion dollar_

10. I bought a forty dollar Windows utility program **10.** _____$40_____
    that removes old programs quickly and efficiently.

B. **Directions:** *Select the correct form of the number, and write it in the space provided.*

1. The product's cost of $839.72 included the   **1.** ___5 percent___
   (*5 percent, five percent*) sales tax.

2. Hutchinson Technology plans to expand its global **2.** _____45_____
   operations to (*45, forty-five*) countries.

3. The next meeting of the Website advertisement   **3.** _February 1999_
   consulting group will be (*February 1999,*
   February, 1999).

4. To mark our (*3d, third*) anniversary, we are offering several new products to our customers.

    4. _____third_____

5. Tonight's meeting of the Internet Marketing Club is at (*7:00 p.m., 7 p.m.*) in (*Building 5, Building Five*).

    5. _____7 p.m._____
             _____Building 5_____

6. Some people have (*3 or 4, three or four*) major credit cards.

    6. ____three or four____

7. (*15, Fifteen*) years ago, Philips and Sony introduced CD-ROM players for PCs that sold for approximately (*$1000, $1,000.00, one thousand dollars*).

    7. _____Fifteen_____
             _____$1000_____

8. Focus groups consisting of (*8 to 12, eight to 12, eight to twelve*) current customers are good sources of product information.

    8. _____8 to 12_____

9. Yields on (*30-year, thirty-year*) Treasury bonds were around (*7, seven*) percent.

    9. ____30-year 7____

10. As a sole proprietor, I file a Schedule C with my federal income tax (*Form 1040, Form No. 1040*).

    10. ____Form 1040____

**GO TO
CD-ROM**
PRACTICE 1
EXERCISES

PRACTICE 2A

Directions: *Underline the errors in number usage in the following sentences. Write the corrections in the space provided. Write* **Yes** *if the numbers in a sentence are written correctly.*

1. I bought a used computer for $200.00 for my daughter who is in her 1st year of college.

$200   first _____

2. Some predict that Internet sales will reach $600 million dollars in the year 2,000 and 1.25 trillion in 2,005.

$600 million (*or* 600 million dollars)   2000 _____

$1.25 trillion (*or* 1.25 trillion dollars)   2005 _____

3. Our team's Website design placed 6th in the regional contest finals.

sixth _____

4. We will be in Booth No. 1,920 at Internet World in Chicago in 6 months.

Booth 1920   six months _____

NAME _____

5. Ninety percent of our home office sales comes through personal contacts, not through the Internet.

    Yes

6. Members of the class of 99 can buy their yearbooks on CD-ROM for twenty-five dollars.

    class of '99 (or 1999) $25

7. A merger will result in an extra 80 cents to 90 cents per share in earnings for shareholders.

    80 to 90 cents

8. How will small companies remain competitive in the 21st century?

    twenty-first

9. My favorite stock closed at fifty-six and three fourths yesterday.

    56³/₄

10. Roberto Hernandez, forty-eight, who has been our Texas manager for the past fifteen years, will be in charge of the plant on Thirteenth Street.

    48   15 years   13th Street

11. For less than $1,000.00 of software and an Internet account, spammers can send e-mail to 1 or to 1,000,000 persons.

    $1000   one   one million

12. Features of the monitor include a 0.27 mm dot pitch and 1024- by 768-pixel resolution at 75 Hz.

    Yes

See Instructor Note 18-24 in IAE.

13. If you pay off a $3,000 credit card debt at 18 percent over 2 years, you will make monthly payments that are approximately $149.00.

    $3000   two years $149

14. 5 Hilton hotels have videoconferencing systems that show life-sized images on ninety-two-inch screens.

    Five   92-inch

15. The first McDonald's in our city opened thirty-eight years ago at 1,513 Hastings Way.

    38   1513 Hastings Way

16. Our agents contacted fifteen clients whose insurance policies had expired, but only eight of these clients renewed.

    15   8

17. The odds of winning the lottery this week are <u>ten to one</u>.

10 to 1   (or 10:1)
_____

18. We are offering Internet workshops for home business owners at <u>11 a.m. in the morning</u> and <u>2:30 p.m. in the afternoon</u>.

11 a.m.   2:30 p.m.
_____

19. The road signs indicated that we still had to travel 150 kilometers before we reached our destination.

Yes   (or 150 km)
_____

20. Some cyberspace merchants require buyers to call an <u>eight hundred</u> number to transmit credit card information.

800 number
_____

**GO TO
CD-ROM**
PRACTICE 2
EXERCISES

PRACTICE 3A

PROOFREADING

*Directions: Proofread and compare the two sentences in each group. If they are the same, write **Yes** in the space provided. If they are not the same, write **No**. Use the first sentence as the correct copy. If you find errors in the second sentence, underline them; insert any omitted words or marks of punctuation.*

1. The U.S. Small Business Administration's Website (http://www.sbaonline.sba.gov) includes a section entitled "Financing Your Business," which provides information on all the SBA's funding programs.

The U.S. Small Business Administration Website (http://www.sbaonline.gov) includes a section entitled Financing Your Business, which provides infomation on all the S.B.A.'s funding programs.

1. __No__

2. Self-service online directories, which are offered free, help users find business or individual phone numbers by entering only a name or a partial address.

Self-service online directories, which are offered free, help users find business or <u>person</u> phone numbers by entering only a name or a partial address.

2. __No__

3. Funds Network offers access to more than 3300 funds and 300 fund families, including more than 700 with 4- or 5-star Morningstar ratings.

Funds Network offers access to more than <u>3500 funds</u>, and <u>330</u> fund families, including more than 700 with 4- or 5-star <u>Morningside</u> ratings.

3. __No__

NAME _____

4. Direct electronic access to social security records jumped from 3000 users a day to 8500 users after the introductory publicity, but access soon was suspended because of the invasion of personal privacy.

4.   No

Direct electronic access to social security records jumped from 3,000 users a day to 8,500 _{users} after the introductory publicity, but access soon was suspended, because of the invasion of personal privacy.

5. Most Internet transmissions are currently encrypted (electronically scrambled), which makes it very difficult for someone to intercept a message and use the personal information illegally.

5.   Yes

Most Internet transmissions are currently encrypted (electronically scrambled), which makes it very difficult for someone to intercept a message and use the personal information illegally.

See Instructor Note 18-25 in IAE.

Proofreading Exercise

Whenever companies offer training, they want to make sure that their announcements are accurate. The following announcement needs proofreading before it is distributed.

Directions: Use proofreaders' marks to correct the copy.

Join us for a series of free seminars to learn how new technology can help you meet your small business goals.

Internet Basics
Tuesday, April 21, 1999
    Learn the language of the internet.
    Identify the possibilities of the Internet.
    Save time and money in your research.
    Discover new solutions for your business problems.
        9:30 a.m. - 12 o'clock noon
        1:30 p.m. - 4:00 p.m.
        5:30 p.m. - 8 p.m.
Networking Basics
Wed., April 22, 1999
    Explore the many types of networks.
    Determine how networks function in different business environments.
    Identify networking solutions that will work for you.
        9 a.m. in the morning to 4 p.m.
Send your registration forms to Ideal Business Concepts, 1 South 10th Street, Bozeman, MT 59715 or call (406) 555-1380.

GO TO
CD-ROM
PRACTICE 3
EXERCISES

PRACTICE 4A

WRITING

You received an unsolicited chain e-mail. You were asked to send $5 to the person's name at the top of the list. Your name would go on the list, and eventually people would start sending you $5. The e-mail claimed that people had made over $10,000. You think this offer sounds too good to be true.

Directions: *Compose a paragraph or two to the Internet Fraud Watch describing the e-mail and asking them for advice on handling the situation.*

Answers will vary.

I received an e-mail requesting that I send $5 to the person's name at the top of a

list. My name would appear on the list and eventually I would start receiving $5 from

others.

This e-mail was unsolicited and appears to be fraudulent. How do you recommend

that I handle this situation?

GO TO CD-ROM
PRACTICE 4
EXERCISES

ONLINE EXERCISES

Direct marketing is integrated into advertising and involves direct mail, catalogs, and telephone marketing. Newspaper, magazine, television, radio, and interactive media are also involved. The Direct Marketing Association closely follows the trends in direct marketing and is particularly interested in interactive Internet marketing.

Objective: *To visit the Direct Marketing Association Web page.*

1. With your Internet browser on screen, key:

    http://www.the-dma.org in the location text box.

    Press the **Enter** key on your keyboard.

2. You will be at the Direct Marketing Association (DMA) Web page. The DMA is a trade association for businesses interested in database marketing.

3. Click on **Consumers.** Read the information posted for consumers.

4. In the Search box, key **Internet.** Click on the Search button. Read the information that the DMA has gathered about doing business on the Internet.

See Instructor Note 18-26 in IAE.

Punctuation
ALERT!

Use exact punctuation when keying an Internet address.

NAME _____

PRACTICE 1B

A. Directions: *Underline the errors in number and word usage in the following sentences. Write the corrections in the space provided. Write* **Yes** *if the numbers and words in a sentence are written correctly.*

1. During the past twelve months, the use of the Internet has increased.

   Yes

2. Our staff meeting is at 12 noon in the cafeteria.

   noon

3. You should hear from a customer service representative by ten a.m.

   10 a.m.

4. Please call 707-555-3999, Ext. 78, for our pricing structure.

   Yes

5. Please get a size six wrist brace from the storage cabinet.

   size 6

6. If you read pages 121-34 of the HTML manual, you can probably troubleshoot the problem. (general use)

   pages 121-134   See Instructor Note 18-27 in IAE.

7. Please proofread pages five, eight, and 12 before posting this information on our Web page.

   pages 5, 8, and 12

8. Harry worked for Oracle during the years 1989-1996.

   Yes

9. James Filmore the second financially supported our Internet venture.

   James Filmore II *or* James Filmore 2d

10. Look on page II, immediately after the title page, to find the table of contents.

    page ii

B. Directions: *Select the correct form of the number, and write it in the space provided.*

1. The number of men in our company outranks the number of women (*two to one, 2 to 1*).   **1.** _____2 to 1_____

2. The technology coalition is working to defeat the (*10th, Tenth*) District representative.   **2.** _____Tenth_____

3. We negotiated a (*ten, 10*) percent discount for the next fiscal year.   **3.** _____10_____

4. We plan a (*.03, 0.03*) increase in the workforce next year.   **4.** _____0.03_____

5. Even though it costs only (*30 to 40, thirty to forty*) cents to mail the letter, we find the delivery time is too long.   **5.** _____30 to 40_____

6. The (*fifty-cent, 50-cent*) coupons were not an incentive to cause me to switch disk brands.   **6.** _____50-cent_____

7. We paid (*$1 million, $1,000,000*) to update our computers and our network.   **7.** _____$1 million_____

8. Our Internet access costs (*$325.00, $325*) a month.   **8.** _____$325_____

9. During the past (*ten, 10*) years, we have seen dramatic declines in the cost of computers.   **9.** _____ten_____

10. Read page (*15, fifteen*) of the contract carefully.   **10.** _____15_____

NAME _____

PRACTICE 2B

Directions: *Underline the errors in number usage in the following sentences. Write the corrections in the space provided. Write* **Yes** *if the numbers in a sentence are written correctly.*

1. A recent Northwest CyberSaver offered a round-trip Detroit-Seattle fare for one hundred and seventy-nine dollars, a savings of sixty-eight percent of the twenty-one-day advance purchase fare of $572.00.

   $179 68 percent 21-day $572 _____

2. Chih-Yuan "Jerry" Yang, twenty-eight, and David Filo, thirty, founders of Yahoo!, were the youngest philanthropists in Stanford University history to give a $2,000,000 gift.

   28 30 $2 million _____

3. We recommend a thirty-three point six kbps or even a fifty-six k modem for a high-speed connection to the Internet.

   33.6 kbps 56 k _____

4. Scott Oki, a retiree from Microsoft, is a member of twenty-three nonprofit boards.

   23 _____

5. 12 national high-tech companies performed poorly last quarter; of the 12, only five were relatively small software companies.

   Twelve 5 _____

6. The policies for a decentralized, global communications network are targeted to be completed by January 1 2000.

   January 1, 2000 _____

7. The stock fell four and three-quarters to seventy-six dollars after it announced the resignation of its chief executive.

   4¾ $76 _____

8. Call (800)555-3784, X38, to find out how the Massachusetts Department of Revenue eliminated two hundred tons of paper.

   (800) 555-3784, Ext. 38 (*or* Extension 38) 200 tons _____   **See Instructor Note 18-28 in IAE.**

9. American Airlines is increasing its 1st-class section from eight seats to fourteen.

   first-class 8 14 _____

10. John was in his 20s when he began working at the plant that is located at 1 Ingram Circle.

    twenties One _____

11. Model No. 40,500 is available at a price of $3099.00 if we order by March 30th.

    Model 40500 $3099 March 30 _____

12. The computer weighs 3/4 of a pound and costs about three thousand dollars.

    three-fourths of a pound *or* 3/4 pound $3000 _____

13. Only about 1/10 of the population has a home computer.

    one-tenth _____

14. We stayed until after 12 a.m. midnight working on the computer problem.

    midnight _____

End-of-Chapter Worksheets

15. I am working this month from 6:00 a.m. until 2:00 p.m.

6 a.m. 2 p.m.

16. If your ZIP code is between 20,000 and 39,999, call (800) 555-4802 to reach Florist Express.

20000 and 39999

17. New Century Network, located on 7th Avenue, sells advertising for about 100 newspapers.

Seventh Avenue

18. If you have a personal computer equipped with a sound card, you can hear music for ninety-nine cents.

99 cents

19. 62 percent of Americans believe a cell phone is a convenience, but not a necessity.

Sixty-two

20. Several decades ago, calendars in computers were set to show only the last 2 digits of years in the 20th century.

two   twentieth century

PRACTICE 3B

PROOFREADING

Directions: *Proofread and compare the two sentences in each group. If they are the same, write **Yes** in the space provided. If they are not the same, write **No**. Use the first sentence as the correct copy. If you find errors in the second sentence, underline them; insert any omitted words or marks of punctuation.*

1. More than four million people visit the National Consumers League Information Center (NFIC) Website, whose goal is to assist fraud victims by relaying reports daily to more than 150 law enforcement agencies in the United States and Canada.

More than four billion people visit the National Consumers League Information Center (NFC) Website, whose goal is to assist fraud victims by relying reports daily to more than 150,000 law enforcement agencies in the United States and Canada.

1. No

2. "Consumers lose between $10 and $10,000 in Internet scams," said National Consumers League president Linda Golodner. "Cybercrooks are in your wallet with a click of the mouse."

"Consumers loose between $100 and $10,000 in Internet scams," said National Consumers League president Linda Goldner. "Cybercrooks are in you wallet with a click of the mouse."

2. No

3. Posting your name in a member directory; posting messages to a bulletin board, automated mailing list, or newsgroup; or participating in chat sessions will make your e-mail address available to strangers.

Posting your name in a member directory; posting messages to a bulletin board, automated mailing list, or newsgroup; or participating in chat sessions will make your e-mail address available to strangers.

3. Yes

4. By the year 2002, interactive sales are forecasted to grow by 74.7 percent per year to reach $31.3 billion and to employ almost 200,000 workers.

By the year 2022, interactive sales are forcasted to grow by 74.7 percent per year to reach $313 billion and to employ almost 200,000,000 workers.

4. No

NAME _____

5. The Interactive Services Association and the Direct Marketing Association have developed guidelines   **5.** __No__
   that outline responsible marketing practices on the Internet (http://www.isa.net).
                                                  the
   The Interactive Services Association and ⟨ Direct Marketing Association have developed guidelines
   that <u>outlines</u> <u>responsable</u> marketing practices on the Internet (http://www.<u>isan</u>.net).

Proofreading Exercise

The National Consumers League launched an Internet Fraud Watch in 1996. The goal of the Internet Fraud Watch is to help consumers use the Internet and online services safely. The following information is from the Internet Fraud Watch Website.

Directions: *Use proofreaders' marks to correct the copy.*

INTERNET FRAUD WATCH
800-876-7060

1. The Internet Fraud Watch (IFW) received ~~thirty-two~~ *32* reports of fraud a month in 1996, compared to ~~one hundred~~ *100* a month in 1997.
2. More than ~~35,000,000~~ *35 million* people visited the IFW Web site, with an average "hit" per week ranging from 70,000–90,000.
3. Emails about fraud have increased from 100 per week in 1996 to 1,500 per week in 1997.
4. IFW lists the top ⑩ Internet scams. No. ~~one~~ *1* on the fraud list is a promise of free Internet services. Examples of the scam include the promise of free Internet access with the purchase of software that is never provided or payment for a password to access pictures that are never received.
5. More than ~~sixty~~ *60* percent of Internet fraud victims pay by check, cash, or money orders, and ~~nineteen~~ *19* percent pay by credit card. Others pay by telephone bills, bank account debits, or wire transfers.
6. Consumers lose between $10.00 and $10,000.00 in Internet scams.

PRACTICE 4B

WRITING

You have decided you are going to do business on the Internet. The following are some criteria that successful marketers use to determine whether their products will sell on the Internet:

- The product appeals to the technologically savvy.
- The product appeals to a wide geographic audience.
- The product is an item otherwise difficult to locate.
- The product can be purchased over the Internet less expensively than otherwise.

Directions: *Select a product that you think would sell well over the Internet. In a paragraph, describe the product and indicate why you think this product is one that would sell well over the Internet.*   **Answers will vary.**

Selling car polish/wax on the Internet would be successful. The car polish/wax provides a durable shine that repels water

and protects the car's finish from pollutants. The wax comes in 16 ounce plastic containers with an application sponge

included. The item sells for $18.50 and includes all shipping, handling, and applicable taxes. You can order this product

over the Internet by using the order blank provided or call 1-800-555-8812.

NAME _____

ONLINE **EXERCISES**

Reports of Internet fraud are steadily increasing. The National Consumers League launched the Internet Fraud Watch (IFW) in 1996. The goal of the IFW is to help consumers use the Internet and online services safely. The IFW lists the latest Internet scams and also provides ways for consumers to report these scams.

Objective: *To visit the National Fraud Information Center Web page.*

1. With your Internet browser on screen, key:

   http://www.fraud.org in the location text box.

   Press the **Enter** key on your keyboard.

2. Click on **Internet Fraud Watch.**

3. Explore the site, clicking on information of interest.

LOOKING BACK

Posttest

Directions: *Underline the errors in number usage in the following sentences. Write the corrections in the space provided. Write* **Yes** *if the numbers in a sentence are written correctly.*

1. The Website for the National Fraud Information Center won 13 awards in just <u>1</u> year of operation.

   1. <u>one</u>

2. Our Website won <u>2nd</u> place from *Home Office Computing* for our interactive ordering procedure.

   2. <u>second</u>

3. Fred Tarkenton, 50, retired from Zipom in <u>January, 1997,</u> and started a Web design business.

   3. <u>January 1997</u>

4. After launching a Web page in January, we saw our sales increase <u>twenty</u> percent by December.

   4. <u>20</u>

5. We paid <u>$1,000.00</u> to a Web designer to modify our order form and link our site to <u>twenty-five</u> other sites.

   5. <u>$1000 25</u>

6. By 2002, interactive marketing is expected to reach <u>$31,300,000,000</u> a year.

   6. <u>$31.3 billion</u>

7. <u>40</u> new clients requested assistance with Website designs.

   7. <u>Forty</u>

8. We must place the order by <u>2 p.m. in the afternoon.</u>

   8. <u>2 p.m.</u>

A

absolute adjective: An adjective that does not allow for comparisons.

absolute adverb: An adverb that does not allow for comparisons.

accent mark: A stress mark indicating the syllable that requires emphasis when the word is pronounced.

action verbs: Verbs that indicate what someone or something does.

active voice: The subject of a sentence performs the action. Used for most business writing.

adjective clause: A group of words that modifies a noun or pronoun; has a subject and predicate but cannot stand by itself.

adjective phrase: A group of words that modifies a noun or pronoun but does not have a subject or predicate and cannot stand by itself.

adjectives: Words that modify (describe) nouns and pronouns. Adjectives answer the questions *What kind? How many? Which one?*

adverb clause: A group of words that modifies verbs, adjectives, and adverbs; has a subject and predicate but cannot stand by itself.

adverbs: Words that usually give additional information about the main verb but also modify adjectives or other adverbs. Adverbs answer the questions *In what manner? Where? When? To what extent?*

antecedent: The word or group of words to which a personal pronoun refers or that a personal pronoun replaces.

antonyms: Words that are opposite in meaning.

application software: Software that tells the computer how to accomplish specific tasks such as word processing.

appositive: A noun that explains or identifies a preceding noun or pronoun.

articles: The adjectives *a, an,* and *the.*

auxiliary verbs: Verbs that assist and precede the main verb. Also called *helping verbs.*

B

brainstorming: A group problem-solving technique characterized by unrestrained, spontaneous discussion.

business etiquette: The accepted requirements for proper professional behavior.

C

cardinal number: Any of the numbers that express an amount (e.g., *1, 2, 3*).

carpal tunnel syndrome: A nerve disorder resulting from pressure on the median nerve that travels through the wrist.

cellular phone: A communications system which uses FM radio waves to transmit conversations.

clause: A sequence of words with both a subject and a predicate.

collective antecedent: A group of people such as a committee, class, board, or jury to which a pronoun refers or that a pronoun replaces. Neuter in gender.

collective noun: A noun which refers to a group as one unit.

comma splice: An error in writing that results when a comma without a coordinating conjunction is placed between two independent clauses.

command sentences: Sentences that express direct commands or express courteous requests that imply action. The pronoun *you* is understood. Also called *imperative sentences.*

common nouns: Words that refer to general names and are not capitalized.

communication: To give information or to exchange thoughts with another.

comparative degree: A form of an adjective or adverb used to compare two things.

complete predicate: Consists of a verb or verbs and all the modifiers that limit or describe the verbs.

complete subject: A simple or compound subject plus any of its modifiers.

complex sentence: A sentence with an independent clause and one or more dependent clauses.

complimentary closing: A parting phrase such as *Sincerely* at the close of a letter.

compound adjective: The combination of two or more words to form one thought when modifying a noun.

compound noun: A noun composed of two or more words. A compound noun may be written as one word, a hyphenated word, or two words.

compound personal pronoun: Consists of a personal pronoun and the suffix *self* or *selves*.

compound predicate: Consists of two or more predicates that are connected by a coordinating conjunction and have the same subject.

compound preposition: A combination of words that is often considered as one preposition.

compound sentence: A sentence with two independent clauses connected by a coordinating conjunction.

compound subject: Two or more subjects connected by a coordinating conjunction.

compound-complex sentence: A sentence with one or more independent clauses and one or more dependent clauses.

conjunctions: Words that connect words, phrases, or clauses.

conjunctive adverbs: Adverbs that function as connectors and show a relationship between two independent clauses of equal weight.

consonants: All letters except the vowels *a, e, i, o,* and *u.*

consumer: A person who uses goods or services.

contraction: A word made up of two words combined into one by the omission of one or more letters. An apostrophe takes the place of the missing letter or letters.

contrasting expression: An expression that often begins with the word *not* or *never* and contradicts the preceding noun or idea.

coordinating conjunctions: Words (*and, or, but, nor*) that join two independent clauses.

coping strategies: Plans or methods for dealing with problems or responsibilities.

copyright: The exclusive right to use software (also literary, musical, or artistic works) protected by law for a specified period of time.

correlative conjunctions: Words such as *neither/nor* or *not only/but also* that appear in pairs and join words, phrases, and sentences of equal importance.

courteous request sentences: Sentences that require actions rather than answers in words. The pronoun *you* is understood. Also called *imperative sentences.*

cover letter: A letter describing one's education, experience, skills, and job qualifications that is submitted to a potential employer.

cultural diversity: Differences among people such as gender, physical size, age, ethnicity, or religion.

cultural heritage: The ways of living transmitted to succeeding generations.

cumulative trauma disorders (CTDs) or **musculoskeletal disorders (MSDs):** Injuries that occur because of mismatches between workers and the physical requirements of jobs. Also known as *repetitive motion injuries* or *illnesses, repetitive strain injuries* or *illnesses,* or *repetitive stress injuries* or *illnesses.*

customer service: Providing help to someone who purchases goods or services.

D

decision-making process: The steps followed in making up one's mind about a situation.

decision-making software: A software program that helps a decision maker organize thoughts, analyze multiple options, and make the best choice.

declarative sentence: A sentence that states a fact, an idea, or an opinion.

demographics: The statistical data of a human population such as age, income, and years of education.

demonstrative adjective: The words *this, that, these,* and *those* that modify nouns. Answers the questions *Which one?* or *Which ones?*

demonstrative pronoun: A pronoun that points out specific persons, places, or things (*this, that, these, those*).

dependent clause: A clause that must be joined to an independent clause to make sense; it cannot stand alone.

derogatory: Detracting from the character or standing of something; belittling.

descriptive adjective: An adjective that answers the question *what kind?*

direct address: A name of an individual who is being addressed directly.

direct object: A noun or pronoun that provides one way to complete the verb by answering the questions *whom?* or *what?* after the verb.

direct question: A question that is expected to have a reply and that ends with a question mark. Also called an *interrogative sentence.*

direct quotation: The exact words spoken or written by someone.

double negative: A sentence construction in which two negative words are used in the same clause when one is sufficient.

download: To transfer data to the user's computer from another computer.

E

electronic mail: The exchange of computer-stored messages by telecommunications links.

ellipsis mark: A mark or series of marks (. . .) to indicate that part of a quoted sentence has been omitted.

em dash: A substitution for a dash (—).

e-mail address: A code or series of letters, numbers, and/or symbols by which the Internet identifies a person or a location where information is stored.

e-mail: Short for *electronic mail.*

emphatic tense: Adds emphasis to a verb when combined with the word *do.*

en dash: A dash longer than a hyphen but not so long as an em dash.

ergonomics: An applied science that coordinates the design of devices and systems in the workplace with the requirements of the workers.

ethical decisions: Decisions made according to the principles of right and wrong.

ethical dilemma: A confusing situation that requires a choice of action based upon ethics.

ethics: A system of moral principles.

ethnicity: Traits of a group sharing a common cultural background.

etymologies: The history of words.

exclamatory sentence: A sentence that expresses strong reactions and that ends with an exclamation mark.

F

fax machine: Abbreviation for *facsimile machine.* A device that can send or receive text or pictures over a telephone line.

first-person pronoun: A pronoun that refers to the one who is speaking.

future perfect progressive tense: The form of a verb tense that expresses a continuing action; used with *will have been* and the present participle of the main verb.

future perfect tense: Indicates an action or condition of a verb that will begin and end before a specific future time. Use *will have* or *shall have* with the past participle of the verb.

future progressive tense: The form of a verb tense that expresses a continuing action; used with *will be* and the present participle of the main verb.

future tense: Indicates an action or condition of a verb that will occur in the future. Uses *will* or *shall* before the present part of the verb.

G

gender: 1. The sex of a person or animal. 2. A set of grammatical categories applied to nouns such as masculine, feminine, or neuter.

gerund phrase: Includes a gerund (word ending in *ing*) and any modifiers that are needed to make the meaning complete.

gerund: A verb form ending in *ing* that functions as a noun.

global communications: Worldwide exchange of information.

global competition: A process in which products are manufactured and/or services performed by competing companies and are made available to customers throughout the world.

H

helping verbs: Verbs that assist and precede the main verb. Also called *auxiliary verbs*.

homonyms: Words that sound alike but have different meanings.

I

idiom: An expression that has evolved from general usage through the years but which has no established rule for this usage.

imperative mood: A verb form used to give instructions and commands or to make courteous requests.

imperative sentences: Sentences that express direct commands or courteous requests that imply action.

indefinite numbers: Numbers that are not easily counted or determined.

indefinite pronoun antecedents: Third-person pronouns which do not refer to masculine or feminine nouns. May be singular or plural.

indefinite pronouns: Pronouns that refer to persons, places, or things in general ways (e.g., *all, any, more, most, none,* and *some*).

independent clause: A group of words that is a complete sentence and can stand alone.

indicative mood: A verb form used to state facts or to ask direct questions.

indirect object: A noun or pronoun that completes a verb by answering the questions *To whom?* or *For whom?*

indirect question: A sentence that sounds like a question but does not require an answer; ends with a period.

indirect quotation: A restatement of the original material; does not require quotation marks.

infinitive: A verbal that consists of the present part of a verb plus the word *to.*

infinitive phrase: The infinitive (*to* and a verb) and its modifiers.

information overload: Too much information is received to be able to effectively sort or use.

inside address: The name and address of the person to whom a letter is written.

intensive pronoun: A compound personal pronoun that adds emphasis.

interactive ordering: Placing an order for goods or services over the Internet.

interjections: One or two words that show emotions or strong reactions to events or things that have occurred.

Internet: A large computer system linking existing computer networks worldwide.

interrogative pronoun: A pronoun that is used to form direct and indirect questions.

interrogative sentence: A sentence that asks a question.

intransitive verb: An action verb that does not require an object to complete the thought.

irregular plurals: The plural forms change within the nouns or at the end of the nouns.

irritability: Easily annoyed.

J

job search: The process used in finding employment.

job targets: Specific occupational goals, kinds of industries, and/or places of employment determined by job candidates.

junk e-mail: Unwanted electronic messages. Also called *spam*.

L

leader: A person who influences the behavior of others.

leadership: The characteristics that a leader possesses which help influence the behavior of others.

limiting adjective: Numbers or words that indicate *How many*; limits the scope of the noun or pronoun.

linking verbs: Show a state of being or a condition and provide a "link" between the subject and a noun, pronoun, or adjective. Do not indicate action.

M

mailbox: An electronic storage space where electronic messages are received or stored.

mnemonic device: A memory device.

modem: An acronym derived from <u>mo</u>dulator/<u>dem</u>odulator. An electronic device or program that makes possible the transmission of data from a computer by telephone or other communication lines.

modifiers: Words that describe.

multilingual: More than one language.

N

Net: Short for *Internet*.

netiquette: The proper behavior in sending and receiving electronic mail messages.

network: A group of two or more computer or telecommunications systems linked together to permit an exchange of information.

networking: The informal sharing of information among individuals, groups, or institutions.

neuter gender: A pronoun (*it, its*) used to refer to an antecedent that represents things.

nominative case: Nouns or pronouns used as subjects of sentences, as appositives, or as subject complements. Also called the subjective case.

nonrestrictive clause: A dependent clause that has a subject and predicate and does not add to the meaning of the sentence.

nouns: Words that name people, places, things, activities, ideas, or qualities.

O

objective case: Nouns or pronouns used as direct objects, indirect objects, objects of a preposition, or objects of infinitives.

Occupational Safety and Health Administration (OSHA): A federal government agency responsible for providing education, research, enforcement, and rulemaking to combat injuries in the workplace.

online: One computer connected to another computer electronically to receive or send data. Also spelled *on-line*.

operating system software: Software that tells the computer how to use its own components.

ordinal numbers: Numbers used to show the order of succession (e.g., *lst, 2d, 3d*).

P

pager: A small telecommunications device that receives short messages, typically a phone number, for the pager user to call. Also called a "beeper."

parallelism: The linking together of similar grammatical parts in a sentence.

parenthetical expression: A side remark that interrupts a sentence and does not add to the clarity of a sentence.

participial phrase: Consists of a present, past, or perfect participle plus any additional modifiers; functions as an adjective.

participle: A verbal that functions as an adjective.

passive voice: The subject of a sentence that receives the action of the verb.

past participle: A verb part formed by adding *ed* to the base form.

past perfect tense: Shows that one action or condition of a verb began and was completed before another action in the past; uses past participle form with the helping verb *had*.

past progressive tense: Involves an action or condition of a verb that was in progress at a time in the past; uses past tense of the verb *be* with the present participle of the main verb.

past tense: Expresses an action or condition of a verb that was started and completed in the past.

permanent record: Written information intended to last for a long, indefinite period.

personal pronouns: Words that can substitute for nouns referring to persons or things.

phrase: A sequence of words with neither a subject nor a predicate that cannot stand alone.

plural nouns: Name two or more persons, places, things, activities, or ideas and qualities.

point-and-click interface: Clicking on a picture or words on an Internet Web page and being automatically connected to another Web page.

positive degree: The base form of an adjective to describe one person, place, thing, quality, idea, or one group of things; the base form of an adverb to describe a verb, adjective, or other adverb; cannot be used to make a comparison.

possessive adjective: A possessive pronoun such as *my, her, his, your, its,* and *our* that functions as an adjective; answers the question *Whose?*

possessive case: Shows that someone or something owns or possesses something else.

predicate: Adds meaning and clarity to the subject and tells what the subject is doing or what the subject is.

predicate noun: Follows a linking verb and renames the subject. Also called a *subject complement.*

prefix: Letters or words placed before a word (e.g., s*elf*-confidence).

prepositional phrase: A group of words that connects nouns and pronouns to other words.

prepositions: Words that connect nouns or pronouns to other words in the sentence.

present participle: A verb part formed by adding *ing* to the base form.

present perfect progressive tense: Describes a continuous action of a verb up to the present time; uses *has been/have been* with the present participle of the main verb.

present perfect tense: Shows that an action or condition of a verb that started in the past has just been completed or continues to take place up to the present; uses *has* or *have* with the past participle of a verb.

present progressive tense: Involves an action or condition of a verb that is in progress at the present time; uses the preset tense of the verb *be* with the present participle of the main verb.

present tense: Expresses a general truth or an action of a verb that is occurring now.

procrastination: The postponement of action.

procrastinator: A person who postpones action.

pronouns: Words that substitute for nouns.

proper adjective: A word derived from a proper noun that functions as an adjective; answers the question *Which?*

proper noun derivatives: Adjectives formed from proper nouns.

proper nouns: Words that refer to specific persons, places, or things.

Q

quality service: Excellent concern and care toward someone who purchases goods or services.

R

reflexive pronoun: A compound personal pronoun that refers to a previously named noun or pronoun.

relative pronoun: A pronoun which begins a dependent clause that cannot stand on its own.

repetitive stress injury (RSI): An injury that occurs because of a mismatch between the worker and the physical requirements of the job. Also known as *repetitive motion injury* or *illness, repetitive strain injury* or *illness,* or *cumulative trauma (or musculoskeletal) disorder.*

restrictive clause: A dependent clause that has a subject and predicate and is necessary to the meaning of the sentence.

résumé: A summary of one's education, experience, skills, and job qualifications submitted to a potential employer.

roman numerals: Any of the numerals in the ancient Roman system of notation (e.g., I, II, III).

run-on sentences: Sentences in which two independent clauses run together. These sentences are not punctuated correctly. They may have comma splices, or they may lack periods, semicolons, or conjunctions.

S

salutation: The opening greeting of a letter (e.g., *Dear Ms. Miller*).

scams: Fraudulent schemes.

search engine: A service that helps organize various Internet sites into categories.

second-person pronoun: A pronoun that refers to the one spoken to.

self-managing teams: People who work together and manage themselves by sharing power, authority, and decision making.

sentence diagramming: Shows the parts of a sentence and the relationship of all the words to one another.

sentence fragments: Words, phrases, or dependent clauses that cannot stand alone.

sentences: Words correctly arranged so the words comprise complete statements or ideas that make sense.

simple predicate: A single verb in a sentence.

simple sentence: A sentence with one complete subject and one complete predicate.

simple subject: Main word of the subject in a sentence.

singular nouns: Words that name one person, place, thing, activity, or idea and quality.

software: Programs for directing the operation of a computer or processing electronic data.

software piracy: The unauthorized copying or use of software.

stress: Emotional tension caused by everyday events in our lives.

subject: Indicates who is speaking, who is spoken to, or who or what is spoken about in a sentence.

subject complements: Predicate nouns or predicate pronouns that follow linking verbs and rename the subject(s).

subjective case: See *nominative case.*

subjunctive mood: A verb used to express a condition that is contrary to fact or subject to an element of doubt.

subordinating conjunctions: Words that introduce a dependent clause and link it to an independent clause.

suffix: Letter(s) added to the end of a word.

superlative degree: A form of an adjective or adverb used to compare more than two things.

surf the Net: Looking at information on the Internet.

suspending hyphens: Hyphens that are used when a series of hyphenated adjectives has a common basic element and this element is shown only with the last item. A "suspended hyphen" is inserted after each incomplete adjective to indicate a relationship with the last term (e.g., *12- to 15-hour project*).

syllable: Represents distinct sound divisions in a word.

synonyms: Words that mean the same or almost the same as another word.

T

tag question: A question that appears at the end of a sentence.

team: A number of persons working together.

teamwork: A cooperative effort by a group of persons acting together as a team.

telecommunications: The science and technology of transmitting all types of data, from voice to video, over great distances in the form of electromagnetic signals.

telecommuting: A term to describe working outside the traditional office or workplace on a computer and transmitting information to a central office over telephone lines.

tension: Mental or emotional strain.

thesaurus: A book that gives suggestions for similar substitute words as well as their parts of speech.

third-person pronoun: A pronoun that refers to the one spoken about.

time management: Identification and completion of tasks and projects within a specified period of time.

transitive verb: An action verb that needs an object to complete the thought.

V

value system: Determination of importance according to personal beliefs.

verb phrase: A helping (auxiliary) verb with a main verb.

verb tense: Identifies the time of an action or a state of being of a verb.

verbal: A gerund, participle, or infinitive that looks like a verb but functions as a noun, adjective, or adverb.

verbs: Words that show action, indicate a state of being, or help main verbs.

vision: A plan or direction for the future.

voice mail: A telephone system which can record and store human voices and play the recording back to the intended person on command.

vowels: The letters *a, e, i, o,* and *u.*

W

Web: Short for *World Wide Web.*

Websites: Locations on the Internet with information about a person, organization, or business.

work climate: The prevailing attitude, atmosphere, or condition of a place of employment.

workers' compensation: A compensation system of wage replacement benefits for and medical treatment of work-related injuries and occupational diseases.

workstation: A work area for one person; it often accommodates a computer.

World Wide Web: A graphical system on the Internet that supports links to other documents.

Z

ZIP Code: A system to facilitate mail delivery by assigning a numerical code to every postal area in the U.S. (*Zone Improvement Program*).

ie/ei Words

The grade school rhyme "*i* before *e* except after *c* or when sounded like *a* as in *neighbor* and *weigh*" helps you spell many words. Study Rules 1-6 carefully.

Rule 1: Most words use *i* before *e*.

friend	audience	variety	scientist
tier	patient		

Rule 2: Use *i* before *e* except after the letter *c*. In many words, the *ie* sounds like *e* (as in *be*).

achieve	brief	field
thief	wield	relieve

Exceptions:

either	neither	leisure
weird	seize	

Rule 3: Use *e* before *i* after the letter *c*. Note that the *ei* sounds like *e* (as in *be*).

ceiling	conceive	deceit	receipt
perceive	receive		

Rule 4: Use *e* before *i* when the *ei* sounds like *a* (as in *weigh*).

freight	their	vein	neighbor
reign	rein		

Rule 5: Use *e* before *i* when the *ei* sounds like *i* (as in *twice*).

height	sleight

Rule 6: Use *e* before *i* when *ei* sounds like *i* (as in *fit*).

foreign	forfeit	counterfeit

Adding Suffixes to Words

A *suffix* added to the *end* of a word changes the form of that word and, in some cases, changes the spelling. *Vowels* consist of the letters *a, e, i, o,* and *u*. The letters *w* and *y* sometimes act like vowels. All other letters are *consonants*. A *syllable* represents distinct sound divisions in a word.

Rule 7: For words that end in a single consonant preceded by a single vowel, double the final consonant when adding a suffix that begins with a vowel or *y*.

One-Syllable Word		Suffix	New Word
bid	+	er	bidder
stop	+	ed	stopped
wrap	+	ing	wrapping
bag	+	age	baggage
sad	+	en	sadden
fun	+	y	funny

Rule 8: For words that end in *w, x,* and *y* preceded by a single vowel, do not double the final consonant when adding a suffix that begins with a vowel.

One-Syllable Word		Suffix	New Word
draw	+	er	drawer
pay	+	able	payable
say	+	ing	saying
show	+	ed	showed
tax	+	ing	taxing

Rule 9: Double the final consonant of a *two-syllable* word that ends in a *single* consonant preceded by a *single* vowel when you add a suffix that begins with a vowel. This rule applies when the accent falls on the last syllable of the root word. An accent mark (') is a stress mark and indicates the syllable that requires emphasis when the word is pronounced.

Two-Syllable Word		Suffix	New Word
re fer'	+	ing	referring
oc cur'	+	ed	occurred
ex cel'	+	ing	excelling
trans fer' (v.)	+	ed	transferred
im pel'	+	ed	impelled
re mit'	+	ance	remittance

Rule 10: If the accent falls on a syllable other than the last when a suffix is added, do not double the final consonant. Memorize these words.

pre fer'	pref' erence (The accent is on the first syllable.)
re fer'	ref' erence (The accent is on the first syllable.)
con fer'	con' ference (The accent is on the first syllable.)

Exception:

ex cel'	ex' cellence (Even though the accent is on the first syllable, the consonant doubles.)

Rule 11: Do not double the final consonant when adding *any* suffix to words ending with two or more consonants.

Word		Suffix	New Word
send	+	ing	sending
consent	+	ed	consented
conform	+	ed	conformed
earn	+	er	earner
back	+	ward	backward
harsh	+	ly	harshly
tempt	+	ed	tempted

Rule 12: Do not double the final consonant when adding *any* suffix to a word ending in one consonant and preceded by two vowels.

Word		Suffix	New Word
mail	+	able	mailable
wear	+	ing	wearing
equal	+	ed	equaled
beat	+	en	beaten
retail	+	er	retailer
equip	+	ment	equipment

Exceptions:

Word		Suffix	New Word
equip	+	ing	equipping
equip	+	ed	equipped
quiz	+	ed	quizzed
quiz	+	ing	quizzing
quit	+	ing	quitting

Rule 13: Do not double the final consonant of a *one-syllable word* ending in *one* consonant and preceded by *one* vowel when adding a suffix beginning with a consonant.

Word		Suffix	New Word
ship	+	ment	shipment
fret	+	ful	fretful
ten	+	fold	tenfold
bad	+	ly	badly
man	+	hood	manhood

Rule 14: Do not double the final consonant of a *multisyllable* word that ends in *one* consonant and is preceded by *one* vowel and is not accented on the last syllable when a suffix beginning with a vowel is added.

Word		Suffix	New Word
can' cel	+	ed	canceled (preferred)
prof' it	+	ed	profited

of' fer	+	ed	offered
ben' efit	+	ed	benefited (preferred)
to' tal	+	ed	totaled (preferred)

Exceptions:

for' mat	+	ed	formatted
pro' gram	+	ed	programmed
hand' icap	+	ed	handicapped

Rule 15: With most words that end with *e*, drop the final silent *e* at the end of the word when adding a suffix beginning with a vowel.

Word		Suffix	New Word
advise	+	able	advisable
reverse	+	ible	reversible
argue	+	ing	arguing
arrive	+	al	arrival
use	+	ed	used
please	+	ant	pleasant
scarce	+	ity	scarcity
hope	+	ing	hoping
procede	+	ing	proceding
base	+	ic	basic

Exceptions:

agree	+	ing	agreeing
mile	+	age	mileage
dye	+	ing	dyeing

Rule 16: With words that end with *e*, do not drop the final silent *e* when adding a suffix beginning with a consonant. See Rule 16 for the suffix *y* exception.

Root Word		Suffix	New Word
absolute	+	ly	absolutely
advertise	+	ment	advertisement
care	+	less	careless
edge	+	wise	edgewise
enforce	+	ment	enforcement
entire	+	ty	entirety
nine	+	ty	ninety
sincere	+	ly	sincerely
use	+	ful	useful

Exceptions:

acknowledge	+	ment	acknowledgment (preferred)
judge	+	ment	judgment (preferred)
argue	+	ment	argument
true	+	ly	truly
nine	+	th	ninth
whole	+	ly	wholly
awe	+	ful	awful

Rule 17: With words that end with *e*, drop the final silent *e* before adding the suffix *y*.

Root Word		Suffix	New Word
ease	+	y	easy
edge	+	y	edgy
ice	+	y	icy
spice	+	y	spicy

Exceptions:

price	+	y	pricey
smile	+	y	smiley

Rule 18: Do not drop the final silent *e* when a word ends in *ce* or *ge* and the suffix begins with an *a* or *o*. The *c* and *g* retain a soft sound.

Word		Suffix	New Word
advantage	+	ous	advantageous
change	+	able	changeable
manage	+	able	manageable
notice	+	able	noticeable
outrage	+	ous	outrageous
peace	+	able	peaceable
replace	+	able	replaceable

Rule 19: Drop the final silent *e* when a word ends in *ce* or *ge* and the suffix begins with *i*.

Word		Suffix	New Word
age	+	ing	aging
judge	+	ing	judging
mortgage	+	ing	mortgaging
finance	+	ial	financial
force	+	ible	forcible

Rule 20: Change the final *y* to *i* before adding a suffix to a word that ends in *y* preceded by a consonant.

Word		Suffix	New Word
envy	+	ous	envious
copy	+	er	copier
easy	+	ly	easily
try	+	ed	tried
heavy	+	est	heaviest
ordinary	+	ly	ordinarily
happy	+	ness	happiness
likely	+	hood	likelihood
merry	+	ment	merriment

Exceptions:

dry	+	ness	dryness
country	+	side	countryside
shy	+	ly	shyly

Rule 21: In most cases, retain the *y* in words ending in *y* preceded by a vowel when adding any suffix.

Word		Suffix	New Word
enjoy	+	ment	enjoyment
employ	+	ment	employment
play	+	er	player
display	+	ing	displaying
convey	+	ing	conveying
pay	+	er	payer
joy	+	ous	joyous

Exceptions:

day	daily	lay	laid
pay	paid	say	said

Appendix: Spelling Review

Words Ending In *able* and *ible*

Word endings are confusing. The lists that follow include words arranged in families according to their endings. When you are not certain about the correct spelling of a word, check your dictionary.

Words Ending in *able*

Most words end in *able*.

advisable	likable	reasonable
comparable	noticeable	receivable
dependable	payable	valuable
movable		

Words Ending in *ible*

Some words end in *ible*.

collectible	flexible	sensible
eligible	legible	terrible
feasible	responsible	

Words Ending in *ence, ent, ant,* and *ance*

Words ending in *ant, ent, ance,* and *ence* do not have rules for spelling. Practice these words so they become familiar. Use a dictionary whenever you are in doubt about a spelling.

ence	ent	ant	ance
existence	incident	irrelevant	attendance
occurrence	obsolescent	sergeant	hindrance
persistence	superintendent	immigrant	surveillance
reference	dependent	resistant	remittance

Words Ending in *ize, ise,* and *yze*

Words ending with *ize, ise,* and *yze* do not have rules for spelling. Most words end in *ize* but some commonly used words end in *ise*. Practice these words so they become familiar. Use a dictionary whenever you are in doubt about a spelling.

Words Ending in *ize*

amortize	economize	penalize	scrutinize
authorize	emphasize	realize	utilize
criticize	modernize	recognize	visualize
capitalize	organize	prize	specialize

Words Ending in *ise*

advise	devise	merchandise	surmise
compromise	exercise	supervise	arise
despise	franchise	advertise	

Words Ending in *yze*

analyze	paralyze

Adding Prefixes to Words

A prefix is a syllable that is attached to the beginning of a word. Misspellings often occur in words because a prefix is added incorrectly. The words below need extra review and practice. Use a dictionary whenever you are in doubt about a spelling. To avoid misspellings, analyze the word before you add a prefix; then add the prefix to the complete word.

Prefix		Word		New Word
dis	+	satisfaction	=	dissatisfaction
dis	+	service	=	disservice
il	+	legal	=	illegal

il	+	legible	=	illegible
il	+	logical	=	illogical
im	+	mature	=	immature
mis	+	statement	=	misstatement
mis	+	spell	=	misspell
over	+	run	=	overrun
over	+	ride	=	override
un	+	necessary	=	unnecessary
un	+	natural	=	unnatural
under	+	rate	=	underrate

Meanings of Prefixes

Prefix		**Meaning**
dis		**lack of, not**
disadvantageous	disagreeable	
distasteful		
im, in, ir		**not**
immeasurable	impractical	
inappropriate	inconceivable	
inexcusable	ineligible	
intangible	irreplaceable	
inter		**between**
intermission	interoffice	
intersection	interstate	
mis		**wrong**
misinformed	misguided	
misinterpret		
pre		**before**
precaution	prerecorded	
re		**again**
recover	recollect	
reemphasize	rewritten	

Meanings of Suffixes

A suffix is a word part that is attached to the end of a word. A suffix added to a word may change the meaning of the word. The words that follow involve several word endings for you to practice.

Suffix		**Meaning**
ful	=	full of
ative	=	inclined to
ous	=	full of
ly	=	in the way or manner mentioned

ful	**ative**	**ous**	**ly**
useful	demonstrative	conscious	immediately
plentiful	talkative	continuous	necessarily
respectful	creative	disastrous	obviously
thoughtful	initiative	envious	patiently
	humorous	undoubtedly	

Use *The Gregg Reference Manual* or any other available reference manual to check the definitions of these commonly misused or confused words or phrases. You may also use your dictionary to look up these words.

insure	overdue	knew	fewer	irregardless	access
assure	overdo	new	less		excess
ensure					
advice	etc.	loose	perspective	to	
advise		lose	prospective	too	
		loss		two	
allot	capital	recent	through	already	in regards
a lot	capitol	resent	threw	all ready	
alot					
addition	bases	council	device	of	set
edition	basis	counsel	devise	have	sit
		consul			
adverse	cite	its	lessee	serve	stature
averse	sight	it's	lesser	servicing	statue
			lessor		statute
close	decent	apportion	cereal	bad	come/go
clothes	descent	portion	serial	badly	come and/come to
cloths	dissent	proportion			
are	principal	quiet	their	among	kind of
hour	principle	quit	there	between	kind of a
our		quite	they're		
accept	affect	coarse	rain	biannual	in
except	effect	course	reign	biennial	in to
			rein	semiannual	into
adapt	bring	lead	pole	precede	raise
adept	take	led	poll	proceed	rays
adopt					raze
defer	lessen	may be	passed	lie	may
differ	lesson	maybe	past	lay	can
brake	detract	medal	shone	learn	let
break	distract	meddle	shown	teach	leave
		metal			
		mettle			
disinterested	marital	miner	suit	anxious	doesn't
uninterested	marshal	minor	suite	eager	don't
	martial		sweet		
foreword	hear	later	respectably	good	real
forward	here	latter	respectfully	well	really
			respectively		
beside	interstate	personal	stationary	every one	than
besides	intrastate	personnel	stationery	everyone	then
	intestate				
complement	different from	leased	plain	role	some time
compliment	different than	least	plane	roll	sometime
					sometimes
any one	eminent	moral	en route	cannot help	could have
anyone	imminent	morale	root	but	should have
			route		would have
appraise	last	precedence	track	try and	vain
apprise	latest	precedents	tract	try to	vane
					vein
cent	disburse	fiscal	reality		
scent	disperse	physical	realty		
sent					

accommodate	adjacent	Albuquerque	analysis	attendance
bankruptcy	beneficiary	bureau	candidate	category
collateral	column	committee	conscience	conscientious
consensus	correspondent	courtesy	deductible	deficit
definite	Des Moines	develop	dilemma	disappoint
dissatisfied	distinguish	eighth	eliminate	embarrass
emphasize	entrepreneur	environment	equally	exaggerate
exhibition	exorbitant	extension	facilitate	familiar
fascinating	February	forty	fourth	government
guarantee	harass	hindrance	impasse	inasmuch as
incredible	indict	interim	itinerary	jeopardy
ledger	liabilities	liable	liaison	library
maintenance	maneuver	manila	mediocre	miniature
miscellaneous	misspell	mortgage	necessary	negotiate
ninety	ninth	obsolescent	omission	pamphlet
parallel	patience	perseverance	persuade	potato, potatoes
practically	prerogative	pronunciation	quantity	questionnaire
recommend	requisition	San Francisco	satellite	secretary
separate	similar	simultaneous	sponsor	subpoena
substantial	succeed	summary	surprise	thoroughly
unanimous	unique	vicinity	warrant	Wednesday
withhold				

Conjunction(s), 39, 418–446, G-2
  cautions in using, 432
  parallelism and, 430–432
  types of
    conjunctive adverbs, 428–430, 485–486, G-2
    coordinating, 424–425
    correlative, 426
    subordinating, 375, 427–428
Conjunctive adverb, 428–430, 485–486, G-2
Consecutive numbers, 527
Consonants, G-2
Consumer, 53, G-2
Contraction, 372–373, G-2
  apostrophe in, 493
  possessive pronouns vs., 185–186
  word division of, 498
Contrasting expression, 466, G-2
Coordinating conjunction, 39, 69, 424–425, 456–457, G-2
Coping strategies, v, 419, G-2
Copyright, 267, G-2
Corporations, names of, 453. *See also* Companies, names of
Correlative conjunctions, 426, G-2
Courteous request, 57
Courteous request sentence, 451, G-2
Cover letter, 449, G-2
Cultural diversity, v, 209, G-2
  Websites, 234, 237
Cultural heritage, 209, G-2
Cumulative trauma disorders (CTDs), 329, G-2
Customer service, v, 53, G-2
  Website, 78

D

Dash, 499–501
Dates, 467–468, 527–528
Days, capitalization rules for, 152
Decades, numbers expressing, 527–528
Decimals, 529
Decision making
  ethical, 361
  suggestions for, 263
Decision-making process, 241, G-3
Decision-making software, 241, 260, G-3
Declarative sentences, 56–57, 451, G-3
Definitions
  in dictionary entries, 7
  italics for, 503–504
Demographics, 519, G-3
Demonstrative adjectives, 334–335, G-3
Demonstrative pronouns, 189, G-3

Dependent clause, 67–68, 375, 421, G-3
  in complex sentence, 69–70
  in compound-complex sentences, 70
  as introductory expressions, commas with, 463
  in sentence fragments, 70
  subordinating conjunction with, 427
Derogatory, 209, G-3
Descriptive adjective, 331–332, G-3
Diagramming sentences, 72–73
  adjective clause, 347–348
  adverb, 378–379
  appositive, 101
  compound adjective,, 435–436
  compound adverb, 435–436
  compound object, 195–196, 434
  compound subject, 195–196, 434
  compound verb, 195–196, 434
  conjunction, 469–470
  gerund, 287–288
  independent clause, 469–470
  indirect object, 125–126
  infinitive phrase, 315–316
  possessive noun, 126
  predicate noun, 100
  prepositional phrase, 406–407
  pronouns as adjective, 227–228
  review, 253–254, 506–507, 540–541
  subject complements, 100
Dictionary
  electronic, 11
  spelling and, 16
  types of, 5–6
  using, 6
  Website, 107
  See also Dictionary entry
Dictionary entry
  abbreviations in, 8
  antonyms in, 8
  compound adjective hyphenation in, 337
  compound noun spellings in, 115
  definitions in, 7
  irregular grammatical forms in, 8
  parts of speech in, 7
  pronunciation in, 6–7
  sample, 6
  spelling in, 6
  status labels in, 7–8
  stress (accent) marks in, 7
  syllabication in, 6
  synonyms in, 8
  word history in, 7
Different from, 401
Direct address, G-3, 92, 466
Direct command, 57

Direct object, 63, 72–73, G-3
  nouns used as, 91
  on sentence diagram
Direct question, 57, 191, G-3
Direct quotation, 467, 490, G-3
Discussion groups, 87
Displays, ellipsis marks in, 505
Documents. *See also* Written communications
Do, 269–271
Double negatives, 373, G-3
Download, 87, G-3
Drafting, 130

E

e.g., 486
Each/every, 307
Each, 189, 221, 308, 500
Each one, 221
Each other/one another, 226–227
Either, 189, 221, 308
Either/or, 426
Electronic dictionaries, 11
Electronic mail, v, 177, G-3. *See also* E-mail
Ellipsis marks, G-3
  for displays, 505
  for omissions, 504
E-mail, 29, 177. *See also* Electronic mail
  capitalization rules for, 160
  guidelines for, 202
  junk, 519
  in workplace, 483
E-mail address, 177, G-3
Em dash, 499, G-3. *See also* Dash
Emphatic tense, G-3
En dash, 499, G-3
Enough, 189, 221
Enumerations, 486
Ergonomics, v, 329, G-3
Ergonomic workstations, 351–352
Errors
  proofreading for format, 12
  sic in brackets to indicate, 505
etc., comma usage with, 459
Ethical decisions, 361, G-3
Ethical dilemma, 361, G-3
Ethics, v, 361, G-3
Ethnicity, 209, G-3
Etiquette, 361
Etymology, 7, G-3
Every, 221
Everybody, 189, 221, 308
Everyone, 189–190, 221, 308
Everyone/Every one, 226
Everything, 189, 221, 308

Exclamation point, 57, 492
Exclamatory sentence, 56–57, G-3
Explanations
    colon with, 488
    semicolon with, 486

F

Farther/further, 346, 376
Fax machine, 29, G-3
Feminine gender, 213–214
Few, 189, 221, 308
Fewer/less, 346
Financial quotes, 530
First-person pronoun, 179, 212, G-3
Footnote, asterisk for, 506
For, 432
For example, 486, 488
Format errors, proofreading for, 12
Fractions
    hyphen with, 496
    numbers in, 530
    subject-verb agreement and, 312
Frequently misspelled words, 15
From/off, 401
Furthermore, 485
Future perfect progressive tense, G-3
Future perfect tense, 276, G-4
Future progressive tense, 278–279, G-4
Future tense, 275, G-4
Futurists, 87

G

Gender, 209, G-4
    feminine, 213–214
    masculine, 213–214
    neuter, 214
    unknown, 214–215
Geographic locations
abbreviations of, 454
capitalization of, 142
Gerund, 283–284, G-4
Gerund phrase, 283, 314–315, G-4
Global communications, 87, G-4
Global competition, 301, G-4
Global workplace, 209
Good/well, 376
Go to, 433
Government
    acts, bills and laws, 150
    titles of officials, 147
    names of units, 145
Grammar check function (electronic), 13
Grammar errors, proofreading, 12
Gregg Reference Manual, The, 10, 17
Groups, collective antecedents with, 219

H

Have
    forms of, 270–271
    as irregular verb, 270–271
He/she, 215
He/she/it, 33
Helping verb, 35, G-4
    list of, 246
    with past participle, 248–251
    See also Auxiliary verbs
Her/hers, 184
Her/his, 332–333
Here, 313
Highway numbers, 524
Him/her/his, 215
Him/her/his/hers/its, 33
His, 184
Holidays, capitalization of, 150
Homonyms, 16–17, G-4
House numbers, 524
However, 485
Hyphen, 495–499
    adverb ending in *ly* and, 367, 497
    with compound adjectives, 337, 496
    with compound nouns, 116, 496
    with compound numbers, 495
    with fractions, 496
    with numbers and nouns, 496
    with prefix *re,* 497
    in range of numbers or letters, 497
    with *self-* prefixes, 497
    suspending, 496
    in title of person with two functions, 497
    in word division, 497

I

I/me, 182
I/me/my/mine, 33
i.e., 486
Identification numbers, 530
Idiom, 403, G-4
Idiomatic expressions, 403–406
Illustrations, colon with, 488
Imperative mood, 281, G-4
Imperative sentence, 56–57, G-4
    period with, 451
    See also Command sentences;
        Courteous request sentence;
        Request sentences
In addition to, 224
In/into, 402
Inclusive figures, 536
Indefinite numbers, 531, G-4
Indefinite pronoun antecedents, 220–222, G-4
Indefinite pronouns, 189–190, G-4
    plural, 221–222

singular, 221–222
    subject-verb agreement and, 308–309
Independent adjectives, comma with, 460
Independent clause, 67–68, 421, G-4
    in complex sentence, 69–70
    in compound-complex sentences, 70
    in compound sentence, 69
    conjunction, 469–470
    conjunctive adverbs and, 428
    diagramming, 469–470
    semicolon with, 485
Indicative mood, 281, G-4
Indirection quotation, 467
Indirect object, 63, 91, G-4
Indirect question, 57, 191, 452, G-4
Indirect quotations, 490–491, G-4
Infinitive, 182, 285–286, G-4
Infinitive phrase, 67–68, 285, G-4
    as adjective phrase, 345
    diagramming sentences with, 315–316
    as introductory expression, 464
    prepositional phrase vs., 396
Inflected forms, 8
Information overload, 113, G-4
Inside addresses, 160, G-4
Institutions
    names of
        capitalization of, 144
        subject-verb agreement with, 311
    titles of officials, 147
Instructions, quotation marks with, 492
Intensive pronoun, 187–188, G-4
Interactive ordering, 519, G-4
Interjections, 41, G-4
Internet, 87, G-4
    address, 46
    doing business on, 519
    electronic postcards, 206
    as writing resource, 3
    See also E-mail; Web pages;
        Websites
Internet Fraud Watch (IFW), 551–552
Interrogative pronouns, 191, G-4
Interrogative sentences, 56–57, G-5.
    See also Questions
Intransitive verb, 244, G-5
Introductory expressions
    dependent clause, 463
    incomplete clause, 488
    infinitive phrase, 464
    participial phrase, 464
    prepositional phrase, 463–464
Inverted sentences, 313–314

to correct run-on sentence, 71
with courteous request sentence, 451
as decimal point, 452
with declarative sentence, 451
at end of command sentences, 57
at end of indirect question, 57
at end of statement sentence, 56–57
with imperative sentence, 451
with indirect question, 191, 452
with measurements, 452
in outlines, 455
shortened word forms and, 455
Permanent record, G-6
Personal names
abbreviations of, 453
capitalizing, 142
Personal pronouns, 32–33, G-6
basic guide for using, 186
defined, 179
nominative case, 179–181
objective case, 181–183
possessive case, 184
See also Pronouns
Phrase, 67–68, G-6
adjective, 344–345
explanatory, 224
gerund, 283, 314–315
infinitive, 67–68, 285, 315–316, 345, 464
modifying, subject-verb agreement and, 305
participial, 284, 345, 464
prepositional, 40, 67–68, 463. *See also* Prepositional phrase
in sentence fragment, 70
Planning, 139, 168
Plural indefinite pronouns, 221–222
Plural noun, 93–97
apostrophe and, 494–495
defined, 93, G-6
subject-verb agreement with, 314
Plural pronoun, 215–216
Plural subject
present tense with, 272–273
subject-verb agreement with, 303
Plural verb
collective nouns requiring, 310
indefinite pronouns requiring, 308–309
p.m., 538
Point-and-click interface, 519, G-6
Political divisions, numbers in, 535
Positive degree, 341–343, G-6
Possessive adjectives, 332–333, G-6
Possessive case, G-6
basic guide for using, 186
defined, 117
See also Possessives

Possessive case nouns, 118–125. *See also* Possessives
Possessive pronouns, 185–186
Possessives
abbreviations, 124
apostrophe with, 494
compound nouns, 123–124
irregular plural nouns, 121
joint ownership, 122
names of associations, companies and organizations, 122–123
plural nouns, 120
separate ownership, 122
singular nouns, 119–120
time, 124
understood possession, 124
See also Possessive case
Predicate, G-6
complete, 62
compound, 61–62
of sentence, 61–62
simple, 61–62, 68–69
Predicate adjectives, 64
Predicate complements, 64
Predicate noun, 64, G-6
diagramming, 100
nouns used as, 91
See also Predicate pronoun; Subject complement
Prefix, G-6
Prepositional phrase, 40, 67–68, 393–394, G-6
as adjective phrase, 345
diagramming, 406–407
functions of, 397–398
as introductory expression, 463
sentences beginning with, 65–66
subject-verb agreement and, 304–305
Prepositions, 39–41, 390–417, G-6
commonly used, 393
compound, 394–395
conjunctions vs., 432
frequently used, 40
identifying, 393–395
infinitive phrases vs. prepositional phrases, 396
objects of prepositions vs. pronouns, 396–397
prepositions vs. adverbs, 396
objects of, nouns used as, 91
placement of, 398–399
special
among/between, 400–401
beside/besides, 400
different from, 401
in/into, 402
like/as, 401
off/from, 401
to/too/two, 402
Present participle, 248–251, 284, G-6

Present perfect progressive tense, 278–279, G-6
Present perfect tense, 276, G-6
Present progressive tense, 278–279, G-6
Present tense, 247–251, 272–273, G-6
Problem solving, 241, 258
Procrastination, 139, G-6
Procrastinator, 139, G-6
Product names, 156
Progressive tenses, 278–279
Pronoun(s), 32–33, 175–207, G-6
adjectives with, 36–37
capitalization of, 142
cases of
contractions, 185
nominative case, 179–181. *See also* Nominative case, personal pronoun
objective case, 181–183
possessive, 118, 184–186
compound personal pronouns, 187–188
demonstrative, 189
feminine gender, 213–214
indefinite, 189–190
intensive, 187–188
interrogative, 191
masculine gender, 213–214
miscellaneous, 187–193
neuter gender, 214
objects of prepositions, 396–397
personal, 32–33, 179
as possessive case noun, 118. *See also* Possessives
in prepositional phrase, 40
reference, 223–225
relative, 191–192
requiring special attention
after *than* and *as,* 226
each other/one another, 226–227
one or two words, 226
reflexive, 187–188
unknown gender, 214–215
Pronoun/antecedent agreement, 208–238
collective antecedents, 219–220
compound antecedents, 217–219
gender and, 213–215
indefinite pronoun antecedents, 220–222
noun as antecedent, 211
number, 215–216
person and, 212–213
pronoun as antecedent, 211
steps for determining, 212
Pronunciation
in dictionary entries, 6–7
misspelling and, 16
Proofreaders' marks, 14, 232, 237, 258, 263, 293, 320, 352, 356. *See also inside back cover of textbook*

Proofreading, 12–14
  electronic, 13–14
  errors in, 12–13
  procedures, 13
  resources to improve, 2–27
Proper adjective, 143, G-7
Proper nouns, 31–32, 89, G-7
  abbreviations of, 155, G-7
  capitalizing, 141, 143
  derivatives of, 143
  substitutions for, 143
Publications
  capitalization rules for, 149
  names of, subject-verb agreement with, 310
  numbers expressing parts of, 535
  parts of, quotation marks and, 491
Punctuation
  apostrophe, 493–495. *See also* Apostrophe
  asterisk, 506
  brackets, 505
  business letter, 489
  colon, 487–488
  comma, 457–469. *See also* Comma
  dash, 499–501
  ellipsis marks for, 504–505
  hyphen, 495–499. *See also* Hyphen
  in Internet address, 46, 107
  parentheses, 501–503
  period, 451–456. *See also* Period
  quotation marks, 490–493. *See also* Quotation marks
  semicolon, 485–487. *See also* Semicolon

Q

Quality service, 53, G-7
Question(s)
  direct, 57, 191
  indirect, 57, 191, 452
  interrogative pronouns and, 191
  as sentence, 57
  subject-verb agreement in, 313
  tag, 467
  word order in, 65
Question mark, 57
  with direct question, 191
  quotation marks and, 492
Quotation marks
  colons with, 493
  direct quotations, 490
  with exclamation point, 492
  indirect quotations, 490–491
  with instructions, 492
  parts of published works and, 491
  with question marks, 492
  semicolons with, 493
  with separated quotations, 491

special effect words in, 492
  in technical or unusual expressions, 491
Quotations
  capitalization rules for, 157
  comma with, 467
  ellipsis marks in, 505
  Internet search for, 3
  within quoted material, 495
  separated, 491

R

Raise/rise, 251–252
Ratios, 535
Real/really, 377
Reference pronouns, 223–225
  explanatory phrases, 224
  they/you/it, 223–224
  unclear reference, 224–225
References, v
  dictionaries, 5–6
  online, 3
  resources, 3
  types of, 5–11
Reflexive pronoun, 187–188, G-7
Regions, capitalization rules for, 153–154
Regular verbs, 248–251
Re-, 497
Relative pronouns, 191–192, 344, G-7
Repetitive stress injury (RSI), 329, G-7
Request sentences, 56–57
Restrictive clause, G-7
  as adjective clause, 344, 465
  defined, 465
Résumé, 449, G-7
Roman numerals, 158, 536, G-7
Run-on sentences, 70–71, G-7

S

Salutation, G-7
  capitalization in, 160
  colon with, 489
Scams, 519, G-7
Search engine, 3, G-7
Seasons, capitalization rules for, 153
Second-person pronoun, 179, 186, 212, G-7
-self/-selves, 187–188
Self-, 340, 497
Self-managing team, 301, 324, G-7
Semicolon
  with conjunctive adverb, 429
  with conjunctive adverbs, 485–486
  to correct run-on sentence, 70–71
  with enumerations, 486
  with explanations, 486
  with independent clauses, 485

with quotation marks, 493
  in series, 486
Seniority titles
  abbreviations of, 454
  roman numerals in, 536
Sense verbs, 245
Sentence(s), G-7
  capitalizing first word in, 141
  colon with interruptions of, 489
  complement of, 63
  complex, 69–70, 422
  compound, 422
  compound-complex, 70, 423
  declarative, 56–57
  defined, 55
  diagramming, 72–73. *See also* Diagramming sentences
  effective, 167–168
  exclamatory, 56–57
  formation, 68–71
  imperative, 56–57
  interrogative, 56–57
  inverted, subject–verb agreement with, 313–314
  number at beginning of, 526–527
  objects of, 63
  order of words in, 65–66
  parts of, 58–62
  predicate of, 61–62
  prepositional phrase at beginning of, 65–66
  purposes of, 56–58
  question, 65
  run-on, 70–71
  simple, 68–69, 422
  as statements, 56–57
  subject of, 58–62
  there/here, 65, 313
  weak, 180
Sentence development, 52–84
Sentence diagramming, 72–73, G-7
  See also Diagramming sentences
Sentence fragments, 70, G-7
Sentence identification, 55–56
Separated quotations, 491
Series
  cents in, 534
  commas in, 425, 458–459
  of compound adjectives, 340
  of percentages, 534
  semicolon in, 486
Set/sit, 251–252
Several, 189, 221, 308–309
Sic, 505
Simple predicate, 61–62, 72–73, G-7
Simple sentence, 68–69, 422, G-7
Simple subject, 59, 72–73, G-7
Since, 432